Culture and Belief
in Europe 1450–1600

An Anthology of Sources

Edited by
David Englander, Diana Norman,
Rosemary O'Day and W. R. Owens
at the Open University

BLACKWELL
Oxford UK & Cambridge USA

in association with
the Open University

Selection and editorial material copyright © The Open University 1990

First published 1990
Reprinted 1990, 1993 (twice)

Blackwell Publishers
108 Cowley Road, Oxford, OX4 1JF, UK

238 Main Street
Cambridge, Massachusetts 02142, USA

British Library Cataloguing in Publication Data

A CIP catalogue record for this book is available from the British Library.

Library of Congress Cataloging in Publication Data

Culture and belief in Europe, 1450–1600: an anthology of sources.
   p. cm.
Edited by David Englander, Diana Norman, Rosemary O'Day and W. R. Owens.
Includes index.
ISBN 0–631–16991–1 (pbk.):
1. Europe—History—1492–1648—Sources.   2. Europe—
Civilization—16th century—Sources.   3. Religious thought—16th
century—Sources.   I. O'Day, Rosemary.
D220.C85   1990
940.2′3—dc20   89–15089
                                                                                                  CIP

Designed by Chase Production Services, Chipping Norton
Typeset in Ehrhardt by Joshua Associates Ltd, Oxford
Printed in Great Britain by T.J. Press Ltd, Padstow

This book is printed on acid-free paper.

CONTENTS

II. Civic Pride and Civic Patronage: Venice and Antwerp

III. Reformation

IV. Religious Reform and Cultural Change: Spain and England   219

V. Europe and the Wider World   269

VI. Print Culture 353

VII. The Crisis of Authority: France 393

VIII. Church, State and Literature in Britain 439

INTRODUCTION

The sixteenth century has long been regarded as a watershed in modern European culture, celebrated as the period of Renaissance and Reformation, Print and Propaganda, Loyola and Luther, Shakespeare and Sachs, Prelates and Princes. Scholars have rejoiced in the sharp contrasts and comparisons afforded by the culture and religion of the period. But how best to study this period has for as long been problematic. Broadly speaking, students have been encouraged to follow one of two paths: either they have followed a traditionally conceived history course, or they have studied individual texts or artefacts using the tools of other disciplines – literary criticism, art history, philosophy or linguistics, for example. Historians have sought to provide a coherent and chronological explanation for the occurrence and development of both Renaissance and Reformation. Indeed, there has been much discussion of the meaning to be attached to these two key terms. On the whole, though, they have concentrated upon those aspects of sixteenth-century culture which have survived to enrich our own, giving most space and attention to a few privileged texts such as Erasmus's *Praise of Folly*, Machiavelli's *The Prince*, or More's *Utopia*, largely penned by members of the European elite. Other scholarly disciplines have stuck equally rigidly to the accepted canon of 'important' sixteenth-century works; that is to say, to works appreciated for their intrinsic worth and for their discernible influence upon the development of later European culture, *not* because they were of overwhelming concern to contemporaries.

In the past two decades or so, some changes in the scholarly attitude to the sixteenth century, as to past cultures in general, have become apparent. There is more concern to study the past on its own terms, to try to understand what was important to contemporaries – all contemporaries, high and low, young and old, male and female. Vernacular and popular cultures have become a valid subject for study in all disciplines. Scholars are attempting to discover why contemporaries thought, felt and expressed themselves as they did, and are finding the answer in in-depth study of '*histoire totale*', even '*culture totale*', as well as of texts and artefacts themselves. There has been a desire to disentangle the many threads of the process of change and to understand its uneven pace and pattern. It is a much more complex society which today's scholar perceives, and it is a much more complex understanding of its changing nature for which the scholar strives.

The Open University has been one of the pioneers of interdisciplinary study in the arts, and the present anthology has been planned as a source book for use by students taking a course entitled *Culture and Belief in Europe 1450–1600*. We as editors believe that this rich selection of texts will also be of much interest and value to general readers and other students of the period. Since the anthology is linked to a particular course, however, it may be helpful to outline its main features, and how they have governed the choice of material reprinted here.

The aim of the course is to achieve a truly integrated study of sixteenth-century Europe, and in so doing to enable students to examine 'evidence' of sixteenth-century culture and belief and to advance hypotheses about it themselves. The course is not chronologically organized. Instead it attempts by means of 'case studies' of particular texts, places and artefacts to offer answers to three broad questions. How far was European society in the sixteenth century dominated by religion, in particular by Christianity? What were the authority relations – political, religious, familial and intellectual – in Europe? How far was it a European society as opposed to a collection of distinct national cultures? Much of the material included in this anthology will be found to relate in some way to one or more of these three questions. In studying the course students will use a textbook account of the period but the main emphasis is upon primary sources. These include such well-known literary texts as Shakespeare's *Richard II*, Marlowe's *Dr Faustus*, Montaigne's *Essays* and Spenser's *Faerie Queene*, in addition to the documents reprinted here.

This, then, is an interdisciplinary anthology, designed to illustrate, and to facilitate the study of, the relationships between religious belief and cultural change in sixteenth-century Europe. Some of the items included are printed here or rendered in English translation or in accessible form for the first time, and the anthology therefore extends significantly the range of sixteenth-century documents available to students. Many different kinds of writing are represented: drama, letters, diaries, parliamentary statutes, works of philosophy and theology, fiction, autobiography, travel literature, poetry and literary criticism.

The book is divided into eight thematic sections. Section I, 'Humanism, Popular Culture and Belief' provides a vivid illustration of the range and complexity of sixteenth-century culture and belief, with documents ranging from medieval plays, ghost stories, and accounts of religious pilgrimages, through to the works of humanists – Erasmus, Machiavelli and Rabelais – who were beginning to call into question many traditional beliefs and ways of thinking. In section II, 'Civic Pride and Civic Patronage: Venice and Antwerp', we move to a case study of two of the leading cities in sixteenth-century Europe. Documents here include inventories, wills, legal documents and descriptions of libraries from which much information can be gleaned concerning the activities of sections of the population – particularly women – about whom little literary evidence survives. With section III, 'Reformation', we plunge into the religious upheavals of the age. The great reformers, Tyndale, Luther and Calvin, are allowed to speak for themselves, and there are also examples of the ways in which the message of the reformers reached the people and of their responses to it. In section IV, 'Religious Reform and Cultural Change: Spain and England', the focus shifts to examine the social and cultural consequences of religious reform in Spain and England, with extracts from the writings of such notable religious personalities as St Teresa of Ávila, St Ignatius de Loyola, founder of the Jesuits, and St Thomas More, a Catholic martyr in England. Section V, 'Europe and the Wider World', is devoted to the impact on European thought and culture of contact with non-European and non-Christian cultures. Extracts here illustrate the development of 'travel literature' and also the intellectual and moral debates to which it gave rise. One of the most far-reaching technological developments of the period was the invention and spread of printing, and section VI, 'Print Culture', reprints selections from three notable examples of early printed literature: Caxton's edition of Sir Thomas Malory's *Le Morte d'Arthur*, a popular sermon by Hugh Latimer, and Cervantes' famous novel *Don Quixote*. In section VII, 'The Crisis of Authority: France', the focus is on political thought in France, and in particular on the debates over the nature of the state and the basis of both secular and religious authority. Finally, in section VIII, 'Church, State and Literature in Britain', we look at the political and ecclesiastical consequences of the move from Catholicism to Protestantism and at the wider cultural traces of both religious reform and humanism in Scottish and English poetry of the period.

Each section has a brief introduction, and each individual document has a headnote which gives details of the source as well as contextual information. The aim of the editors has been not to produce definitive scholarly editions but to present each item in a form which is as accessible and easy to understand as possible. Some documents are presented in modern English, either in a translation made specially for this book or in one taken from a modern printed edition. Explanatory annotation has been provided where it was thought this would assist the reader. All editorial deletions are indicated by ellipses (three points; or, for a long deletion, ellipses on a new line, followed by a line space) while editorial additions are enclosed in square brackets.

The production of this anthology has been a team effort, involving not only the four editors but also the members of the Open University course team who chose documents and in many cases abridged or translated them: Joan Bellamy, Tim Benton, Dinah Birch, Stuart Brown, Angus Calder, John Fauvel, David Goodman, Cicely Havely, Lucille Kekewich, Catherine King, Anne Laurence, Tony Lentin, John Purkis, Angela Scolar, Keith Whitlock, Kevin Wilson, Susan Khin Zaw. We are also grateful to scholars outside the Open University for help with translation: S. J. Brander, Francis Clark, Marga Emlyn Jones, R. Niall D. Martin, and Wendy Scase. We wish to thank A. G. Dickens, Claire Cross and J. Lynch for their valuable advice. Finally, we are extremely grateful to Lydia Chant for her invaluable assistance, and, for secretarial help, to Wendy Clarke, Laura Dimmock, Barbara Humphry and Adele Sheffer.

The task of editing the volume was divided between the editors as follows: sections I and III were edited by Rosemary O'Day, who drafted the general introduction; sections II and VII were edited by David Englander; sections IV and V were edited by Diana Norman, who also handled the illustrations; and sections VI and VIII were edited by W. R. Owens, who chaired the editorial group.

The Open University   D. E.
                                                                       D. N.
                                                                       R. O'D.
                                                                       W. R. O.

ACKNOWLEDGEMENTS

The editors and publishers wish to thank the following for permission to use copyright material: A. Asher & Co. B.V. for material from Gasparo Contarini, *The Commonwealth and Government of Venice*, trans. by Lewis Lewkenor, 1599, Theatrum Orbis Terraru, 1969; Basil Blackwell Ltd for material from Jean Bodin, *Six Books of the Commonwealth*, abridged and trans. by M. J. Tooley, 1955; Bodleian Library for material from 'The Pilgrimage of William Wey', MS Bodl. 565; The Borthwick Institute of Historical Research for material from W. J. Sheils, ed., *Archbishop Grindal's Visitation*, *Camperta and Detecta*, 1575, 1977; Burns & Oates Ltd. for material from St Thomas Aquinas, *Summa Theologica*, Illa Ilae Question 88, Article 6; Cambridge University Press for material from G. R. Elton, ed., *The Tudor Constitution*: *Documents and Commentary*, 2nd edition, 1982; and François Hotman, *Francogallia*, trans. by J. H. M. Salmon, 1972; J. M. Cohen for material from *The Four Voyages of Christopher Columbus*, edited and trans. by J. M. Cohen; Collins Publishers for material from E. Newby, ed. *A Book of Travellers' Tales*, trans. by G. Tyler Northup, 1936; Columbia University Press for material from Jean Bodin, *Method for the Easy Comprehension of History*, trans. by B. Reynolds, 1945; Duke University Press for material from H. Cline, 'The *Relaciones Geograficas* of the Spanish Indies 1577–1586', *Hispanic American Historical Review*, Vol. 44, 3, 1964. Copyright © 1964 by Duke University Press; Edinburgh University Press for material from John McQueen, ed., *Ballattis of Luve*, 1970; Eyre & Spottiswoode for material from W. E. Campbell, ed., *The English Works of Sir Thomas More*, Vol. II, 1931; Gower Publishing Group for material from Edward Peters, ed. and trans., *Heresy and Authority in Medieval Europe: Documents in Translation*, Scolar Press, 1980; Harper & Row, Publisher, Inc. for material from John C. Olin, ed., *Autobiography of Ignatius Loyola*, trans. by Joseph F. O'Callaghan. Copyright © 1974 by John C. Olin and Joseph F. O'Callaghan; and Charles Gibson, ed., *The Spanish Tradition in America*. Copyright © 1968 by Charles Gibson; The Huguenot Society of Great Britain and Ireland, University College, London, for material from *Actes du Consistoire de l'Église Française de Threadneedle Street, Londres*, XXXVIII, 1937; Lichfield Joint Record Office and J. P. Thorneycroft for material from Marston, B/C/5/1599 (sic), and Sudbury, B/C/5/1601; Longman Group Ltd. for material from Sally J. Brander, trans., 'Ghost Stories',

English Historical Review, July 1922; and Daniel Waley, *Later Medieval Europe*, 1975; Lund Humphries Publishers Ltd. for material from Albrecht Dürer, *Diary of his Journey to the Netherlands* for the English translation rights by P. Trou, eds. J. A. Goris and G. Marlier, 1971; Penguin Books Ltd. for material from *The Life of Saint Theresa of Ávila by Herself*, trans. by J. M. Cohen. Translation copyright © 1957 by J. M. Cohen; Niccolò Machiavelli, *The Prince*, trans. by George Bull. Copyright © 1961, 1975, 1981 by George Bull; Baldesar Castiglione, *The Book of the Courtier*, trans. by George Bull. Copyright © 1967 by George Bull; François Rabelais, *The Histories of Gargantua and Pantagruel*, trans. by J. M. Cohen. Copyright © 1955 by J. M. Cohen; Bernal Díaz, *The Conquest of New Spain*, trans. by J. M. Cohen. Copyright © 1963 by J. M. Cohen; Miguel de Cervantes Saavedra, *The Adventures of Don Quixote*, trans. by J. M. Cohen. Copyright © 1950 by J. M. Cohen; and *The Autobiography of Benvenuto Cellini*, trans. by George Bull. Copyright © 1956 by George Bull; Oxford University Press for material from W. L. Renwick, ed., *A View of the Present State of Ireland*, Clarendon Press, 1970; D. B. and A. M. Quinn, eds., *The Virginia Voyages from Hakluyt*, 1973; William J. Ringler, Jr., ed., *The Poems of Sir Philip Sidney*, Clarendon Press, 1962; Katherine Duncan-Jones and Jan Van Dorsten, eds., *Miscellaneous Prose of Sir Philip Sidney*, Clarendon Press, 1973; J. MacQueen and T. Scott, eds., *The Oxford Book of Scottish Verse*, Clarendon Press, 1966; and *The Turkish Letters of Ogier Ghiselin de Busbecq*, trans. by E. S. Forster, Clarendon Press, 1927; Princeton University Press for material from Isa Ragusa and Rosalie B. Green, eds., *Meditations on the Life of Christ: An Illustrated Manuscript of the Fourteenth Century*, trans. by Isa Ragusa. Copyright © 1961 by Princeton University Press; Routledge for material from Dorothy M. Meads, ed., *Diary of Lady Margaret Hoby*, George Routledge & Sons, 1930; State University of New York Press for material from C. Barnstone Willis, ed. and trans., *The Unknown Light: The Poems of Fray Luis de Leon*, 1979; Gerald Strauss, for material from *Nuremberg in the Sixteenth Century*, extracted and trans. by G. Strauss, John Wiley Inc., 1966; Trustees for Roman Catholic Purposes Registered for material from T. Corbishley, S.J., trans., *The Spiritual Exercises of Saint Ignatius*, Anthony Clarke Books, 1973; The University of California Press for material from Sir Thomas Malory, *Caxton's Malory: A New Edition of Sir Thomas Malory's 'Le Morte d'Arthur*, ed. and trans. by James W. Spisak and William Matthews. Copyright © 1983 by The Regents of the University of California; The University of Chicago Press for material from Craig R. Thompson, ed. and trans., *The Colloquies of Erasmus*, 1965; and Ernst Cassirer et al., eds., *Renaissance Philosophy of Man*, 1948; University of Toronto Press for material from *Collected Works of Erasmus*, Vols I, II, III and XXV, 1985; Unwin Hyman Ltd. for material from M. Mullett, *Radical Religious Movements in Early Modern Europe*, George Allen & Unwin, 1980; Viking Penguin Inc. for material from Mary McLaughlin and James Bruce Ross, eds., *The Portable Renaissance Reader*. Copyright © 1953 by The Viking Press, Inc., renewed 1981 by Viking Penguin Inc.; Yale University Press for material from Claude de Seyssel, *The Monarchy of France*, trans. by J. H. Hexter, ed. Donald R. Kelley. Copyright © 1981 by Yale University.

NOTE TO THE READER

The documents are presented here in English, mostly with modernized spelling. Punctuation has not, as a rule, been altered. The vocabulary and syntax of early modern writing can seem strange to the modern reader and where this is the case you might find it helpful to your understanding to read an extract aloud. We have provided headnotes to each document which offer useful contextual information. In addition, we have explained difficult words in the text where these cannot be found in the *Concise Oxford Dictionary* and have provided annotation to assist you. For ease of reference we speak throughout of the sixteenth century, but a number of texts from the later fifteenth century fall within the scope of this work.

The Editors

SECTION I

An old peasant couple
wood engraving by Hans Sebald Beham.
Reproduced by kind permission of the Trustees of the British Museum.

SECTION I

Humanism, Popular Culture and Belief

It is a truism to say that early modern European society was religious – that it was impossible for people in the sixteenth century to extricate secular from religious matters, to see political affairs, for example, in other than religious terms. Yet it is also often asserted by scholars that this was an age of increasing secularization, in which religion mattered less and less. It would be instructive to be able to pinpoint that moment in time when today's 'secular' society came into being – when the turning point occurred.

One essential step along this way is that of establishing the nature of sixteenth-century culture and belief – what thoughts, activities and beliefs preoccupied Europeans? In order to find out, a thorough acquaintance with the surviving remains of sixteenth-century society is required.

Unfortunately life is too short for any individual to explore all the writings and works of art which sixteenth-century people have left behind. Most of us have to rely upon digests of the knowledge acquired by scholars and interpretations of this knowledge. But we need to know which scholarly works and interpretations to trust and we must have a yardstick to measure them against. Some route must be found through the mass of surviving printed texts, manuscripts, artefacts and accounts of events to give the interested reader the 'confidence' to accept or challenge the work of scholars. We hope that we have devised a strategy to allow you to do just this.

Secondary works are, then, of vital importance to the student of sixteenth-century Europe. We should not scorn the diligent research and considered opinions and interpretations of others. But equally crucial is a study of texts, manuscripts, artefacts and 'events' for ourselves. Traditionally, studies of culture and belief have concentrated almost exclusively upon works produced by educated elites. This is partly because it was such works which were put into print and into collections of art and sculpture or repertoires of music, and which had the most discernible influence upon our own vernacular cultures and beliefs. It is partly because the affairs of princes and elites have become the 'stuff' of modern history courses, for a number of reasons – patriotism and the support of established regimes being but two of these. There is absolutely no doubt that such culture was and is important. Elites were influential and we need to study what they thought, said, wrote and did.

We need to find out whether elite culture was the dominant culture in sixteenth-century Europe. Did the 'people' (over 90 per cent of the population) share the same concerns as the rich and the educated? What acquaintance with and sympathy for elite culture did the mass of the people have? But the influence might not necessarily have been one-way – to what extent did popular culture and beliefs influence the educated elites?

No single document can provide an answer to questions as complex as these but many documents can afford clues. Elite texts are thicker on the ground than popular ones but there are some surviving evidences of the culture and beliefs of the 90 per cent. Reading such evidence does require a degree of critical awareness which must be encouraged. Here we offer some short texts as 'raw material' for your explorations (documents I.1, 2, 3, 4 and 13).

Individuals in the sixteenth century could think, believe, write and do only certain things. On the one hand, there were structures of authority which sought to impose orthodoxies upon the people and to enforce them – the Catholic Church; the Universities; the Monarchies. Documents I.5, 6, 7, 12 and 13 permit further study of these structures in two areas – philosophy and Church discipline. On the other hand, there were less visible boundaries which militated against 'free' thinking: traditional roles (such as those within the family, community and state), inborn and cultivated fears (such as those of death, of purgatory, of disorder), opportunities or rather the lack of them (for example, for education, travel, social mobility), environment (whether rural or urban, rich or poor, for instance) – the list is seemingly endless. People were obligated to believe some beliefs, dream some dreams, do some deeds; they were permitted or allowed to act and think only in certain ways. Many extracts in this section can be used to explore this idea (documents I.1, 2, 3, 4, 13).

True though this may be, some individuals of this era did challenge contemporary orthodoxies. Their works were atypical of their age – the products of a new movement or movements – humanism (which can be divided conveniently into secular and Christian humanism). We should consider how it came to be that some individuals were able to burst the bonds of traditional permissions and obligations – More, Erasmus, Machiavelli, Rabelais, Castiglione, Valla, Pico, Leonardo, Michelangelo, Luther, Calvin, Loyola among others – and cause Europeans to think anew. Further, we must consider to what extent their views influenced contemporaries and near-contemporaries throughout society (documents I.6, 7, 8, 9, 10, 11, 12). For example, the colloquies of

♯ 4

Erasmus grouped as document 9 show the great Christian humanist both reflecting and challenging the values and views of many of his peers. The role of woman is explored in documents I.9.A and B. In document I.9.C Erasmus challenges the popular view of the importance of pilgrimages and relics.

1 The Spicers' Play (c.1463–1477)

a Guild's 'art + mystery'

Source: British Library MS Additional 35290. That portion of the play which shows the annunciation and the visitation of the Virgin Mary has been printed here. The extract has been modernized and edited by Dr Wendy Scase.

The sole surviving manuscript, which contains over forty plays of the York cycle of plays, was compiled between 1463 and 1477, but the cycle was established by 1415. The plays continued to be performed until the second half of the sixteenth century. Each play was staged and performed by members of a specific craft or trade guild. For this reason the plays have been called mystery plays – the mystery being the specialized skills of the guild. Scholars prefer to call them the Corpus Christi plays because they were performed during the Church's midsummer festival of Corpus Christi between 23 May and 24 June.

The plays were written in the northern dialect of late medieval English, with 'stage directions' and character designations added in Latin. In order to make the plays more accessible to student readers, in this edition marginal glosses have been provided where necessary to give the meanings of words and unfamiliar grammatical forms and constructions, and words still current in modern English have been printed in their modern spellings.

In this manuscript *The Annunciation and the Visitation* includes a prologue in which a Doctor, that is, a learned man, recounts the sayings of the prophets concerning the birth of Jesus. This has not been included here.

. . .

Angelus:
    [*Tunc cantat angelus*]
Hail Mary, full of grace and bliss!   1
Our Lord God is with thee
And has chosen thee for his;
Of all women blest mot thou be.
Maria:
What manner of halsyng is this   5
Thus privily comes to me?
For in my heart a thought it is,
The tokening that I here see.
    [*Tunc cantat angelus 'ne timeas Maria'*]

Ang:
Ne dread thee not, thou mild Mary,
For nothing that may befall;   10

[*Angelus*: Angel (Gabriel)]
Tunc cantat angelus: Then the angel sings
4 *mot*: shall
Maria: Mary
5 *halsyng*: greeting
7 *thought*: concern
8 *tokening*: sign
ne timeas Maria: fear not, Mary

For thou has found sovereignly
At God a grace over other all.
In chastity of thy body
Conceive and bear a child thou shall;
This bodword bring I thee forthy: 15
His name 'Jesus' shall thou call.

Mekill of might then shall he be;
He shall be God and called 'God son'.
David sege his father free
Shall God him give to sit upon.   20
As king for ever reign shall he
In Jacob house ay for to wonne:
Of his kingdom and dignity
Shall no man earthly know ne con.

Mar:
Thou God's angel meek and mild,   25
How should it be, I thee pray,
That I should conceive a child
Of any man by night or day?
I know no man that should have fyled
My maidenhood, the sothe to say,   30
Without will of works wild
In chastity I have been ay.

Ang:
The Holy Ghost in thee shall light;
High virtue shall to thee hold.
The holy birth of thee so bright,   35
'God son' he shall be called.
Lo! Elizabeth thy cousin ne might
In elde conceive a child for alde;
This is the sixth month full right
To her that barren has been talde!   40

Mar:
Thou angel, blessed messenger,
Of God's will I hold me paid.
I love my Lord with heart clear,
The grace that he has for me laid.
God's handmaiden lo, me here,   45
To his will all ready grayd.
Be done to me of all manner
Through thy word as thou hast said.

[*Ang*:]*
Now God that all our hope is in,
Through the might of the Holy Ghost,   50

11 *found sovereignly*: received surpassingly
12 *At*: From
over other all: above all others
15 *bodword*: message
forthy: therefore
17 *Mekill of might*: Powerful
18 *God son*: God's son
[*line 19*] The throne of his worthy forefather David
[*line 22*] Always to dwell in Jacob's house
24 *know ne con*: ?know the full extent; ?enjoy
29 *should have fyled*: has defiled
30 *the sothe to say*: to speak the truth
31 *wild*: impure
32 *ay*: always
33 *light*: alight
35 *The holy birth of thee*: the holy child born of you
38 *elde*: old age
alde: age
[*lines 39–40*] She that has been reputed barren is now in her sixth month [of pregnancy]
[*line 42*] I am content with God's will
44 *has for me laid*: directed at me
[*line 46*] Prepared to do his will
[*line 47*] In every way let it be for me
[*line 48*] As you have spoken

*[*lines 49–52*] A change of speaker is not marked in the manuscript; sometimes these lines are attributed to Mary.

Save thee, dame, from sak of sin
And wisse thee from all works waste.

[*Mar:*]
Elizabeth my own cousin,
Me thought I covet always most
To speak with thee of all my kin,   55
Therefore I come thus in this haste.

Elizabeth:
Ah! welcome mild Mary,
My own cousin so dear!
Joyful woman am I,
That I now see thee here.   60
Blessed be thou only
Of all women in feere,
And the fruit of thy body
Be blessed far and near!

This is joyful tiding   65
That I may now here see:
The mother of my Lord King
Thus gate come to me!
Soon as the voice of thine haylsing
Might my ears enterand be,   70
The child in my womb so young
Makes great mirth unto thee.

Mar:
Now Lord blest be thou ay
For the grace thou hast me sent.
Lord I love thee, God verray.   75
The sande thou has me sent
I thank thee night and day,
And pray with good intent
Thou make me to thy pay;
To thee my will is went.   80

Eliz:
Blessed be thou, grathely grayed
To God through chastity!
Thou trowed and held thee paid
At his will for to be.
All that to thee is said,   85
From my Lord so free,
Swilke grace is for thee laid,
Shall be fulfilled in thee.

Mar:
To his grace I will me ta,
With chastity to deal,   90

51 *sak*: charge
52 *wisse*: guide
   waste: idle
54 *Me thought I covet*: It has
   seemed I desire
61 *only*: singularly
[*line 62*] among all women
68 *Thus gate*: In this way
69 *haylsing*: greeting
70 *enterand*: entering
75 *verray*: true
76 *sande*: message
79 *pay*: pleasure
80 *went*: directed
81 *grathely grayed*: worthily
   made ready
[*line 83*] You believed and held
   yourself rewarded
86 *free*: gracious
87 *Swilke*: Such
   is for thee laid: as is directed
   at you
89 *me ta*: commit myself

That made me thus to go
Among his maidens feele.

My soul shall loving ma
Unto that Lord so lele,
And my ghost make joy also   95
In God that is my hele!
    [*Tunc cantat Magnificat*]

92 *feele*: many
93 *ma*: more
94 *lele*: true
95 *ghost*: spirit
96 *hele*: salvation
[*Tunc cantat Magnificat*: Then she sings the Magnificat]

2 The Pewterers' and Founders' Play (*c.* 1463–1477)

Source: British Library MS Additional 35290. The play, *Joseph's Trouble about Mary*, has been modernized and edited by Dr Wendy Scase.

Joseph:
Of great mourning may I me mene   1
And walk full wearily by this way;
For now then wende I best have been
At ease and rest by reason ay.
For I am of great elde,   5
Weak and all unwelde,
As ilke man see it may.
I may nowther buske ne belde,
But owther in frithe or field.
For shame what shall I say,   10

That thus gates now on my old days
Has wedded a young wench to my wife –
And may not well tryne over two straws!
Now Lord, how long shall I lead this life?
My bones are heavy as lead   15
And may not stand in stead,
As kende it is full rife.
Now Lord, thou me wisse and read,
Or soon me drive to death:
Thou may best stint this strife.   20

For bitterly then may I ban
The way I in the temple went;
It was to me a bad bargain –
For reuthe I may it ay repent!
For therein was ordained   25
Unwedded men should stand,
All sembled at asent,
And ilke one a dry wand
On height held in his hand;
And I ne wist what it meant.   30

[*line 1*] I shall make known my great distress
2 *full*: very
[*line 3*] For then, I expected now to have been most completely
[*line 4*] Always, at ease and rest in accordance with reason
5 *elde*: age
6 *unwelde*: feeble
[*line 7*] as each man may see
8 *nowther buske ne belde*: neither rush about nor settle
[*line 9*] except either in woods or in fields
11 *thus gates*: in this way
13 *tryne over two straws*: stride over two straws (i.e. can hardly walk)
16 *stand in stead*: stay in position
17 *kende*: known
full rife: very widely
18 *wisse*: guide
read: advise
20 *stint*: stop
21 *ban*: curse
[*line 22*] The path I took to the temple
[*line 24*] I shall always repent of it sorrowfully
25 *was ordained*: it was customary
27 *All sembled*: all assembled
at asent: ? at the appointed time
28 *wand*: rod
30 *ne wist*: did not know

In mange all other one bore I;
It flourished fair and flowers on spread,
And they said to me forthy
That with a wife I should be wed.
The bargain I made there   35
That rues me now full sore:
So am I straytely sted.
Now casts it me in care,
For well I might ever more
Anlepy life have led!   40

Her works me works my wonges to wet;
I am beguiled; how, wate I not.
My young wife is with child full great:
That makes me now sorrow unsought,
That reproof near has slain me.   45
Forthy if any man frayne me
How this thing might be wrought,
To gab if I would pain me,
The law stands hard against me:
To death I mon be brought.   50

And loath me thinketh, on the other side,
My wife with any man to defame.
And whether of there two that I bide
I mon not scape without shame.
The child, certis, is not mine: 55
That reproof does me pine
And gars me flee from home.
My life if I should tyne,
She is a clean virgin,
For me without blame.   60

But well I wate through prophecy,
A maiden clean should bear a child . . .
But it is not she, sekirly!
Forthy I wate I am beguiled.
And why ne would some young man take
    her?   65
For certis I think overgo her
Into some woods wild;
Thus think I to steal from her –
God shield ther wild beasts slay her
She is so meek and mild!   70

Of my wending will I none warn;
Nevertheless it is my intent
To ask her who got her that bairn;
Yet would I wate fain ere I went.

All hail, God be herein!   75

31 *In mange all other one*: among
   all the others
33 *forthy*: on that account
[*line 36*] I now regret very sorely
37 *straytely sted*: placed in
   difficulties
40 *Anlepy life*: A single life
[*line 41*] her deeds make my
   cheeks become moist [with
   tears]
42 *wate*: know
43 *great*: large
46 *Forthy*: Therefore
   frayne: ask
47 *be wrought*: have come
   about
48 *gab*: lie
50 *mon*: must
51 *loath me thinketh*: it is
   loathsome to me
53 *whether of there two*:
   whichever of these two
   bide: suffer
54 *scape*: escape
55 *certis*: certainly
56 *me pine*: distresses me
57 *gars me*: causes me to
58 *tyne*: lose [i.e. I would
   wager my life]
63 *sekirly*: for sure
65 *ne would*: would not
66 *overgo her*: to depart with
   her
69 *shield ther*: forbid that these
71 *warn*: tell
[*line 74*] I would like to know
   before leaving

Prima Puella:
Welcome by God's dear might!
Jos:
Where is that young virgin,
Mary my berde so bright?

Pr. Plla:
Certis, Joseph, ye shall understand
That she is not full far you from.
She sits at her book full fast prayand
For you and us and for all tha
That aught has need.
But for to tell her will I go
Of your coming, without dread.
Have done and rise up dame,
And to me take good heed:
Joseph he is comen home.
Maria:
Welcome, as God me speed,

Dreadless, to me he is full dear.
Joseph my spouse, welcome are ye!
Jos:
Gramercy Mary. Say, what cheer?
Tell me the soth, how is't with thee?
Who has been there?
Thy womb is waxen great think me;
Thou art with bairn, alas for care!
Ah, maidens, woe worth you
That let her lere swilke lore!
Secunda Puella:
Joseph, ye shall not trowe
In her no feeble fare.

Jos:
Trowe it not harm? Lefe wench, do way!
Her sides shows she is with child.
Whose is't Mary?
Mar:
    Sir, God's and yours.
Jos:
       Nay, nay!
Now wate I well I am beguiled,
And reason why:
With me fleshly was thou never fylid
And I forsake it here forthy.
Say, maidens, how is this?
Tells me the sothe, rede I,
And but ye do, i-wisse,
The bargain shall ye aby!

80
85
90
95
100
105
110

[*Prima Puella*: First Maiden]
78 *berde*: lady
79 *Certis*: Indeed
80 *not full far you from*: not very far from you
81 *prayand*: praying
82 *tha*: those
83 *That aught has*: Who have any
87 *to me take good heed*: pay attention to me
88 *is comen*: has come
89 *speed*: help
92 *Gramercy*: Thank you
    what cheer?: how are you?
93 *soth*: truth
95 *is waxen great*: has grown large
97 *woe worth you*: ill luck befall you
98 *lere swilke lore*: learn such a lesson
[*Secunda Puella*: Second Maiden]
    trowe: believe
[*line 100*] of her any weakness of conduct
101 *Trowe it not harm?*: Not believe it evil?
    Lefe: dear
102 *Her sides shows*: Her shape shows
106 *fylid*: defiled
107 *forsake*: reject
    forthy: therefore
109 *Tells me the sothe*: Tell me the truth
    rede I: I advise
110 *but*: unless
    i-wisse: for sure
    aby: pay for [i.e. you'll pay the penalty]

Sec. Plla:
If ye threte as fast ye can,
There is nought to say there till;
For truly here come never no man
To waite the body with none ill   115
Of this sweet wight.
For we have dwelt ay with her still
And was never from her day nor night;
Her keepers have we been
And she ay in our sight.   120
Come here no man between
To touch that berde so bright.

Pr. Plla:
No, here come no man in there wanes,
And that ever witness will we –
Save an angel ilke a day once,   125
With bodily food her fed has he –
Other come none.
Wherefore we ne wate how it should be,
But through the Holy Ghost alone.
For truly we trowe this: 130
His grace with her is gone;
For she wrought never no miss,
We witness, ever ilkane.

Jos:
Then see I well your meaning is
The angel has made her with child.   135
Nay, some man in angel's likeness
With somkyn gaud has her beguiled,
And that trow I!
Forthy needs not swilke words wild
At carp to me dissayuandly.   140
We, why gab ye me so,
And feigns swilk fantasy?
Alas, me is full woe,
For dule why ne might I die?

To me this is a care-full case;   145
Reckless I rave, refte is my read,
I dare look no man in the face.
Derfely for dole, why ne were I dead?
Me loathes my life.
In temple and in other stead   150
Ilke man till hethyng will me drive.
Was never wight so woe,
For ruthe I all to-ryff,
Alas, why wrought thou so,
Mary, my wedded wife?   155

[*line 112*] however much you threaten
113 *there till*: thereto [i.e. there is no case to answer]
114 *come*: came
[*line 115*] to treat the body with any evil
116 *wight*: creature
117 *ay*: always
118 *was*: were
123 *in there wanes*: within these walls
125 *ilke a day*: each day
127 *Other come none*: No one else has come
[*line 128*] therefore we cannot explain how it could have happened
132 *she wrought never no miss*: she never committed any crime
133 *ilkane*: each one [of us]
137 *somkyn gaud*: some kind of trick
139 *swilke*: such
[*line 140*] to speak deceivingly to me
[*line 141*] Fie, why do you tell me such fibs?
[*line 142*] and make such a pretence?
144 *dule*: sorrow
[*line 146*] I am out of my mind
148 *Derfely*: wretchedly
    dole: sorrow
    ne were I: am I not
149 *Me loathes*: I hate
150 *in other stead*: elsewhere
[*line 151*] everyone will make me a laughing-stock
[*line 153*] I am torn apart by grief
154 *wrought*: behaved

Mar:
To my witness great God I call
That i mind wrought never no miss.
Jos:
Whose is the child thou art with all?
Mar:
Yours sir, and the King's of bliss.
Jos:
Ye, and how then?   160
No! Selcouthe tythandis then is this!
Excuse them well there women can!
But Mary, all that sees thee
May wit thy works are wan;
Thy womb all way it wreyes thee   165
That thou has met with man.

Whose is it, as fair mot thee befall?
Mar:
Sir, it is yours and God's will.
Jos:
Nay, I ne have nought ado with all,
Neme it no more to me, be still!   170
Thou wate as well as I
That we two same fleshly
Wrought never swilk works with ill.
Look thou did no folly
Before me privily   175
Thy fair maidenhead to spill.

But who is the father? Tell me his name!
Mar:
None but yourself.
Jos:
      Let be for shame!
I did it never! Thou dotist, dame, by
      books and bells!
Full sakles should I bear this blame after thou
      tells.   180
For I wrought never in word nor deed,
Thing that should mar thy maidenhead,
To touch me till –
For of slyk note war little need!
Yet for my own I would it feed,   185
Might all be still.

Therefore the father, tell me, Mary!
Mar:
But God and you I know right none.

[*line 157*] [I] who never
      intended any crime
160 *Ye*: Yes
161 *Selcouthe tythandis*:
      Marvellous news
162 *them*: themselves
      there women: these women
164 *wit*: know
      wan: evil
165 *wreyes*: betrays
167 *fair mot*: prosperity may
169 *I ne have nought ado with all*:
      I've nothing to do with it
170 *Neme*: Mention
172 *same fleshly*: together
173 *swilk works*: such deeds
179 *Thou dotist, dame*: You
      prattle, lady
180 *sakles*: guiltless
      after thou tells: that you
      impute
182 *Thing*: Anything
[*line 183*] to make sexual
      contact
[*line 184*] For there was little
      desire for that sort of thing
185 *for my own*: as my own
      [child]
188 *But*: Except for

Jos:
Ah, slike sawes make me full sorry,
With great mourning to make my moan.   190
Therefore be not so bold,
That no slike tales be told,
But hold thee still as stone.
Thou art young and I am old –
Slike works if I do would   195
Those games from me are gone!

Therefore tell me in privity,
Whose is the child thou is with now?
Sertis there shall none wit but we
I dread the law as well as thou.   200
Mar:
Now great God of his might,
That all may dress and dight,
Meekly to thee I bow.
Rue on this weary wight,
That in his heart might light   205
The soth to ken and trowe.

Jos:
Who had thy maidenhead, Mary, has
    thou aught mind?
Mar:
For soth, I am a maiden clean.
Jos:
Nay, thou speaks now against kind,
Slike thing might never no man of
    mean   210
A maiden to be with child!
Those works from thee are wild;
She is not born, I wene.
Mar:
Joseph, ye are beguiled:
With sin was I never filed;   215
God's sande is on me seen.

Jos:
God's sande! Yha, Mary, God help!
But certis that child was never ours two!
But womankind if them liste help,
Yet would they no man wiste their woe.   220
Mar:
Sertis it is God's sande

[There is probably a line missing here: one is
needed to complete the rhyme scheme.]

That shall I never go from.

189 *slike sawes*: such words
192 *slike tales*: such stories
[*line 195*] even if I wanted to do
    such deeds
197 *in privity*: privately
199 *Sertis*: Certainly
    wit: know
202 *dress and dight*: arrange and
    dispose
205 *light*: alight
207 *aught mind*: any recollection
209 *kind*: nature
210 *mean*: imagine
213 *wene*: believe
215 *filed*: defiled
216 *sande*: message
217 *Yha*: Yes
219 *if them liste*: even if they
    wish for
220 *wiste*: knew

Jos:
Yha Mary, draw thy hande,
For further yet will I frande   225
I trowe not it be so.

The soth from me if that thou layne,
The child-bearing may thou not hide!
But sit still here till I come again;
Me bus an errand here beside.   230
Mar:
Now great God, he thou wisse
And mend you of your miss,
Of me what so betide.
As he is king of bliss,
Send you some seand of this,   235
In truth that ye might bide.

Jos:
Now Lord God that all thing may
At thy own will both do and dress,
Wisse me now some ready way
To walk here in this wilderness.   240
But ere I pass this hill –
Do with me what God will,
Owther more or less –
Here bus me bide full still,
Till I have slepid my fill: 245
My heart so heavy it is.

Angelus:
Waken Joseph, and take better keep
To Mary that is thy fellow fast.
Jos:
Ah! I am full weary, lefe, let me sleep –
Forwandered and walked in this forest.   250
Ang:
Rise up and sleep no more,
Thou makist her heart full sore
That loves thee alther best.
Jos:
We! Now is this a farly fare,
Forto be cached both here and there,   255
And nowhere may have rest!

Say, what arte thou? Tell me this thing.
Ang:
I Gabriel God's angel full even
That has taken Mary to my keeping,
And sent is thee to say with steven,   260
In lele wedlock thou lead thee;

224 *draw thy hande*: draw breath
    [i.e. be quiet]
225 *frande*: ?enquire
[*line 227*] even if you keep the
    truth from me
230 *Me bus*: I have to do
231 *he thou wisse*: may he guide
    you
[*line 233*] whatever happens to
    me
235 *seand of this*: message
    concerning this
237 *thing*: things
243 *Owther*: Either
244 *Here bus me bide*: Here I
    must remain
245 *slepid*: slept
249 *lefe*: sir
250 *Forwandered and walked*:
    Worn out with wandering
    and walking
253 *alther best*: best of all
254 *farly fare*: wonderful thing
255 *cached*: chased
260 *thee*: to thee
    steven: voice
261 *lele*: true

Leave her not, I forbid thee;
No sin of her thou neven,
But tille her fast thou speed thee
And of her nought thou dread thee: 265
It is God's sande of heaven.

The child that shall be born of her,
It is conceived of the Holy Ghost.
All joy and bliss then shall be after,
And to all mankind now althir most.   270
'Jesus' his name thou call,
For slike happe shall him fall
As thou shall see in haste.
His people save he shall
Of evils and angers all   275
That they are now enbraste.

Jos:
And is this soth, angel, thou says?
Ang:
Yha, and this to token right:
Wend forth to Mary thy wife always,
Bring her to Bethlehem this ilke night;   280
There shall a child born be,
God's son of heaven is he
And man ay most of might.
Jos:
Now, Lord God, full well is me,
That ever that I this sight should see;   285
I was never ere so light!

For for I would her thus refused
And sakles blame that ay was clear;
Me bus pray her hold me excused,
As some men does with full good cheer.   290
Say, Mary, wife how fares thou?
Mar:
The better, sir, for you.
Why stand ye there? Come near.
Jos:
My back fain would I bow
And ask forgiveness now   295
Wiste I thou would me hear.

Mar:
Forgiveness, sir? Let be, for shame!
Slike words should all good women lack.
Jos:
Yha, Mary, I am to blame
For words long ere I to thee spoke.   300
But gather same now all our gear,

263 *neven*: mention
264 *tille*: to
270 *althir most*: most of all
272 *happe*: good fortune
     fall: befall
275 *Of*: From
     angers: troubles
276 *That*: With which
     enbraste: beset
286 *light*: happy
[*line 287*] For previously I
     would have rejected her
[*line 288*] And blamed the guilt-
     less one who was always
     pure
[*line 289*] I must pray her to
     excuse me
290 *does*: do
298 *lack*: be without
[*line 300*] For the words that I
     long ago spoke to you
301 *gather same*: gather together

Slike poor wede as we wear,	302 *wede*: garments
And prick them in a pack.	304 *bus me it bear*: I must carry it
Till Bethlehem bus me it bear,	305 *will women dere*: will harm
For little thing will women dere; 305	women
Help up, now, on my back!	

3 Late Medieval Ghost Stories

Source: *English Historical Review*, 38 (1923), 85–6; 37 (1922), 419. Translated by Sally J. Brander.

Ghost stories were often used by medieval preachers. There were collections of stories in circulation for their use. The threat of retribution from beyond the grave would encourage the laity to follow the Church's dictates. Preachers would add local colour to make the stories more convincing and effective. The stories printed here involve much circumstantial detail about real people and places.

The first two tales below appear in a preacher's manuscript commonplace book of the fifteenth century from Ely, preserved in Trinity College, Oxford. A monk of Byland Abbey, Yorkshire, entered the third story, with eleven others, into the blank leaves of a fine volume of the twelfth and thirteenth centuries containing tracts from Cicero belonging to Byland. He probably wrote them in or shortly before 1400. The book is now in the British Library. All three stories were originally in medieval Latin and have been translated.

I. FROM Master Richard de Puttes etc. A story about the celebration of the mass. In the year of our Lord 1373: A certain man from Haydock in the county of Lancashire had a mistress who bore his sons. After the death of this woman the man took another woman as his wife. It so happened that this man went on a certain day to a certain smithy where iron ploughs were sharpened or repaired, presumably to procure a blade or a ploughshare. The smith was residing at another estate called Hulme which is two miles distant from the above-mentioned Haydock. As he was returning at night he came to a certain cross standing in the road, the one known as Newton Cross, and there he experienced a terrible fright. Terrified out of his wits, he looked around him and saw what looked like a dark shadow which he implored not to harm him, but to identify itself. And a voice replied from out of the shadow and said to him, 'Do not be afraid. I am the woman who was once your lover and I am given leave to come to you to ask for your help.' The man asked her how she was faring. To this she replied, 'Poorly. But if you wish, you can help me.' The man replied, 'Willingly. I will do what I can, if you tell me how.' Whereupon she said, 'I can be freed from the punishment I am suffering, if masses are celebrated for me by good priests.'[1]

---

[1] It was widely believed that masses said for the departed would be efficacious in shortening the bitter pains of their punishment in purgatory. Stipendiary priests serving in the chantries of churches and cathedrals spent their days reading masses for the dead for a fee. A Christian making a last will and testament would leave a sum of money to pay for a given number of masses. The poor unfortunate in this story had had no opportunity so to do. The story is clearly a reinforcement of the teaching that masses are necessary and that individual Christians should

To which he replied 'And I will celebrate masses for you even if it costs me all my goods, right down to my last penny.' And then she said, 'Do not fear, but place your hand on my head and take what you find there.' So he put his hand on her head and took from there about half a handful of very black hair. But during her lifetime the woman had beautiful golden hair upon her head. Then the woman said, 'If you celebrate as many masses for me as the number of these hairs, then I will be liberated from my punishment.' This he agreed to do. And then the woman said, 'Come to this place at such and such a time and you will then know about my circumstances.' And with that she disappeared. And he fastened the said hairs with a nail in a hole in his door and immediately sold a considerable number of his goods and raised money and went looking for a priest near and far and had many masses celebrated. That done, he looked again at the above-mentioned hair and found much of it had turned gold according to the number of masses celebrated. And thus he had many masses celebrated again and thus again all of those above-mentioned hairs had turned gold. After that he came at the arranged time to the above-mentioned cross and waited for a little while and saw a shining light coming towards him, moving fast. And when it reached him, a voice spoke from it, thanking him again and said, 'May you be blessed amongst all men for liberating me from the most dreadful punishment and now I am going happily.' And after a short conversation, she left him swiftly. Praise be the power of the mass etc.

II. In the year 1389 [in . . .] the reign of King Richard II, a certain Thomas of Ely, recently the servant of a certain deceased Adam Sporlam, was visited for 13 nights in succession by a spirit who on the last night, viz. Sunday 20 June, threw him and his son out of bed. Upon which the child began to cry in a loud voice, at which crying the said Thomas, the father of this child, picked up the child from his disturbed sleep. Thomas got into bed again with the child; but the spirit returned and summoned him to wait upon his mistress, St Ethelreda. Thomas unwillingly followed the spirit to a most delightful place, unknown to him, in the presence of a certain lady, dressed in a religious fashion,[2] who told him that as he had loved her and honoured her by his prayers, she had decided to warn him, and that he was to tell his confessor to warn certain people of Ely, whose names the woman told him, that they were to put themselves right before God and Holy Church in the matter of unpaid tithes and unproved wills.[3] He was also to warn the Prior and Convent of Ely to hold processions every Wednesday and Friday for five weeks, to implore God that a fierce heatwave now threatening the population should not harm the crops in the future, because the heat will be so

---

make provision for masses for the dead. There is some evidence that belief in purgatory and in the efficacy of satisfactory masses was already declining in England by the early sixteenth century.

[2] i.e. as a nun or member of one of the regular orders (known as religious).

[3] Every person was expected to pay a tithe – one tenth of his or her income to the church, either in money or in kind, according to custom. At the time of this story, personal tithes were also payable – a per capita sum.

great that the lead on the churches will melt. Thomas, replying that being poor and of modest reputation he would not be believed, was told to go back to bed, and stay there until the feast of St Ethelreda, on which he would recover his health; and to meet his objection that he was not ill, he was afflicted with a curvature of both his legs and was in that condition seen, touched and manipulated by many faithful people, until he was restored on the day and at the tomb of the saint by the words, 'Get up and walk.' And as soon as he woke, his health was restored. Whereupon Brother Roger of Norwich, a Master of Theology, that day performed a good Collect, declaring the aforesaid miracle to all the people. And accordingly a solemn procession was held on Friday, 25 June; and Thomas swore to the truth of his story on the Holy Gospels and the relics of St Ethelreda.

. . .

III. ABOUT a certain Canon of Newbury, who was captured after his death and whom —— [unnamed] caught: It happened that he was walking in a field, talking to the Head Ploughman. And suddenly the aforesaid Head Ploughman fled in great fear and the other man was fighting with a certain spirit which shamefully tore his clothes. But at last he was the winner and conjured it up. And when it was conjured up, it confessed it was the said Canon of Newbury, excommunicated[4] for stealing some silver spoons from a certain place. Thus it beseeched the living man to take them and go to the above-mentioned place, and having returned them to his prior, to ask for absolution. This he did, and found the said silver spoons in the place he remembered. After that, absolved from his sins, it rested in peace. However, the aforesaid man grew sick and was ill for many days. And he asserted that it was true that it appeared to him in the dress of a canon.

4 The Pilgrimage of William Wey (c.1456)

Source: Bodleian Library, Oxford, MS Bodl. 565. Extracts translated by M. L. Kekewich (with advice from Chris Emlyn Jones).

William Wey (d. 1476), a priest and fellow of Eton College, went on three pilgrimages during his life – once to Santiago in 1456 and twice to the Holy Land in 1458 and 1462. He retired from Eton College to the Augustinian Community at Edington, Wiltshire. On his death he left to this religious community his manuscript account of his travels. His account reads, in many ways, like a guidebook and he certainly intended it to be of practical benefit to future Augustinian pilgrims. He did explain that Christ and the saints had recommended that the faithful undertake pilgrimages and he repeated the view of Pope Leo that pilgrimages strengthened faith.

---

[4] Literally: out of the communion of. An individual who was banished from the communion of the church by the courts was excluded from the life of the community (social and economic as well as religious association being forbidden); the sentence could be removed when the individual performed penance and received absolution.

In the name of God I, William Wey, fellow of the royal college at Eton by the inspiration of divine grace, undertook a pilgrimage to St James in Compostela in Spain on 6 April, in the year of our Lord 1456. I had a licence to do so from my king, the founder of the college, Henry VI. I arrived at the port of Plymouth on the last day of April and remained there until the seventeenth of May. On that day six ships departed at the same time on pilgrimage: one from Portsmouth, another from Bristol, another from Weymouth, another from Lymyngton, another called Cargryne and a ship from Plymouth called Marywhyte. We were at sea until the twenty first of May on which day we came to the port of Corunna at around the ninth hour, and then went on to St James in Compostela on the vigil of the Holy Trinity.

Whilst I was there I heard that there is an archbishop in the church of St James of Compostela, under him in the same church he has seven cardinals, a deacon, a cantor,[1] five archdeacons, one scholar and two judges who all have mitres and staffs. There are eighty canons in that church and twelve porcionarii.[2] The cardinals and bishops receive fifty ducats a year and, if he is resident, each canon receives twenty ducats a year. These cardinals wear neither amices[3] nor hooded cloaks in the choir but only surplices. On the vespers of the Holy Trinity six rectors were in the choir in red caps, they held long staffs in their hands covered in silver and they sang a verse of the Bible and Benedicamus. Two mitred cardinals in pontificals[4] with pastoral staffs and holding censers in their right hands poured incense over the high altar with one hand, and afterwards did the same to the ministers in the choir. On the day of the Holy Trinity nine bishops and cardinals in pontificals walked in procession before Mass. The ministers of the church asked whether any English gentlemen were present and, when told that there were, they chose them in preference to all other nations and asked them to carry the canopy above the body of Christ. There were six who carried the canopy, the names of four of them were Austile, Gale, Lile and Fulford.

The archbishop of St James of Compostela has twelve bishops under him, besides those who are in his church. There are three archbishops in the whole kingdom: first the archbishop of Compostela, second the archbishop of Seville which is the great city of Spain, the third is the archbishop of Toledo; the last two have canons and not cardinals under them. Offerings to St James of Compostela are divided into three parts: the archbishop has one, another is for the canons, cardinals and bishops and the third is devoted to the fabric of the church.

I afterwards returned to the port of Corunna where we waited for three days. There were eighty ships belonging to Englishmen, Welshmen, Irishmen, Normans, Frenchmen, Bretons and other nationalities which had topcastles and four were without them, the English ships totalled thirty

---

[1] A leading singer.

[2] Members of a cathedral chapter who enjoyed only half the revenues of their prebends (their allocated livings).

[3] Hoods lined with grey fur.

[4] The vestments of a bishop.

two. We left Corunna on 28th of May, on the 3rd of June we returned to the port and on the 5th we again left Corunna and arrived at Plymouth on the 9th of June.

There are five kingdoms in Spain: the kingdom of Spain, of Castille and Leon, of Portugal which are Christian and Almeria and Granada which are Saracen. Lord Henry, king of Castille and Leon, captured the king of Granada in the year of our Lord 1456. He took possession of the greatest city of Granada called Malaga, whence come the figs called 'figs of Malike'. He held the Saracen king prisoner in his own kingdom and wrote using his own seal to the inhabitants of his captive's cities and towns. In sign of victory lord Henry sent the king of Granada's golden or gilded crown to St James of Compostela and it was placed on the head of the statue of St James seated in the middle of the high altar on the day of the Holy Trinity in the year of our Lord above said and the year of indulgence at St James. In the same year the great tower made by the French at Bordeaux for their defence from the fabric of the bell tower of St Peter was swallowed up by the earth.

In the same year a man from Somerset, who had promised to make a pilgrimage to St James on account of a grave illness from which he suffered, came to me at Plymouth. He asked my advice about whether, after he had taken his vow, he should return home immediately for he feared that he would die of his illness. He preferred to die on the way home rather than on the way to St James. I advised him that he should go on with his pilgrimage as it would be better to die on the route and receive an indulgence than whilst he was on his way home. Despite this advice he turned back and travelled twenty miles in one day with great pain and difficulty. When he arrived at a hospice where he intended to spend the night he was suddenly relieved of the illness from which he had suffered for such a long time. Realizing that he was completely cured he returned to Plymouth, covering nearly as great a distance in the next half day as he had accomplished during the whole previous day. Again he took ship for St James and I met him at Corunna in the home of the Friars Minor on the day of Corpus Christi.

Another miracle: a person on our ship had his purse cut from his belt, losing his jewels and all the money he had. He immediately promised St James that should he get his goods back he would visit his shrine without baggage or extra clothing. After his promise a Breton who had taken his purse was caught in the act of cutting another; the pilgrim's property was found in his clothing. He had regained the purse with the help of St James and immediately made his way to his shrine as he had promised.

The song of the Spanish children who dance in front of the pilgrims for small coins:

> St James bring you from your land to Compostela;
> St James, a good man, gives you a good pardon,
> Good weather, a good road, a fair wind, a good journey;
> Give those who are here a coin by your grace.

I HEARD THE FOLLOWING IN SPAIN:

All Catholics know that the most holy apostle James Zebedee was disposed by divine grace to travel to Spain. Undoubtedly he thought that it should be visited by its patron during his lifetime so that he might introduce and divulge the faith to the unbelieving people who lived there at the time. The said apostle stayed there, preaching and delivering sermons, but converted only a few on account of the great heresy that was rooted in their hearts. He therefore returned again to Judaea and preached the passion of Christ and his most holy faith in Jerusalem even to Jews, to Gentiles and other pagans. He submitted to earthly death and took the way of all flesh for the love of our Saviour Jesus Christ. After his death his disciples, guided by divine grace, took up his most blessed body and carried it to the port of Jaffa where, by divine grace, they found a ship which had been made ready in every respect. They placed the body of the most blessed apostle in it and passed over the sea with great joy, blessing the name of the Lord. In seven days they arrived here at that very place which was the port where the aforesaid apostle had tried to introduce the faith, as I said above. By divine will on account of his death, all Spain was instructed in the faith to which it could not be converted during his life.

The disciples of the same apostle when they arrived at the abovesaid port removed the most holy body from the ship constantly singing the refrain: 'Your way is in the sea and you move through many waters.' Praising the name of the Lord, they placed the body on a stone which is called Barca, and also on another which was lying there called Padron. Romipete[5] and pilgrims visiting the body broke these stones and needlessly took part of them away. The most holy Pope Gregory III, noting the most holy truth and recognizing the most fortunate advent, provided a formula by which the life and death of the apostle should be investigated. He conceded universal and singular benefits and other gifts to true penitents who had confessed and who might visit the said places so that the memory of the said advent should not perish and the pilgrims might achieve a reward for their great labours.

THESE ARE THE RELICS THAT ARE KEPT IN THE SAID PLACES:

First and principally there is the holy stone called Padron upon which the body of blessed James Zebedee rested which now stands under the altar of St James in the church of Padron.

Item, there is the most holy Barca, which is in the river to which pilgrims go so they may touch it in summertime because the water is low and the river dry. There is a fountain on mount Padron where St James placed his staff and a great stone on which he stood when he first preached in Spain.

These following relics are kept in the church of Compostela. First and principally the body of the blessed James Zebedee, nephew of the Virgin

---

[5] Another word for 'pilgrim'.

Mary, brother of the blessed John the apostle and evangelist, it is whole and uncorrupted.

Item, the body of the blessed bishop Fructuosus, item, the body of the blessed Athanasius, item, the body of the blessed Cucufatus, item, the body of the blessed Theodorus, a disciple of the apostle himself, item, the body of the blessed martyr Silvestris, a companion of the apostle himself. Item, in the treasure of the said church the head of blessed apostle James Alpheus is most clearly on show to everybody.

THESE ARE THE INDULGENCES CONCEDED BY THE HOLY FATHERS TO THE SAID CHURCH OF COMPOSTELA:

A third part of all their sins are remitted for anyone who makes a pilgrimage to the church of the blessed James Zebedee at whatever time. If they die on the way there, or at the shrine or returning, if they have repented of their sins, these are all remitted. Item, those who go every Sunday to the procession of the church of St James are given for the procession and consecration forty days of indulgence and are given the same throughout the week. If it is a feast day they are given three hundred more days in addition to the indulgence for a third part of all their sins. Item, on the vigil of St James and on the feast for the dedication of his church they are given six hundred days in addition to the indulgence for a third part of all their sins.

Item, it was conceded by the bull of the pope St Calixtus, who was truly devoted to St James, to all pilgrims to the metropolitan church of Compostela in Galicia that when the feast of St James fell on a Sunday, they should have plenary indulgence for all their sins on the vigil and on the feast day. It would be given throughout the whole year from the first day of January to the last day of December. Item, it has been ordered by the bull of the said pope St Calixtus, ratified and confirmed by his successors, that anyone who doubts and does not firmly believe those remissions or privileges or indulgences of the said church of Compostela will incur the greater penalty of excommunication by apostolic authority. Item, it was graciously conceded to the same church by the supreme pontiffs that on the feast of the same apostle and the feast of his translation and at all times all pilgrims from the day they left home should be able to choose a confessor who would have jurisdiction by papal authority to absolve them from all papal cases whilst they were on their journey or staying at Compostela.

5 Pico: A Young Philosopher Defends His Right to Dispute in Public (1486)

Source: *Renaissance Philosophy of Man*, edited by Ernst Cassirer et al. (Chicago: Chicago University Press, 1948), pp. 237–254. Extracts from Giovanni Pico della Mirandola, *On the Dignity of Man*, abridged by Stuart Brown.

Giovanni Pico della Mirandola (1463–94) studied at the University of Ferrara. In 1479 he began friendships with Girolamo Savonarola, Marsilio Ficino and Lorenzo (II) de'Medici. In 1480 Pico transferred to the University of Padua where, until 1482, he studied Aristotle and Averroes. Eventually in 1484 he moved to Florence. He determined to produce a new synthesis of the ideas of Plato and Aristotle built around scholastic philosophy and using his Arabic and Hebrew studies. In December 1486 Pico completed 900 theses and published them as the *Conclusiones*. He invited scholars to join him in a public disputation of them. A Papal Commission examined the theses in 1487 and thirteen were found to be 'unorthodox' or 'dubious'. In the meantime Pico had prepared the speech he would have given. In 1487 Pope Innocent VIII condemned all the theses and had Pico imprisoned at Vincennes. The King of France released him and Pico lived in Florence under Lorenzo's protection. In 1496 his nephew Gianfrancesco published for the first time the prefatory oration *On the Dignity of Man* (the above-mentioned speech), extracts from which are given below. The extracts relate particularly to two contentious aspects of Pico's philosophy: his defence of natural magic and his belief in the Cabbala.

The Cabbala, a type of Jewish theosophy, using a system of cyphers, was believed to reveal to its initiates hidden doctrines within the Old Testament – for example the creation of the world by means of emanations from the Divine Being. It achieved the height of its influence during the later Middle Ages and Renaissance. A Christian form of the Cabbala was in vogue during the Renaissance, favoured by scholars such as Reuchlin and Paracelsus who professed, through its use, to deduce the doctrines of the Trinity, the Atonement and the Divinity of Christ.

23. For my part, reverend Fathers, I was not unaware that this very disputation of mine would be as grateful and pleasing to you who favour all good sciences, and have been willing to honour it with your most august presence, as it would be offensive and annoying to many others. And I know there is no lack of those who have heretofore condemned my project, and who condemn it at present on a number of grounds. Enterprises that are well and conscientiously directed toward virtue have been wont to find no fewer – not to say more – detractors than those that are wickedly and falsely directed toward vice. There are, indeed, those who do not approve of this whole method of disputation and of this institution of publicly debating on learning, maintaining that it tends rather to the parade of talent and the display of erudition than to the increase of learning. There are those who do not indeed disapprove this kind of practice, but who in no wise approve it in me because I, born I admit but twenty-four years ago, should have dared at my age to offer a disputation concerning the lofty mysteries of Christian theology, the highest topics of philosophy and unfamiliar branches of knowledge, in so famous a city, before so great an assembly of very learned men, in the presence of the apostolic senate. Others, who give me leave to offer this disputation, are unwilling to allow me to debate nine hundred theses, and misrepresent it as being a work as unnecessary and as ostentatious as it is beyond my powers. I would have yielded to their objections and given in immediately if the philosophy I profess had so instructed me; and I should not now be answering them, even with philosophy as my preceptress, if I believed that this debate between us had been undertaken for the purpose of quarrelling and scolding. Therefore, let

the whole intention to disparage and to exasperate depart from our minds, and malice also, which Plato writes is ever absent from the heavenly choir. Let us in friendly wise try both questions: whether I am to debate and whether I am to debate about this great number of theses.

24. First, as to those who revile this custom of debating in public I shall certainly not say a great deal, since this crime, if it is held a crime, is shared with me not only by all of you, excellent doctors, who have rather frequently engaged in this office not without the highest praise and glory, but also by Plato, also by Aristotle, and also by the most worthy philosophers of every age. For them it was certain that, for the attainment of the knowledge of truth they were always seeking for themselves, nothing is better than to attend as often as possible the exercise of debate. For just as bodily energy is strengthened by gymnastic exercise, so beyond doubt in this wrestling-place of letters, as it were, energy of mind becomes far stronger and more vigorous.

. . .

What were it to have dealt with the opinions of others, no matter how many, if we are come to a gathering of wise men with no contribution of our own and are supplying nothing from our own store, brought forth and worked out by our own genius? It is surely an ignoble part to be wise only from a notebook (as Seneca says)[1] and, as if the discoveries of our predecessors had closed the way to our own industry and the power of nature were exhausted in us, to produce from ourselves nothing which, if it does not actually demonstrate the truth, at least intimates it from afar.

. . .

For this reason I have not been content to add to the tenets held in common many teachings taken from the ancient theology of Hermes Trismegistus,[2] many from the doctrines of the Chaldaeans and of Pythagoras, and many from the occult mysteries of the Hebrews. I have proposed also as subjects for discussion several theses in natural philosophy and in divinity, discovered and studied by me. I have proposed, first of all, a harmony between Plato and Aristotle, believed to exist by many ere this but adequately proved by no one.

. . .

32. I have also proposed theorems dealing with magic, in which I have indicated that magic has two forms, one of which depends entirely on the

---

[1] Seneca was a Roman Stoic philosopher of the first century AD. The reference is to his *Moral Letters* xxxiii. 7.

[2] Hermes Trismegistus was a mythical Egyptian sage whose ideas represented, in the mind of Pico and others, an ancient wisdom comparable to that of Moses and Plato. Hermes Trismegistus was supposed to have taught Pythagoras who in turn was the teacher of Plato. Pico's Neoplatonist mentor Marsilio Ficino had translated the *Corpus Hermeticum* as well as various Platonic texts into Latin.

work and authority of demons, a thing to be abhorred, so help me the God of truth, and a monstrous thing. The other, when it is rightly pursued, is nothing else than the utter perfection of natural philosophy. While the Greeks make mention of both of them, they call the former γοητεία, in no wise honouring it with the name of magic; the latter they call by the characteristic and fitting name of μαγεία, as if it were a perfect and most high wisdom. For, as Porphyry says,[3] in the Persian tongue *magus* expresses the same idea as 'interpreter' and 'worshipper of the divine' with us. Moreover, Fathers, the disparity and unlikeness between these arts is great, nay, rather, the greatest possible. The former not only the Christian religion but all religions and every well-constituted state condemn and abhor. The latter all wise men, all peoples devoted to the study of heavenly and divine things, approve and embrace. The former is the most deceitful of arts; the latter a higher and more holy philosophy. The former is vain and empty; the latter, sure, trustworthy and sound . . .

33. If we ask Plato what the magic of both these men was, he will reply, in his *Alcibiades*, that the magic of Zoroaster was none other than the science of the Divine in which the kings of the Persians instructed their sons, to the end that they might be taught to rule their own commonwealth by the example of the commonwealth of the world . . . Plotinus also mentions it when he demonstrates that a *magus* is the servant of nature and not a contriver.[4] This very wise man approves and maintains this magic, so hating the other that, when he was summoned to the rites of evil spirits, he said that they should come to him rather than that he should go to them; and surely he was right. For even as the former makes man the bound slave of wicked powers, so does the latter make him their ruler and their lord. In conclusion, the former can claim for itself the name of neither art nor science, while the latter, abounding in the loftiest mysteries, embraces the deepest contemplation of the most secret things, and at last the knowledge of all nature. The latter, in calling forth into the light as if from their hiding-places the powers scattered and sown in the world by the loving-kindness of God, does not so much work wonders as diligently serve a wonder-working nature. The latter, having more searchingly examined into the harmony of the universe . . . and having clearly perceived the reciprocal affinity of natures, and applying to each single thing the suitable and peculiar inducements . . . brings forth into the open the miracles concealed in the recesses of the world, in the depths of nature, and in the storehouses and mysteries of God, just as if she herself were their maker, and, as the farmer weds his elms to vines, even so does the *magus* wed earth to heaven, that is, he weds lower things to the endowments and powers of higher things. Whence it comes about that the latter is as divine and as salutary as the former is unnatural and harmful, for this reason especially, that in subjecting man to the

[3] Porphyry was a Greek Neoplatonist of the third century and a student of Plotinus (see n. 4).
[4] Plotinus (AD 205–269/70) was the most important of the Greek Neoplatonists. The works of Plotinus were translated into Latin by Ficino in the late fifteenth century.

enemies of God, the former calls him away from God, but the latter rouses him to the admiration of God's works which is the most certain condition of a willing faith, hope, and love. For nothing moves one to religion and to the worship of God more than the diligent contemplation of the wonders of God; if we have thoroughly examined them by this natural magic we are considering, we shall be compelled to sing, more ardently inspired to the worship and love of the Creator: 'The heavens and all the earth are full of the majesty of thy glory.' And this is enough about magic. I have said these things about it, for I know there are many 'who, just as dogs always bark at strangers, in the same way often condemn and hate what they do not understand.

34. I come now to the things I have elicited from the ancient mysteries of the Hebrews and have cited for the confirmation of the inviolable Catholic faith. Lest perchance they should be deemed fabrications, trifles, or the tales of jugglers by those to whom they are unfamiliar, I wish all to understand what they are and of what sort, whence they come, by what and by how illustrious authors supported, and how mysterious, how divine, and how necessary they are to the men of our faith for defending our religion against the grievous misrepresentations of the Hebrews. Not only the famous doctors of the Hebrews, but also from among men of our opinion, Esdras, Hilary, and Origen,[5] write that Moses on the mount received from God not only the Law, which he left to posterity written down in five books, but also a true and more occult explanation of the Law. It was, moreover, commanded him of God by all means to proclaim the Law to the people but not to commit the interpretation of the Law to writing or to make it a matter of common knowledge. He himself should reveal it only to Iesu Nave,[6] who in his turn should unveil it to the other high priests to come after him, under a strict obligation of silence. It was enough through guileless story to recognize now the power of God, now his wrath against the wicked, his mercy to the righteous, his justice to all; and through divine and beneficial precepts to be brought to a good and happy way of life and the worship of true religion. But to make public the occult mysteries, the secrets of the supreme Godhead hidden beneath the shell of the Law and under a clumsy show of words – what else were this than to give a holy thing to dogs and to cast pearls before swine? Therefore to keep hidden from the people the things to be shared by the initiate, among whom alone, Paul says, he spoke

[5] Esdras: This is the Greek and Latin form of Ezra. The Books of Ezra form two books of the Septuagint, the most influential of the Greek versions of the Old Testament. Hilary: This is Hilary of Poitiers (c. AD 315–67) who, as Bishop of Poitiers, was involved in the Arian disputes about the divinity of Christ. He was the most respected Latin theologian of his time. His chief works were De Trinitate (Against the Arians), De Synodis and Opus Historicum. Origen: He was an Alexandrian biblical critic and theologian (c. AD 185–254). His De Principiis presented a systematic exposition of Christian doctrine. There was a strong element of mysticism in his thought.

[6] Iesu Nave: A reference to Joshua Ben Nun, who succeeded Moses not only as leader of the Jewish nation but, according to Ecclesiasticus 46: 1, 'in the prophetic office'. (See New English Bible, Apocrypha, 1970, p. 183.)

wisdom, was not the part of human deliberation but of divine command. This custom the ancient philosophers most reverently observed, for Pythagoras wrote nothing except a few trifles, which he entrusted on his deathbed to his daughter Dama. The Sphinxes carved on the temples of the Egyptians reminded them that mystic doctrines should be kept inviolable from the common herd by means of the knots of riddles . . .

. . .

35. In exactly the same way, when the true interpretation of the Law according to the command of God, divinely handed down to Moses, was revealed, it was called the Cabbala, a word which is the same among the Hebrews as 'reception' among ourselves; for this reason, of course, that one man from another, by a sort of hereditary right, received that doctrine not through written records but through a regular succession of revelations. But after the Hebrews were restored by Cyrus from the Babylonian captivity, and after the temple had been established anew under Zorobabel, they brought their attention to the restoration of the Law. Esdras, then the head of the church, after the book of Moses had been amended, when he plainly recognized that, because of the exiles, the massacres, the flights, and the captivity of the children of Israel, the custom instituted by their forefathers of transmitting the doctrine from mouth to mouth could not be preserved, and that it would come to pass that the mysteries of the heavenly teachings divinely bestowed on them would be lost, since the memory of them could not long endure without the aid of written records, decided that those of the elders then surviving should be called together and that each one should impart to the gathering whatever he possessed by personal recollection concerning the mysteries of the Law and that scribes should be employed to collect them into seventy volumes (about the number of elders in the Sanhedrin). That you may not have to rely on me alone in this matter, Fathers, hear Esdras himself speak thus: 'And it came to pass, when the forty days were fulfilled, that the Most High spake unto me, saying, The first that thou hast written publish openly, and let the worthy and the unworthy read it: but keep the seventy last books, that thou mayst deliver them to such as be wise among thy people: for in them is the spring of understanding, the fountain of wisdom, and the stream of knowledge. And I did so.' And these are the words of Esdras to the letter. These are the books of cabbalistic lore. In these books principally resides, as Esdras with a clear voice justly declared, the spring of understanding, that is, the ineffable theology of the supersubstantial deity; the fountain of wisdom, that is, the exact metaphysic of the intellectual and angelic forms; and the stream of knowledge, that is, the most steadfast philosophy of natural things. Pope Sixtus the Fourth who last preceded the pope under whom we are now fortunate to be living, Innocent the Eighth, took the greatest pains and interest in seeing that these books should be translated into the Latin tongue for a public service to our faith, and, when he died, three of them had been done into Latin. Among the Hebrews of the present day these books are cherished with such devotion that it is permitted no man to touch them unless he be forty years of age.

36.   When I had purchased these books at no small cost to myself, when I had read them through with the greatest diligence and with unwearying toil, I saw in them (as God is my witness) not so much the Mosaic as the Christian religion. There is the mystery of the Trinity, there the Incarnation of the Word, there the divinity of the Messiah; there I have read about original sin, its expiation through Christ, the heavenly Jerusalem, the fall of the devils, the orders of the angels, purgatory, and the punishments of hell, the same things we read daily in Paul and Dionysius,[7] in Jerome and Augustine. But in those parts which concern philosophy you really seem to hear Pythagoras and Plato, whose principles are so closely related to the Christian faith that our Augustine gives immeasurable thanks to God that the books of the Platonists have come into his hands. Taken altogether, there is absolutely no controversy between ourselves and the Hebrews on any matter, with regard to which they cannot be refuted and gainsaid out of the cabbalistic books, so that there will not be even a corner left in which they may hide themselves. I have as a most weighty witness of this fact that very learned man Antonius Chronicus who, when I was with him at a banquet, with his own ears heard Dactylus, a Hebrew trained in this lore, with all his heart agree entirely to the Christian idea of the Trinity.

6 Thomas Aquinas, *Summa Theologica* (thirteenth century)

Source: St Thomas Aquinas, *Summa Theologica*, translated by Fathers of the English Dominican Province (London: Burns, Oates & Washbourne, 1922), pp. 116–18. Abridged by Susan Khin Zaw.

Thomas Aquinas (*c*.1225–74), Dominican philosopher and theologian, was canonized in 1323. His theology and his method dominated the universities of Europe throughout the later Middle Ages. *Summa Theologica* was the last of his works, unfinished at his death. It has been described as 'the highest achievement of medieval theological systematization'. His thought is characterized by a sharply drawn distinction between reason and faith. Many of the great Christian truths lie outside the province of reason – but the revealed truth of, for example, the Incarnation is not contrary to reason. Aquinas thought that reason could aid faith by providing arguments in favour of Christian doctrine and making clearer what has been revealed. A premise would be drawn from the Church's authorities (Scripture or the writings of the Early Fathers) and a conclusion was reached through the application of formal logic to this premise. This was a way of reaching new truths and extending knowledge. The extract below demonstrates the scholastic method in operation.

---

[7] Dionysius the Areopagite (Saint) revered as first Bishop of Athens and disciple of St Paul, who was confused in the Middle Ages with an author (*c*. AD 500) of whom little is now known apart from his name, Dionysius, but whose writings enjoyed enormous authority in the Middle Ages because of the confusion!

QUESTION 88, ARTICLE 6

WHETHER IT IS MORE PRAISEWORTHY AND MERITORIOUS TO DO SOMETHING IN
FULFILMENT OF A VOW THAN WITHOUT A VOW.

. . .

Objection I. It would seem that it is more praiseworthy and meritorious to do a thing without a vow than in fulfilment of a vow. Prosper says (*De Vita Contempl*. [*Of the Contemplative Life*]): 'We should abstain or fast without putting ourselves under the necessity of fasting, lest that which we are free to do be done without devotion and unwillingly.' Now he who vows to fast puts himself under the necessity of fasting. Therefore it would be better for him to fast without taking the vow.

. . .

ON THE contrary: A gloss on the words of Psalm 75: 12, 'Vow ye and pay', says, 'Vows are counselled to the will'. But a counsel is about none but a better good. Therefore it is better to do a deed in fulfilment of a vow than without a vow: since he that does it without a vow fulfils only one counsel, viz. the counsel to do it, whereas he that does it with a vow, fulfils two counsels, viz. the counsel to vow and the counsel to do it.

I ANSWER that: For three reasons it is better and more meritorious to do one and the same deed with a vow than without. First, because to vow, as stated above (Article 5), is an act of religion which is the chief of the moral virtues.[1] Now the more excellent the virtue the better and more meritorious the deed. Wherefore the act of an inferior virtue is the better and the more meritorious for being commanded by a superior virtue, whose act it becomes through being commanded by it, just as the act of faith or hope is better if it be commanded by charity. Hence the works of the other moral virtues (for instance, fasting, which is an act of chastity) are better and more meritorious, if they be done in fulfilment of a vow, since thus they belong to the divine worship, being like sacrifices to God. Whereon Augustine says (*De Virg*. [*Of Virginity*] viii) that 'not even is virginity honourable as such, but only when it is consecrated to God, and cherished by godly continence.'

Secondly, because he that vows something and does it, subjects himself to God more than he that only does it; for he subjects himself to God not only as to the act, but also as to the power, since in future he cannot do something else. Even so he gives more who gives the tree with its fruit, than he that gives the fruit only, as Anselm (Eadmer) observes (*De Simil*. viii). For this reason, we thank even those who promise, as stated above (Article 5).

[1] Here is Aquinas's earlier explanation of this: 'It is evident from what has been said above that a vow is a promise made to God, and that a promise is nothing else than a directing of the thing promised to the person to whom the promise is made. Hence a vow is a directing of the thing vowed to the worship or service of God. And thus it is clear that to take a vow is properly an act of . . . religion.'

Thirdly, because a vow fixes the will on the good immovably and to do anything of a will that is fixed on the good belongs to the perfection of virtue, according to the Philosopher (*Ethic*. ii. 4),[2] just as to sin with an obstinate mind aggravates the sin, and is called a sin against the Holy Ghost, as stated above (Question 14, Article 2).

Reply to Objection I. The passage quoted should be understood as referring to necessity of coercion which causes an act to be involuntary and excludes devotion. Hence he says pointedly: 'Lest that which we are free to do be done without devotion and unwillingly.' On the other hand the necessity resulting from a vow is caused by the immobility of the will, wherefore it strengthens the will and increases devotion. Hence the argument does not conclude.

7 Lorenzo Valla, *The Profession of the Religious* (1439–1440)

Source: Lorenzo Valla, *The Profession of the Religious* and *The Falsely Believed and Forged Donation of Constantine*, translated and edited by Olga Zorzi Pugliese (Toronto: Centre for Reformation and Renaissance Studies, 1985), pp. 18–34. Abridged by Susan Khin Zaw.

Lorenzo Valla (1407–57) was the son of an ecclesiastical advocate at Rome. After a brief lecturing career in Pavia, Milan and Genoa (1431–5) Valla became secretary to King Alfonso of Naples (1435–48). Employed by the Papal Curia, 1448–57, he was Apostolic Secretary 1455–7. His *De Elegantiae Linguae Latinae*, a major study of Latin usage completed in 1440 and later revised and published, served as a basic humanist text throughout the fifteenth, sixteenth and seventeenth centuries. The *Collatio Novi Testamenti* of 1443, revised in the 1450s, had a profound influence on Erasmus, who adopted Valla's method of biblical criticism. Valla criticized the Vulgate translation and demonstrated his awareness of the theological implications of varying translations. It was Valla who laid the foundations for a philological scriptural theology which eventually replaced scholastic theology. These activities exposed him to charges of heresy in 1444. Although rescued by the intervention of Alfonso I, Valla became wary of the authorities. As a consequence he later restricted the circulation and therefore the influence of the *De Professione Religiosorum* (1439–40) which criticized the claim of the religious bound by vows to greater merit than other Christians, whether members of the laity or the secular clergy. Extracts of this critique of the religious are printed below.

Among historical writings ... is there not yet such diversity due to the unevenness of the authors, that you read and reread one with an attentive,

---

[2] Aristotle (384–322 BC), Greek philosopher. He was a disciple of Plato but one with a very different philosophical position. He asserted that an idea exists only as expressed in the individual object or 'matter'. Aristotle's *Ethics* has had enormous influence. He saw the ideal life as one of moderation between extremes – courage, for example, strikes a happy medium between cowardice and foolhardiness.

engrossed, and engaged mind, whereas you skim through the other negligently and sleepily, unable to read it through to the end? Why is this so? Because in the former it appears that great, important and critical matters are described; in the latter, petty, commonplace, and unimportant ones. Now, in truth, do you not see how even in judicial cases one orator's speech is passionate, while another's is cold, and when the first declaims, the judges and the audience first become angry, then calm down; at one point they rejoice, cheer and laugh, at another feeling pity and sorrow, they weep; whereas when the other delivers his speech, they can hardly resist sleep or even succumb to it?

Leaving aside countless examples of this, I shall proceed to theology, which is the subject I am going to write about. Who, I ask, does not dare to compose works in this field, even in the most difficult branches of it? Thus, not without reason Horace said: 'We all write poems, whether we know how to do it or not.' What he says of poets I apply to theologians. There is such a difference among writers of theology that, when I compare those who treat a common theme, they do not appear to be speaking on the same subject even; rather, one deals with the most weighty matters, another with the most insignificant; one with the stars, another with little flowers. One appears to creep listlessly, to sleep, snore, and dream, the other moves in a felicitous flight, now, as it were, ranging the sky, then frolicking in a circle, at one time plunging in a headlong descent and, at another, returning on high with the same speed.

I am not saying this, of course, as though I myself possessed these laudable qualities, but simply in order to illustrate the diversity of talents that exert themselves in the same field. Clearly, those who discourse sublimely, eloquently, and with grandeur, do not necessarily owe their success to their subject matter, nor do those who express themselves aridly, feebly, and poorly derive these results from the dryness of their theme. The cause lies in the writer rather than in that which is written about . . .

It has been my custom up to now, and it will be even more so in the future, to follow the style and the opinions of both the Greek and Latin ancients, and to speak frankly, according to their practice.

[Valla then explains the origin of the ensuing dialogue. In the course of a discussion with friends, among whom is a friar, about a political conspiracy in which priests were involved, one of the company suggests jeeringly that treachery is just the sort of thing one would expect friars to engage in. The friar defends the dignity of his order, claiming, among other things, that 'although both you and I conduct our lives in a similar manner, I, nevertheless, shall receive a greater reward from God than you.' The company express some scepticism about this, and urge Valla and the friar to debate the matter, which they do as follows; 'Laurentius' is the Latin form of Valla's Christian name 'Lorenzo'.]

Laurentius: In order to remove all trace of ambiguity from our discussion, I ask, first of all, for a clarification. You were saying that, although you and our friend Paulus may lead similar lives, you will receive a greater reward from God. Does this mean that although two persons may not differ at all with respect to the nature of their minds and bodies, and even though the same external things that befall mankind await both of them, and both their lives are engaged in the same activities, yet a greater gift from God is owing to him who professes your sect (which you call 'religion' [*religio*], and hence you call yourselves 'religious') than to him who has not professed, nor wishes to profess, any sect, neither yours nor that of the monks nor any other?

Friar: Before I can answer you on this point, you oblige me to express astonishment at your manner of speaking. You think that our Rule should be called a 'sect' and not a 'religious order' and that we should not be called 'religious', as though either we *are not* religious or certain other persons *are* religious. Thereby you call into question not only the merits of our profession, which constitute the subject of our discussion, but indeed the name itself. Stripping us even of our title, in spite of the fact that it is by now long established, you disgrace us with another, and a shameful, one. Consequently you are more abusive towards us than Paulus was, for he said ours is a religious order, not a sect.

Laur: Indeed my purpose was not to quarrel over words, especially since we have established another topic for our debate, or to divert our discussions into a different channel. But since you bid me to account for this, I shall answer you. When I engage in disputations in the company of learned men like those here present, I am not in the habit of using terms that are approved by the masses rather than by experts, unless a preliminary explanation or some evidence is given. Otherwise it would seem that, in adopting them, I accept them, and thus I could be refuted on the grounds of the terminology I use, as we see happening in judicial trials. I could cite examples of this if I were not afraid of dwelling too long on such a pedantic matter. Indeed one should not only speak with precision out of mere necessity, as I have had to do now, but also for the sake of the beauty of the language. Restricting myself to your vocabulary, should I say, according to your usage, *observantia* instead of *observatio*, *guardianus* instead of *custos*, *claustrum* instead of *atrium* or *porticus*, *ecclesia* instead of *templum*; *sacristia* instead of *sacrarium*; *libraria* instead of *biblioteca*; *stola* instead of *vitta*; *indulgentia* instead of *venia*; *confessor* instead of *the person who hears the confessions of sinners*; *antiphana* instead of *antiphóna*, a word which you friars corrupt both in spelling and pronunciation, and so on?[1]

Nevertheless, as for your wondering at my having preferred to say 'sect' instead of 'religious order', you should know that I have been concerned not only with the question of elegance of expression, but also with the logic of the matter. Since I do not think, as you do, that so much store should be set by your way of life, it seemed excessive that you should ascribe such a sacred and venerable name to it. If this were not the case, there would be nothing

---

[1] Valla is here urging a return to classical Latin usage, instead of the medieval Latin terms then current. The shifts in meaning of the words he cites have been used to draw up the table at the end of this document. The final word he cites, *antíphana*, is a Latinized version of a Greek word. *Antiphóna* is nearer the original Greek.

for us to debate. For, if you friars alone are religious, one will have to concede that you are the best of all men. That this is not so, as I believe, is what I shall be discussing. First, therefore, I shall comment on the two terms that you have asked me to explain.

The term *sect* is used properly in connection with philosophers although there were sects even in the field of rhetoric among the followers of Theodorus and Apollodorus.[2] They can be found in law and in other disciplines as well. Sects, which in Greek are called αἱρέσεις [*hairéseis*],[3] are different ways of teaching, acquiring, and practising wisdom. For the Stoics think and live in one manner, the Cyrenaics in another, the Peripatetics, Academics and the rest in different ways.[4] You too do something similar, and not just because some of you are monks and friars, some hermits and some spiritual brothers, but also because there are thousands of such individual groups, as the variety of habits you wear indicates. Sometimes I laugh, sometimes I become angry when I see such vastly diverse attire on display throughout the city. Indeed, scarcely more types and colours are to be found among the uniforms of the military. Therefore if the philosophers themselves have termed their different ways of thinking and living 'sects', you must not be surprised if I too call those varying styles of life of yours 'sects'. Nevertheless I am not concerned whether you accept this term or not, nor am I discussing what name ought to be bestowed on you. I do question though the name already given you, and the second part of my argument was whether you should be called 'religious'.

On this subject, then, let me continue the comparison with philosophers. These thinkers are insufferable when they claim for themselves exclusively the appellation 'seekers of wisdom' and refuse to share it with any others, whether they be legislators, illustrious senators, supreme orators, or most just sovereigns. Nevertheless, cities were governed through the wisdom of these groups both before and after the appearance of philosophers. Similarly who can put up with you when you state that none save yourselves are religious, not priests, popes, nor anyone else? It is a claim that makes you look not merely presumptuous on your own account, but also insolent toward all others. For what more lavish praise can I receive, or, on the other hand, more severe reproof, than to be called 'religious' or 'irreligious'? Now, what does it mean to be religious, if not to be a Christian, and indeed a true Christian? I am not referring to the sense in which tombs are called 'religious' and judges and other persons are said to be 'religious'.[5] I am talking now of divinely-inspired religion. Although there are many religions, yet those that are false are not termed 'religious', but are considered and called 'superstitions', at least by those who are acquainted with true religion.

---

[2] Theodorus and Apollodorus were rhetoricians of classical times. Apollodorus taught Augustus, Theodorus Tiberius. They are mentioned in this capacity by Quintilian (*Institutio oratoria* III. i. 17–18).

[3] The word 'heresy' is derived from the Greek *hairéseis*.

[4] Stoics, Cyrenaics, Peripatetics, Academics: these were all schools of ancient philosophy.

[5] The tomb of a saint, for instance, might be called a religious site, in the sense of 'venerable' or 'holy'. A judge might be said to be religiously honest, in the sense of 'scrupulously'.

True religion itself should actually be designated simply 'religion' without the attribute 'true', and, moreover, without the qualification 'of Christ', since religion and faith are one and the same, as is a religious and a faithful person. For I describe as 'faithful' not the person who is like a dead man incapable of works, but one who is active and can truly be called a Christian. As James says:

> If any man among you seem to be religious, and bridleth not his tongue, but deceiveth his own heart, this man's religion is vain. Pure religion and undefiled before God and the Father is this, To visit the fatherless and widowed in their affliction, and to keep himself unspotted from the world. (James 1: 26–7)

Therefore when you judge only yourselves to be religious, because you have made a religious profession, whereas you deny that others are religious, are you not in essence indicating that you alone are Christians, you alone are good, pure and untainted, and thus you condemn and disdain others and cast them down into Tartarus [hell]
. . .

Many others who have not professed your 'sect' or 'Rule', must be called religious since they live the purest of lives, whereas many of you can not be called religious, since you live most sinfully.
    Friar: There are arguments I could adduce in answer to your speech.[6] However . . . let us now proceed on the path by which we started.
    Laur: Then answer the questions I asked. Do you recall what they were?
    Friar: Why should I not remember them since both you and I are saying the same thing? That is, all else being equal, we who have professed religion acquire more merit than others who may practise the same behaviour in their lives. For example, I am more meritorious than you, even though we deem ourselves to be very similar in spirit, body, conduct, and in all else, except for this one thing.
    Laur: That is precisely the point. We cannot be similar at all, since we differ in opinion so radically.
. . .

Laur: . . . the issue itself is badly put.
    Friar: Why?
    Laur: How can we be equal with respect to our conduct when we lead lives that are so different? You are bound to poverty, chastity and obedience while I am not. Thus your behaviour differs from mine, your virtues from mine, and neither of us has anything in common with the other. It is as though you were a good painter and I a good architect. No comparison between the two is possible, and it would be very foolish to declare one superior to the other, especially if each is perfect in his kind.

---

[6] The friar's claim about the greater merit of the religious life would follow from Aquinas's conclusion that it is better and more meritorious to do something with a vow than without a vow.

Friar: Suppose that, being equal in everything else, we differ in these things only.

Laur: But this amounts, so to speak, to praising you friars for architecture too, and not praising us laymen even for painting. You wish to defeat us with those three virtues, but you certainly must not be allowed to do so, since you can be surpassed by us in qualities which are different from those. It is a virtue to endure poverty, but it is also a moral act to distribute wealth. Chastity is good, but marriage is equally so. Obeying is a virtue, but so is ruling wisely. Thus some persons possess the latter qualities, some the former; no one possesses both.

Friar: You may have virtues that are different from ours, but they are by no means commensurate with ours, since we have taken vows.

Laur: The question will be reversed then.

Friar: How is that?

Laur: We were investigating whether you and I deserve the same reward for the same deeds. As things stand, our conduct cannot be the same. What will our point of contention be then?

Friar: Let us modify it thus, if it seems appropriate: between two persons who lead most holy lives, like you and me, I am more deserving by the mere fact that I have pronounced vows. However, even if the rest of our virtues are different in kind, they can be equal in magnitude.

Laur: I must confess to you already that you are saying an astonishing thing. Certainly everyone will at once refuse to concede it, recalling the holiest of men who are already enthroned in the Kingdom of Heaven. Why do you think that professing vows is so efficacious?

Friar: I can recall, or think of, three reasons. The first is that we promise to obey the following three rules at all times and in all places: to obey our superiors, to live in poverty and in chastity. The second is that we bind ourselves by the vow, from which we are not allowed to retreat. The third is that, since a more severe punishment awaits us if we sin, there will be a more generous reward if we refrain from sin. Indeed one can see that other men do not wish to undertake these things, either because they are reluctant to do without human goods, or, indeed, because they fear the harsher penalty they will receive if they break their pact. This is why those who profess religion deserve praise for their magnanimity in facing those difficulties and for their tolerance in enduring them . . .

[Valla objects that the friar has advanced not three reasons, but one, since the first two are identical and are connected with the third. The friar accepts this, thinking nothing much hangs on it, and Valla proceeds:]

Laur: You argue that, by the very fact that, if you sin, a more severe chastisement awaits you, it follows that, if you do not sin, your rewards will be more numerous. This, say you, necessarily befalls you who have professed religion.

It seems to me that, just as something is worthy of the greatest reward when it is done properly, so too it is deserving of the lightest penalty when it is badly done; on the other hand, that which merits a harsh punishment if it turns out badly, by the same token deserves a minimal prize if it does not go amiss. For the highest reward is owing to the greatest virtue and the severest punishment to the gravest offence. Similarly, the most paltry reward is due to the least degree of virtue and the lightest punishment is required by the most venial of sins. Thus, if your virtue is not considerable, it does not merit a large recompense. To make this clearer, it will be necessary to support it with illustrations and weigh it, as it were, against the testimony of men and the decisions of the courts. Which, then, if I may put the question to you, is worthy of greater praise and greater reward, that is to say, which showed more virtue: the person who, at some risk to his own person, snatched his parent, who was in deadly peril, from a shipwreck, for example, or from a fire, or a collapsing building, or he who saved a fellow citizen or a stranger?

Friar: He who saved a fellow citizen or a stranger.

Laur: I also ask: if one of the two, the son or the stranger, should neglect to save the person who, as I said, is in danger, although he is able to do it without great effort, which would be more guilty and more deserving of censure?

Friar: Certainly the son, and not only should he be rebuked but should also be given a very severe penalty, whereas the other does not even deserve to be reproached, let alone chastised.

Laur: You are right. And so that an authority will not be lacking in our discussion, let us recall what that old man in Quintilian says against his son: 'It is not a favour to support one's father; rather, it is a crime to deny support'.[7] One can cite endless examples of this type; if a doctor cures or fails to cure a most serious illness; if in a terrible storm a captain arrives in port having saved the ship or if he is shipwrecked; if in a war a group of young boys put an equal number of grown men to flight or flee before them; if a beautiful woman is chaste or unchaste; if, without a teacher, one becomes learned or remains ignorant. The principle is the same in the opposite case, namely, if a doctor is faced with a very slight disease or a captain with a calm sea; if mature men in war encounter the same number of boys; if a woman is ugly; or if one has a teacher. These are all circumstances in which those who are found to be most at fault, if they neglect virtue, merit only the slightest commendation if they have not neglected to act virtuously.

The same can be said in your case. You friars who, if we are to believe you, are subject to a greater penalty for your sins, are therefore rewarded for your virtuous action with a lesser prize, as I have shown, just like a physician who receives hardly any praise for curing a simple disease but, on the other hand, the sharpest reproof if he does not know how to treat it. Oh how excellent and desirable is the life of friars and monks, who are granted more meagre rewards and more abundant punishments than others! If this is so, I shall not ask with what countenance you dare to exhort others to join a similar

---

[7] Quintilian: Roman lawyer and teacher of rhetoric, born *c*. AD 35. Not a Christian. He founded the first school of rhetoric, and one work by him survives – an exhaustive manual of rhetoric called *Institutio oratoria*. It teaches the art of presenting a convincing case to a law court. Logic is only one of the skills necessary for this purpose, and not the most important one. Quintilian was much revered by Valla both as a Latin stylist and as a rhetorician.

institution, but rather what can prompt you to be able to endure such a mode of existence.

Friar: There you go condemning religious orders with your words, not just by saying their activities are useless and completely unproductive, but also by making the members of those orders out to be exerting themselves to their own disadvantage, since they subject themselves to graver dangers and cheat themselves of more ample rewards.

Laur: You understand, then, that your mode of reasoning is inappropriate. It is against this that I am arguing, not against your Order. I maintain that reason supports my position rather than yours. So, if you are not satisfied with my conclusion you will have to reproach yourself, not me, because you introduced this argument. You will have to retract it, even if I were to let it stand.

Friar: I will certainly not retract it; on the contrary, I uphold and defend it as being true, well-founded, and evident, even though you are trying to create confusion with your discourse. Would I not receive harsher punishment than you if I were to give myself over to wanton pleasures?

Laur: Later I show whether you would be sinning or not; but now, since you want me to grant this, I shall.

Friar: Then why should I not receive a greater reward too?

Laur: Have I not already answered that this is not at all a logical consequence?

[In further exchanges, the friar continues to fail to get the point, and Valla continues to reiterate it. Then:]

Laur: . . . thus far, you have not demonstrated at all why we should believe you deserve a greater reward. This is why I ask repeatedly for what reasons you have so exalted an opinion of your religious profession.

Friar: Do you not see that it is because of the act of professing itself which, constrained through its vows, involves the obligation to observe such difficult rules?

Laur: No, I do not, especially since you admit you have been refuted on the subject we have been debating. And what you now assert is another question, namely whether religious vows in themselves have merit or not.

Friar: I certainly have not been refuted on the former point. But let us postpone it for a moment while we examine this second question. On this topic I cannot be brought to believe that you will have anything to urge against myself, that is to say, against mankind at large.

Laur: Do you say you cannot be persuaded? But watch with what fervour I am going to speak against you. I maintain that from the very first words you friars utter, you do not know what you are talking about at all. You employ ignorantly the term '*votum*' ['vow'] which has two significations: according to the first, it is taken to stand for 'greed' and 'desire', as in Virgil: 'That crop, which twice has felt the sun's heat and the frost twice, will answer at last the *prayers* [*votis*] of the never-satisfied farmer' [Virgil, *Georgics* tr. C. Day Lewis]. The second meaning is that of a promise made to God, that we shall do something to please him, if, in return, he will first grant the favour

we beg of him, provided it is not something unjust, of course. In Virgil again we read: 'and sailors ashore shall pay their *vows* [*vota*] for a safe return.'
. . .

However that so-called 'vow' of yours cannot be taken to be such in either of the two accepted senses, although you would like to adopt it in its second meaning. This you will absolutely not be allowed to do. For what vow can we find, either in false religions or the true one, that can be taken without the condition I mentioned? Did Jacob perhaps make an unconditional promise when, as he travelled toward Mesopotamia, he said:

> If God will be with me, and will keep me in this way that I go, and will give me bread to eat, and raiment to put on, so that I come again to my father's house in peace; then shall the Lord be my God: and this stone, which I have set for a pillar, shall be God's house: and of all that thou shalt give me I will surely give the tenth unto thee. (Genesis 28: 20–2)

[Valla gives two more biblical examples in support of his case.]

But why do I mention these examples, as if the matter were not perfectly clear? You cite a single vow that has no condition and you will have won.

Friar: None comes to mind now. Is our taking vows meaningless then? Or how do you define what we call a 'vow'?

Laur: What else if not a promise or an oath?

Friar: Why is it not also a vow? He who binds himself with a vow makes a promise.

Laur: But not all who make promises bind themselves by a vow. You yourselves are separating the promise from the vow when you say 'I promise and vow'.

Friar: Let us divide vows into two types, conditional and unconditional.

Laur: You are taking refuge in the permissiveness, or rather fatuousness, of distinctions. How do you dare to call a 'vow' what no man of learning has designated as such? To put it bluntly, you speak that way out of ignorance.

Friar: Were the many learned men who have left books written on the subject not allowed to speak that way and to call every promise made under oath a 'vow'?

Laur: Are you saying that they were allowed what is inadmissable? Try saying that before the Greeks, Hebrews and ancient Latins. Let one of them rise up now and prove that all those you judge to be worthy of imitation lack preparation and knowledge. He would silence you in a severe tone thus: 'O you ignorant souls, should we allow ourselves to be guided by men rather than by God? For God separated vows from promises made under oath.'

[Valla supports his claim with another biblical quotation. He then goes on to argue that there is no special merit in accompanying a promise with an oath, (1) because of a point he raised earlier, in an omitted passage, that if I promise to accompany you and confirm it by swearing, I do you one favour not two, (2) because oaths are inappropriate between man and God, indeed are expressly forbidden in the New

Testament. He then shifts the topic of debate again, to whether the things promised by the religious orders – obedience, poverty and chastity – have special merit; and claims that they do not, developing the point already made on p. 35: 'It is a virtue to endure poverty, but it is also a moral act to distribute wealth. Chastity is good, but marriage is equally so. Obeying is a virtue, but so is ruling wisely.' Finally he points out that a man who endures an operation without being held down is more virtuous than one who has to be held down for the operation, and compares entrants to the religious orders to the man who has to be held down: 'What else induced you to make the pledge, or what was the point of promising, if not the possibility that, in using your own free will, some cause would make you deviate from the worship of God? This is why almost all who join your community are evil, abominable, destitute, and alone. They despair of being able to serve God or their own body well in any other way. Thus it is not improper to say that a convent is a refuge like that of Romulus, where all the rabble of the city and the dregs of humanity converged.' However, he follows this with a paragraph in praise of friars who fulfil their vocation worthily.]

Latin word	Classical Latin meaning	Medieval Latin meaning
observantia	divine worship	religious order
observatio	observance	
guardianus	(the word is medieval Latin of Germanic origin)	warden
custos	guard	
claustrum	lock	cloister
atrium	court	
porticus	colonnade	
ecclesia	assembly of the people	church
templum	temple	
sacristia	sacrarium	sacristy
biblioteca	library	
libraria	bookshop	library
stola	garment worn by women	stole worn by priests
vitta	band worn by priests	
indulgentia	gentleness	remission of sins
venia	pardon	

8 Erasmus and John Colet (1499–1516)

Desiderius Erasmus (c.1466–1536) was educated by the Brethren of the Common Life at Deventer in Holland, where he early came under humanist influence. In 1486 he became an Augustinian Canon at Steyn near Gouda and began to read the Classics and the Fathers. In 1492 he was ordained priest and in 1495 began to study at Paris, residing in the College of Montaigu. Here his dislike of scholasticism became established. He took pupils in order to make a living and produced his own teaching materials for them. Among these pupils was William Lord Mountjoy, whom Erasmus accompanied to England in 1499. During this visit Erasmus was received by John Colet (*c*.1466–1519) who encouraged his dislike of scholasticism and directed him towards Old and New Testament study. In 1497 Colet had delivered his famous series of lectures on the Epistles of St Paul which called for a return to the discipline of the primitive Church. From this meeting of true minds arose a lively correspondence over the next few years, from which we print extracts below. Erasmus always exhibited a great interest in letter-writing as a literary form. See, for example, his treatise *De Conscribendis Epistolis* (*On the Writing of Letters*) of 1499, which was first published in 1521.

A. Erasmus to John Colet, October 1499

Source: *Collected Works of Erasmus*, translated by R. A. B. Mynors and D. F. S. Thompson; annotated by Wallace K. Ferguson (Toronto: University of Toronto Press, 1974), I. 203–7 abridged.

In this letter, written from St Mary's College, Oxford, Erasmus expresses his distaste for scholasticism and his praise for Colet's attempts to restore the ancient theology. He notes Colet's advice that he, Erasmus, should work on the Old Testament but professes his unworthiness for such a task. Nevertheless, Erasmus says, he is not interested in continuing to profess secular learning. Yet devotion to Scriptural study requires a technical expertise which he does not yet possess. Colet, an eminent English humanist, was Dean of St Paul's Cathedral and founder of St Paul's School, 1509.

Oxford, 1499

... Now let me briefly turn to your letter, in order to make sure that the boy who brought it shall not return to you empty-handed. When you tell me that you dislike the modern class of theologians, who spend their lives in sheer hair-splitting and sophistical quibbling, you have my emphatic agreement, dear Colet. It is not that I condemn their learned studies, I who have nothing but praise for learning of any sort, but these studies are isolated, and not seasoned with references to any well-written works of an older age, and so they seem to me likely to give a man a smattering of knowledge or a taste for arguing. But whether they can make him wise, others may judge; for they exhaust the intelligence by a kind of sterile and thorny subtlety, in no way quickening it with vital sap or breathing into it the breath of life; and, worst of all, by their stammering, foul, and squalid style of writing, they render unattractive that great queen of all sciences, theology, enriched and adorned as she has been by the eloquence of antiquity. In this way they choke up, as it were with brambles, the way of a science that early thinkers had cleared and, attempting to settle all questions, so they claim, merely envelop all in darkness. Thus you can see her, once supremely revered and full of majesty, today all but silent, impoverished, and in rags; while we are seduced by the attractions of a perverted and insatiable passion for quibbling. One quarrel leads to another, and with extraordinary arrogance we quarrel over insignificant trifles.

Moreover, lest we seem to have made no progress beyond the discoveries of the early Fathers, we have had the effrontery to lay down a number of fixed procedures that God used, we claim, in working out his hidden purposes, though it would sometimes be more pious to believe in the fact while conceding to the omnipotence of God alone the knowledge of how it comes to be. Further, in our eagerness to show off our knowledge, we sometimes debate questions of a sort intolerable to truly religious men, as when we ask whether God could have taken the form of the Devil or an ass. Perhaps one ought to put up with such things when a youth dabbles in them slightly for the sake, as it were, of whetting his mind's edge; but these are the things over which we grow old – even die – as upon the rocks of the Sirens, relegating all literature to an inferior place in comparison with them. And moreover, nowadays practically no one devotes himself to the study of theology, the highest branch of learning, except such as, having sluggish or disordered wits, are scarcely fit for letters at all.

Now, I would wish to say these things not of good and scholarly professors of divinity, for whom I have an especially warm regard and respect, but only of the squalid mob of carping theologues, who hold all men's culture worthless save their own. Inasmuch as you, Colet, have undertaken to do battle with this invincible tribe, for the sake of restoring to as much of its early splendour and dignity as you can that ancient true theology, overgrown as it is with the entanglements introduced by the modern school, as God loves me, you have assumed a responsibility of the most creditable sort, one that is a true labour of love towards theology herself, and will enormously benefit every studious person, and this most flourishing university of Oxford in particular, yet nevertheless is, to be quite honest, an extremely difficult and unpopular undertaking. Your difficulties, indeed, will be surmounted by a combination of scholarship and hard work; as for unpopularity, your generous nature will manage without trouble to overlook that. Even among divines themselves there are, too, not a few who could and would offer assistance to endeavours as honourable as yours; or rather, everyone will lend a hand, since there is not a soul, even among the doctors, in this famous university who has not listened with the greatest attention to the lectures you have given on the Pauline epistles for the past three years. In regard to this, which should one praise more: the modesty of the professors, who are not abashed to appear merely as audience at the lectures of a man who is young in years and unprovided with the authority of the doctorate, as it is called, or your own unequalled combination of learning, eloquence, and moral integrity, which they judge to be worthy of this honour?

What surprises me, however, is not that you have taken so heavy a burden upon your shoulders – your strength is fit to match it – but that you are inviting my insignificant self to share in this grand undertaking. For you urge, or rather almost demand with threats, that, just as you are doing by your lectures on Paul, so I should try this winter to set alight the enthusiasms of this university, which you say are cooling down, by lecturing either on old Moses or on that eloquent stylist, Isaiah. However, I have learned to live with myself, and am well aware how scanty my equipment is; and I can neither lay claim to scholarship enough for the prosecution of such high aims, nor suppose myself to possess strength of character enough to be able to endure the ill-will of all those determined defenders of their own. This is no assignment for a recruit, but for a highly experienced general. Please, however, do not call me shameless for declining the tasks you suggest; I should be utterly shameless did I not do so. It is you, dear Colet, who are less than wise in demanding water from a stone, as Plautus puts it. How could I ever be so brazen as to teach what I myself have not learned? How can I fire the cool hearts of others, when I myself am trembling and shivering all over? I should think myself more irresponsible than irresponsibility itself if in a matter of such importance I plunged in wholeheartedly at a venture and, as the Greek proverb has it, began to learn pottery on the largest size of jar. But, you will say, I had relied on you; and you will complain that I have disappointed your hopes. If so, you should reproach yourself and not me; for I have not deceived you, inasmuch as I never promised, or even held out a prospect of, anything of the kind; it is you who have deceived yourself, in refusing to believe me when I told you the truth about myself. And I have not come to these shores to teach literature, in verse or in prose. Literature ceased to have its charms for me as soon as it ceased to be necessary to me. As I reject this task because it falls below my purpose, so I reject your proposal because it is too great for my powers. In the one case, dear Colet, I do not deserve your reproaches, because I never intended to become a professor of what is called secular learning; in the other case your exhortations are wasted on me, since I am only too well aware of my inadequacy.

But even were I fully adequate to the task, I should still be in no position to undertake it, for I am shortly returning to Paris, whence I came. As I am kept here for the present, partly by the winter season and partly because the recent flight of a certain duke prevents my leaving safely,[1] I have betaken myself to this celebrated university in order to spend a month or two in the company of men like yourself rather than of those decorated gentlemen at court. And so far am I from wishing to oppose your honourable and pious endeavours, that I promise I shall diligently encourage and support them, since I am not yet qualified to work with you. For the rest, as soon as I feel myself to possess the necessary stamina and strength, I shall come personally to join your party, and will give devoted, if not distinguished, service in the defence of theology. Meanwhile, nothing could afford me greater pleasure than daily debates between us on the subject of holy writ,

---

[1] The 'certain duke' was Edmund de la Pole, Earl of Suffolk, eldest son of Elizabeth the sister of King Edward IV. Edmund was found guilty of treason in 1499 and fled to Calais in the summer. On 20 August a royal proclamation forbade anyone to leave the kingdom (hence Erasmus's problem) but de la Pole was soon allowed to return.

continued as we have begun either face to face or by means of letters. Farewell, dear Colet.

ps My host and our common friend Richard Charnock, that kind and reverend gentleman, has asked me to add warm greetings on his own behalf.

B. Erasmus to John Colet, December 1504

Source: *Collected Works of Erasmus*, translated by R. A. B. Mynors and D. F. S. Thompson; annotated by Wallace K. Ferguson (Toronto: University of Toronto Press, 1974), II. 85–9.

In this letter, written in Paris, Erasmus urges Colet to publish his work on Paul and the Gospels in the public interest. He describes his own scholarly preoccupations – his study of Greek and Hebrew; his views about these languages and his writings – especially the *Enchiridion* (published in 1503).

Paris, 1504

If our friendship, most learned Colet, had arisen from commonplace causes, or if your character had ever appeared to me to have a tinge of the common about it, I should be somewhat anxious in case it might have, not died perhaps, but at least cooled off, when we were so far and so long apart in place and time. As it is, since it was admiration for your extraordinary learning and love of your piety that drew me to you and since you too were perhaps attracted to me by hopes of finding similar qualities in me, or a fancy that I had them, I do not think we need fear that, as generally seems to happen, I have been out of sight, out of mind. If I have not received a line from you for many years past, I would rather think that this was due to your busy life, or your lack of information about my precise whereabouts, or in a word anything other than forgetfulness of a dear friend. But though I ought not to reproach you for your silence, nor should I wish to do so, still I beg and beseech you all the more earnestly sometimes to steal from your studies and public concerns just the tiny amount of spare time required to write me a letter. I am astonished that none of your commentaries on Paul and the Gospels has yet been published. Though I know your modesty well, yet you must sooner or later overcome even this, and shed it out of consideration for the general good. My congratulations on your doctorate, on attaining the office of dean, and certain other honours with which I hear your distinguished qualities have been rewarded without any effort on your part;[1] congratulations not so much for you who will, I am certain, claim nothing for yourself except the work involved, as for those for whose sake you propose to shoulder those responsibilities; congratulations indeed to the very honours you have won, which do not become honours in fact as well as name, until they are bestowed on one who deserves, yet does not court them.

[1] Colet had been appointed Dean of St Paul's, London.

I am now eager, dear Colet, to approach sacred literature full sail, full gallop; I have an extreme distaste for anything that distracts me from it, or even delays me. But the ill will of Fortune, which has ever regarded me with steadfast hostility, is the reason why I have not been able to free myself from these vexations; and so it was in order to shake them off as best I could, even if I proved unable to abolish them altogether, that I withdrew to France. Hereafter I intend to address myself to the Scriptures and to spend all the rest of my life upon them. Three years ago, indeed, I ventured to do something on Paul's Epistle to the Romans, and at one rush, as it were, finished four volumes; and would have gone on, but for certain distractions, of which the most important was that I needed the Greek at every point. Therefore for nearly the past three years I have been wholly absorbed by Greek; and I do not think my efforts have been altogether wasted. I began to take up Hebrew as well, but stopped because I was put off by the strangeness of the language, and at the same time the shortness of life and the limitations of human nature will not allow a man to master too many things at once. I have gone through a good part of Origen's works; under his guidance I think I have achieved worthwhile results, for he reveals some of the well-springs, as it were, and demonstrates some of the basic principles, of the science of theology.

I am sending you a small literary gift . . . The *Enchiridion*[2] I composed not in order to show off my cleverness or my style, but solely in order to counteract the error of those who make religion in general consist in rituals and observances of an almost more than Jewish formality, but who are astonishingly indifferent to matters that have to do with true goodness. What I have tried to do, in fact, is to teach a method of morals, as it were, in the manner of those who have originated fixed procedures in the various branches of learning . . .

If you would like to have any of your works printed, merely send me the manuscript and for the rest I will see to it that the printed version is quite accurate. Lately I sent a letter, as I believe you recall, about the hundred copies of the *Adagia* sent to England at my own expense, and three years ago at that. Grocyn had written to me, saying that he would take the utmost pains to see that they were sold as I wished; and I have no doubt he kept his promise, for he is the most upright, excellent man now living in England. So will you please oblige me by lending me your help in this matter, admonishing and goading into action those by whom you think the business ought to be concluded; for it must be that over such a long period all the books have been sold and the purchase price paid to someone; and it would be more useful to me to have the money now than ever before, since I have somehow to provide myself with several months' complete leisure in order to discharge the commitments I have entered into with respect to secular literature; I hoped it might be possible to do so this winter, and so it would

---

[2] *Enchiridion Militis Christiani* (*The Handbook of the Christian Soldier*), written at St Omer in 1501 but not published until 1503. It was translated into English and published as *The Manuell of the Christen Knyght* (London: Wynkyn de Worde, 1533).

have been had not so many of my prospects proved false. But I can still purchase this liberty not too expensively – for a few months at any rate.

So I beseech you to help me as far as you can in my burning zeal for sacred studies by releasing me from the kind of literature which has now ceased to give me pleasure ... Now, though for the present I am concerned with what may be a rather mundane subject, still while I linger within the garden of the Greeks I am gathering by the way many flowers that will be useful for the future, even in sacred studies; for experience teaches me this, at any rate, that we can do nothing in any field of literature without a knowledge of Greek, since it is one thing to guess, another to judge; one thing to trust with your own eyes, and another again to trust those of others. See how long my letter has grown! But it is affection, not a fault of character, that makes me so talkative. Farewell, Colet, my learned and good friend.

C. Erasmus to John Colet, October 1511

Source: Collected Works of Erasmus, translated by R. A. B. Mynors and D. F. S. Thompson; annotated by Wallace K. Ferguson (Toronto: University of Toronto Press, 1974), II. 183–7 abridged.

When he wrote this letter in Cambridge in 1511 Erasmus was evidently finishing his De Copia, which he dedicated to Colet on 29 April 1512. He knew that in Colet, founder in 1509 of St Paul's School, he would find a sympathetic audience for his views on the importance of educating children. In the final part of the letter Erasmus demonstrates his conviction that the return to Scripture meant a return to living according to the moral norms of the Sermon on the Mount – the essence of the 'philosophia Christi'.

Cambridge, 1511

... At the moment I am completely absorbed in finishing off my *Copia*;[1] so much so that I might seem to make a riddle of it – at once in the midst of abundance and also in utter penury. And how I wish I could put an end to both alike! – for presently I will be writing finis to the *Copia*, provided only that the Muses give better fortune to my studies than Fortune has hitherto given to my purse.

This was the reason why I have answered your letters somewhat briefly and carelessly.

As for the Scotists,[2] the most unbeatable and most successfully complacent class of men there is, I am not seriously campaigning against

[1] *De Duplici Copia Verborum* (1512), a study of stylistic richness in the Latin language and how to achieve it. This was revised in 1516.

[2] John Duns Scotus, late thirteenth/early fourteenth-century theologian and logician. Famous for lectures on the *Sentences* of Peter Lombard. It was this commentary on the *Sentences* which his followers (Scotists) revived and used as a framework for the study of speculative theology at Oxford University.

them for fear of wasting lamp-oil and labour and only stirring up a hornets' nest. I have virtually lost interest in translating Basil, not only because certain conjectures suggest that the work is not genuine, but also because the bishop of Rochester[3] seemed rather unenthusiastic after I sent him a sample of my projected translation, explaining in a letter that I intended that Basil should be presented to readers of Latin under the bishop's auspices and from his own university: also, as I have learnt from a friend, he suspects that I am polishing up a previous version and not translating from the Greek. What won't men think of?

. . .

Something occurs to me that I know you will laugh at. When I put forth a suggestion about a second master for your school in the presence of several university people, a person of some reputation smiled and said: who would bear to spend his life in that school, among children, if he could make some sort of a living anywhere else? I replied with a good deal of modesty that this function of bringing up youth in good character and good literature seemed to me one of the most honourable; that Christ did not despise the very young, and that no age of man was a better investment for generous help and nowhere could a richer harvest be anticipated, since the young are the growing crop and material of the commonwealth. I added that all who are truly religious hold the view that no service is more likely to gain merit in God's eyes than the leading of children to Christ. He grimaced and sneered: if anyone wished to serve Christ properly he should enter a monastery and live as a religious. I replied that St Paul defines true religion in terms of works of love; and love consists in helping our neighbours as best we may. He spurned this as a foolish remark. 'Lo,' said he, 'we have left all; there lies perfection.' That man has not left all, said I, who, when he could help very many by his labours, refuses to undertake a duty because it is regarded as humble. And with this I took my leave of the fellow, to avoid starting a quarrel. Here you see a sample of the Scotists' wisdom and the way in which they talk. Farewell again.

D. John Colet to Erasmus, June 1516

Source: *Collected Works of Erasmus*, translated by R. A. B. Mynors and D. F. S. Thompson; annotated by Wallace K. Ferguson (Toronto: University of Toronto Press, 1974), III. 311–12 abridged.

On 20 June John Colet addressed this letter of fulsome praise to Erasmus, commenting on many of his works. He expresses his agreement with Erasmus's interpretation of the 'philosophia Christi' and begs Erasmus to produce detailed commentaries on his translations of Holy Scripture to make the teaching clear.

---

[3] John Fisher, Bishop of Rochester 1504–35. He was deprived of his see on 2 January 1535 and died on 22 June 1535.

You cannot easily believe, dear Erasmus, how delighted I was to get your letter, which our one-eyed friend has lately delivered. I learnt from it where you are, which I did not know; and also you seem in it to expect to return to us here, which will be most welcome both to me and to the many friends you have here. I understand what you say about the New Testament. The copies of your new edition sell here like hot cakes and are read everywhere, and many approve your labours and marvel at them; some however disapprove and find fault, making the same criticisms that Maarten van Dorp makes in his letter to you.[1] But these are theologians, of the kind you describe with as much truth as wit in your *Moria*[2] and elsewhere, to be praised by whom is a discredit, and whose dispraise is praise. Personally I like your work and welcome your new edition, but in a way that rouses mingled feelings. At one time I am sorry that I never learnt Greek, without some skill in which we can get nowhere; and then again I rejoice in the light which is shed by your genius like the sun. In fact, Erasmus, I am astonished at the fertility of your intellect – you conceive so much, have so much in gestation, and bring forth some perfectly finished offspring every day – especially as you have no certain abode, and lack the support of any fixed, substantial endowment. Your Jerome is awaited here; he owes you a great debt, and so do we all, who can henceforth read him corrected and explained by you. You did well to write *Institutio principis christiani*.[3] I wish all Christian princes would follow excellent principles. Their madness upsets everything. I want a copy of that book very badly, for I well know that, like everything else of yours, it will be a really finished performance.

. . .

Your remarks about the pursuit of a Christian philosophy are perfectly just. There is no one, I think, in the Christian world of our own day better fitted for this business and profession than yourself, with the wide range of your learning; you do not say so yourself, I say it, because I really mean it. I have read what you have written on the first psalm, and I admire your *Copia*;[4] I long to see the result of your work on the Epistle to the Romans. Do not hesitate, my dear Erasmus, but when you have given us the New Testament in better Latin, go on to elucidate it with your explanations, and let us have a really long commentary on the Gospels. Length from you will

---

[1] Martin Dorp (1485–1525) was a professor of theology at the University of Louvain who wrote to Erasmus in September 1514 criticizing his famous satire *The Praise of Folly* and his boldness in correcting the Latin of the Vulgate text of the Bible. There ensued a controversy with letters exchanged between Dorp and Erasmus during 1515. Thomas More is said to have brought Dorp to Erasmus's point of view.

[2] Abbreviated Latin title of *The Praise of Folly* (1509, first published 1511). Erasmus wrote the book for the amusement of Thomas More while he was More's house-guest for a week. He remarked that More's name was very like the Latin word for folly but that More himself was very unlike folly. It was a satirical attack on the condition of the Church.

[3] Otherwise known as *The Education of a Christian Prince* (1516). While writing this work on government, Erasmus was in correspondence with Thomas More, who was engaged on his *Utopia*.

[4] *De Duplici Copia Verborum* (1512), a study of stylistic richness in the Latin language and how to achieve it. This was revised in 1516.

seem short. In those who love Holy Scripture the appetite can only grow, provided their digestion is sound, as they read what you have written. If you make the meaning clear, which no one will do better than you, you will confer a great benefit on us all, and make your name immortal. Immortal, did I say? The name of Erasmus shall never perish, but you will win for your name eternal glory, and as you toil in Jesus, you will win for yourself eternal life.

9 Erasmus: Colloquies and Writings (1523–1526)

The Colloquies had their beginnings in a textbook of conversational Latin penned in 1497 for the use of his students when Erasmus was supporting himself by tutoring at the University of Paris. This was revised and published in 1519. Over the years Erasmus added new colloquies to and revised the old colloquies in fresh editions. They were popular teaching materials in contemporary school and university curricula. For the most part, Erasmus drew upon his own experiences and sixteenth-century events and attitudes for his subject matter, which had, therefore, a compelling immediacy and relevance for his readers.

A. Courtship

Source: *The Colloquies of Erasmus*, translated and edited by Craig R. Thompson (Chicago and London: University of Chicago Press, 1965), pp. 88–98.

Courtship was first published in an August 1523 edition (Basel: Johannes Froben) and is sometimes known as 'The Lover and the Maiden'. It is one of five colloquies in this edition which treated various aspects of love and marriage. The others are: *The Girl with no Interest in Marriage*, *The Repentant Girl*, *The Young Man and the Harlot* and *Marriage*. Three others appeared later: *The New Mother* (1526), *A Marriage in Name Only* (1529) and *The Lower House* (1529). In *Courtship* Maria is receptive to the advances of Pamphilus but wary of binding herself by the exchange of vows or a kiss which might constitute a contract under Church law. Erasmus met with contemporary criticism both for Pamphilus's free language and for the implicit suggestion that marriage is superior to virginity.

PAMPHILUS, MARIA

Pamphilus: Hello – you cruel, hardhearted, unrelenting creature!
Maria: Hello yourself, Pamphilus, as often and as much as you like, and by whatever name you please. But sometimes I think you've forgotten my name. It's Maria.
Pamph: Quite appropriate for you to be named after Mars.
Maria: Why so? What have I to do with Mars?
Pamph: You slay men for sport, as the god does. Except that you're more pitiless than Mars: you kill even a lover.
Maria: Mind what you're saying. Where's this heap of men I've slain? Where's the blood of the slaughtered?

Pamph: You've only to look at me to see one lifeless corpse.

Maria: What do I hear? You speak and walk about when you're dead? I hope I never meet more fearsome ghosts!

Pamph: You're joking, but all the same you're the death of poor me, and you kill more cruelly than if you pierced with a spear. Now, alas, I'm just skin and bones from long torture.

Maria: Well, well! Tell me, how many pregnant women have miscarried at the sight of you?

Pamph: But my pallor shows I've less blood than any ghost.

Maria: Yet this pallor is streaked with lavender. You're as pale as a ripening cherry or a purple grape.

Pamph: Shame on you for making fun of a miserable wretch!

Maria: But if you don't believe me, bring a mirror.

Pamph: I want no other mirror, nor do I think any could be brighter, than the one in which I'm looking at myself now.

Maria: What mirror are you talking about?

Pamph: Your eyes.

Maria: Quibbler! Just like you. But how do you prove you're lifeless? Do ghosts eat?

Pamph: Yes, but they eat insipid stuff, as I do.

Maria: What do they eat, then?

Pamph: Mallows, leeks, and lupines.

Maria: But you don't abstain from capons and partridges.

Pamph: True, but they taste no better to my palate than if I were eating mallows, or beets without pepper, wine, and vinegar.

Maria: Poor you! Yet all the time you're putting on weight. And do dead men talk, too?

Pamph: Like me, in a very thin, squeaky voice.

Maria: When I heard you wrangling with your rival not long ago, your voice wasn't so thin and squeaky. But I ask you, do ghosts even walk? Wear clothes? Sleep?

Pamph: They even sleep together – though after their own fashion.

Maria: Well! Witty fellow, aren't you?

Pamph: But what will you say if I demonstrate with Achillean proofs that I'm dead and you're a murderer?

Maria: Perish the thought, Pamphilus! But proceed to your argument.

Pamph: In the first place, you'll grant, I suppose, that death is nothing but the removal of soul from body?

Maria: Granted.

Pamph: But grant it so that you won't want to take back what you've given.

Maria: I won't want to.

Pamph: Then you won't deny that whoever robs another of his soul is a murderer?

Maria: I allow it.

Pamph: You'll concede also what's affirmed by the most respected authors and endorsed by the assent of so many ages: that man's soul is not where it animates but where it loves?

Maria: Explain this more simply. I don't follow your meaning well enough.

Pamph: And the worse for me that you don't see this as clearly as I do.

Maria: Try to make me see it.

Pamph: As well try to make adamant see!

Maria: Well, I'm a girl, not a stone.

Pamph: True, but harder than adamant.

Maria: But get on with your argument.

Pamph: Men seized by a divine inspiration neither hear nor see nor smell nor feel, even if you kill them.

Maria: Yes, I've heard that.

Pamph: What do you suppose is the reason?

Maria: You tell me, professor.

Pamph: Obviously because their spirit is in heaven, where it possesses what it ardently loves, and is absent from the body.

Maria: What of it?

Pamph: What of it, you unfeeling girl? It follows both that I'm dead and that you're the murderer.

Maria: Where's your soul, then?

Pamph: Where it loves.

Maria: But who robbed you of your soul? – Why do you sigh? Speak freely; I won't hold it against you.

Pamph: Cruellest of girls, whom nevertheless I can't hate even if I'm dead!

Maria: Naturally. But why don't you in turn deprive her of *her* soul – tit for tat, as they say?

Pamph: I'd like nothing better if the exchange could be such that her spirit migrated to my breast, as my spirit has gone over completely to her body.

Maria: But may I, in turn, play the sophist with you?

Pamph: The sophistress.

Maria: It isn't possible for the same body to be living and lifeless, is it?

Pamph: No, not at the same time.

Maria: When the soul's gone, then the body's dead?

Pamph: Yes.

Maria: It doesn't animate except when it's present?

Pamph: Exactly.

Maria: Then how does it happen that although the soul's there where it loves, it nevertheless animates the body left behind? If it animates that body even when it loves elsewhere, how can the animated body be called lifeless?

Pamph: You dispute cunningly enough, but you won't catch me with such snares. The soul that somehow or other governs the body of a lover is incorrectly called soul, since actually it consists of certain slight remnants of soul – just as the scent of roses remains in your hand even if the rose is taken away.

Maria: Hard to catch a fox with a noose, I see! But answer me this: doesn't one who kills perform an act?

Pamph: Of course.

Maria: And the one who's killed suffers?

Pamph: Yes indeed.

Maria: Then how is it that although the lover is active and the beloved passive, the beloved is said to kill – when the lover, rather, kills himself?

Pamph: On the contrary, it's the lover who suffers; the beloved does the deed.

Maria: You'll never win this case before the supreme court of grammarians.

Pamph: But I'll win it before the congress of logicians.

Maria: Now don't begrudge an answer to this, too: do you love willingly or unwillingly?

Pamph: Willingly.

Maria: Then since one is free not to love, whoever loves seems to be a self-murderer. To blame the girl is unjust.

Pamph: Yet the girl doesn't kill by being loved but by failing to return the love. Whoever can save someone and refrains from doing so is guilty of murder.

Maria: Suppose a young man loves what is forbidden, for example another man's wife or a Vestal Virgin? She won't return his love in order to save the lover, will she?

Pamph: But *this* young man loves what it's lawful and right, and reasonable and honourable, to love; and yet he's slain. If this crime of murder is trivial, I'll bring a charge of poisoning too.

Maria: Heaven forbid! Will you make a Circe of me?[1]

Pamph: Something more pitiless than that. For I'd rather be a hog or a bear than what I am now, a lifeless thing.

Maria: Well, just what sort of poison do I kill men with?

Pamph: You charm them.

Maria: Then you want me to keep my poisonous eyes off you hereafter?

Pamph: Don't say such things! No, turn them on me more and more.

Maria: If my eyes are charmers, why don't the other men I look at languish too? So I suspect this witchcraft is in your own eyes, not in mine.

Pamph: Wasn't it enough to slay Pamphilus without mocking him besides?

Maria: A handsome corpse! But when's the funeral?

Pamph: Sooner than you think – unless you rescue me.

Maria: Have I so much power?

Pamph: You can bring a dead man back to life, and that with little trouble.

Maria: If someone gave me a cure-all.

Pamph: No need of medicines; just return his love. What could be easier or fairer? In no other way will you be acquitted of the crime of homicide.

Maria: Before which court shall I be tried? That of the Areopagites?

Pamph: No, the court of Venus.

Maria: She's an easygoing goddess, they say.

Pamph: Oh, no, her wrath's the most terrible of all.

Maria: Has she a thunderbolt?

[1] Circe was a goddess, very powerful in magic, who turned men into animals.

Pamph: No.

Maria: A trident?

Pamph: By no means.

Maria: Has she a spear?

Pamph: Not at all, but she's goddess of the sea.

Maria: I don't go sailing.

Pamph: But she has a boy.

Maria: Boys don't scare me.

Pamph: He's vengeful and wilful.

Maria: What will he do to me?

Pamph: What will he do? Heaven avert it! I wouldn't want to predict calamity to one whose welfare I have at heart.

Maria: Tell me anyway. I'm not superstitious.

Pamph: Then I'll tell you. If you reject this lover – who, unless I'm mistaken, is not altogether unworthy of having his love returned – the boy may, at his mother's bidding, shoot you with a dreadfully poisonous dart. As a result you'd fall desperately in love with some low creature who wouldn't return your love.

Maria: You tell me of a horrible punishment. For my part, I'd rather die than be madly in love with a man who's ugly or wouldn't return love for love.

Pamph: Yet there was recently a much publicized example of this misfortune, involving a certain girl.

Maria: Where?

Pamph: At Orleans.

Maria: How many years ago was this?

Pamph: How many years? Scarcely ten months ago.

Maria: What was the girl's name? Why do you hesitate?

Pamph: Never mind. I knew her as well as I do you.

Maria: Why don't you tell me her name, then?

Pamph: Because I don't like the omen. I only wish she'd had some other name! Hers was the very same as yours.

Maria: Who was her father?

Pamph: He's still living. Eminent lawyer and well-to-do.

Maria: Give me his name.

Pamph: Maurice.

Maria: Family name?

Pamph: Bright.

Maria: Is the mother living?

Pamph: Died recently.

Maria: What illness did she die of?

Pamph: What illness, you ask? Grief. And the father, though one of the hardiest of men, was in mortal danger.

Maria: May one know the mother's name too?

Pamph: Of course. Everybody knew Sophronia. But why this questioning? Do you think I'm spinning some yarn?

Maria: Would I suspect that of *you*? More commonly this suspicion is directed against our sex. But tell me what happened to the girl.

Pamph: She was a girl of respectable, wealthy background, as I said, and extremely beautiful; in short, worthy to marry a prince. She was courted by a certain young man whose social standing was similar to hers.

Maria: What was his name?

Pamph: Alas, a bad omen for me! Pamphilus was his name too. He tried everything, but she obstinately turned him down. The young man wasted away with sorrow. Not long afterwards she fell desperately in love with one who was more like an ape than a man.

Maria: What's that you say?

Pamph: So madly in love it's inexpressible.

Maria: So attractive a girl in love with so hideous a man?

Pamph: He had a peaked head, thin hair – and that torn and unkempt, full of scurf and lice. The mange had laid bare most of his scalp; he was cross-eyed, had flat, wide-open nostrils like an ape's, thin mouth, rotten teeth, a stuttering tongue, pocky chin; he was hunchbacked, potbellied, and had crooked shanks.

Maria: You describe some Thersites to me.[2]

Pamph: What's more, they said he had only one ear.

Maria: Perhaps he lost the other in war.

Pamph: Oh, no, in peace.

Maria: Who dared do that to him?

Pamph: Denis the hangman.

Maria: Maybe a large family fortune made up for his ugliness.

Pamph: Not at all; he was bankrupt and head over heels in debt. With this husband, so exceptional a girl now spends her life and is often beaten.

Maria: A wretched tale you tell.

Pamph: But a true one. Thus it pleased Nemesis to avenge the injury to the youth who was spurned.[3]

Maria: I'd rather be destroyed by a thunderbolt than put up with such a husband.

Pamph: Then don't provoke Nemesis: return your lover's love.

Maria: If that's enough, I do return it.

Pamph: But I'd want this love to be lasting and to be mine alone. I'm courting a wife, not a mistress.

Maria: I know that, but I must deliberate a long time over what can't be revoked once it's begun.

Pamph: *I've* thought it over a very long time.

Maria: See that love, who's not the best adviser, doesn't trick you. For they say he's blind.

Pamph: But one who proceeds with caution is keen-sighted. You don't appear to me as you do because I love you; I love you because I've observed what you're like.

Maria: But you may not know me well enough. If you'd wear the shoe, you'd feel then where it pinched.

---

[2] Thersites was in classical mythology an ugly, foul-tongued fellow who railed at Agamemnon (in Homer's *Iliad*) until beaten into silence by Odysseus.

[3] Nemesis was the goddess personifying divine retribution for human presumption.

Pamph: I'll have to take the chance; though I infer from many signs that the match will succeed.

Maria: You're a soothsayer too?

Pamph: I am.

Maria: Then by what auguries do you infer this? Has the night owl flown?

Pamph: That flies for fools.

Maria: Has a pair of doves flown from the right?

Pamph: Nothing of the sort. But the integrity of your parents has been known to me for years now. In the first place, good birth is far from a bad sign. Nor am I unaware of the wholesome instruction and godly examples by which you've been reared; and good education is better than good birth. That's another sign. In addition, between my family – not an altogether contemptible one, I believe – and yours there has long been intimate friendship. In fact, you and I have known each other to our fingertips, as they say, since childhood, and our temperaments are pretty much the same. We're nearly equal in age; our parents, in wealth, reputation, and rank. Finally – and this is the special mark of friendship, since excellence by itself is no guarantee of compatibility – your tastes seem to fit my temperament not at all badly. How mine agree with yours, I don't know.

Obviously, darling, these omens assure me that we shall have a blessed, lasting, happy marriage, provided you don't intend to sing a song of woe for our prospects.

Maria: What song do you want?

Pamph: I'll play 'I am yours'; you chime in with 'I am yours.'

Maria: A short song, all right, but it has a long finale.

Pamph: What matter how long, if only it be joyful?

Maria: I 'hate' you so that I wouldn't want you to do something you might regret later!

Pamph: Stop looking on the dark side.

Maria: Maybe I'll seem different to you when illness or old age has changed this beauty.

Pamph: Neither will I always be as handsome as I am now, my dear. But I don't consider only this dwelling place, which is blooming and charming in every respect. I love the guest more.

Maria: What guest?

Pamph: Your mind, whose beauty will forever increase with age.

Maria: Truly you're more than a Lynceus if you see through so much make-up!

Pamph: I see your thought through mine. Besides, we'll renew our youth repeatedly in our children.

Maria: But meantime my virginity will be gone.

Pamph: True, but see here: if you had a fine orchard, would you want it never to bear anything but blossoms, or would you prefer, after the blossoms have fallen, to see the trees heavy with ripe fruit?

Maria: How artfully he argues!

Pamph: Answer this at least: which is the prettier sight, a vine rotting on the ground or encircling some post or elm tree and weighing it down with purple grapes?

Maria: *You* answer *me* in turn: which is the more pleasing sight, a rose gleaming white on its bush or plucked and gradually withering?

Pamph: In my opinion the rose that withers in a man's hand, delighting his eyes and nostrils the while, is luckier than one that grows old on a bush. For that one too would wither sooner or later. In the same way, wine is better if drunk before it sours. But a girl's flower doesn't fade the instant she marries. On the contrary, I see many girls who before marriage were pale, run-down, and as good as gone. The sexual side of marriage brightened them so much that they began to bloom at last.

Maria: Yet virginity wins universal approval and applause.

Pamph: A maiden is something charming, but what's more naturally unnatural than an old maid? Unless your mother had been deflowered, we wouldn't have this blossom here. But if, as I hope, our marriage will not be barren, we'll pay for one virgin with many.

Maria: But they say chastity is a thing most pleasing to God.

Pamph: And therefore I want to marry a chaste girl, to live chastely with her. It will be more a marriage of minds than of bodies. We'll reproduce for the state; we'll reproduce for Christ. By how little will this marriage fall short of virginity! And perhaps some day we'll live as Joseph and Mary did. But meantime we'll learn virginity; for one does not reach the summit all at once.

Maria: What's this I hear? Virginity to be violated in order to be learned?

Pamph: Why not? As by gradually drinking less and less wine we learn temperance. Which seems more temperate to you, the person who, sitting down in the midst of dainties, abstains from them or the one secluded from those things that invite intemperance?

Maria: I think the man whom abundance cannot corrupt is more steadfastly temperate.

Pamph: Which more truly deserves praise for chastity, the man who castrates himself or the one who, while sexually unimpaired, nevertheless abstains from sexual love?

Maria: My vote would go to the latter. The first I'd regard as mad.

Pamph: But don't those who renounce marriage by a strict vow castrate themselves, in a sense?

Maria: Apparently.

Pamph: Now to abstain from sexual intercourse isn't a virtue.

Maria: Isn't it?

Pamph: Look at it this way. If it were a virtue per se not to have intercourse, intercourse would be a vice. Now it happens that it *is* a vice *not* to have intercourse, a virtue to have it.

Maria: When does this 'happen'?

Pamph: Whenever the husband seeks his due from his wife, especially if he seeks her embrace from a desire for children.

Maria: What if from lust? Isn't it right for him to be denied?

Pamph: It's right to reprove him, or rather to ask him politely to refrain. It's not right to refuse him flatly – though in this respect I hear few husbands complain of their wives.

Maria: But liberty is sweet.

Pamph: Virginity, on the other hand, is a heavy burden. I'll be your king, you'll be my queen: we'll rule a family at our pleasure. Or does this seem servitude to you?

Maria: The public calls marriage a halter.

Pamph: But those who call it that really deserve a halter themselves. Tell me, I beg you, isn't your soul imprisoned in your body?

Maria: Evidently.

Pamph: Like a little bird in a cage. And yet ask him if he desires to be free. He'll say no, I think. Why? Because he's willingly confined.

Maria: Our fortune is modest.

Pamph: So much the safer. You'll increase it at home by thrift, which is not unreasonably called a large source of income; I'll increase it away from home by my industry.

Maria: Children bring countless cares with them.

Pamph: But they bring countless delights and often repay the parents' devotion with interest many times over.

Maria: Loss of children is a miserable experience.

Pamph: Aren't you childless now? But why expect the worst in every uncertainty? Tell me, which would you prefer, never to be born or to be born to die?

Maria: I'd rather be born to die, of course.

Pamph: As those who have lived are more fortunate than those who never were born and never will be born, so is childlessness the more miserable in never having had and never expecting to have offspring.

Maria: Who are these who are not and will not be?

Pamph: Though one who refuses to run the risks of human life – to which all of us, kings and commoners alike, are equally liable – ought to give up life, still, whatever happens, you'll bear only half. I'll take over the larger share, so that if we have good luck the pleasure will be double; if bad, companionship will take away half the pain. As for me, if heaven summons, it will be sweet to die in your arms.

Maria: Men bear more readily what Nature's universal laws decree. But I observe how much more distressed some parents are by their children's conduct than by their death.

Pamph: Preventing that is mostly up to us.

Maria: How so?

Pamph: Because, with respect to character, good children are usually born of good parents. Kites don't come from doves. We'll try, therefore, to be good ourselves. Next, we'll see that our children are imbued from birth with sacred teachings and beliefs. What the jar is filled with when new matters most. In addition, we'll see that at home we provide an example of life for them to imitate.

Maria: What you describe is difficult.

Pamph: No wonder, because it's lovely. (And you're difficult too, for the same reason!) But we'll labour so much the harder to this end.

Maria: You'll have tractable material to work with. See that you form and fashion me.

Pamph: But meanwhile say just three words.

Maria: Nothing easier, but once words have flown out they don't fly back. I'll give better advice for us both: confer with your parents and mine, to get the consent of both sides.

Pamph: You bid me woo, but in three words you can make success certain.

Maria: I don't know whether I could. I'm not a free agent. In former times marriages were arranged only by the authority of elders. But however that may be, I think our marriage will have more chance of success if it's arranged by our parents' authority. And it's your job to woo; that isn't appropriate to our sex. We girls like to be swept off our feet, even if sometimes we're deeply in love.

Pamph: I won't be backward in wooing. Only don't let your decision alone defeat me.

Maria: It won't. Cheer up, Pamphilus dear!

Pamph: You're more strait-laced toward me in this business than I should like.

Maria: But first ponder your own private decision. Judge by your reason, not your feeling. What emotions decide is temporary; rational choices generally please forever.

Pamph: Indeed you philosophize very well, so I'm resolved to take your advice.

Maria: You won't regret it. But see here: a disturbing difficulty has turned up.

Pamph: Away with these difficulties!

Maria: You wouldn't want me to marry a dead man?

Pamph: By no means; but I'll revive.

Maria: You've removed the difficulty. Farewell, Pamphilus darling.

Pamph: That's up to you.

Maria: I bid you good night. Why do you sigh?

Pamph: 'Good night,' you say? If only you'd grant what you bid!

Maria: Don't be in too great a hurry. You're counting chickens before they're hatched.

Pamph: Shan't I have anything from you to take with me?

Maria: This scent ball, to gladden your heart.

Pamph: Add a kiss at least.

Maria: I want to deliver to you a virginity whole and unimpaired.

Pamph: Does a kiss rob you of your virginity?

Maria: Then do you want me to bestow my kisses on others too?

Pamph: Of course not. I want your kisses kept for me.

Maria: I'll keep them for you. Though there's another reason why I wouldn't dare give away kisses just now.

Pamph: What's that?

Maria: You say your soul has passed almost entirely into my body and that there's only the slightest particle left in yours. Consequently, I'm afraid this particle in you would skip over to me in a kiss and you'd then become quite lifeless. So shake hands, a symbol of our mutual love; and farewell. Persevere in your efforts. Meanwhile I'll pray Christ to bless and prosper us both in what we do.

B. *Marriage*

Source: *The Colloquies of Erasmus*, translated and edited by Craig R. Thompson (Chicago and London: University of Chicago Press, 1965), pp. 115–27.

Once again, this colloquy first appeared in the August 1523 edition. It was later given the subtitle 'The Discontented Wife'. By 1557 this dialogue had been translated into German, Spanish, French, Italian and English. Xanthippe complains to Eulalia of her husband's debauchery. In the colloquy Eulalia gives sound traditional advice to Xanthippe. The first story Eulalia uses to convey her advice is said to refer to Sir Thomas More and Jane Colt, his first wife, who was More's junior by ten years. Xanthippe is named after the shrewish wife of Socrates, the Ancient Greek philosopher. She was noted for her bad temper.

EULALIA, XANTHIPPE

Eulalia: Greetings, Xanthippe! I've been dying to see you.
Xanthippe: Same to you, my dearest Eulalia. You look lovelier than ever.
Eul: So you greet me by making fun of me right away?
Xan: Not at all: I mean it.
Eul: Maybe this new dress flatters my figure.
Xan: Of course it does. I haven't seen anything prettier for a long time. British cloth, I suppose?
Eul: British wool with Venetian dye.
Xan: Softer than satin. What a charming shade of purple! Where did you get such a marvellous gift?
Eul: Where should honest wives get them except from their husbands?
Xan: Lucky you to have such a husband! As for me – I might as well have married a mushroom when I married my Nicholas.
Eul: Why so, if you please? Are you falling out so soon?
Xan: I'll never fall in with the likes of him. You see I'm in rags: that's how *he* allows his wife to appear. Damned if often I'm not ashamed to go out in public when I see how well dressed other women are who married husbands much worse off than mine.
Eul: Feminine finery, as St Peter the apostle teaches (for I heard this in a sermon recently), consists not of clothes or any other adornment of the person but of chaste and modest sentiments and embellishments of the mind. Harlots are decked out for vulgar eyes. We're sufficiently well dressed if we please one husband.

Xan: But meanwhile that fine gentleman, so stingy toward his wife, squanders the dowry he got from me – no slight one – as fast as he can.

Eul: On what?

Xan: On whatever he pleases: wine – whores – dice.

Eul: That's no way to talk.

Xan: But it's the truth. Besides, when he comes home drunk in the middle of the night, after being long awaited, he snores all night and sometimes vomits in bed – to say no worse.

Eul: Hush! You bring reproach on yourself when you reproach your husband.

Xan: Hope to die if I wouldn't rather sleep with a brood sow than with such a husband!

Eul: Don't you welcome him with abuse then?

Xan: Yes – as he deserves. He finds I'm no mute!

Eul: What does he do to counter you?

Xan: At first he used to talk back most ferociously, thinking he'd drive me away with harsh words.

Eul: The bickering never came to actual blows?

Xan: Once, at least, the argument grew so hot on both sides that it very nearly ended in a fight.

Eul: You don't say so!

Xan: He was swinging a club, yelling savagely all the while and threatening terrible deeds.

Eul: Weren't you scared at that?

Xan: Oh, no. When it came to my turn, I grabbed a stool. Had he laid a finger on me, he'd have found I didn't lack arms.

Eul: A new sort of shield! You should have used your distaff for a lance.

Xan: He'd have found he had an Amazon to deal with.

Eul: My dear Xanthippe, this won't do.

Xan: What *does* do? If he won't treat me as a wife, I won't treat him as a husband.

Eul: But Paul teaches that wives should be obedient to their husbands in all subjection. And Peter sets before us the example of Sarah, who would call her husband Abraham 'lord'.

Xan: So I've heard. But this same Paul teaches that husbands should cherish their wives as Christ has cherished his spouse the Church. Let him remember his duty and I'll remember mine.

Eul: All the same, when things have come to such a pass that one person must yield to the other, the wife should give way to the husband.

Xan: Provided he deserves to be called husband. He treats me like a servant.

Eul: But tell me, my dear Xanthippe, did he stop threatening to beat you after that?

Xan: Yes – and he was wise to do so or he'd have got a cudgelling.

Eul: But haven't you stopped brawling with him?

Xan: No, and I won't stop.

Eul: What does he do all this time?

Xan: Do? Sometimes he sleeps, the lazy loafer. Occasionally he just laughs; and at other times grabs his guitar, which has hardly three strings, and plays it as loud as he can to drown out my screaming.

Eul: That infuriates you?

Xan: More than I could say. At times I can hardly keep my hands off him.

Eul: Xanthippe, my dear, may I speak rather frankly with you?

Xan: You may.

Eul: You may do the same with me. Our intimacy – which goes back almost to the cradle – surely demands this.

Xan: That's true. You've always been my dearest friend.

Eul: Whatever your husband's like, bear in mind that there's no exchanging him for another. Once upon a time divorce was a final remedy for irreconcilable differences. Nowadays this has been entirely abolished; you must be husband and wife until the day you die.

Xan: May heaven punish whoever robbed us of this right!

Eul: Mind what you're saying. Christ so willed.

Xan: I can scarcely believe it.

Eul: It's the truth. There's nothing left now but to try to live in harmony by adjusting yourselves to each other's habits and personalities.

Xan: Can I reform him?

Eul: What sort of men husbands are depends not a little on their wives.

Xan: Do you get along well with your husband?

Eul: Everything's peaceful now.

Xan: There was some turmoil at first, then?

Eul: Never a storm, but slight clouds appeared occasionally: the usual human experience. They could have caused a storm had they not been met with forbearance. Each of us has his own ways and opinions, and – to tell the truth – his own peculiar faults. If there's any place where one has a duty to recognize these, not resent them, surely it's in marriage.

Xan: Good advice.

Eul: It frequently happens, however, that good will between husband and wife breaks down before they know each other well enough. This above all is to be avoided, for once contention arises love is not easily recovered, especially if the affair reaches the point of harsh abuse. Things glued together are easily separated if you shake them immediately, but once the glue has dried they stick together as firmly as anything. Hence at the very outset no pains should be spared to establish and cement good will between husband and wife. This is accomplished mainly by submissiveness and courtesy, for good will won merely by beauty of person is usually short-lived.

Xan: But tell me, please, by what arts you draw your husband to your ways.

Eul: I'll tell you in order that you may imitate them.

Xan: If I can.

Eul: It will be very easy if you want to; and it's not too late, for he's a young man and you a girl, and the marriage isn't a year old, I believe.

Xan: You're correct.

Eul: I'll tell you, then, but only if you'll keep it secret.

Xan: Of course.

Eul: My first concern was to be agreeable to my husband in every respect, so as not to cause him any annoyance. I noted his mood and feeling; I noted the circumstances too, and what soothed and irritated him, as do those who tame elephants and lions or suchlike creatures that can't be forced.

Xan: That's the sort of creature I have at home!

Eul: Those who approach elephants don't wear white, and those who approach bulls don't wear red, because these beasts are known to be enraged by such colours. Likewise tigers are driven so wild by the beating of drums that they tear their own flesh. And trainers of horses have calls, whistles, caresses, and other means of soothing mettlesome animals. How much more fitting for us to use those arts on our husbands, with whom, whether we like it or not, we share bed and board for our entire lives!

Xan: Go on with what you've begun.

Eul: When these matters were looked after, I would adapt myself to him, taking care to avoid any unpleasantness.

Xan: How could you do that?

Eul: First of all, I was vigilant in my management of household affairs, the special province of wives. I made certain not only that nothing was omitted but that everything was suited to his taste, even in the slightest details.

Xan: What details?

Eul: For example, if my husband was unusually fond of this or that dish, or if he liked his food cooked, or the bed made, in a certain way.

Xan: But how could you adapt yourself to one who wasn't at home or was drunk?

Eul: Just a moment; I was coming to that. If my husband seemed quite depressed and I had no chance to appeal to him, I wouldn't laugh or joke, as some women like to do, but I too put on a sombre, worried look. As a mirror, if it's a good one, always gives back the image of the person looking at it, so should a wife reflect her husband's mood, not being gay when he's sad or merry when he's upset. But whenever he was more upset than usual, I'd either soothe him with pleasant conversation or defer to his anger in silence until he cooled off and an opportunity came to correct or advise him. I'd do the same whenever he came home tipsy: at the time I'd say nothing except what was agreeable; I'd just coax him to bed.

Xan: Wives have an unhappy lot for sure if they must simply put up with husbands who are angry, drunk, and whatever else they please.

Eul: As if this putting up with things didn't work both ways! Husbands have much to endure from our habits as well. On occasion, however – in a serious matter, when something important's at stake – it's right for a wife to reprove her husband; trivial matters are better winked at.

Xan: What occasion, pray?

Eul: When he's at leisure and not disturbed, worried, or tipsy, then she should admonish him politely, or rather entreat him – in private – to take better care of his property, reputation, or health in one respect or another. And this very admonition should be seasoned with wit and pleasantries.

Sometimes I'd make my husband promise in advance not to be angry if I, a foolish woman, reproved him about something that seemed to concern his honour, health, or welfare. After reproving him as I intended, I'd break off that talk and turn to other, more cheerful topics. For as a rule, my dear Xanthippe, our mistake is that once we've started to talk we can't stop.

Xan: So they say.

Eul: Above all I was careful not to scold my husband in the presence of others or to carry any complaint farther than the front door. Trouble's sooner mended if it's limited to two. But if something of this sort does prove intolerable, or can't be cured by the wife's reproof, it's more polite for her to take her complaint to her husband's parents and relatives than to her own, and to state her case with such restraint that she won't seem to hate her husband but his fault instead. She should refrain from blurting out everything, though, so that her husband may tacitly acknowledge and admire his wife's courtesy.

Xan: Whoever could do all this must be a philosopher.

Eul: Oh, no; by such practices we'll entice our husbands to similar courtesy.

Xan: There are some no courtesy would improve.

Eul: Well, I don't think so, but suppose there are. In the first place, remember you must put up with your husband, whatever he's like. Better, therefore, to put up with one who behaves himself or is made a little more accommodating by our politeness than with one who's made worse from day to day by our harshness. What if I were to cite examples of husbands who improved their wives by courtesy of this kind? How much more fitting for us to do the same for our husbands!

Xan: Then you'd tell me of an example very different from *my* husband!

Eul: I'm well acquainted with a certain nobleman, a learned and remarkably clever man. He married a girl of seventeen who had been reared wholly in her parents' country home (since nobles generally like to live in the country, for the sake of hunting and hawking). Her lack of sophistication recommended her, because he would fashion her to his tastes the more readily. He undertook to teach her literature and music and gradually to accustom her to repeating what she had heard in a sermon; and by other devices to train her in what would be of later use. Since this was all new to the girl, who had spent her time in her own home in complete idleness and had been brought up amidst the chatter and pranks of servants, she began to grow bored. She became balky, and when her husband became insistent she would cry and cry, sometimes throwing herself down and dashing her head against the floor as though she wished she were dead. Because there was no end to this, her husband, hiding his vexation, invited his wife to accompany him on a visit to the country, to his father-in-law's house, for a holiday. She accepted eagerly. When they arrived there the husband left his wife with her mother and sisters; he himself went hunting with his father-in-law. Then, when they're out of hearing, he tells his father-in-law he had hoped for an amiable partner but now had one who was forever weeping and tormenting herself and could not be corrected by any reproofs. He begs for help in curing the daughter's fault. The father-in-law replies that he gave him his daughter once and for all; that if she refused to obey his commands, he should exercise his rights and correct her by blows. 'I know my rights,' says the son-in-law, 'but rather than resort to this desperate remedy I'd prefer to have her cured by your skill or authority.' The father-in-law promised to attend to the matter. A day or so later he seizes an opportunity to be alone with his daughter. Then, putting on a stern look, he begins to recall how homely she was, how ill-mannered, how often he had feared he would be unable to find her a husband. 'But,' he says, 'with the greatest difficulty I've found you a husband such as any girl, however favoured, would long for. And yet, not recognizing what I've done for you, nor realizing that you have such a husband – who would scarcely think you fit for one of his maidservants if he weren't the kindest of men – you rebel against him.' To make a long story short, the father's speech grew so heated that he seemed barely able to keep his hands off her. (For he's a man of marvellous cunning, capable of playing any comedy without a mask.) Moved partly by fear, partly by the truth, the girl promptly went down on her knees before her father, begging forgiveness for the past and swearing she would be mindful of her duty in the future. He pardoned her, promising to be a most affectionate father if she carried out her promise.

Xan: Then what happened?

Eul: After the conversation with her father, the girl went to her bedroom, met her husband privately, fell on her knees before him, and said, 'Husband, up to this time I have known neither you nor myself. Hereafter you shall see me a changed person; only forget the past.' Her husband received this speech with a kiss and promised her everything if she kept her word.

Xan: Well? Did she keep it?

Eul: As long as she lived. And there was nothing, however lowly, that she did not do promptly and willingly when her husband wished. So strong was the love born and confirmed between them. After some years the girl often congratulated herself on her luck in marrying such a husband. 'If it hadn't been for this,' she said, 'I'd have been the unhappiest woman in the world.'

Xan: Husbands like that are as scarce as white crows.

Eul: If you don't mind, I'll tell you something about a husband reformed by his wife's kindness: something that happened recently in this very city.

Xan: I've nothing to do and I enjoy your conversation very much.

Eul: There's a certain man of no mean rank who, like most of his class, used to hunt a good deal. In the country he came across some girl, the daughter of a poor peasant woman, with whom he – a man already fairly well along in years – fell passionately in love. On her account he'd often spend the night away from home, his excuse being his hunting. His wife, a woman of exceptional goodness, suspected something, investigated her husband's secret doings, and, after discovering the facts (I don't know how), went to their rude cottage. She found out everything: where he slept, what he drank out of, what dinner-ware he had. No furniture there – just sheer poverty. The wife went home but soon came back, bringing with her a comfortable bed and furnishings and some silver vessels. She added money, too, advising the girl to treat him more handsomely on his next visit – all the while concealing the fact that she herself was his wife and pretending to be his sister. Some days later the husband returns there secretly. Noticing the new furniture and the more expensive household utensils, he asks where this uncommon luxury comes from. Some good lady (he's told), a relative of his, had brought it and had left orders to entertain him more properly thereafter. He suspected at once that his wife had done this. Back home, he asks her; she doesn't deny it. And why, he asks finally, had she sent the furniture to him? 'My dear husband,' she replies, 'you're used to a pretty comfortable life. I saw you were shabbily treated there. I thought that since you're so fond of the place, I ought to see that you're entertained more elegantly.'

Xan: Too good a wife! I'd sooner have made him a bed of nettles and thistles.

Eul: But hear the conclusion. In view of so much gentleness and kindness on the part of his wife, the husband never again engaged in secret amours but enjoyed himself at home with his own wife.

. . .

Eul: First of all, keep to yourself any wrong your husband does you and win him over gradually by favours, cheerfulness, gentleness. Either you'll triumph at last or certainly you'll find him much more affable than you do now.

Xan: He's too savage to soften under any favours.

Eul: Oh, don't say that. No creature's so fierce that he can't be tamed. Don't despair of the man. Try for several months; blame me if you don't find this advice has helped you. There are even some failings you ought to wink at. Above all, in my judgement, you must be careful not to start an argument in the bedroom or in bed, but try to see that everything there is pleasant and agreeable. If that place, which is dedicated to dispelling grudges and renewing love, is profaned by any contention or bitterness, every means of recovering good will is clean gone. Some women are so peevish that they even quarrel and complain during sexual intercourse and by their tactlessness render disagreeable that pleasure which ordinarily rids men's minds of whatever vexation may be therein – spoiling the very medicine that could have cured their ills.

Xan: That's often happened to me.

Eul: Yet, even though a wife should always be careful not to offend her husband on any occasion, she should take special pains to show herself wholly complaisant and agreeable to him in that union.

Xan: Husband! My business is with a monster.

Eul: Do stop talking in that horrid fashion. Usually it's our fault that husbands are bad. But to return to the subject. Those well read in ancient poetry say that Venus, whom they make the patroness of married love, has a girdle fashioned by Vulcan. Woven in it is some drug to arouse love. She puts on this girdle whenever she's going to sleep with her husband.

Xan: That's a mere story.

Eul: A story, yes, but hear what the story signifies.

Xan: Tell me.

Eul: It teaches that a wife must take every precaution to be pleasing to her husband in sexual relations, in order that married love may be rekindled and renewed and any annoyance or boredom driven out of mind.

Xan: But where shall I get that girdle?

Eul: You don't need sorcery or charms. No charm is more effective than good behaviour joined with good humour.

Xan: I can't humour such a husband.

Eul: Yet it's important to you that he stop being such. If by Circe's arts you could turn your husband into a swine or a bear, would you do it?

Xan: I don't know.

Eul: Don't know? Would you rather have a swine than a man for a husband?

Xan: I'd prefer a man, of course.

Eul: Well, now, what if by Circe's arts you could change him from drunk to sober, spendthrift to thrifty, idler to worker? Wouldn't you do it?

Xan: Indeed I would, but where can I find those arts?

Eul: But you've those very arts in yourself if only you're willing to make use of them. He's yours whether you like it or not; *that*'s settled. The better you make him, the better off you'll be. You have eyes only for his failings. These intensify your disgust, and with this handle you're simply catching him where he can't be held. Mark the good in him, rather, and by this means take him where he *can* be held. The time to weigh his faults was before you married him, since a husband should be chosen not only with eyes, but with ears too. Now's the time for improving him, not blaming him.

Xan: What woman ever picked a husband by ear?

Eul: The one who sees nothing but good looks chooses him with her eyes. The woman who chooses by ear is the one who considers his reputation carefully.

Xan: Good advice – but too late!

Eul: But it's not too late to try to improve your husband. If you present your husband with a child, that will help.

Xan: I've already had one.

Eul: When?

Xan: Long ago.

Eul: How many months ago?

Xan: Almost seven.

Eul: What do I hear? Are you reviving the old joke about the three-month baby?

Xan: Not at all.

Eul: You must be if you count the time from your wedding day.

Xan: Oh, no, we had some conversation before marriage.

Eul: Are children born from conversation?

Xan: Chancing to find me alone, he began to play, tickling me under the arms and in the sides to make me laugh. I couldn't stand the tickling, so I fell back on the bed. He leaned over and kissed me – I'm not sure what else he did. I *am* sure my belly began to swell soon afterwards.

Eul: Go on! Belittle a husband who begot children in sport? What will he do when he goes to work in earnest?

Xan: I suspect I'm pregnant now, too.

Eul: Fine! A good ploughman's found a good field.

Xan: He's better at this than I would like.

Eul: Few wives join you in *that* complaint. But were you engaged?

Xan: Engaged, yes.

Eul: Then your sin was the lighter. Is the child a boy?

Xan: Yes.

Eul: That will reconcile you two if you meet him halfway . . . You must not even think of divorce.

Xan: But I've often thought of it.

Eul: Whenever the notion comes into your head, consider with yourself, first of all, what a paltry thing a woman is if separated from her husband. A woman's highest praise is to be obedient to her husband. It's the order of Nature, the will of God, that woman be entirely dependent on man. Only think what the situation is: he's your husband; you can't get a different one. In the second place, think about the little boy you two have. What will you do about him? Take him with you? You'll rob your husband of his possession. Leave him with your husband? You'll deprive yourself of the one dearest to you . . .

Xan: What should I do?

Eul: I've already told you. See that everything at home is neat and clean and there's no trouble that will drive him out of doors. Show yourself affable to him, always mindful of the respect owed by wife to husband. Avoid gloominess and irritability. Don't be disgusting or wanton. Keep the house spick and span. You know your husband's taste; cook what he likes best. Be cordial and courteous to his favourite friends, too. Invite them to dinner frequently, and see that everything is cheerful and gay there. Finally, if he strums his guitar when he's a bit tipsy, accompany him with your singing. Thus you'll get your husband used to staying at home and you'll reduce expenses. At long last he'll think, 'I'm a damned fool to waste my money and reputation away from home on a drab when I have at home a wife much nicer and much fonder of me, from whom I can get a more elegant and more sumptuous welcome.'

Xan: Do you think I'll succeed if I try?

Eul: Look at me. I'll vouch for it.

C. *A Pilgrimage for Religion's Sake*

Source: *The Colloquies of Erasmus*, translated and edited by Craig R. Thompson (Chicago and London: University of Chicago Press, 1965), pp. 287–91.

It was first published in the February 1526 edition (Basel: Johannes Froben). In 1536 or 1537 an anonymous English translation of the colloquy was published as *The Pilgrimage of Pure Devotion*, probably commissioned by Thomas Cromwell.

In *A Pilgrimage for Religion's Sake* Erasmus treats three topics: the spiritual value or harm of pilgrimages; the false claims made for relics; and iconoclasm. This colloquy was based upon Erasmus's actual experiences. He had visited the shrine of Our Lady of Walsingham in the summer of 1512 and perhaps in 1514. He had, like Ogygius, composed a poem in honour of the Blessed Virgin. Between summer 1512 and summer 1514 he visited the shrine of St Thomas Becket at Canterbury. Other characters in the colloquy, not represented in this extract, were also based on real people. Gratianus Pullus, his companion who was indignant about relics, is John Colet. Robert Aldridge, the interpreter, was a Cambridge scholar and associate of Erasmus who later became Provost of Eton and Bishop of Carlisle. The letter of Mary to Glaucoplutus (the Greek form of Ulrich) lamenting the destruction of images was suggested by iconoclasm in Ulrich Zwingli's Zurich.

The names of the speakers in this colloquy are significant. Menedemus means 'Stay-at-home'; it was also the name of an ancient Cynic philosopher who rejected convention and taught independence and simplicity of mind. Ogygius means 'Simpleminded' or 'Stupid'. Ogygius was the mythical founder of Thebes in Boeotia and the adjective Boeotian came to mean stupid.

MENEDEMUS, OGYGIUS

Menedemus: What marvel is this? Don't I see my neighbour Ogygius, whom nobody's laid eyes on for six whole months? I heard he was dead. It's his very self, unless I'm losing my mind completely. I'll go up to him and say hello. – Greetings, Ogygius.

Ogygius: Same to you, Menedemus.

Men: Where in the world do you return from, safe and sound? A sad rumour spread here that you'd sailed in Stygian waters.[1]

Ogyg: No, thank heaven; I've seldom enjoyed better health.

Men: I hope you'll always be able to refute silly rumours of that sort! But what's this fancy outfit? You're ringed with scallop shells,[2] choked with tin and leaden images on every side, decked out with straw necklaces, and you've snake eggs on your arms.[3]

Ogyg: I've been on a visit to St James of Compostela and, on my way back, to the famous Virgin-by-the-Sea, in England; or rather I revisited her, since I had gone there three years earlier.

Men: Out of curiosity, I dare say.

Ogyg: On the contrary, out of devotion.

Men: Greek letters, I suppose, taught you that devotion.

Ogyg: My wife's mother had bound herself by a vow that if her daughter gave birth to a boy and he lived, I would promptly pay my respects to St James and thank him in person.

Men: Did you greet the saint only in your own name and your mother-in-law's?

Ogyg: Oh, no, in the whole family's.

---

[1] A reference to the poisonous qualities of the River Styx, which in Greek mythology was one of the rivers of the underworld.

[2] Shells, traditional symbols of pilgrims, were particularly associated with St James and the pilgrimage to Compostela, Spain.

[3] Snake eggs are beads, i.e. a rosary.

Men: Well, I imagine your family would have been no less safe even if you had left James ungreeted. But do please tell me: what answer did he make when you thanked him?

Ogyg: None, but he seemed to smile as I offered my gift, nodded his head slightly, and at the same time held out these scallop shells.

Men: Why does he give these rather than something else?

Ogyg: Because he has plenty of them; the sea nearby supplies them.

Men: Generous saint, who both delivers those in labour and gives presents to callers! But what new kind of vowing is this, that some lazy person lays the work on others? If you bound yourself by a vow that, should *your* affairs prosper, *I* would fast twice a week, do you think I'd do what you had vowed?

Ogyg: No, I don't, even if you'd sworn in your own name. For you enjoy mocking the saints. But she's my mother-in-law; custom had to be kept. You're acquainted with women's whims, and besides *I* had an interest in it too.

Men: If you hadn't kept her vow, what risk would there have been?

Ogyg: The saint couldn't have sued me at law, I admit, but he could have been deaf thereafter to my prayers or secretly have brought some disaster upon my family. You know the ways of the mighty.

Men: Tell me, how is the excellent James?

Ogyg: Much colder than usual.

Men: Why? Old age?

Ogyg: Joker! You know saints don't grow old. But this newfangled notion that pervades the whole world results in his being greeted more seldom than usual. And if people do come, they merely greet him; they make no offering at all, or only a very slight one, declaring it would be better to contribute that money to the poor.

Men: A wicked notion!

Ogyg: And thus so great an apostle, accustomed to shine from head to foot in gold and jewels, now stands a wooden figure with hardly a tallow candle to his name.

Men: If what I hear is true, there's danger that other saints may come to the same pass.

Ogyg: More than that: a letter is going round which the Virgin Mary herself wrote on this very theme.

Men: Which Mary?

Ogyg: The one called Mary a Lapide.[4]

Men: At Basel, unless I'm mistaken.

Ogyg: Yes.

Men: Then it's a stony saint you tell me of. But to whom did she write?

Ogyg: She herself gives the name in the letter.

Men: Who delivered the letter?

---

[4] Means 'Mary of the Stones' – the Latin word *lapis*, *lapidis* can mean several types of stone, including a precious stone or gem (particularly pearl) or a stone which symbolized justice. A pun on the title occurs three lines later.

Ogyg: Undoubtedly an angel, who placed it on the pulpit from which the recipient preaches. And to prevent suspicion of fraud, you shall see the very autograph.

Men: So you recognize the hand of the angel who is the Virgin's secretary?

Ogyg: Why, of course.

Men: By what mark?

Ogyg: I've read Bede's epitaph,[5] which was engraved by an angel. The shape of the letters agrees entirely. Also I've read the manuscript message to St Giles.[6] They agree. Aren't these facts proof enough?

Men: Is one allowed to see it?

Ogyg: Yes, if you'll promise to keep your mouth shut about it.

Men: Oh, to tell me is to tell a stone.

Ogyg: But some stones are notorious for giving secrets away.

Men: Then tell it to a deaf man if you don't trust a stone.

Ogyg: On that condition I'll read it. Lend me your ears.

Men: I've lent them.

Ogyg: 'Mary, Mother of Jesus, to Glaucoplutus: greetings. Know that I am deeply grateful to you, a follower of Luther, for busily persuading people that the invocation of saints is useless. Up to this time I was all but exhausted by the shameful entreaties of mortals. They demanded everything from me alone, as if my Son were always a baby (because he is carved and painted as such at my bosom), still needing his mother's consent and not daring to deny a person's prayer; fearful, that is, that if he did deny the petitioner something, I for my part would refuse him the breast when he was thirsty. And sometimes they ask of a virgin what a modest youth would hardly dare ask of a bawd – things I'm ashamed to put into words. Sometimes a merchant, off for Spain to make a fortune, commits to me the chastity of his mistress. And a nun who has thrown off her veil and is preparing to run away entrusts me with her reputation for virtue – which she herself intends to sell. A profane soldier, hired to butcher people, cries upon me, "Blessed Virgin, give me rich booty." A gambler cries, "Help me, blessed saint; I'll share my winnings with you!" And if they lose at dice, they abuse me outrageously and curse me because I wouldn't favour their wickedness. A woman who abandons herself to a life of shame cries, "Give me a fat income!" If I refuse anything, they protest at once, "Then you're no mother of mercy."

'Some people's prayers are not so irreverent as absurd. An unmarried girl cries, "Mary, give me a rich and handsome bridegroom." A married one, "Give me fine children." A pregnant woman, "Give me an easy delivery." An old woman, "Give me a long life without a cough or a thirst." A doddering old man, "Let me grow young again." A philosopher, "Give me power to contrive insoluble problems." A priest, "Give me a rich benefice." A bishop, "Preserve my church." A sailor, "Give me prosperous sailings." A governor,

---

[5] In the abbey church at Durham.

[6] When St Giles asked God for the remission of a king's sins, an angel placed on the altar a scroll declaring that the king's sins were forgiven.

"Show me thy Son before I die." A courtier, "Grant that at the point of death I may confess sincerely." A countryman, "Send me a heavy rain." A countrywoman, "Save the flock and herd from harm." If I deny anything, straightaway I'm cruel. If I refer to my Son, I hear, "He wills whatever you will." So am I alone, a woman and a virgin, to assist those who are sailing, fighting, trading, dicing, marrying, bearing children; to assist governors, kings, and farmers?

'What I've described is very little in comparison with what I endure. But nowadays I'm troubled less by these matters. For this reason I would give you my heartiest thanks, did not this advantage bring a greater disadvantage along with it. I have more peace but less honour and wealth. Formerly I was hailed as "Queen of Heaven, mistress of the world"; now I hear scarcely an "Ave Maria" even from a few.[7] Formerly I was clothed in gold and jewels; I had many changes of dress; I had golden and jewelled offerings made to me. Now I have hardly half a cloak to wear, and that one is mouse-eaten. My annual income is scarcely enough to keep the wretched sacristan who lights the little lamp or tallow candle. And yet all these hardships I could have borne if you weren't said to be plotting even greater ones. You're trying, they say, to remove from the churches whatever belongs to the saints. Now just consider what you're doing. Other saints have means of avenging injuries. If Peter is ejected from a church, he can in turn shut the gate of heaven against you. Paul has a sword. Bartholomew is armed with a knife. Under his monk's robe William is completely armed, nor does he lack a heavy lance. And what could you do against George, with his horse and his coat of mail, his spear and his terrible sword? Antony's not defenceless either: he has his sacred fire. Others likewise have weapons or mischiefs they direct against anybody they please. But me, however defenceless, you shall not eject unless at the same time you eject my Son whom I hold in my arms. From him I will not be parted. Either you expel him along with me, or you leave us both here, unless you prefer to have a church without Christ. I wanted you to know this. Think carefully what to answer, for my mind is absolutely made up.

'From our stony house, on the Calends of August, in the year of my Son's passion 1524, I, the Virgin a Lapide, have signed this with my own hand.'

Men: A dreadful, threatening letter indeed! Glaucoplutus will take warning, I imagine.

Ogyg: If he's wise.

Men: Why didn't the excellent James write to him on this same subject?

Ogyg: I don't know, except that he's rather far away, and all letters are intercepted nowadays.

Men: But what fortune brought you back to England?

Ogyg: An unexpectedly favourable breeze carried me there, and I had virtually promised the Virgin-by-the-Sea that I would pay her another visit in two years.

---

[7] Ave Maria or Hail Mary, sometimes known as the Angelic Salutation, is the form of prayer to the Blessed Virgin Mary based upon the greetings of the angel Gabriel and Elizabeth in St Luke's Gospel (Luke 1: 28 and 42).

Men: What were you going to ask of her?

Ogyg: Nothing new, just the usual things: family safe and sound, a larger fortune, a long and happy life in this world, and eternal bliss in the next.

Men: Couldn't the Virgin Mother here at home see to those matters? At Antwerp she has a church much grander than the one by the sea.

Ogyg: I can't deny that, but different things are bestowed in different places, either because she prefers this or (since she is obliging) because she accommodates herself to our feelings in this respect.

10 Machiavelli, *The Prince* (1513)

Source: Niccolò Machiavelli, *The Prince*, edited and translated by George Bull (Harmondsworth: Penguin Books, 1961), pp. 29–30; 87–92; 95–8.

Niccolò Machiavelli (1469–1527) was the son of a Florentine lawyer (Bernardo Machiavelli). His was a strong Republican family, and therefore Machiavelli was shunned by the Medici. He openly opposed the Friar Savonarola's rule in Florence (1494–8). Machiavelli was Florentine ambassador to various courts (including France) and personal aide in military affairs to Piero Soderini, who was Gonfalonier for life and virtual head of the government of Republican Florence (1498–1512). With the return of the Medici in 1512 he lost his position as secretary and second chancellor and spent the remainder of his life out of favour and office. The corpus of his works includes *The Discourses* (1515–17), *The Art of War* (1519–20) and *The History of Florence* (1520–25). Below are printed several short extracts from the most famous of his works, *The Prince* (1513). In the first extract he explains his reasons for writing the book. In the others he offers advice to the prince.

A. Letter from Niccolò Machiavelli to Lorenzo de' Medici

Lorenzo de' Medici (1492–1519) was the son of Piero de' Medici and the nephew of Giovanni de' Medici (Pope Leo X), who made him Duke of Urbino in 1516. This dedicatory letter from Machiavelli formed the Preface to *The Prince*.

Men who are anxious to win the favour of a prince nearly always follow the custom of presenting themselves to him with the possessions they value most, or with things they know especially please him; so we often see princes given horses, weapons, cloth of gold, precious stones, and similar ornaments worthy of their high position. Now, I am anxious to offer myself to Your Magnificence with some token of my devotion to you, and I have not found among my belongings anything as dear to me or that I value as much as my understanding of the deeds of great men, won by me from a long acquaintance with contemporary affairs and a continuous study of the ancient world; these matters I have very diligently analysed and pondered for a long time, and now, having summarized them in a little book, I am sending them to Your Magnificence.

And although I consider this work unworthy to be put before you, yet I am fully confident that you will be kind enough to accept it, seeing that I could not give you a more valuable gift than the means of being able in a very short space of time to grasp all that I, over so many years and with so much affliction and peril, have learned and understood. I have not embellished or crammed this book with rounded periods or big, impressive words, or with any other charm or superfluous decoration of the kind which many are in the habit of using to describe or adorn what they have produced; for my ambition has been either that nothing should distinguish my book, or that it should find favour solely through the variety of its contents and the seriousness of its subject-matter. Nor I hope will it be considered presumptuous for a man of low and humble status to dare discuss and lay down the law about how princes should rule; because, just as men who are sketching the landscape put themselves down in the plain to study the nature of the mountains and the highlands, and to study the low-lying land they put themselves high on the mountains, so, to comprehend fully the nature of the people, one must be a prince, and to comprehend fully the nature of princes one must be an ordinary citizen.

So, Your Magnificence, take this little gift in the spirit in which I send it; and if you read and consider it diligently, you will discover in it my urgent wish that you reach the eminence that fortune and your own accomplishments promise you. And if, from your lofty peak, Your Magnificence will sometimes glance down to these low-lying regions, you will realize the extent to which, undeservedly, I have to endure the great and unremitting malice of fortune.

B. Chapter 14. How a prince should organize his militia

A prince, therefore, should have no other object or thought, nor acquire skill in anything, except war, its organization, and its discipline. The art of war is all that is expected of a ruler; and it is so useful that besides enabling hereditary princes to maintain their rule it frequently enables ordinary citizens to become rulers. On the other hand, we find that princes who have thought more of their pleasures than of arms have lost their states. The first way to lose your state is to neglect the art of war; the first way to win a state is to be skilled in the art of war.

Francesco Sforza,[1] because he was armed, from being an ordinary citizen rose to be duke of Milan; his sons, because they fled the hardships involved, sank to being ordinary citizens after being dukes. You are bound to meet misfortune if you are unarmed because, among other reasons, people despise you, and this, as I shall say later on, is one of the infamies a prince should be on his guard against. There is simply no comparison between a man who is unarmed and one who is not. It is unreasonable to expect that an

---

[1] A *condottiere* (mercenary soldier) who in 1450 came to power as Duke of Milan on the crest of popular support, after serving the city in a war against Venice.

armed man should obey one who is unarmed, or that an unarmed man should remain safe and secure when his servants are armed. In the latter case, there will be suspicion on the one hand and contempt on the other, making cooperation impossible. So a prince who does not understand warfare, as well as the other misfortunes he invites, cannot be respected by his soldiers or place any trust in them.

So he should never let his thoughts stray from military exercises, which he should pursue more vigorously in peace than in war. These exercises can be both physical and mental. As for the first, besides keeping his men well organized and trained, he should always be out hunting, so accustoming his body to hardships and also learning some practical geography: how the mountains slope, how the valleys open, how the plains spread out. He should study rivers and marshes; and in all this he should take great pains. Such knowledge is useful in two ways: first, if he obtains a clear understanding of local geography he will have a better understanding of how to organize his defence; and in addition his knowledge of and acquaintance with local conditions will make it easy for him to grasp the features of any new locality with which he may need to familiarize himself. For example, the hills and valleys, the plains, the rivers, and the marshes of Tuscany have certain features in common with those of other provinces; so with a knowledge of the geography of one particular province one can easily acquire knowledge of the geography of others. The prince who lacks the ability to do this lacks the first qualification of a good commander. This kind of ability teaches him how to locate the enemy, where to take up quarters, how to lead his army on the march and draw it up for battle, and lay siege to a town, to the best advantage.

Philopoemen, the leader of the Achaeans, has been praised by the historians for, among other things, having never in peacetime thought of anything else except military strategy. When he was in the country with his friends, he would often stop and invite a discussion: If the enemy were on top of that hill, and we were down here with our army, which of us would have the advantage? How would one engage them without breaking ranks? If we wanted to retreat, how would we have to set about it? If they retreated, how would we best pursue them?

And, as they went along, he expounded to his friends all the contingencies that can befall an army; he heard their opinion, gave his own, and corroborated it with reasons. As a result, because of these continuous speculations, when he was leading his armies he knew how to cope with all and every emergency.

As for intellectual training, the prince should read history, studying the actions of eminent men to see how they conducted themselves during war and to discover the reasons for their victories or their defeats, so that he can avoid the latter and imitate the former. Above all, he should read history so that he can do what eminent men have done before him: taken as their model some historical figure who has been praised and honoured; and always kept his deeds and actions before them. In this way, it is said, Alexander the Great imitated Achilles; Caesar imitated Alexander; and

Scipio, Cyrus. And anyone who reads the life of Cyrus, written by Xenophon, will then see how much of the glory won by Scipio can be attributed to his emulation of Cyrus, and how much, in his high moral standards, courtesy, humanity, and generosity, Scipio conformed to the picture which Xenophon drew of Cyrus.[2]

A wise prince should observe these rules; he should never take things easy in times of peace, but rather use the latter assiduously, in order to be able to reap the profit in times of adversity. Then, when his fortunes change, he will be found ready to resist adversity.

C. Chapter 15. The things for which men, and especially princes, are praised or blamed

It now remains for us to see how a prince should govern his conduct towards his subjects or his friends. I know that this has often been written about before, and so I hope it will not be thought presumptuous for me to do so, as, especially in discussing this subject, I draw up an original set of rules. But since my intention is to say something that will prove of practical use to the inquirer, I have thought it proper to represent things as they are in real truth, rather than as they are imagined. Many have dreamed up republics and principalities which have never in truth been known to exist; the gulf between how one should live and how one does live is so wide that a man who neglects what is actually done for what should be done learns the way to self-destruction rather than self-preservation. The fact is that a man who wants to act virtuously in every way necessarily comes to grief among so many who are not virtuous. Therefore if a prince wants to maintain his rule he must learn how not to be virtuous, and to make use of this or not according to need.

So leaving aside imaginary things, and referring only to those which truly exist, I say that whenever men are discussed (and especially princes, who are more exposed to view), they are noted for various qualities which earn them either praise or condemnation. Some, for example, are held to be generous, and others miserly (I use the Tuscan word rather than the word avaricious: we call a man who is mean with what he possesses, miserly, and a man who wants to plunder others, avaricious). Some are held to be benefactors, others are called grasping; some cruel, some compassionate; one man faithless, another faithful; one man effeminate and cowardly, another fierce and courageous; one man courteous, another proud; one man lascivious, another pure; one guileless, another crafty; one stubborn, another flexible; one grave, another frivolous; one religious, another sceptical; and so forth. I know everyone will agree that it would be most laudable if a prince possessed all the qualities deemed to be good among those I have

[2] These are all cases from the history of ancient Greece and Rome with which contemporaries with a classical education would have been familiar.

enumerated. But, human nature being what it is, princes cannot possess all those qualities, or rather they cannot always exhibit them. So a prince should be so prudent that he knows how to escape the evil reputation attached to those vices which could lose him his state, and how to avoid those vices which are not so dangerous, if he possibly can; but, if he cannot, he need not worry so much about the latter. And then, he must not flinch from being blamed for vices which are necessary for safeguarding the state. This is because, taking everything into account, he will find that some of the things that appear to be virtues will, if he practises them, ruin him, and some of the things that appear to be wicked will bring him security and prosperity.

D. Brief extracts from Chapter 17. Cruelty and compassion; and whether it is better to be loved than feared, or the reverse ¹

I say that a prince should want to have a reputation for compassion rather than for cruelty: nonetheless, he should be careful that he does not make bad use of compassion. Cesare Borgia was accounted cruel;¹ nevertheless, this cruelty of his reformed the Romagna, brought it unity, and restored order and obedience . . . So a prince should not worry if he incurs reproach for his cruelty so long as he keeps his subjects united and loyal. By making an example or two he will prove more compassionate than those who, being too compassionate, allow disorders which lead to murder and rapine. These nearly always harm the whole community, whereas executions ordered by a prince only affect individuals. A new prince, of all rulers, finds it impossible to avoid a reputation for cruelty . . .

From this arises the following question: whether it is better to be loved than feared, or the reverse. The answer is that one would like to be both the one and the other; but because it is difficult to combine them, it is far better to be feared than loved if you cannot be both. One can make this generalization about men: they are ungrateful, fickle, liars, and deceivers, they shun danger and are greedy for profit; while you treat them well, they are yours. They would shed their blood for you, risk their property, their lives, their children, so long, as I said above, as danger is remote; but when you are in danger they turn against you. Any prince who has come to depend entirely on promises and has taken no other precautions ensures his own ruin; friendship which is bought with money and not with greatness and nobility of mind is paid for, but it does not last and it yields nothing. Men worry less about doing an injury to one who makes himself loved than to one who makes himself feared. The bond of love is one which men, wretched creatures that they are, break when it is to their advantage to do so; but fear is strengthened by a dread of punishment which is always effective.

The prince should nonetheless make himself feared in such a way that, if he is not loved, at least he escapes being hated. For fear is quite compatible

¹ Cesare Borgia: son of Pope Alexander VI. With the help of the French army and the Vatican treasury, Cesare built a kingdom for himself in the Romagna in the period 1499–1502.

with an absence of hatred; and the prince can always avoid hatred if he abstains from the property of his subjects and citizens and from their women. If, even so, it proves necessary to execute someone, this should be done only when there is proper justification and manifest reason for it. But above all a prince should abstain from the property of others; because men sooner forget the death of their father than the loss of their patrimony . . .

However, when a prince is campaigning with his soldiers and is in command of a large army then he need not worry about having a reputation for cruelty; because, without such a reputation, he can never keep his army united and disciplined. Among the admirable achievements of Hannibal is included this: that although he led a huge army, made up of countless different races, on foreign campaigns, there was never any dissension, either among the troops themselves or against their leader, whether things were going well or badly. For this, his inhuman cruelty was wholly responsible. It was this, along with his countless other qualities, which made him feared and respected by his soldiers. If it had not been for his cruelty, his other qualities would not have been enough. The historians, having given little thought to this. on the one hand admire what Hannibal achieved, and on the other condemn what made his achievements possible.

11 Castiglione, *The Courtier* (1528)

Source: Baldesar Castiglione, *The Book of the Courtier*, edited and translated by George Bull (Harmondsworth: Penguin Books, 1967), pp. 42–6, 48–9, 211–15.

Baldesar (variously Balthasar, Baldassare) Castiglione (1478–1529) was an Italian courtier, author and diplomat. In 1507 he wrote about the court of the Duchy of Urbino in *Il Cortegiano* (*The Courtier*), first published in 1528. It appeared in an English translation by Sir Thomas Hoby in 1561.

The Courtier was the most influential courtly manual of the period. It was a book of courtesy in the best medieval tradition and was not notable for its originality of thought. The book owed its influence to its political nature: it provided a convenient and elegantly presented defence of the role of the courtier in the new-style Renaissance court. In 1531 its influence was already apparent in Sir Thomas Elyot's *The Governor*, and in 1570 Roger Ascham's *The Schoolmaster* recommended it as the model for the behaviour of an English gentleman. The extracts below describe life at court and consider the desirable attributes of the lady courtier.

A. Life at the Court of Urbino

So all day and every day at the Court of Urbino was spent on honourable and pleasing activities both of the body and the mind. But since the Duke always retired to his bedroom soon after supper, because of his infirmity, as a rule at that hour everyone went to join the Duchess, Elisabetta Gonzaga,[1] with whom was always to be found signora Emilia Pia,[2] a lady gifted with such a lively wit and judgement, as you know, that she seemed to be in command of all and to endow everyone else with her own discernment and goodness. In their company polite conversations and innocent pleasantries were heard, and everyone's face was so full of laughter and gaiety that the house could truly be called the very inn of happiness. And I am sure that the delight and enjoyment to be had from loving and devoted companionship were never experienced elsewhere as they once were in Urbino. For, apart from the honour it was for each of us to be in the service of a ruler such as I described above, we all felt supremely happy whenever we came into the presence of the Duchess; and this sense of contentment formed between us a bond of affection so strong that even between brothers there could never have been such harmonious agreement and heartfelt love as there was among us all. It was the same with the ladies, whose company we all enjoyed very freely and innocently, since everyone was allowed to talk and sit, make jokes and laugh with whom he pleased, though such was the respect we had for the wishes of the Duchess that the liberty we enjoyed was accompanied by the most careful restraint. And without exception everyone considered that the most pleasurable thing possible was to please her and the most displeasing thing in the world was to earn her displeasure. So for these reasons in her company the most decorous behaviour proved compatible with the greatest freedom, and in her presence our games and laughter were seasoned both with the sharpest witticisms and with a gracious and sober dignity. For the modesty and nobility which informed every act, word and gesture of the Duchess, in jest and laughter, caused even those seeing her for the first time to recognize that she was a very great lady. It seemed, from the way in which she influenced those around her, that she tempered us all to her own character and quality, so that everyone endeavoured to imitate her personal way of behaviour, deriving as it were a model of fine manners from the presence of so great and talented a woman, whose high qualities I do not intend to describe now, since this is not to my purpose and they are well known to all the world, apart from being beyond the reach of whatever I could say or write. But I must add that those qualities in the Duchess which might have remained somewhat hidden, Fortune, as if admiring such rare virtues, chose to reveal through many adversities and harsh blows, in order to demonstrate that in the tender soul of a woman, and accompanied by singular beauty, there may also dwell prudence and a courageous spirit and all those virtues very rarely found even in the staunchest of men.

To continue, let me say that it was the custom for all the gentlemen of the

---

[1] Elisabetta Gonzaga (1471–1526), second daughter of Federico Gonzaga of Mantua, married Duke Guidobaldo da Montefeltro in 1488. The two were driven from Urbino by Cesare Borgia but were restored to power in 1504. Elisabetta was renowned for her virtuous and childless life. She imprinted her personality on the Urbino court. Guidobaldo died in 1508.

[2] Emilia Pia (d. 1528) was the daughter of Marco Pia of Carpi and faithful companion of Elisabetta Gonzaga. She was married to an illegitimate brother of Duke Guidobaldo and widowed in 1500. She too was praised as a model of gaiety and virtue.

house to go, immediately after supper, to the rooms of the Duchess; and there, along with pleasant recreations and enjoyments of various kinds, including constant music and dancing, sometimes intriguing questions were asked, and sometimes ingenious games played (now on the suggestion of one person and now of another) in which, using various ways of concealment, those present revealed their thoughts in allegories to this person or that. And occasionally, there would be discussions on various subjects, or there would be a sharp exchange of spontaneous witticisms; and often 'emblems',[3] as we call them nowadays, were devised for the occasion. And everyone enjoyed these exchanges immensely, since, as I have said, the house was full of very noble and talented persons ... So gathered together at the Court of Urbino there were always to be found poets, musicians, buffoons of all kinds, and the finest talent of every description anywhere in Italy.

Now after Julius II[4] had by his presence and with the help of the French brought Bologna under the rule of the Apostolic See, in the year 1506, he passed through Urbino on his way back to Rome ... And there were some who were so drawn by the charm of the company they found at Urbino that, when the Pope and his Court went their way, they stayed on for many days. During this time, not only were the customary amusements and entertainments continued in the usual style but everyone did his best to contribute something more, and especially in the games that were played nearly every evening. As far as these were concerned, the rule was that as soon as anyone came into the presence of the Duchess he would take his place in a circle, sitting down wherever he wished or wherever he happened to find himself; the group was arranged alternately one man and one woman, as long as there were women, for invariably they were outnumbered by the men. Then the company was governed according to the wishes of the Duchess, who usually left this task to signora Emilia. So the day after the Pope's departure, they all assembled in the customary place at the usual time, and after many pleasant discussions, the Duchess decided that signora Emilia should begin the games; and she, after resisting the suggestion for a little while, spoke as follows: 'Madam, since it is your wish that I should be the one to begin the games this evening, as I cannot rightly refuse to obey you, I want to suggest a game which I think will cause me little criticism and even less trouble. And this is that each one of us should suggest some game he likes that has not been played before; and then the choice will be made of the one that seems worthiest of us.'

Saying this, she turned to signor Gaspare Pallavicino[5] and told him to say what his proposal would be; and he immediately replied: 'It is for you, madam, to tell yours first.'

---

[3] The emblems, consisting of a picture and a Latin motto, were worn on clothing or armour. They were popular with sixteenth-century courtiers.

[4] Pope Julius II.

[5] Gaspare Pallavicino (1486–1511) from Lombardy was one of the youngest taking part in the court conversations. He was chronically ill and died young.

'But I've already done so,' she answered, 'so now,' (turning to the Duchess) 'you, my lady, order him to do what he is told.'

At this the Duchess laughed and said: 'So that everyone will obey you, I make you my deputy and give you all my authority.'

'It really is remarkable,' said signor Pallavicino, 'that women are always allowed this exemption from work, and it would only be reasonable to insist on knowing just why. However, as I don't want to be the first to disobey, I shall leave this matter for another time and do what I am supposed to.'

And then he began as follows: 'It seems to me that in love, just as in everything else, we all judge differently. Therefore it often happens that what one person finds adorable another finds most detestable. Despite this, we are all alike in cherishing the one we love, and quite often the blind devotion of the lover makes him think the person he loves is the only one in the world possessing every virtue and completely without defect. Yet since human nature does not allow such complete perfection, and since there is no one who is wholly without defect, it cannot be said that such people do not deceive themselves, or that love is not blind. So the game I would like played this evening is that each of us should say what quality he would most like the person he loves to possess; and then, since everyone must have some defect, what fault he would choose as well. This is so that we can see who will think of the most commendable and useful qualities and of the faults that are the most excusable and the least harmful to either the lover or the one he loves.'

After signor Gaspare had spoken, signora Emilia made a sign to the lady Costanza Fregoso,[6] as it was her turn, to speak next; and madam Costanza was about to do so when the Duchess suddenly remarked: 'Since signora Emilia is unwilling to give herself the trouble of thinking of a game, it is only right for the other ladies to enjoy the same privilege and also be exempt from making any effort this evening, especially as we have so many men with us that there is no danger of running out of games.'

'Very well, then,' said signora Emilia. And imposing silence on madam Costanza, she turned to Cesare Gonzaga,[7] who sat by her side, and told him to speak next. So he began . . .

[Cesare Gonzaga proposes 'that each one of us should answer the question: "If I had to be openly mad, what kind of folly would I be thought likely to display, and in what connection, going by the sparks of folly which I give out each day?"' This is enthusiastically received by the company, until:]

Fra Serafino,[8] laughing as usual, said: 'This suggestion would take too long, but if you want a really fine game get everyone to give his opinion why it is that almost all women hate rats and love snakes; and you'll discover that no

[6] Costanza Fregoso, granddaughter on the wrong side of the blanket of Duke Federico da Montefeltro of Urbino. When she was exiled from Genoa, she made her home at Urbino and married Count Marcantonio Landi of Piacenza.

[7] Cesare Gonzaga (1475–1512), cousin and close friend of Castiglione. After studying at Mantua, he served the Dukes of Urbino as soldier and diplomat.

[8] Fra Serafino, traveller, correspondent and frequent visitor at Urbino. In 1507 his crude humour got him into trouble: he was assaulted in Rome because of his disrespect for the Pope.

one will hit upon the truth except myself, for I have discovered this secret in a strange way.'

And he had already launched into his usual nonsense when signora Emilia ordered him to keep quiet and, passing over the lady who sat next in line, made a sign to the Unico Aretino,[9] whose turn it now was. And without waiting for anything more, he said: 'I would like to be a judge with the authority to employ any kind of torture in order to extract the truth from criminals. This is so that I could reveal the deceits of a certain ungrateful woman who, with the eyes of an angel and the heart of a serpent, never says what she is thinking in her mind and who, with a feigned and deceitful compassion, does nothing but cut open human hearts. And I tell you, there is no venomous serpent in all the sands of Libya as avid of human blood as this deceiver, who is a veritable Siren not only in the sweetness of her voice and her honeyed words but also in her eyes, her smiles, her looks and in all her ways. However, since I am not allowed, as I would wish, to make use of chains, rope or fire to learn the truth about a certain thing, I would like to find it out through a game, which is as follows: namely, that each one of us should say what he believes is the meaning of the letter "S" that the Duchess is wearing on her forehead.[10] Although this is certainly only another cunning subterfuge, someone may chance to give an explanation for it which she has not perhaps been expecting, and it will be found that Fortune, who looks at men's sufferings with such compassion, has led her unwittingly to reveal by this little sign her secret plan to smother with calamities and kill whoever gazes at her or serves her.'

The Duchess burst out laughing; and then Aretino, seeing that she wished to protest her innocence, went on: 'No, madam, it is not your turn to speak now.'

So then signora Emilia turned to him and said: 'Sir, there is no one among us who does not yield to you in everything, and especially in your knowledge of what is in the Duchess's mind. And just as you know her mind better than the rest of us, because of your inspired understanding, so you love it more than we, who are like those weak-sighted birds which cannot look at the sun and therefore cannot know how perfect it is. So, apart from what you yourself decided, every effort we made to resolve this problem would be useless. Therefore you must undertake the task on your own, as the only one who can carry it through successfully.'

Aretino stayed silent for a little while, and then, when he was again asked to speak, he eventually recited a sonnet on the subject he had raised, describing what was the meaning of the letter 'S', which many of those present thought he had made up on the spot but which others decided must have been composed beforehand since it was more ingenious and polished than seemed possible in the time.

---

[9] Bernardo Accolti (1458–1535), nicknamed Unico Aretino, son of the lawyer and historian Benedetto Accolti. He grew up in Florence. Served as peripatetic court poet at Milan, Urbino, Mantua, Naples, Ferrara and Rome. He thought very well of his own abilities as a poet.

[10] Probably a golden emblem signifying a scorpion.

B. Attributes of a lady courtier

The Magnifico[1] continued: 'Then, madam, to make it clear that your commands can induce me to attempt what I do not even know how to do, I shall describe this excellent lady as I would wish her to be. And when I have fashioned her to my own liking, since I may have no other I shall, like Pygmalion, take her for my own. And although signor Gaspare[2] has stated that the rules laid down for the courtier also serve for the lady, I am of a different opinion; for although they have in common some qualities, which are as necessary to the man as to the woman, there are yet others befitting a woman rather than a man, and others again which befit a man but which a woman should regard as completely foreign to her. I believe this is true as regards the sports we have discussed; but, above all, I hold that a woman should in no way resemble a man as regards her ways, manners, words, gestures and bearing. Thus just as it is very fitting that a man should display a certain robust and sturdy manliness, so it is well for a woman to have a certain soft and delicate tenderness, with an air of feminine sweetness in her every movement, which, in her going and staying and whatsoever she does, always makes her appear a woman, without any resemblance to a man. If this precept be added to the rules that these gentlemen have taught the courtier, then I think that she ought to be able to make use of many of them, and adorn herself with the finest accomplishments, as signor Gaspare says. For I consider that many virtues of the mind are as necessary to a woman as to a man; as it is to be of good family; to shun affectation: to be naturally graceful; to be well mannered, clever and prudent; to be neither proud, envious or evil-tongued, nor vain, contentious or clumsy; to know how to gain and keep the favour of her mistress and of everyone else; to perform well and gracefully the sports suitable for women. It also seems to me that good looks are more important to her than to the courtier, for much is lacking to a woman who lacks beauty. She must also be more circumspect and at greater pains to avoid giving an excuse for someone to speak ill of her; she should not only be beyond reproach but also beyond even suspicion, for a woman lacks a man's resources when it comes to defending herself. And now, seeing that Count Lodovico[3] has explained in great detail what should be the principal occupation of a courtier, namely, to his mind, the profession of arms, it seems right for me to say what I consider ought to be that of the lady at Court. And when I have done this, then I shall believe that most of my task has been carried out.

'Leaving aside, therefore, those virtues of the mind which she must have in common with the courtier, such as prudence, magnanimity, continence and many others besides, and also the qualities that are common to all kinds

---

[1] Giuliano de' Medici (1479–1516), youngest son of Lorenzo the Magnificent, exiled from Florence *c*.1494.

[2] Gaspare Pallavicino (1486–1511) of Lombardy.

[3] Lodovico Pia (d. 1512), distant relative of Emilia Pia.

of women, such as goodness and discretion, the ability to take good care, if she is married, of her husband's belongings and house and children, and the virtues belonging to a good mother, I say that the lady who is at Court should properly have, before all else, a certain pleasing affability whereby she will know how to entertain graciously every kind of man with charming and honest conversation, suited to the time and the place and the rank of the person with whom she is talking. And her serene and modest behaviour, and the candour that ought to inform all her actions, should be accompanied by a quick and vivacious spirit by which she shows her freedom from boorishness; but with such a virtuous manner that she makes herself thought no less chaste, prudent and benign than she is pleasing, witty and discreet. Thus she must observe a certain difficult mean, composed as it were of contrasting qualities, and take care not to stray beyond certain fixed limits. Nor, in her desire to be thought chaste and virtuous, should she appear withdrawn or run off if she dislikes the company she finds herself in or thinks the conversation improper. For it might easily be thought that she was pretending to be straitlaced simply to hide something she feared others could find out about her; and in any case, unsociable manners are always deplorable. Nor again, in order to prove herself free and easy, should she talk immodestly or practise a certain unrestrained and excessive familiarity or the kind of behaviour that leads people to suppose of her what is perhaps untrue. If she happens to find herself present at such talk, she should listen to it with a slight blush of shame. Moreover, she should avoid an error into which I have seen many women fall, namely, eagerly talking and listening to someone speaking evil of others. For those women who when they hear of the immodest behaviour of other women grow hot and bothered and pretend it is unbelievable and that to them an unchaste woman is simply a monster, in showing that they think this is such an enormous crime, suggest that they might be committing it themselves. And those who go about continually prying into the love affairs of other women, relating them in such detail and with such pleasure, appear to be envious and anxious that everyone should know how the matter stands lest by mistake the same thing should be imputed to them; and so they laugh in a certain way, with various mannerisms which betray the pleasure they feel. As a result, although men seem ready enough to listen, they nearly always form a bad opinion of them and hold them in very little respect, and they imagine that the mannerisms they affect are meant to lead them on; and then often they do go so far that the women concerned deservedly fall into ill repute, and finally they come to esteem them so little that they do not care to be with them and in fact regard them with distaste. On the other hand, there is no man so profligate and brash that he does not respect those women who are considered to be chaste and virtuous; for in a woman a serious disposition enhanced by virtue and discernment acts as a shield against the insolence and beastliness of arrogant men; and thus we see that a word, a laugh or an act of kindness, however small, coming from an honest woman is more universally appreciated than all the blandishments and caresses of those who without reserve display their lack of shame, and who, if they are not unchaste, with their wanton laughter, loquacity, brashness and scurrilous behaviour of this sort, certainly appear to be.

'And then, since words are idle and childish unless they are concerned with some subject of importance, the lady at Court as well as being able to recognize the rank of the person with whom she is talking should possess a knowledge of many subjects; and when she is speaking she should know how to choose topics suitable for the kind of person she is addressing, and she should be careful about sometimes saying something unwittingly that may give offence. She ought to be on her guard lest she arouse distaste by praising herself indiscreetly or being too tedious. She should not introduce serious subjects into light-hearted conversation, or jests and jokes into a discussion about serious things. She should not be inept in pretending to know what she does not know, but should seek modestly to win credit for knowing what she does, and, as was said, she should always avoid affectation. In this way she will be adorned with good manners; she will take part in the recreations suitable for a woman with supreme grace; and her conversation will be fluent, and extremely reserved, decent and charming. Thus she will be not only loved but also revered by all and perhaps worthy to stand comparison with our courtier as regards qualities both of mind and body.'

Having said this, the Magnifico fell silent and seemed to be sunk in reflection, as if he had finished what he had to say. And then signor Gaspare said: 'You have indeed, signor Magnifico, beautifully adorned this lady and made her of excellent character. Nevertheless, it seems to me that you have been speaking largely in generalities and have mentioned qualities so impressive that I think you were ashamed to spell them out; and, in the way people sometimes hanker after things that are impossible and miraculous, rather than explain them you have simply wished them into existence. So I should like you to explain what kind of recreations are suitable for a lady at Court, and in what way she ought to converse, and what are the many subjects you say it is fitting for her to know about; and also whether you mean that the prudence, magnanimity, purity and so many other qualities you mentioned are to help her merely in managing her home, and her family and children (though this was not to be her chief occupation) or rather in her conversation and in the graceful practice of those various activities. And now for heaven's sake be careful not to set those poor virtues such degraded tasks that they come to feel ashamed!'

The Magnifico laughed and said: 'You still cannot help displaying your ill-will towards women, signor Gaspare. But I was truly convinced that I had said enough, and especially to an audience such as this; for I hardly think there is anyone here who does not know, as far as recreation is concerned, that it is not becoming for women to handle weapons, ride, play the game of tennis, wrestle or take part in other sports that are suitable for men.'

Then the Unico Aretino[4] remarked: 'Among the ancients women used to

---

[4] Bernardo Accolti (1458–1535), court poet, nicknamed Unico Aretino.

wrestle naked with men; but we have lost that excellent practice, along with many others.'

Cesare Gonzaga[5] added: 'And in my time I have seen women play tennis, handle weapons, ride, hunt and take part in nearly all the sports that a knight can enjoy.'

The Magnifico replied: 'Since I may fashion this lady my own way, I do not want her to indulge in these robust and manly exertions, and, moreover, even those that are suited to a woman I should like her to practise very circumspectly and with the gentle delicacy we have said is appropriate to her. For example, when she is dancing I should not wish to see her use movements that are too forceful and energetic, nor, when she is singing or playing a musical instrument, to use those abrupt and frequent *diminuendos* that are ingenious but not beautiful. And I suggest that she should choose instruments suited to her purpose. Imagine what an ungainly sight it would be to have a woman playing drums, fifes, trumpets or other instruments of that sort; and this is simply because their stridency buries and destroys the sweet gentleness which embellishes everything a woman does. So when she is about to dance or make music of any kind, she should first have to be coaxed a little, and should begin with a certain shyness, suggesting the dignified modesty that brazen women cannot understand. She should always dress herself correctly, and wear clothes that do not make her seem vain and frivolous. But since women are permitted to pay more attention to beauty than men, as indeed they should, and since there are various kinds of beauty, this lady of ours ought to be able to judge what kinds of garments enhance her grace and are most appropriate for whatever she intends to undertake, and then make her choice. When she knows that her looks are bright and gay, she should enhance them by letting her movements, words and dress incline towards gaiety; and another woman who feels that her nature is gentle and serious should match it in appearance. Likewise she should modify the way she dresses depending on whether she is a little stouter or thinner than normal, or fair or dark, though in as subtle a way as possible; and keeping herself all the while dainty and pretty, she should avoid giving the impression that she is going to great pains.

12 Rabelais, *Gargantua* (1534) and *Pantagruel* (1532)

Source: François Rabelais, *The Histories of Gargantua and Pantagruel*, edited and translated by J. M. Cohen (Harmondsworth: Penguin Books, 1955), pp. 86–91; 159–60; 136–7; 192–6; 554–8; 563–5 abridged.

François Rabelais (*c.* 1483–1553) was a friar and a priest whose interest in humanism began in the 1520s when he and a fellow monk studied Greek. When their superiors objected and took away their books Rabelais transferred to the Benedictine

---

[5] Cesare Gonzaga (1475–1512), cousin and close friend of Castiglione.

monastery at Maillezais where the abbot, Bishop Geoffrey d'Estissac, was sympathetic to humanist scholarship and appointed Rabelais as his secretary. In the late 1520s Rabelais went to Paris to study medicine. In 1530 he moved to the University of Montpellier where he lectured on Galen and Hippocrates. From June 1532 he worked as physician at the hospital in Lyons and began to publish medical editions and popular stories. *Pantagruel* was published in 1532, followed in 1534 by *Gargantua*. Both were written in French. In them Rabelais displayed his desire for ecclesiastical reform and satirized religious abuses. Although Rabelais enjoyed considerable patronage and protection for the remainder of his life (for example, from Jean du Bellay, Bishop of Rome and from Francis I) he spent much time evading persecution. (When the Affair of the Placards (17–18 October 1534) identified Protestantism with popular rebellion, official attitudes to Protestants and evangelical humanists became sterner.) In 1546 he published under royal licence the *Tiers Livre* and dedicated it to Margaret of Navarre. This was, however, listed as a censured book and Rabelais left France until 1549 – prudently given the burning of Étienne Dolet the printer in 1546. When he returned in 1549 he occupied himself in writing.

The characters in *Gargantua* and *Pantagruel* are in more ways than one larger than life! Gargantua was the son of the giant king and landowner, Grandgousier. Gargantua, already as well known in contemporary legend as Tom Thumb is to us, was a childish, petulant, fun-loving sort going nowhere until he was taken in hand by his humanist tutor, Ponocrates. Thereafter Gargantua became the model Renaissance prince, ready to assume his responsibilities and discharge his duties to those dependent upon him.

Pantagruel was the son of Gargantua and, like his forebears, of gigantic dimensions. He had the additional power of inducing thirst in those he met. From a 'good time guy' in his youth he grew up to become a wise, prudent and temperate sort; an amiable and engaging person who thought ill of none.

Panurge is initially presented as the cunning, cheeky servant, a foil to his high-minded master, Pantagruel. Subsequently he undergoes something of a transformation into a selfish egotist, indecisive, stupid, fearful and superstitious. Many of the funniest moments in the work centre on Panurge and his antics. Panurge's religion is very orthodox: he does not pray to God but pleads with the Saints and the Virgin Mary. His religion is really superstition and fear. He provides a challenge to Pantagruel's religious evangelism.

Ugly, dirty and ignorant, Friar John epitomized the worst features of the 'monking world' as Rabelais put it. But he was not without virtue. He was honest, energetic and courageous, a man whose fundamental goodness was submerged by an unreformed monastic system. He was excellent company, full of good conversation and bawdy jokes. Above all he was loyal. It was Friar John who first conceived the Abbey of the Thelemites. This Abbaye de Thélème represented the ideals of the progressive humanists. The Thelemite life, devoid of rules except 'Do what you will', forms a striking contrast to the oppressive medieval monasticism that still obtained in sixteenth-century France.

Pantagruel's comrade in arms was Epistemon. The episode of his resurrection and of his view of the underworld (Book 2, chapter 30) parodies the Gospel text.

Greatclod was the Bishop of Papimania. This forms part of a relentless parody of the unreformed Papacy.

A. Rabelais' conception of a humanist education

When Ponocrates saw Gargantua's vicious manner of living, he decided to educate him differently. But for the first days he bore with him, knowing that Nature cannot without great violence endure sudden changes. Therefore, to make a better beginning of his task, he entreated a learned physician of that time, Master Theodore by name, to consider if it would be possible to set Gargantua on a better road. Theodore purged the youth in due form with black hellebore, and with this drug cured his brain of its corrupt and perverse habits. By this means also Ponocrates made him forget all that he had learnt from his old tutors, as Timotheus did for his pupils who had been trained under other musicians. The better to do this, Ponocrates introduced him into the society of the learned men of the region, in emulation of whom his wit increased, as did his desire to change his form of study and to show his worth; and after that the tutor subjected his pupil to such a discipline that he did not waste an hour of the day, but spent his entire time on literature and sound learning.

Gargantua now woke about four o'clock in the morning and, whilst he was being rubbed down, had some chapter of Holy Writ read to him loudly and clearly, with a pronunciation befitting the matter; and this was the business of a young page called Anagnostes, a native of Basché. Moved by the subject and argument of that lesson, he often gave himself up to worship and adoration, to prayers and entreaties, addressed to the good God whose majesty and marvellous wisdom had been exemplified in that reading. Then he went into some private place to make excretion of his natural waste-products, and there his tutor repeated what had been read, explaining to him the more obscure and difficult points. On their way back they considered the face of the sky, whether it was as they had observed it the night before, and into what sign the sun, and also the moon, were entering for that day.

This done, Gargantua was dressed, combed, curled, trimmed, and perfumed, and meanwhile the previous day's lessons were repeated to him. Next, he himself said them by heart, and upon them grounded some practical examples touching the state of man. This they sometimes continued for as long as two or three hours, but generally stopped as soon as he was fully dressed. Then for three full hours he was read to.

When this was done they went out, still discussing the subjects of the reading, and walked over to the sign of the Hound or to the meadows, where they played ball or tennis or the triangle game, gaily exercising their bodies as they had previously exercised their minds. Their sports were entirely unconstrained. For they gave up the game whenever they pleased, and usually stopped when their whole bodies were sweating, or when they were otherwise tired. Then they were well dried and rubbed down, changed their shirts, and sauntered off to see if dinner was ready; and whilst they were waiting there they clearly and eloquently recited some sentences remembered from their lesson. In the meantime my lord Appetite came in, and when the happy moment arrived they sat down at table.

At the beginning of the meal there was a reading of some pleasant tale of the great deeds of old, which lasted till Gargantua had taken his wine. Then, if it seemed good, the reading was continued. Otherwise, they began to converse gaily together, speaking in the first place of the virtues, properties, efficacy, and nature of whatever was served to them at table: of the bread, the wine, the water, the salt, the meats, fish, fruit, herbs, and roots, and of their dressing. From this talk Gargantua learned in a very short time all the relevant passages in Pliny, Athenaeus, Dioscorides, Julius Pollux, Galen, Porphyrius, Oppian, Polybius, Heliodorus, Aristotle, Aelian, and others. As they held these conversations they often had the afore-mentioned books brought to table, to make sure of their quotations; and so well and completely did Gargantua retain in his memory what had been said that there was not a physician then living who knew half as much of this as he.

Afterwards they discussed the lessons read in the morning; and as they concluded their meal with a confection of quinces, he picked his teeth with a mastic branch, and washed his hands and eyes with good fresh water. Then they gave thanks to God by reciting some lovely canticles, composed in praise of the Divine bounty and munificence. After this cards were brought in, not to play with, but so that he might learn a thousand little tricks and new inventions, all based on arithmetic. In this way he came to love this science of numbers, and every day, after dinner and supper, whiled away the time with it as pleasantly as formerly he had done with dice and cards; and so he came to know the theory and practice of arithmetic so well that Tunstal, the Englishman who had written so copiously on the subject, confessed that really, in comparison with Gargantua, all that he knew of it was so much nonsense. And Gargantua did not only become skilled in that branch, but also in such other mathematical sciences as geometry, astronomy, and music. For while they waited for his meal to be prepared and digested they made a thousand pretty instruments and geometrical figures, and also practised the astronomical canons.

After this they amused themselves by singing music in four or five parts or on a set theme, to their throats' content. With regard to musical instruments, he learned to play the lute, the spinet, the harp, the German flute, the nine-holed flute, the viol, and the trombone. After spending an hour in this way, his digestion being complete, he got rid of his natural excrements, and then returned to his principal study for three hours or more, during which time he repeated the morning's reading, went on with the book in hand, and also practised writing, drawing, and shaping the Gothic and Roman letters.

This done, they left their lodging in the company of a young gentleman of Touraine, named Squire Gymnaste, who taught Gargantua the art of horsemanship; and after changing his clothes, the pupil mounted in turn a charger, a cob, a jennet, a barb, and a light horse, and made each run a hundred courses, clear the ditch, leap over the barrier, and turn sharp round to the right and to the left. He did not break his lance. For it is the greatest nonsense in the world to say: 'I broke ten lances at tilt or in battle' – a carpenter could do it easily – but it is a glorious and praiseworthy thing with one lance to have broken ten of your enemies'. So with his lance steel-tipped, tough, and strong, he would break down a door, pierce a harness, root up a tree, spike a ring, or carry off a knight's saddle, coat of mail, and gauntlets; and all this he did armed from head to foot.

As for riding to the sound of trumpets and chirruping to encourage his horse, he had no master; the vaulter of Ferrara was a mere ape by comparison. He was singularly skilled also at leaping rapidly from one horse to another without touching the ground – these horses were called *desultories* – at getting up from either side, lance in hand and without stirrups, and at guiding his horse wherever he would without a bridle. For such feats are helpful to military discipline.

Another day he practised with the battle-axe, which he wielded so well, so lustily repeating his cutting strokes, so dexterously swinging it round his head, that he was passed as a knight-at-arms in the field and at all trials. Then he brandished the pike, played with the two-handed sword, the thrusting sword, the Spanish rapier, the dagger, and the poniard, in armour or without, with a buckler, a rolled cape, or a handguard.

He would hunt the stag, the roebuck, the bear, the boar, the hare, the partridge, the pheasant, and the bustard. He would play with the great ball, and make it fly into the air either with his foot or his fist. He wrestled, ran, and jumped, not at three steps and a leap, not with a hop or with the German action – for, as Gymnaste said, such leaps are useless and serve no purpose in war – but with one bound he would clear a ditch, sail over a hedge, or get six foot up a wall, and in this way climb into a window a lance-length high.

He would swim in deep water on his belly, on his back, on his side, with his whole body, or only with his legs, or with one hand in the air holding a book. Indeed, he would cross the whole breadth of the Seine without wetting that book, dragging his cloak in his teeth, as Julius Caesar did. Then with one hand he would powerfully lift himself into a boat, from there dive head foremost back into the water, sound the depths, explore the hollows of the rocks, and plunge into the gulfs and abysses. Then he would turn the boat, steer it, row it quickly, slowly, with the stream, against the current, check it in full course, guide it with one hand while flourishing a great oar with the other, hoist the sail, climb the mast by the shrouds, run along the spars, fix the compass, pull the bowlines to catch the wind, and wrench at the helm.

Coming out of the water, he sturdily scaled the mountain-side and came down as easily; he climbed trees like a cat, jumped from one to another like a squirrel, and tore down great branches like another Milo. With two stout poniards, as sharp as tried bodkins, he would run up the wall of a house like a rat, and then drop down from the top to the bottom with his limbs in such a posture that he suffered no hurt from the fall. He threw the dart, the bar, the stone, the javelin, the boar-spear, and the halbert; drew a bow to the full, bent by main force great rack-bent cross-bows, lifted an arquebus to his eye to aim it, planted the cannon, shot at the butts, at the popinjay, riding uphill, riding downhill, frontways, sideways, and behind him, like the Parthians. They tied a cable for him to the top of some high tower, with the end hanging to the ground, up which he climbed hand over hand, and then came down so firmly and sturdily that no one could have done better on a level plain. They put up a great pole for him, supported by two trees; and from this he would hang by his hands, moving up and down along it without touching anything with his feet, so fast that you could not catch up with him if you ran at full speed. And to exercise his chest and lungs, he would shout like all the devils. I heard him once calling Eudemon from the Porte St Victor to Montmartre; never had Stentor such a voice at the battle of Troy.

Then, for the strengthening of his sinews, they made him two great sows of lead, each weighing eight hundred and seventy tons, which he called his dumb-bells. These he lifted in either hand, and raised in the air above his head, where he held them without moving for three-quarters of an hour and more, an inimitable feat of strength. He fought at the barriers with the strongest, and when the tussle came, his foothold was so firm that he would let the toughest of them try to move him, as Milo did of old; and in imitation of that champion he would hold a pomegranate in his hand and give it to whoever could get it from him.

After these pastimes and after being rubbed, washed, and refreshed by a change of clothes, he returned quietly; and as they walked through the meadows, or other grassy places, they examined the trees and the plants, comparing them with the descriptions in the books of such ancients as Dioscorides, Marinus, Pliny, Nicander, Macer, and Galen; and they brought back whole handfuls to the house. These were in the charge of a young page called Rhizotome, who also looked after the mattocks, picks, grubbing-hooks, spades, pruning-knives, and other necessary implements for efficient gardening.

Once back at the house, while supper was being prepared, they repeated some passages from what had been read, before sitting down to table. And notice here that Gargantua's dinner was sober and frugal, for he only ate enough to stay the gnawings of his stomach. But his supper was copious and large, for then he took all that he needed to stay and nourish himself. This is the proper regimen prescribed by the art of good, sound medicine, although a rabble of foolish physicians, worn out by the wrangling of the sophists, advise the contrary. During this meal the dinner-time lesson was continued for as long as seemed right, the rest of the time being spent in good, learned, and profitable conversation. After grace had been said, they began to sing melodiously, to play on tuneful instruments, or to indulge in those pleasant games played with cards, dice, or cups; and there they stayed, making good cheer and amusing themselves sometimes till bedtime. But sometimes they went to seek the society of scholars or of men who had visited foreign lands.

B. Rabelais' delight in the New Learning and the authority of the ancients

As you may well suppose, Pantagruel studied very hard. For he had a double-sized intelligence and a memory equal in capacity to the measure of twelve skins and twelve casks of oil. But while he was staying in Paris, he one day received a letter from his father [Gargantua] which read as follows:

Most dear Son,

Among the gifts, graces, and prerogatives with which the Sovereign Creator, God Almighty, endowed and embellished human nature in the beginning, one seems to me to stand alone, and to excel all others; that is the one by which we can, in this mortal state, acquire a kind of immortality and, in the course of this transitory life, perpetuate our name and seed; which we do by lineage sprung from us in lawful marriage. By this means there is in some sort restored to us what was taken from us by the sin of our first parents, who were told that, because they had not been obedient to the commandment of God the Creator, they would die, and that by death would be brought to nothing that magnificent form in which man has been created.

But by this method of seminal propagation, there remains in the children what has perished in the parents, and in the grandchildren what has perished in the children, and so on in succession till the hour of the Last Judgement, when Jesus Christ shall peacefully have rendered up to God His Kingdom, released from all danger and contamination of sin. Then all generations and corruptions shall cease, and the elements shall be free from their continuous transformations, since peace, so long desired, will then be perfect and complete, and all things will be brought to their end and period.

Not without just and equitable cause, therefore, do I offer thanks to God, my Preserver, for permitting me to see my grey-haired age blossom afresh in your youth. When, at the will of Him who rules and governs all things, my soul shall leave this mortal habitation, I shall not now account myself to be absolutely dying, but to be passing from one place to another, since in you, and by you, I shall remain in visible form here in this world, visiting and conversing with men of honour and my friends as I used to. Which conversation of mine has been, thanks to God's aid and grace, although not free from sin, I confess – for we all sin, and continually pray to God to wipe out our sins – at least without evil intention.

If the qualities of my soul did not abide in you as does my visible form, men would not consider you the guardian and treasure-house of the immortality of our name; in which case my pleasure would be small, considering that the lesser part of me, which is my body, would persist, and the better part, which is the soul, and by which our name continues to be blessed among men, would be bastardized and degenerate. This I say not out of any distrust of your virtue, which I have already tried and approved, but in order to encourage you more strongly to proceed from good to better. For what I write to you at present is not so much in order that you may live in this virtuous manner as that you may rejoice in so living and in so having lived, and may strengthen yourself in the like resolution for the future. For the furtherance and perfection of these ends I have, as you will easily remember, spared no expense. Indeed, I have helped you towards them as if I treasured nothing else in this world but to see you, in my lifetime, a perfect model of virtue, honour, and valour, and a paragon of liberal and high-minded learning. I might seem to have desired nothing but to leave you, after my death, as a mirror representing the person of me your father, and if not as excellent and in every way as I wish you, at least desirous of being so.

But although my late father Grandgousier, of blessed memory, devoted all his endeavours to my advancement in all perfection and political knowledge, and although my labour and study were proportionate to – no, even surpassed – his desire; still, as you may well understand, the times were not as fit and favourable for learning as they are to-day, and I had no supply of tutors such as you have. Indeed the times were still dark, and mankind was perpetually reminded of the miseries and disasters wrought by those Goths who had destroyed all sound scholarship. But, thanks be to God, learning has been restored in my age to its former dignity and enlightenment. Indeed I see such improvements that nowadays I should have difficulty in getting a place among little schoolboys, in the lowest class, I who in my youth was reputed, with some justification, to be the most learned man of the century. Which I do not say out of vain boastfulness, although I might commendably do so in writing to you – for which you have the authority of Marcus Tullius [Cicero][1] in his work on Old Age, and Plutarch's statement in his book entitled: *How a Man may Praise Himself without Reproach* – but in order to inspire you to aim still higher.

Now every method of teaching has been restored, and the study of languages has been revived: of Greek, without which it is disgraceful for a man to call himself a scholar, and of Hebrew, Chaldean, and Latin. The elegant and accurate art of printing, which is now in use, was invented in my time, by divine inspiration; as, by contrast, artillery was inspired by diabolical suggestion. The whole world is full of learned men, of very erudite tutors, and of most extensive libraries, and it is my opinion that neither in the time of Plato, of Cicero, nor of Papinian[2] were there such facilities for study as one finds today. No one, in future, will risk appearing in public or in any company, who is not well polished in Minerva's workshop. I find robbers, hangmen, freebooters, and grooms nowadays more learned than the doctors and preachers were in my time.

Why, the very women and girls aspire to the glory and reach out for the celestial manna of sound learning. So much so that at my present age I have been compelled to learn Greek, which I had not despised like Cato, but which I had not the leisure to learn in my youth. Indeed I find a great delight in reading the *Morals* of Plutarch, Plato's magnificent *Dialogues*, the *Monuments* of Pausanias, and the *Antiquities* of Athenaeus, while I wait for

---

[1] Marcus Tullius Cicero (106–43 BC).
[2] Rabelais' invented figure in Papimania, land of the unreformed Papacy.

the hour when it will please God, my Creator, to call me and bid me leave this earth.

Therefore, my son, I beg you to devote your youth to the firm pursuit of your studies and to the attainment of virtue. You are in Paris. There you will find many praiseworthy examples to follow. You have Epistemon for your tutor, and he can give you living instruction by word of mouth. It is my earnest wish that you shall become a perfect master of languages. First of Greek, as Quintilian advises; secondly, of Latin; and then of Hebrew, on account of the Holy Scriptures; also of Chaldean and Arabic, for the same reason; and I would have you model your Greek style on Plato's and your Latin on that of Cicero. Keep your memory well stocked with every tale from history, and here you will find help in the Cosmographes of the historians. Of the liberal arts, geometry, arithmetic, and music, I gave you some smattering when you were still small, at the age of five or six. Go on and learn the rest, also the rules of astronomy. But leave divinatory astrology and Lully's art alone,[3] I beg of you, for they are frauds and vanities. Of Civil Law I would have you learn the best texts by heart, and relate them to the art of philosophy. And as for the knowledge of Nature's works, I should like you to give careful attention to that too; so that there may be no sea, river, or spring of which you do not know the fish. All the birds of the air, all the trees, shrubs, and bushes of the forest, all the herbs of the field, all the metals deep in the bowels of the earth, the precious stones of the whole East and the South – let none of them be unknown to you.

Then scrupulously peruse the books of the Greek, Arabian, and Latin doctors once more, not omitting the Talmudists and Cabbalists, and by frequent dissections gain a perfect knowledge of that other world which is man. At some hours of the day also, begin to examine the Holy Scriptures. First the New Testament and the Epistles of the Apostles in Greek; and then the Old Testament, in Hebrew. In short, let me find you a veritable abyss of knowledge. For, later, when you have grown into a man, you will have to leave this quiet and repose of study, to learn chivalry and warfare, to defend my house, and to help our friends in every emergency against the attacks of evil-doers.

Furthermore, I wish you shortly to show how much you have profited by your studies, which you cannot do better than by publicly defending a thesis in every art against all persons whatsoever, and by keeping the company of learned men, who are as common in Paris as elsewhere.

But because, according to the wise Solomon, Wisdom enters not into the malicious heart, and knowledge without conscience is but the ruin of the soul, it befits you to serve, love, and fear God, to put all your thoughts and hopes in Him, and by faith grounded in charity to be so conjoined with Him that you may never be severed from Him by sin. Be suspicious of the world's deceits and set not your heart on vanity; for this life is transitory, but the

[3] The art of Raimon Lull condemned here was a form of derivative Cabbalistic magic using a lettered wheel. It had been officially condemned in the fifteenth century but remained popular with many Renaissance magicians.

word of God remains eternal. Be helpful to all your neighbours, and love them as yourself. Respect your tutors, avoid the company of those whom you would not care to resemble, and do not omit to make use of those graces which God has bestowed on you. Then, when you see that you have acquired all the knowledge to be gained in those parts, return to me, so that I may see you and give you my blessing before I die.

My son, the peace and grace of our Lord be with you. Amen.

From Utopia, this seventeenth day of the month of March,

Your father, GARGANTUA

After receiving and reading this letter, Pantagruel took fresh courage and was inspired to make greater advances than ever. Indeed, if you had seen him studying and measured the progress he made, you would have said that his spirit among the books was like fire among the heather, so indefatigable and ardent was it.

C. Rabelais: critic of the Church

When the Mass was over Greatclod drew a huge bundle of keys out of a trunk beside the high altar, and with them opened the thirty-two locks and fourteen padlocks of a strongly barred iron window above it. Then he most mysteriously enveloped himself in damp sackcloth and, pulling back a curtain of crimson satin, showed us an image, which I thought very crudely painted. This he touched with a longish stick, and made us all kiss the point that had touched it. He then asked us: 'What do you think of this image?'

'It represents a Pope,' answered Pantagruel. 'I know it by the tiara, the furred stole, the surplice, and the slipper.'

'You are perfectly right,' said Greatclod. 'It is the archetype of that good God upon earth whose coming we devotedly await, and whom we hope to see one day in our land. O happy, yearned-for, long-expected day! Happy and thrice-happy you also, to whom the stars have been so favourable that you have actually seen that good God on earth in life and face-to-face! For we, by the mere sight of his image, gain full remission of all our sins that we can remember, together with the third part and eighteen fortieths of the sins we have forgotten. We are only shown it, to be sure, on the great annual festivals.'

Thereupon Pantagruel said that it was a work in the great tradition of Daedalus, the first sculptor; and that though ill-proportioned and badly made, still, latently and occultly, it contained a certain divine efficacy in the matter of pardons.

'It was like that at Seuilly,' said Friar John. 'The beggars were supping one high feast day in the hospital, and boasting, one that he had made six farthings, another two halfpennies, and a third seven threepenny bits. Then a fourth fat rascal got up and proclaimed that he had made three whole shillings. "Oh yes," replied his companions; "but you've got God's lucky leg." – as if there were some divine and fortunate power concealed in a leg that was all ulcerated and decayed.'

'When you are going to tell us stories like that,' said Pantagruel, 'please remember to bring a basin. That one nearly made me sick. Fancy using the name of God in such a filthy, abominable context! Ugh, I say ugh! If such a misuse of words is the habit in your monkery, please leave it there, and don't bring it with you out of the cloister.'

'Physicians do say,' said Epistemon, 'that there is a certain divine participation in certain ailments. You remember how Nero used to praise mushrooms, and call them in the Greek phrase, *the food of the Gods*, because he had poisoned his predecessor, the Emperor Claudius, with them.'

'I don't think this statue is much like our last Popes,' put in Panurge. 'I have never seen them in stoles, but with helmets on their heads, and a Persian tiara on top; and while the whole Christian realm was in peace and quiet, they alone carried on furious and most cruel wars.'

'But that,' said Greatclod, 'was against rebels, heretics, and desperate Protestants, who disobeyed this great and holy God upon earth. It is not only permissible and lawful for him to wage such wars, but he is commanded to by the sacred Decretals.[1] It is his duty to put to the fire and sword Emperors, Kings, Dukes, Princes, and Republics the moment they transgress his commandments by so much as a jot. He must spoil them of their goods, dispossess them of their realms, proscribe them, and anathematize them, and not only kill their bodies and those of their children and other relatives, but also damn their souls to the bottom of the hottest cauldron in all Hell.'

'But here, in all the devils' names,' protested Panurge, 'there are no such heretics as Raminagrobis was, and as there are now among the Germans and the English. You are proved and sifted Christians.'

'Yes, we are indeed,' said Greatclod, 'and so we shall all be saved. Let us go and take some holy water. Then we will have dinner.'

. . .

Now note, fellow boozers, that while Greatclod was saying his dry Mass, three church bell-ringers, each with a great bowl in his hand, were passing among the crowd, crying: 'Don't forget the happy people who have seen him face-to-face.' As we came out of the temple, they brought Greatclod their basins, which were quite full of Papimaniac money.

Greatclod told us that this collection was for convivial purposes, and that, in accordance with a miraculous gloss, hidden in a certain corner of their holy Decretals, one half of the contribution would be spent on good drink, the other on good food. This was done, in a very fine tavern, which rather reminded me of Guillot's at Amiens. Believe me, the viands were copious and the drinks numerous.

I made two memorable observations at this dinner: first, that no dish was brought in that had not a great deal of canonical stuffing; whether it was kid,

---

[1] Collections of papal pronouncements, issued periodically to enforce the Papacy's secular power; they are parodied and lampooned relentlessly by Rabelais.

capon, or hog – which is very plentiful in Papimania – pigeon, rabbit, leveret, turkey, or any other meat, it was all the same. Secondly, that the whole of the first and second courses was served by the young marriageable maidens of the place. They were pretty, I promise you, and most appetizing; sweet little fair creatures, and most graceful. They wore long, white, loose robes with double girdles. Their heads were bare, and their hair plaited with little bands and ribbons of violet silk, embellished with roses, pinks, marjoram, fennel, orange blossom, and other scented flowers, and each time we put down our glasses they invited us to drink again with the neatest and daintiest of curtseys. Friar John took sideways glances at them, like a dog who has stolen a chicken.

As they cleared the first course these maidens sang a melodious epode[2] in praise of the sacrosanct Decretals; and as the second course was brought in Greatclod, in high good cheer, called to one of these master-butlers: 'Here, clerk, bring some light!' At these words one of the girls promptly presented him with a full beaker of *Supplementary* wine. Then, holding it in his hand and sighing deeply, he said to Pantagruel: 'My Lord, and you, my good friends, I drink to you all from the bottom of my heart. You are all very welcome.' When he had drunk and handed the beaker back to the pretty maiden, he exclaimed most ponderously: 'O divine Decretals, it is thanks to you that wine is found to be so good, so very good.'

'That's the best joke yet,' exclaimed Panurge.

'It would be better still,' said Pantagruel, 'if they could turn poor wine into good.'

'O seraphic *Sixth*,' continued Greatclod, 'how vital that book is for the salvation of humanity! O cherubic *Clementines*, how neatly the perfect life of a true Christian is contained and described in that fourth book! O angelic *Supplementaries*, without you all poor souls would perish, who wander aimlessly here in mortal bodies, about this vale of tears! Alas, when will this gift of special grace be vouchsafed to men, that they may forsake all other studies and occupations only to read you, blessed Decretals, to understand you, know you, use you, put you into practice, incorporate you, absorb you into their blood, and draw you into the deepest lobes of their brains, the very marrow of their bones, and the tortuous labyrinths of their arteries? Then, and not till then, so and not otherwise, will the world be a happy place.'

At this Epistemon got up and said quite clearly to Panurge: 'For want of a close stool I'm forced to retire. This stuffing has relaxed my bumgut. I shan't be long.'

'Then,' continued Greatclod, 'there will be no more hail, frost, fogs, or natural disasters! Then there will be an abundance of all good things on earth! Then there will be perpetual and inviolable peace throughout the Universe, an end of all wars, plunderings, forced labour, brigandage, and assassination, except against heretics and accursed rebels! Then there will be joy, happiness, jollity, gladness, sport, pleasures, and delights throughout all human kind! Oh what great learning, what inestimable erudition, what

---

[2] A lyric poem in which a long line is followed by a short.

godlike precepts, are packed into the divine chapters of these immortal Decretals! Oh, when you read only half a canon, a small paragraph, a single sentence of these sacrosanct Decretals, you feel the furnace of divine love kindle in your hearts; and of charity towards your neighbour as well, providing that he is not a heretic. You feel a fixed contempt for all fortuitous and earthly things, an ecstatic elevation of your spirits, even to the third heaven, and firm contentment in all your affections.'

D. Rabelais parodies the Papacy

'As for you, my good people, [said Greatclod] if you wish to be called good Christians and to have that reputation, I beseech you with clasped hands to believe no other thing, to have no other thought, to say, undertake, or do nothing, except what is contained in our sacred Decretals and their corollaries: the fine *Sextum*, the magnificent *Clementines*, the splendid *Supplementaries*. What deific books! So you will be glorified, honoured, exalted, and rich in dignities and preferments in this world. You will be universally revered and dreaded, and preferred, chosen, and elected above all others. For there is no class of men beneath the cope of heaven in which you will find persons fitter for all undertakings and affairs than those who, by divine foreknowledge and eternal predestination, have applied themselves to the study of the holy Decretals. Should you wish to select a bold commander, a good captain and leader of an army in time of war, a man capable of foreseeing all difficulties, of avoiding all dangers, of leading his men boldly to the attack, and gaily into battle, of taking no risks, but always winning without loss of life and turning his victories to good account, then, believe me you must take one who knows the Decrees. No, no, I mean the Decretals.'

'That was a big gaffe,' said Epistemon.

'Should you wish in time of peace to find a man fit and capable of undertaking the government of a republic, a kingdom, an empire, or a principality; of maintaining the Church, the nobility, the senate, and the people in riches, friendship, concord, obedience, virtue, and dignity, believe me, you must choose a Decretalist. Should you wish to find one capable, by means of his exemplary life, his rare eloquence, and his holy admonitions, of rapidly conquering the Holy Land without bloodshed, and converting the unbelieving Turks, Jews, Tartars, Muscovites, Mamelukes, and Sarra-bovites, then, believe me, you must choose a Decretalist.

'Why is it that in many lands the people are rebellious and uncontrolled, the pages cheeky and mischievous, and the students frivolous dunces? Why, because their governors, squires, and teachers were not Decretalists! But tell me, on your conscience, what was it that founded, strengthened, and gave authority to those splendid religious houses which you now see everywhere, adorning, decorating, and doing honour to the Christian world as the stars do to the firmament? The divine Decretals. What was it that founded, underpropped, and shored up, that now maintains, supports, and nourishes, the devout monks and nuns in their convents, monasteries, and abbeys? To what do we owe these holy folk, without whose continuous prayers, day and night, the world would be in evident danger of returning to its ancient chaos? To the holy Decretals.

'What is it that endowed the famous and celebrated patrimony of St Peter with such abundance of all goods, temporal, corporeal, and spiritual, and what is it that daily increases that abundance? The sacred Decretals. What makes the holy apostolic See of Rome so powerful throughout the Universe, that at all times even to this day, willy-nilly, all kings, emperors, potentates, and lords depend on it, pay homage to it, are crowned, confirmed, and lent authority by it? What is it that forces them to come and kiss it, and prostrate themselves before its miraculous slipper, of which you have seen the picture? Why, God's blessed Decretals. I'll tell you a great secret. The Universities of your world generally bear on their crests and coats-of-arms a book, sometimes open, sometimes closed. Now what book do you think it can be?'

'I'm sure I don't know,' said Pantagruel. 'I've never read a word of it.'

'Why, the Decretals, of course,' proclaimed Greatclod, 'without which all the privileges of all the Universities would decay. I've taught you something there! Ha, ha, ha, ha!'

Here Greatclod began to belch, fart, laugh, dribble, and sweat. He handed his great, greasy bonnet with its four codpiece-like corners to one of the girls, who placed it on her head in great delight, having first kissed it most lovingly. For she took this as a sign and promise that she would be the first to marry.

'Hurrah,' cried Epistemon, 'hurrah! *Hoch! Trinken wir!* Let us drink! That was an apocalyptic secret.'

'Clerk,' cried Greatclod, 'Clerk, some light here, and make it two lanterns. Bring in the dessert, girls! ... As I was saying, if you devote yourself in this way to the exclusive study of the blessed Decretals, you'll be rich and honoured in this world. I say therefore, that in the next world, you will infallibly be brought safely into the blessed kingdom of Heaven, the keys of which are in the hands of our good God the Arch-Decretalist. O my good God, whom I adore but have never seen, open to us, of your especial grace, at least at the hour of our death, that most sacred treasure house of our most holy mother Church, of which you are the guardian, preserver, dispenser, administrator, and steward. Give orders that those precious works of supererogation, those goodly pardons, do not fail us in our need. Then the devils will find no purchase for their teeth in our poor souls, and the dread jaws of hell will not engulf us. If we must pass through purgatory, so be it! It is in your power and discretion to deliver us when you will!'

Here Greatclod began to weep huge hot tears, to beat his breast, to cross his thumbs and to kiss them.

E. Rabelais, Plato and princely power

Meanwhile Grandgousier questioned the pilgrims, asking them of what country they were, where they had come from, and where they were going; and Wearybones answered for them all: 'My lord, I'm from Saint-Genou in Berry, this fellow is from Palluau, this one from Onzay, this one from Argy, and this one here from Villebrenin. We have come from Saint-Sebastien near Nantes, and we are returning by our usual short stages.'

'Yes,' said Gargantua, 'but what was your purpose in going to Saint-Sebastien?'

'We went,' said Wearybones, 'to offer up our vows to that saint against the plague.'

'Oh,' said Grandgousier, 'you poor creatures. Do you imagine that the plague comes from Saint Sebastian?'

'Yes, of course,' replied Wearybones, 'our preachers assure us that it does.'

'Indeed?' said Grandgousier. 'Do the false prophets tell you such lies, then? Do they blaspheme God's holy saints in this fashion, making them seem like devils who do men nothing but harm? It is like Homer's story that the plague was introduced into the Grecian army by Apollo, and the poets' invention of a whole host of Anti-joves and other maleficent gods. There was a canting liar preaching at Cinais to the same tune, that St Anthony sent fire into men's legs, and St Eutropius sent the dropsy, and St Gildas sent madness, and St Genou the gout. But I made such an example of him, although he called me a heretic, that not a single hypocrite of that kidney has ventured to enter my territories to this day. I'm surprised that your king allows them to preach such scandalous doctrine in his kingdom. Why, they deserve worse punishment than those practitioners of magical arts and suchlike who, they say, actually did bring the plague into this country. Pestilence only kills the body, but these impostors poison the soul.'

As he was speaking these words, the monk entered most briskly and asked them: 'Where do you come from, you poor wretches?'

'From Saint-Genou,' they said.

'And how is that great boozer Abbot Tranchelion?' asked the monk. 'And the monks, what cheer are they keeping? God's body, they'll be having a fine fling at your wives while you're out on your pilgrimage!'

'H'm, h'm!' exclaimed Wearybones. 'I'm not afraid about mine. For anyone who has seen her by day won't break his neck to go and visit her by night.'

'You've spoken out of your turn!' said the monk. 'She may be as plain as Proserpine. But, by God, she'll be turned over, seeing that there are monks about. For a good workman finds a use for all timber alike. Pox take me if you don't find them considerably plumper when you get back, for even the shadow of an abbey-steeple is fruitful.'

'It's like the Nile water in Egypt, if you believe Strabo,' said Gargantua, 'and Pliny, in the third chapter of his seventh book. Why, their crumbs, their clothes, or their bodies will serve to get a woman with child.'

Then said Grandgousier: 'Go your ways, poor men, in the name of God the creator. May he be a perpetual guide to you, and don't be so ready to undertake these idle, useless journeys in future. Look after your families, work, each man at his vocation, instruct your children, and live as the good apostle St Paul directs you. If you do so you'll have God's protection, the angels and saints will be with you, and no plague or evil will bring you harm.'

Then Gargantua led them into the hall to take their meal. But the pilgrims could not stop sighing. 'Oh, how happy is the country,' they said to him, 'that has such a man for its lord! We have been more edified and instructed by his conversation than by all the sermons that were ever preached to us in our town.'

'That,' said Gargantua, 'is what Plato says, in the fifth book of his *Republic*, where he says that states will only be happy when the kings shall be philosophers and the philosophers kings.'

F. Rabelais on freedom, education and Christian virtue

All their life [i.e. the Thelemites'] was regulated not by laws, statutes, or rules, but according to their free will and pleasure. They rose from bed when they pleased, and drank, ate, worked, and slept when the fancy seized them. Nobody woke them; nobody compelled them either to eat or to drink, or to do anything else whatever. So it was that Gargantua had established it. In their rules there was only one clause:

DO WHAT YOU WILL

because people who are free, well-born, well-bred, and easy in honest company have a natural spur and instinct which drives them to virtuous deeds and deflects them from vice; and this they called honour. When these same men are depressed and enslaved by vile constraint and subjection, they use this noble quality which once impelled them freely towards virtue, to throw off and break this yoke of slavery. For we always strive after things forbidden and covet what is denied us.

Making use of this liberty, they most laudably rivalled one another in all of them doing what they saw pleased one. If some man or woman said, 'Let us drink', they all drank; if he or she said, 'Let us play', they all played; if it was 'Let us go and amuse ourselves in the fields', everyone went there. If it were for hawking or hunting, the ladies, mounted on fine mares, with their grand palfreys following, each carried on their daintily gloved wrists a sparrow-hawk, a lanneret, or a merlin, the men carrying the other birds.

So nobly were they instructed that there was not a man or woman among them who could not read, write, sing, play musical instruments, speak five or six languages, and compose in them both verse and prose. Never were seen such worthy knights, so valiant, so nimble both on foot and horse; knights more vigorous, more agile, handier with all weapons than they were. Never were seen ladies so good-looking, so dainty, less tiresome, more skilled with the fingers and the needle, and in every free and honest womanly pursuit than they were.

For that reason, when the time came that anyone in that abbey, either at his parents' request or for any other reason, wished to leave it, he took with him one of the ladies, the one who had accepted him as her admirer, and they were married to one another; and if at Thélème they had lived in devotion and friendship, they lived in still greater devotion and friendship when they were married. Indeed, they loved one another to the end of their days as much as they had done on their wedding day.

13 The Church and Discipline (fourteenth to sixteenth centuries)

The Church, whether Catholic or Protestant, whether pre- or post-Reformation, established and sought to maintain orthodoxy in matters of doctrine, ceremonial, morals and religious observance. This is not the place for an exhaustive description of the machinery of Church discipline: we have selected several documents which illustrate differing aspects of this machinery which can provide the basis for further exploration. Document 13.A is taken from the records of Jacques Fournier's Inquisition into the Cathar heresy in his diocese. Inquisition was a normal instrument of Church discipline but it was not often used before the introduction of the Inquisition in many European countries in the sixteenth century. Document 13.B moves from the disciplinary procedures against heretics of the late medieval Church to the attempts by Protestant Churches to control their membership. The selection from the *Actes du Consistoire de l'Église Française de Threadneedle Street* (London) has been specially translated to demonstrate the all-pervasive attempts by the Stranger Church to influence its members' lives. An enormous variety of offences were brought before the court and dealt with by the godly. But this court, like those in the other Protestant communities of Europe, acted as an administrative arm of the Church as well as a disciplinary instrument. The late medieval and early modern Churches, Catholic and Protestant, were organized as well as ordered through the courts of their law. Document 13.C shows part of the visitation system in operation in the diocese of York. The visitation was the normal and ordinary means in the medieval Church of seeking out nonconformity among both clergy and laity to the Church's rules and regulations, of dispensing punishment and of enforcing conformity. Bishops normally visited their dioceses triennially; archdeacons visited their jurisdictions more frequently and archbishops less frequently. A list of clergy and church officials, variously known as *liber cleri* or a call book, was drawn up for the visitors to work from. Churchwardens would bring presentments to the visitation court – that is charges of irregular behaviour of clergy and laity, non-maintenance of the fabric, non-attendance at church and so forth. Composite books of *comperta* (inquiries) and *detecta* (findings) noted the presentments and recorded the inquiries and findings of the visitation. Visitations were continued in England and in many other Protestant states after the Reformation. The brief extracts are from the *comperta* and *detecta* books of the Archbishop's 1575 visitation of his diocese – they show the process of uncovering irregularities and offences within the Church's life. Over a three-month period the commissioners moved from ruri-decanal church to ruri-decanal church receiving presentments from parishes in that area. The next stage in the process was to hear these cases in the correction courts in the Minster at York two or three months later. Serious and obdurate cases would be heard in the Bishop's consistory court. Document 13. D is selected from the Lichfield cause (meaning case) papers to illustrate the operation of the consistory court in its role of disciplining church personnel.

A. Extracts from an inquisitorial register

Source: *Heresy and Authority in Medieval Europe: Documents in Translation*, edited and translated by Edward Peters (London: Scolar Press, 1980), pp. 254–5; 257–8; 261; 264.

Jacques Fournier, Cistercian monk and Bishop of Pamiers (later Pope Benedict XII), conducted a rigorous inquisition in his diocese from 1318 to 1325. This was largely to root out Catharism in the area. Inquisitions were part of the normal apparatus of the Church in the medieval period. The excellent records of the inquisition were later copied out at Fournier's request and were deposited in the Papal Library at Avignon after he died. Emmanuel LeRoy Ladurie's *Montaillou* is based upon an edited version of these records. The extracts here demonstrate some of the evidence which such records yield about the nature of popular, and especially peasant, beliefs. The unorthodox beliefs of one of the Cathars have been set along-side the orthodox Catholic positions. The Cathar or Albigensian heresy had spread throughout Languedoc by about 1200. Its adherents believed in a dualism between God and Satan, good and evil, pure spiritual world and corrupt material world. A crusade by the northern French barons rooted out the heresy here by the mid-thirteenth century but the heresy lingered in the mountains of southern France and underwent something of a revival in Montaillou in the Ariège in the first quarter of the fourteenth century.

TESTIMONY OF ARNAUD DE SAVINHAN, OF TARASCON, A STONECUTTER

He believed that 'there was no other world except this present one'. For this and other unorthodox beliefs he was imprisoned for sixteen months and thereafter had to wear crosses. He did not perform this latter penance and was arrested again. He complained of the severity of his earlier punishment, since 'he felt that he was without blame ... because he had not seen [Albigensian] heretics.' He endured five and a half more years of strict imprisonment as punishment for his failure to perform his earlier penance, and after his release he had to wear crosses.

TESTIMONY OF GUILLAUME AUSTATZ, OF ORNOLAC, A FARMHAND

'He said that he believed that if each soul had its own body, then the world would hardly be able to contain so many souls, because although they are small quantities, nevertheless since there were so many of them they would fill up the world. From this he appeared to believe that souls are corporeal, having hands, feet, and other members, and he was asked if he believed this. He answered that at the time he was talking about he believed that human souls had the corporeal form of men and women and members just like the members of the human body.'

On another occasion Guillaume was talking to other men in the village square in Ornolac about the place where dead souls go. Guillaume said that paradise 'was as big as if the area from Toulouse up to Merens were made into one house that would occupy the whole area, and many souls can fit into it'.

TESTIMONY OF PETER MAURY, OF MONTAILLOU

'Asked if he had heard from heretics or believed that the human soul has members separate from the body, as well as a form and figure and flesh and bones just like the human body, he responded that he had not heard this from heretics but that he nevertheless believed that the human soul separated from the body has all these attributes and is like a person. He had always believed this from the time when he had gained the use of reason, although he was amazed at how this could be; for if the soul of a human going out of his body is in the figure of a man, how could it be that no one sees it leaving the body in human figure and form? . . .'

TESTIMONY OF JEAN MAURY, OF MONTAILLOU

'Likewise he believed that although God was a good heavenly Father, he had never descended from heaven nor did he accept the body of a worldly human; nevertheless existing in himself in heaven, he has a heavenly rather than a terrestrial body similar in form and figure to the terrestrial human body; and he has flesh and bones, although spiritual, not earthly, ones; and in the likeness and figure of his own celestial body he made Adam out of earth. And he believed likewise concerning all spirits that remained in heaven with the Father . . . But he nevertheless did not believe that the Father of the spirits and the spirits that stayed with him ate anything or drank, but that they lived by the grace of God; and even less did he believe that they brought forth any wastes because he did not believe that there were any filthy things in heaven but rather that all things were beautiful there.'

TESTIMONY OF ARNAUD SICRE, OF TARASCON

'And once, he said, he heard Peter Maury and his brother Jean talking about human souls: where they might be able to be received, because so many men were living and so many had already died. And the priest [with whom they were talking] said that all human souls which exist are able to be received in the space of a single finger of a man's hand. And when the witness [Arnaud] and Peter and Jean Maury were amazed at this, the priest added that all souls are able to fit in the place of one button; and when they were even more amazed at this, the priest said, "We others do not wish to say to you, who are beasts [heretics?], what the human soul is lest you err greatly." '

TESTIMONY OF GUILLAUME FORT, OF MONTAILLOU

'He believed that the souls of good men go to heavenly paradise, but that the souls of bad men, both now and after the last judgment, will go among the cliffs and precipices and that demons will throw them down from the cliffs onto the rocks below.

'Asked who taught him these errors, he said that he himself had thought up the idea that after death human bodies do not revive and are not resurrected. He came to the conclusion that souls without bodies will appear at the last judgment and will be judged by Christ, but that the souls of evil men both now and after the judgment will wander among the cliffs and be thrown down from the heights. And he believed this and believes it still, informed, as he said, in this by the common talk in the lands of Aillon and Saltu [the area where Montaillou lies] . . .'

PRACTICES PERFORMED ON THE DEAD TO BRING GOOD FORTUNE: TESTIMONY OF FABRISSA RIBA

'She also said that when Ponclus Clergue, father of the priest [of Montaillou], died, many people from Alliou came to the priest's house. The body was placed in the room called the *foganhu* [kitchen] and had not yet been wrapped in cloth. The priest [Pierre Clergue] made everyone leave the house except Alamainis Ademeria, and Bruna, wife of Guillelm Porcell and the natural daughter of Prades Tavernier, the heretic. They remained with the priest and the corpse. And she heard that the women along with the priest then took off the hair and [finger- and toe-] nails of the dead man; and they were said to have done this for this reason: so that good fortune would remain in that house.'

INVOCATION OF THE DEVIL: TESTIMONY OF ARNAUD LAUFRE

'He also said that Guillelm Carreria said to him that he had heard that Bor (Raimund de l'Aire) was ploughing in a field in Bodiers . . . with two untamed oxen. When the oxen moved out of alignment, the yoke that was over their necks was brought down under the necks. Seeing this Raimund said, "Devil, put back that yoke in its proper place!" And when this was said, the yoke was reversed up over the necks of the oxen.'

TESTIMONY OF ARNAUD GELIS, OF PAMIERS

Arnaud's beliefs

1. The souls of dead people do not do any other penance except to wander from church to church,

Roman Catholic orthodoxy

1. All souls of dead people go to purgatory, where they do the penance they had not completed on

some faster, some slower according to their sinfulness.

2. After they are finished going around to churches through the streets, the souls go to the place of rest, which is on this earth. They stay there until the judgment day.

3. No soul of any man except the most saintly goes directly to heaven or the heavenly kingdom. Souls do this on the day of judgment.

4. Souls of children who died before baptism go to an obscure place until the judgment day. There they feel neither pain nor pleasure. After the judgment day they enter paradise.

5. No soul of a dead person, no matter how evil, has entered or will enter hell.

6. At the last judgment God will have mercy on all who held the Christian faith and no one will be damned, no matter how evil he was.

7. Christ will have mercy on the souls of all heretics, Jews, and pagans; therefore none of them will be damned.

8. Human souls, both before the body's death and after, have their own bodily form just like their external body. And the souls have

earth. And when this is done they go to the heavenly paradise where Christ, Mary, the angels, and the saints reside.

2. When their penance is done, the souls of the dead go to the joy of the celestial paradise, which is no place of rest on earth, but rather in heaven.

3. All souls of the dead, when their penance is done in purgatory (if they had need of it), enter the heavenly kingdom.

4. The souls of unbaptized children will never be saved or enter the kingdom of heaven.

5. The souls of all evil persons – i.e., those who perpetrate great crimes that they do not confess or do penance for – go immediately after death to hell, where they stay and are punished for their sins.

6. All souls that held the Christian faith and accepted its sacraments and obeyed its commandments will be saved; but those who, even though holding the faith and accepting the sacraments, did not live according to the commandments will be damned.

7. All souls of heretics, pagans, and Jews, who did not want to believe in Christ, will be damned. They will be punished eternally in hell.

8. Human souls, both while in the body and after its death, because they are spirits, are not corporeal, nor do they have corporeal mem-

| distinct members like hands, eyes, feet, and the rest. | bers, nor do they eat or drink, nor do they suffer such corporeal necessities. |
| 9. Hell is a place only for demons. | 9. Hell is a place for demons and for wicked people, where each is punished eternally as he deserves. |

Some other beliefs imputed to Arnaud by witnesses:

10. The souls of the dead do not eat, but they do drink good wine and warm themselves at fires. The wine is not, however, diminished by their drinking it.

11. 'Those who move their arms and hands from their sides when they walk along do great evil . . . [since] such moving arms throw down many souls of the dead to the earth . . .'

DISBELIEF IN INDULGENCES: TESTIMONY OF GUILLELME CORNELHANO

'He also said that about two years before around the feast of Pentecost . . . a seller of indulgences passed by [him and Guillelma Vilara, wife of Arnald Cuculli] who had with him many indulgences. And after he had left them, Guillelma said, "Do you believe that any man is able to indulge or absolve anyone of his sins? Don't believe it, because no one can absolve anyone except God." And when he himself said that the pope and all priests could absolve man from sins, Guillelma answered that it was not so, only God could [do that].'

BELIEF AND DISBELIEF IN MARY'S POWER TO INTERVENE IN A CASE OF THEFT: TESTIMONY OF GUALHARDA, WIFE OF BERNARD ROS OF ORNOLAC

She said that 'this year around the feast of the birth of John the Baptist, a certain quantity of money and other things were stolen from her; she had been keeping them in a box which had been broken into. She went to Guillelm, the bailiff of Ornolac, and requested him to perform his office and seek out the thief and make it so that she would get her things back. He turned a deaf ear to her request; so she, grieving and crying, went to the church of Blessed Mary of Montgauzy in order to obtain a miracle from her, namely the recovery of the money and goods. The better to obtain this [miracle], she fixed candles around the altar of Blessed Mary. And when she returned to Ornolac and again petitioned Guillelm about the theft and he refused to intervene, she reminded him that just as he had tracked down some grain stolen from himself that year, he was obligated to search for her stolen money and goods. Guillelm responded that he searched for the grain because he would know it when he found it, but that he would not recognize her money and goods. And Gualharda then said, "I confided in the Blessed Mary of Montgauzy when I visited the church there, and I asked her to return to me the money and the goods stolen from me; and she will vindicate me against those who have stolen these things if she cannot restore the goods." Then Guillelm said . . . that Blessed Mary did not have the power to recover the money and goods of Gualharda; and when she replied that of course Mary had that power and that he was speaking evil things and that Mary would vindicate her, Guillelm answered that Blessed Mary did not kill men or perpetrate death.'

B. The Consistory of the French Congregation in London

Source: *Actes du Consistoire de l'Église Française de Threadneedle Street, Londres*. The Huguenot Society of London, 38; (London: Huguenot Society, 1937); extracts selected by Rosemary O'Day and translated by R. Niall D. Martin.

The French and Dutch Stranger Churches, which under Edward VI possessed a church discipline (modelled on that of Zwingli at Zurich) which was totally outside the control of the Bishop of London, went into exile or hiding under Mary I. In 1559 Elizabeth permitted their re-establishment but on less favourable terms. The Bishop of London was appointed their superintendent and it was expected that the rites and ceremonies practised should not be 'contrary or derogatory to our laws'. The appointment of the erstwhile Marian exile, Edmund Grindal, as Bishop of London neutralized any immediate ill-effects. Under his indulgent protection the Stranger Church came to enjoy a wide measure of independence. By 1570 the congregation stood at 4,000 (perhaps half the alien population of London).

The consistory or court was the typical instrument of godly discipline in the new Protestant Churches. The extracts selected show how the consistory of the French Church functioned both as a court in which recalcitrant members stood accused and were judged and as the policy-making and administrative arm of the Church – appointing officials, determining, defining and executing policy, and so forth. The extracts show the consistory officials acting as moral police but they do much more than that – they show how resistant the members of the Church could be to the censure and sanctions of the congregation to which they belonged.

On Tuesday 13 [August 1560] Nicolas Volandrel, a native of Bordeaux in the Diocese of Rouen, appeared before us with certain divorce letters issued in Berne, written in German with a Latin translation and dated 18 October 1559. They stated that Anne de Boyr his wife had deserted him and how much she had been searched and called for. Since nevertheless she was not to be found or caught, permission therefore was granted him by the said letters to marry another. He also produced other letters, issued at Payerne [on 20 October 1559] . . . testifying to his good conduct . . . He requested that . . . we should be willing to . . . give him permission to marry.

On this he was questioned on his conduct both before and after his return to this country and, so as to be sure, he should within a week bring to us people worthy of trust who have known him to testify to it. Also, to check if there was an exception in the said letters of divorce, saying that if he had no relationship with anyone else, it was necessary to know how he had controlled himself.

In addition he was admonished that even before asking this permission and licence of us he had made a promise to a certain woman. Which he did not deny . . .

On the assigned day . . . [Volandrel] came and with him appeared . . . [several witnesses]. These all agreed in affirming and testifying to his integrity and good conduct, both in this city in the time of King Edward, and out of this country where he has lived, as in Geneva, Lausanne and Payau. With the exception of Jehan, none opposed this divorce, but he, however, had known him as a good man and alleged no sufficient reason for opposing it [the divorce].

The decision of the consistory was that in view of the diligence that the said Volandrel showed in the search for his wife, the judgement he had obtained against her, the good testimony given for him by the letters and by witnesses, the divorce obtained by him in Berne ought rightly to be approved here and freedom to marry granted him. The whole of this matter must be communicated to the Lord Bishop of London our superintendent,[1] to enable him to provide as necessary. On 27 [August] Piere Alexandre gave his report to the consistory on the decision on this matter of the Lord Bishop of London . . . This was that we ought to proceed in all equity in accordance with the liberty given us in the gospel.

. . .

On Tuesday 27 August, Joachin le Loup appeared before our consistory requesting that his marriage might be celebrated the following Sunday. This was granted and he was questioned on his faith, and enjoined to learn the principal articles of our faith so that he could make a public confession on the day of his marriage for the edification of the church.

. . .

On Tuesday 10 September it was agreed by the whole of the consistory that from then on, before the Sunday and Thursday sermon some of the elders and deacons would give readings from Holy Scripture for the purpose of avoiding the conversations that take place in the church before the service time, and the congregation was gathered. Readings to begin at the first chapter of the New Testament, continuing in order until the end. The other purpose was to enable everyone to be better prepared and ready to receive the exposition of the Holy Scriptures given by the minister . . .

. . .

On the said Tuesday 17 September 1560 Jehan le Bugle, a young man and a native of Rockfort [?Roquefort] in Normandy was called before the consistory concerning the tennis game. He confessed having played with Jehan le Gallois, losing 4 écus. This was on the incitement of the said le

---

[1] The Bishop of London concerned was Edmund Grindal (see document I.13.C).

Gallois. However, when the said Gallois appeared before us . . . he excused himself saying that he did not incite him to do it, and even that it was the said Bugle who did not let him play in peace. Nonetheless the said Gallois was admonished in view of the fact that he was the older and that he had long since made profession of the Word and had sinned in this and that henceforth he should better fulfil his duty before such young persons when he sees them thus dissipating themselves.

. . .

On Thursday [26 September] Master Jehan Wacquerie schoolmaster was called before the consistory. He was admonished to do better his duty to bring the children to the church, and also to teach them to intone the psalms with him, so that there should be no confusion in the singing of the psalms

. . .

On . . . Tuesday 1 October 1560, it was decided . . . that . . . promises of marriage were not to be made unless the minister was present, or at least the elder of the district, in cases where they wanted to be married in church.

. . .

On Tuesday 15 October anno 1560 we had to consider the case of a girl who used to lodge with the ambassador of Sweden, and was the niece of the wife of the late Master Piere du Val. She had once before been found pregnant by the said ambassador and now was so again. It was decided that Mr Alixandre and Mr du Mas will go to the said ambassador to admonish him and beg him to keep order so that the said girl should not go and ruin herself in this way, as he was bound to do by the Word of God.

Further on the said day Jehan Saloe, chaplain of St Catherine's and member of the church, brought his wife to have her brought to acknowledge her sin and the whoredom she had committed against him. She did not show any great repentance but, nonetheless, in consideration of the change she promised to make, and the need of her husband, he was permitted to take her again and retain her as his wife, after she had made public penitence before the whole church. This she promised to do the following Thursday.

. . .

On Thursday 17 October . . . Jehanne the wife of Jehan Saloe made public penitence in the face of the whole church as she had been ordered to . . . Many received this with tears and crying as they saw her truly displeased at her sin and ask for pardon from God and his Church. The whole church pardoned her and then she was received as a member of the church by the ministers and elders.

. . .

On [Thursday 29 May 1561] Mr de Solles mentioned to the consistory that he was considering whether people would come to him to do two Latin lessons each week, that is Monday and Wednesday at 8 in the morning. He said that he had already mentioned it to the Bishop our superintendent. Everyone thought this good and edifying since he was so good as to take such pains.

. . .

The following Monday Mr de Solles began his Latin classes and is planning to continue . . . The following Tuesday the 3rd of June Jaques Lambert's wife was received into the church.

. . .

On the said day it was decided by the consistory that from now on those who did not communicate at the Sacrament should be questioned on what hindrances held them back, and each elder and deacon was charged with this in the district committed to him.

On the same day it was also decided to publish in the name of the consistory that all under its discipline were not to suborn each other's servants, and also not to receive any without first knowing whether their previous master was happy with their move . . .

. . .

[12 June 1561] . . . Nicholas Binet and Paul Tetellet were together at the consistory, to be reconciled over the insults they had given each other, and even Binet acknowledged having sinned in using some lies . . .

At the 17 June consistory Piere Joeuron was called to be admonished over his drunkenness. He had been seen drunk by some of the brothers of the church. He nonetheless strongly excused himself. However he did not deny he had been locked up on account of his lack of self-control. He was admonished to abstain.

On the same day . . . Master Jehan le Telier called de Guines requested at the consistory a letter of recommendation from the church. This was not found good by all members of the consistory . . .

On the said 17th day Jean Rock reported that people who lived in the house of the temple building complained that they cannot get into their house because of the books being sold in front of their lodging. Jaques de Chalon was charged with pointing this out to the seller of the said books.

. . .

[1 August 1564] Jaques Caillon, ropemaker, complains against the widow Anthoine Typrey. He says she refuses to come to the consistory.

On the said day agreement was established in our presence between Robert and Jehan Mary and Anthoine Perioau who had accused each other to the official procurators.

Hans van Hulsten was questioned on his abstention from the sacrament. He replied that it was because of some argument that de Glaude's wife had with his, and other quarrels. He said that it was because of the maidservant, and . . . that there had been a reconciliation.

. . .

[19 September 1564] Didier Bonaer presented himself to hear what he was ordered to do by way of satisfaction for his sin and the scandal he caused the church. He was told that he had to acknowledge his fault publicly, and his wife likewise.

The said Didier requested to be excused by some means if possible, such as by giving some fine to the poor, and that the matter be not put before the whole congregation, for he well knows that some will only laugh and make fun of him, and as for his wife it seems to him that she too could well go without acknowledging her fault publicly in view of the fact that she had not yet become a member of the church. The answer was that being excused for money was in no way permissible, and that he should consider his position between now and Thursday and then give us a final answer.

. . .

[31 October 1564] . . . Nicholas le Roy came to beg the consistory to admonish his daughter because she wants to marry against the wishes of him and her mother, i.e. to a young man called Jehan Gramer of Lorraine whom nobody knew and could give a reference for. The girl who is a young widow replies that she does not want to act against the will of her father and her mother but that she really wants them to accept this because they have already stopped another suitor. She was told that it would be good if he went to his country to Metz to obtain testimonials from his relatives and friends. She said that he . . . [would be happy to] and that she agreed.

Nonetheless when the following day the said friend was called to the consistory and was admonished to make the said journey before he got married, he replied that the matter was too far advanced for such a journey and that it would cost much money.

He made it sufficiently clear that they wanted to accept no other advice than their own and that they were already engaged to each other.

On Wednesday 1 November 1564, Jehan Dehors came to say that he was content to follow the order of the church and submit himself to what the consistory thought good for him to do.

He was told that he had to acknowledge his sin publicly on the next Sunday morning.

He accepted this with great difficulty. Nevertheless he went as if decided to do it, but when he was outside he returned and asked for so much favour as to be allowed to do it on a weekday or tomorrow [Thursday] . . . The only answer given was that the acknowledgement would give more edification on a Sunday than on another day.

[April 1565] It was also ordained that Piere Chastelain would be sent with brothers of the church to warn yet again Nicolas Lancre and Jaenne Wateble to stop living together in accordance with the advice the church gave them. Otherwise we were to proceed the following Sunday to their excommunication. This they refused. So the following Sunday after the sermon they were both declared by the minister to be barred from the communion of this congregation and that as long as they stayed in such a state they were taken for Gentiles and Heathens.

. . .

On Thursday 12 April two of the brothers living in St Martins presented themselves in the consistory to declare that they had been summoned before the Dean of Westminster who had ordered them to come to communion on Easter Day in their parish, which was given for the hands once a year. They had answered the said dean that they belonged to the church of the French and that they would speak to their minister and elders. So they had come to seek advice on the matter.

C. Archbishop Grindal's second visitation of the diocese of York, 1575

Source: Archbishop Grindal's Visitation, Comperta and Detecta, 1575, edited by W. J. Sheils (York: Borthwick Institute of Historical Research, 1977), pp. 2–5.

Edmund Grindal, Bishop of London (1559–70), Archbishop of York (157c–6), Archbishop of Canterbury (1575–83), was a former Marian exile and conscientious Protestant.

THE DEANERY OF THE CHRISTIANITY OF THE CITY OF YORK

ALL HALLOWS PARISH UPON THE PAVEMENT

The churchyard is not cleanly kept. 5.[1]
The curate doth not every holy day read the Lord's Prayer, the Articles of Faith, and Ten Commandments. 12.
The people on the Pavement do commonly open their shops on Sundays and holy days if fairs and markets fall on such days. 46.

SAINT GEORGE'S PARISH

They want the book of the Paraphrases of Erasmus. 2.[2]
The chancel of the church is in decay in the default of Mr Criplinge, farmer of the parsonage there.[3]

SAINT MAURICE'S PARISH

Nil mali.[4]

[1] The numerals following various of the entries are a cross-reference to the number of the relevant article in Archbishop Grindal's Visitation Articles of 1575.
[2] Erasmus's commentaries on the New Testament.
[3] The chancel (that part of the church containing the choir and the high altar) was the responsibility of the rector of a parish – i.e. he who held the great (corn) tithes (a tax of a tenth on corn produced in the parish). This might be an ecclesiastic (clerical rector) or a lay parson (lay impropriator) or, as in this case, someone who leased (farmed) the right to the tithes.
[4] 'Nothing wrong'.

CRUXE [ST CROSS] PARISH

They lack Erasmus' Paraphrase. 2.

SAINT NICHOLAS' PARISH

William Clarkson, John Clarkson and Robert Clarkson, executors of John Clarkson, late of Grimston deceased, do refuse to pay xxd, to the parish for the ground where their father was buried.
Mr Nicholas Valentine refuseth to pay ordinary duties for a house which he hath in this parish, viz. clerk wages for ii years and more.

TRINITY IN MICKLEGATE

John Edwin cometh not to the church but twice or thrice in the year, and since Easter was twelvemonth neither he nor his wife did communicate at their parish church aforesaid.
Mr Christopher Asheburne, John Alderson, John Edwin [and 11 other men] do refuse to contribute to the repairing of the church and other necessaries thereunto belonging. 54.

SAINT MARTIN'S IN MICKLEGATE

The chancel is very ruinous and like to fall. 5.
The Lady Wilstropp received not the Communion this year, neither cometh to this her parish church.

SAINT JOHN'S PARISH

Nil mali saving that they present Janet Williamson, wife of Cuthbert Williamson, to be a notorious scold, a slanderer of her neighbours, a common bawd and such as permitteth naughty persons to repair to her house.

SAINT MICHAEL'S PARISH

Their curate doth serve two cures, viz. he is vicar of Askham Richarde and serveth here by sequestration.

SAINT SAVIOUR'S PARISH

Nil mali.

ALL HALLOWS IN PEASHOLME

The church is in decay. 5.
No sermons. 10.
Anthony Iveson, clerk, parson there, is also parson of Burghwalles and vicar in the cathedral church of York, having yet showed no dispensation for the holding of them all. 27.[5]

SAINT SAMPSON'S PARISH

They lack the Book of Common Prayer with the new calendar, two psalters, two tomes[6] of the Homilies, the Paraphrases of Erasmus, a coffer with two locks and keys for keeping the register books and a box for the poor. 2.

D. Henry Trickett in the Lichfield Consistory Court

Source: Original records of the case survive in Lichfield Joint Record Office, BC/5/1598/9.

A case was brought by officials against Henry Trickett, Vicar of Marston and Dovebridge, Derbyshire, in the consistory court of the diocese of Coventry and Lichfield. The case was heard between October and March 1599. In the following extracts, modernized by Rosemary O'Day, an attempt has been made to retain some of the flavour of the original language.

[THE ALLEGATIONS]

6. Item, it is objected and alleged against you that you the said Henry Trickett by public fame of the countries[1] of Derby and Stafford adjoining have attained to[2] the possession of the vicarage of Dovebridge aforesaid by unlawful bargain and compact for money with one Richard Barber of Tutbury in the county of Stafford aforesaid: which money was paid either by yourself, or by some other person for you and in your name or by your consent and knowledge . . .[3]
7. . . . you the said Henry Trickett were never known or supposed to be a

[5] Pluralism was forbidden without licence granted by the authorities.
[6] Volumes (of set sermons or homilies, in this case).

[1] Counties.
[2] Acquired.
[3] Simony, or the purchase or sale of spiritual things with money, was against Church law. Clergymen were not permitted to buy benefices, i.e. positions in the Church. But traffic in benefices was very common and the Canons of the Church of England in 1604 required all ordinands and recipients of benefices to declare on oath that they had not purchased their offices.

favourer of the Gospel. In regard you never endeavoured yourself to read, study or give ear to the preaching of the same . . .[4]

8. . . . that you . . . never preached one sermon, nor ever expounded one text of Scripture to the parishioners of or in either of your cures: and yet you have from time to time denied and repelled God's ministers, that have offered themselves to preach in the said cures . . .[5]

9. . . . that you . . . in all your time never entertained any curate able or sufficient to preach or instruct the people of God in either your said cures, neither have you yourself been diligent or careful by reading of homilies to teach or instruct the same people. But all your time you have robbed the people of God of his sacred word in two great congregations and parishes . . .

10. . . . that you . . . in time of divine service sitting in the chancel of the church of Marston did nevertheless turn your back to the congregation and so thereby and by lowness of your voice do very unChristianly hide and obscure divine service and prayer now by public authority set forth: As it well does appear in this, for that you have never used openly or distinctly to read the same, but lewdly to omit some part thereof: And hastily to mumble up the rest in such sort that the more part of the congregation know not when service is ended but by departure of some of their neighbours. And so depart themselves (as long time they have done, to the great grief of their consciences and slander of the ministry . . .)[6]

12. . . . that you . . . have not in all your time once catechized the youth of or in either your said cures:[7] nor never trained up any scholars in learning but have consumed your time in all careless security, at no time and in no wise respecting or regarding the duty and calling of a Christian minister . . .

13. . . . that you . . . have not in all your time used or frequented the company of any Godly or learned preacher, nor associated yourself with any such. But in all odious and unreverent manner have disdained them and their sermons and termed them 'Minishers' or 'Minish Jacks' . . .

15. . . . that you . . . have spent and consumed your time as a layman in

[4] All ministers were required to spend a proportion of their time in study of the Scriptures.
[5] If a minister was unqualified to preach to the people himself, he was required either to provide a suitably qualified curate or to employ a licensed preacher to visit the parish. Every minister, licensed or no, was able to read to his congregation the set homilies of Christian instruction provided in the Book of Common Prayer.
[6] Protestantism emphasized the participation of the laity in divine service. The minister turned to face the people and spoke distinctly so that they could follow the service. It was considered a mark of a Catholic priest, if the priest turned away from the people, seeking to exclude the laity and to make a mystery of the service. This applied especially to the celebration of the communion, which should be not a sacrificial act from which the people were excluded but a shared supper. There were varying opinions within the Church of England concerning this matter: the allegations against Trickett adopt a Protestant viewpoint.
[7] Oral instruction, using the question and answer method, given to both adults and children in the principal Christian doctrines accepted by the Church of England, was required of the pastoral ministry. Catechizing covered the Creed (or declaration of belief), the Lord's Prayer and the Ten Commandments. It would often be given by the assistant curate rather than the vicar or rector. Ministers were also expected to talent spot – to recruit able boys for the ministry and help nurture them.

purchasing of land. In buying and taking of leases. In troubling and vexing poor men at the law to their undoing. In lending money upon usury.[8] In hunting, fishing and breeding beasts as oxen, mares and colts and selling them your own self at fairs and markets wherein you daily exercise your self still nothing regarding your charge and calling . . .[9]

16. . . . that you . . . have heretofore been presented to be a favourer of the Romish religion. And to have obstinately maintained the doctrine of justification by works:[10] for the which and for other notable crimes and errors in you noted, whereunto you have obstinately refused to give answer, being lawfully cited thereunto you have long time stood excommunicate . . .[11]

17. . . . that you . . . have been and are a harbourer and fosterer of one Margaret Wathoe, a woman that resorts not to church but is much inclined to papistry, carrying a pair of beads continually and praying upon them openly from the which she has not been dissuaded by you . . .

19. . . . that you . . . by colour of naming fairs and markets have and do yearly admonish the people of abrogate holy days, as namely of the feasts of St Lawrence and the feasts of the nativity and assumption of the Virgin Mary and such like . . .[12]

28. . . . that you . . . were suspended and excommunicated five or six times before you sought or obtained any absolution . . .

[FURTHER ALLEGATIONS]

Item . . . you . . . by public fame have committed adultery with Dorothy the wife of John Wright of Dovebridge . . . at such time as the said Dorothy dried peas on a kiln at and in the vicarage house . . . to whom you . . . gave twelve pence to have your pleasure of her: And the said John Wright having notice thereof you . . . did give unto the said Wright twenty shillings to conceal the matter . . .

Item . . . one Anne Dakin a maid servant was begotten with child in your vicarage at Dovebridge . . . which bastard child one Sir Richard Traverse

---

[8] Lending money at interest.

[9] Ministers were not permitted by the rules of state and of the Church to conduct themselves 'as laymen'. While a clergyman might teach, practise medicine and serve as an ecclesiastical lawyer, he was not permitted to follow a trade or to farm for profit (*Statutes of the Realm*: 21 Henry VIII, c. 13; reinforced by Canon 76 of 1604). He was required to wear distinctive, sober clerical attire and to adopt a serious demeanour. Frivolous clothing and behaviour were forbidden.

[10] That salvation can be earned by good works and performing the rituals of the Church.

[11] He had been cited before the bishop's court for this offence, had refused to appear and explain himself, had been declared excommunicate and had not sought absolution from the court. Excommunication (which literally meant being thrust out of the community and communion of the Church) was the chief means of enforcing Church discipline. By ignoring this sanction Trickett appeared to be scorning flagrantly the authority of the courts.

[12] At the Reformation the number of saints' days in the calendar of the Church of England was much reduced. Trickett is charged with using the advertising of secular fairs and markets (held on particular saints' days) as a covert means of advising the people of the forbidden red letter days.

then curate of . . . Dovebridge did instantly affirm to be begotten by you the said Henry Trickett.

Item . . . you . . . of late time have been vehemently suspected of having lived incontinently with one Helen or Eleanor Creswell the wife of George Creswell a woman of very evil name and fame, who is reported to have had two bastards before the said Creswell married her. Which said Creswell is entertained by you . . . to be your curate not for any sufficiency in the man, being neither minister nor preacher nor otherwise learned but for the liking and desire you are deemed to have had to the said Helen or Eleanor.

Item . . . the said George Creswell your curate being no minister did enterprise to marry one John Collins and one Jane Shingleton together on the feast day of St Bartholomew at night last past in the mansion house of one John Wright of Dovebridge . . . which was then and still is an alehouse. And took of the married persons two shillings for the said marriage.

[Several witnesses were called to make depositions concerning the truth or otherwise of these allegations. Opinion was divided. There was agreement that Trickett was no preacher and an indifferent performer in church but a variety of opinions were expressed concerning his inclinations towards Roman Catholicism, his relationships with women and his general bearing.]

[TRISTRAM DAYNTRIE, AGED 46, OF MARSTON, WHO HAD KNOWN TRICKETT FOR 20 YEARS]

13. . . . he this deponent having been a parishioner of Marston about twenty years together did never hear . . . Henry Trickett make any one sermon, neither having procured any quarterly sermons to be made . . . but sayeth that now and then he readeth homilies and sayeth the communion is not administered but once in the year unless it be upon some special occasion . . .

15. . . . his voice is so low and soft when he readeth divine service the people in the nether end of the church cannot hear what he says. And when he readeth the psalms he turns his face up the church but when he readeth the chapters and the epistle and gospels he turns his face towards the people . . .

16. . . . he never useth to catechize the youth at Marston but he useth diverse times to read homilies . . .

18. . . . he has heard the said Henry Trickett at such time as he useth to bid holy days and fasting days tell unto the people when the days of the nativity and assumption of the blessed virgin Mary do come but he does not bid them holy days . . .

19. . . . [he] hath kept in his house the said Wathow mentioned . . . being a poor woman not otherwise able to live unless by begging, but whether she be a papist or useth to pray upon beads he knows not . . .

28. . . . [he] hath executed divine service continually . . .

29. . . . the said Ursula Curtis dwelleth in the said vicarage of Marston with the said Mr Trickett being his housekeeper . . .

30. . . . Ursula was once thrust off a little bridge . . . and so fell into [the] Dove but he never heard her called the vicar's whore . . .

[One witness, 37-year-old William Mansfield of Marston, described how he and another parishioner had sought to persuade Trickett to continue the employment of a particular curate, who was well liked in the parish. His comments reveal how Trickett was thought to be influenced by his housekeeper Ursula Curtis.]

[Mansfield reported] . . . that Ursula could not abide him or any other since she was robbed. Whereupon this deponent said 'Why Mr Vicar, she is your servant, you may rule your servant.' Whereupon, he replied, 'Can you rule your wife?' and this deponent told him that was not a like reason and told him a man might put away a servant and he answered again he would put away five or six such as he was rather than put away her and called the said curate a knave . . .

SECTION II

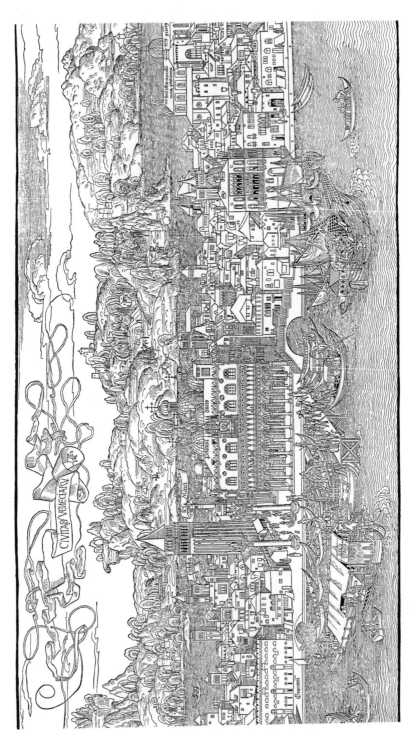

The ducal palace and church of San Marco detail of the view of Venice from Bernhard von Breydenbach's Pilgrimage in the Holy Land (Peregrinatio in Terram Sanctam) printed by Erhard Renwich (Maintz 1486). Reproduced by kind permission of The British Library.

SECTION II

Civic Pride and Civic Patronage: Venice and Antwerp

Centres of trade and industry, banking and finance, Venice and Antwerp occupied a pivotal position in the world economy of the sixteenth century. In terms of social structure and social arrangements there was a good deal of similarity between them. Cosmopolitan and corporatist in character, both were patrician in government. In terms of cultural and artistic activity, too, Venice and Antwerp had much in common. Neither was a university town, but as centres of conspicuous consumption and book production, both were magnets for scholars, writers and artists. For all that, there were significant differences in the situations of the two cities which ultimately made Antwerp more susceptible to religious radicalism and social unrest.

Venice, by contrast, was famous for the perfection of its political arrangements, the marvels of its mixed constitution and the harmonious social relations arising therefrom. The myth of Venice is here represented in the classic statement of Gasparo Contarini (document II.1). His treatise, though, is more than a celebration of Venetian state-craft; the passages printed below indicate how the mass of the population was excluded from the political process but integrated into the commonwealth. From this account it is clear that the Venetian social order was essentially the outcome of a process of negotiation. Guicciar-dini's analysis suggests that similar considerations informed the governing process in Antwerp (document II.2). In both cities relations between rulers and ruled were mediated by trade guilds and confrater-nities; without these props the civic order could not have been sustained.

Moving from institutions to individuals and from the public to the private sphere immediately brings us up against the intractability of the sources, the gendered nature of historical scholarship – for so long written by men about men – and the fact that in general nobody saw fit to record the activities, interests and aspirations of ordinary folk. Women, for example, were invariably written about in prescriptive rather than descriptive terms; rarely do we know what women thought and did, particularly women of the middle and lower orders. This makes all the more valuable the information about domestic arrangements and household and personal effects that can be teased out of inventories, wills and other legal documents (documents II.3, 4, 5, 6).

Women, though the largest, were not, of course, the only disadvantaged group in these urban centres; and while patriarchy was an important buttress to the civic order, it is equally true that the prosperity of Venice and Antwerp depended in no small measure upon an unusual latitude in matters of faith allowed to the resident foreign merchant communities of both cities. Here it is the situation of the Jewish minority which is most engaging. Notwithstanding the discrimination to which they were subject, Jews performed an important role in the intellectual and religious life of the host community, as well as in its economic development. Of Antwerp's clandestine community we know comparatively little; it maintained a low profile and appears to have been largely Marrano in make-up.* Venetian Jewry, by contrast, was socially more diverse, larger in numbers and much better documented. The orthodox belief that Judaism was a degenerate faith destined to be superseded by Christianity was not one to which all Christian intellectuals subscribed. Some were particularly interested in Jewish culture and learning. Francesco Giorgi, the Venetian friar and philosopher, was one of them. The ways in which the ancient wisdom contained in the Cabbala sustained their Neoplatonism and Christian concerns are represented in document II.10.

The rich cultural life of Venice and Antwerp, the variety of scholarly activity and the development of their civic consciousness, can also be approached through the growth of public and private libraries. The donation of Cardinal Bessarion to the Venetian Republic and the more humble legacy of Pensionary Pauwels to the citizens of Antwerp supply the basis for a number of instructive comparisons and fruitful contrasts (documents II.7, 8, 9).

1 Contarini: Governing Venice (1534)

Source: Gasparo Contarini, *The Commonwealth and Government of Venice*, translated by Lewis Lewkenor, London 1599 (Amsterdam and New York: Theatrum Orbis Terrarum and Da Capo Press, 1969), pp. 15–19, 68–71, 78–9, 138–49. Spelling modernized by David Englander.

Gasparo Contarini (1483–1542), a Venetian political writer, theologian, humanist and diplomatist, was the scion of a patrician household. He was created Cardinal in 1535 and worked hard for conciliation and reunion between Catholic and Protestant.

---

* Marrano is a Spanish term meaning 'swine' applied to those Jews who, compelled to adopt Christianity in consequence of the persecutions of 1391 and later, remained faithful at heart to Judaism. The concept is, however, a contested one.

Contarini is best remembered for his treatise on Venetian government. His argument that the Venetian constitution presented the wisest and happiest combination of democratic, aristocratic and monarchic forms of government was subsequently criticized by Bodin, but remained influential. This celebrated study was written in 1534 and published in Paris in 1543.

But now finally to come to the institution of our Venetian commonwealth, the whole authority of the city from whose whole decrees and laws as well as the senate as all other magistrates derive their power and authority, is in that council, into which all the gentlemen of the City being once past the age of 25 years are admitted ... Now first I am to yield you a reckoning how and with what wisdom it was ordained by our ancestors, that the common people should not be admitted into this company of citizens, in whose authority consisteth the whole power of the commonwealth ... Because many troubles and popular tumults arise in those cities, whose government is swayed by the common people, which we have also read, hath been observed in sundry commonwealths, and also delivered in way of precept by many and great philosophers, yet many were of contrary opinion, deeming that it would do well, if this manner of governing the commonwealth should rather be defined by ability and abundance of riches: but here again they fell into great absurdities and no small inconveniences: for it happeneth often that those of the basest sort, yea of the very scum of the people, do scrape together great wealth, as those that apply themselves to filthy arts, and illiberal occupation,[1] never sparing the toilsome and careful wearing out of their lives, but with an intolerable saving, defrauding themselves of the comforts of life, thereby to increase their substance. Contrariwise the honest citizens, and those that are liberally brought up, oftentimes fall to poverty ... Therefore our wise and prudent ancestors ... ordered that this definition of the public rule should go rather by the nobility of lineage, than by the estimation of wealth: yet with that temperature [proviso], that men of chief and supreme nobility should not have this rule alone (for that would rather have been the power of a few than a commonwealth) but also every other citizen whosoever not ignobly born: so that all which were noble by birth, or ennobled by virtue, or well deserving of the commonwealth, did ... obtain this right of government ... This ... great council (upon whose authority the whole power of this commonwealth, as also the dignity of the senate and of all the magistrates dependeth) representeth in this commonwealth the form of a popular state. The Duke who ... ruleth during life, beareth the show of a kingly power ... But the Senate, the ten, the college of elders or chief counsellors ... carry with them a certain show of an Aristocracy or government of the nobility ...
...
Our elders were not ignorant, that if every Senator should confusedly make report unto the Senate, and then deliver his opinion without limitation

---

[1] i.e. those pursuits or occupations considered servile, mechanical and unworthy of a free man.

or restriction of that office to some particulars: there must of necessity follow great trouble and intricateness in the Senate. Besides, it is by experience approved, that the thing which dependeth generally alike upon the care of all, is generally alike in a manner of all neglected.

Therefore it was by our laws ordained, that there should be chosen sixteen citizens out of the senate, which in respect of their further knowledge and sufficiency above the rest ... counsel the senate in those things that are to be handled ... This magistrate doth not continue in office any longer than six months.

. . .

Calling therefore to mind, that among the Lacedemonians the Ephores were mighty and of great authority, and among the Athenians the Areopagites, and so likewise among the Romans the Decemviri or ten men,[2] insomuch that they made laws: they thought it not amiss by imitation of their example, though in an unlike cause, to create in this our city some magistrate of authority and power, whose office above all other things should be, to have especial care to see that among the citizens should not arise any strife or dissension, whereby there might ensue any scandal or uproar: and to prevent factions, or the attempts of any wicked citizen that should conspire against the liberty of the commonwealth: of which sort of mischief if there should by evil destiny any creep into the commonwealth, they then to have absolute authority to punish and chasten the same, lest otherwise the commonwealth might thereby receive harm ...

. . .

It remaineth that we show you the manner whereby our most prudent ancestors have retained the common and meaner people in duty: a matter surely strange and scarcely credible, that the people being so many years deprived of the public government, did never yet refuse nor unwillingly support the government of the nobility, neither yet did ever attempt anything whereby the form of the commonwealth might be altered, and they received into the fellowship of rule, but have always hitherto faithfully loved and willingly obeyed the Nobility. But ... whosoever ... will consider ... shall find that the people hath not been wholly rejected, but received into such offices and charges, as might be committed unto them without detriment or hindrance of the general good ...

Among the Venetians this always hath been most constantly observed, that justice should be equally administered to all, and that it be not lawful for any how great soever, to do wrong or injury to the least of the lower or meanest people, insomuch that it has always been held as a heinous abomination, and detestable sacrilege, for any gentleman to misuse a Plebeian ... Besides, there is not any thing more carefully provided for by the Senate, than that there may be plenty of corn and of all other things that are necessary either for the sustenance or safety and healthiness of the

---

[2] These references are to variant forms of magistracies in the Greco-Roman world that combined executive, judicial and disciplinary powers.

people: insomuch that to preserve the people from want and famine, the common treasure is sometimes exceedingly spent and wasted . . . But many things besides added, whereby the commodities of the people are exceeding respected, and their poverty carefully relieved, especially of such that either presently do, or at any time have employed themselves in honest trades of use and service to the commonwealth, and grow at length either by age or weakness unable to pursue therein: for in Venice there are built infinite many houses fitly and commodiously, which are frankly given to such kinds of men, wherein during their lives they may live and their Families without charge: besides within the Arsenal . . . there is a determinate stipend and yearly allowance given to a great multitude of men unable either through age, impotency, or weakness to do any work, only in regard, that when in their better times they were able, they had employed their labour in doing service to the commonwealth . . .

But now besides these good institutions and means to retain the common people in duty, there are also certain laws, which were as me seemeth established with exceeding wisdom of our ancestors; such as thereby both the people's ambition, and desire of honour being a humour inseparably possessing the minds of men, may be thoroughly satisfied, and yet the government of the Nobility no way disturbed.

The whole people are divided into two parts, the one of the honester and best respected sort, the other of the very base common people, as mechanical, and handicrafts men . . . either of these in my opinion are both fitly and commodiously provided for, because to this meaner people . . . there are . . . granted certain mean degrees, and dignities: for they are divided into so many companies as there are several trades and occupations, and every company hath certain peculiar laws, under which they are in the exercise thereof directed and governed, over every of these companies there are chosen by suffrage of the whole company certain, that they may well be called as it were masters of that company: for by their commandment many things are prescribed, and many small controversies by their arbitrament ended, whence it cometh, that all such artificers as can once attain to that honour, do exceedingly content and please themselves therewith, and do think themselves not smally advanced when they once are come so far, that they are by the rest of their condition and company thought worthy of that pre-eminence, there are besides in every Company certain other Officers elected, though inferior to the masters thereof, yet notwithstanding of good credit, and much respected among the rest, in some sort therefore you see that this desire of honour, which seemeth to be settled even in the minds of the lowest and meanest people, is satisfied and provided for. The other better kind of people obtaineth also in the City of Venice, a better and more honourable place, enjoying certain particular offices and degrees, of especial reckoning and account, into which no gentleman may be admitted . . . the office of the Secretaries is honest, and of great regard. They sit at the tribunals with every magistrate, the same is only given to plebeians, and not to any gentleman . . . of these Secretaries to the Senate one is above the rest, and is called Chancellor of Venice, a name of great dignity and honour . . . , he is acquainted with every secret of the commonwealth, and hath great rents allowed him out of the common treasure, and when he dieth, his obsequies are honoured with a funeral oration, which dignity is not in Venice yielded to any, unless it be to the Duke or to some Citizen of extraordinary desert, and to none else. The Chancellor representing as it were the prince of the common people, he only is chosen in the Sessions of the great Council, the other Secretaries are created by the College of ten, and are subject to their censure, if they make any fault in the public office which they execute. Likewise the popular assemblies and companies of artificers and masters of every occupation, and some others of whom we will speak hereafter, depend upon the arbitrament of the ten, and are subject to their authority, being by the same instituted at the first, and now still ordered and maintained, and surely the creation of this officer being at the first only to avoid the danger of these popular meetings and assemblies, was not done without exceeding providence and foresight, lest otherwise their fraternities and assemblies, being at the first ordained for the common good, might in time under colour of assembling, to do their duty, have tempted something prejudicial to the commonwealth's quietness.

There are besides these five fellowships and societies in Venice protected under the name and religion of certain saints, in which there are innumerable numbers of men both plebeians and Patricians, of which every one hath his peculiar kind of attire, ornament, and ensign, which they nevertheless do not use at all times but only when they go in procession, or to honour any man's funeral, or else to any solemn service, they do usually assemble every holyday, first hearing divine service, and then going about unto the churches of the Saints, honouring the high and immortal God, with pompous solemnity of supplication and prayer.

Every of these fellowships hath his particular house, and in the same a goodly and spacious hall, in which upon appointed days they do all meet to perform the duties which they do owe unto religion, sometimes they have Mass there solemnly celebrated, sometimes they go altogether to visit the church of some Saint: oftentimes they solemnize the obsequy and funeral of one of their deceased brothers, offering oblations and dirges for his sins: besides those spacious halls every of them hath an appointed several room, wherein both the heads and presidents of these fellowships do meet. Their office continueth but a year, and is among the Plebeians of especial dignity and prerogative; their meetings are to consult and take care for such things as are necessary and fit for the good of the fellowship, and likewise there is committed to their trust a great quantity of money, which is to be bestowed upon the poor: for such and so exceeding, in times past, was the estimation of these fellowships, that many who by testament had ordained and bequeathed the distribution of their goods to the use of the poor, would make these to be their executors, and wholly refer the bestowing thereof to their discretion ... these fellowships ... are all restrained under the power and authority of the Council of ten, so that they may not in any thing make any alteration, nor assemble together, unless it be at appointed seasons, without their leave and permission. Such honours do the plebeians of either sort attain unto in this commonwealth of ours, to the end that they should not altogether think themselves deprived of public authority, and civil offices, but should also in some sort have their ambition satisfied, without having occasion either to hate or perturb the estate of nobility . . .

2 Guicciardini: Antwerp (1567)

Source: Description de touts les Païs-bas, autrement appellés la Germanie inférieure, ou Basse Allemagne; par Messire Louis Guicciardin . . . Maintenant reveue, & augmentée plus que la moictiée par le mesme autheur. Avec toutes les cartes géographiques des dicts païs & plusieurs pourtraicts de villes, etc (Traduict d'Italien en langue françoise par F. de Belle Forest) (Antwerp: Plantin, 1582), translated and corrected against the 1582 Italian edition by R. Niall D. Martin, and checked by Dr T. J. Hermans, Department of Dutch, University College London.

Ludovico Guicciardini (1523–89) came from a distinguished Florentine family, and was a nephew of Francesco, the diplomat, historian and scholar. His *Description* of the city forms part of a wider study of the Low Countries; it was first published in Antwerp in 1567 and in many editions thereafter. In it Guicciardini presents a sharp-eyed account of the city at the height of its success. The extracts below, which are concerned with the structure of urban government, point up the discrepancy between its formal and its real status in relation to the Holy Roman Empire and indicate the extent of popular participation in the governing process.

Antwerp has always been an Imperial City, and not only that, but also capital of the Margravate of the Holy Empire . . . For this reason it enjoys many privileges . . .
. . .

Antwerp also has an honour or pre-eminence . . . known in Flemish as Burgravate and in Walloon and Italian as a Viscounty. This honour and title of Burgrave or Viscount was formerly given to the commander of the castle of Antwerp along with some provision for a pension and lodging, and other possessions and lands since given as fiefs to one person or another. Out of that was instituted a feudal court and civil jurisdiction which still sits every fortnight under the lieutenant of the lord of the fief . . . The function of the Burgrave was to be lord and guardian of the castle and its inhabitants, a fact that can be decisively proved. In particular, to this day, when someone is admitted as a Freeman, he is made to take the oath at the Vierscale in the form of words and terms of the past, that is that he will be faithful and loyal to the Duke of Brabant as Margrave of the Holy Roman Empire, promising to guard and defend loyally, in the company of the Burgrave and the other Freemen, the castle and fort (which is now taken as the city), and the whole of the territory of Antwerp. After falling into the hands of the Duke of Cleves . . . this title finally came into the hands of the Prince of Orange . . . This title is certainly worthy of honour, but hardly profitable, inasmuch as today it operates more in name than in reality and function.

. . .

So then, to resume, let us have a brief look at how this noble city is ruled and governed. In the first place, Antwerp has for Lord and Prince the Duke of Brabant in his capacity of Margrave of the Holy Empire, but with such great privileges of such a character, obtained and granted from time immemorial, that it now rules and governs itself, as if autonomous, almost like a free city and republic, while always respecting the rights and suzerainty of the Prince. Hence, this mode of government is (in my judgement), if all of it were kept and observed, hardly different from the form of polity given and prescribed for the true and happy republic by the sage philosopher and historian Polybius. In it he wants the three states, monarchy, aristocracy and democracy, to be intermingled, so that the Prince has his empire and majesty, the Aristocracy their authority, and the people their power and their arms. This is the arrangement of the body politic that preserved the Lacedaemonian power for several centuries. This is the arrangement that has long preserved the city of Antwerp, and will (please God) preserve its happiness. It has always had its own prince and nobles to govern it, and these have been accompanied and followed by the consent and power of the people. Now this governing system has four parts. The first, to take the Flemish word in its true sense and meaning, could be expressed in our language as the New Magistracy: it includes the sovereign Magistracy, of Burgomasters and Aldermen, Treasurers and Collector. We shall call the second limb the Old Magistracy: this includes all those who have been Burgomasters or Aldermen and those still currently filling lesser offices. The third constituent part is called the Freemen, and consists of the twenty-six commanders of the citizens of the thirteen quarters of the city, together with the four gentlemen, called captains [*Hooftmannen*], who are their chiefs. The fourth is named the Deans, of whom there are fifty-four in Antwerp, and are the chiefs of the twenty-seven trade guilds of the city. These four constituent parts make up the Corporation and State of the city, although there are some who claimed that there are only three branches, since they make the second and third to be one only: but on this there is a very old dispute not till this day resolved: up to now, however, people ordinarily proceed as if there were four branches. But before moving on, let us be more precise about how they are appointed, and their duties.

The Supreme Magistracy is newly appointed every year, usually in the month of May . . . in the following manner: The Magistrates there present nominate nine gentlemen from those they consider worthy of attaining this degree, while the chiefs of the thirteen quarters of the city nominate another nine, giving eighteen in all. To these is added the body of Magistrates currently in office, equal in number to those newly nominated, because the External Burgomaster is not included. Thus by this means there are thirty-six gentlemen capable of entering the ranks of the New Magistracy, and their names are then sent to the court, for it is up to it to make the election.

Thus the Prince or his Lieutenant, after seeing and consulting the council on the qualities of the men written on the nomination paper, then makes the election from them, though he can only change half of those nominated, and cannot install two brothers or two cousins . . . Now in truth these new Magistrates have the privilege and prerogative of electing the Burgomasters, but inasmuch as the Prince is accustomed to recommend to the electors two such that he desires, his will is the most often obeyed if those he presents can rightly be so accepted. Thus, preserving due order, the Magistrates appoint the Internal Burgomaster from among themselves, and the External Burgomaster from the Old Magistracy, or even from other former Magistrates. It is thus that the Supreme Magistracy is elected, comprising, as stated above, two Burgomasters, and eighteen Aldermen, the former including the Internal Burgomaster who is also an Alderman – the name for a Magistrate of the city currently in office . . .

The most senior Burgomaster, with the most authority, is the external, in so far as his main duties consist in travelling to treat with the court and the States of the country on the affairs of the city that arise. The other is called the Internal Burgomaster, since his office is properly to stay in the city to look after its government and administration, and give audience to both burgesses and foreigners in the city. This Magistrate has great authority and power in the whole of the city's territory as should clearly appear in what follows. But in the administration of justice he yields to the two Lieutenants of the Prince, the one in civil cases and the other in criminal cases, offices the Prince usually fills, and whose authority is so great that their holders have precedence over all the other Magistrates.

The Criminal Lieutenant, whose standing is the highest, is properly and most usually called the Sheriff, but in virtue of the fact that he also has jurisdiction over some villages near the city, composing the Margravate of Rien, . . . he also is commonly called the Margrave (or in our language marquis), in contrast to his deputy, a man of standing, who is commonly called the Sheriff . . . Besides his deputy, the Margrave has several ministers and other officers, all likewise subject to the Prince and swearing fealty to him. His duties are to arrest malefactors and call for judgement on them from the Supreme Magistracy, and thereafter to carry out the resulting sentences, as will be explained more fully below in its place.

In Flemish the Civil Lieutenant is called the *Amman*, a Germanic word I will translate into our language as First Magistrate. He takes his seat on the prescribed dates at the places and times where civil cases are heard. His function is to summon or require the Magistrates to do justice and give sentence (as will be explained later on) on the cases. It is then up to him to carry out these sentences.

The Supreme Magistracy has many important chief officers, but only the most important will be mentioned. In the first place it has two Treasurers and a Collector, who to please and content people, are elected triennially as follows: Those in office that year nominate three gentlemen who have previously been Magistrates, and so report to the Deans of the Guilds in writing. At a meeting for this purpose, the latter elect one of these three

members of the Old Magistracy by a majority of votes, as they see fit, to be the Principal Treasurer. However in the election of the other Treasurer it is up to the Deans and Masters of the Trade Guilds to choose three of the most prominent and best qualified citizens in the city, and nominate them to the Magistrates. The latter select one of these as is agreeable to them for the Second Treasurer. In the same way, in appointing the Collector, the same Deans nominate three burgesses from the best qualified in their trades, passing these names in writing to the Magistrates, who elect to be Collector the one who meets with their approval. Thus are the said three officers elected and appointed. Now the duties of the Treasurers are to have the care and administration of the public treasury, to collect the revenues and authorize the ordinary payments, though only after first communicating with the Burgomasters and Aldermen ... The Collector is, so to speak, their cashier, paying and collecting the revenues as they instruct, although in the ordinary course of events he can pay them on his own authority. He also keeps the ledgers and account books.
. . .

The Supreme Magistracy then appoints annually, on its own authority and without the presence or other consent of the Commissioners of the court the lesser magistrates. In the first place it chooses and elects twelve Counsellors, the most suitable and best qualified it can find from among the Deans of the trade guilds. However, to provide a Counsellor is not granted to all the twenty-seven guilds; since, like the Porters and others, some of them of the lowest standing have never had this distinction, and of those that have, one has it triennially, others biennially, in accordance with their standing. But the Seamen, the Drapers and the Gardeners, the most ancient and important, have a Counsellor every year, that is one Counsellor continuously from each guild. These Counsellors come to Council every Monday, where they sit with dignity and authority, hearing the petitions of the supplicants, and transacting every other matter relating to the administration and republic raised that day, vigorously voicing their opinions on every matter. If they should chance to have to report to the Council some evil word or murmur or other matter concerning the public good they report it diligently to the Council, but in matters of greater consequence recourse is had to an assembly of the superior Council known as the *Breedenraedt*.

The same Council appoints the Market Authority, which consists of two Deans (the chiefs), two Wardens, and six Elders [*Oudemannen*], two of whom must be Aldermen of the Supreme Magistracy. It then also appoints a Clerk, and other officers for that Authority. Before this Magistracy are brought all actions relating to wool and everything to do with wool, such as draperies, camlets, serges, tapestries, alum, woad, madder and the like, but there is an appeal to the Council of the Supreme Magistracy ...

It also appoints two Procurators called in their language *Keurmeesters*: it is appropriate that they should be Aldermen. To these is added a third, appointed by the Prince. Their main duties are the supervision of the food supply, as by ensuring that bread is sold at the correct weight, wine and beer at honest prices, and that meat and other foods are fresh and pure. For example, every Saturday, the main market day for grain and rye, they set the weight for the bread for the whole of that week, according to the price at which wheat and rye are sold in the said market, and if thereafter, on a visit, they find short weight or other fraud at the bakers, they impose a fine. Thus on returning to the palace, the *Keurmeester* enters the price ruling on the market for grain and the other commodities in an ordinary public register. This register can be consulted to check the prices followed in the past and to provide for some necessary matters. However, apart from ordinary bread, wine and beer, prices are not entered for meat or any other kind of foodstuff, in truth a great failing, for even if everything is in abundance, everything is expensive there. They excuse themselves on the ground of the number and multitude of foreigners in the city.

It also appoints over the affairs of orphans four Judges, of whom two must be Aldermen. These judges are known as Orphan Masters since the entire protection, nurture and defence of them is theirs.

It appoints annually four Judges and one *Greffier* [clerk of the court] to reconcile and compose insults and enmities. For this reason they are known as the peacemakers.

Every year it chooses two Almoners, to make up their number to the four who normally fill this office, highly regarded rich people, Freemen of the city. With great diligence and a good heart they go daily collecting alms in the churches and everywhere, particularly on solemn feast days. All that they collect from the good people for the honour of God (at the present day a sum in excess of 30,000 ducats annually), they themselves, in accordance with custom, and their conscience and judgement, distribute to the poor, the hospitals and other pious places in the city, and carry out truly pious and holy works. They always add substantial sums of their own money to meet needs. Hence, with these funds, with the help of the legacies of many pious wealthy deceased persons, and some assigned revenues used for this purpose, the poor are provided for in such sort that they are forbidden to beg in the streets or solicit alms except at certain festivals and certain times. In addition they feed up to a certain fixed age around two or three thousand children of poor people and other innocents given to them or abandoned, and make them learn various skills and trades, and then commend and place them all, both male and female, something that redounds greatly to their honour and praise.

In the same way the Supreme Magistracy elects and appoints in each quarter of the city, for the following two years, two Commanders, known as *Wijckmeesters*. Since there are thirteen quarters, these Commanders are twenty-six in number. Over them the Council allows as chiefs and protectors four gentlemen of the city, called in their language *Hooftmannen* [captains]. When the need arises the latter direct and assist the *Wijckmeesters* and speak on their behalf in the Council, so that in many respects the authority of their office truly resembles (if it is permissible to liken the minor to the great) that of the ancient Tribunes of the people of Rome. Besides these four *Hooftmannen*, each quarter has in the same way two other gentlemen as superiors to give assistance to the *Wijckmeesters* on all occasions of importance. Thus these Commanders and their Chiefs make up the third constituent part of the constitution. But although the Commanders are elected for two years the system is nonetheless organized so that every year half of them are replaced in the following manner: the thirteen of these twenty-six *Wijckmeesters* (i.e. one for each quarter) who have already served two years must on the expiry of their term give the said Magistracy in writing a number of men from their quarter apt and suitable for this office. Of these, the Magistrates on their authority then elect thirteen for the two years to come, and so they proceed annually in order that those remaining in office hand in hand train those coming in.

The main duties of the *Wijckmeesters* and their *Hooftmannen* are to keep a count of the number of men in their quarters who are fit for service, and to assemble and raise them as need arises. The citizens of these quarters are obliged to arm themselves whenever required, and at all times, by night or day, to follow them with their banners and standards. Hence this office is of very great importance, and the third constituent part (as stated) of governance under the constitution of Antwerp. Each of these captains has his Centurions, Decurions, and other corporals with the best and strictest discipline.

The Supreme Magistracy also appoints annually the fifty-four Deans of the twenty-seven trade guilds of the city, who, as stated above, form the fourth and final constituent part of its constitution. Here is how they are appointed. The men of each guild assemble at its assigned place. There they nominate six of their number, the most suitable and prominent in the guild, and pass the names in writing to the said Magistracy. Of these six it selects two acceptable to it from each guild. After election in this manner these are the Deans and chiefs of that guild for one year. But then they are to choose two more from the principals of that trade to assist them and support them. They carry out the same duties as the Deans and therefore like the Deans must take the oath at the hands of the Burgomaster, swearing fealty and obedience. The duties of the Deans and their assistants are to be at the town hall for a general council, to treat with the other constituent parts and confer with those of their craft, to see that entrants to the trade are proven able and loyal, to ensure harmony between them, to take cognizance of debits and credits and settle them, and in addition to protect them by reason from any violence. For the present, these trades are divided into twenty-seven groups each including many types of artisan. The oldest trade, and highest in precedence, is that of the Seamen, who own the majority of the ships and barques ordinarily to be seen in front of the city, ready to sail, not only to this or that region of the country and of England, but also to every other province. The richest and most numerous trade is the Drapers', which includes also the dealers and artisans retailing cloth of gold, silver and silk, drapes and so on, of whatever kind, by measure and by weight on the small balance. At the end of their period of office, the chiefs of the trades are obliged to render account and reason for their administration of it in the presence of two Aldermen and one Secretary. Thus if it happens that one of the trade guilds complains about a chief, or there is some other disorder, these Aldermen try to sort it out and resolve the differences, and if they cannot or will not do so, they report to the Council, which decides it on the spot. These, then, are the principal Magistrates and offices appointed by the Supreme Magistracy. There are also some lesser ones, but since they are of little importance, they are omitted.

3 The Civic Inventory of Household Goods: a Sample for the Antwerp Notary (1582)

Source: Die Rechten ende Costumen van Antwerpen (Antwerp: Plantin, 1582), translated by Marga Emlyn Jones.

Legal documents, besides their expression of formal relationships, sometimes disclose useful information on moral values and material conditions. The digest of the laws of the city of Antwerp, printed by Plantin in 1582, with its detailing of provisions respecting the allocation of communal property at the death of the spouse, supplies an insight into the domestic arrangements of well-to-do Antwerpers at the close of the sixteenth century.

CITY PRIVILEGE:
RIGHTS PERTAINING TO PERSONS

The wife or widow of a merchant may not enjoy her inheritance before all her husband's creditors have been satisfied and paid in full, according to the decrees of His Imperial Highness Charles V, in the year 1550.

The same, in all the cases where the surviving spouse enjoys the usufruct, the usufruct must be totally, and solely, paid for from the inherited goods.

The privilege according to the city rights of Antwerp, due to the surviving husband or wife, as far as household goods are concerned (excluding any craft tools with which he has followed a trade, or with which he has traded or made a profit; these do not carry privileges or dues, these things comprised therein); the household goods are as follows.

First of all a frying pan with an iron handle
A rotating spit and weights
A basting spoon
A chopping knife
An iron skewer with a handle
An iron hoist
An iron rack
A trivet or a hanging-iron
A grid-iron

A round iron saucepan, with a handle
A coal shovel
A waffle iron
A pronged fork
A branding iron, of metal or iron
A pair of tongs
A saucepan lid of metal or iron
A chestnut roaster
An iron spade with a wooden handle

A pair of scissors/because it has not been used to earn a living
A grater
A pair of scales with a pound-weight, or hoist
A candle snuffer
A lavender press
A urine pot
A pair of bellows
A dishcloth
A spice box
A ham dish
A tray to remove things
A board game
A press for tablecloths or serviettes
A hemp comb
A wooden hammer
A glass plate
A woman's footwarmer
A wooden salt vat
A table-edging of metal or tin
A pulpit
A screen
A spinning wheel with a reel
A halberd/or other defensive weapon
A spindle
A meat board
A tool for scraping hides with straps and iron pivot
The best chair
A candle basket
A cheese board
A mirror with its accessories, decorated either with gilt, or, if it is found to be upholstered, with some other drapery
A spice canister
A mustard mill
A stone hand-mill, in order that one does not have to pay money for grinding
A chopping board
A stone oil jar
A ladder
A draining board without a lock
An axe

An iron hammer
A saw
A clothes brush
A ledger
A shoe horn
A whetting board
A wind vane
A chopping knife
A tape measure
A bowl
The best kettle, but not a stewing pot, or roasting dish
A warming pan
The pot containing the most metal or iron
A metal, copper or wooden bucket
A storm or fire bell of metal or pottery
A metal candlestick or candelabrum
A brazier of metal, iron, or pottery
A metal ladle or scoop
A market bucket of metal or of wood/or a market basket, or two-handled basket
A fish-slice of metal or of iron
A pastry bowl of metal or pottery
A bowl, tin or pottery, or a glass bottle
A tapered basket
A metal cooler or a cooling tub
A mortar, made of metal, pottery or wood, with a pestle
A blood-letting bowl
A holy water basin of tin or metal
A winestoop, pot, or jug, leaded or unleaded
A tin dish
A tin bowl with a ewer, or of metal, or a washing-tub, tin or lead jug with a bowl under it
A tin or wooden plate
A tin salt cellar
A tin bowl or metal bucket
A trivet of tin or metal
A vomit bowl of tin or metal
An oil bowl, or a bowl to eat from
A mustard pot of tin or pottery

A chamberpot, tin or pottery
A tin or wooden whisk
A lamp of tin, metal or stone
A tin beaker, when there is no silver one
A tin butter dish
A bedspread of linen, wool or velvet
The best pair of sheets
A shroud, the cloth in which the deceased is laid
The best tablecloth
The best serviette
The best towel

A pillow case
A long woven floor-cloth
A drying cloth
A blue or white linen apron
A faggot sack
A flour sack
A peat sack
The best vest either for men or women
The best kerchief
The best head-scarf
The best hood, hair ribbons, handkerchiefs, hairbands and suchlike

THEN THE CLOTHES DUE TO THE MAN

First his best saddle-horse (because then he does not have to hire one, because it does not save money) with his best weapons, belonging to his body.
The same with his best tabard: And if he is an ordinary fellow, belonging to an ordinary guild: then his silver ensign belongs to him, or if that is so, the same tabard to which it is attached belongs to him: And if he is not a guild-brother of any of the above guilds: his ensign of his craft belongs to him, which he attaches to his sleeve when he takes part in the procession to a Eucharist: and if he does not have a tabard, then he shall have his best coat or cape.

The best tail-coat or jacket, without gold or silver attached to it
The best doublet
The best sweatband

The best pair of stockings
The best garters
The best shoes and slippers
The best hat

The best belt with a silver buckle, if he has worn it in this way; and if this belt weighs more than eight ounces, then he must pay for it, and if it weighs less, that is his loss
His best purse or pouch, without silver attached to it
The best rosary that he has used, without silver attached to it
His best seal, if it be gold, silver or iron, just as it shall be found

CONCERNING WOMEN'S CLOTHES AND JEWELS

The best tabard/braided skirt/or long dress
The best bodice
The best corset

The best pair of stockings
The best slippers or shoes
A pinafore apron

The best pair of sleeves without beaten gold, or silver, or stones, but braided borders are allowed

The best collar without beaten gold, silver or stones attached to it, as above

The best coat or cloak of serge or wool

The best belt or chain, weighing eight ounces, without beaten gold or stone; but silver, or even gold-plated silver is allowed, if it, or a gold chain, is present in the form described above: and if that belt or chain weighs more than the aforesaid eight ounces the widow will have to pay for it, and if it weighs less, that is her loss

The best rosary, as long as it is not silver; but allowed are coral, amber, jet; but if it is unmarked, or gilded in silver, or if there is any gold on it, then the widow must pay, either in money or in kind

The best purse or pouch, without any gold or silver attached

The best pair of knives, without any silver attached

The best book-pouch, with one book, without any gold or silver attached

THEN THE SILVER ARTICLES

A silver drinking utensil, either a cup, bowl, or beaker, weighing one mark or eight ounces of silver or gold-plated silver, if it is present there; and if it weighs more than eight ounces, the surviving spouse will have to pay, and if it weighs less, that is their loss

A silver spoon weighing up to an ounce, and not more than that; in that case it will have to be seen as the drinking utensil described above

THEN THE WOODEN ARTICLES

The best bedstead with curtains, or a box bed with its curtains and valance

A wooden chest or box with a lock

The best table, if it has no lock

The best mantlepiece runner

The best chest cloth or cover

The best tablecloth

The best painting with frame or moulding, decorated with painter's gold, silver or suchlike, which are suitable for the painting

The best woollen blanket

The best cushion

A seat cushion

A pillow with a pillow case

The best bed with a pillow

A mattress or straw bag under the bed

A square linen chest

A lantern

A winnow

A wooden corn spade

A corn container, but not more

A straw corn basket

A flour bin

A candle box

A chicken run without a provision cupboard

A clothes basket

A peat basket

A tub for dishes

A plate- or sewing-basket

A pull-cart or wheelbarrow

A barrow

A meat container

A washing tub

A mill with bowl and utensils

A cast-iron bowl

A storage basket
A quarter or half-size beer barrel
A beer container
A chamber jug, without tin bowl
A wooden commode containing copper or basin, if it is present
A blue stone with wooden hammer or stick with which one beats the laundry, when it has been washed
A writing slate, with a gold weight
A wooden butter churn
A ladle
A suitcase for travel
A fan

A cake tin
A beer tankard
A metal tap or wooden tube/to put into the barrel
A rat trap
A mouse trap
A pulley with rope

PERTAINING TO WOMEN ONLY

A steel hairclip
A halberd or other defensive weapon

PRIVILEGE ACCORDING TO LAND RIGHTS IN THE CITY OF ANTWERP

First of all the best horse, with a good harness, with a long wagon, or cart, suitable to be drawn by a horse

The best cow with its wooden collar
The best calf
The best pig
The best sheep
The best goose
A cock with a hen
A duck
A manure fork
A wooden pitchfork
A dung rake
The best plough with good tools
A harrow
A bean or pea drill
The best sieve with tools
The best pick-axe with tools
The best spade
An iron shovel for digging and planting
The best flagstaff
A winnow
A flail
A measuring basket

A pair of handpliers
A strickle
A kettle for boiling cattle-feed
The best stove
A butter-stand with tools
A flour bin, metal or pottery
A milk bucket, metal or pottery
A cream vat
A wooden dish/in which to make butter with a wooden spoon
A wooden corn shovel
The best corn sack
The best axe with a wooden hammer, and an iron chisel
A scale for milled corn
A chopping block
A pull-cart or wheelbarrow
A hay fork
A frame for hay carts
A hand barrow
A millrind
A sickle

4 Inventory of Michiel van der Heyden (1552)

Source: J. Denucé, *Inventories of the Art Collections of Antwerp 1500–1800* (Antwerp, *c*..1932), pp. 1–5, translated by Marga Emlyn Jones.

Antwerp's commanding position in the world economy of the sixteenth century affected the market for art. The private collection of art objects, though a rich man's pastime, influenced the production, presentation, commissioning and sale of works of art. By the second half of the century the collecting habit in the city was established. The first Antwerp collection to be inventoried, that of Michiel van der Heyden in 1552, is reprinted below.

MICHIEL VAN DER HEYDEN – 24 JUNE 1552

Inventory of the furnishings or moveable goods – located in a gaming-house (named Crauwels) situated on the outskirts of Antwerp – which were left by the late Master Michiel van der Heyden, Knight of blessed memory, and now belonging to his widow Lady Margriet Salomon and their children . . .

IN A DOWNSTAIRS ROOM, LEADING OFF THE DOORWAY:

A beautiful burnished-mirror, with a square cover, in which one can see or look at, people the wrong way round

Two large, and two smaller Italian dishes with people painted on them

A picture of Eel Sunday, oil paint

A picture, in oil, showing our dear Lord carrying his cross

An alabaster relief of Venus and Cupid

IN THE ROOM ABOVE THE DOORWAY WAS FOUND:

Three Moorish head-covers and another figure of a woman

A large picture, painted in oil on canvas, framed, of Venus and Cupid, with a white linen cloth in front of it

Three small square pictures of the Scriptures, oil paint

IN THE ROOM NEXT TO THE ABOVE, AND NEXT TO THE ROOM CALLED CHAPEL:

A picture in oil of Adam and Eve

A picture on canvas, framed, of Antaeus and Hercules

Two paper maps, framed – one of Brabant, the other of Flanders

IN THE ROOM ABOVE THE AFORESAID:

A picture of St Jerome

A portrait of the person of the late Master Michiel van der Heyden, painted on a square board, in oil

A picture, embroidered, of Our Lady

FOUND IN THE ROOM, NEXT TO THE ABOVE, UPSTAIRS:

A large picture of Jacob, in oil

A statue of Mary in front of the fireplace

IN THE SUMMERHOUSE OR IN THE GALLERY:

A large map in a frame, made of landscapes

IN THE ROOM ABOVE THE DOWNSTAIRS ROOM ADJOINING THE GARDEN:

In front of the fireplace: a large picture in oil of the Seven Works of Charity

Another picture in oil, containing the story of Lot and his daughters

A small picture in oil of the two disciples who went to the city of Emmaus

A framed mirror with a round glass

A square picture, in oil, of a female figure

A square picture, in oil, of a male figure, and on it is written: QUINTINUS METZIJS ME FECIT ANNO XVe ENDE XIIe

A small picture, in oil, of Our Lady in Egypt

Another picture in oil, of two people

A portrait of Jacop Noosen, according to my notary

IN THE ROOM NEXT DOOR:

In front of the fireplace: a picture in oil of three children with a little sheep

Two tapestries of the old kind, green in colour

A portrait of the person of the late Master Michiel van der Heyden

A portrait of my lady, the widow of Master Michiel

A small square crystal little mirror

IN THE LARGE DOWNSTAIRS ROOM AT THE BACK OF THE HOUSE:

A beautiful square picture, in oil, of the Resurrection of our Lord

Eight figures painted on canvas in water-colour, and framed; the figures are called: Charitas, Spes, Fides, Justicia, Temperantia, Prudentia, Fortitudo, Cognitio

In front of the fireplace: a large picture, painted on canvas in water-colour, of Venus and Cupid

A square metal mirror built into a hardwood cupboard

IN THE FRONT ROOM ABOVE THE HALL FACING THE STREET:

A large beautiful chest with two locks of lute[?] wood

On the above chest: a picture on the lid, in oil, of our Lord Salvator Mundi and of Our Lady

A square picture, in oil, of Joseph and Mary in the Flight to Egypt

A large triangular mirror

IN THE ROOM NEXT DOOR:

A large picture on linen, framed, by Hieronymus Bosch

Another clothes chest, made of hardwood and with a lock, in which were found:

First tapestry: a piece with people hunting, and birds, four yards long and three yards wide

A flowered piece, to hang around or at the sides of a table, three yards wide and seven yards long less a quarter

A piece of large dyed flowers, four and a quarter yards long and four yards wide, less a *taille* [a unit of measurement]

A small piece of embroidery, four yards wide, less half a quarter, and four yards long

A small piece of the same, four and a half, plus half a quarter long, and three yards and a quarter wide

A beautiful piece of tapestry, worked in silk, representing two figures, to wit a man and a woman, four yards minus half a quarter long, and three yards minus half a quarter wide

A small flowered piece, four yards long, and three yards minus half a quarter wide.

A piece with dyed flowers, almost four yards long, and almost three yards wide

A woven carpet or tablecloth

A velvet tablecloth with coloured stripes etc.

IN THE NURSERY:

A picture, painted in oil, with figures and landscapes, and a doll's house

IN A LITTLE ROOM ON THE STAIRS . . .

A figure representing ''groot Gielken', painted on canvas in water-colour

IN THE LARGE HALL FACING THE STREET:

In front of the fireplace: a large wooden figure and other representations made on canvas by Hieronymus Bosch

A framed map of High Germany

A coat of arms, containing that of my Lord

IN AN OFFICE NEXT TO THE DOWNSTAIRS ROOM BY THE GARDEN:

A beautiful picture on canvas, framed, of the Judgement of Paris

A small picture of Isaac, in oil

A beautiful little picture with doors, our Lord having been painted on it with a sceptre in his hand, and on the doors on both sides having been written . . .

A little statue of Our Lady Mary, in the sun, with a cover

An alabaster Lucretia, standing in a wooden cabinet, painted black

Another wooden cabinet, painted black, containing Mars and Amor

Another wooden cabinet, painted black, of three women, all alabaster

A statue of Our Lady, carved in palm-wood, standing in a black wooden cabinet

Another carved wooden statue of Mary

Three woodprints and another woodprint

Three crystal glasses, made in the manner of Noesens

A statue of Mary, Our Lady of everlasting help, placed in an antique frame

IN THE DOWNSTAIRS ROOM NEXT TO THE HALL FACING THE STREET:

The widow of the late Master Michiel van der Heyden has told us that there used to be a picture of our Lord blessing the children, paid for after the death of her husband

[The same has also declared] that there used to be a civet that excreted musk bringing an annual profit of at least a hundred guilders

A picture of an adulterous woman, paid for after the death of her husband

A picture of Hercules spinning

Signed: The Duke's Notary

5 The Inventory of Margaretta Boge (1574)

Source: J. Denucé, *Inventories of the Art Collections of Antwerp 1500–1800* (Antwerp, *c*.1932), pp. 5–7, translated by Marga Emlyn Jones.

Sixteenth-century Antwerp was a man's world in the sense that women were largely excluded from participation in the public life of the city and from the ownership and management of property. Exceptions were made for spinsters and widows: the former could own goods and houses; the latter had the first choice of the deceased husband's household goods. Margaretta Boge was more fortunate than most women of the period.

Margaretta Boge – 1574

Inventory of all the . . . goods of the lady Margaretta Boge, widow of Signor Joris Veselaer, in his lifetime General of the Coinage here of our blessed Lord the King; these goods were found in the house where she died; the house is named The Red Saucer, situated on the Steenhouwers [Masons'] wall; this inventory is written down at the request of Mr Jacques Hoefnagel and Elias Boudaens . . .

Paintings

A picture by Hieronymus Bosch of the Seven Deadly Sins
A Jerome on panel
A Bacchus on panel
A Pomona without a frame
A Mars and Venus on canvas by Mabuse
A sermon of St John on panel by Merten van Cleve
A sower and a little boat on panel
A Temptation of St Anthony on canvas
A Narcissus on canvas
A Flood on canvas
A Crucifixion with a Mary Magdalene on panel
A peasant wedding on canvas
The city of Antwerp on canvas
A fire on canvas
The siege of Argel on canvas
A piece of swaggery of Jupiter on canvas by Peter van Aelst
A foreshortened man on canvas
A Flora on canvas in oil
A portrait of the young Joris Veselaer on canvas
The story of the paterfamilias on panel
A Naked Venus on panel by Anthonie Moor
An Adam and Eve on canvas by Peter van Aelst
A Last Judgement on panel
A Christmas night on panel
A round picture by Carolus Quintus
A Mars and Venus with a little boat, on panel
A landscape on panel by Todias
Seven round pictures of princes and princesses
A portrait of Joris Veselaer and the lady Margriet [Margaretta] Boge his
    wife, on two doors

A picture of Abraham on panel
A picture of the Separation of the Apostles on panel
A small illuminated painting behind glass, of David and Bathsheba
Nineteen drawings on plates
A Magdalene playing the harpsichord
A portrait of Maximilian
Another Magdalene on panel
A small statue of Mary with the Child
A picture of a fisherman
A large St Christopher
A picture of Rebecca
A poor devil
A fire on canvas
An Orpheus on canvas
The city of Antwerp, with people dancing
A piece by Geert Martens
A picture of two doors, on one St Barbara, St Katherine on the other
A picture of the Descent from the Cross

6 Marcantonio Michiel's Description of the Collection of Andrea Odoni, Venice (c.1530)

Source: Notes on the Pictures and Works of Art in Italy made by an Anonymous Writer in the Sixteenth Century, translated by Paolo Musi, edited by G. C. Williamson (London, 1903), pp. 95–102.

Marcantonio Michiel (the Anonimo or 'Anonymous Writer') went around houses in the Veneto listing the contents of rich men's collections during the 1520s and 1530s. His records show how alert he was to individual attribution and how keen collectors were on antique art, and on collecting the work of local Italian artists.

IN THE HOUSE OF MESSER ANDREA DI ODONI – 1532

IN THE COURT DOWNSTAIRS:
The colossal marble head of Hercules, with a garland of oak leaves, is by Antonio Minello
The colossal marble head of Cybele, crowned with towers, is by the same
The marble figure of a woman entirely draped, headless and handless, is antique, and it used to be in the studio of Tullio Lombardo, who reproduced it several times in his many works[1]
The life-size marble bust without either hands or head is antique
The many other marble heads and figures, mutilated and shattered, are antique

[1] Tullio Lombardo died in the year 1532

The entire marble foot upon a base was executed by Simone Bianco[2] The nude marble figure of a man, represented in the act of walking, handless and headless, near the door, is antique

IN THE LITTLE STUDY UPSTAIRS:
The porphyry cup was made by Piero Maria Fiorentino,[3] and it is the one which formerly belonged to Francesco Zio
The inlaid crystal cup was made by Cristoforo Romano, and formerly belonged to Francesco Zio
The cup of petrified root was made by Vittore di Arcangeli
The four headings of the small Book of Hours, which formerly belonged to Francesco Zio, were painted by Giacometto
The David at the beginning of the other small Book of Hours was painted by Benedetto Bordone[4]
The five small vases of gems and gold are modern, and formerly belonged to Francesco Zio, as well as the porcelain vases and plates, the antique vases and medals, and the animals, that is to say, the petrified crabs, fishes and snakes, a dried chameleon, some small rare lizards, crocodiles and quaint fishes
The small wood statuette on horseback is by ...
The small dog in bronze is by ...

IN THE ROOM UPSTAIRS:
The oil picture with the two half-length figures of a girl and an old woman behind her is by Jacopo Palma
The portrait of Messer Andrea himself, in oil, half-length, represented looking at some antique marble fragments, was painted by Lorenzo Lotto
The picture representing Our Lady with the Divine Infant, St John as a child, and a female saint in a landscape, is by Titian
The chests in the same room, the bedstead and the doors, were painted by Stefano, a pupil of Titian's
The large figure of a woman, nude, lying down, painted on the back of the bed, is by Gerolamo Savoldo of Brescia
The numerous bronze statuettes are modern works by different artists

IN THE PORTICO:
The picture on canvas representing the episode of the girl brought into the presence of Scipio was painted by Gerolamo Bresciano
The Transfiguration of St Paul is by Bonifacio Veronese
The canvas representing the Infernal Regions, in which is Cupid holding his bow, is by Giovanni del Zanin Comandador, and

---

[2] This Florentine sculptor, who worked mainly in Venice, was noted by Vasari and also by Aretino who wrote to Simone Bianco: 'That I, dear Messer Simone, have seen in my days many figures of both gods and men, I know you will believe, without my taking my oath for it; but of all I have ever seen none has given me so much pleasure and wonder as the portrait in which your chisel and genius rendered the celestial features of her who was joined in marriage to His Magnificence, Messer Niccolò Molino, master and friend of us both ... Sansovino and Titian agree in my judgement.'
[3] Piero Maria Fiorentino, better known as Pietro da Pescia, was an engraver of gems and cameos who is mentioned by Vasari.
[4] Bordone was a native of Padua and a noted miniaturist; also known as Benedetto Miniatore.

belonged formerly to Francesco Zio

The History of Trajan, with many figures and ancient buildings, was painted by the same Giovanni del Comandador; but the buildings were drawn by Sebastiano Bolognese

The canvas, representing various monsters in the Infernal Regions, in the Flemish manner, is by . . .

The St Jerome, naked, sitting in the desert by moonlight, was painted by . . . from a picture on canvas of Giorgio da Castelfranco

The marble statuette, two feet high, of Mars, nude, with his helmet on his shoulder, was executed by Simone Bianco

In the room upstairs, the half-length

portrait of Francesco Zio is by Vincenzo Catena

The small portrait, in three-quarter length, of the same Zio, armed, is by the same Catena

The portrait of the little child, wearing a white cap in the French fashion and holding four rosary beads in its hand, was painted by . . . and is the portrait of the boy named . . . who was seized by our soldiers at the battle of Taro, together with the royal baggage[5]

The small pictures, on tempera, are by . . .

The Ceres, on the door halfway up the stairs, is by Jacopo Palma, and is the same which Francesco Zio used to keep at the door of his room

7 The Inventory of Willem Pauwels (1481)

Source: Letter of discharge to the executors of Master Willem Pauwels from the Mayor and Aldermen of the city of Antwerp, containing an inventory of the books he had left to the city, April 1481, in Bibliotheca Antverpiensis, *Catalogue Méthodique de la Bibliothèque Publique d'Anvers* (Antwerp: F. H. Mertens, 1846), II, ii–iii.

Pensionary Pauwels, who died in 1481, was the chief municipal magistrate of the city of Antwerp and its principal legal adviser. His bequest tells us something about private and public book-collecting, scholarly activity, civic pride and civic consciousness.

With regard to the books which Master Willem Pauwels, erstwhile Counsellor of the city of Antwerp, has bequeathed in his will to that same city.

The Mayors and Aldermen of the city of Antwerp send greetings to all those who will read this letter or hear it read out. We hereby give notice publicly that we have accepted and received from H. Cornelis den Hout, priest, Costene van Halmale and Peter de Bot, executors of the will of the late Master Willem Pauwels, in his lifetime lawyer of the city and environs,

[5] This battle, which took place on the River Taro in north Italy, was fought by Charles VIII of France in 1495. In the course of a rapid retreat the king left his baggage with its many precious articles of furniture and works of art.

the books of the same Master Willem, deceased; we have proceeded by making an inventory of them, checking thoroughly with the executors and inserting each book item by item; Master Willem has generously stipulated in his will that these books should be placed in a room for the benefit and use of the counsellors, secretaries and clerks serving the city, without lending or selling them, or hiring them out. And according to the conditions laid down in his will, we hereby, in the name of the late Master Willem, relieve his widow, executors and all those requiring a receipt, of all that he possessed at the time of his decease in the city, for the benefit of the city and its environs. The inventory that was drawn up reads as follows:

INVENTORY OF THE BOOKS FORMERLY BELONGING TO MASTER WILLEM PAUWELS, BEQUEATHED TO THE CITY OF ANTWERP AND FOUND IN HIS HOUSE

The *Decretum* of Jorimo [Jerome] with a commentary

Item, Decretals, Sextus [Clementine][1]

Panormitanus on the fourth and fifth Decretals[2]

A small volume. Printed on paper

A Codex on parchment[3]

An old Digest on parchment

A Digest, the *Infortiatum*, printed on paper

A new Digest on paper

The *Institutes* glossed[4]

Other *Institutes* written on paper without a gloss

A lecture by Bartolus [of Sassoferato][5] on nine books of the Codex written on paper

A lecture by the same author on the first part of the old Digest

A lecture by the same author on the second part of the old Digest

Two volumes by Bartolus on the ninth part of the Digest

A brief critique by Bartolus on the Codex

Cases of Ferrara written on paper

[Jacobus] Alvarotus *On Feudal Estates*, on paper, unbound

The *Summa* of Tancredus, without a gloss, on parchment

A printed tract by Panormitanus, *On the Order of Judges*

A commentary by Lewis of the Romans on the fifth Decretal, printed on paper

A tract on the clauses in contracts which have been re-written etc. produced by Master Vitalis of Cambano

Catholicon [of Balbis] printed on paper

Bible printed on paper

The *Etymologies* of Isidore [of Seville][6]

---

[1] Decretals: collection of papal pronouncements that bear the force of law within the jurisdiction of the papacy. The item enumerated here refers to the collection issued by Clement V (1317).

[2] Panormitanus (1386–1445): Canonist whose principal writings include commentaries on the decretals of Gregory IX, and Boniface VIII and others.

[3] Codex: code of Canon Law.

[4] *Institutes*: the *Institutes of Justinian* (533) were the basis of Roman Law and a major influence upon the development of Canon Law in the West. 'Gloss' was a word often used for 'commentary' in the Middle Ages.

[5] See document II.9, n. 41.

[6] See document II.9, n. 36.

Lorenzo Valla[7]
Vegetius,[8] *On Military Affairs*, written by hand
Terence with a commentary by Donatus, printed[9]
A tract *On the Great Fall of Troy*, written by hand
Valerius Maximus, written by hand but not complete[10]
A commentary on Valerius Maximus in print
Letters to His Friends by Tullius [Cicero][11]
Letters and prefaces by Gasparini

Tullius, *On Duties* in print
Letters of Carolus
The letters of Seneca *To Lucilius*, written on paper[12]
Quintilian's *Exercises in Oratory*[13]
Sallust, *To Lucius* with other tracts[14]
A Mirror for Kings and Princes
The Paradoxes of Tullius, *On Old Age*
Eneas, *Of Two Lovers* with other tracts, in one volume
The Rhetoric of Cicero revised by the precepts and elegant phrases of Gasparini

In witness thereof we Mayors and Aldermen of the city and environs put a seal to this letter, written in the year of Our Lord a thousand, four hundred and eighty, having been written by the scribe Shoefs van Cameryck, on the fifth day before Easter in April [1481].

8 Bessarion's Act of Donation (1468)

Source: L. Labowsky, *Bessarion's Library and the Biblioteca Marciana* (Sussidi Eruditi, 31; Rome: Edizioni di storia e letteratura, 1979), pp. 147–56, translated from the Latin by Francis Clark.

[7] See document I.7.

[8] Flavius Vegetius, author of the best-known manual of Roman military institutions to have survived intact, written between AD 383 and 450; it exerted great influence upon military thinking in the Middle Ages and the Renaissance.

[9] Donatus: fourth-century grammarian whose pupils included St Jerome. His commentary remains a key source on the plays of Terence.

[10] Valerius Maximus: first-century AD Roman historian of a strong rhetorical and philosophical orientation. The sheer variety of his sources, their uncritical usage notwithstanding, made him popular down to the Middle Ages.

[11] Cicero (106–43 BC), Marcus Tullius, Roman orator, politician and prolific writer. His prose style and concept of civic virtue were formative influences upon Renaissance humanism.

[12] Seneca, tutor and political adviser to Emperor Nero; committed suicide in AD 65; author of ten ethical treatises and other works, the bulk of it philosophical in character and a prime source for the history of Stoicism. His *Epistulae Morales* (*Moral Letters*) consists of 124 letters addressed to Lucilius. The letters, though, are not a genuine correspondence but merely a device for philosophizing and declamation. His exemplary prose style long remained influential.

[13] Quintilian (b. *c.* AD 35 in Spain); teacher, advocate and rhetorician. His *Institutio oratoria*, which traces the training of an orator from the cradle to manhood, profoundly influenced medieval and Renaissance writers like Erasmus and Vives. It is still worth reading.

[14] Sallust (*c.* 86–35 BC), annalist and historian whose work is more important for its presentation than its content.

John Bessarion (*c*.1400–72), Cardinal, Greek scholar and statesman; his patronage of humanist scholars and promotion of scholarship played an important part in the revival of Greek studies in the Italian Renaissance. The first of the two sub-documents printed below includes extracts from a Papal Bull issued by Paul II in 1467 authorizing Bessarion to revoke his earlier donation of his library of Greek books to the island monastery of St George, Venice, and to give it instead (with many other works) to the Cathedral Church of St Mark, Venice. It is followed by Bessarion's Act of Donation, dated 30 May 1468.

A. Papal Bull authorizing the donation (1467)

[PRELIMINARY DESCRIPTION OF THE DOCUMENT]

In the name of the Lord, amen. This is a copy or transcription of a certain Apostolic Letter, or Bull, with a leaden seal affixed, on which there appears the impressed image of the Pope seated on the papal throne, with two Cardinals assisting him and some other persons kneeling around. There is also an inscription on the seal which reads: *Paulus Papa Secundus*. On the reverse there is an impressed image of Saint Peter and Saint Paul, seated, with the inscription: *S. Pet*[*rus*], *S. Pau*[*lus*]. There is a silken cord coloured saffron and red. The wording of the document is as follows:

[THE PAPAL DECREE]

Paul, Bishop and servant of the servants of God, wishes health and imparts the apostolic blessing to Bessarion, Bishop of Tusculum. If, by virtue of our apostolic office, we ought to accord our favour and aid to any of the faithful who are engaged in pious and holy works, how much more ought we to give such assistance to our venerable brothers the Cardinals of the Holy Roman Church, who stand constantly at our side. It is right that we should enable them to effect beneficial changes in the statutes they have made for noble and beneficial purposes, especially where those statutes will be of benefit to posterity and will serve to develop the talents of many. We recall that you have recently put before us, in our presence, a petition which is as follows:

You explained that at a former time, having many volumes of Greek books in your possession, and desiring those books to be publicly available and to serve the good of posterity, you bestowed all those books (namely your Greek books only), by a donation *inter vivos*, on the Venetian monastery of St George the Greater, belonging to the Congregation of St Justina, of the Order of St Benedict. You reserved to yourself the use of the books during your lifetime . . .

You went on to explain that [you had been moved to reconsider the form of your donation] for a number of good reasons. In particular, there is the disadvantage that, since the aforesaid monastery is on an island, it is not possible to go thither from the city of Venice except by boat. In order therefore to provide easier access to your library for those who wish to read or study there, you desire that the aforementioned books, together with many others (both Greek books acquired by you after your previous donation and also your Latin books), should, under the care of the

Procurators of St Mark, be in [the possession of] the Church of St Mark in Venice. Access to that church is easy from the city itself, without need of boats, and there, through the action of the aforesaid Procurators,[1] the books can evidently be more diligently preserved and more securely kept ...

We, then, having in mind the holy and beneficial fruits which will follow, for the education of countless scholars, from your intended donation and bequest, and from the preservation of those books which were composed by their authors with great pains in order that they should be publicly available and should serve the common good; and therefore highly commending your good intent and wishing to encourage it by our opportune favour, accede to your petitions. That is, by our apostolic authority, we do hereby concede to Your Fraternity full and free licence, faculty and power, enabling you to make valid provision as follows:

To revoke the aforementioned donation made by you to the said monastery, even for no other reason than that which you have expressed to us;

to give, by a donation *inter vivos*, the aforementioned books, both Latin and Greek, to the aforesaid Church of St Mark, in order that they be diligently preserved in a suitable place through the care of the Procurators of St Mark holding office for the time being, in order that those books may be publicly available for the use of any students who may wish to study or read there;

to attach or add to the said donation any conditions or qualifications, or to make any other kind of provisions, concerning the custody and preservation of the books and easier access to them; such conditions may include the following: that the Procurators of St Mark for the time being should locate the books in some secure library in the vicinity of St Mark's; that there should be public access to the library for all who wish to study or read there; that it will not be permissible to the Procurators to sell or dispose of any of the said books, or to lend them to anyone, except in the city of Venice and then with adequate pledge of security (in no circumstances, however, may they be lent to anyone outside the city);

to reserve to yourself the use of the same books, or any of them, during your lifetime;

to do, dispose or execute, freely and licitly, anything at all which you consider to be necessary or in any way opportune concerning these matters.

This permission will have force notwithstanding the previous donation mentioned above, or any contrary apostolic constitutions and decisions, or other legal titles or any other provision whatsoever. No one at all may impair this document of our concession and will, nor temerariously oppose it. If however someone should presume to attempt to do so, let him know that he

[1] Procurators: trustees for the fabric and possessions of the church.

will incur the wrath of Almighty God and of the blessed apostles Peter and Paul.

Given in Rome, at St Mark's, in the year of the Lord 1467, on the 17th day of October, in the fourth year of our pontificate.

B. The Act of Donation

Bessarion, Cardinal and Patriarch of Constantinople, wishes health to the most illustrious and glorious prince and lord, the Doge Christopher Maurus, and to the renowned Senate of Venice.

From my youth, even from childhood, I have always endeavoured, with all my energy, care and diligence, to acquire as many books as I could, in every field of scholarly study. Wherefore in those years of my youth I not only transcribed many texts with my own hand, but I also spent on buying books whatever small sums of money I could set aside by frugal saving. I deemed that I could provide for myself no more worthy and noble household adornments, no more useful and distinguished treasure, than books.

Books are full of the voices of the wise, full of lessons from antiquity, full of moral and legal wisdom, full of religion. Books live, they discourse and speak directly to us, they teach and instruct us, they bring us consolation. They show us things far remote from our times, and, as it were, place them before our eyes as if they were present today. So great is the power of books, so great their dignity, their grandeur, even their divinity, that without them we should all be rude and ignorant. Without books, we should have almost no memory of the past, no examples to follow, no knowledge of either human or divine affairs. Were it not for books, the same tombs that consume men's bodies would likewise bury their very names in oblivion.

I have always engaged myself wholeheartedly in this quest; but after the overthrow of Greece and the grievous captivity of Byzantium,[2] I have, with still more ardent zeal, devoted all my strength and solicitude, all my labours, resources and diligence, to seeking out books in the Greek language. I was moved by anguished concern lest so many excellent books, the fruit of the labours and vigils of so many men of genius, books which are lanterns for the whole world, thus threatened with extinction, might abruptly perish in the general destruction. Even in times past we have suffered so great a loss in this respect that out of the two hundred and twenty thousand books that, as Plutarch related,[3] were once in the library of Apamea, hardly a thousand have survived to our age. To the best of my ability, I have tried to collect the best books, rather than a multitude of books, and to procure single copies of each work. In this way I have brought together a collection of almost all the

---

[2] The capture of Constantinople by the Turks in 1453 marked the end of the Christian Empire based there.

[3] Plutarch (Mestrius Plutarchus) of Chaeronea, AD 46–120, philosopher and biographer, was a popular educational writer in medieval times, and was a major influence on the Renaissance in general and Shakespeare and Montaigne in particular.

works of the great Greek thinkers, especially those which are rare and difficult to find.

As I constantly reflected on this matter, it seemed to me that I should fail to achieve my purpose unless I could ensure that the books which I have brought together with such great diligence and effort should during my lifetime be assigned to a secure location, in such a way that even after my death they could not be dispersed and disposed of. I desired that they should serve to the common benefit of both Greeks and Latins, in a place that would be both safe and convenient. I pondered on this question, and considered in my mind many towns of Italy; but your renowned and honourable city was the only one in which my mind found complete assurance.

I did not see what safer place I could choose than one in which equity holds sway, which is preserved by its laws, which is governed with uprightness and wisdom; which is the home of virtue, self-restraint, dignity, justice and faith; a state where the exercise of authority is sovereign and far-reaching, yet at the same time fair and moderate. There, men of prudence, impartial in counsel and untouched by base desire or crime, hold the keys of empire. There, the good are set above the wicked. Forgetful of their own private advantage, they seek the good of the whole body politic, with common purpose and with the highest integrity. For these reasons there is well-founded hope – and this is my prayer – that your city may ever increase its power and fame.

Hence I realized that I could choose no place more suitable, or more appropriate for my fellow countrymen in particular. The peoples of almost the whole world come together in great numbers in your city, but especially the Greeks, whose first port of call as they sail from their own lands is Venice. They have besides a familiar relationship with you; when they put ashore at your city it seems to them that they are entering another Byzantium. I ask, furthermore, in what place could I more honourably establish this benefaction than among those men to whom I am already bound in obligation because of their manifold goodness to me? Where better than in that city which, when Greece was subjugated, I chose as my fatherland, and into which I was admitted by you and welcomed with the greatest honour?

Wherefore, conscious that death lies ahead of me, and mindful of the weight of my years, of bodily afflictions and of other eventualities that might arise, I have given and dedicated all my books, in both languages, to the most sacred temple of Saint Mark in your renowned city. I feel that thereby I am paying a debt that I owe to your distinguished merit, to my own sense of gratitude, and to the city that, thanks to your goodwill, is our common fatherland. I am firmly and devotedly bound to you by your virtue, your wisdom and your many kindnesses to me. My chief wish is that you, and your children and descendants, may enjoy bountiful and lasting fruit from my labours. It is also my wish to extend this benefit to others associated with you who will in future time devote themselves to sound learning.

We are therefore sending to Your Excellencies the act of donation itself, together with an inventory of the books and a decree of the Sovereign Pontiff. We offer our prayers to God that all the affairs of your republic may prosper and succeed, and that it may have perpetual peace, tranquillity, leisure and concord. May Your Excellencies enjoy health and happiness.

[signed and sent] from the baths of Viterbo,
in the year of salvation 1468, on the last day of May

9 Bessarion's Library (1474)

Source: L. Labowsky, *Bessarion's Library and the Biblioteca Marciana* (Sussidi Eruditi, 31; Rome: Edizioni di storia e letteratura, 1979), pp. 41–2, 191–243, translated from the Latin by Francis Clark.

The following extracts are from the inventory of Bessarion's library made in 1474 when the Cardinal's remaining books had arrived in Venice, two years after his death. Although the number of volumes in each of the chests referred to is given, details are only provided of one or two books from each. The titles and authors cited are intended to represent the scope and nature of the collection, i.e. a preponderance of works on theology and philosophy.

Chest number and number of volumes in the chest	Subject(s)	Contents
GREEK		
1 (18)	Philosophy (Aristotle)	Simplicius'[1] commentary on the *Categories* of Aristotle,[2] and the commentary of another author on the first and second books of Aristotle's *On the Soul*. On parchment, beautiful.
2 (18)	Philosophy, History	Some discourses of Plotinus[3] and of Hermes Trismegistus.[4] On paper.
3 (13)	Philosophy, Poetry	(i) Three comedies of Aristophanes[5]

[1] Simplicius (sixth century AD), Aristotelian commentator.
[2] Aristotle (384–322 BC), Greek philosopher who created the science of logic and supplied the foundation of Aquinas's thought.
[3] Plotinus (AD 205–269/70), Neoplatonist philosopher and mystic; author of series of essays published as the *Enneads*, the most complete corpus of philosophical teachings to have come down to us from antiquity other than that of Aristotle.
[4] See document II.10, n. 8.
[5] Aristophanes (*c*.448–*c*.380 BC), poet and playwright.

Chest number and number of volumes in the chest	Subject(s)	Contents
		and four tragedies of Sophocles.[6] On paper. (ii) All the *Moral Works* of Plutarch[7] [i.e. all his writings except the *Lives*] in the same volume, on paper.
4 (17)	Philosophy (Plato), History	Commentary of Proclus on Plato's *Timaeus*.[8] A new and beautiful book.
5 (18)	History, Rhetoric	All the speeches of Demosthenes.[9] On parchment; a very beautiful book.
6 (22)	Rhetoric, Mathematics	Euclid's *Geometry*, on paper.
7 (16)	Mathematics, Astronomy, Law	The *Almagest* of Ptolemy,[10] with an exposition of Theon [of Smyrna].[11] On paper, a precious book.
8 (16)	Law, Medicine	*On the care of horses*, by many authors. On parchment.
9 (18)	Theology, Canon Law	*Acts* of the Council of Florence.[12]
10 (23)	Mixed	*Dialogue concerning Grammar* of Planudes, and the *Metamorphoses* of Ovid.[13] In Greek, on paper.
11 (10)	Theology	*Homilies* of Chrysostom,[14] made up from an anthology of his sermons.

[6] Sophocles (c.496–406 BC), tragic poet and dramatist.
[7] See document II.8, n. 3.
[8] Plato (c.427–c.347 BC), Greek philosopher. The *Timaeus* comprises that part of the dialogues dealing with cosmology and natural science; it presents Plato's principal discussions of theology.
[9] Demosthenes (c.384–322 BC), the most famous Athenian orator, noted for his lucid and convincing exposition of arguments and capable of producing maximum effect with a few simple words. Unsurpassed as a stylist.
[10] Ptolemy of Alexandria, astronomer, mathematician and geographer of the second century AD. His major work, the *Almagest*, is a complete textbook of astronomy in 13 books. In it is elaborated a set of astronomical doctrines which explained the apparent motions of the sun, moon and planets on the assumption that the earth was stationary. He remained an authority for over one thousand years.
[11] Theon of Smyrna (fl. c.AD 115–40), Platonist, author of commentaries on the *Republic* and a lost work on the order of Plato's writings.
[12] Council of Florence (1438–65), whose chief object was reunion with the Greek Church. In this it failed.
[13] Ovid (Publius Ovidius Naso, 43 BC–AD 17), poet, who possessed extraordinary linguistic and metrical dexterity.
[14] St John Chrysostom (c.347–407), Bishop of Constantinople. His *Homilies*, delivered in Antioch in the years 386–98, establish him as the most celebrated of Christian expositors.

Chest number and number of volumes in the chest	Subject(s)	Contents
12 (12)	Theology	The *Hexaemeron* and *Moralia* of St Basil.[15] On parchment.
13 (11)	Theology, Church History	Many sermons of St Gregory of Nazianzen.[16] On paper.
15 (9)	Theology	Discourses of many doctors on the lives of the saints, [whose feasts are] in the months of July and August. On parchment.
16 (12)	Theology	*Against the Jews* by the monk Aristobulus. On paper.
17 (10)	Theology	Commentary of Origen on Matthew and John.[17] On paper.
19 (13)	Theology, Bible	Discourses of St Ephraem on the monastic life.[18] On parchment.
21 (14)	Theology, Bible	The four Gospels, in a very beautiful volume, covered with silk. On parchment.
31 (16)	Bible, Theology	The Pentateuch [the first five books of the Old Testament], with some other texts. A new translation; beginning at the end of the book, in the Jewish manner.
32 (17)	Theology, Liturgy	The Latin Missal translated into Greek. On paper.
33 (24)	Theology, Canon Law, Philosophy	Commentary of Chrysostom on all the epistles of Paul. On paper.
34 (23)	Philosophy (Plato)	(i) The work of the Most Reverend Lord [Cardinal Bessarion] *Against the Calumniator of Plato*. On parchment. (ii) *Against Plato*, Scolaris. On paper.
35 (21)	Philosophy (Aristotle)	The *Logic* of Aristotle. On parchment. Excellent.

[15] St Basil, 'the Great' (c.330–79), an eloquent, learned and statesmanlike figure, and author of an important treatise on *The Holy Spirit* and other theological writings.

[16] St Gregory of Nazianzus (329–89), contemporary of St Basil with whom he prepared a selection of the writings of Origen; an eloquent preacher and theologian of distinction.

[17] Origen (c.185–c.254), Alexandrian biblical interpreter, theologian and spiritual writer.

[18] St Ephraem Syrus (c.306–73), Syrian biblical interpreter and ecclesiastical writer. His voluminous writings, mostly in verse, are described by the *Oxford Dictionary of the Christian Church* as 'repellent to modern readers'.

Chest number and number of volumes in the chest	Subject(s)	Contents
36 (30)	Mathematics, Rhetoric etc.	*Arithmetica*, with commentary of Asclepius;[19] *Musica*, with commentaries of Porphyry,[20] Briennius, Nicomachus[21] and Bacchius Senex.[22] On paper, an excellent book.
37 (22)	History, Philosophy	Historical books of Herodotus,[23] Thucydides[24] and Xenophon.[25] On parchment.
38 (30)	History, Rhetoric, Poetry	Homer's *Iliad*.[26] On parchment, beautiful.
39 (28)	Medicine, Grammar	The *Aphorisms* of Hippocrates,[27] with a commentary of Galen.[28] On paper.
52 (18)	Bible, personal papers	The Books of Kings, and Paralipomenon, Ezra, Tobit, Maccabees. On paper, cover lacking.
55 (29)	Mixed	Josephus, *The Jewish War*.[29] In quinternios [sets of five folios], not bound; very ancient.

[19] Asclepius, god of healing, in Greek mythology son of Apollo and Coronis. The name of several classical writers.

[20] Porphyry (AD 232/3–c.305), scholar, philosopher and student of religions; a prolific polymath, author of what became the standard medieval textbook on logic. He also wrote on grammar, rhetoric and history of scholarship.

[21] Nicomachus, son of Aristotle to whom, allegedly, the *Nicomachean Ethics* was dedicated.

[22] Bacchius Senex, otherwise Baccheius Geron, musical theorist who lived in the time of Constantine (AD 274–337).

[23] Herodotus (c.484–c.425 BC), historian of ancient Greece; one of the founding fathers of the Western historical tradition.

[24] Thucydides (c.460–c.400 BC) author of (unfinished) *History* of the war between Athens and Sparta 431–404 BC, in 8 books.

[25] Xenophon (c.428/7–c.354 BC) author of history of Greek affairs from 411 to 362, in 7 volumes.

[26] Homer, Greek poet, biographical details unknown or uncertain; traditionally supposed to be the author of the *Iliad* and the *Odyssey*.

[27] Hippocrates, contemporary of Socrates; most famous Greek physician, the founder of scientific medicine and a major influence on the Renaissance.

[28] Galen of Pergamum (AD 129–?199), physician, philosopher, anatomist (who proved that the arteries as well as the veins carry blood) and teacher.

[29] Flavius Josephus, Jewish historian, born AD 37/8; involved in Jewish revolt of 66; author of multi-volumed study *Jewish War*, which he translated into Greek.

p146

Chest number and number of volumes in the chest	Subject(s)	Contents
LATIN		
22 (15)	History, Rhetoric	(i) All the speeches of Cicero,[30] in a very beautiful volume, on parchment. (ii) Vitruvius, *On Architecture*,[31] and Vegetius, *On Military Affairs*.[32] On parchment.
23 (24)	History, Poetry, Rhetoric	Virgil's *Bucolics, Georgics, Aeneid*.[33] On parchment.
25 (16)	Science, Logic, Medicine	St Thomas Aquinas,[34] commentary on Aristotle's *On the Soul* (II and III), *On Memory and Remembering*, *On Sensation*; and another commentary on *On the Soul*. On parchment.
26 (22)	Theology	(i) Augustine's *City of God*.[35] On parchment. (ii) Isidore's *Etymologies*.[36] On parchment.
27 (17)	Theology	One part (namely 16 books) of the *Moralia* [Commentary on Job] of St Gregory. On parchment.
28 (17)	Canon Law, Philosophy, Theology	Sextus [Empiricus],[37] Decretals. On parchment.
29 (26)	Mixed	The whole Bible. On parchment. A very beautiful scroll with silver gilt clasps and rollers.

[30] Cicero – See document II.7, n.11.

[31] Vitruvius, Roman architect and military engineer, active by 40 BC and early in Augustus's reign; his fame rests on a treatise *De architectura*, the only work of its kind to have survived. Subjects included are town-planning, architecture in general and the qualifications proper in an architect, building materials, civic buildings, domestic buildings, pavements, water supplies, machines, military and civil, etc.

[32] See document II.7, n. 8.

[33] Virgil (Publius Vergilius Maro) (70–19 BC), poet; peerless in style and metre, in command of resources, artistic expression, range and tone.

[34] Aquinas, see document I.6.

[35] St Augustine of Hippo (354–430), one of the 'Doctors of the Church', *The City of God* deals with the fundamental contrast between Christianity and the world and is one of the most influential texts of all time.

[36] St Isidore (c.560–636), Archbishop of Seville. The most important of his works, *The Etymologies*, is an encyclopaedia of the knowledge of his time encompassing grammar, rhetoric, mathematics, medicine, history and theology.

[37] Sextus Empiricus (c.AD 200), Greek doctor of medicine and sceptical philosopher, a valuable source of information on earlier philosophy.

Chest number and number of volumes in the chest	Subject(s)	Contents
41 (36)	Theology, Philosophy, Bible	A beautiful Breviary covered with cloth of gold.
42 (19)	Canon Law	Jean Gerson, *On the Power of the Church*.[38] On paper.
44 (21)	Mixed	Leonardus [Aretinus], *On the War in Italy*. On paper.
46 (9)	Mixed (some printed books)	The Master of the Sentences [the *Sentences* of Peter Lombard].[39] On parchment.
47 (18)	Grammar, classical authors	*Catholicon* [Latin dictionary of John Balbis]. On parchment.
48 (26)	Mixed	Quintilian [rhetorical works].[40] On paper.
49 (14)	Canon and Civil Law	Bartolus [of Sassoferato],[41] commentary on the second part of the *Infortiatum* [a part of the *Pandects* of Justinian]. On paper.
50 (32)	Mixed	George of Trebizond,[42] *Against Plato*, without index. Paper.
51 (16)	Mixed	Procedure for the election of the Doge of Venice. In one quinternion.

[38] Jean Gerson (1363–1429), French churchman and spiritual writer. *On the Power of the Church* (1417) developed the Conciliar theory without rejecting the primacy of the Pope, and was a potent influence on the development of Gallicanism.

[39] Peter Lombard (*c.* 1100–60). His *Sentences* became the standard textbook of Catholic theology during the Middle Ages.

[40] Quintilian (Marcus Fabius Quintilianus), see document II.7, n. 13.

[41] Bartolus of Sassoferato (1314–1357), founder of school of Roman Law studies, dominant in the fourteenth and fifteenth centuries, which sought to assimilate secular and Canon Law principles into a code for all Christendom. Humanist scholars subsequently rejected its ahistorical perspective and procedures.

[42] George of Trebizond (*c.* 1396–1488), friend and compatriot of Cardinal Bessarion; taught Greek and rhetoric in Venice, Florence and Rome; an Aristotelian who readily engaged Platonists like Bessarion and Gemistus Plethon; translated Plato and Aristotle into Latin.

10 Giorgi, *Harmony of the World* (1525)

Source: Francesco Giorgi, *De Harmonia Mundi Totius* (Venice, 1525), translated by Stuart Brown in consultation with R. Niall D. Martin.

Francesco Giorgi (1466–1540) was a Franciscan friar interested in Jewish culture as a source for the revitalization of Christianity. Giorgi, in common with Pico and other Neoplatonists, believed that Man was a microcosm of the universe. He argues for this conclusion in the extract below both by his interpretation of passages of the Bible and by appealing to the agreement between ancient philosophical authorities. The passage is from canto I, vol. IV, ch. 5.

A GENERAL ARGUMENT, THAT ALL THINGS ARE CONTAINED IN MAN

Our Moses, an entirely sound philosopher, has shown us with how much fullness and harmony the supreme Workman has included and assembled all things in Man. He did this in a single mysterious sentence, when he said: 'The Lord God formed Man from the dust of the earth and breathed into his face and nostrils the Breath of Life.'[1] He touched both extremes of every thing, so that whatever comes in between the extremes should be understood as included in Man. By this means He has ordered things so that the highest and the lowest degree are brought together. For the lowest and least of all things is the element of the earth, and the highest is He who says: 'I am the life':[2] as if to say: 'I am He who diffuses the rays of life into everything.' And when Moses declared all the degrees of living things to be included in Man, he did not say 'Breath of Life' without reason. For Man's life spans all the degrees of living things. He shows then that the extremes and the middle come together in Man when he says that the earth, the dust and the Breath of Life come together in him. And just as in the Great World the divine things, which exert their influence through the Heavens, are united with the terrestrial so [in the Lesser World] the divine, the celestial and the dust are united in Man. This was indicated secretly by the name 'Adam',[3] which first meant 'Man'. For 'A' signifies divinity, 'D' signifies celestial nature and 'M' signifies corruptible corporeal nature. Thus there are in Man the corruptible, the celestial and the divine, or every kind of living thing.[4] For Man lives by the life of the elements and stones, to which is ceaselessly given the strength to be, to grow, to alter or change. With the metals he lives a higher life, for their spirit is deeply hidden, and is rarely or never found by artisans or alchemists, however carefully they have searched. With the

---

[1] Genesis 2: 7 is the source; Moses is not the speaker.

[2] John 11: 25, 14: 6, and *passim*. The notion of 'eternal life' is a recurring theme of this Gospel and one that made it a favourite with Giorgi. The author identifies the Messiah (Jesus) both with life and, less mystically, as the provider of 'eternal life'. See nn. 5 and 6 below.

[3] The argument is a Cabbalistic one about the significance of the three letters that make up the Hebrew word for 'Adam', אדם

[4] Giorgi here supposes, as the Neoplatonists characteristically did, that everything in the chain of created things, even down to stones and metals, has life.

plants Man lives a vegetative life, with the animals a mobile life, with the separated intelligences a rational life or one with understanding, and with the true God a life divine and eternal, of which [St] John says: 'The life was the light of men.'[5] And again, according to the Highest Truth: 'I am come that they might have life and have it more abundantly.'[6]

Thus it was well said that the Breath of Life, of every kind of living thing, was breathed into Man. And what Moses showed secretly by means of the two extremes and the middle, Solomon, or perhaps Philo,[7] expresses openly by saying: 'God took Man from the silt of the earth and gave him the power to contain all things.' Trismegistus agrees with this.[8] To his son's question about how Man was brought into being he replied: 'Man is a whole, a totality within the whole', that is, within God. Man consists of an aggregate of the powers of all things whereas God, who contains all powers, is not an aggregate.

Augustine was thinking of this inclusion of all things[9] not only in Man as a totality but also in the soul by itself when he said: 'The soul, being the semblance of all wisdom, carries within itself the image of all things.' For this reason the philosopher has defined the soul as the likeness of all things. For it has within itself the powers by which it includes all things, investigates all things and is the likeness of all things. Though it is only one thing, through the senses it is like the earth, through its imagination like the water, through its reason like the air, through its understanding like the firmament and through its intelligence it is like the Heaven of Heavens. Just as God may be received by and participate in all things, so the soul is capable of all things.

[5] John 1: 4.

[6] John 10: 10.

[7] Philo Judaeus, an important Jewish philosopher (c. 30 BC–AD 45), who sought to harmonize the teachings of Greek philosophy, particularly of Plato, with those of the Bible.

[8] Hermes Trismegistus, mythical founder of an ancient Egyptian tradition of magic and mystical philosophy, who was supposed to match Moses and Plato in antiquity and wisdom. Giorgi's source would probably have been the edition of the Hermetic writings that Ficino had edited and translated from the Greek – the existence of original Egyptian manuscripts is itself doubtful – into Latin: *Mercurii Trismegisti Liber de Potestate et Sapientia Dei*, Venice, 1483.

[9] Augustine (354–430) was one of the great Christian philosophers. The idea of the soul as made in the image of God is one that Christian Platonists made much of, since it is authorized both by the Bible and by the writings of Plato himself.

SECTION III

SECTION III

Reformation

Studies of the Reformation at undergraduate level traditionally have equated *Reformation* with *Protestantism* and even with *Lutheranism* and have seen Luther as the Reformation's hero. Scholars today do not question the importance of the Protestant Reformation nor of Luther himself but they are interested in setting both within the context of a wider reformation. Was the Catholic Reformation, for example, simply a reaction to the Protestant schism or was it the bedfellow of the Lutheran Reformation? Were the other Protestant Reformers (Melanchthon, Bucer, Zwingli, Calvin, Bullinger, Knox) simply Luther's successors, to be measured against the yardstick of his heroic stand, or did they have equally or more important contributions to make to the cause of reform? Modern scholars seek, moreover, to establish and explain the appeal and the impact of both the Protestant and the Catholic Reformations upon society as a whole.

Before we can even attempt to consider these questions we have to come to some understanding of the religious climate into which the Protestant and Catholic Reformations of the sixteenth century were born. Luther's was certainly not the first attempt to reform the Catholic Church in Europe. Christian humanists such as Erasmus, More and Colet all criticized aspects of the Church and advocated reform. In fifteenth-century Europe there had been a strong Conciliar movement, which challenged the supreme authority of the Pope within the Church – a movement which persisted in some of the universities. There were movements for reform within some of the religious orders. And there were individuals – John Wycliffe, for example – who boldly attacked the dogmas of the Church and who inspired, directly or indirectly, a popular following.

Just how much Protestantism had in common with these earlier expressions of dissatisfaction within the Church is debatable. This is at least in part because Protestants were eager to claim antecedents for their revolutionary positions. The sixteenth century, unlike our own age, did not rate originality and individuality highly. Contemporaries were ever searching for a precedent to lend authority to their views and actions. In this section several extracts have been included which can be used to shed further light on the common origins of Lutheran and reformed Protestant and late medieval attempts at reform (documents III.1, 2, 3, 4).

When we are placing early Protestantism within the context of reform movements in the later medieval Church we do need an understanding of what it was that Protestants were trying to reform. The doctrinal thought of the Reformation is complicated and to many people offputting. Nevertheless, it is vital that we appreciate what the principles of Protestantism were. The supreme authority of Scripture; justification by faith alone; predestination; the accessibility of Scripture; the priesthood of all believers; the nature of the sacraments – an understanding of the Reformers' basic doctrines on these matters is essential. The texts are not as forbidding as they may sound: extracts from works of Martin Luther, John Calvin and William Tyndale have been selected to offer opportunities for such an appreciation (documents III.6, 7, 8).

The message of the Reformers was spread by a variety of methods – sermons, catechisms, books, pamphlets, songs, plays, broadsheets, woodcuts. In section VI we have printed an example of a sermon; here documents III.6, 7, 8, 9 show other ways in which the new teachings were spread. Document 9 can be used to exemplify one of the reasons for the welcoming of the Reformation – its message was one of consolation, of lifting the burden of anxiety from the shoulders of men and women.

The Protestant Reformation was not welcomed by all states or by all individuals. Large parts of Europe rejected Luther and the other Reformers for a variety of reasons – political, religious, economic. Individuals – some of whom, like Erasmus, shared many of the concerns of Luther – ultimately stayed in the Catholic fold. Such states and individuals did not necessarily positively embrace Reformed Catholicism. The manifestations of the Catholic Reformation belong largely to the seventeenth century but some consideration of its implementation is given in section IV.

A number of states and myriad individuals did embrace Protestantism and it has often been claimed that Protestantism had a profound influence upon them. The position of women was changed in Protestant communities, we are told. This contention is subjected to detailed scrutiny elsewhere and here we have the opportunity to examine the diary of one elite Englishwoman and determine the extent to which her Protestant convictions shaped her life (document III.11). Document III.5 can be used as an indication of the relationships between husbands and wives in Reformation Nuremberg. Compare this with documents I.9.A and I.9.B by Erasmus. There are many other ways in which Protestantism is said to have broken with the old ways. Protestants, for example, are said to have rejected an instrumental view of religion – good works, ritual and magic were to no avail, man could not alone effect his own salvation. Document III.10 allows us to study the views of Henry

Cornelius Agrippa who, not a Protestant, shared the desire for a Christianity rooted in the Scriptures and rejected most kinds of magic. Protestantism was not a necessary condition for questioning the power of the occult. We hope that you will approach these and other texts presented in section IV to decide for yourselves whether there were distinctive Reformed Protestant, Reformed Catholic and Medieval Catholic world views and whether the acceptance of Protestantism 'changed' more than an individual's or a state's religion.

1 Articles of Tabor (*c.* 1420)

Source: Daniel Waley, *Later Medieval Europe* (London: Longman, 1975), pp. 136–7, slightly adapting the translation in Josef Macek, *The Hussite Movement in Bohemia*, translated by Vilem Fried and Ian Milner, 2nd edn (Prague: Orbis, 1958), pp. 130–3.

Hussites were the followers of the Bohemian religious reformer John Hus, who was condemned at the Council of Constance and burned at the stake in 1415. The Hussites broke with Rome by using a Czech liturgy and administering both the consecrated bread and wine to the laity. Under King Wenceslas IV of Bohemia the Hussite movement spread widely. In 1419, Wenceslas was succeeded by his half-brother Sigismund, King of the Romans and Hungary, who was a bitter enemy of the Hussites.

The Taborites were the extreme party of the Hussites, and drew their name from Mount Tabor, their fortified stronghold to the south of Prague. The Articles of Tabor summarized the radical tenets of the Taborites. They scorned all accepted theology, rejecting churches, festivals, transubstantiation, oaths and court discipline. Under their leader Žižka they began to spread their vision of the kingdom of God by force of arms after Wenceslas's death in 1419. None of the superior armies ⟨ ? ? . sent to oust them by King and Pope could be defeated. When Žižka died in 1424 the Taborites split into two groups: moderates, who joined the Catholics in 1533; and radicals, who suffered a crushing defeat in 1534.

First, that in our time there shall be an end of all things, that is, all evil shall be uprooted on this earth.

That this is the time of vengeance and retribution on wicked men by fire and sword so that all adversaries of God's Law shall be slain by fire and sword or otherwise done to death.

So that in this time whoever will hear the Word of Christ, then let them that be Jews [*sic*][1] flee to the mountains, and those that will not leave the towns, villages and hamlets for the mountains or for Tabor shall all be guilty of mortal sin.

Everyone that will not go to the mountains shall perish amidst the towns, villages and hamlets by the blows of God.

In this time nobody can be shielded from God's blows but on the mountains.

[1] Waley adds: 'The intention was to quote Mark 13: 14 "let them that be in Judaea ...".'

The Taborite brethren are in this time of vengeance the messengers of God sent to purge away all offences and evil from Christ's kingdom, all wickedness from good people and from the Holy Church.

The Taborite brethren shall take revenge by fire and sword on God's enemies and on all towns, villages and hamlets.

Every church, chapel or altar built to the honour of the Lord God or of any saint shall be destroyed and burnt as a place of idolatry.

Every house of a priest, canon, chaplain or other cleric shall be destroyed and burnt.

In this time of vengeance only five towns shall remain and those who flee to them shall be saved . . .

As in Hradiště or in Tabor nothing is mine and nothing thine, but all is common, so everything shall be common to all forever and no one shall have anything of his own; because whoever owns anything himself commits a mortal sin.

Debtors who flee to the mountains or the aforesaid five towns shall be acquitted of paying their debts.

Even now, at the end of the ages, all shall see Christ bodily descend from Heaven to accept His kingdom here on earth . . .

In this time no king shall reign nor any lord rule on earth, there shall be no serfdom, all dues and taxes shall cease, nor shall any man force another to do anything, because all shall be equal, brothers and sisters.

Holy Mass shall not be sung or read in the Latin tongue, but only in the language of the people.

Missals sung in Latin, prayer books and other books, priestly vestments, surplices, silver or golden monstrances and chalices, silver or golden belts, ornamented or richly embroidered garments, finely made or costly robes: all these things shall not exist and must therefore be spoilt and destroyed.

Priests shall have no payments nor hamlets nor cattle nor estates nor houses in which to dwell nor anything of the like, even if they were given such things as alms, even if they held them by secular law and governance.

2 Lollard Documents (sixteenth century)

Source: Michael A. Mullett, *Radical Religious Movements in Early Modern Europe* (London: Allen & Unwin, 1980), pp. 113–15 abridged.

A Lollard was initially one who followed the teachings of John Wycliffe (*c*.1329–84) but the term came to be used to describe people in England who were critical of the Church in a variety of ways. The Lollards who followed Wycliffe based their teachings on personal faith, on divine election and on the centrality of the Scriptures. The Scriptures were the sole religious authority. The Lollards attacked transubstantiation, clerical celibacy, indulgences, pilgrimages and the Church hierarchy. The extent of Lollard survival and revival in early sixteenth-century England has given rise to a lively debate among historians. The thorny question of the degree to which Lollardy fed into early English Protestantism has prompted several detailed studies.

The first of the two documents here is an account of the trial for heresy of John Florence in 1424, as recorded in John Foxe's *Acts and Monuments* (1563); the second is the confession of faith of a sixteenth-century Lollard, John Tyball, taken from John Strype's *Ecclesiastical Memorials* (first published 1722).

A. The examination of John Florence

John Florence, a turner in Shelton, in the diocese of Norwich, was attached for that he held and taught these heresies (as they called them) here under written, contrary to the determination of the Church of Rome;

Imprimis, That the Pope and cardinals have no power to make or constitute any laws.

Item, That there is no day to be kept holy but only the Sunday, which God hath allowed.

Item That men ought to fast no other time, but the *Quatuor Temporum*.

Item That images are not to be worshipped, neither that people ought to set up any lights before them in the churches; neither to go on pilgrimages, neither to offer for the dead, nor with women that are purified.

Item That curates should not take tithes of their parishioners, but that such tithes should be divided among the poor parishioners.

Item That all such as swear by their life or power shall be damned, except they repent.

On Wednesday, August 2nd AD 1424, the said John Florence personally appeared before William Bernham, Chancellor to William Bishop of Norwich, where he, proceeding against him, objected the first article, touching the power of the Pope and cardinals; to which article the said John Florence answered in this manner, 'If the Pope lived uprightly as Peter lived he hath power to make laws. Otherwise I believe he hath no power.' But being afterwards threatened by the judge he acknowledged that he had erred and submitted himself to the correction of the Church and was abjured; taking on oath that from that time forward he should not hold, teach, preach, or willingly defend any error or heresy contrary to the determination of the Church of Rome; neither maintain, help, nor aid any such that shall teach or hold any such errors or heresies, either privily or apertly, and for his offence in this behalf done he was enjoined this penance following: Three Sundays in a solemn procession, in the cathedral church of Norwich, he should be disciplined before all the people. The like also should be done about his parish church of Shelton . . .

B. The confession of a Lollard

THE CONFESSION of John Tyball, a Lollard; charged with heresy. Examined he saith that about seven or eight years past, he had certain books of the four Evangelists in English, of one holy John, and certain Epistles of Peter and Paul; which he burned the same day at night (as he saith) that Sir Richard

Fox was attached. And so in continuance of time, by reading of the said books, and especially by a chapter of Paul, which he wrote to the Corinthians . . . he fell into those errors and heresies. That for some time he had thought that the Blessed Sacrament of the Altar is not the very body of Christ, but bread and wine, and done for a remembrance of Christ's passion. And he thought and believed that a priest had no power to consecrate the body of Christ.

Also he confesseth that he hath said, affirmed and believed that every priest and bishop ought to have a wife upon the chapter of Paul, where he saith these words: 'every bishop ought to be husband of one wife, and to bring forth children.'

Also he saith that he hath said, affirmed and believed that it was as good for man to confess himself alone to God, or else to any other layman, as to a priest – upon the saying of Saint James, where he saith: 'Show your sins one to another.' Which error he shewed and taught Robert Faire of Steeple Bumstead about a twelvemonth past.

Also he saith that he hath taught that priesthood was not necessary. For he thought that every layman might minister the sacraments of the Church as well as any priest.

Also he confesseth that pilgrimages to images were not profitable; and that men should not worship or kneel to images in the church, nor set up candles or lights before them, for they be but stocks and stones.

Also he saith that he hath for some time doubted whether the pope or bishop had power to grant pardon. For some time he thought that they had power, and for some time he thought the contrary, because they had so much money for it. And, he said, he thought that it were better that their mitres, crosses, rings and other precious stones should be given to poor and needy people than so to wear them – according to the saying of Paul where he saith, 'wear ye no gold, silver nor pearls, nor precious stones.'

Also he saith that saints as Peter, Paul and others, be in heaven; but as for other souls of good men which departeth this world, he thinketh that they go not to heaven before the general resurrection; but be in some place of joy and pleasure, except they be helped to heaven by good prayer.

3 The Council of Trent and Religious Art (1563)

Source: *A Documentary History of Art*, edited by E. Gilmore Hall (New York: Doubleday, 1958), pp. 63–5 abridged.

This extract is taken from the proceedings of the 25th session of the Council of Trent on 3 and 4 December 1563. The Council of Trent, after false starts, sat from 1545 to 1563. Its sessions fell into distinct periods: (1) 1545–7; (2) 1551–2; (3) 1562–3. During the last period all hopes of conciliation with the Protestants were gone and the Jesuits were a strong force. Session 25 dealt cursorily with several issues – purgatory, invocation of saints, indulgences and veneration of relics and images. The Council ended on 4 December 1563. Its decrees were confirmed by Pope Pius IV on 26 June 1564. In the same year Pius published the *Profession of the Tridentine Faith*, known as the 'creed of Pius IV', which was a brief summary of the doctrine promulgated by the Council. The extract printed here contains what can be regarded as the definitive teaching of the Catholic Reformation regarding religious art and its purpose.

CANONS AND DECREES OF THE COUNCIL OF TRENT

ON SACRED IMAGES

The holy council commands all bishops and others who hold the office of teaching and have charge of the *cura animarum*, that in accordance with the usage of the Catholic and Apostolic Church, received from the primitive times of the Christian religion, and with the unanimous teaching of the holy Fathers and the decrees of sacred councils, they above all instruct the faithful diligently in matters relating to intercession and invocation of the saints, the veneration of relics, and the legitimate use of images ... Moreover, that the images of Christ, of the Virgin Mother of God, and of the other saints are to be placed and retained especially in the churches, and that due honour and veneration is to be given them; not, however, that any divinity or virtue is believed to be in them by reason of which they are to be venerated, or that something is to be asked of them, or that trust is to be placed in images, as was done of old by the Gentiles who placed their hope in idols; but because the honour which is shown them is referred to the prototypes which they represent, so that by means of the images which we kiss and before which we uncover the head and prostrate ourselves, we adore Christ and venerate the saints whose likeness they bear. That is what was defined by the decrees of the councils, especially of the Second Council of Nicaea,[1] against the opponents of images.

Moreover, let the bishops diligently teach that by means of the stories of the mysteries of our redemption portrayed in paintings and other representations the people are instructed and confirmed in the articles of faith, which ought to be borne in mind and constantly reflected upon; also that great profit is derived from all holy images, not only because the people are thereby reminded of the benefits and gifts bestowed on them by Christ, but also because through the saints the miracles of God and salutary examples are set before the eyes of the faithful, so that they may give God thanks for those things, may fashion their own life and conduct in imitation of the saints and be moved to adore and love God and cultivate piety. But if anyone should teach or maintain anything contrary to these decrees, let him be anathema.[2] If any abuses shall have found their way into these holy and

---

[1] The Second Council of Nicaea (AD 787) was called to end the iconoclastic controversy of that time.

[2] To declare someone anathema meant a curse and separation from the Church's communion and community altogether. After the Council of Elvira (*c*.306) it became the regular procedure against heretics and was associated with a solemn service. It is often called major excommunication.

salutary observances, the holy council desires earnestly that they be completely removed, so that no representation of false doctrines and such as might be the occasion of grave error to the uneducated be exhibited. And if at times it happens, when this is beneficial to the illiterate, that the stories and narratives of the Holy Scriptures are portrayed and exhibited, the people should be instructed that not for that reason is the divinity represented in picture as if it can be seen with bodily eyes or expressed in colours or figures. Furthermore, in the invocation of the saints, the veneration of relics, and the sacred use of images, all superstition shall be removed, all filthy quest for gain eliminated, and all lasciviousness avoided, so that images shall not be painted and adorned with a seductive charm, or the celebration of saints and the visitation of relics be perverted by the people into boisterous festivities and drunkenness, as if the festivals in honour of the saints are to be celebrated with revelry and with no sense of decency. Finally, such zeal and care should be exhibited by the bishops with regard to these things that nothing may appear that is disorderly or unbecoming and confusedly arranged, nothing that is profane, nothing disrespectful, since holiness becometh the house of God. That these things may be the more faithfully observed, the holy council decrees that no one is permitted to erect or cause to be erected in any place or church, howsoever exempt, any unusual image unless it has been approved by the bishop; also that no new miracles be accepted and no relics recognized unless they have been investigated and approved by the same bishop, who, as soon as he has obtained any knowledge of such matters, shall, after consulting theologians and other pious men, act thereon as he shall judge consonant with truth and piety. But if any doubtful or grave abuse is to be eradicated, or if indeed any graver question concerning these matters should arise, the bishop, before he settles the controversy, shall await the decision of the metropolitan[3] and of the bishops of the province in a provincial synod; so, however, that nothing new or anything that has not hitherto been in use in the Church shall be decided upon without having first consulted the most holy Roman pontiff.[4]

4 Luther, *Against the Heavenly Prophets* (1525)

Source: *Luther's Works*, edited by H. T. Lenman (Philadelphia: Muhlenberg Press, 1958), XL, 84–100 abridged.

These extracts from Martin Luther's work *Against the Heavenly Prophets* have been selected to show the Protestant Reformer's attitude to images and religious art.

---

[3] i.e. the archbishop.
[4] i.e. the Pope.

ON THE DESTRUCTION OF IMAGES

I approached the task of destroying images by first tearing them out of the heart through God's Word and making them worthless and despised. This indeed took place before Dr Karlstadt ever dreamed of destroying images.[1] For when they are no longer in the heart, they can do no harm when seen with the eyes ... Which of these two forms of destroying images is best, I will let each man judge for himself.

For where the heart is instructed that one pleases God alone through faith, and that in the matter of images nothing that is pleasing to him takes place, but is a fruitless service and effort, the people themselves willingly drop it, despise images, and have none made. But where one neglects such instruction and forces the issue, it follows that those blaspheme who do not understand and who act only because of the coercion of the law and not with a free conscience. Their idea that they can please God with works becomes a real idol and a false assurance in the heart. Such legalism results in putting away outward images while filling the heart with idols.

. . .

Furthermore, I have allowed and not forbidden the outward removal of images, so long as this takes place without rioting and uproar and is done by the proper authorities. In the world it is considered foolish to conceal the true reason for a good venture out of fear that it may fail. However, when Karlstadt disregards my spiritual and orderly putting away of images and makes me out to be only a 'protector of images', this is an example of his holy and prophetic art, though I only resisted his factious, violent, and fanatical spirit. Now since the evil spirit sits so firmly in his mind I am less inclined than ever to yield to obstinacy and wrong. I will first discuss images according to the law of Moses, and then according to the gospel. And I say at the outset that according to the law of Moses no other images are forbidden than an image of God which one worships. A crucifix, on the other hand, or any other holy image is not forbidden. Heigh now! you breakers of images, I defy you to prove the opposite!

In proof of this I cite the first commandment [Exodus 20: 3]: 'You shall have no other gods before me.' Immediately, following this text, the meaning of having other gods is made plain in the words: 'You shall not make yourself a graven image, or any likeness . . .' [Exodus 20: 4]. This is said of the same gods, etc. And although these spirits cling to the little word 'make' and stubbornly insist, 'Make, make is something else than to worship,' yet they must admit that this commandment basically speaks of nothing else than of the glory of God. It must certainly be 'made' if it is to be worshipped, and unmade if it is not to be worshipped. It is not valid, however, to pick out one word and keep repeating it. One must consider the meaning of the whole

---

[1] Andrew Karlstadt (1480–1541), a radical reformer who incited image breaking in Wittenberg and welcomed the Zwickau prophets. Luther was called back to Wittenberg to restore order and did so by preaching eight sermons.

text in its context. Then one sees that it speaks of images of God which are not to be worshipped. No one will be able to prove anything else. From subsequent words in the same chapter [Exodus 20: 23], 'You shall not make gods of silver to be with me, nor shall you make for yourselves gods of gold,' it follows that 'make' certainly refers to such gods.

. . .

Now that we are under our princes, lords, and emperors, we must outwardly obey their laws instead of the laws of Moses. We should therefore be calm and humbly petition them to put away such images . . .

However, to speak evangelically of images, I say and declare that no one is obligated to break violently images even of God, but everything is free, and one does not sin if he does not break them with violence. One is obligated, however, to destroy them with the Word of God, that is, not with the law in a Karlstadtian manner, but with the gospel. This means to instruct and enlighten the conscience that it is idolatry to worship them, or to trust in them, since one is to trust alone in Christ. Beyond this let the external matters take their course. God grant that they may be destroyed, become dilapidated, or that they remain. It is all the same and makes no difference, just as when the poison has been removed from a snake.

Now I say this to keep the conscience free from mischievous laws and fictitious sins, and not because I would defend images. Nor would I condemn those who have destroyed them, especially those who destroy divine and idolatrous images. But images for memorial and witness, such as crucifixes and images of saints, are to be tolerated. This is shown above to be the case even in the Mosaic law. And they are not only to be tolerated, but for the sake of the memorial and the witness they are praiseworthy and honourable, as the witness stones of Joshua [Joshua 24: 26] and of Samuel [1 Samuel 7: 12].

. . .

I have myself seen and heard the iconoclasts read out of my German Bible. I know that they have it and read out of it, as one can easily determine from the words they use. Now there are a great many pictures in those books, both of God, the angels, men and animals, especially in the Revelation of John and in Moses and Joshua. So now we would kindly beg them to permit us to do what they themselves do. Pictures contained in these books we would paint on walls for the sake of remembrance and better understanding, since they do no more harm on walls than in books. It is to be sure better to paint pictures on walls of how God created the world, how Noah built the ark, and whatever other good stories there may be, than to paint shameless worldly things. Yes, would to God that I could persuade the rich and the mighty that they would permit the whole Bible to be painted on houses, on the inside and outside, so that all can see it. That would be a Christian work.

Of this I am certain, that God desires to have his works heard and read, especially the passion of our Lord. But it is impossible for me to hear and bear it in mind without forming mental images of it in my heart. For whether I will or not, when I hear of Christ, an image of a man hanging on a cross takes form in my heart, just as the reflection of my face naturally appears in the water when I look into it. If it is not a sin but good to have the image of Christ in my heart, why should it be a sin to have it in my eyes?

5 Hans Sachs, *The Old Game* (1554)

Source: E. U. Ouless, *Seven Shrovetide Plays* (London: The Year Book Press, 1930), pp. 38–46.

Hans Sachs (1494–1576) was a shoemaker, poet and playwright. He is perhaps best known in his guise as one of the master-singers of Nuremberg in Wagner's opera *Die Meistersinger von Nürnberg*. Sachs wrote more than 4,000 master-songs. He also wrote many farces and at least eighty *Fastnachtspiele* or Shrovetide plays for performance during the popular festivities associated with that season. Each lasted for about a quarter of an hour and they were enacted in halls, taverns, courtyards and private houses by bands of amateur players. Some of Sachs's religious plays were presented in the churches of Nuremberg. The plays were written in octosyllabic couplets. The play which is reprinted here, *The Old Game* (originally *Der dot Man wur Lebentig*), was written in 1554. It has been modified for use by English theatre companies and is at best a free translation from the German original. In the original, Master Hans Sachs and his neighbours did not appear: the modern version has attributed the moralizing of the last speech directly to Sachs. Nevertheless, it does offer a good example of the type of play which remained current and popular in Reformation Germany, of the subject matter, the views expressed, and the values upheld.

CHARACTERS

Hans, a Farm Labourer
His Wife
A Village Woman
The Farmer
Master Hans Sachs, a Cobbler
Neighbours

Interior of Hans's kitchen. Entrances R. and L. A large kitchen table and two chairs are the only furniture in the room. An empty washing-basket stands near the door R., and an old pig-skin and some sacks lie rolled up in one corner. A long red cloak hangs on a nail on the door R. Hans *is sitting on the table swinging his legs.* His Wife *is sweeping the floor. A lively discussion is going on.*

Hans: You did, I seen you!
Wife: I didn't.
Hans: You did.
Wife: I didn't.

Hans: But I says as you did! [*He thumps the table.*]

Wife: And I say as I didn't – leastways if I did, it was all for the best. [*She flourishes with her broom round the table, and Hans draws up his legs in alarm.*] And if I say it once, Hans, I say it a hundred times, that whatsoever I may do that puts you in a rage, 'tis all that good may come out of it! Trust me, dear husband and be sure I love you well.

Hans [*gloomily*]: No woman's to be trusted till she's in her grave!

Wife [*pausing and leaning on her broom*]: Why husband, don't you love me?

Hans: Times I do. More often I don't.

Wife: In truth I would fain know how much you *do* love me. Answer me, husband.

Hans: But I can't answer, not in sober truth. You're that round-a-bout in your goings on.

Wife: Then, when is it you love me best?

Hans [*readily*]: Why to be sure, when you do as I bids you, like a humble, willing and obedient wife. Then I'm ready enough to share my last crust of sour bread with you, and to see you lack no clothing nor finery. Then it's a pleasure to look after you, and give you good counsel. If I'm a bit cold and stern at times, why 'tis your own fault entirely.

Wife: And how is it my own fault pray? When is it I act as you don't like?

Hans: I can give a short answer to that. When you go against my wishes, either behind of my back, or in front of my eyes.

Wife: But tell me just what it is I do.

Hans: Oh, no end of things. Every day I suffer torments from what you say and do.

Wife [*very persistently*]: And what is it I says and does?

Hans [*peevishly*]: Aren't I telling you? You don't manage the house as it ought to be managed, and when I points it out, you are angry and answer me back. You are always crossing me. I can't never do nothing right. Why anyone would think I was the wife and you the husband! That's not right! It puts a man against you!

Wife: Now husband, if you let such petty things upset you, your love is worth no more than that! [*She snaps her fingers.*] If you was as fond of me as I am of you, 'twouldn't flicker in and out, but get stronger and brighter every day.

Hans [*moodily*]: Times I sit and wonder if you ever cared at all about me.

Wife: My dear husband, whatever makes you say a silly thing like that?

Hans: Well, I can't say as I've seen many signs.

Wife [*hurt*]: Why, I'm always calling you 'dear Hans'.

Hans [*scornfully*]: 'Dear Hans'! That sort of love is naught but talk. If you showed it in your actions now! But it's contradictions, contradictions, morning, noon and night!

Wife: Dear Hans! [*He snorts in contempt.*] I have loved you for many a year, but I don't always show it. Let me tell you this, if you was sick unto death, I would die in your place right willingly. And if you was to die before me, mark my words I wouldn't live a moment longer, nor take a second husband, but I'd bury you with all honour in my red cloak, so as all the world should vow there was never a more loving wife. I pledge you my solemn word!

Hans [*impressed in spite of himself*]: If you'd do all that, your love must be as strong as mine. Why didn't you tell me afore?

Wife: If I'd spoken out sooner you'd have grown slack in caring for me. But believe me, it's the truth. [*She picks up the basket.*] Well, well, after that I'm off down to the river to wring out the washing. You can stay and mind the house.

Hans: You go and get the washing, wife, and I'll stay and kill time by the fireside.

[*The Wife goes out R. with the basket, leaving the door open.*]

Hans: She's mighty proud of her love for me, and I believe that if I did die, she'd show her grief right enough. But what's the good of that? How will her tears and groans help a man when he's gone? I'd sooner have 'em when I'm alive, I might get a better time of it! There's one way I could get to the root of this, and find out if she's speaking truth. Supposing I was to stretch myself out on this very spot [*He doubles up a bit of old sacking on the table as a pillow, and lies down on the table*] and breathe all trembly and gaspy like as though it hurted! [*He gasps.*] Then when she comes back and finds me gone, what about the tears and sorrowing, and a costly burial in the red cloak she's always promised me? We shall see! Meantime, I'll put her to the test, and prove her words. She loves me? She loves me not? She loves me? She –

[*Re-enter the Wife R. with her basket filled with washing. Hans begins to draw his breath in short, sharp gasps. The Wife puts down the basket with a bang.*]

Wife [*irritably*]: Now fool, what are you lying on the table for, like a stable-boy? Get up, and give me a hand with the washing. [*Anxiously seeing he does not move*] Oh, Hans, what is it? Are you ill? [*She shakes him vigorously. The gasps cease, and he lies quite still.*] Come now, get up, dear Hans! [*She leans over him and feels his pulse. Hans opens one eye, and moves one foot slightly. The Wife smiles, as she realizes what has happened.*] I fear in truth you must be dead! Alas, I see clearly that you are dead! [*She goes to the door, closes it with a bang, and comes back wringing her hands.*] Alack-the-day! What shall I do to begin with? Weep, or have a bit of supper? Supper will be best, for if I start crying and making a to-do, the neighbours will come running, and here I shall be mourning all night long without bite or sup! Moreover I am wet through with the washing. First I'll put on dry things, then break five eggs in the frying-pan to help me cry the better. Maybe, too, I'll fetch out a cask of wine to comfort me in my great sorrow, for as the old saying goes:

> Neither dance nor mourn the dead,
> Till you feasted be and fed.

[*She goes, singing L. Hans sits up very indignant.*]

Hans: She's no more concerned over my death than the loss of a spoon! A cold love forsooth! [*Knock on door R.*] Come – [*He claps his hand over his mouth, and lies down again hurriedly. The knocking continues at intervals till the Wife re-enters L. with a tankard in her hand.*]

Wife: Now I am somewhat refreshed and ready for the mourning when company comes. [*Knocking grows more insistent. She puts down the tankard on the table by Hans's feet, and begins to lament loudly*.] Woe is me! Who's that a-knocking? Woe is me! Woe is me!

[*She goes to the door R., and opens it. As soon as her back is turned, Hans lifts his head and watches her. Enter the first neighbour, a woman from the village, who peers round inquisitively.*]

Village Woman: Why, neighbour, what's the matter? Why have you shut your door? [*She sees Hans and gives a scream.*] Mercy me! What's that on the table? It's never your husband?

[*The Wife winks, and makes violent signs. Then she draws the Neighbour nearer the table.*]

Wife: Look, dear neighbour, while I was away down at the washing, my husband passed away. Misery me! I am stricken to the heart.

Woman [*looking at Hans, then turning away smiling*]: Ah, my dear neighbour, to think he's really dead! Him that did no ill to no one, a good neighbour, and a pious man withal. Alas and alack, I am sore grieved to hear of this. How did it come about?

[*The two women sit down for a chat.*]

Wife: Well, only yesterday he cut his finger. But then he was a poor weak creature at the best of times. [*Hans wriggles.*] It's a pretty penny he's cost me of late, what with drugs and herbs and roots for hot baths. I've grudged him naught.

Woman [*bracingly*]: Well, neighbour, 'tis an everlasting pity he's dead, but since it can't be otherwise, you must resign yourself. What's done by Providence is well done.

Wife: That's true enough. But now that I have no husband, who will look after me?

Woman [*briskly*]: Why, take a second to be sure, who'll do as well for you as this good neighbour.

Wife: That cannot be yet awhile, for tomorrow Lent begins, and parson has decreed there's to be no marriages in Lent. What shall I do? I never thought to keep house without a husband, so hard as 'twill be!

Woman [*soothingly*]: There, there, let sorrow take its course. Go, fetch down your red cloak from behind the door, and wrap up the corpse, so that it'll be out of our sight.

Wife: No, no, neighbour. I must keep the old red cloak against the time I get married again. I have nothing else. [*She picks up the pig-skin.*] Here, let us sew up my husband in this pig-skin. 'Tis useless for the tannery, seeing the pig died of something catching.

[*Hans wriggles again.*]

Woman: But the pig-skin is far too little. 'Twouldn't near cover the body. Come, let him have your red cloak. You always promised it him for a shroud.

Wife [*covering Hans with the skin, but leaving his feet uncovered*]: If his feet do stick out, what matter? My husband'll never heed. I have but one shroud, and that my mother gave me for a dowry. 'Tis worth at least five florins.

Woman: Oh lay him in the ground with honour! The cloak will be your last gift to him in this world. Count it not too dear. The good man is worth it! [*Loud knocking at door R. The Wife begins to moan and cry.*]

Wife: Woe, woe is me! There's someone at the door. Woe, woe is me! Go see who 'tis.

[*The Neighbour opens the door R., and the second neighbour enters. He is a middle-aged* Farmer *of prosperous appearance, evidently a man of standing in the village, and a churchwarden. He is followed by four or five other* Neighbours, *both men and women from the village, and by* Hans Sachs, *an old man with a white beard, wearing the leather apron of a cobbler, and a half-finished shoe sticking out of his pocket.*]

Farmer: Good dame, as we come down the street, we heard a weeping and a wailing within, so we are come straight to find out the cause.

Wife: Come right in, good neighbours, you're welcome. Come over here and see where my husband lies dead! [*The Neighbours recoil in horror, but the Wife reassures them smiling and nodding and winking.*] I am undone! I'd sooner all my livestock sickened and died!

Farmer: On my oath you must have held him dear if you'd give all that to have him back again. [*He stifles a laugh, and the Neighbours make sympathetic noises.*] What livestock have you got, neighbour?

Wife [*counting on her fingers*]: In the house alone, there's a dog, two cats, a bird, two dozen mice, one dozen rats, not to speak of the black-beetles! I'd give 'em all if only he was alive!

Farmer [*solemnly*]: The love betwixt you two must have been powerful strong. Now how would it be, if you was to give a promise of three pounds of wax candles and an offering in silver in memory of him in the green grave? That might bring him to life again. I did hear t'other day of a man being fetched back by something of that sort!

Wife: Good neighbour, be silent! My husband has gone to heaven. It would be wicked and shameful to bring him down to earth again.

Farmer [*going to door*]: Then I'd best get a barrow right away, and we'll carry him down to the church.

Woman: See that the candles be not forgotten, nor the tolling of the bell.

Chorus of Neighbours: And we'll follow the corpse in procession!

Wife: Oh, neighbours, neighbours, I pray you leave me in peace! My Hans was never a man for show. Bear him to the church on the barrow, but go secretly and after dark. Let the parson and the clerks stay at home! What need has he of candles, when he'll not see them, nor of the tolling of bells when he'll never hear more? 'Twould be sinful waste of money!

Farmer [*coming back*]: But, good dame, if we bury him tonight, we must have a silver collection on the morrow among both young and old in the village, so that his soul may fare the better.

[*The Neighbours shake their heads in disapproval.*]

Wife: When my man was alive, he never gave willing to the collection, so why start now he's dead driving other folks to the alms-giving, and all for the sake of a few pence? [*She appeals to Hans.*] Oh, my dear husband, what will happen to me? Shall I never see you alive no more? Oh Hans, husband of my heart, whatever shall I do next?

[*Hans sits up suddenly, kicking over the tankard, and throwing aside the pig-skin.*]

Hans: I'll tell you what to do next. You listen, wife. First you go and break five eggs in the frying-pan; then you pour a cask of my wine down your throat; next you try to sew me up in a pig-skin, though you swore I should be buried in your red cloak. You better lie down quiet till you've got your wits about you again!

Wife [*showing surprise*]: Why, husband, you're talking in your old way!

Hans [*bitterly*]: And what way would I be talking? Is this the love you boasted of so brazen? It's little I've heard nor seen of loving words and deeds this day!

Wife: Dear Hans –

Hans: You wicked woman! You'll do for me in death same as you've done for me in life. You prize me only for what I can give you, the clothes to your back, and the roof over your head. Without them you wouldn't so much as look at me over a hedge! Bah!

Wife: Good gracious, husband mine! Now you must despise me into the bargain. [*She laughs.*] Why I knew all the time you wasn't dead!

Hans [*amazed*]: You knew?

Wife: Now Hans, didn't you make believe to die just to see how I should act? That was why I played the trick on you.

Hans: You knew all the time I laid on this yere table I wern't dead? Oh, the artfulness of it!

Wife [*putting her arm around him*]: If you was really to die, you know well I should behave very different.

Hans [*still hurt*]: How'd I know what you'd do? Didn't I do my best to find out?

Wife: You ask the neighbours, they'll tell you.

Neighbours: Ay, ay, she's fond of you right enough!

Woman: Truth is Hans, you've mauled your hand in your own trap.

Farmer [*taking him by the arm*]: Come, come, friend, your wife's so full of cunning there's no curing her. Soon as ever she opened her eyes on this world, she was at her tricks. But bless you, my wife's as bad! Let 'em be, and come along down to the ale-house.

Woman: 'Twas for the best she done it. Isn't that so, Master Cobbler?

[*Hans Sachs comes forward and stands in the centre of the crowd.*]

Hans Sachs:

> I say, a joke's a joke, my friend,
> Like all good things, must have an end.
> Wives will be wives, they're all the same!
> So let them play the ancient game
> In their own way; nor seek to test
> A woman's love by questions, lest
> Grey hairs and bitter sorrows wax
> 'Twixt man and wife; so says Hans Sachs!

All [*repeating*]: So says Hans Sachs!

CURTAIN

6 Martin Luther (1520s)

Source: E. G. Rupp and B. Drewery, *Martin Luther* (London: Arnold, 1970), pp. 1–2, 4–7, 47–54, 95–7, 107–12, 121–6 abridged.

Martin Luther (1483–1546) was the son of Hans Luther of Eisleben, Saxony. He studied law at the University of Erfurt, but abandoned his studies to join a religious order of Augustinian hermits. Selected for further studies at the University of Wittenberg, he was taught by Johann von Staupitz, whom he succeeded as Professor of Biblical Studies at Wittenberg. In November 1517 his ninety-five theses questioning the value of indulgences led to a public debate which drew Luther into sharper and deeper criticism of moral and doctrinal abuses in the Church. He was condemned by the Pope in 1520 and by the Imperial Diet in 1521. From then onwards he fought both the Roman Church and radicals within the ranks of the Reformers. By 1524, when the Peasants' War erupted, Luther was playing a less and less prominent role in the shaping of the Reformation. We have selected brief extracts from some of his more important writings, which reflect the preoccupations of Luther during his most influential years.

A. 'On the Babylonish Captivity of the Church', 1520

This theological treatise was addressed to scholars and originally written in Latin, unlike many of Luther's writings.

I must deny that there are seven Sacraments,[1] and must lay it down, for the time being, that there are only three, baptism, penance and the bread,[2] and that by the court of Rome all these have been brought into miserable bondage, and the Church despoiled of all her liberty. And yet, if I were to speak according to the usage of scripture, I should hold that there was only one Sacrament, and three Sacramental signs. I shall speak on this point more at length at the proper time; but now I speak of the Sacrament of the bread, the first of all . . .

Formerly, when I was imbibing the scholastic theology, my lord the Cardinal of Cambray gave me occasion for reflection by arguing most acutely, in the fourth book of the *Sentences*, that it would be much more probable, and that fewer superfluous miracles would have to be introduced, if real bread and real wine, and not only their accidents, were understood to be upon the altar, unless the Church had determined the contrary. Afterwards, when I saw what the Church was which had thus determined – namely, the Thomistic, that is, the Aristotelian Church – I became bolder;

---

[1] Sacrament: the outward and visible sign of an inward and spiritual grace. By the sixteenth century a long list of such signs had been reduced by the Catholic Church to seven: Baptism, Confirmation, Eucharist, Penance, Extreme Unction, Orders, Marriage.

[2] In the Catholic communion the consecrated bread was offered to the laity and the priest alone partook of the consecrated wine.

and whereas I had been before in great straits of doubt, I now at length established my conscience in the former opinion, namely, that there is real bread and real wine, in which is the real flesh and real blood of Christ, in no other manner and in no less degree than the other party asserts them to be under the accidents . . .

I quite consent, then, that whoever chooses to hold either opinion should do so. My only object now is to remove scruples of conscience, so that no man may fear being guilty of heresy if he believes that real bread and real wine are present on the altar . . .

But why should not Christ be able to include His body within the substance of bread, as well as within the accidents? Fire and iron, two different substances, are so mingled in red-hot iron that every part of it is both fire and iron. Why may not the glorious body of Christ much more be in every part of the substance of the bread? . . .

The third bondage of this same Sacrament is that abuse of it – and by far the most impious – by which it has come about that at this day there is no belief in the Church more generally received or more firmly held than that the mass is a good work and a sacrifice. This abuse has brought in an infinite flood of other abuses, until faith in the Sacrament has been utterly lost, and they have made this divine Sacrament a mere subject of traffic, huckstering, and money-getting contracts . . .

Concerning the sacrament of baptism

. . . This doctrine ought to have been studiously inculcated upon the people by preaching; this promise ought to have been perpetually reiterated; men ought to have been constantly reminded of their baptism; faith ought to have been called forth and nourished. When this divine promise has been once conferred upon us, its truth continues even to the hour of our death; and thus our faith in it ought never to be relaxed, but ought to be nourished and strengthened, even till we die, by perpetual recollection of the promise made to us in baptism . . .

From what has been said we may clearly distinguish between man, the minister, and God, the Author, of baptism. Man baptizes, and does not baptize: he baptizes, because he performs the work of dipping the baptized person; he does not baptize, because in this work he does not act upon his own authority, but in the place of God. Hence we ought to receive baptism from the hand of man just as if Christ himself, nay, God himself, were baptizing us with his own hands. For it is not a man's baptism, but that of Christ and God, though we receive it by the hand of a man . . .

Baptism then signifies two things: death and resurrection; that is, full and complete justification. When the minister dips the child into the water, this signifies death; when he draws him out again, this signifies life.

Concerning the sacrament of penance[3]

... When Christ says, 'Whatsoever ye shall bind', etc., he means to call forth the faith of the penitent man, so that, on the strength of this work of promise, he may be sure that, if he believes and is absolved, he will be truly absolved in heaven. Evidently nothing is said here of power, but it is the ministry of absolution which is spoken of. It is strange enough that these blind and arrogant men have not arrogated to themselves some tyrannical power from the terms of the baptismal promise. If not, why have they presumed to do so from the promise connected with penitence? In both cases there is an equal ministry, a like promise, and the same character in the Sacrament; and it cannot be denied that, if we do not owe baptism to Peter alone, it is a piece of impious tyranny to claim the power of the keys for the Pope alone ...

Of confirmation

It is surprising how it should have entered anyone's mind to make a Sacrament of confirmation out of that laying on of hands which Christ applied to little children, and by which the Apostles bestowed the Holy Spirit, ordained presbyters, and healed the sick, as the Apostle writes to Timothy, 'Lay hands suddenly on no man' ...

I do not say this because I condemn the seven Sacraments but because I deny that they can be proved from the scriptures. . . .

Of matrimony

It is not only without any warrant of scripture that matrimony is considered a Sacrament, but it has been turned into a mere mockery by the very same traditions which vaunt it as a Sacrament ...

Of orders

Of this Sacrament the Church of Christ knows nothing: it was invented by the Church of the Pope. It not only has no promise of grace, anywhere declared, but not a word is said about it in the whole of the New Testament. Now it is ridiculous to set up as a Sacrament of God that which can nowhere be proved to have been instituted by God. Not that I consider that a rite practised for so many ages is to be condemned; but I would not have human invention established in sacred things, nor should it be allowed to bring in anything as divinely ordained which has not been divinely ordained, lest we should be objects of ridicule to our adversaries ...

---

[3] Although Luther argued here for the retention of Baptism, Eucharist and Penance as Scripturally ordained sacraments, eventually the Reformers rejected Penance. Penance was a tripartite sacrament comprising confession, penance and absolution.

Let every man then who has learnt that he is a Christian recognize what he is, and be certain that we are all equally priests, that is that we have the same power in the word, and in any Sacrament whatever, although it is not lawful for any one to use this power, except with the consent of the community.

B. Concerning Christian liberty, 1520

This work, *The Liberty of a Christian Man* written in German, was intended for a wide public. It presented the doctrines of justification by faith and the priesthood of all believers in conciliatory terms in a last attempt to win over his enemies.

I first lay down these two propositions, concerning spiritual liberty and servitude: a Christian man is the most free lord of all, and subject to none; a Christian man is the most dutiful servant of all, and subject to everyone . . .

Man is composed of a twofold nature, a spiritual and a bodily. As regards the spiritual nature, which they name the soul, he is called the spiritual, inward, new man; as regards the bodily nature, which they name the flesh, he is called the fleshly, outward, old man. The Apostle speaks of this: 'Though our outward man perish, yet the inward man is renewed day by day' [2 Corinthians 4: 16]. The result of this diversity is that in the scriptures opposing statements are made concerning the same man, the fact being that in the same man these two men are opposed to one another; the flesh lusting against the spirit, and the spirit against the flesh [Galatians 5: 17] . . .

And so it will profit nothing that the body should be adorned with sacred vestments, or dwell in holy places, or be occupied in sacred offices, or pray, fast and abstain from certain meats, or do whatever works can be done through the body and in the body. Something widely different will be necessary for the justification and liberty of the soul, since the things I have spoken of can be done by any impious person, and only hypocrites are produced by devotion to those things. On the other hand, it will not at all injure the soul that the body should be clothed in profane raiment, should dwell in profane places, should eat and drink in the ordinary fashion, should not pray aloud, and should leave undone all the things above mentioned, which may be done by hypocrites.

And, to cast everything aside, even speculations, meditations, and whatever things can be performed by the exertions of the soul itself, are of no profit. One thing, and one alone, is necessary for life, justification and Christian liberty; and that is the most holy word of God, the Gospel of Christ . . .

Let us therefore hold it for certain and firmly established that the soul can do without everything except the word of God, without which none at all of its wants are provided for. But, having the word, it is rich and wants for nothing . . .

Hence it is clear that as the soul needs the word alone for life and justification, so it is justified by faith alone, and not by any works ...

Meanwhile it is to be noted that the whole scripture of God is divided into two parts: precepts and promises. The precepts certainly teach us what is good, but what they teach is not forthwith done. For they show us what we ought to do, but do not give us the power to do it. They were ordained, however, for the purpose of showing man to himself, that through them he may learn his own impotence for good and may despair of his own strength. For this reason they are called the Old Testament, and are so ...

Hence the promises of God belong to the New Testament; nay, are the New Testament.

Now, since these promises of God are words of holiness, truth, righteousness, liberty, and peace, and are full of universal goodness, the soul, which cleaves to them with a firm faith, is so united to them, nay, thoroughly absorbed by them, that it not only partakes in, but is penetrated and saturated by, all their virtues ...

From all this it is easy to understand why faith has such great power, and why no good works, nor even all good works put together, can compare with it, since no work can cleave to the word of God or be in the soul. Faith alone and the word reign in it.

C. Preface to the Epistle to the Romans, 1522

The Preface explained the meaning of the Epistle to the Romans and its importance. See document III.8.B for a beautiful English rendering of this Preface.

Luther based his German translation upon Erasmus's revision (1518) of the Greek text. He adopted the German of the Saxon Chancery to make it comprehensible to both High and Low Germans and he sought to make it intelligible to the people: 'My teachers were the housewife in her home, the children at their games, the merchant in the market places; I tried to learn from them how to express and explain myself.'

This Epistle is really the chief part of the New Testament and the very purest Gospel, and is worthy not only that every Christian should know it word for word, by heart, but occupy himself with it every day, as the daily bread of the soul. It can never be read or pondered too much, and the more it is dealt with the more precious it becomes, and the better it tastes ...

It is, in itself, a bright light, almost enough to illume all the scripture.

To begin with we must have knowledge of its language and know what St Paul means by the words, law, sin, grace, faith, righteous, flesh, spirit, etc., otherwise no reading of it has any value ...

Faith is not that human notion and dream that some hold for faith. Because they see that no betterment of life and no good works follow it, and yet they can hear and say much about faith, they fall into error, and say, 'Faith is not enough; one must do works in order to be righteous and be saved.' This is the reason that, when they hear the Gospel, they fall to – and make for themselves, by their own powers, an idea in their hearts, which says, 'I believe.' This they hold for true faith. But it is a human imagination and idea that never reaches the depths of the heart, and so nothing comes of it and no betterment follows it.

Faith, however, is a divine work in us. It changes us and makes us to be born anew of God [John 1]; it kills the old Adam and makes altogether different men, in heart and spirit and mind and powers, and it brings with it the Holy Ghost. O, it is a living, busy, active, mighty thing, this faith; and so it is impossible for it not to do good works incessantly. It does not ask whether there are good works to do, but before the question arises it has already done them, and is always at the doing of them. He who does not these works is a faithless man. He gropes and looks about after faith and good works, and knows neither what faith is nor what good works are, though he talks and talks, with many words, about faith and good works.

Faith is a living, daring confidence in God's grace, so sure and certain that a man would stake his life on it a thousand times. This confidence in God's grace and knowledge of it makes men glad and bold and happy in dealing with God and with all his creatures; and this is the work of the Holy Ghost in faith. Hence a man is ready and glad, without compulsion, to do good to everyone, to serve everyone, to suffer everything, in love and praise of God, who has shown him this grace; and thus it is impossible to separate works from faith, quite as impossible as to separate heat and light from fire

. . .

Righteousness, then, is such a faith and is called 'God's righteousness', or 'the righteousness that avails before God', because God gives it and counts it as righteousness for the sake of Christ, our mediator, and makes a man give to every man what he owes him. For through faith a man becomes sinless and comes to take pleasure in God's commandments; thus he gives to God the honour that is his and pays him what he owes him; but he also serves man willingly, by whatever he can, and thus pays his debt to everyone. Such righteousness nature and free will and all our powers cannot bring into existence. No one can give himself faith; and no more can he take away his own unbelief; how, then, will he take away a single sin, even the very smallest? Therefore, all that is done, apart from faith, or in unbelief, is false; it is hypocrisy and sin, no matter how good a show it makes [Romans 14].

You must not so understand flesh and spirit as to think that flesh has to do only with unchastity and spirit only with what is inward, in the heart; but Paul, like Christ, in John 3[:6], calls 'flesh' everything that is born of the flesh; that is, the whole man, with body and soul, mind and senses, because everything about him longs for the flesh. Thus you should learn to call him 'fleshly' who thinks, teaches, and talks a great deal about high spiritual matters, but without grace. From the 'works of the flesh', in Galatians 5[:19-21], you can learn that Paul calls heresy and hatred 'works of the flesh', and in Romans 8[:3], he says that 'the law was weak through the flesh', and this does not refer to unchastity, but to all sins, above all to unbelief, which is the most spiritual of all vices. On the other hand, he calls him a spiritual man who is occupied with the most external kind of works, as Christ, when he washed the disciples' feet, and Peter, when he steered his boat, and fished.

Thus 'the flesh' is a man who lives and works, inwardly and outwardly, in the service of the flesh's profit and of this temporal life; 'the spirit' is the man who lives and works, inwardly and outwardly, in the service of the Spirit and the future life . . .

But do you follow the order of this Epistle? Worry first about Christ and the Gospel, that you may recognize your sin and his grace; then fight your sin, as the first eight chapters here have taught; then, when you have reached the eighth chapter, and are under the cross and suffering, that will teach you the right doctrine of predestination, in the ninth, tenth and eleventh chapters, and how comforting it is. For in the absence of suffering and the cross and the danger of death, one cannot deal with predestination without harm and without secret wrath against God. The old Adam must die before he can endure this subject and drink the strong wine of it. Therefore take heed not to drink wine while you are still a suckling. There is a limit, a time, an age for every doctrine . . .

Thus in this Epistle we find most richly the things that a Christian ought to know; namely, what is law, Gospel, sin, punishment, grace, faith, righteousness, Christ, God, good works, love, hope, the cross, and also how we are to conduct ourselves towards everyone, whether righteous or sinner, strong or weak, friend or foe. All this is ably founded on scripture and proved by his own example and that of the prophets. Therefore it appears that St Paul wanted to comprise briefly in this one Epistle the whole Christian and evangelical doctrine and to prepare an introduction to the entire Old Testament; for, without doubt, he who has this Epistle well in his heart, has the light and power of the Old Testament with him. Therefore let every Christian exercise himself in it habitually and continually. To this may God give His grace. Amen.

D. 'On the Appointment of Ministers', November 1523

This work offers important insights into Luther's understanding of the Eucharist, the public ministry of the Word, the priesthood of all believers and ministers as 'stewards of the mysteries of God'.

1. DECLARATION

In the first place I freely confess that if there are any who expect they are to receive from me, intact or improved, the rite and custom hitherto observed in shaving and anointing priests, then the contents of this little book will have no relevance for them. They are welcome to enjoy their own religion – or superstition, popularized as it is from ancient and widespread tradition. Our concern, however, is to seek the pure and genuine system [*rationem*] prescribed in holy scripture, and not to trouble ourselves with what custom or the Fathers have given us or done in this matter; once and for all we have learned that our duty is . . . so far from obeying human traditions, openly to dominate them, as our purpose and our Christian liberty require . . .

2. Dissuasion from accepting Papal ordinations

... For the time being I will overlook the fact that in Papal ordinations these whom they call priests are anointed and appointed by the sole authority of the bishop; the consent or election of the people over whom they are to be placed is neither sought nor given ... Also, the majority are ordained only to what they call 'benefices'; their only duty will be to offer masses ... As I say, however, I am willing to overlook this monstrous abuse in Papal ordinations for the time being.

Anyone who loves Christ must needs recoil from such a state of affairs, and endure any suffering rather than submit to Papal ordinations, since everything about them is transacted with the utmost ... perversity ... For since ordination was instituted on the authority of scripture ... in order to provide for the people ministers of the Word, it is (I maintain) this public ministry of the Word, by which are dispersed the mysteries of God, which ought to be instituted through holy ordination ..., since without the Word nothing stands in the Church, and everything in it stands by the Word alone. But these Papists I am talking about do not even dream of a ministry like this in their ordinations ... Instead of ministers of the Word they ordain petty sacrificers, who offer masses and hear confessions. For this is what the bishop intends when he gives the chalice into their hand and confers the power of consecrating and sacrificing for the living and the dead ... In this way ... he breathes the spirit into their ears and makes them confessors, saying 'Receive the Holy Spirit'. Such is this most resplendent power of consecration and absolution ...

But since it is quite certain that the mass is not a sacrifice, and that such confessions, which they would make obligatory, are nothing, both alike being the sacrilegious and lying inventions of men, it clearly follows that such sacred ordinations make nobody a priest or a minister in the sight of God [*coram Deo*] ... Therefore faith and conscience urge us, under penalty of the anathema of God, to beware of being ordained by them; indeed, the plan of our salvation enforces our abstention from their hateful and damnable ordinations.

3. A priest is not the same as a presbyter or minister: the former is born, the latter made

And here the prime need is unswerving faith ... Hence, first of all, let it be to you as an immovable rock, that the New Testament knows nothing of any priest who is or can be anointed externally. If there are such, they are masks [*larvae*] and idols ... For a priest ... is not made but born; not ordained but created. His birth indeed is not of the flesh but of the Spirit, by water and Spirit in the bath of regeneration [John 3: 5; Titus 3: 5]. In a word, all Christians are priests and all priests Christians ...

But let us proceed, and show from what they call the priestly offices themselves that all Christians are equally priests. I have sufficiently treated elsewhere[1] the words of 1 Peter 2 [: 9] and Revelation 5 [: 10]. The offices of a priest are, in the main, the following: to teach, to preach and proclaim the Word of God, to baptize, to consecrate or administer the Eucharist, to bind and loose sins, to pray for others, to sacrifice, to judge the doctrines and the spirits of all men . . .

But all these things of which we have been speaking concern the common right of Christians: for since, as we have proved, all these things are common to all Christians, no man can step forward on his own authority and arrogate to himself what belongs to all . . . But the rights of the community demand that one, or as many as the community decides, shall be chosen or accepted to perform these offices publicly in the place and the name of all, who have the same rights. Otherwise there would be shameful confusion among the people of God and another Babylon would arise in the Church . . . For it is one thing to exercise a right in public, another to use it in emergency; and public exercise is only authorized by the consent of the whole community or the Church, whereas in emergency whoever is willing may use it . . .

All this, I believe, confirms the conclusion that those who preside over the Sacraments or the Word among the people neither can nor ought to be called priests. The fact that they are called priests is a borrowing from heathen ritual or a relic of Jewish practice . . . According to the Gospel writings, they would be better named ministers, deacons, bishops, stewards (more frequently called presbyters on account of their age). As Paul says in 1 Corinthians 4:[1]: 'We must be regarded as ministers of Christ and stewards of the mysteries of God.' He does not say 'as priests of Christ', because he would know that the name and office of priest are the common possession of all . . .

If ministers are as we say, then the 'indelible character' vanishes and the perpetuity of the priesthood is a mere fiction. A minister may be deposed if he ceases to be faithful, or reinstated as long as he deserves it or the community of the Church desires, just as any civil administrator among brethren of equal rights . . .

By these . . . impregnable stays[2] of scripture (if we believe the Word of God) that most dreadful need is overcome which hitherto has forced Bohemia to beg for a shaven priesthood and accept the most unworthy specimens it received. For here we have clearer than day . . . the source of priests or ministers of the Word: that is, from the very flock of Christ and no other source. For when clear proof has been given that everyone has the right of ministering the Word, and that he is even commanded to do so if he sees either a deficiency of teachers or wrongful teaching by those he has – as Paul lays down in 1 Corinthians 14, to ensure the proclamation of the power

[1] *Address to the Christian Nobility* (1520), in which Luther appealed to the German nation to summon a General Council to reform the Church.
[2] Stays: in the sense of 'supports'.

of God among us all – how much more does a whole Christian community have the right and duty to commit this office by common vote to one or more in their stead? And these one or more in turn to others, if the common vote likewise approves? . . .

Necessity and the common mind of the faithful force the same conclusion. For since the Church is . . . nourished by the Word of God, it is patent that without the Word it cannot exist; if it loses the Word it ceases to be the Church. Hence if a man is born from his baptism for the ministry of the Word, and papal bishops are unwilling to bestow the ministry of the Word . . . the only thing left is either to let the Church of God perish without the Word or to allow the propriety of a church meeting to cast its votes and choose from its own resources one or as many as are necessary and suitable, and commend and confirm these to the whole community by prayer and the laying-on of hands. These should then be recognized and honoured as lawful bishops and ministers of the Word, in the assured faith that God himself is the author of what the common consent of the faithful has so performed – of those, that is, who accept and confess the Gospel . . .

This, then, is what you should do . . . Let those be called and come together freely whose heart God has so touched that they think and judge as you do yourselves: go forward in the name of the Lord to choose him or those whom you desire, and who are seen to be worthy and suitable. Then let those who have influence among you lay hands on them, and confirm and commend them . . . to the Church . . . and let them on this showing be your bishops, ministers, pastors. Amen.

E. 'Secular Authority: To What Extent it Should be Obeyed', 1523

A key document in Luther's political thought. Christians live simultaneously in two kingdoms: the spiritual (Church) and the temporal. The secular authorities alone have coercive powers; claims to worldly jurisdiction over Church or State by Pope or Church are a usurpation.

LETTER OF DEDICATION [TO JOHN, DUKE OF SAXONY][1]

Again, illustrious, high-born Prince, gracious Lord, necessity is laid upon me, and the entreaties of many and above all your Grace's wishes impel me, to write concerning the secular authorities and the sword they bear; how it should be used in a Christian manner and in how far men are bound to obey it . . .

---

[1] John, Elector of Saxony, 1525–32, was, unlike his father Frederick the Wise, an uncompromising Lutheran.

I hope, however, to instruct the princes and the secular authorities in such a way that they shall remain Christians and that Christ shall remain Lord, yet so that Christ's commandments need not for their sake be changed into counsels . . .

Your Princely Grace's obedient servant, MARTIN LUTHER

WITTENBERG, *New Year's Day*, 1523

THE TREATISE

. . . We must divide all the children of Adam into two classes; the first belong to the kingdom of God, the second to the kingdom of the world. Those belonging to the kingdom of God are all true believers in Christ and are subject to Christ. For Christ is the King and Lord in the kingdom of God, as the second Psalm and all the scriptures say . . .

Now observe, these people need no secular sword or law. And if all the world were composed of real Christians, that is, true believers, no prince, king, lord, sword or law would be needed. For what were the use of them, since Christians have in their hearts the Holy Spirit, who instructs them and causes them to wrong no one, to love everyone, willingly and cheerfully to suffer injustice and even death from everyone. Where every wrong is suffered and every right is done, no quarrel, strife, trial, judge, penalty, law or sword is needed. Therefore, it is not possible for the secular sword and law to find any work to do among Christians, since of themselves they do much more than its laws and doctrines can demand . . .

Why is this? Because the righteous does of himself all and more than all that the laws demand. But the unrighteous do nothing that the law demands, therefore they need the law to instruct, constrain, and compel them to do what is good. A good tree does not need any teaching or law to bear good fruit, its nature causes it to bear according to its kind without any law and teaching. A man would be a fool to make a book of laws and statutes telling an apple tree how to bear apples and not thorns, when it is able by its own nature to do this better than man with all his books can define and direct. Just so, by the Spirit and by faith all Christians are throughout inclined to do well and keep the law, much more than anyone can teach them with all the laws, and need so far as they are concerned no commandments nor law . . .

All who are not Christians belong to the kingdom of the world and are under the law. Since few believe and still fewer live a Christian life, do not resist the evil, and themselves do no evil, God has provided for non-Christians a different government outside the Christian estate and God's kingdom, and has subjected them to the sword, so that, even though they would do so, they cannot practise their wickedness, and that, if they do, they may not do it without fear nor in peace and prosperity . . .

If anyone attempted to rule the world by the Gospel, and put aside all secular law and the secular sword, on the plea that all are baptized and Christian, and that according to the Gospel, there is to be among them neither law nor sword, nor necessity for either, pray, what would happen? He would loose the bands and chains of the wild and savage beasts, and let them tear and mangle everyone, and at the same time say they were quite tame and gentle creatures; but I would have the proof in my wounds . . .

It is indeed true that Christians, so far as they themselves are concerned, are subject to neither law nor sword and need neither; but first take heed and fill the world with real Christians before ruling it in a Christian and evangelical manner. This you will never accomplish; for the world and the masses are and always will be unchristian, although they are all baptized and are nominally Christian. Christians, however, are few and far between, as the saying is. Therefore it is out of the question that there should be a common Christian government over the whole world, nay even over one land or company of people, since the wicked always out-number the good. Hence a man who would venture to govern an entire country or the world with the Gospel would be like a shepherd who should place in one fold wolves, lions, eagles and sheep together and let them freely mingle with one another and say, Help yourselves, and be good and peaceful among yourselves; the fold is open, there is plenty of food; have no fear of dogs and clubs. The sheep, forsooth, would keep the peace and would allow themselves to be fed and governed in peace, but they would not live long; nor would any beast keep from molesting another.

For this reason these two kingdoms must be sharply distinguished, and both be permitted to remain; the one to produce piety, the other to bring about external peace and prevent evil deeds; neither is sufficient in the world without the other. For no one can become pious before God by means of the secular government, without Christ's spiritual rule. Hence Christ's rule does not extend over all, but Christians are always in the minority and are in the midst of non-Christians . . .

Christians, among themselves and by and for themselves, need no law or sword, since it is neither necessary nor profitable for them. Since, however, a true Christian lives and labours on earth not for himself, but for his neighbour, therefore the whole spirit of his life impels him to do even that which he need not do, but which is profitable and necessary for his neighbour. Because the sword is a very great benefit and necessary to the whole world, to preserve peace, to punish sin and to prevent evil, he submits most willingly to the rule of the sword, pays tax, honours those in authority, serves, helps and does all he can to further the government, that it may be sustained and held in honour and fear. Although he needs none of these things for himself and it is not necessary for him to do them, yet he considers what is for the good and profit of others . . .

You are under obligation to serve and further the sword by whatever means you can, with body, soul, honour or goods. For it is nothing that you need, but something quite useful and profitable for the whole world and for your neighbour. Therefore, should you see that there is a lack of hangmen, beadles, judges, lords or princes, and find that you are qualified, you should offer your services and seek the place, that necessary government may by no means be despised and become inefficient or perish. For the world cannot and dare not dispense with it . . . Now, it should be quite unchristian to say that there is any service of God in which a Christian ought not and dare not take part, when such a service belongs to no one so much as to Christians. It would indeed be good and profitable if all princes were real and good Christians, for the sword and the government, as a special service of God, belong of right to Christians, more than to all other men on earth. Therefore you should cherish the sword or the government, even as the state of matrimony, or husbandry, or any other handiwork which God has instituted . . .

But you ask further, whether the beadles, hangmen, jurists, advocates, and their ilk, can also be Christians and in a state of salvation. I answer: If the state and its sword are a divine service, as was proved above, that which the state needs in order to wield the sword must also be a divine service. There must be those who arrest, accuse, slay and destroy the wicked, and protect, acquit, defend and save the good. Therefore, when such duties are performed, not with the intention of seeking one's own ends, but only of helping to maintain the laws and the state, so that the wicked may be restrained, there is no peril in them and they may be followed like any other pursuit and be used as one's means of support. For, as was said, love of neighbour seeks not its own, considers not how great or how small, but how profitable and how needful for neighbour or community the works are . . .

How far secular authority extends

. . . If then your prince or temporal lord commands you to hold with the Pope, to believe this or that, or commands you to give up certain books, you should say, It does not befit Lucifer to sit by the side of God.[2] Dear lord, I owe you obedience with life and goods; command me within the limits of your power on earth, and I will obey. But if you command me to believe, and to put away books, I will not obey; for in this case you are a tyrant and overreach yourself, and command where you have neither right nor power, etc. Should he take your property for this, and punish such disobedience, blessed are you. Thank God that you are worthy to suffer for the sake of the divine Word, and let him rave, fool that he is. He will meet his judge . . .

You must know that from the beginning of the world a wise prince is a rare bird indeed; still more so a pious prince. They are usually the greatest fools or the worst knaves on earth; therefore one must constantly expect the worst from them and look for little good from them, especially in divine matters, which concern the salvation of souls. They are God's jailers and hangmen, and his divine wrath needs them to punish the wicked and preserve outward peace . . .

---

[2] It is not appropriate for Lucifer (i.e. the Devil) to sit by the side of God.

What, then, are the priests and bishops? I answer, their government is not one of authority or power, but a service and an office; for they are neither higher nor better than other Christians. Therefore they should not impose any law or decree on others without their will and consent; their rule consists in nothing else than in dealing with God's Word, leading Christians by it and overcoming heresy by its means. For, as was said, Christians can be ruled by nothing but by God's Word . . .

[The Christian prince or lord] should picture Christ to himself, and say, 'Behold, Christ the chief ruler came and served me, sought not to have power, profit and honour from me, but only considered my need, and did all he could that I might have power, profit and honour from him and through him. I will do the same, not seek mine own advantage in my subjects, but their advantage, and thus serve them by my office, protect them, give them audience and support, that they, and not I, may have the benefit and profit by it.' Thus a prince should in his heart empty himself of his power and authority, and interest himself in the need of his subjects, dealing with it as though it were his own need. Thus Christ did unto us; and these are the proper works of Christian love.

You say, Who then would be a prince? For that would make the position of a prince the worst on earth, full of trouble, labour and sorrow. Where would there be room for the princely pleasures, such as dancing, hunting, racing, gaming and similar worldly enjoyments? I answer, We are not prescribing now how a temporal prince shall be a Christian, in order that he also may reach heaven. Who does not know that a prince is a rare bird in heaven? . . .

But when a prince is in the wrong, are his people bound to follow him then too? I answer, No, for it is no one's duty to do wrong; we ought to obey God who desires the right, rather than men. How is it, when the subjects do not know whether the prince is in the right or not? I answer, As long as they cannot know, nor find out by any possible means, they may obey without peril to their souls . . .

Therefore we will close by saying briefly that a prince's duty is fourfold: first, that towards God consists in true confidence and in sincere prayer; second, that towards his subjects consists in love and Christian service; third, that towards his counsellors and rulers consists in an open mind and unfettered judgement; fourth, that towards evil doers consists in proper zeal and firmness. Then his state is right, outwardly and inwardly, pleasing to God and to the people. But he must expect much envy and sorrow – the cross will soon rest on the shoulders of such a ruler.

F. 'Against the Robbing and Murdering Hordes of Peasants', May 1525

The Peasants' War had started in June 1524. Luther eventually took fright and denounced the action of the lower orders at the height of the rebellion. The tract was published after the suppression of the revolt.

In the former book I did not venture to judge the peasants, since they had offered to be set right and to be instructed, and Christ's command, in Matthew 7[:1], says that we are not to judge. But before I look around they go on, and, forgetting their offer, they betake themselves to violence, and rob and rage and act like mad dogs. By this it is easy to see what they had in their false minds, and that the pretences which they made in their twelve articles,[1] under the name of the Gospel, were nothing but lies. It is the devil's work that they are at, and in particular it is the work of the archdevil who rules at Mühlhausen,[2] and does nothing else than stir up robbery, murder and bloodshed; as Christ says of him in John 8[:44], 'He was a murderer from the beginning.' Since, then, these peasants and wretched folk have let themselves be led astray, and do otherwise than they have promised, I too must write of them otherwise than I have written, and begin by setting their sin before them, as God commands Isaiah and Ezekiel, on the chance that some of them may learn to know themselves. Then I must instruct the rulers how they are to conduct themselves in these circumstances.

The peasants have taken on themselves the burden of three terrible sins against God and man, by which they have abundantly merited death in body and soul. In the first place they have sworn to be true and faithful, submissive and obedient, to their rulers, as Christ commands, when he says, 'Render unto Caesar the things that are Caesar's,' [Matthew 22:21] and in Romans 13[:1], 'Let everyone be subject unto the higher powers.' Because they are breaking this obedience, and are setting themselves against the higher powers, wilfully and with violence, they have forfeited body and soul, as faithless, perjured, lying, disobedient knaves and scoundrels are wont to do. St Paul passed this judgement on them in Romans 13[:2] when he said, that they who resist the power will bring a judgement upon themselves. This saying will smite the peasants sooner or later, for it is God's will that faith be kept and duty done.

In the second place, they are starting a rebellion, and violently robbing and plundering monasteries and castles which are not theirs, by which they have a second time deserved death in body and soul, if only as highwaymen

[1] The Twelve Articles of Memmingen, formal demands made by the Swabian peasants of their rulers, in March 1525.
[2] Thomas Müntzer, c. 1489–1525, a university-educated priest with a living in Swabia, who originally followed Luther but broke with him in 1521 when he thought Luther had sold out to the powers that be. A genuine revolutionary, he was exiled for preaching inflammatory sermons. In 1525 he led the peasantry of Franconia against the princes, lost, was tortured and killed.

and murderers. Besides, any man against whom it can be proved that he is a maker of sedition is outside the law of God and Empire, so that the first who can slay him is doing right and well. For if a man is an open rebel every man is his judge and executioner, just as when a fire starts, the first to put it out is the best man. For rebellion is not simple murder, but is like a great fire, which attacks and lays waste a whole land. Thus rebellion brings with it a land full of murder and bloodshed, makes widows and orphans, and turns everything upside down, like the greatest disaster. Therefore let everyone who can, smite, slay and stab, secretly or openly, remembering that nothing can be more poisonous, hurtful or devilish than a rebel. It is just as when one must kill a mad dog; if you do not strike him, he will strike you, and a whole land with you.

In the third place, they cloak this terrible and horrible sin with the Gospel, call themselves 'Christian brethren', receive oaths and homage, and compel people to hold with them to these abominations. Thus they become the greatest of all blasphemers of God and slanderers of his holy Name, serving the devil, under the outward appearance of the Gospel, thus earning death in body and soul ten times over. I have never heard of a more hideous sin. I suspect that the devil feels the Last Day coming and therefore undertakes such an unheard-of-act, as though saying to himself, 'This is the last, therefore it shall be the worst; I will stir up the dregs and knock out the bottom.' God will guard us against him! See what a mighty prince the devil is, how he has the world in his hands and can throw everything into confusion, when he can so quickly catch so many thousands of peasants, deceive them, blind them, harden them and throw them into revolt, and do with them whatever his raging fury undertakes.

It does not help the peasants, when they pretend that, according to Genesis 1 and 2, all things were created free and common, and that all of us alike have been baptized. For under the New Testament Moses does not count; for there stands our Master, Christ, and subjects us, with our bodies and our property, to the emperor and the law of this world, when he says, 'Render to Caesar the things that are Caesar's.' Paul, too, says, in Romans 13[:1], to all baptized Christians, 'Let every man be subject to the power', and Peter says, 'Be subject to every ordinance of man' [1 Peter 2:13]. By this doctrine of Christ we are bound to live, as the Father commands from heaven, saying, 'This is My beloved Son; hear him.' For baptism does not make men free in body and property, but in soul; and the Gospel does not make goods common, except in the case of those who do of their own free will what the apostles and disciples did in Acts 4. They did not demand, as do our insane peasants in their raging, that the goods of others – of a Pilate and a Herod – should be common, but only their own goods. Our peasants, however, would have other men's goods common, and keep their own goods for themselves. Fine Christians these! I think there is not a devil left in hell; they have all gone into the peasants. Their raving has gone beyond all measure.

Since the peasants, then, have brought both God and man down upon them and are already so many times guilty of death in body and soul, since they submit to no court and wait for no verdict, but only rage on, I must instruct the worldly governors how they are to act in the matter with a clear conscience.

First, I will not oppose a ruler who, even though he does not tolerate the Gospel, will smite and punish these peasants without offering to submit the case to judgement. For he is within his rights, since the peasants are not contending any longer for the Gospel, but have become faithless, perjured, disobedient, rebellious murderers, robbers and blasphemers, whom even heathen rulers have the right and power to punish; nay, it is their duty to punish them, for it is just for this purpose that they bear the sword, and are 'the ministers of God upon him that doeth evil'.

But if the ruler is a Christian and tolerates the Gospel, so that the peasants have no appearance of a case against him, he should proceed with fear. First he must take the matter to God, confessing that we have deserved these things, and remembering that God may, perhaps, have thus aroused the devil as a punishment upon all Germany. Then he should humbly pray for help against the devil, for 'we are battling not only against flesh and blood, but against spiritual wickedness in the air', and this must be attacked with prayer. Then, when our hearts are so turned to God that we are ready to let his divine will be done, whether he will or will not have us to be princes and lords, we must go beyond our duty, and offer the mad peasants an opportunity to come to terms, even though they are not worthy of it. Finally, if that does not help, then swiftly grasp the sword.

For a prince and lord must remember in this case that he is God's minister and the servant of his wrath (Romans 13), to whom the sword is committed for use upon such fellows, and that he sins as greatly against God, if he does not punish and protect and does not fulfil the duties of his office, as does one to whom the sword has not been committed when he commits a murder. If he can punish and does not – even though the punishment consist in the taking of life and the shedding of blood – then he is guilty of all the murder and all the evil which these fellows commit, because, by wilful neglect of the divine command, he permits them to practise their wickedness, though he can prevent it, and is in duty bound to do so. Here, then, there is no time for sleeping; no place for patience or mercy. It is the time of the sword, not the day of grace.

The rulers, then, should go on unconcerned, and with a good conscience lay about them as long as their hearts still beat. It is to their advantage that the peasants have a bad conscience and an unjust cause, and that any peasant who is killed is lost in body and soul and is eternally the devil's. But the rulers have a good conscience and a just cause; and can, therefore, say to God with all assurance of heart, 'Behold, my God, thou hast appointed me prince or lord, of this I can have no doubt; and thou hast committed to me the sword over the evildoers (Romans 13). It is thy Word, and cannot lie. I must fulfil my office, or forfeit thy grace. It is also plain that these peasants have deserved death many times over, in thine eyes and the eyes of the world, and have been committed to me for punishment. If it be thy will that I be slain by them, and that my rulership be taken from me and destroyed, so be it: thy will be done. So shall I die and be destroyed fulfilling thy commandment and thy Word, and shall be found obedient to thy commandment and my office. Therefore will I punish and smite as long as my heart beats. Thou wilt judge and make things right.'

Thus it may be that one who is killed fighting on the ruler's side may be a true martyr in the eyes of God, if he fights with such a conscience as I have just described, for he is in God's Word and is obedient to him. On the other hand, one who perishes on the peasant's side is an eternal brand of hell, for he bears the sword against God's Word and is disobedient to him, and is a member of the devil. And even though it happens that the peasants gain the upper hand (which God forbid!) – for to God all things are possible, and we do not know whether it may be his will, through the devil, to destroy all order and rule and cast the world upon a desolate heap, as a prelude to the Last Day, which cannot be far off – nevertheless, they may die without worry and go to the scaffold with a good conscience, who are found exercising their office of the sword. They may leave to the devil the kingdom of the world, and take in exchange the everlasting kingdom. Strange times, these, when a prince can win heaven with bloodshed, better than other men with prayer!

Finally, there is another thing that ought to move the rulers. The peasants are not content to be themselves the devil's own, but they force and compel many good people against their wills to join their devilish league, and so make them partakers of all of their own wickedness and damnation. For anyone who consents to what they do, goes to the devil with them, and is guilty of all the evil deeds that they commit; though he has to do this because he is so weak in faith that he does not resist them. A pious Christian ought to suffer a hundred deaths, rather than give a hair's breadth of consent to the peasant's cause. O how many martyrs could now be made by the bloodthirsty peasants and the murdering prophets! Now the rulers ought to have mercy on these prisoners of the peasants, and if they had no other reason to use the sword, with a good conscience, against the peasants, and to risk their own lives and property in fighting them, there would be reason enough, and more than enough, in this – that thus they would be rescuing and helping these souls, whom the peasants have forced into their devilish league and who, without willing it, are sinning so horribly, and who must be damned. For truly these souls are in purgatory; nay, in the bonds of hell and the devil.

Therefore, dear lords, here is a place where you can release, rescue, help. Have mercy on these poor people [whom the peasants have compelled to join them]. Stab, smite, slay, whoever can. If you die in doing it, well for you! A more blessed death can never be yours, for you die in obeying the divine Word and commandment in Romans 13, and in loving service of your neighbour, whom you are rescuing from the bonds of hell and of the devil. And so I beg everyone who can to flee from the peasants as from the devil himself; those who do not flee, I pray that God will enlighten and convert. As for those who are not to be converted, God grant that they may have neither fortune nor success. To this let every pious Christian say Amen! For this prayer is right and good, and pleases God; this I know. If anyone think this too hard, let him remember that rebellion is intolerable and that the destruction of the world is to be expected every hour.

G. A hymn of Luther

The translation is by Thomas Carlyle (1795–1881).

> A safe stronghold our God is still,
> A trusty shield and weapon,
> He'll help us clear from all the ill
> That hath us now o'ertaken.
> The ancient prince of hell
> Hath risen with purpose fell;
> Strong mail of craft and power
> He weareth in this hour;
> On earth is not his fellow.
>
> With force of arms we nothing can,
> Full soon were we down-ridden;
> But for us fights the proper Man,
> Whom God himself hath bidden.
> Ask ye: Who is this same?
> Christ Jesus is his name,
> The Lord Sabaoth's Son;
> He, and no other one,
> Shall conquer in the battle.
>
> And were this world all devils o'er,
> And watching to devour us,
> We lay it not to heart so sore;
> Not they can overpower us.
> And let the prince of ill
> Look grim as e'er he will,
> He harms us not a whit:
> For why? His doom is writ;
> A word shall quickly slay him.
>
> God's word, for all their craft and force
> One moment will not linger,
> But, spite of hell, shall have its course;
> 'Tis written by his finger.
> And though they take our life,
> Goods, honour, children, wife,
> Yet is their profit small:
> These things shall vanish all;
> The city of God remaineth.

7 John Calvin (1536)

Source: *The Portable Renaissance Reader*, edited by James Bruce Ross and Mary Martin McLaughlin (Harmondsworth: Penguin Books, 1977), pp. 704–11.

John Calvin (1509–64), French reformer and theologian, was born in Noyon in Picardy and was early prepared for an ecclesiastical career. After studying theology at Paris (1523–7) he seems to have had some doubts about his vocation and studied law at Orleans and then at Bourges. He broke with the Catholic Church in 1533 after a religious experience in which he believed he had been commissioned by God to restore the Church to its original purity. In 1535 he fled possible persecution under Francis I to Basel. In March 1536 he published the first edition of his famous *Institutes of the Christian Religion* in Latin. From 1536 to 1538 he served as preacher and professor of theology at Geneva. After his expulsion he served the French congregation in Strasbourg (1538–41) and the second edition of the *Institutes* came under Bucer's influence. Calvin returned to Geneva in 1541 and spent the next fourteen years establishing a theocratic regime in that city through a series of Ordinances. By 1555 all resistance to the regime had ceased. Calvin's influence far exceeded his work in Geneva, however. His teaching, as formulated in the *Institutes*, was accepted by most of the non-Lutheran reformed churches. We include here a brief extract from the *Institutes* which treats the doctrines of free will and predestination.

Since we have seen that the domination of sin, from the time of its subjugation of the first man,[1] not only extends over the whole race, but also exclusively possesses every soul; it now remains to be more closely investigated, whether we are despoiled of all freedom, and, if any particle of it yet remain, how far its power extends. But that we may the more easily discover the truth of this question, I will first set up by the way a mark, by which our whole course must be regulated. The best method of guarding against error is to consider the dangers which threaten us on every side. For when man is declared to be destitute of all rectitude, he immediately makes it an occasion of slothfulness; and because he is said to have no power of himself for the pursuit of righteousness, he totally neglects it, as though it did not at all concern him. On the other hand, he cannot arrogate anything to himself, be it ever so little, without God being robbed of His honour, and himself being endangered by presumptuous temerity. Therefore to avoid striking on either of these rocks, this will be the course to be pursued: that man, being taught that he has nothing good left in his possession, and being surrounded on every side with the most miserable necessity, should nevertheless be instructed to aspire to the good of which he is destitute, and to the liberty of which he is deprived; and should be roused from indolence with more earnestness than if he were supposed to be possessed of the greatest strength. The necessity of the latter is obvious to everyone. The former, I perceive, is doubted by more than it ought to be. For this being

---

[1] Adam.

placed beyond all controversy, that man must not be deprived of anything that properly belongs to him, it ought also to be manifest how important it is that he should be prevented from false boasting. For if he was not even then permitted to glory in himself, when by the divine beneficence he was decorated with the noblest ornaments, how much ought he now to be humbled, when on account of his ingratitude he has been hurled from the summit of glory to the abyss of ignominy? At that time, I say, when he was exalted to the most honourable eminence, the Scripture attributes nothing to him, but that he was created after the image of God; which certainly implies that his happiness consisted not in any goodness of his own, but in a participation of God. What then remains for him now, deprived of all glory, but that he acknowledge God, to whose beneficence he could not be thankful when he abounded in the riches of His favour? And that he now at least by a confession of his poverty glorify Him, whom he glorified not by an acknowledgement of His blessings? It is also no less conducive to our interest than to the divine glory that all the praise of wisdom and strength be taken away from us; so that they join sacrilege to our fall, who ascribe to us anything more than truly belongs to us. For what else is the consequence, when we are taught to contend in our own strength, but that we are lifted into the air on a reed, which being soon broken, we fall to the ground. Though our strength is placed in too favourable a point of view, when it is compared to a reed. For it is nothing but smoke, whatever vain men have imagined and pretend concerning it. Wherefore it is not without reason that that remarkable sentence is so frequently repeated by Augustine,[2] that free will is rather overthrown than established even by its own advocates. It was necessary to premise these things for the sake of some who, when they hear that human power is completely subverted in order that the power of God may be established in man, inveterately hate this whole argument, as dangerous and unprofitable: which yet appears to be highly useful to us, and essential to true religion . . .

Now when I assert that the will, being deprived of its liberty, is necessarily drawn or led into evil, I should wonder if anyone considered it as a harsh expression, since it has nothing in it absurd, nor is it unsanctioned by the custom of good men. It offends those who know not how to distinguish between necessity and compulsion. But if anyone should ask them whether God is not necessarily good, and whether the devil is not necessarily evil, what answer will they make? For there is such a close connection between the goodness of God and His divinity that His deity is not more necessary than His goodness. But the devil is by his fall so alienated from communion with all that is good that he can do nothing but what is evil. But if anyone should sacrilegiously object that little praise is due to God for His goodness, which He is constrained to preserve, shall we not readily reply that His inability to do evil arises from His infinite goodness and not from the impulse of violence? Therefore if a necessity of doing well impairs not the

<hr>

[2] St Augustine of Hippo, AD 354–430, a Father of the early Church. His later years were occupied by the Pelagian controversy, in which he adopted a predestinarian stance.

liberty of the divine will in doing well; if the devil, who cannot but do evil, nevertheless sins voluntarily; who then will assert that man sins less voluntarily, because he is under a necessity of sinning? This necessity Augustine everywhere maintains, and even when he was pressed with the cavils of Celestius,[3] who tried to throw an odium on this doctrine, he confidently expressed himself in these terms: 'By means of liberty it came to pass that man fell into sin; but now the penal depravity consequent on it, instead of liberty, has introduced necessity.' And whenever the mention of this subject occurs, he hesitates not to speak in this manner of the necessary servitude of sin. We must therefore observe this grand point of distinction, that man, having been corrupted by his fall, sins voluntarily, not with reluctance or constraint; with the strongest propensity of disposition, not with violent coercion; with the bias of his own passions, and not with external compulsion: yet such is the pravity of his nature that he cannot be excited and biased to anything but what is evil ... From these passages the reader clearly perceives that I am teaching no novel doctrine, but what was long ago advanced by Augustine with the universal consent of pious men, and which for nearly a thousand years after was confined to the cloisters of monks. But [Peter] Lombard,[4] for want of knowing how to distinguish necessity from coaction, gave rise to a pernicious error ...

It has now, I apprehend, been sufficiently proved that man is so enslaved by sin as to be of his own nature incapable of an effort or even an aspiration towards that which is good. We have also laid down a distinction between coaction and necessity, from which it appears that while he sins necessarily, he nevertheless sins voluntarily. But since, while he is devoted to the servitude of the devil, he seems to be actuated by his will rather than by his own, it remains for us to explain the nature of both kinds of influence. There is also this question to be resolved, whether anything is to be attributed to God in evil actions, in which the Scripture intimates that some influence of His is concerned. Augustine somewhere compares the human will to a horse, obedient to the direction of his rider: and God and the devil he compares to riders. 'If God rides it, He, like a sober and skilful rider, manages it in a graceful manner: stimulates its tardiness, restrains its immoderate celerity, represses its wantonness and wildness, tames its perverseness, and conducts it into the right way. But if the devil has taken possession of it, he, like a foolish and wanton rider, forces it through pathless places, hurries it into ditches, drives it down over precipices, and excites it to obstinacy and ferocity.' With this similitude, as no better occurs, we will at present be content. When the will of a natural man is said to be subject to the power of the devil, so as to be directed by it, the meaning is, not that it resists and is compelled to a reluctant submission, as masters

---

[3] Celestius was a fifth-century British heretic who, while in Rome, allied with Pelagius to preach the doctrine of free will. Celestius thought men responsible for their own actions and even went so far as to deny the existence of original sin.

[4] Peter Lombard (d. Aug. 21/22 1160) was Bishop of Paris. His *Four Books of Sentences* (1148–51) was the standard medieval theological text. He was known as the Master of the Sentences. Book I dealt with God, the Trinity, Divine Guidance, evil and predestination.

compel slaves to an unwilling performance of their commands; but that, being fascinated by the fallacies of Satan, it necessarily submits itself to all his directions. For those whom the Lord does not favour with the government of His Spirit, He abandons in righteous judgement to the influence of Satan . . .

The covenant of life not being equally preached to all, and among those to whom it is preached not always finding the same reception, this diversity discovers the wonderful depth of the divine judgement. Nor is it to be doubted that this variety also follows, subject to the decision of God's eternal election. If it be evidently the result of the divine will that salvation is freely offered to some and others are prevented from attaining it, this immediately gives rise to important and difficult questions, which are incapable of any other explication than by the establishment of pious minds in what ought to be received concerning election and pre-destination: a question, in the opinion of many, full of perplexity; for they consider nothing more unreasonable than that of the common mass of mankind some should be predestinated to salvation and others to destruction. But how unreasonably they perplex themselves will after-wards appear from the sequel of our discourse. Besides, the very obscurity which excites such dread not only displays the utility of this doctrine, but shows it to be productive of the most delightful benefit. We shall never be clearly convinced as we ought to be, that our salvation flows from the fountain of God's free mercy, till we are acquainted with his eternal election, which illustrates the grace of God by this comparison, that He adopts not all promiscuously to the hope of salvation, but gives to some what He refuses to others. Ignorance of this principle evidently detracts from the divine glory and diminishes real humility. But, according to Paul, what is so necessary to be known never can be known, unless God, without any regard to works, chooses those whom He has decreed. 'At this present time also, there is a remnant according to the election of grace. And if by grace, then it is no more of works: otherwise, grace is no more grace. But if it be of works, then it is no more grace: otherwise, work is no more work' [Romans 11: 5]. If we need to be recalled to the origin of election to prove that we obtain salvation from no other source than the mere goodness of God, they who desire to extinguish this principle do all they can to obscure what ought to be magnificently and loudly celebrated, and to pluck up humility by the roots. In ascribing the salvation of the remnant of the people to the election of grace, Paul clearly testifies that it is then only known that God saves whom He will of His mere good pleasure, and does not dispense a reward to which there can be no claim. They who shut the gates to prevent anyone from presuming to approach and taste this doctrine do no less injury to man than to God; for nothing else will be sufficient to produce in us suitable humility, or to impress us with a due sense of our great obligations to God. Nor is there any other basis for solid confidence, even according to the authority of Christ, who, to deliver us from all fear, and render us invincible amidst so many dangers, snares, and deadly conflicts, promises to preserve in safety all whom the Father hath committed to His care. Whence we infer that they who know not themselves to be God's peculiar people will be tortured with continual anxiety; and therefore that the interest of all the faithful, as well as their own, is very badly consulted by those who, blind to the three advantages we have remarked, would wholly remove the foundation of our salvation. And hence the Church rises to our view; which otherwise, as Bernard justly observes,[5] could neither be discovered nor recognized among creatures, being in two respects wonderfully concealed in the bosom of a blessed predestination, and in the mass of a miserable damnation. But before I enter on the subject itself, I must address some preliminary observations to two sorts of persons. The discussion of predestination, a subject of itself rather intricate, is made very perplexed, and therefore dangerous, by human curiosity, which no barriers can restrain from wandering into forbidden labyrinths and soaring beyond its sphere, as if determined to leave none of the divine secrets unscrutinized or unexplored. As we see multitudes everywhere guilty of this arrogance and presumption, and among them some who are not censurable in other respects, it is proper to admonish them of the bounds of their duty on this subject. First, then: let them remember that when they inquire into predestination they penetrate the inmost recesses of divine wisdom, where the careless and confident intruder will obtain no satisfaction to his curiosity, but will enter a labyrinth from which he will find no way to depart. For it is unreasonable that man should scrutinize with impunity those things which the Lord hath determined to be hidden in Himself; and investigate, even from eternity, that sublimity of wisdom which God would have us to adore and not comprehend, to promote our admiration of His glory. The secrets of His will which He determined to reveal to us He discovers in His Word; and these are all that He foresaw would concern us, or conduce to our advantage . . .

Predestination, by which God adopts some to the hope of life and adjudges others to eternal death, no one, desirous of the credit of piety, dares absolutely to deny. But it is involved in many cavils, especially by those who make foreknowledge the cause of it. We maintain that both belong to God; but it is preposterous to represent one as dependent on the other. When we attribute foreknowledge to God, we mean that all things have ever been, and perpetually remain, before His eyes, so that to His knowledge nothing is future or past, but all things are present: and present in such a manner that He does not merely conceive of them from ideas formed in His mind, as things remembered by us appear present to our minds, but really beholds and sees them as if actually placed before Him. And this foreknowledge extends to the whole world and to all the creatures. Predestination we call the eternal decree of God, by which He hath determined in Himself what He would have to become of every individual of mankind. For they are not all created with a similar destiny; but eternal life

[5] St Bernard of Clairvaux (1090–1153), whose thought was heavily influenced by Augustine.

is foreordained for some, and eternal damnation for others. Every man, therefore, being created for one or the other of these ends, we say, he is predestinated either to life or to death.

8 William Tyndale and the Principles of Protestantism (1530, 1526)

Source: *Doctrinal Treatises and Introductions to Different Portions of the Holy Scriptures by William Tyndale, Martyr, 1536*, edited by H. Walter (The Parker Society; Cambridge: Cambridge University Press, 1848), pp. 392–5; 484–5; 492–9.

William Tyndale (between 1490 and 1500–1536) was educated at Oxford, where he took his MA in 1515. He transferred to Cambridge in 1515 and remained there until 1521. In 1522 he took a position as tutor to the children of Sir John Walsh and translated Erasmus's *Enchiridion* into English (this was not published until 1533; see document I.8.B, n. 2). In 1523 he moved to London and became acquainted with and converted by the works of Luther. Between 1524 and 1535 he travelled in Europe while translating the New Testament. He used the Greek and Latin translations of Erasmus to produce an English New Testament. In 1535 Tyndale was captured in Flanders, was tried for heresy by the officers of the Holy Roman Empire and was executed.

A. Tyndale's Preface to the Pentateuch

The extract here is taken from Tyndale's Preface to the Pentateuch (the first five books of the Bible) of 1530. It demonstrates Tyndale's conviction that the Scriptures must be made available and accessible to the laity – by means of a vernacular Bible. Erasmus had already expressed this view in 1516 but the English bishops remained steadfast against it, fearing that it would encourage the spread of Lollardy. Tyndale translated the Pentateuch and the whole of the New Testament into English. His follower Miles Coverdale translated the remains of the Old Testament. Their Bible became the Great Bible (1538–9) which was printed by Thomas Cromwell and sanctioned by Henry VIII. Much of this translation (about 90 per cent) was incorporated in the Authorized Version.

When I had translated the New Testament, I added an epistle unto the latter end, in which I desired them that were learned to amend if ought were found amiss. But our malicious and wily hypocrites, which are so stubborn and hard-hearted in their wicked abominations, that it is not possible for them to amend any thing at all (as we see by daily experience, when both their livings and doings are rebuked with the truth), say, some of them, that it is impossible to translate the scripture into English; some, that it is not lawful for the lay-people to have it in their mother-tongue; some, that it would make them all heretics; as it would, no doubt, from many things which they of long time have falsely taught; and that is the whole cause wherefore they forbid it, though they other cloaks pretend: and some, or rather every one, say that it would make them rise against the king, whom they themselves (unto their damnation) never yet obeyed. And lest the temporal rulers should see their falsehood, if the scripture came to light, causeth them so to lie.

And as for my translation, in which they affirm unto the lay-people (as I have heard say) to be I wot[1] not how many thousand heresies, so that it cannot be mended or correct; they have yet taken so great pain to examine it, and to compare it unto that they would fain have it, and to their own imaginations and juggling terms, and to have somewhat to rail at, and under that cloak to blaspheme the truth; that they might with as little labour (as I suppose) have translated the most part of the bible. For they which in times past were wont to look on no more scripture than they found in their Duns,[2] or such like devilish doctrine, have yet now so narrowly looked on my translation, that there is not so much as one *i* therein, if it lack a tittle over his head, but they have noted it, and number it unto the ignorant people for an heresy. Finally, in this they be all agreed, to drive you from the knowledge of the scripture, and that ye shall not have the text thereof in the mother-tongue, and to keep the world still in darkness, to the intent they might sit in the consciences of the people, through vain superstition and false doctrine, to satisfy their filthy lusts, their proud ambition, and unsatiable covetous-ness, and to exalt their own honour above king and emperor, yea, and above God himself.

A thousand books had they lever[3] to be put forth against their abominable doings and doctrine, than that the scripture should come to light. For as long as they may keep that down, they will so darken the right way with the mist of their sophistry,[4] and so tangle them that either rebuke or despise their abominations, with arguments of philosophy, and with worldly similitudes and apparent reasons of natural wisdom, and with wresting the scripture unto their own purpose, clean contrary unto the process, order, and meaning of the text; and so delude them in descanting upon it with allegories, and amaze them, expounding it in many senses before the unlearned lay-people (when it hath but one simple, literal sense, whose light the owls cannot abide), that, though thou feel in thine heart, and art sure, how that all is false that they say, yet couldst thou not solve their subtle riddles.

Which thing only moved me to translate the new Testament. Because I had perceived by experience, how that it was impossible to establish the lay-people in any truth, except the scripture were plainly laid before their eyes

---

[1] Know.

[2] John Duns Scotus (b. *c*.1266 in Duns, Lothian, Scotland; d. 8 Nov. 1308 in Cologne), who was a Franciscan Realist philosopher and scholastic theologian. He pioneered the defence of the doctrine of the Virgin Mary's Immaculate Conception. He was unpopular amongst the English Reformers because of his strong defence of the Papacy against the Divine Right of Kings. Among Roman Catholics, however, his following in the universities rivalled that of Aquinas in sixteenth-century Europe.

[3] Rather.

[4] An attack on scholastic theology.

in their mother-tongue, that they might see the process, order, and meaning of the text: for else, whatsoever truth is taught them, these enemies of all truth quench it again, partly with the smoke of their bottomless pit, whereof thou readest in Apocalypse, chap. ix[5] (that is, with apparent reasons of sophistry, and traditions of their own making, founded without ground of scripture) and partly in juggling with the text, expounding it in such a sense as is impossible to gather of the text, if thou see the process, order, and meaning thereof.

B Tyndale's Prologue to the Epistle to the Romans

Tyndale's Prologue to his translation of St Paul's Epistle to the Romans of 1526 was for the most part an English translation of Martin Luther's earlier Preface of 1522 to the Epistle (see document III.6.C). Tyndale thus acquainted the English reader with the Lutheran interpretation of the Pauline message. The law of God must be followed with a loving, joyful heart. This attitude can only be attained by faith. Paul denies that our own good works can contribute anything to our justification and salvation but a person who has faith will inevitably do good works.

Forasmuch as this epistle is the principal and most excellent part of the new Testament and most pure evangelion, that is to say, glad tidings, and that we call gospel, and also is a light and a way unto the whole scripture; I think it meet that every christian man not only know it, by rote and without the book, but also exercise himself therein evermore continually, as with the daily bread of the soul. No man verily can read it too oft, or study it too well; for the more it is studied, the easier it is; the more it is chewed, the pleasanter it is; and the more groundly[1] it is searched, the preciouser things are found in it, so great treasure of spiritual things lieth hid therein. I will therefore bestow my labour and diligence, through this little preface or prologue, to prepare a way in thereunto, so far forth as God shall give me grace, that it may be the better understood of every man: for it hath been hitherto evil darkened with glosses and wonderful dreams of sophisters, that no man could spy out the intent and meaning of it; which nevertheless of itself is a bright light, and sufficient to give light unto all the scripture . . .

But right faith is a thing wrought[2] by the Holy Ghost in us, which changeth us, turneth us into a new nature, and begetteth us anew in God, and maketh us the sons of God, as thou readest in the first of John; and killeth the old Adam, and maketh us altogether new in the heart, mind, will, lust, and in all our affections and powers of the soul; the Holy Ghost ever accompanying her, and ruling the heart. Faith is a lively thing, mighty in working, valiant, and strong, ever doing, ever fruitful; so that it is impossible

---

[5] Revelation 9.

---

[1] Thoroughly.
[2] Worked.

that he who is endued[3] therewith should not work always good works without ceasing. He asketh not whether good works are to be done or not, but hath done them already, ere[4] mention be made of them; and is always doing, for such is his nature; for quick faith in his heart, and lively moving of the Spirit, drive him and stir him thereunto. Whosoever doth not good works, is an unbelieving person, and faithless, and looketh round about him, groping after faith and good works, and wotteth not[5] what faith or good works mean, though he babble never so many things of faith and good works.

Faith is, then, a lively and a steadfast trust in the favour of God, wherewith we commit ourselves altogether unto God; and that trust is so surely grounded, and sticketh so fast in our hearts, that a man would not once doubt of it, though he should die a thousand times therefor. And such trust, wrought by the Holy Ghost through faith, maketh a man glad, lusty, cheerful, and true-hearted unto God and unto all creatures: whereof, willingly and without compulsion, he is glad and ready to do good to every man, to do service to every man, to suffer all things, that God may be loved and praised, which hath given him such grace; so that it is impossible to separate good works from faith, even as it is impossible to separate heat and burning from fire. Therefore take heed to thyself, and beware of thine own fantasies and imaginations; which to judge of faith and good works will seem wise, when indeed they are stark blind and of all things most foolish. Pray God, that he will vouchsafe to work faith in thine heart, or else shalt thou remain evermore faithless; feign thou, imagine thou, enforce thou, wrestle with thyself, and do what thou wilt or canst.

Righteousness is even such faith; and is called God's righteousness, or righteousness that is of value before God. For it is God's gift, and it altereth a man, and changeth him into a new spiritual nature, and maketh him free and liberal to pay every man his duty . . . Such righteousness can nature, free-will, and our own strength, never bring to pass . . .

In the second chapter the apostle proceedeth further, and rebuketh all those holy people also, which, without lust and love to the law, live well outwardly in the face of the world, and condemn others gladly; as the nature of all hypocrites is, to think themselves pure in respect of open sinners; and yet they hate the law inwardly, and are full of covetousness, and envy, and of all uncleanness (Matthew 23). These are they which despise the goodness of God, and according to the hardness of their hearts heap together for themselves the wrath of God. Furthermore, St Paul, as a true expounder of the law, suffereth no man to be without sin; but declareth that all they are under sin, who of free-will and of nature will live well, and suffereth them not to be better than the open sinners, yea, he calleth them hard-hearted and such as cannot repent.

In the third chapter he mingleth both together, both the Jews and the

---

[3] Endowed.
[4] Before.
[5] Knows not.

Gentiles; and saith, that the one is as the other, both sinners, and no difference between them, save in this only, that the Jews had the word of God committed unto them. And though many of them believed not thereon, yet is God's truth and promise thereby neither hurt nor diminished; and he taketh in his way, and allegeth the saying of Psalm 51, 'that God might abide true in his words, and overcome when he is judged.' After that he returneth to his purpose again, and proveth by the scripture, that all men, without difference or exception, are sinners; and that by the works of the law no man is justified; but that the law was given to utter and to declare sin only. Then he beginneth and sheweth the right way unto righteousness, by what means men must be made righteous and safe; and saith, they are all sinners and without praise before God, and must, without their own deserving, be made righteous through faith in Christ; who hath deserved such righteousness for us, and is become unto us God's mercy-seat, for the remission of sins that are past: thereby proving that Christ's righteousness, which cometh upon us through faith, helpeth us only. Which righteousness, saith he, is now declared through the gospel, and was 'testified of before by the law and the prophets'. Furthermore, saith he, the law is holpen[6] and furthered through faith; though that the works thereof, with all their boast, are brought to nought, and are proved not to justify.

In the fourth chapter, after that now, by the three first chapters, sins are opened, and the way of faith unto righteousness laid, he beginneth to answer unto certain objections and cavillations.[7] And first, he putteth forth those blind reasons, which commonly they that will be justified by their own works are wont to make, when they hear that faith only, without works, justifieth; saying, 'Shall men do no good works? Yea, and if faith only justifieth, what need a man to study for to do good works?' He putteth forth therefore Abraham for an example, saying, What did Abraham with his works? Was all in vain? Came his works to no profit? And so he concludeth that Abraham, without and before all works, was justified and made righteous; insomuch that, before the work of circumcision, he was praised of the scripture, and called righteous by his faith only (Genesis 15): so that he did not the work of circumcision, for to be helped thereby unto righteousness, which yet God commanded him to do, and was a good work of obedience. So in like wise, no doubt, none other works help any thing at all unto a man's justifying: but as Abraham's circumcision was an outward sign, whereby he declared his righteousness which he had by faith, and his obedience and readiness unto the will of God; even so are all other good works outward signs and outward fruits of faith and of the Spirit; which justify not a man, but shew that a man is justified already before God, inwardly in the heart, through faith, and through the Spirit purchased by Christ's blood.

Herewith St Paul now establisheth his doctrine of faith, rehearsed afore in chapter 3, and bringeth also the testimony of David, Psalm 32, which

[6] Helped, strengthened.
[7] Legal quibbles, sophistry.

calleth a man blessed, not of works, but in that his sin is not reckoned, and in that faith is imputed for righteousness, although he abide not afterward without good works, when he is once justified. For we are justified, and receive the Spirit, for to do good works; neither were it otherwise possible to do good works, except we first had the Spirit.

. . .

Now have we then that faith only, before all works, justifieth, and that it followeth not yet therefore, that a man should do no good works, but that the right shapen works abide not behind, but accompany faith, even as brightness doth the sun; and they are called by Paul the fruits of the Spirit. Where the Spirit is, there it is always summer, and there are always good fruits, that is to say, good works. This is Paul's order, That good works spring of the Spirit; the Spirit cometh by faith; and faith cometh by hearing the word of God, when the glad tidings and promises, which God hath made unto us in Christ, are preached truly, and received in the ground of the heart, without wavering or doubting, after that the law hath passed upon us, and hath condemned our consciences. Where the word of God is preached purely, and received in the heart, there is faith, and the Spirit of God; and there are also good works of necessity, whensoever occasion is given. Where God's word is not purely preached, but men's dreams, traditions, imaginations, inventions, ceremonies, and superstition, there is no faith; and consequently no spirit that cometh from God. And where God's Spirit is not, there can be no good works, even as where an apple-tree is not, there can grow no apples; but there is unbelief, the devil's spirit, and evil works.

9 Hans Sachs, 'The Wittenberg Nightingale' (1523)

Source: Hans Sachs, 'The Wittenberg Nightingale', extracted and translated in G. Strauss, *Nuremberg in the Sixteenth Century* (New York: John Wiley & Sons, 1966), pp. 167–8.

Hans Sachs (see document III.5 above) wrote the song 'The Wittenberg Nightingale' during the summer of 1523 when Luther had a secure popular following in the German city of Nuremberg. When he wrote the song Sachs possessed over forty sermons and tracts by Luther. It represents another way in which Luther's message was disseminated widely (compare document III.8.B). The Nightingale which can be heard, explains Sachs, is Martin Luther. His song rouses us from a long sleep induced by the moon (the scholastics whose appeals to reason have lured men away from the true Gospel message). The evil rule of the Church hierarchy is now at an end. Luther has revealed in plain German the true meaning of the Gospel. The extracts speak of the message and its effect upon the faithful. They are part of a very long chronicle of events. Sachs wrote more than 4,000 songs. Many of the tunes for these songs were taken over as the melodies for Lutheran hymns.

. . .

> First Luther tells us that we all
> Inherit sin from Adam's fall,
> In evil lust and foul intent
> And avid pride our lives are spent;
> Our hearts are black and unrefined,
> Our wills to horrid sins inclined,
> And God, who judges soul and mind
> Has cursed and damned all human kind.
> In our hearts we know this state,
> Feel burdened with a dreadful weight
> Of anguish, fear, bewilderment
> That we should be so impotent.
> Sure of man's inability
> We change pride to humility
> And then, and only then, we see
> The Gospel, sent to make us free,
> For in it we find Christ, God's son
> Who for us men has so much done,
> Fulfilled the law, wiped clean the stain
> And won God's grace for us again.

[The lamb of God has taken upon itself all mankind's sin. He has come for the sake of sinners. Whoever believes in him shall have everlasting life. The message is one of consolation.]

> So Jesus speaks. All who have heard
> His comforting, consoling word,
> Who trust him without doubt or scorn,
> Such men, we say, are newly born.
> Quit of all fear, no longer prone
> To sin, they live God's word alone.
> In total love they turn to God,
> Submit themselves in deed and thought,
> Accept his judgment and decree
> In sorrow and adversity,
> Trust and revere Him, come what may,
> 'God gives, God takes' is what they say,
> Because they know, God's on their side
> Through Christ, His Son, the crucified,
> Whom God grants such a faith, he is
> Already saved, he lives in bliss;
> His deeds are good, his efforts right
> His works find favour in God's sight.

. . .

10 Agrippa, *The Vanity and Uncertainty of the Arts and Sciences* (1530)

Source: Henry Cornelius Agrippa, *De Vanitate et Incertitudine Omnium Scientiarum et Artium* (Antwerp, 1530), translated and abridged by Stuart Brown.

Henry Cornelius Agrippa of Nettesheim (1486–1535) was the son of a citizen of Cologne. He studied at Cologne and Paris, where he demonstrated a deep interest in the occult and magic. He wanted a Christianity founded upon the Bible and the writings of Fathers of the Church. In 1510 Agrippa studied the Pauline Epistles with John Colet and in 1515 he lectured at Pavia and Turin on the Hebrew Cabbala. Between 1516 and 1518 he wrote three treatises on the role of the Cabbala in human knowledge. The years 1518 to 1530 saw him moving from position to position throughout Europe. In 1530 he published *De Vanitate* and fled from the court of Margaret of Austria to Cologne when he feared subsequent persecution. He corresponded with Erasmus, whom he admired, between 1531 and 1533. Erasmus approved of his ideas but feared the consequences of Agrippa's attacks on the scholastics. He died in poverty in Grenoble.

These extracts are from a work that subjects the accepted branches of knowledge, as well as some of the accepted institutions, to a comprehensive attack. Most forms of magic are rejected and the section on 'natural magic' stands out as one of the few passages where Agrippa makes an exception. His defence of 'natural magic' may be compared with that of Pico in document I.5. The second extract provides a contemporary and informed, if highly critical, view of the Inquisition from the standpoint of one who undertook the defence of women charged with witchcraft.

CHAPTER 42. NATURAL MAGIC

Men think that natural magic is nothing but a special power of all the natural sciences and therefore they call it the apex and highest perfection of natural philosophy. Natural magic reveals the active side of natural philosophy ... its public manifestations are exceedingly wonderful. This magic was much cultivated by the Egyptians and the Indians, where there was an abundance of herbs, stones and other pertinent things ... And this is the sort of magician that those Magi were,[1] who went to worship Christ when he was born and presented him with gifts ...

Magic, then, is natural when, after considering well the powers of all natural and celestial things and having found their pattern by careful inquiry, the magician brings into the open the hidden and secret power of Nature ... when he entices it out by coupling the inferior things with the qualities of the superior and by a natural joining of them together. Remarkable wonders frequently arise in this way, not so much by art but as by Nature working these things, the art being no more than a servant. For

[1] The *New English Bible* refers to these as 'astrologers from the east' (Matthew 2: 1). Other translations speak vaguely of 'wise men'. The reference appears to be to a sacred Persian caste, known as Magians, who were possessed of certain occult skills. Agrippa's claim seems, therefore, to be partially correct.

the Magicians, as very careful inquirers into Nature, by applying and setting active things to passive, very often bring out the things that are prepared by Nature before the time that She appointed for these effects to be produced. These are commonly taken to be miracles but for all that they are no more than natural works, nothing else coming into it than the speeding up of time, as if a man in the month of March should produce roses, ripe grapes or beans or make parsley seed grow within a few hours into a perfect plant. There are also greater things that Roger Bacon is said to have often done,[2] with natural magic, with clouds, rain, thunder, various sorts of beasts and infinitely many transformations of things . . .

CHAPTER 96. THE ART OF THE INQUISITORS

To this company [of thieves and robbers] also belong the Inquisitors of heretics of the order of preaching friars.[3] Though their authority ought to be based on theological traditions and the Holy Scriptures, they most cruelly exercise this whole art rather in accordance with the Canon Law and the decrees of the Popes, as if the Pope were infallible.[4] They neglect the Holy Scripture as if it were a dead letter and a shadow of the truth. Indeed they cast it aside, saying it is the shield and bulwark of heretics. They dismiss the traditions of the ancient Doctors and Fathers [of the Church], saying that it is possible for them to be deceived and deceive. They accept only the Church of Rome, whose head is the Pope – who, according to what they say, is infallible and whose office they make the object of their faith.

When they conduct an Inquisition, they demand nothing else as the mark of faith than that the offender believe in the Church of Rome. If the offender professes this belief they say straightaway that the Church of Rome condemns something he has said as either heretical, sinful, offensive to pious ears or subversive of ecclesiastical authority. And immediately they compel him to recant and revoke what he said. But if the person who is the subject of Inquisition sets about defending his opinion with the evidence of Scripture or other reasons, they interrupt him with great noise and verbal abuse, saying that he was not answering before a conference of Bachelors [of Arts] or scholars but before a tribunal of judges. He must not be contentious and engage in disputation but must answer plainly, whether he will abide by the judgement of the Church of Rome and renounce his opinion. If he will not, they show him faggots and fire, saying that in the case of heretics they are not allowed to contend with arguments and appeals to Scripture but only with faggots and fire. Even where the man has not been convicted of

---

[2] Roger Bacon (c.1214–94) was an English philosopher and scientist who laid much emphasis on experiment and applied science. He worked on lenses, navigational aids and gunpowder. Like Agrippa he was credited with magical powers and suspected of being in league with the Devil.

[3] The Dominicans, the order most involved in Inquisitorial activities.

[4] The Church had its own laws and courts. Canon Law is distinguished from Civil Law, that exercised by the secular authorities.

obstinacy, they force him against his conscience to deny his opinions under oath. If he will not do it, they deliver him into the hands of the secular power to be burned, saying with the Apostle:[5] 'Take away mischief from among you.'

So great was the gentleness of the Church and the clemency of the bishops in times past that, as Gratian has recorded[6] ..., they did not put to death those that lapsed into Judaism, nor did they punish blasphemers. Berengarius fell into abominable heresy but was not only not put to death but not even deprived of his status as an archdeacon.

But nowadays it is more than someone's life is worth even to fall into the smallest error. Sometimes, for even a small offence, a person is delivered by these Inquisitors to be burned. Perhaps it is now in the Church's interests to impose such severe punishments, to prevent the loss of its traditional piety.

The fact that Inquisitors of heresy are sometimes wicked and may be heretics themselves prompted [Pope] Clement[7] to make a new decree: that Inquisitors ought not to dispute the Catholic faith with heretics by obscure arguments and wrangling syllogisms but by the word of God. They were to convince a heretic by Holy Scriptures. The outcome was to be determined in accordance with the requirements of the Canon Laws and the regulations of the holy Councils. They were to bring whoever was the subject of Inquisition to the Catholic faith, or else to declare him a heretic. For he is no heretic who is not obstinate. Nor is he a supporter of heretics who tries to defend an innocent person charged with heresy and to prevent his being handed over to be butchered for no reason by these cruel and ravenous Inquisitors.

It is expressly provided by the Laws that the Inquisitors have no power, nor any jurisdiction, to proceed upon a case of heresy ... except where there is explicit heresy that is obviously to be condemned. But these bloodthirsty vultures nonetheless exceed the powers of the office of Inquisition granted to them. Contrary to what is right and to the Canon Laws themselves, they meddle in the jurisdiction of the judges of the Ordinaries Court,[8] they usurp the authority of the bishops in such matters as are not heretical but only offensive to pious ears, sinful or in some other manner erroneous (without being heretical).

In this way they show their stern and extreme cruelty towards poor countrywomen who are accused of witchcraft or sorcery and condemned without first being examined by a lawful judge. They put these women to atrocious and frightful suffering, till they are forced to confess what it had

[5] Paul, the supposed author of many of the letters (to the early Christian groups) included in the New Testament.

[6] Gratian was a twelfth-century monk who compiled a large collection of texts and commentaries on Canon Law, known as the *Decretum*.

[7] Clement VII was Pope, 1523–34.

[8] An Ordinaries Court was one with a territorial jurisdiction, authorized to try certain cases under Canon Law.

never crossed their minds to believe and they ['these bloodthirsty vultures'] have the means to condemn them. They really suppose they are fulfilling the role of Inquisitors when they do not cease from their duty until the defenceless woman is burned or has put gold into the Inquisitor's hand, on account of which he takes pity on her and releases her as sufficiently purged by tortures. For often the Inquisitor can change the pain of the body into the punishment of the purse and apply it to his Inquisitorial office. Because of this they accumulate no small profit and not a few of these unfortunate women are obliged to pay them an annual fee so that they will not be punished again. And when the goods of heretics are confiscated, the Inquisitor gets no small part. The very accusation, or barest suspicion of heresy, even the citation by the Inquisitor, is enough to bring up the question of how much a woman is worth. The Inquisitor makes no small gain from the money given to him. Thus, when I was in Milan, several Inquisitors tormented a number of honest matrons, including some of high social standing, and privately milked very large sums from the poor frightened women, till eventually their cheating was discovered and they were severely treated by the nobility, only just escaping fire and sword.

In the past, when I was an advocate and counsellor of the commonwealth of Metz,[9] I had a very troublesome case against an Inquisitor. He, being a wicked man, dragged a poor countrywoman, on the strength of certain unsupported and most unjust accusations, to his prison – the wrong place – not so much to examine as to torment her. When I had undertaken to defend her and had demonstrated that there was no evidence or proof of her having done anything that could justify her being tortured, he stoutly denied it, saying that it was sufficient proof that her mother had previously been burned as a witch. I replied and showed him that this consideration was irrelevant and that the law did not allow one person to be condemned for what was done by someone else. He promptly answered me – to prevent it seeming that what he had previously said was not thought out – by appealing to details of the *Malleus maleficarum* and to the bases of Peripatetic Theology.[10]

He argued that it was quite right [to arrest the daughter of a witch], since witches were accustomed to dedicate their children to the Devil as they burn. Also it often happened that they would be made pregnant by spirits that had taken the form of a man. Thus (he concluded) it comes about that the wickedness is deeprooted in the child, like an inherited disease.

Then I said to him: 'O wicked father, is this the kind of divinity you study? Are these the concocted arguments by which you get the poor innocent

[9] Metz, now in northern France, was at the time a free city within the Holy Roman Empire. Agrippa was there 1518–20 and the story he narrates presumably relates to events that took place then.
[10] The *Malleus maleficarum* ('Hammer of Witches') was a textbook on how to deal with witches used by Inquisitors. It was written by the Dominicans Henry Institoris and Jacob Sprenger and first published in 1487. Peripatetic Theology: Aristotelian theology.

women to the rack? Are these the sophisms by which you judge others to be heretics? Are you with this opinion not yourself as much of a heretic as Faustus and Donatus?[11] If the child sacrificed by its wicked mother should remain, as you say, in the power of the Devil, do you not make the grace of baptism empty? And do you not make the priest's words vain when he says "Depart you unclean spirit, give way to the Holy Ghost!" if the children are devils because of the impiety of their parents?

'But I say to you, in faith, that we are all a mass of sin and eternal wrongdoing in virtue of our [fallen] human nature. We are the sons of the Devil, sons of the wrath of God and heirs of hell. But by the grace of baptism, Satan is cast out from us, and we are made new creatures in Jesus Christ, from whom no man can be separated but by his own sin: for it is far from the truth that one person should suffer for the sin of another. Do you not see how even your strongest argument is invalid in law, how utterly indefensible in reason and indeed how completely heretical it is?'

At these words the cruel hypocrite was very angry and threatened that he would charge me as a supporter of heretics. But I did not stop defending that unfortunate soul and finally, through the power of the law, I delivered her safely from the mouth of that lion. In consequence that bloody monk stood rebuked and disgraced in the eyes of everyone and was forever notorious on account of his cruelty. Moreover both he and the unjust accusers who attacked the woman's reputation were fined a large sum of money by the chapter of the Church of Metz, whose subjects they were.

11 The Diary of Lady Margaret Hoby (1599–1605)

Source: *Diary of Lady Margaret Hoby, 1599—1605*, edited by Dorothy M. Meads (London: Routledge, 1930), pp. 62–225. Extracts selected and spelling modernized by Rosemary O'Day.

Margaret Dakins (*c*.1567–1633) of Linton in Yorkshire was educated in the household of the Countess of Huntingdon in York. Her Protestant credentials were unimpeachable. In 1596, when she was still under 30, she was married for a third time, at the wish of the dying Earl of Huntingdon, to Sir Thomas Posthumous Hoby, son of Lady Elizabeth Russell and grandson of Sir Anthony Cooke. They set up household in the village of Hackness, near Scarborough, which had previously been noted for its staunch Catholicism. Lady Hoby and her personal chaplain organized the religious life and instruction of the extended household and the village itself. There were family prayers, during which her servants read from John Foxe's *Acts and Monuments*, sermons, Bible study and private meditation using the devotional works

---

[11] Faustus, a contemporary of Augustine, associated with the heresy known as Manichaeism. The Manichees held that matter is essentially evil and that Christ was a man only in appearance. Donatus was leader of a heretical sect in the fourth century. The Donatists held that the validity of the mass could be vitiated by the bad character of the officiating priest.

of William Perkins and Richard Greenham. She died in 1633 and her husband built a chapel in her memory and pledged his descendants to support an educated preacher to serve it on Sundays. The brief extracts printed here have been chosen to show the extent of Lady Hoby's religious commitment and the manner in which women exercised influence and authority within the domestic and religious spheres.

[AUGUST 1599]

Friday 10. After I was ready I betook myself to private prayer, wherein it pleased the Lord to deal mercifully [. . . page torn]: after, I went about the house, and instructed Tomson's wife in some principles of religion,[1] and then ate my breakfast, and then walked abroad till almost :11: of the clock: and after I had read :2: chapters of the bible, I went to dinner: after dinner I went to work, at which [. . . page torn] Continued till :4:, then I took order for supper [. . . page torn] went to prayer to write some notes in my testament,[2] from which I was called to walk with Mr Hoby, talking of sundry business, and so to supper: immediately after prayer and lector,[3] for the diligent attention of which the Lord did hear my prayer by removing all wanderings which use to hurt me so that I received much comfort, I went to bed.

Sunday 12. After I was ready, I went to private prayers, then to breakfast: then I walked till church time with Mr Hoby, and after to dinner: after which I walked and had speech of no serious matters till :2: a clock: then I wrote notes into my bible till :3: and after :4: I came again from the church, walk, and meditated a little, and again wrote some other notes in my bible of that I had learned till :5: at which time I returned to examination and prayer: and after I had read some of Bond of the Sabbath,[4] I walked abroad: and so to supper, after to prayers, and Lastly to bed.

Monday 13. In the morning after private prayers and order taken for dinner, I wrote some notes in my testament till :10: a clock: then I went to walk, and, after I returned home, I prayed privately, read a chapter of the Bible, and wrought till dinner time:[5] after I walked a while with Mr Rhodes[6] and then I wrought, and did some things about the house till :4: then I wrote out the sermon into my book preached the day before, and, when I had again gone about in the house and given order for supper and other things, I returned to examination and prayer: then I walked till supper time, and, after catechizing[7] meditated awhile of that I had heard, with mourning to

---

[1] As with many of the people mentioned in the diary, Tomson and his wife are now unidentifiable.

[2] It was usual to annotate readings from the Bible. Writing notes in a personal copy of the New Testament was both a common and an encouraged practice.

[3] Used variously as either a reading or a brief oral exhortation of a spiritual nature.

[4] This is Nicholas Bownde (d. 1613), *Doctrine of the Sabbath*, 1595.

[5] Wrought in the sense of embroidery or sewing tasks.

[6] Richard Rhodes was Lady Hoby's private chaplain. He had recently come down from the University of Cambridge. He presumably 'set' the books mentioned in these passages for Lady Hoby to work on. As a rule they are books written in the previous two decades.

[7] Instruction in the fundamental tenets of the Christian religion by rote question and answer.

god for pardon both of my omission and commission wherein I found my self guilty, I went to bed.

. . .

Wednesday 15. In the morning at :6: a clock, I prayed privately: that done, I went to a wife in travail of child[8] about whom I was busy [. . . torn] till :1: a clock, about which time, she being delivered and I having praised god, returned home and betook myself to private prayer :2: several times upon occasion: then I wrote the most part of an examination or trial of a christian, framed by Mr Rhodes, in the doing where[?of] I again fell to prayer, and after continued writing . . . after :3: a clock: then I went to work till after :5:, and then to examination and prayer: the Lord make me thankful, who hath heard my prayers and hath not turned his face from me: then I talked with Mrs Brutnell till supper time, and after walked a little into the fields, and so to prayers, and then to bed.

Thursday 16. After I was ready in the morning I prayed privately and wrote out the rest of those positions[9] which I left uncopied the day before: then I went take order for dinner and went to work till breakfast came, and, after I had broken my fast, I examined that I had written with Mr Rhodes, read some thing in the Bible, and so to work till Comring came for dinner . . .

Friday 17. After private prayers I went about the house and read of the Bible and wrought till dinner time: and, after dinner, it pleased [God] for a just punishment to correct my sins, to send me feebleness of stomach and pain of my head, that kept me upon my bed till :5: a clock:[10] at which time I arose, having release of my sickness, according to the wonted[11] kindness of the Lord, who, after he had Let me see how I had offended, that so I might take better heed to my body and soul hereafter, with a gentle correction let me feel he was reconciled to me: at which time I went to private prayer, and praises, examination, and so to work till supper time: which done I heard the Lector and, after I had walked an hour with Mr Hoby, I went to bed.

. . .

Sunday 19. After I was ready I betook me private prayer: . . . then, because Mr Hoby was not well,[12] I kept him company till the sermon time, and did eat my breakfast: that done, I thank God who gave him will and ability, we went to church, where we received the sacraments . . .

Monday 20. After I was ready I prayed privately: then I walked with Mr Hoby till :8: a clock, [. . . breakfasted, worked till 11] I took a lector of Mr Rhodes, and went to dinner: after dinner I wound yarn till :3:, and then walked with Mr Hoby about the town to spy out the best places where

[8] In labour; the customary duty of the 'lady of the manor'.
[9] Positions taken by given writers.
[10] She saw her sickness as a punishment by God for her sins.
[11] Accustomed.
[12] This conviction that sickness was a divine punishment was not, apparently, reduced by the fact that her husband suffered a like affliction two days after she was stricken down.

cottages might be built: after I came home and wrought till :6: and gave order for supper . . .

[SEPTEMBER]

Friday 7. [. . . day spent as usual until dinner time]: after which I talked a little with some of my friends, and exercised my body at bowls a while, of which I found good . . . then I came home and wrought till :4:.
. . .

Monday 24. After I had prayed, I went to breakfast to my cousin Bouser's house: after that I went to Gremston, to my Cousin Stanhopes, where I prayed privately before supper,[13] and soon after went to bed.

Tuesday 25. After I had prayed I walked in the garden till breakfast time:[14] after breakfast I came to York, then I went to the manor[15] after I had prayed privately, and supped there, and took my leave of my Lady Burghley, Came to my lodging and went to bed.
. . .

Thursday 27. After I had prayed privately I went to breakfast: I took my coach and came home to Hackness safe, I thank god, and, after I had prayed privately and supped, I heard Mr Rhodes catechize, and, soon after, went to bed.

Friday 28. In the morning, after private prayer, I took order for things about the house, and at :8: I did eat my breakfast: then I heard Mr Rhodes read till almost dinner time: after dinner I talked with Thomas Addison about the purchasing his own farm: then I wrought till almost supper time and, after I had privately prayed, I went to supper: after that I walked till Lector time, and after that I heard one of the men read of the book of martyrs,[16] and so went to bed . . .

[OCTOBER 1599]
. . .

Tuesday 2. After private prayer I wrote notes into my testament, then I went to church: after I came home, I prayed, and so went to dinner: after, I talked with Mr Bell and his wife: when they were gone, I gave out corn, wrote more notes in my testament, took order for supper, took a lector, and then went to meditation & prayer: then I went to supper: after which I heard the sermon repeated, and Mr Rhodes read a sermon of the Rule: and so went to bed.
. . .

---

[13] *c.*5.30 p.m.
[14] Usually 8 a.m.
[15] King's Manor.
[16] John Foxe, *Acts and Monuments*, English edition first published in 1563. This was popularly known as *The Book of Martyrs*.

Thursday 4. After I had prayed I wrote notes in my testament, then I walked abroad, then I came home and dined: and after dinner I went again awalking: then I wrote in my sermon book, then I went about the house with Mrs Ormston, then I went to examination and prayer, then to supper: after to the lector, and then heard one of the men read the book of martyrs, and so went to bed.

Friday 5. After private prayer I went about the house, then I wrote notes in my testament: then Mr Hoby came home, with whom I talked till dinner time: after dinner I was busy about preserving quinces, and, a little before supper time, I walked about the house: then I examined myself[17] and prayed, then I went to supper: after to the lector, and, soon after that, to bed.

Saturday 6. After private prayers I did walk about and eat my breakfast: then I went abroad with Mr Hoby: then I came home and dined: after, I wrote notes in my testament, then I went in to the Granary, and other places in the house, and so came to examine myself and prayed: and then I went to supper, and so to lector, and then to bed.

Sunday 7. After private prayers I did eat my breakfast, and then to the church, where, after the hearing of the word and receiving the sacraments,[18] I came home and did pray: and so to dinner: after which I walked and talked with Mr Rhodes: then, soon after, I went to church again, and, after the sermon ended, I came home, where I did little good but talked of many matters, little concerning me, with Mrs Ormston, to whom I read a while of the Bible: and after I returned in to my heart, examined myself, and craved pardon for my several omissions and commissions: the Lord strengthen me with his grace that I may sin no more in the like sort, amen: then I went to supper, after to the repetition and prayers, and so to bed.

Tuesday 9. After private prayers I did eat my breakfast with Mr Hoby: then I walked abroad, and took a lector: after, I came in and prayed, and then went to dinner: then I went about and delivered corn: then I came into my chamber, & wrote notes in my testament, and after received rents, and walked a while: and then examined myself and prayed: after, I walked a while, and read of Babington,[19] and then went to supper, and, soon after, went to bed, Mr Hoby coming home late.

Wednesday 10. After private prayers I went about and did eat my breakfast: then I wrote some notes in my bible, then went to dinner: after, I walked, and preserved some sweet meat: then I wrote notes again in my bible, then I walked, and then came in and examined myself and prayed: then I went to supper, and, after, paid servants wages, and so went to bed.

---

[17] In the sense of a spiritual examination by precise question and answer. Precise Protestants, popularly known as puritans, such as Lady Hoby, undertook a rigorous daily examination of their conduct and thoughts. Some used a diary as a vehicle of self-examination.

[18] Holy Communion.

[19] Gervase Babington. The book could be any of the following: *A Very Fruitful Exposition of the Commaundements*, 1583; *A Briefe Conference Betwixt Mans Frailtie and Faith*, 1583; *A Profitable Exposition of the Lord's Prayer*, 1588; or *A Sermon Preached at Paul's Crosse*, 1591.

Friday 12. After private prayer I went about the house and did eat my breakfast: then I wrote some notes in my testament, and then walked about: then I prayed and read of the bible, and so went to dinner: after, I walked abroad, and, at my coming home, I took a Lector, and wrote a while: and, after I had gone about the house, I returned to prayer and examination, my self, and then read of Bright of Mallincocolie,[20] and then went to supper: after, to prayers, and so to bed.

. . .

Sunday 14. After private prayers I did eat my breakfast, and then I did read of the Testament, and so went to church: after I came from thence, I meditated a while of that I had heard, and then prayed, and so went to dinner: after, I walked till church time and then, after the sermon, I walked and read and talked with Mrs Ormston of that was delivered: after, I examined myself and prayed: after I went to supper and, after that, to prayers, and lastly to bed.

. . .

Sunday 21. After private prayer I did eat my breakfast and then I went to church: after, I came home and prayed, then dined, and after went to Catechism and after none[21] sermon: and then came home, and wrote something, then prayed, and so went to supper; after, I heard prayers and, not long after that, having talked with the workime,[22] I went to bed.

Monday 22. After private prayer I did write: then, I did eat my breakfast: then I went about the house and then I wrote out my sermon: after, I prayed, and so went to dinner: after dinner I walked about and had a Lector, and then came to private prayer and meditation: after, I wrote some notes in my testament and then went to supper: after, to the Lector, and then I wrote a letter to my mother, and so to bed.

Tuesday 23. After private prayer I did walk about the house and then write note [*sic*] in my testament: after, I went to breakfast, and, after, talked awhile with Mr Langdall of his son, and then went to Skabye to visit Mrs Bell: then, after 2 hours, I came home and took order for things in the house, and then examined myself and prayed: after, I walked a while and then went to supper, and after that to the Lector, and, when I had dispatched some to York and Scarborough, I went to bed.

Wednesday 24. After private prayer I went about the house a while, then I wrote notes in my testament, and, after I had eaten my breakfast, I went abroad: after I came home I prayed, and, soon after, when I had read of the Bible, I dined: after, I dispatched some business in the house, then I took a Lector: after, I wrote in my Commonplace book,[23] and then prayed with Mr

---

[20] Timothy Bright, *A Treatise of Melancholy, containing the causes thereof*, 1586.

[21] The 'ninth hour' (modern 3 p.m.), the fifth canonical hour of prayer.

[22] ?workwomen, as below.

[23] Educated people made collections of extracts from their reading, conversations and observations in a commonplace book.

Rhodes, and went about the house a while, and then returned to meditation and private prayer: then I studied awhile for my Lector, and, after, went to supper: after I heard a Lector, and then read of the book of martyrs and so went to bed.

Friday 26.   After private prayer I did eat my breakfast, Read a Long Letter and wrote an other, then prayed, and after went to dinner: after which I heard a great disputation between 2 preachers, then took a lector: after, talked with one that came to see me, and then went to prayer and examination: after, I went to supper, then to the Lector, and so to bed.

Saturday 27.   . . . after dinner I went about the house, and then took my coach and went abroad: after I came home and took order for supper, I prayed privately & examined myself: then I looked and wrote in the household book, and so went to supper, after to Lector, and then to bed.

Sunday 28.   After private prayers I wrote notes in my testament, and did eat my breakfast: then to church, after I came honne[24] to prayer and so to dinner: after which, I talked with a woman that was to be divorced from her husband with whom she lived incestuously: then, I went to church, and, after catechizing and sermon, I walked abroad: then I meditated of the sermons, and read and spoke to Mrs Ormston of the chapter that was read in the morning, and so went to private prayer: after, to supper, then to prayers, and soon after to bed.

Monday 29.   After private prayer I did eat my breakfast, then I did go about the house till almost dinner time, then I prayed and then dined: after I had rested awhile, I wrote my sermon, and then took a lector, and after, I heard prayer and a lector, because, in regard of men's dullness after meat and being winter, it was thought more convenient to be before supper: after, I prayed privately and then of the testament and so went to bed.

Tuesday 30.   After private prayer I did eat my breakfast, then I was busy to dye wool till almost dinner time . . .

[NOVEMBER 1599]
. . .

Friday 3.   . . . after dinner I walked about the house, and did pray with Mr Rhodes: then I did read a while to my workwomen, and then to the Lector: after, to supper, and, after that, I did walk a while, and then I prayed privately and examined myself, and so to bed.

Saturday 4.   After private prayer I read a while of the Bible, then I took a Lector: after, I prayed, and then went to dinner: after that I performed . . .

---

[24] ?home.

SECTION IV

The engraved title page of the Polyglot Bible printed by
Christopher Plantin at Antwerp, 1569, and dedicated to Philip II of Spain.
Reproduced by kind permission of The British Library (6h. 4–11, Vol. I 6h. 4).

Religious Reform and Cultural Change: Spain and England

In section III of this anthology, the collection of documents provided an insight into the range and variety of religious activities, debates and issues that the process of religious reformation – both Catholic and Protestant – initiated and encouraged to flourish. In this section the documents chosen illustrate further aspects of the wideranging cultural ferment of the period – a period which, indeed, witnessed remarkable developments in all branches of cultural and intellectual endeavour.

This selection of documents seeks to demonstrate, moreover, the diversity of ways in which the processes of religious reform interacted with the broader cultural process. Thus a number of extracts come from the work of various sixteenth-century Spanish writers – writers, moreover, who were either major religious figures or who belonged to a major religious order and were thus party to the intellectual programme of the reforming Catholic Church.

While the principal focus of the documents in section IV is upon sixteenth-century Spanish culture, three sets of extracts from literary works produced in England have also been included. The documents in section VIII, 'Church, State and Literature in Britain', are designed to provide a wider and more broadly based introduction to the kinds of political, religious and cultural issues prominent in sixteenth-century Britain. In this section, however, the English documents act as a useful foil to the Spanish ones. In particular, they demonstrate some of the more pressing intellectual and cultural issues that preoccupied English scholars at that time – many of which they shared with their continental counterparts. They also represent the cultural production of a society in which the question of religious allegiance (whether the state would be officially Catholic or Protestant) was both hotly debated and for a long time of uncertain outcome. By contrast, the documents issuing from sixteenth-century Spain represent the production of a culture whose Catholic identity was never seriously in doubt.

Each of the English documents addresses the central issue of education and, therefore, what form of knowledge should be accessible to the educated layman and woman. Thus, to a greater or lesser degree, the authors are engaged with the issue of whether or not the Church and clergy should have an exclusive monopoly over education itself and over the various branches of learning. Moreover, all three documents refer specifically to the production of works in English and are therefore concerned with promoting the development of the vernacular – the very vehicle that allowed for greater accessibility to learning.

In the extract from Caxton's Prologue to the *Aeneid* (document IV.1), the printer-publisher highlights some of the advantages and some of the problems attendant upon the development of the English vernacular. Thus, he indicates how his translation would bring this seminal classical text to a wider audience, who would thereby enjoy some of the educational advantages already current in the 'schools in Italy'. He also provides an insight into the complexity of his task as a translator, faced as he was with a vernacular which comprised a bewildering variety of dialects.

In the extract from Thomas More's *Dialogue Concerning Heresies* (document IV.2), the scholar-statesman engages directly with one of the most crucial issues concerning the development of the vernacular and one that directly impinged upon the processes of religious reform. Was it or was it not legitimate to translate the Bible into the vernacular, and if it was, was it safe to allow the laity to have access to it without the intervention and guidance of the clergy? More, using the dialogue form, mounts a measured, cautious and authoritative examination of the pros and cons of the case. As such, the extract provides an insight as to why certain sixteenth-century Catholic thinkers shared the view of their Protestant counterparts that the Bible should be translated into the vernacular. In this respect, More exhibits something of the spirit of certain sixteenth-century Spanish writers who shared his wish to make their readers' religious experience more immediate and who, as often as not, used the Spanish vernacular in order to achieve such ends. Concomitant with such intentions was the wish that such personal spiritual experience should be conducted firmly within the controlling framework of orthodox Catholic religious belief, practice, pastoral oversight and guidance.

The extracts from the Preface to a much later English translation of another seminal classical text – Euclid's *Elements* – reveal the author, John Dee, mounting a detailed and lengthy apologia for this translation (document IV.3). The fact that Dee perceived the need for such an introductory preface is itself indicative of the slow progress of the development of the vernacular: a cultural process which met with opposition, not only from the Church but also from the universities, who were anxious to maintain Latin as the universal language of scholarship, with all the exclusivity attendant upon such an arrested development. The Preface also demonstrates something of the sheer variety and complexity of the mix of intellectual traditions which constituted Renaissance knowledge at this time, with its diverse branches of inquiry.

The intrinsic variety and complexity of the overall body of Renaissance knowledge was, moreover, enhanced by the development of the vernacular – and thus provided both the Catholic and Protestant Churches with a constant and ongoing challenge to control and channel such knowledge to their own ends.

The extracts drawn from the writings of several major sixteenth-century Spanish writers in turn demonstrate very well the rich variety of impulses which gave Spanish Renaissance culture its particular colour and character. They also provide a compelling example of the ways in which religious reform, and more particularly Catholic reform, might impinge upon a specific country's literary culture. Three of the sets of extracts originate from two of the country's major religious figures – Ignatius de Loyola and Teresa of Ávila. They are highly personalized autobiographical accounts which provide graphic descriptions of different kinds of religious experience. The extracts from Ignatius de Loyola's *Autobiography* (document IV.4) offer a description of the young soldier's experience of religious conversion. The extracts from Teresa of Ávila's *Life* (document IV.6) furnish a graphic account of the saint dealing with the personal challenges of her spirituality, her mysticism and her self-doubt – challenges exacerbated by the suspicion and resistance of her male religious superiors and mentors.

The extracts from Ignatius de Loyola's *Spiritual Exercises* (document IV.5) – a highly influential handbook outlining to the reader a structured programme of private meditation – offer another example of the highly committed and personal nature of the type of religious belief that both Ignatius and Teresa espoused and sought to communicate to others. Nevertheless, despite the emphasis of both these authors upon the importance of individual commitment and belief, both also return, time and time again, to the crucial importance of the authority of the Church and to the essentiality of obedience to the tenets and beliefs of the Catholic faith – the personally intense and committed spiritual life of the individual Catholic is to be lived firmly within the boundaries and discipline of her or his Church.

It was not only innovation in the realm of the spiritual life, however, which was subject to the constraints and controls of ecclesiastical authority and discipline. Such regulatory authority and discipline also extended to innovation in theological and literary scholarship and to the holders of chairs of theology engaged in such work. Thus, when the Augustinian theologian and scholar Luis de León criticized the Vulgate it transpired that his criticism fell foul of the Church authorities, notably of the Spanish Inquisition. Possibly for this reason, if for no other, León's poems, which he wrote in the Spanish vernacular, were never published (under his name) during his lifetime and therefore attained only a limited circulation in the sixteenth century. Nevertheless, the form in which León chose to write his poems provides compelling evidence of the impact and influence of Italian Renaissance poetry upon Spanish culture. In terms of content, the poems treat of religious themes but utilize the poetic form in order to communicate central tenets of Catholic belief and doctrine in an immediate and highly emotive way (documents IV.7.A, B and C). They thus share, at one level at least, a similar kind of intention to the devotional writings of both Ignatius de Loyola and Teresa of Ávila.

The extract from the treatise *The King and the Education of the King* by the Jesuit philosopher Juan de Mariana (document IV.8) provides a notable and interesting example of the ways in which the highly organized and effective educational programme encouraged by the Jesuit Order founded by Ignatius de Loyola developed. In its teaching, this order firmly espoused the fundamentally traditional philosophy of Aristotle and St Thomas Aquinas, but tended to utilize this body of orthodox knowledge in a number of progressive and even distinctly revolutionary ways. Thus, in this treatise, the Jesuit philosopher discusses political theory, addressing the rights and duties of a monarch towards his subjects and in so doing engages with the more controversial issue of the legitimacy of regicide. This extract, therefore, illustrates a paradoxical dimension of late sixteenth-century Spanish culture: a member of a leading reform order writes on an essentially secular, political issue but in doing so deploys the formidable panoply of sixteenth-century philosophical and theological knowledge and learning.

1 Caxton's Prologue to Virgil's *Aeneid* (1490)

Source: *The Pelican Book of English Prose*, edited by R. Sharrock (Harmondsworth: Penguin Books, 1970), I, 106–7; spelling modernized by D. Norman.

William Caxton (*c*.1422–91) is justly celebrated as the first English printer. In this Prologue to his 1490 edition of the English translation of Virgil's epic poem the *Aeneid*, Caxton refers to his work as a translator and publisher. He also makes clear his interest in the English language and his acute awareness of the problems of linguistic change.

After diverse works made, translated and achieved, having no work in hand, I sitting in my study where lay many diverse pamphlets and books, [it] happened that to my hand came a little book in French which late was translated out of Latin by some noble clerk of France, which book is named Eneydos [the *Aeneid*], made in Latin by that noble poet and great clerk Virgil, which book I saw over and read therein: how after the general destruction of the great Troy, Aeneas departed bearing his old father

Anchises upon his shoulders, his little son Yolus[1] on his hand, his wife with much other people following, and how he shipped and departed with all the story of his adventures that he had before he came to the achievement of his conquest of Italy as all along shall be shown in this present book. In which book I had great pleasure, by cause of the fair and pleasant terms and words in French, which I never saw the like before, nor none so pleasant nor so well ordered. Which book as me seemed should be much requisite to noble men to see as well for the eloquence as to the histories, how well that many hundred years passed was the said book of Eneydos with other works made and learned daily in schools specially in Italy and other places, which history the said Virgil made in metre. And when I advised me in this said book, I deliberated and concluded to translate it into English. And forthwith took a pen and wrote a leaf or twain, which I oversaw again to correct it. And when I saw the fair and strange terms therein, I doubted that it should not please some gentlemen which late blamed me saying that in my translations I had over curious terms which could not be understood of common people and desired me to use old and homely terms in my translations. And fain would I satisfy every man, and so to do took an old book and read therein, and certainly the English was so rude and broad that I could not well understand it. And also my lord abbot of Westminster did do show me late certain evidences written in old English for to reduce it to our English now used. And certainly it was written in such wise that it was more like to Dutch than English; I could not reduce nor bring it to be understood, and certainly our language now used varies far from which was used and spoken when I was born. For we Englishmen being born under the domination of the moon, which is never steadfast, but ever wavering, waxing one season, and wanes and decreases another; and that common English that is spoken in one shire varies from another. In so much that in my day happened that certain merchants were in a ship in [the] Thames for to have sailed over the sea into Zeeland, and for lack of wind they tarried at a foreland, and went to land for to refresh them. And one of them named Sheffelde a mercer came into a house and asked for meat; and specially he asked after eggs. And the good wife answered that she could speak no French. And the merchant was angry, for he also could speak no French but would have had eggs, and she understood him not. And then at last another said that he would have eyren. Then the good wife said that she understood him well. Lo what should a man in these days now write, eggs or eyren? Certainly it is hard to please every man, by cause of diversity and change of language.

---

[1] Aeneas' son Iulus (also known as Ascanius).

2 Sir Thomas More, *Dialogue Concerning Heresies* (1528)

Source: *The English Works of Sir Thomas More*, edited by W. E. Campbell (London and New York: Eyre & Spottiswoode, 1931), II, 242–50, abridged and some spellings modernized by D. Norman.

This dialogue was written in 1528 by Sir Thomas More (1477–1535), English humanist and statesman, and first published in 1557 by William Rastell, More's nephew and printer. More was commissioned by Cuthbert Tunstall, Bishop of London, to write this piece as a means of reply and refutation to the so-called heretical books and pamphlets which were being imported into England at that time. In this dialogue the author writes as if to a correspondent, providing a record of a debate between himself and a young man of Lutheran sympathies. The correspondent (the Messenger), has apparently sent the young man to discuss religious questions with More, who refers to his visitor as 'your friend'.

Sir, quoth your friend . . . [I can] see no cause why the clergy should keep the bible out of laymen's hands, that can [know] no more but their mother tongue.

I had went [thought], quoth I, that I had proved you plainly that they keep it not from them. For I have shewed you that they keep none from them but such translation as be either not yet approved for good or such as be already reproved for nought, as Wiclif's was, and Tyndale's.[1] For as for other old ones, that were before Wiclif's days, remain lawful, and be in some folks' hands had and read . . .

I am sure, quoth your friend, ye doubt not but that I am full and whole of your mind in this matter that the bible should be in our English tongue. But yet that the clergy is of the contrary, and would not have it so, that appeareth well, in that they suffer it not to be so. And over that I hear in every place almost, where I find any learned man of them, their minds all set thereon to keep the scripture from us. And they seek out for that part every rotten reason that they can find, and set them forth solemnly to the show, though five of those reasons be not worth a fig. For they begin as far as our first father Adam, and shew us that his wife and he fell out of paradise with desire of knowledge and cunning [skill]. Now if this would serve, it must from the knowledge and study of scripture drive every man, priest and other, lest it drive all out of paradise. Then say they that God taught his disciples many things apart, because the people should not hear it. And therefore they would the people should not now be suffered to read all. Yet they say further that it is hard to translate the scripture out of one tongue into another, and specially, they say, into ours which they call a tongue vulgar and barbarous. But of all thing specially they say that scripture is the food of the soul. And

[1] References to the translations of the Bible into the English vernacular by John Wycliffe and William Tyndale.

that the common people be as infants that must be fed but with milk and pap. And if we have any stronger meat, it must be chammed [chewed] afore by the nurse, and so put into the babe's mouth. But methink though they make us all infants, they shall find many a shrewd brain among us that can perceive chalk from cheese well enough; and, if they would once take us our meat in our own hand, we be not so evil toothed but that within a while they shall see us cham it ourself as well as they. For let them call us young babes and [if] they will, yet, by God, they shall for all that well find in some of us that an old knave is no child.

Surely, quoth I, such things as ye speak, is the thing that as I somewhat said before putteth good folk in fear to suffer the scripture in our English tongue. Not for the reading and receiving, but for the busy chamming thereof, and for much meddling with such parts thereof as least will agree with their capacities. For undoubtedly, as ye spake of our mother Eve, inordinate appetite of knowledge is a mean to drive any man out of paradise. And inordinate is the appetite, when men unlearned, though they read it in their language, will be busy to ensearch and dispute the great secret mysteries of scripture, which, though they hear, they may be not able to perceive. This thing is plainly forbode us that be not appointed nor instructed thereto. And therefore holy Saint Gregory Nazianzenus, that great solemn doctor,[2] sore toucheth and reproveth all such bold busy meddlers in the scripture, and sheweth that it is in Exodie, by Moses ascending up upon the hill where he spake with God, and the people tarrying beneath,[3] signified that the people be forboden to presume to meddle with the high mysteries of holy scripture, but ought to be content to tarry beneath, and meddle none higher than is meet for them; but receiving from the height of the hill by Moses that that is delivered them – that is to wit, the laws and precepts that they must keep, and the points they must believe, look well thereupon, and often, and meddle well therewith – not to dispute it; but to fulfil it. And as for the high secret mysteries of God and hard texts of his holy scripture, let us know that we be so unable to ascend up so high on that hill, that it shall become us to say to the preachers appointed thereto, as the people said unto Moses, 'Hear you God, and let us hear you.' ... And therefore, as I said before, the special fear in this matter is, lest we would be so busy in chamming of the scripture our self (which ye say we were able enough to do) which undoubtedly, the wisest, and the best learned, and he that therein hath by many years bestowed his whole mind, is yet unable to do. And then far more unable must he needs be that boldly will, upon the first reading because he knoweth the words, take upon him therefore to teach other men the sentence, with peril of his own soul, and other men's too, by the bringing men into mad ways, sects and heresies, such as heretics have of old brought up, and the church hath condemned. And thus in these matters, if the common people might be bold to cham it, as

---

[2] Gregory of Nazianzus, one of the early Church Fathers (*c*.329–*c*.389) and a staunch opponent of schism and heresy.

[3] As recounted in Exodus 24: 1–2.

ye say, and to dispute it; then should ye have the more blind the more bold, the more ignorant the more busy, the less wit the more inquisitive, the more fool the more talkative of great doubts and high questions of holy scripture, and of God's great and secret mysteries – and this, not soberly of any good affection, but presumptuously and unreverently at meat and at meal. And there, when the wine were in and the wit out, would they take upon them with foolish words and blasphemy to handle holy scripture in more homely manner than a song of Robin Hood. And some would, as I said, solemnly take upon them like as they were ordinary readers to interpret the text at their pleasure, and therewith fall themself, and draw down other with them, into seditious sects and heresies whereby the scripture of God should lose his honour and reverence, and be, by such unreverent and unsuitable demeanour, among much people quite and clean abused unto the contrary of that holy purpose that God ordained it for. Whereas, if we would no further meddle therewith; but well and devoutly read it and, in that that is plain and evident as God's commandments and his holy counsels, endeavour ourself to follow with help of His grace, asked thereunto; and in his great and marvellous miracles consider his godhead; and in his lowly birth, his godly life, and his bitter passion, exercise ourself in such meditations, prayer, and virtues, as the matter shall minister us occasion, knowledgeing [acknowledging] our own ignorance where we find a doubt, and therein leaning to the faith of the church, wrestle with no such text as might bring us in a doubt and perplexity of any of those articles wherein every good Christian man is clear. By this manner of reading can no man nor woman take hurt in holy scripture . . .

Now as touching the harm that may grow by such blind bayardes[4] as will when they read the bible in English be more busy than will become them, they that touch that point harp upon the right string, and touch truly the great harm that were likely to grow to some folk. Howbeit, not by the occasion yet of the English translation, but by the occasion of their own lewdness and folly, which yet were not in my mind a sufficient cause to exclude the translation and to put other folk from the benefit thereof; but rather to make provision against such abuse, and let a good thing go forth . . .

There is no treatise of scripture so hard but that a good virtuous man, or woman either, shall somewhat find therein that shall delight and increase their devotion. Besides this that every preaching shall be the more pleasant and fruitful unto them when they have in their mind the place of scripture that they shall there hear expowned [expounded]. For though it be, as it is indeed, great wisdom for a preacher to use discretion in his preaching, and to have a respect unto the qualities and capacities of his audience, yet letteth that nothing but that the whole audience may without harm have read and have ready the scripture in mind that he shall in his preaching declare and expowne. For no doubt is there but that God and his holy spirit hath so prudently tempered Their speech through the whole corps of scripture that every man may take good thereby and no man harm but he that will in the

---

[4] Men blind and reckless in their self-confidence.

study thereof lean proudly to the folly of his own wit. For albeit that Christ did speak to the people in parables, and expowned [expounded] them secretly to his especial disciples, and sometime forbare to tell some things to them also, because they were not as yet able to bear them, and the apostles in likewise did some time spare to speak to some people the things that they did not let plainly to speak to some other, yet letteth all this nothing the translation of the scripture into our own tongue no more than in the Latin

. . .

Finally, methinketh, that the constitution provincial of which we spake right now, hath determined this question already. For when the clergy therein agreed that the English bibles should remain which were translated afore Wiclif's days, they consequently did agree that to have the bible in English was none hurt. And in that they forbade any new translation to be read till it were approved by the bishops, it appeareth well thereby that their intent was that the bishop should approve it if he found it faultless, and also of reason amend it where it was faulty, but if the man were an heretic that made it or the faults such and so many as it were more easy to make it all new than mend it – as it happed for both points in the translation of Tyndale. Now if it so be that it would haply be thought not a thing meetly to be adventured to set all on a flush[5] at once, and dash rashly out holy scripture in every lewd fellow's teeth, yet, thinketh me, there might such a moderation be taken therein as neither good virtuous lay folk should lack it nor rude and rash brains abuse it. For it might be with diligence well and truly translated by some good catholic and well learned man, or by divers, dividing the labour among them, and after conferring their several parts together each with other. And after that might the work be allowed and approved by the ordinaries,[6] and by their authorities so put unto print, as all the copies should come whole unto the bishop's hand. Which he may after his discretion and wisdom deliver to such as he perceiveth honest, sad [serious], and virtuous, with a good monition and fatherly counsel to use it reverently with humble heart and lowly mind, rather seeking therein occasion of devotion than of discussion. And providing as much as may be that the book be, after the decease of the party, brought again and reverently restored unto the ordinary. So that, as near as may be devised, no man have it but of the ordinary's hand, and by him thought and reputed for such as shall be likely to use it to God's honour and merit of his own soul. Among whom, if any be proved after to have abused it, then the use thereof to be forboden him, either for ever, or till he be waxen wiser.

---

[5] To let down a volume of water.
[6] Ecclesiastics who had, of their own right, jurisdictional powers.

3 John Dee, Preface to Euclid's *Elements* (1570)

Source: Euclid's *Elements*, translated by H. Billingsley (London, 1570), pp. i–Aii (idiosyncratic pagination) abridged. Spelling modernized by J. Fauvel.

John Dee (1527–1608), English alchemist, astrologer and mathematician, used his expertise to good effect in his lengthy Preface to Henry Billingsley's 1570 translation of Euclid's *Elements* – the canonic work of the most celebrated mathematician of antiquity. The impact of Dee's Preface was very strong in Elizabethan England particularly amongst those of a more practical bent who could utilize his recommendations to advance their own technological skills. Dee's interests also extended to Neoplatonic philosophy and the occult and it is of interest that in these extracts he admits to being an admirer of the work of Henry Cornelius Agrippa, whose unorthodox views had gained this German philosopher a certain notoriety amongst Dee's contemporaries.

A. John Dee on number

How immaterial and free from all matter Number is, who doth not perceive? Yea, who doth not wonderfully wonder at it? . . . O comfortable allurement! O ravishing persuasion! To deal with a science whose subject is so ancient, so pure, so excellent, so surmounting all creatures, so used of the almighty and incomprehensible wisdom of the Creator in the distinct creation of all creatures: in all their distinct parts, properties, natures, and virtues, by order and most absolute Number brought from nothing to the formality of their being and state. By Number's property therefore . . . we may both wind and draw ourselves into the inward and deep search and view of all creatures' distinct virtues, natures, properties and forms: and also, farther, arise, climb, ascend and mount up (with speculative wings) in spirit, to behold in the Glass of Creation the Form of Forms, the Exemplar Number of all things numerable, both visible and invisible, mortal and immortal, corporal and spiritual.

B. John Dee on music

Music is a Mathematical Science, which teacheth by sense and reason perfectly to judge and order the diversity of sounds, high and low. *Astronomy* and *Music* are Sisters, saith Plato. As for Astronomy the eyes: so for Harmonious motion the ears were made. But as Astronomy hath a more divine Contemplation and commodity than mortal eye can perceive: so is Music to be considered, that the mind may be preferred before the ear. And from audible sound, we ought to ascend to the examination: which numbers are harmonious, and which not; and why either the one are: or the other are not. I could at large, in the heavenly motions and distances, describe a marvellous harmony, of Pythagoras Harp with eight strings . . . And what is the cause of the apt bond and friendly fellowship of the intellectual and mental part of us with our gross & corruptible body: but a certain mean and harmonious spirituality, with both participating, & of both (in a manner) resulting: in the tune of man's voice, and also the sound of instrument, what might be said, of harmonie: no common musician would lightly believe.

C. John Dee on anthropography

Anthropography is the description of the number, measure, weight, figure, situation, and colour of every diverse thing contained in the perfect body of MAN . . . If the description of the heavenly part of the world had a peculiar art, called *Astronomy*: if the description of the earthly globe hath his peculiar art, called *Geography*: if the matching of both hath his peculiar art, called *Cosmography*: which is the description of the whole and universal frame of the world: Why should not the description of him who is the less world, and from the beginning called *Microcosmos* (that is, *The Less World*) [Dee's marginal note: MAN is the less world] and for whose sake and service all bodily creatures else were created – who also participates with spirits and angels, and is made to the image and similitude of God – have his peculiar art? . . . Whereby good proof will be had of our harmonious and micro-cosmical constitution. The outward image and view hereof, to the art of painting, to sculpture, and architecture (for church, house, fort or ship) is most necessary and profitable: for that, it is the chief base and foundation of them. Look in Vitruvius,[1] whether I deal sincerely for your behoof, or no. Look in Albert Durer, *De Symmetria humani Corporis*.[2] Look in the 27 and 28 chapters of the second book, [of Agrippa's] *De occulta Philosophia*.[3] Consider the Ark of Noah. And by that, wade further. Remember the Delphic Oracle NOSCE TE IPSUM (*Know thy self*),[4] so long ago pronounced, of so many a philosopher repeated, and of the wisest attempted: and then you will perceive how long ago you have been called to the school where this art might be learned. Well. I am nothing afraid of the disdain of some such as think Sciences and Arts to be but seven.

---

[1] Marcus Vitruvius Pollio (active 46–30 BC), a Roman architect whose treatise *De architectura* was enormously influential in the sixteenth century.

[2] The theoretical treatise on human anatomy and its proportions composed by the German artist, Albrecht Dürer, based on his admiration for ancient canons of beauty and his awareness of contemporary Italian artists' work where such standards were adopted.

[3] The philosophical work by the German scholar Henry Cornelius Agrippa of Nettesheim, extracts from which are given in document III.10.

[4] On the ancient temple of Apollo at Delphi were inscribed several maxims attributed to seven statesmen, lawgivers and philosophers. One of the most famous was this one.

D. John Dee on navigation

The art of navigation demonstrateth how by the shortest good way, by the aptest direction, & in the shortest time, a sufficient ship between any two places (in passage navigable) assigned, may be conducted: and in all storms, & natural disturbances chancing, how to use the best possible means whereby to recover the place first assigned. What need the master pilot hath of other arts, here before recited, it is easy to know: as, of *hydrography*, *astronomy*, *astrology*, and *horometry*.[5] Presupposing continually the common base and foundation of all: namely *arithmetic* and *geometry*. So that he be able to understand and judge his own necessary instruments and furniture necessary, whether they be perfectly made or no, and also can (if need be) make them himself. As quadrants, the astronomer's ring, the astronomer's staff, the astrolabe universal, an hydrographical globe, charts hydrographical (true – not with parallel meridians), the common sea compass, the compass of variation, the proportional and paradoxal compasses (of me invented for our two Muscovy master pilots, at the request of the Company) . . . And also be able to calculate the planets' places for all times.

. . . In navigation, none ought to have greater care to be skilful than our English pilots. And perchance some would more attempt, and other some more willingly would be aiding, if they wist certainly what privilege God had endued this island with, by reason of situation most commodious for navigation, to places most famous and rich. And though of late a young gentleman [Dee's marginal note: Anno. 1567 S[ir].H[umphrey].G[ilbert].], a courageous captain, was in a great readiness, with good hope and great causes of persuasion, to have ventured for a discovery (either westerly, by Cape de Paramantia: or easterly, above Nova Zemla and the Cyremisses)[6] and was, at the very near time of attempting, called and employed otherwise (both then and since) in great service to his country, as the Irish rebels have tasted [Dee's marginal note: Anno. 1569]: yet, I say, though the same gentleman do not hereafter deal therewith, someone or other should listen to the matter: and by good advice and discreet circumspection, by little and little win to the sufficient knowledge of that trade and voyage, which now I would be sorry through carelessness, want of skill, and courage, should remain unknown and unheard of . . . Thereof, verily, might grow commodity, to this land chiefly and to the rest of the Christian Common wealth, far passing all riches and worldly treasure.

---

[5] The measurement of time.

[6] A reference to the English navigator's search for the North-West or the North-East Passage to the Far East via the Arctic Circle.

E. John Dee affirms the purity of his endeavours

Ought any honest student and modest Christian philosopher be counted & called a conjuror? Shall the folly of idiots and the malice of the scornful so much prevail, that he who seeketh no worldly gain or glory at their hands, but only of God, the treasure of heavenly wisdom & knowledge of true verity: shall he (I say) in the mean space be robbed and spoiled of his honest name and fame? . . . Shall that man be (in hugger mugger) condemned as a companion of the hellhounds, and a caller and conjuror of wicked and damned spirits? . . . Well: well. O (you such) my unkind countrymen. O unnatural countrymen. O brainsick, rash, spiteful, and disdainful countrymen. Why oppress you me thus violently, with your slandering of me: . . . Have I so long, so dearly, so far, so carefully, so painfully, so dangerously fought & travailed for the learning of wisdom & attaining of virtue: and in the end (in your judgement) am I become worse than when I began? Worse than a madman? A dangerous member in the Common Wealth, and no member of the Church of Christ?

4 Ignatius de Loyola, *Autobiography* (1553/1555)

Source: *The Autobiography of Saint Ignatius Loyola*, translated by J. O'Callaghan and edited by J. C. Olin (New York: Harper Torch Books, 1974), pp. 21–32 abridged.

Ignatius de Loyola (1491–1556) was one of the most influential figures in the Catholic Reformation of the sixteenth century and founder of the Jesuits. Ignatius dictated the material for his autobiography in Rome towards the end of his life, calling his amanuensis – a young Portuguese Jesuit, Luis Goncalves de Câmara – to him when quiet moments presented themselves during a hectic round of engagements. The original manuscript no longer survives but there are several very old copies on the basis of which a number of modern critical editions have been made.

Until the age of twenty-six he was a man given over to vanities of the world; with a great and vain desire to win fame he delighted especially in the exercise of arms.[1] Once when he was in a fortress that the French were attacking,[2] although all the others saw clearly that they could not defend themselves and were of the opinion that they should surrender provided their lives were spared, he gave so many reasons to the commander that he persuaded him at last to defend it; this was contrary to the views of all the knights, but they were encouraged by his valour and energy. When the day arrived on which the bombardment was expected, he confessed to one of his companions in arms. After the bombardment had lasted a good while, a shot

---

[1] It is likely that Ignatius was 29–30 at the time of his conversion.
[2] The French attack on the citadel of Pamplona, May 1521.

hit him in the leg, breaking it completely; since the ball passed through both legs, the other one was also badly damaged.

When he fell, the defenders of the fortress surrendered immediately to the French who, having taken possession of it, treated the wounded man very well, with courtesy and kindness. After he had been in Pamplona for twelve or fifteen days, they carried him on a litter to his own country where he was very ill. All the doctors and surgeons who were summoned from many places decided that the leg ought to be broken again and the bones reset because they had been badly set the first time or had been broken on the road and were out of place and could not heal. This butchery was done again; during it, as in all the others he suffered before or since, he never spoke a word nor showed any sign of pain other than to clench his fists.

Yet he continued to get worse, not being able to eat and showing the other indications that are usually signs of death. When the feast of St John came, because the doctors had very little confidence in his health, he was advised to confess; he received the sacraments on the vigil of Sts Peter and Paul. The doctors said that if he did not feel better by midnight, he could consider himself dead. As the sick man had devotion to St Peter, Our Lord willed that he should begin to improve that very midnight. His improvement proceeded so quickly that some days later it was decided that he was out of danger of death.

As his bones knit together, one bone below the knee remained on top of another, shortening his leg. The bone protruded so much that it was an ugly sight. He was unable to abide it because he was determined to follow the world and he thought that it would deform him; he asked the surgeons if it could be cut away. They said that indeed it could be cut away, but that the pain would be greater than all those that he had suffered, because it was already healed and it would take some time to cut it. Yet he was determined to make himself a martyr to his own pleasure. His older brother was astounded and said that he himself would not dare to suffer such pain, but the wounded man endured it with his customary patience.

After the flesh and excess bone were cut away, means were taken so the leg would not be so short; many ointments were applied to it, and, as it was stretched continually with instruments, he suffered martyrdom for many days. But Our Lord was restoring his health, and he was getting well. In everything else he was healthy except that he could not stand easily on his leg and had to stay in bed. As he was much given to reading worldly and fictitious books, usually called books of chivalry, when he felt better he asked to be given some of them to pass the time. But in that house none of those that he usually read could be found, so they gave him a Life of Christ and a book of the lives of the saints in Spanish.[3]

As he read them over many times, he became rather fond of what he found written there. Putting his reading aside, he sometimes stopped to think about the things he had read and at other times about the things of the world

---

[3] *The Life of Christ* by the fourteenth-century German Carthusian Ludolph of Saxony, and *The Golden Legend* by the thirteenth-century Dominican writer Jacopo de Voragine.

that he used to think about before . . . Yet there was this difference. When he was thinking about the things of the world, he took much delight in them, but afterwards, when he was tired and put them aside, he found that he was dry and discontented. But when he thought of going to Jerusalem, barefoot and eating nothing but herbs and undergoing all the other rigours that he saw the saints had endured, not only was he consoled when he had these thoughts, but even after putting them aside, he remained content and happy. He did not wonder, however, at this; nor did he stop to ponder the difference until one time his eyes were opened a little, and he began to marvel at the difference and to reflect upon it, realizing from experience that some thoughts left him sad and others happy. Little by little he came to recognize the difference between the spirits that agitated him, one from the demon, the other from God.

From this reading he obtained not a little insight, and he began to think more earnestly about his past life and about the great need he had to do penance for it. At this point the desire to imitate the saints came to him, though he gave no thought to the circumstances, but only promised with God's grace to do as they had done. All he wanted to do was to go to Jerusalem as soon as he recovered . . . performing all the disciplines and abstinences which a generous soul, inflamed by God, usually wants to do.

[After his conversion, Ignatius journeyed in March 1522 to the famous shrine of Our Lady at Montserrat in Catalonia.]

As he was going on his way . . . a Moor riding on a mule came up to him, and they went on talking together. They began to talk about Our Lady, and the Moor said it seemed to him that the Virgin had indeed conceived without a man, but he could not believe that she remained a virgin after giving birth. In support of this he cited the natural reasons that suggested themselves to him. The pilgrim,[4] in spite of the many reasons he gave him, could not dissuade him from this opinion. The Moor then went on ahead so rapidly that he lost sight of him, and he was left to think about what had transpired with the Moor. Various emotions came over him and caused discontent in his soul, as it seemed to him that he had not done his duty. This also aroused his indignation against the Moor, for he thought that he had done wrong in allowing the Moor to say such things about Our Lady and that he was obliged to defend her honour. A desire came over him to go in search of the Moor and strike him with his dagger for what he had said. He struggled with this conflict of desires for a long time, uncertain to the end as to what he was obliged to do. The Moor, who had gone on ahead, had told him that he was going to a place on the same road a little farther on, very near the highway, though the highway did not pass through the place.

Tired of examining what would be best to do and not finding any guiding principle, he decided as follows, to let the mule go with the reins slack as far as the place where the road separated. If the mule took the village road, he would seek out the Moor and strike him; if the mule did not go toward the

---

[4] At this point in the biography Ignatius refers to himself as the pilgrim.

village but kept on the highway, he would let him be. He did as he proposed. Although the village was little more than thirty or forty paces away, and the road to it was very broad and very good, Our Lord willed that the mule took the highway and not the village road. Coming to a large town before Montserrat, he wanted to buy there the clothing he had decided to wear when he went to Jerusalem. He bought cloth from which sacks were usually made, loosely woven and very prickly. Then he ordered a long garment reaching to his feet to be made from it. He bought a pilgrim's staff and a small gourd and put everything up front on the mule's saddle.

He went on his way to Montserrat, thinking as always about the deeds he would do for the love of God. As his mind was full of ideas from Amadis of Gaul[5] and such books, some things similar to those came to mind. Thus he decided to watch over his arms all one night, without sitting down or going to bed, but standing a while and kneeling a while, before the altar of Our Lady of Montserrat where he had resolved to leave his clothing and dress himself in the armour of Christ. Leaving this place then he went on, thinking as usual about his intentions. After arriving at Montserrat, he said a prayer and arranged for a confessor. He made a general confession in writing which lasted three days. He arranged with the confessor[6] to take his mule and to place his sword and his dagger in the church on the altar of Our Lady. This was the first man to whom he revealed his decision, because until then he had not revealed it to any confessor.

On the eve of the feast of Our Lady in March in the year 1522, he went at night as secretly as he could to a poor man, and stripping off all his garments he gave them to the poor man and dressed himself in his desired clothing and went to kneel before the altar of Our Lady. At times in this way, at other times standing, with his pilgrim's staff in his hand he spent the whole night. He left at daybreak so as not to be recognized. He did not take the road that led straight to Barcelona, where he would encounter many who would recognize and honour him, but he went off to a town called Manresa. There he decided to stay in a hospice a few days and also to note some things in his book that he carefully carried with him and by which he was greatly consoled. After he had gone about a league from Montserrat, a man who had been hurrying after him caught up to him and asked if he had given some clothing to a poor man, as the poor man said. Answering that he had, the tears ran from his eyes in compassion for the poor man to whom he had given the clothes – in compassion, for he realized they were threatening him, thinking he had stolen them. Yet as much as he avoided esteem, he could not remain long in Manresa before people were saying great things, as the story of what happened at Montserrat spread. Eventually they said more than the truth, that he had given up much wealth and so forth.

---

[5] A knight and hero of a prose romance which was very popular in sixteenth-century Spain.
[6] Jean Chanon, a French Benedictine, noted for his austere spirituality.

5 Ignatius de Loyola, *Spiritual Exercises* (1522–1538)

Source: *The Spiritual Exercises of Saint Ignatius*, translated by T. Corbishley, S J (Wheathampstead: A. Clarke, 1973), pp. 12–124 abridged.

Between 1522 and 1523 Ignatius Loyola lived an ascetic life at Manresa and began work on *The Spiritual Exercises*, which was completed in Paris in 1538. A revised version was approved by Pope Paul III in 1548. The Spanish original of this text is lost but there survives a manuscript copy with the author's corrections. The first printed edition appeared in 1548 (Rome). This programme of meditation with its structured, well ordered procedure for prayer, meditation and self-examination, had an enormous impact amongst sixteenth-century Catholics, with figures such as St Teresa of Ávila (see below, document IV.6) adopting them as part of their spiritual devotions.

The work begins with an explanation of the nature of the Spiritual Exercises:

1. The name 'Spiritual Exercises' means every form of examination of conscience, of meditation, contemplation, prayer (vocal and mental) and the spiritual activities mentioned later. Going for long or short walks and running are physical exercises; so we give the name of spiritual exercises to any process which makes the soul ready and able to rid itself of all irregular attachments, so that, once rid of them, it may look for and discover how God wills it to regulate its life to secure its salvation.

2. The person who gives another the method and outline for meditation or contemplation must faithfully recount the historical subject of such a contemplation or meditation, just running over the headings in a brief and summary explanation; the reason for this is that when the person making the contemplation is given the basic facts of the story and then goes over it and thinks about it for himself, any discovery he makes which sheds light on the story, or brings it home to him more, will give him greater delight and more benefit of soul. Such discoveries may be due to his own reflection or to the divine action, but they are better than if the giver of the exercises had gone into great detail and expounded at length the significance of the story. Nor does the soul's full satisfaction come from wide knowledge so much as from the personal appreciation of and feeling for things.

3. In all the following spiritual exercises we make acts of the understanding in reasoning and acts of the will in being moved to action; we must be careful to note that, in those acts of the will in which we hold converse (in word or thought) with our Lord God or His Saints, greater reverence is required of us than when we are employing our reasoning faculties.

4. Four weeks are assigned to the following exercises, corresponding with their four divisions: first, reflection on and contemplation of sins; second, the life of Christ our Lord, up to and including Palm Sunday; third, the sufferings of Christ our Lord; fourth, the Resurrection and Ascension, with three ways of Praying, as an appendix. But these four weeks are not to be understood as each consisting of seven or eight days. In the first week some

may be slower to find what they want, namely contrition and tears of sorrow for their sins, whilst some are more earnest, or more disturbed and tried by different spiritual influences: so sometimes the first week will have to be shortened, sometimes lengthened, and so with the following weeks, having in mind all the time what the given subject-matter is meant to effect. Still, the whole course should be completed in approximately thirty days.

5. The retreatant will benefit greatly if he starts with a largehearted generosity towards his Creator and Lord, surrendering to Him his freedom of will, so that His Divine Majesty may make that use of his person and possessions which is in accordance with His most holy will . . .

[A number of additional recommendations are made for the reader to follow out in the first week.]

82. (10) *Penance*. This is divided into interior and exterior penance. Interior penance means sorrow for one's sins, with a firm intention of not committing them or any others.

Exterior penance, which is the outcome of this interior penance, consists in inflicting punishment on ourselves for the sins we have committed. It is of three main kinds:

83. (a) The first kind concerns food. When we cut out what is excessive, this is temperance, not penance.

We do penance when we cut down what is normal. The more we do this, the greater and the better is the penance, provided that the constitution is not undermined and no obvious weakness ensues.

84. (b) The second kind concerns sleep. Here again, it is not penance to do away with anything excessively luxurious or soft. Penance consists in cutting down what is normal in our sleeping habits, and the more we cut down the better, provided the constitution is not undermined and no obvious weakness ensues. But we should not shorten our normal time for sleeping, unless perhaps to reach the mean, if we have got into a bad habit of sleeping too much.

85. (c) The third form is to chastise the body by inflicting actual pain on it. This is done by wearing hairshirts or cords or iron chains, by scourging or beating ourselves and by other kinds of harsh treatment.

86. (1) The safest and most suitable form of penance seems to be that which causes pain in the flesh but does not penetrate to the bones, that is, which causes suffering but not sickness. So the best way seems to be to scourge oneself with thin cords which hurt superficially, rather than to use some other means which might produce serious internal injury.

87. (2) The chief purpose in external penances is to produce three results:

(a) satisfaction for former sins;

(b) to overcome oneself, i.e. to subject the sensual nature to reason, and in general to ensure that all our lower appetites are under the control of our higher powers;

(c) to ask for and to obtain some favour or gift which one earnestly desires: for example, one may wish to have true sorrow for sins and to grieve over them; or over the pains and sorrows which Christ our Lord endured in His Passion, or to solve some doubt one is experiencing . . .

89. (4) When the retreatant has not yet found what he is looking for, e.g., grief, comfort, etc., it often helps if he makes some change in his penances, as regards sleep, food or other things. Thus we can modify our practice by doing penance for two or three days and then omitting it for two or three more, because it suits some to do more penance, others less. Moreover, we often leave off penance out of love of bodily comfort, judging wrongly that our constitution cannot stand it without serious illness; on the other hand, we sometimes go too far, thinking that the body can bear it. As our Lord God understands our nature infinitely better than we do, He very often enables each one, through these variations, to realize what best suits him.

90. (5) The particular examination of conscience is to be made to eliminate faults and slackness in the performance of the exercises and the additional practices. This applies also to the second and third weeks . . .

[On the fourth day of the second week the reader is advised to conduct a meditation on two standards:]

136. One is that of Christ our Lord, our Commander-in-Chief; the other that of Lucifer, our human nature's deadly enemy.

The usual preparatory prayer.

137. *First preliminary.* The story. Christ invites all men, desiring them to rally to His standard, whilst Lucifer, on the other side, invites them to join his.

138. *Second preliminary.* The picture. A great plain, comprising the entire Jerusalem district, where is the supreme Commander-in-Chief of the forces of good, Christ our Lord: another plain near Babylon, where Lucifer is, at the head of the enemy.

139. *Third preliminary.* Prayer for my special need. This time it is to ask for an understanding of the tricks of the wicked leader, and for help to guard against them: also for an understanding of the life of truth exemplified by our true Commander-in-Chief; also for grace to imitate Him.

140. *First heading.* Imagine that leader of all the enemy, in that great plain of Babylon, sitting on a sort of throne of smoking flame, a horrible and terrifying sight.

141. *Second heading.* Watch him calling together countless devils, to despatch them into different cities till the whole world is covered, forgetting no province or locality, no class or single individual.

142. *Third heading.* Study the harangue he makes to them, telling them to have their traps and fetters in position, tempting men first with eagerness for money (his usual procedure) as the easiest means to acquiring some worthless position in the world, and eventually to overweening pride. Notice the three steps, money, position, pride: from these three steps he leads men on to all other vices.

143. By contrast we must make a parallel application of the imagination to our true Commander-in-Chief, Christ our Lord.

144. *First heading.* Study the attitude of Christ our Lord in that great plain

in the Jerusalem country, his unostentatious manner, his attractive and delightful appearance.

145. *Second heading*. Watch the Lord of the entire world choosing so many as apostles, disciples and so on, and sending them out through the whole world, sowing the seed of His sacred teaching in the hearts of men of every rank and condition.

146. *Third heading*. Study the sermon which Christ our Lord preaches to all who serve Him and are His friends, as He sends them out on this expedition. He exhorts them to make it their aim to help everybody, leading them first to perfect poverty in the spirit, and even to poverty in reality, if this be His Divine Majesty's pleasure and He should, of His graciousness, so choose them; then to want to be laughed at and looked down on. From these two comes humility. Notice the three steps: poverty, as against money: being laughed at and looked down on as against being looked up to by men of the world: humility, as against pride. From these three steps men can be led on to all the virtues.

147. *Colloquy*. One colloquy with our Lady, asking her to get me from her Son and Lord the favour of being admitted under His standard, at first in perfect poverty in the spirit, and then in real poverty, should this be His Divine Majesty's pleasure and He should, of His graciousness, so choose me; next, in putting up with being laughed at and treated unjustly, so that I may be more like Him – so long as I can have these to bear without sin on anybody's part and offence to the Divine Majesty. I will then say a Hail Mary.[1]

Second colloquy. I will ask the Son too to get me the same favour from the Father. I will then say the Anima Christi.[2]

Third colloquy. I will ask the Father to give me the same favour and will say the Our Father.[3]

148. *Note*. This exercise is to be made at midnight and again in the early morning. Two repetitions of it should be made at the times for Mass and Vespers, always finishing with the three colloquies with our Lady, the Son and the Father . . .

[On the seventh day of the third week the reader is given a number of recommendations aimed at achieving self-control with regard to eating:]

210. (1) There is not much point in cutting down on bread, which is not a food about which the appetite is usually so irregular or temptation so strong as it is about other foods.

211. (2) There is more point in cutting down on drink than on bread. So one should look carefully to see what is beneficial and to be taken, and what is bad for one and to be given up.

---

[1] A prayer to the Virgin Mary based on the salutations to Mary of the angel Gabriel at the Annunciation and of Elizabeth at the Visitation (Luke 1: 28 and 42).

[2] The prayer, beginning 'Soul of Christ, sanctify me', used especially as a private Eucharistic devotion.

[3] The prayer taught by Jesus Christ to his disciples (Matthew 6: 9–13; Luke 11: 2–4).

212. (3) Food, other than bread, calls for greater and more perfect abstinence. For it is here that the appetite inclines to excess more easily and temptation is liable to be more violent. To avoid disorder, then, in food there are two ways of practising abstinence: one, by making a practice of eating plainer foods; two, delicacies, if eaten at all, should be taken in small amounts . . .

[The work concludes with a set of rules reminding the reader of the mind of the Church:]

352. The following rules are to be observed in order that we may hold the opinions we should hold in the Church militant.

353. (1) We should put away completely our own opinion and keep our minds ready and eager to give our entire obedience to our holy Mother the hierarchical Church, Christ our Lord's undoubted Spouse.

354. (2) We should speak with approval of confession to a priest, of the reception of Holy Communion once a year, still more once a month, most of all once a week, the requisite conditions being duly fulfilled.

355. (3) We should openly approve of the frequent hearing of Mass, and also of hymns, psalms and lengthy prayers both inside and outside the church, as well as the set times for the divine office as a whole, for prayer in general and for all the canonical hours.

356. (4) We should speak with particular approval of religious orders, and the states of virginity and celibacy, not rating matrimony as high as any of these.

357. (5) We should express approval of the vows of religion, poverty, obedience, and chastity, as well as of vows to perform other counsels of perfection. It is to be noted that a vow concerns activities conducive to the perfection of the Gospels; hence a vow should not be taken in matters far removed from those activities, such as going into business or getting married, and so on.

358. (6) We should approve of relics of the saints, showing reverence for them and praying to the saints themselves; visits to Station churches, pilgrimages, indulgences, jubilees, Crusade bulls, the lighting of candles in churches should all be commended.

359. (7) We should approve of the laws of fasting and abstinence in Lent, on Ember Days, vigils, Fridays and Saturdays, as well as mortifications both interior and exterior.

360. (8) We should praise church decoration and architecture, as well as statues, which we should venerate in view of what they portray.

361. (9) Finally, all the Church's commandments should be spoken of favourably, our minds being always eager to find arguments in her defence, never in criticism.

362. (10) We should be more inclined to approve and speak well of the regulations and instructions as well as the personal conduct of our superiors. It may well be that these are not or have not been always praiseworthy; but to criticize them, whether in public utterances or in dealing with ordinary people, is likely to give rise to complaint and scandal

rather than to do good. This would arouse popular hostility towards authority both temporal and spiritual. Of course, whilst it does harm to speak ill of superiors behind their backs in the hearing of ordinary people, it can do good to point out their failings to these superiors themselves, who can correct them.

363. (11) Theology, both positive and scholastic, should be praised by us; on the one hand, the positive doctors, like St Jerome, St Augustine and St Gregory, have the special gift of moving men's hearts to a general love and service of God our Lord; the scholastics, on the other hand, like St Thomas, St Bonaventure, the Master of the Sentences and the rest, have their special gift, which is rather to give precision to and clarify, in a way suited to our age, those truths which are necessary for eternal salvation. These scholastic doctors, being nearer to our own times, not only have the advantage of a correct understanding of the Sacred Scriptures and of the positive doctors and saints but, whilst being also enlightened and assisted themselves by the power of God, they have the further assistance of the Councils, Canons and decrees of our Holy Mother the Church.

364. (12) We must be careful not to institute comparisons between our present generation and the saints of former times, for this can be a source of great error. We should not, for example, say: 'He knows more than St Augustine'; 'He is another St Francis or even greater'; 'He is another St Paul in goodness, holiness', etc.

365. (13) To arrive at complete certainty, this is the attitude of mind we should maintain: I will believe that the white object I see is black if that should be the decision of the hierarchical Church, for I believe that linking Christ our Lord the Bridegroom and His Bride the Church, there is one and the same Spirit, ruling and guiding us for our souls' good. For our Holy Mother the Church is guided and ruled by the same Spirit, the Lord who gave the Ten Commandments.

366. (14) Whilst it is absolutely true that no man can be saved without being predestined and without faith and grace, great care is called for in the way in which we talk and argue about all these matters.

367. (15) Nor should we make a habit of talking about predestination. If we have to talk about it to some extent on occasion, our language should be such as not to lead ordinary people astray, as can happen if a man says: 'It is already settled whether I am to be saved or damned; my good or bad conduct cannot make any difference.' So they lose heart and cease to bother about the activities which make for their souls' health and spiritual profit.

368. (16) Again we must be careful lest, by over-much emphasis in talking about faith, without the necessary qualifications and clarifications, we give occasion to people to become indifferent and lazy about what they do, either before or after the acquisition of faith informed by charity.

369. (17) Nor should we talk so much about grace and with such insistence on it as to give rise to the poisonous view that destroys freedom. Thus, with the help of God, we should take every opportunity of talking about faith and grace, having in view the greater praise of His Divine Majesty; but our language and way of speaking should not be such that the

value of our activities and the reality of human freedom might be in any way impaired or disregarded, especially in times like these which are full of dangers.

370. (18) It is of course true that we must esteem above all else the entire service of God out of sheer love; yet we should often speak in praise of the fear of His Divine Majesty. Not only is a childlike fear a good and holy attitude; so also is the fear proper to servants, which helps greatly to get men out of mortal sin when they are not capable of rising to the better and more effective form of love. Once they have got rid of mortal sin they can more easily rise to the childlike fear which is wholly acceptable and pleasing to God our Lord, since it is in accordance with His own love.

6 St Teresa of Ávila, *Life* (1565)

Source: *The Life of Saint Teresa of Ávila*, translated by J. M. Cohen (Harmondsworth: Penguin Books, 1957), pp. 76–267 abridged.

Teresa of Ávila (1515–82) was one of the great mystics of the Catholic Church and originator of the Carmelite reform order. The autobiographical *Life* which conveys her remarkable personality so well and provides an insight into her moral and spiritual values, was dictated to her confessor and edited for publication by Luis de León. It was first published in 1611.

In chapters 11 and 12 the author explains the quality of successful prayer and of a valid spiritual life:

Now to speak of those who are beginning to be the servants of love – for this, I think, is what we become when we decide to follow along the way of prayer Him who loved us so greatly. It is so high an honour that even the thought of it brings a strange joy. Servile fear vanishes immediately, if we act as we should in this first stage . . . For the perfect possession of this true love of God brings all blessings with it. We are so niggardly and so slow to give ourselves entirely to God that we do not prepare ourselves to secure that precious thing, which His Majesty does not wish us to enjoy if we have not paid a high price first . . .

We resolve to be poor, and that is a great merit. But very often we resume our precautions and take care not to be short of necessities, also of superfluities, and even to collect friends who will supply us. In this way we take greater pains and, perhaps, expose ourselves to greater danger in our anxiety not to go short than we did before, when we had possession of our estates. Presumably we also gave up all thought of our own importance when we became nuns, or when we began to lead a spiritual life and to pursue perfection. Yet the moment our self-importance is wounded we forget that we have given ourselves to God. We want to snatch it up and tear it out of His very hands, as they say, even after we have, to all appearances, made Him lord over our will. And it is the same with everything else.

That is a fine way of seeking God's love! We expect it by the handful, as they say, and yet we want to keep our affections for ourselves! We make no attempt to carry our desires into effect, and fail to raise them above the earth, and yet we want great spiritual comforts. This is not good, for the two aims are, as I see it, irreconcilable. So, since we do not manage wholly to give ourselves up, we never receive the whole of this treasure. May it please the Lord to give it us drop by drop, even though receiving it may cost us all the labours in the world . . .

Here I shall have to make use of a comparison though, being a woman and writing only what I have been commanded to write, I should like to avoid it. But this spiritual language is so difficult to use for those like myself who have no learning, that I must find some other means of expression. It may be that my comparisons will not very often be effective, in which case your Reverence will be amused at my stupidity. It strikes me that I have read or heard this one before. But as I have a bad memory I do not know where it occurred or what it illustrated. But for the present it will serve my purpose.

A beginner must look on himself as one setting out to make a garden for his Lord's pleasure, on most unfruitful soil which abounds in weeds. His Majesty roots up the weeds and will put in good plants instead. Let us reckon that this is already done when a soul decides to practise prayer and has begun to do so. We have then, as good gardeners, with God's help to make these plants grow, and to water them carefully so that they do not die, but produce flowers, which give out a good smell, to delight this Lord of ours. Then He will often come to take His pleasure in this garden and enjoy these virtues.

Now let us see how this garden is to be watered, so that we may understand what we have to do, and what labour it will cost us, also whether the gain will outweigh the effort, or how long it will take. It seems to me that the garden may be watered in four different ways. Either the water must be drawn from a well, which is very laborious; or by a water-wheel and buckets, worked by a windlass – I have sometimes drawn it in this way, which is less laborious than the other, and brings up more water – or from a stream or spring, which waters the ground much better, for the soil then retains more moisture and needs watering less often, which entails far less work for the gardener; or by heavy rain, when the Lord waters it Himself without any labour of ours; and this is an incomparably better method than all the rest.

Now to apply these four methods of watering, by which this garden is to be maintained and without which it will fail. This is my purpose, and will, I think, enable me to explain something about the four stages of prayer, to which the Lord has, in His kindness, sometimes raised my soul. May he graciously grant that I may speak in such a way as to be of use to one of the persons who commanded me to write this,[1] whom the Lord has advanced in four months far beyond the point that I have reached in seventeen years. He prepared himself better than I, and therefore, without any labour on his part, his garden is watered by all these four means; although it only receives

---

[1] Father Pedro Ibañez.

the last water drop by drop. But, as things are going, with the Lord's help, his garden will soon be submerged. If my way of explaining all this seems crazy to him, he is welcome to laugh at me.

We may say that beginners in prayer are those who draw the water up out of the well; which is a great labour, as I have said. For they find it very tiring to keep the senses recollected, when they are used to a life of distraction. Beginners have to accustom themselves to pay no attention to what they see or hear, and to put this exercise into practice during their hours of prayer, when they must remain in solitude, thinking whilst they are alone of their past life. Although all must do this many times, the advanced as well as the beginners, all need not do so equally, as I shall explain later. At first they are distressed because they are not sure that they regret their sins. Yet clearly they do, since they have now sincerely resolved to serve God. They should endeavour to meditate on the life of Christ, and thus the intellect will grow tired. Up to this point we can advance ourselves, though with God's help of course, for without it, as everyone knows, we cannot think one good thought.

This is what I mean by beginning to draw water from the well – and God grant there may be water in it! But at least this does not depend on us, who have only to draw it up and do what we can to water the flowers. But God is so good that when for reasons known to His Majesty – and perhaps for our greater profit – He wishes the well to be dry, we, like good gardeners, must do what we can ourselves. Meanwhile He preserves the flowers without water, and in this way He makes our virtues grow. Here by water I mean tears, or if there be none, a tenderness and inward feeling of devotion. But what shall a man do here who finds that for many days on end he feels nothing but dryness, dislike, distaste and so little desire to go and draw water that he would give it up altogether if he did not remember that he is pleasing and serving the Lord of the garden; if he did not want all his service to be in vain, and if he did not also hope to gain something for all the labour of lowering the bucket so often into the well and bringing it up empty? It will often happen that he cannot so much as raise his arms to the task, or think a single good thought. For by this drawing of water I mean, of course, working with the understanding ...

It is of especial note – and I say this because I know it from experience – that the soul which begins resolutely to tread this path of mental prayer, and can manage not greatly to care about consolations and tenderness in devotion, neither rejoicing when the Lord gives them nor being discouraged when He withholds them, has already gone a large part of the way. Though it may often stumble, it need have no fear of falling back, for its building has been begun on firm foundations. The love of the Lord does not consist in tears or in these consolations and tendernesses which we so much desire and in which we find comfort, but in our serving Him in justice, fortitude, and humility. Anything else seems to me rather an act of receiving than of giving on our part.

As for a poor woman like myself, a weak and irresolute creature, it seems right that the Lord should lead me on with favours, as He now does, in order that I may bear certain afflictions with which He has been pleased to burden me. But when I hear servants of God, men of weight, learning, and understanding, worrying so much because He is not giving them devotion, it makes me sick to listen to them. I do not say that they should not accept it if God grants it to them, and value it too, for then His Majesty will see that it was good for them, but they should not be distressed when they do not receive it. They should realize that since the Lord does not give it to them they do not need it. They should exercise control over themselves and go right ahead. Let them take it from me that all this fuss is a mistake, as I have myself seen and proved. It is an imperfection in them; they are not advancing in freedom of spirit but hanging back through weakness . . .

I repeat my warning that it is most important not to raise the spirit if the Lord does not raise it for us; and if He does, we know it immediately. This straining is especially harmful to women, because the devil can delude them. I am quite certain, however, that the Lord will never allow anyone to be harmed who endeavours to approach Him with humility. On the contrary, such a person will derive great gain and advantage from the attack by which Satan intended to destroy him.

I have dwelt for so long on this way of prayer because it is the commonest with beginners and because the advice I offer is very important. I admit that it has been better expressed by others in other places, and that I have felt some shame and confusion in writing this, though not enough. Blessed be the Lord for it all, whose will and pleasure it is that a woman like myself should speak of things that are His, and of such a sublime nature . . .

[In chapters 20 and 26 Teresa describes her experience of 'rapture' and discusses its implications:]

I wish that I could explain, with God's help, the difference between union and rapture, or elevation, or flight of the spirit or transport – for they are all one. I mean that these are all different names for the same thing, which is also called ecstasy. It is much more beneficial than union, its results are much greater, and it has very many other effects as well. Union seems to be the same at the beginning, the middle, and the end, and is altogether inward. But the ends of rapture are of a much higher nature, and their effects are both inward and outward . . .

In these raptures, the soul no longer seems to animate the body; its natural heat therefore is felt to diminish and it gradually gets cold, though with a feeling of very great joy and sweetness. Here there is no possibility of resisting, as there is in union, in which we are on our own ground. Against union, resistance is almost always possible though it costs pain and effort. But rapture is, as a rule, irresistible. Before you can be warned by a thought or help yourself in any way, it comes as a quick and violent shock; you see and feel this cloud, or this powerful eagle rising and bearing you up on its wings.

You realize, I repeat, and indeed see that you are being carried away you know not where. For although this is delightful, the weakness of our nature makes us afraid at first, and we need a much more determined and courageous spirit than for the previous stages of prayer. Come what may, we must risk everything and leave ourselves in God's hands. We have to go willingly wherever we are carried, for in fact, we are being borne off whether we like it or not. In this emergency very often I should like to resist, and I exert all my strength to do so, especially at such times as I am in a public place, and very often when I am in private also, because I am afraid of delusions. Sometimes with a great struggle I have been able to do something against it. But it has been like fighting a great giant, and has left me utterly exhausted. At other times resistance has been impossible; my soul has been carried away, and usually my head as well, without my being able to prevent it; and sometimes it has affected my whole body, which has been lifted from the ground.

This has only happened rarely. Once, however, it took place when we were all together in the choir, and I was on my knees, about to take Communion. This distressed me very much, for it seemed a most extraordinary thing and likely to arouse considerable talk. So I ordered the nuns – for it happened after I was made prioress – not to speak of it. On other occasions, when I felt that the Lord was about to enrapture me again, and once in particular during a sermon – it was our patron's feast and some great ladies were present – I lay on the ground and the sisters came to hold me down, but all the same the rapture was observed. Then I earnestly beseeched the Lord to grant me no more favours if they must have outward and visible signs. For worries on this score exhausted me, and whenever He gave me these raptures I was observed. It seems that, of His goodness, He has been pleased to hear me. For I have never had them since, although it is true that this was not long ago.

It seemed to me when I tried to resist that a great force, for which I can find no comparison, was lifting me up from beneath my feet. It came with greater violence than any other spiritual experience, and left me quite shattered. Resistance requires a great struggle, and is of little use in the end when the Lord wills otherwise, for there is no power that can resist His power.

What power the soul has when the Lord raises it to a height from which it looks down on everything and is not enmeshed in it! How ashamed it is of the time when it was so enmeshed! It is indeed amazed at its own blindness, and feels pity for those who are still blind, especially if they are men of prayer to whom God is granting consolations. It longs to cry aloud and call their attention to their delusions; and sometimes it actually does so, only to bring down a storm of persecutions on its head. Particularly if the person in question is a woman, it is accused of lacking humility, and of wishing to teach those from whom it should learn. So they condemn it, and not without reason, for they know nothing of the force that impels it. At times it cannot help itself, or refrain from enlightening those whom it loves and wishes to see freed from the prison of this life. For the state in which it has once been living is neither more nor less than a prison, and this it realizes.

The soul is weary of the time when it was concerned with points of honour, and of the delusion which led it to believe that what the world calls by that name is honour at all. It sees that this is just a great lie, and that we are all taken in by it. It understands that true honour is not illusory but real; that it esteems what has value, and despises what has none. For all transitory things are as nothing or less than nothing, and are displeasing to God. The soul laughs at itself when it thinks of the time when it valued money and desired it; though, for myself, I really do not think that I ever had to confess to being covetous. It was quite bad enough that I should have given any thought to money at all. If the blessing that I now see within me could be bought with money I should set great store by it. But I know that it can only be gained by abandoning everything . . .

Whenever the Lord told me in prayer to do one thing and my confessor said something else, the Lord would speak again and tell me to obey him. Then His Majesty would change that confessor's mind, so that he would come back and tell me to do the opposite. When a number of books in Spanish were taken away from us, and we were told not to read them,[2] I felt it deeply because some of them gave me recreation and I could not go on reading them, since now I only had them in Latin. Then the Lord said to me: 'Do not be distressed, for I will give you a living book.' I could not understand why this had been said to me, for I had not yet had visions. But a very few days afterwards I understood perfectly. What I saw before me gave me so much to think about and so many subjects for recollection, and the Lord showed me such love and taught me in so many ways, that I have had very little or no need of books since. His Majesty has been a veritable book in which I have read the truth. Blessed be this book, which imprints on our minds in an unforgettable way what we must read and do . . .

[In chapter 27 Teresa offers the example of the Franciscan mystic Peter of Alcántara (who was for a time her confessor and adviser) as a model for self-denial and poverty:]

What a grand illustration God has just taken from us in the shape of the blessed friar, Peter of Alcántara. The world is not yet fit to bear such perfection. They say that people's health is poorer nowadays, and that times are not what they were. But this holy person was a man of our day, and yet he had as robust a spirit as those of the olden times, and so he trampled on the world. Now although everyone does not go about barefoot or perform such severe penances as he did, there are many ways, as I have said elsewhere, of treading the world underfoot, and the Lord teaches them to those in whom He sees courage. And what great courage His Majesty gave to this holy man, that he could perform, as is common knowledge, such severe penances for forty-six years. I should like to say something about this, for I know that it is all true.

He spoke of it to me, and to another person from whom he concealed very little. In me he confided out of love, for the Lord was pleased that he should feel love for me, and should stand up for me, and encourage me at a time when I was in great need. This I have spoken of and shall speak of again. He said, I think, that for forty years he had never slept more than an hour and a

[2] By decree of the Inquisition, 1559.

half between nightfall and morning, and that at the beginning the hardest part of his penance had been the conquering of sleep. For this reason he always remained standing or on his knees. Such sleep as he had, he took sitting down, with his head propped against a piece of wood, which he had fixed to the wall. He could not lie down to sleep even if he wished to, for his cell, as is well known, was only four and a half feet long. During all those years, however hot the sun or heavy the rain, he never wore his hood or anything on his feet. He was always clothed in a sackcloth habit with nothing between it and his skin; and this he wore as tight as he could bear it, with a cloak of the same material over it. He told me that in the bitterest cold he would take off his cloak and leave the door and window of his cell open, so as to gain some physical relief afterwards from the increased warmth, when he put it on again and closed the door. He usually ate only once in three days, and he wondered why this surprised me. He said that it was perfectly possible once one got used to it, and a companion of his told me that sometimes he would go eight days without food. This must have been when he was at prayer, for he used to have great raptures and transports of love for God, of which I was once a witness.

His poverty was extreme, and so, even in his youth, was his mortification. He told me that he had lived for three years in a house of his Order, and had not known a single friar except by his voice. For he never raised his eyes, and so when he had to go to any part of the house, he could only do so by following the other friars; it was the same thing out of doors. For many years he had never looked at a woman. He told me that it was all one to him whether he looked at things or not; but he was very old when I came to know him, and so extremely thin that he looked like nothing more than a knotted root. With all his holiness, he was very courteous, though he used very few words except when answering questions. Then he was a delight, for he had a very lively intelligence. There are many other things about him that I should like to say, but I am afraid that your Reverence will ask me what this has to do with me – I have been afraid of that even as I have been writing. So I will stop here, adding only that he died as he had lived, preaching and admonishing his friars. As he saw that his end was approaching, he recited the psalm, *I was glad when they said unto me*.[3] Then he fell on his knees and died . . .

[In chapters 32, 33 and 36 Teresa describes her belief in Hell, her determination to save Lutherans from that fate and her commitment to achieving reform within the Carmelite Order:]

One day when I was at prayer, I found myself, without knowing how, plunged, as I thought, into hell. I understood that the Lord wished me to see the place that the devils had ready for me there, and that I had earned by my sins. All this happened in the briefest second; but even if I should live for many years, I do not think I could possibly forget it. The entrance seemed to me like a very long, narrow passage, or a very low, dark, and constricted

[3] Psalm 122: 1.

furnace. The ground appeared to be covered with a filthy wet mud, which smelt abominably and contained many wicked reptiles. At the end was a cavity scooped out of the wall, like a cupboard, and I found myself closely confined in it. But the sight of all this was pleasant compared with my feelings. There is no exaggeration in what I am saying.

I do not think that my feelings could possibly be exaggerated, nor would anyone understand them. I felt a fire inside my soul, the nature of which is beyond my powers of description, and my physical tortures were intolerable. I have endured the severest bodily pains in the course of my life, the worst, so the doctors say, that it is possible to suffer and live, among them the contraction of my nerves during my paralysis, and many other agonies of various kinds, including some, as I have said, caused by the devil. But none of them was in any way comparable to the pains I felt at that time, especially when I realized that they would be endless and unceasing. But even this was nothing to my agony of soul, an oppression, a suffocation, and an affliction so agonizing, and accompanied by such a hopeless and distressing misery that no words I could find would adequately describe it. To say that it was as if my soul were being continuously torn from my body is as nothing. The fact is that I can find no means of describing that inward fire and that despair which is greater than the severest torments or pains. I could not see my torturer, but I seemed to feel myself being burnt and dismembered; and, I repeat, that interior fire and despair were the very worst of all.

In that pestilential spot, deprived of all hope of comfort, it was impossible for me to sit or lie down; there was no room to do so. I had been put in what seemed a hole in the wall, and the very walls, which are hideous to behold, pressed in on me and completely stifled me. There is no light there, only the deepest darkness. Yet, although there was no light, it was possible to see everything that brings pain to the sight; I do not know how this can be. It was not the Lord's will that I should at that time see more of hell itself; since then I have seen another vision of frightful things that are the punishment for certain vices. But although these seemed to me a much more dreadful sight, yet they alarmed me less, for then I felt no physical pain. In the first vision, however, it was the Lord's will that I really should feel these torments and afflictions of spirit, just as if my body were actually suffering them. I do not know how it was, but I quite clearly realized that this was a great favour, and that the Lord wished me to see with my very eyes the place from which His mercy had delivered me . . . I was terrified, and though this happened six years ago, I am still terrified as I write; even as I sit here my natural heat seems to be drained away by fear. I can think of no time of trial or torture when everything that we can suffer on earth has not seemed to me trifling in comparison with this . . .

It was this vision that filled me with the very deep distress which I feel on account of the great number of souls who bring damnation on themselves – of the Lutherans in particular, since they were members of the Church by baptism. It has also given me a fervent desire to help other souls . . .

I tried to think what I could do for God, and decided that the first thing was to follow the call to a religious life that the Lord had given me, by

keeping my Rule with every possible perfection. Although in the house
where I was there were many servants of God and He was well served there,
yet, because it was very poor, we nuns often left it for other places where we
could live decently and keep our vows. Moreover the Rule was not observed
there in its original strictness but, as throughout the Order, in the relaxed
form permitted by the Bull of Mitigation. There were other drawbacks too,
among them what seemed to me the excessive comfort that we enjoyed, for
the house was a large and pleasant one. Now this habit of going on visits,
though I was one who frequently indulged in it, was a serious inconvenience
to me, because many people whom my superiors could not refuse liked to
have me with them, and when I was invited they ordered me to go. Things
reached such a pitch, indeed, that I was able to be in the convent very little;
the devil must have had a hand in these frequent departures of mine, though
at the same time I would always pass on to some of the nuns what I learnt
from the people I met, and this was of great benefit to them.

One day, in conversation with myself and one or two other nuns, a certain
person[4] asked whether we were prepared to follow the practice of the
Barefoot Orders, for it would be quite possible to found a convent of
Discalced nuns.[5] I had desired something of the sort myself, and so I
discussed the idea with a companion who was of the same mind, that
widowed lady whom I have already mentioned. She began to think out ways
of finding the necessary revenue. But, as I can see now, this would not have
got us very far. For my part, however, I was very happy in the house where I
was. The place was pleasing to me, and so was my cell, which suited me
excellently; and this held me back. Nevertheless we agreed to commend the
matter most fervently to God.

One day, after Communion, the Lord earnestly commanded me to pursue
this aim with all my strength. He made me great promises; that the house
would not fail to be established, that great service would be done Him there,
that its name should be St Joseph's; that He would watch over us at one of
its doors and Our Lady at the other; that Christ would be with us; that the
convent would be a star, and that it would shed the most brilliant light . . .
He told me to convey His orders to my confessor,[6] with the request that he
should not oppose them or in any way hinder my carrying them out . . . So I
dared not do otherwise than speak to my confessor and give him a written
account of all that had taken place.

He did not venture definitely to tell me to abandon the project, though he
saw that, humanly speaking, there was no way of carrying it out, since my
companion who was to undertake it all had very small resources – indeed
almost none. He told me to discuss the matter with my director, and to do as

[4] María de Ocampo, the daughter of Teresa's cousin.
[5] The order that St Teresa founded within the Carmelite Order was called the Discalced
Carmelites in contrast to the Calced Carmelites, who followed a more relaxed discipline.
'Discalced' was the name traditionally given to those religious orders and congregations whose
members either went barefoot or wore sandals rather than shoes as a sign of their commitment
to observe a degree of asceticism.
[6] Father Balthasar Alvarez.

he advised me. I did not discuss these visions of mine with my director, but the lady who wanted to found the convent had a talk with him, and the Provincial,[7] who is a friend of the religious Orders, took the idea very well. He offered her all the necessary support, and told her that he would give the house his sanction. They discussed what income it would require, and for many reasons we decided that it must never contain more than thirteen nuns. Before we began these discussions, we had written to the blessed friar Peter of Alcántara, and told him all that was happening. He advised us to stick to our plans, and gave us his opinion on the whole subject.

Hardly had news of this begun to spread around the place than there fell upon us a persecution so severe that it would not be possible to describe it in a few words. They talked, they laughed at us, and they declared that the idea was absurd. Of me they said that I was in the right place where I was, and they subjected my companion to such a persecution that it quite wore her out. I did not know what to do, for they seemed to me partly right . . . There was hardly anyone among the prayerful, or indeed in the whole place, who was not against us, and did not consider our project absolutely absurd.

There was so much chatter and fuss in my own convent that the Provincial thought it would be difficult to oppose everybody, and so changed his mind. He now withdrew his backing, saying that the income was not assured, that in any case it would be insufficient, and that the plan was meeting with heavy opposition. In all this he seemed to be right. So he put the matter aside and refused to sanction it . . .

As the Provincial now refused to sanction the foundation, my confessor at once told me to let it drop, though the Lord knows what great labours and afflictions it had cost me to bring it so far. Once it was discontinued and abandoned, people were even more certain that it had all been an absurd feminine whimsy, and gossip at my expense increased, even though up to that time I had been acting on my Provincial's orders.

I was very unpopular throughout the convent for wanting to found a more strictly enclosed house. The nuns said that this was an insult to them; that I could serve God just as well where I was, since there were others there better than myself; that I had no love for my own house, and that I should have been better employed raising money for it than for founding another. Some said that I ought to be put in the prison-cell; but others, though only a few, came out on my side. I saw quite well that in many respects my opponents were right, and sometimes I could make allowances for them. But as I could not tell them my principal argument – that I had been obeying the Lord's commands – I did not know what to do and was therefore silent . . . It seemed to me that I had done everything in my power to fulfil the Lord's commands, and that I had now no further obligation. So I remained in my house, where I was quite content and happy, though at the same time I was never able to give up the conviction that the task would be fulfilled. How, when, and by what means this would be I could not say, but of its eventual accomplishment I was certain.

[7] Father Nicolás de Jesús María Doria, head of the unreformed Carmelite Order in Spain.

What greatly distressed me was that my confessor wrote to me on one occasion as if I had been acting against his instructions . . . In his letter he said that, as I ought to have realized by now, the whole matter was just a dream. He advised me henceforth to lead a better life, and not to attempt anything more of the kind or even to talk about it, since I now saw what a scandal I had raised. He said some other things too, all of them most painful. This distressed me more than everything else put together, for I wondered whether I had been guilty of leading others into sin, whether these visions were illusory, whether all my prayer had been a deception, and whether I was not utterly lost and deceived. These thoughts so weighed on me that I became quite upset and was plunged into the deepest affliction . . .

For five or six months I kept quiet, making no move towards it and not even speaking about it, and the Lord did not give me a single command. I could not guess the reason for this, but was unable to rid myself of the belief that the foundation would eventually take place. At the end of that time, the then Rector of the Society of Jesus having left, His Majesty replaced him by a very spiritual man of great courage, understanding, and learning,[8] just at the moment when I was in the greatest need. For the priest who was hearing my confessions was subject to a superior, and in the Company they attach great importance to the practice of never taking the slightest action except in conformity with the will of their superiors . . .

I went to see this Rector, and my confessor told me to talk to him with all freedom and frankness. I used very much to dislike speaking about these things, and yet when I entered the confessional I felt something in my spirit that I never remember having felt before or since in the presence of anyone else. I cannot possibly describe its nature, or compare it with anything at all. It was a spiritual joy; my soul recognized that here was a soul which would understand and be in harmony with mine . . . When I began to have conversations with him, I immediately recognized what type of director he was, and saw that he had a pure and holy soul, endowed with a special gift from the Lord for the discernment of spirits. This gave me great comfort. Soon after I came under his direction, the Lord began to impress on me again that I must return to the project of the convent, and explain all my reasons and intentions to my confessor, and to the Rector as well, so that they should not stand in my way. Some of the things I said frightened them, but the Rector never doubted that I was prompted by the spirit of God, for he had considered the probable results of such a foundation with very great care. In short, after hearing my many arguments, they dared not risk standing in my way.

My confessor now gave me leave to resume the project with all my might, and I clearly saw what a task I was taking on, for I was quite alone and could do very little. We agreed that things should be done with the utmost secrecy, and so I arranged that a sister of mine,[9] who lived outside the town, should buy the necessary house and furnish it as if it were for herself, with purchase

[8] The Jesuit Father Gaspar de Salazar.
[9] Doña Juana, St Teresa's married sister.

money that the Lord had provided in various ways. It would be a long story
to tell how He looked after us. I made a great point of doing nothing to
violate my obedience. But I knew that if I spoke of the project to my
superiors all would be lost, as it had been on the last occasion; and this time
things might be even worse. Getting the money, finding a house, arranging
for its purchase and furnishing it was a very trying process, a part of which I
had to carry through alone . . .

Once when I was in a difficulty and could not think what to do or how to
pay certain workmen, St Joseph, my true lord and father, appeared to me,
and told me to proceed with my arrangements, for the money would not be
lacking. So I went on, without a farthing, and the Lord did provide it in ways
that astonished all who heard of them. I thought the house very small, so
small indeed that it did not seem possible to turn it into a convent. I wanted
to buy another, but had not the means. So there was no way of buying it, and
I did not know what to do. There was a little house close to ours, however,
also very small, which would have made a chapel. But one day, after I had
taken Communion, the Lord said to me, 'I have told you already to move in
as best you can', and then added, as a sort of exclamation, 'O the greed of
humankind, to imagine that there will not be enough room for you! How
often did I sleep in the open air, having nowhere else to lay My head!' I was
amazed, and saw that He was right. So I went to survey the little house and
found that it would just do for a convent, though a very small one. I did no
more about adding to the property, but arranged to have the little house
equipped so that we could live in it. It was very rough and ready, and no
more was done to it than was necessary to make it healthy to live in. This is
always the proper way of doing things.

On St Clare's day, as I was going to Communion, that saint appeared to
me in great beauty and told me to take courage. She promised that she
would help me if I went forward with what I had begun. I conceived a great
devotion for her, and she has truly kept her word. For a convent of her
Order, which is close to ours, is at present helping to maintain us. What is
more, she has gradually brought this plan of mine to such perfection that the
same Rule of poverty which obtains in her house is also observed in ours,
and we live on alms. It was essential to get the Holy Father's approval for
our existing without any revenue, and the procuring of that cost me no small
labour. But the Lord is doing even greater things for us, and it may be at the
request of this blessed saint that He is doing them. Without any demand on
our part, His Majesty is providing most amply for our needs. May He be
blessed for it all. Amen . . .

O how great God is! I am often astounded when I reflect on this, and think
how particularly anxious His Majesty was to help me deal with the business
of this little corner of God's kingdom – for such I think it is – or of this
dwelling in which His Majesty takes His delight, as He once told me in
prayer, when He spoke of this house as the paradise of His delight. So it
seems that His Majesty has chosen the souls he has drawn to Himself, in
whose company I live in very deep shame. For I could never have asked for
better companions with whom to live this life of strict enclosure, poverty,

and prayer. They live it so joyfully and contentedly that not one of them thinks herself deserving of her place in this house; and this is especially true of some whom the Lord has called from all the show and vanity of the world, whose customs they might have followed and in which they might have been happy. But here the Lord has so multiplied their happiness that, as they clearly recognize, in exchange for one thing forsaken He has rewarded them a hundredfold, and they can never give His Majesty enough thanks. Others who were good, He has made better. To those who are young He gives fortitude and knowledge, so that they may desire nothing else and understand that to live apart from all the things of this life is to live in greater peace, even here upon earth. To those who are older and poor in health, He has given – and continues to give – strength to endure the same austerities and penances as the rest . . .

When everything had been arranged, the Lord was pleased that some of the sisters should take the habit on St Bartholomew's Day, and on that day too the Most Holy Sacrament was brought to the convent. So with full sanction and authority, this convent of our most glorious father St Joseph was founded in the year 1562. I was there myself to give the habit, with two other nuns of our own house who happened to be absent from it. As the house which thus became a convent belonged to my brother-in-law – for as I have said, it was he who purchased it in order to keep things secret – my special permission allowed me to be there. I did nothing without the approval of some learned men, so as in no way to infringe my obedience. But as they saw what a benefit this was in so many ways to the whole Order, they told me to follow my wishes, even though everything was being done in secret and was being kept from my superiors' knowledge. Had they pointed to a single imperfection in all this, I would, I believe, have willingly given up a thousand convents, let alone one. I am certain of this; for although I desired the foundation to be made in order to withdraw more completely from activities and to fulfil my profession and vocation more perfectly under conditions of greater enclosure, I desired it only in so far as I believed the Lord would not be better served by my abandoning it. If I had thought that He would, I should have given it up with complete peace and tranquillity, as I had done before.

Well, it was like heaven to me to see the Blessed Sacrament in its place, and for us to be supporting four poor orphans, who were taken without dowry and were great servants of God. It was our aim from the beginning to accept only persons whose examples would be a basis on which we could effectively develop our scheme for a community of great perfection and true prayer, and perform a work which I believed would be for God's service, and would honour the habit of His glorious Mother. This is what I yearned for. But I was greatly comforted also, to have done what the Lord had so firmly commanded me, and that there was now one more church in the town than there had been, dedicated to my glorious father, St Joseph.

7 Three Poems by Luis de León (1572–1577)

Source: *The Unknown Light: The Poems of Fray Luis de León*, edited and translated by C. Barnstone Willis (Albany: State University of New York Press, 1979), pp. 84–111.

Luis de León (1527–91) was one of the great Spanish prose writers of the sixteenth century and one of the greatest poets in that language. Educated in Salamanca, he joined the Augustinian Order and in 1561 held the theological chair at the University of Salamanca. From 1572 until 1576, he was imprisoned on a charge of alleged criticism of the Vulgate but later was exonerated. During his lifetime his poems were either circulated by hand or appeared anonymously in collections published by others. Towards the end of his life he prepared for publication an edition of his poetry which circulated privately for some forty years before publication in 1631.

A. 'On the Ascension'

Written either in 1572 or 1578, this is a meditative ode that describes Jesus Christ's ascent into heaven according to the biblical account (Luke 24: 50–2 and Acts 1: 9–11).

> Do you leave, shepherd saint,[1]
> your flock here in this valley, deep, obscure,
>   in loneliness and plaint,
>   and rise piercing the pure
> high air – to that immortal refuge sure?
>
>   Those who were formerly
> lucky are melancholy and grieving too.
>   You nourished them. Suddenly
>   they are deprived of you.
> Where can they go? What can they now turn to?
>
>   What can those eyes regard
> (which one time saw the beauty of your face)
>   that is not sadly scarred?
>   After your lips' sweet grace
> what can they hear that isn't blunt and base?
>
>   And this tumultuous sea,
> who can hold it in check? Who can abort
>   the gale's wild energy?
>   If you're a sealed report,
> then what North Star will guide our ship to port?

---

[1] An allusion to Jesus Christ at the moment of his ascension into heaven.

O cloud, you envy us
even brief joy! What pleasure do you find
   fleeing, impetuous?
   How rich and unconfined
you go! How poor you leave us and how blind!

B. 'Dwelling Place of Heaven'

Written in 1577. This ode has two alternative titles: 'From Life to Heaven', and 'On
the Heavenly Life'.

   O sweet region of light,[1]
meadows of happiness which never fail,
   neither in flaming white
   thunder or ice or hail:
the fertile soil where last rewards prevail.

   Crowned in flowering snow
and purple, the Good Shepherd moves his dear flock
   to sweet pastures that grow
   in you, and he can walk
about with no need for sling, staff or crook.[2]

   Leading the way he goes
followed by his happy sheep; these he feeds
   with the immortal rose,
   a flower that blooms and needs
only to be enjoyed to make more seeds.[3]

   And now into the mountain
of perfect goodness, leading them ahead,
   he bathes them in the fountain
   of full joy. Food is spread
by him the pastor, pasture on which we're fed.[4]

   And when the sun is at
its highest rise, it touches the round steep
   peak of its sphere. Lying flat
   and resting near his sheep,
his music to the holy ear is deep.

[1] In the Ptolemaic system, in its Christian guise, the Empyrean was the abode of God and of
the select, the stable, the incorruptible and the eternal. The Copernican system was optional at
Salamanca from 1561.

[2] The basic metaphor is of Jesus Christ the Good Shepherd.

[3] Erotic imagery possibly drawn from the Song of Songs.

[4] An explicit reference to the eucharistic sacrament: Jesus Christ is both shepherd and
pasture, feeder and fodder.

He lets the rebec sound[5]
and the immortal sweetness stabs their soul,
   hurling gold to the ground.
   Burning, they hurdle whole,
transcendent, to that free and stainless goal.

   O sound! O voice! If but
the slightest echo were to tumble down
   to my ear, my soul cut
   free from itself would drown
wholly in you, O love, and near your crown

   it[6] would know your home, thoughts,
sweet Husband;[7] liberated from the den
   of prison where it rots,
   and near your flock, it then
would never wander wrong and lost again.

C. 'To Our Lady'

Possibly written in prison, August 1572. This ode to the Virgin Mary is probably
modelled on the Petrarchan *canzone* 'Vergine bella che di sol vestita . . .' ('Beautiful
Virgin dressed in sun . . .'). It therefore draws upon both religious and courtly
traditions.

   Virgin purer than the sun,
glory of mortals, light of heavenly skies,
in whom mercy is of a sovereign height,
   toward the earth turn your eyes
and see this wretched man in awful prison,
entombed in melancholy and half light.
   And if no deeper plight
or one like mine has been known in our land
(a state I'm in because of those who reign),
   with your powerful hand
O Queen of heaven, break apart this chain.

   Virgin, upon whose breast
the deity in dignity reposed,
whose harshness became love; and unforeseen,[1]

---

[5] Medieval stringed instrument resembling the violin but having a lute-shaped body.

[6] i.e. the speaker's soul, referred to in the previous stanza.

[7] Husbandman, shepherd.

---

[1] On becoming Mother of the Redeemer (Jesus Christ), Mary became an instrument
expressing change from severe justice (Old Testament) to love and compassion (New
Testament).

if harshness you transposed
to ease, surely my heart, which is beset
   by clouds, might be serene.
   Reveal that face unseen,
desired, that heaven admires and earth adores.
The clouds will flee; the day will glitter white.
   Lady, let your rays pour
and overcome my blind and mournful night.

   Virgin and Mother one,
the happy engenderer of your Creator,
at whose breasts the flowering of life was made,
   see how the crater
of my pain increased, and now is overrun
with time. Hatred digs in and friendships fade.[2]
   If you do not give aid
to truth and justice, which were your creation,
where will they find a safe environment?
   As a Mother your station
should let you witness my abandonment.

   Virgin, clothed in the sun,
crowned with inextinguishable stars,
who walks with holy feet upon the moon;
   poison of envy's scars,
cutting deceit, false tongues in unison,
cruel hatred, lawless power with no bars
   all aim at me, make wars.
Yet against an army of murky fame,
where can a poor, unarmed person reside,
   if your most blessed name,
Mary, is not found working at my side?

   Virgin, by whom the snake
was vanquished, still mourning its bleak perdition,
its everlasting pain, its failed intent,
   from the shore, in safe condition
many people see me fall and nearly break
in violent waters, lost and almost spent.
   While some are quite content,
others are horrified. The kindest of all
wear out their voice with pity, foolishly grave.
   I lean my head, tearful,
near you, and thread my way through hostile waves.

---

[2] Fray Luis was accused of having written a Spanish translation of the Song of Songs and of being a Judaizer because he pointed out errors in Saint Jerome's Vulgate and affirmed the superiority of the Hebraic text.

Virgin, the Father's Wife,
sweet Mother of the Son, the holy shrine
of an immortal Love, the shield of man:
    I see only a line
of terror: danger if I see my life.
My escape is doubtful and my luck is wan,
    the enemy a harsh clan.
The truth is naked; lies are well supplied
with very strong supporters and with arms.
    Life is like suicide.
I breathe only when I regain your arms.

Virgin, whose sure consent[3]
to the supreme request was no less pure
than humble, whom the heavens want to see,
    like a target I endure,
my eyes blindfolded, my arms bound and bent
against the hundred arrows facing me,
    wounding me brutally.
I feel the pain but cannot see the hand;[4]
I cannot run and cannot lift my shield.
    May your sovereign Son command,
Mother of love, and free me on this field!

Virgin, beloved star,
a shining beacon on a raging sea,
whose sacred brightness silences the wind:
    a thousand waves compete
to sink an unarmed galley sailing into depths, undisciplined,
through the water. Night is heavy, gales moan,
now it dives for bottom, touches the sky,
    broken riggings groan.
Help, before it founders where cruel rocks lie!

Virgin, who is apart
from universal stain and primal sin
contaminating all the human race:
    you know my hope lies in
your hands since childhood; if evil forces start
to conquer me, if I've become too base
    to merit your good grace,
your mercy – all the more – will be revealed

---

[3] A reference to the Annunciation (Luke 1: 38).

[4] During his imprisonment, Luis complained (May 1573) that he could not defend himself effectively if he did not know who his accusers were.

to me (whose sinful life is much displayed);
    the more pain goes unhealed,
the less I'm worthy of your precious aid.

    Virgin, a profound grief
knots up my tongue, won't let my voice declare
out loud the things it wants to say or do.
    But hear my soul, it's there,
suffering, and constantly calls out to you.

8 Juan de Mariana, 'Whether it is Right to Destroy a Tyrant' (1599)

Source: Juan de Mariana, *The King and the Education of the King*, translated by G. A. Moore (Washington, DC: County Dollar Press, 1947), pp. 142–9.

Juan de Mariana (1535–1624) was one of a remarkable group of Spanish Jesuit philosophers of the late sixteenth and early seventeenth centuries who wrote on topical and controversial questions. Their political theory, deriving its inspiration from Thomas Aquinas, tended against acceptance of absolute obedience to the sovereign and towards the view that sovereignty could only rest on the consent of the people. The extract from his treatise *The King and the Education of the King* (*De Rege et Regis Institutione*), published in Latin in Toledo in 1599, and dedicated to the Spanish king, Philip III, contains one of the most provocative passages in the book, in which Mariana describes the assassin of the French king Henry III as 'an eternal honour to France'. His own Order required him to remove this phrase from later editions. After the assassination of Henry IV of France in 1610, copies of Mariana's book were publicly burned in Paris.

Such are the character and habits of a tyrant, hated equally by Heaven and men. Though he may seem very fortunate, his shameful acts become his punishment. Like bodies cut with the whip, his distorted mind and conscience are tortured by his savagery, caprice and fear. Those whom the vengeance of Heaven pursues and presses on to destruction it deprives of mind and counsel.

Many examples, both ancient and modern, are available to demonstrate how great is the strength of a multitude angered with hatred for a ruler, and that the ill will of the people results in the destruction of the prince.

Lately in France a well-known example occurred, from which it may be seen how important it is that the spirits of the people be pacified, which are ruled not exactly as their bodies – a remarkable calamity to be kept in mind. Henry III, King of France,[1] lies dead, stabbed by a monk in the intestines with a poisoned knife, a detestable spectacle and one especially to be remembered; but also by this princes are taught that impious attempts by no

---

[1] King of France (1574–89), assassinated in 1589 by a Dominican friar, Jacques Clément.

means go unpunished, and that the power of princes is weak once reverence has departed from the minds of the subjects.

Henry III was planning, since he had no heir, to leave the kingdom to Henry of Vendôme,[2] husband of his sister, although the brother-in-law from an early age had been infected with wrong ideas of religion, being at that time under an excommunication from the Roman Pontiffs and cut off from the succession by law; though now he is King of France, after a change of heart.

When the plan became known a great part of the nobles, after the matter had been talked over with the other princes, both in France and abroad, took up arms for the safety of the fatherland and for their religion; from everywhere came aid. The leader was Guise,[3] in whose manliness and family the hopes and fortunes of France in this storm were resting.

The designs and plans of kings remain constant. Henry, preparing to punish the attempts of the nobles, resolved on killing Guise, and called him to Paris. Since the plan did not go well, as the people were enraged and incited to take up arms, he quickly departed from the city, and after a short interval he pretended that he was won over to better counsels and wanted a public consultation on the common safety.

After all classes had come together at his summons, he killed at Blois on the Loire, in his palace, Guise and his brother the cardinal,[4] who felt safe in the good faith of the meeting. Nevertheless after the killing the crimes of treason were imputed to them, in order that it might seem to have been done justifiably. They were accused with no one defending them, and it was decreed that they were punished under the law of treason. He seized others, among them the Bourbon cardinal, upon whom, although in an advanced age, the next hope of ruling rested by the law of blood.

This matter stirred up the minds of a large part of France; and many cities, after having renounced Henry, publicly renewed the fight for the common safety. At the head was Paris, to which no city in Europe is comparable in resources, extent and pursuit of wisdom. But the insurrection of a people is like a torrent; it is swollen for but a short time.

As the people were quieting down, while Henry had his camp about four miles out, still looking forward to punishing the city, and though matters were almost despaired of, the audacity of one young man in a short time definitely restored them.

Jacques Clement . . . was studying theology in the Dominican college of his order. He was told by the theologians, whom he had consulted, that a tyrant may be killed legally. He then obtained letters from people in the city whom he had ascertained by investigation to be loyal to Henry privately or openly; and keeping his own counsel, he resolved to kill the king. He then went out into his camp on July 31, in the year of our Lord 1589.

---

[2] Henry, Prince of Navarre and a Protestant, heir to the French throne. After the assassination of Henry III, he was crowned Henry IV (1589–1610) and converted to Catholicism in 1593.

[3] Henry, Duke of Guise (1550–88), head of the Catholic League in France.

[4] Louis of Guise, Cardinal, brother and ally of Henry, Duke of Guise.

There was no delay. On the ground that he wished to tell secrets of the citizens to the king, he was admitted at once. After he had delivered the letters that he was carrying, he was directed to wait till the next day.

So, on the very first day of August, which is sacred to the feast of Peter the Apostle in Chains, after Clement performed the service, he was summoned by the king. He went in as the king was arising and was not yet fully dressed. They had some conversation. As he approached under colour of handing over some letter into his hands, he inflicted a deep wound above the bladder with a knife treated with poison which he was concealing in his hand – a deed of remarkable resolution and an exploit to be remembered. Grievously wounded, the king struck back at the murderer, wounding him in the eye and breast with the same knife, crying out against the traitor and king-killer.

The courtiers break in, aroused by this unusual occurrence. Though Clement is prostrate and senseless, they inflict many wounds on him in their wildness and savagery. He says nothing, rather is glad, as appears from his countenance, because with the deed accomplished he missed the other tortures which he feared would be due him. At the same time he rejoiced that by his own blood the liberty of the common fatherland and nation had been redeemed, though, alas, at the great cost of his blows and wounds.

By the death of the king he made a great name for himself. A killing was expiated by a killing, and at his hands the betrayal and death of the Duke of Guise were avenged with the royal blood.

Thus Clement died, an eternal honour to France, as it has seemed to very many, twenty-four years of age, a young man of simple temperament and not strong of body; but a greater power strengthened his normal powers and spirit.

The king breathed his last the next night, in the second hour after midnight – though he had great hope of recovery and therefore had been administered no sacraments – pronouncing these words of David: 'Behold, I was shapen in iniquity; and in sin did my mother conceive me.'[5] He would have been lucky, if he had made his latter acts correspond with his earlier life, and if he had proved himself to be such a prince as in the reign of his brother Charles he was believed to have been, when leading troops in war against traitors. This rank was his in the kingdom of Poland by the choice of the chiefs of this nation. But his character deteriorated as he grew older, and his later life blotted out the good deeds of his youth by shameful crime. After the death of his brother he was recalled to his native land and proclaimed King of France. He turned everything into a mockery; with the result that he seemed to have been raised to the pinnacle of things for no other reason than that he might crash down in greater disaster.

Thus fortune, or a mightier force, makes sport of human affairs.

There was no unanimity of opinion about the deed of the monk. While many praised him and deemed him worthy of immortality, others, eminent in their reputations for wisdom and learning, condemned him, denying that it is right for anyone on his own private authority to kill a king who has been

---

[5] Psalm 51: 5.

proclaimed by the agreement of the people and anointed and sanctified according to the custom with the holy oil, even though he be profligate in his morals and also has degenerated into tyranny. This they assert positively with many arguments and examples.

Think how great, they say, was the wickedness of Saul, the King of the Jews, in the olden times, and how dissolute was his life and morals! His mind was agitated with his evil plans, and as the punishments of his crimes drove him on he swayed along blindly in his course. After he had been disclaimed by the authority of God, the right of ruling was transferred to David, along with the mystical anointing. Nevertheless, though Saul was ruling unjustly and had slipped down into folly and crimes, his rival, David, did not dare to injure him and he was put back into power time and again. Yet David seemed to be in a position to do it legally either by making rightful claim to the dominion, or on the grounds of looking out for his own safety; while Saul, unprovoked by any wrongs, was plotting in every way to take even his life, and dogging the footsteps of the innocent man wherever he presented himself. Now, not only did David himself spare his enemy; but he slew with the sword, as impious and imprudent, the young Amalechite, who told him that he had killed Saul, at the latter's request, when he was conquered in battle and leaning on his sword, because the Amalechite had dared to injure the Prince sacred to God (for that is what the ceremony of anointing signifies).[6]

Who ever judged that the monstrousness of the Roman emperors, at the time of the birth of the Church, ought to be avenged and punished with the sword, although in hunting down the pious folk they indulged in savage tortures throughout the provinces and employed every bodily torment; but did they not rather urge that they must fight cruelty with patience and challenge evil-doing with submission, especially since Paul teaches that whoever resists a magistrate resists the will of God? And if it is unlawful to raise hands against a praetor although he is in the act of assaulting someone unjustly and inconsiderately, how much less may one assault Kings, though they have profligate morals? These God and the commonwealth have placed at the head of things, to be viewed by the subjects as divinities, as more than mortals.

Further, they who try to change princes often bring great misfortune to the state; nor is government overturned without serious disturbance, during which the instigators themselves generally are crushed. The histories are full of examples; ordinary life is replete with them.

For what did it profit the Shechemites to form a conspiracy against Abimelech with the object of avenging, as they wished it to appear, the seventy brothers, whom Abimelech impiously and monstrously killed, though he was born of an inferior mother?[7] He was led on by the evil ambition of ruling – than which there is no purer evil. The result was that all

[6] An Old Testament reference to Saul and David who, as kings of Israel, fought the Amalekites (2 Samuel 1: 15).

[7] An Old Testament reference: Abimelech became king of the Shechemites by the unlawful murder of his brothers (Judges 9).

perished at one blow, the city was completely destroyed, and the site was sowed over with salt.

And to pass over the most ancient cases, after Domitius Nero was overthrown, what did the citizens of Rome do except to bring on Otho and Vitellius, not lesser plagues to the commonwealth? So, to make the butcheries fewer their reigns were made shorter.[8]

Therefore, people conclude that the unjust prince must be accepted like the just, and that the rule of the former must be alleviated by passive obedience. The mildness of kings and leaders depends not only on their own characters but also on that of their subjects. Quite a number think that was the case when Peter was King of Castile, and that the name Cruel was commonly given him not so much through his own fault as that the intemperate nobles, greedy in every way, imposed on him the necessity of punishing wrongs and restraining their impudence.[9] But this is the way with human affairs. Unfortunately virtue is now considered as a fault; and we judge plans by their results.

Moreover, how will respect for princes (and what is government without this?) remain constant, if the people are persuaded that it is right for the subjects to punish the sins of the rulers? The tranquillity of the commonwealth will often be disturbed with pretended as well as real reasons. And when a revolt takes place every sort of calamity strikes, with one section of the populace armed against another part. If anyone does not think these evils must be avoided by every means, he would be heartless, wanting in the universal commonsense of mankind. Thus they argue who protect the interests of the tyrant.

The protectors of the people have no fewer and lesser arguments. Assuredly the republic, whence the regal power has its source, can call a king into court, when circumstances require and, if he persists in senseless conduct, it can strip him of his principate.

For the commonwealth did not transfer the rights to rule into the hands of a prince to such a degree that it has not reserved a greater power to itself; for we see that in the matters of laying taxes and making permanent laws the state has made the reservation that except with its consent no change can be made. We do not here discuss how this agreement ought to be effected. But nevertheless, only with the desire of the people are new imposts ordered and new laws made; and, what is more, the rights to rule, though hereditary, are settled by the agreement of the people on a successor.

Besides, we reflect, in all history, that whoever took the lead in killing tyrants was held in great honour. What indeed carried the name of Thrasybulus in glory to the heavens unless it was the fact that he freed his country from the oppressive domination of the Thirty Tyrants? Why should I mention Harmodius and Aristogiton? Why the two Brutuses, whose praise is most gratefully enshrined in the memory of posterity and is borne witness

[8] Here Mariana cites a number of Roman emperors (reg. AD 54–69) as historical precedents for rulers who were notorious for their unrestrained brutality.

[9] Pedro II of Castile (reg. 1349–69) and for Mariana yet another example of a tyrannical ruler.

to with the people's approval? Many conspired against Domitius Nero with luckless result, and yet without censure, but rather with the praise of all ages. Thus Gaius, a grievous and sinful monster, was killed by the conspiracy of Charea; Domitian fell by the sword of Stephen, Caracalla, by Martial's. The praetorians slew Elagabalus, a monstrosity and disgrace of the empire – his sin atoned for by his own blood.[10]

Whoever criticized the boldness of these men, and not rather considered it worthy of the highest commendations? Also, commonsense, like the voice of nature, has been put into our minds, a law sounding in our ears, by which we distinguish the honest from the base.

You may add, that a tyrant is like a beast, wild and monstrous, that throws himself in every possible direction, lays everything waste, seizes, burns, and spreads carnage and grief with tooth, nail and horn.

Would you be of the opinion that anyone who delivered the state safely at the peril of his own life ought to be ignored, or rather would you not honour him? Would you determine that all must make an armed fight against something resembling a cruel monster that is burdening the earth? And that an end to butchery would not be reached so long as he lived? If you should see your most dear mother or your wife misused in your presence, and not aid her if you were able, you would be cruel and you would incur the opprobrium of worthlessness and impiety. Would you leave to the tyrant your native land, to which you owe more than to your parents, to be harassed and disturbed at his pleasure? Out with such iniquity and depravity! Even if life, safety, fortune are imperilled, we will save our country free from danger, we will save our country from destruction.

These are the arguments of both sides; and after we have considered them carefully it will not be difficult to set forth what must be decided about the main point under discussion. Indeed in this I see that both the philosophers and theologians agree, that the Prince who seizes the state with force and arms, and with no legal right, no public, civic approval, may be killed by anyone and deprived of his life and position. Since he is a public enemy and afflicts his fatherland with every evil, since truly and in a proper sense he is clothed with the title and character of tyrant, he may be removed by any means and got rid of by as much violence as he used in seizing his power.

Thus meritoriously did Ehud, having worked himself by gifts into the favour of Eglon, King of the Moabites, stab him in the belly with a poniard and slay him; he snatched his own people from a hard slavery, by which they had been oppressed for then eighteen years.[11]

It is true that if the prince holds the power with the consent of the people or by hereditary right, his vices and licentiousness must be tolerated up to the point when he goes beyond those laws of honour and decency by which he is bound. Rulers, really, should not be lightly changed, lest we run into

[10] Further examples taken from both ancient Greek and Roman history in order to make Mariana's case the more persuasive.
[11] An Old Testament reference: Eglon, king of the Moabites who enslaved the Israelites, was slain by the Benjamite Ehud (Judges 3).

greater evils, and serious disturbances arise, as was set forth at the beginning of this discussion.

But if he is destroying the state, considers public and private fortunes as his prey, is holding the laws of the land and our holy religion in contempt, if he makes a virtue out of haughtiness, audacity, and irreverence against Heaven, one must not ignore it.

Nevertheless, careful consideration must be given to what measures should be adopted to get rid of the ruler, lest evil pile on evil, and crime is avenged with crime.

Now, if the opportunity for public meeting exists, a very quick and safe way is to deliberate about the issue in an atmosphere of public harmony, and to confirm and ratify what has developed as the common sentiment.

In this the procedure should be by the following steps: First the Prince must be warned and invited to come to his senses. If he complies, if he satisfies the commonwealth, and corrects the error of his ways, I think that it must stop there, and sharper remedies must not be attempted. If he refuses to mend his ways, and if no hope of a safe course remains, after the resolution has been announced, it will be permissible for the commonwealth to rescind his first grant of power. And since war will necessarily be stirred up, it will be in order to arrange the plans for driving him out, for providing arms, for imposing levies on the people for the expenses of the war. Also, if circumstances require, and the commonwealth is not able otherwise to protect itself, it is right, by the same law of defence and even by an authority more potent and explicit, to declare the Prince a public enemy and put him to the sword.

Let the same means be available to any individual, who, having given up the hope of escaping punishment and with disregard for his personal safety, wishes to make the attempt to aid the commonwealth.

You would ask what must be done, if the practicability of public assembly is taken away, as can often happen. There will be, truly, in my opinion at least, no change in the decision, since, when the state is crushed by the tyranny of the ruler and facility for assembly is taken away from the citizens, there would be no lack of desire to destroy the tyrant, to avenge the crimes of the ruler, now plainly seen and intolerable, and to crush his destructive attempts. And so, if the sacred fatherland is falling in ruins and its fall is attracting the public enemies into the province, I think that he who bows to the public's prayers and tries to kill the tyrant will have acted in no wise unjustly. And this is strengthened enough by those arguments against the tyrant which are put at a later place in this discussion.

So the question of fact remains, who justly may be held to be a tyrant, for the question of law is plain that it is right to kill one.

Now there is no danger that many, because of this theory, will make mad attempts against the lives of princes on the pretext that they are tyrants. For we do not leave this to the decision of any individual, or even to the judgement of many, unless the voice of the people publicly takes part, and learned and serious men are associated in the deliberation.

Human affairs would be very admirably carried on, if many men of brave heart were found in defence of the liberty of the fatherland, contemptuous of life and safety; but the desire for self-preservation, often not disposed to attempt big things, will hold back very many people.

Therefore out of so great a number of tyrants, such as existed in the ancient times, one may count only a few that have perished by the swords of their own people; in Spain, hardly more than one or two; though this may be due to the loyalty of the subjects and the mildness of the princes, who got their power with the best right and exercised it modestly and kindly.

Nevertheless it is a salutary reflection that the princes have been persuaded that if they oppress the state, if they are unbearable on account of their vices and foulness, their position is such that they can be killed not only justly but with praise and glory. Perhaps this fear will give some pause lest they deliver themselves up to be deeply corrupted by vice and flattery; it will put reins on madness.

This is the main point, that the prince should be persuaded that the authority of the commonwealth as a whole is greater than that of one man alone.

SECTION V

The Tupinamba Indians with a captive
from Jean de Léry's history of exploration in Brazil,
Historia navigationis . . . in Brasiliam (Paris 1586).

Reproduced by kind permission of the Syndics of Cambridge University Library (Vol. II, after p. 192).

SECTION V

Europe and the Wider World

The sixteenth century was an age of exploration and, in consequence, of colonial expansion as various European powers, and in particular Spain and Portugal, first discovered new continents and subsequently established colonies there.

Contact – and indeed interaction – between the culture of Christian Europe and other, non-European and non-Christian cultures was, of course, already part of the experience of pre-sixteenth century Europe: Christian Europe had long been faced with the challenge of Islamic culture, for example. Moreover, the existence of cultural diversity within 'Christian' Europe itself and the long-established tradition of travel literature generated by, amongst others, merchants and pilgrims, provided a further example of European cultural interaction prior to the discovery of the New World.

However, the encounters with other cultures which resulted from the discovery, exploration and colonization of the Americas, in particular, led to a marked increase in the range and variety of European travel literature. The traditional genre of travel literature – with its vivid descriptions of journeys by land and sea and encounters with peoples whose physiques, deportment, style of dress (or undress), social and religious customs and economies were often alien to the norms and values of the observer/author – was now subjected to a remarkable expansion with the introduction of an entirely new range of places, peoples, cultures and societies hitherto unobserved and hence unrecorded by European observers.

The development of such a literature also raised a variety of questions as sixteenth-century authors attempted to offer explanations for what they had seen or heard of these foreign locations and peoples – a set of questions whose impact and implications were often exacerbated by the attempt to incorporate this new-found knowledge within an already existing body of ideas concerning geography and anthropology inherited from classical antiquity. The attempt to integrate new and traditional perceptions of other cultures and peoples then initiated an intellectual process which, in turn, began to question the usefulness of such classical authorities.

The extracts within section V reflect both the emergence of such travel literature and the debates to which it gave rise. Four pieces

illustrate aspects of the nature of Europeans' observations of and attitudes towards one another. Three reflect the experience of travel within
Germany, Austria, Switzerland, Italy and France. The particular
motives of the authors for travel varied. Thus the extract from the
German artist Dürer's so-called *Diary* (document V.1), with its careful
itemization of expenditure, indicates the professional nature of the
author's journey to the Netherlands. By contrast the extracts from the
travel journal of the French essayist Montaigne (document V.2) and the
Itinerary of the English gentleman Fynes Moryson (document V.3)
represent the records of two travellers motivated largely by intellectual
curiosity about foreign countries and their peoples. All three accounts
are remarkable for the quality of lively observation of places, peoples
and local custom and each author shows an acute awareness of the
increasingly prominent and crucial religious divisions within Europe
and reveals his particular interest in and attitude towards such matters
as the styles of devotional practice in the regions which he visited.

Dürer, Montaigne and Moryson all also, apparently, regard the
countries that they visit as 'civilized' – even if occasionally hazardous for
purposes of travel. In marked contrast, the extract from the English poet
Spenser's dialogue *A View of the Present State of Ireland* (document V.4)
openly describes the Irish people and their culture as savage and un-
civilized. Spenser thus provides an indication of the degree of cultural
and racial prejudice which might be extended by sixteenth-century
Europeans even towards other Europeans – particularly if, as in the case
of the English and Irish, the issue at stake was not merely the recording
of travel experiences but, rather, that of the colonization of one country
and culture by another and, therefore, the wish to denigrate the subject
country's own Celtic culture.

The extracts in the second group in section V reflect European
Christian perceptions of Islamic communities living either in Spain or
in the Ottoman Empire, on the borders of Europe. Two official
documents reveal the shift which occurred over a period of some
seventy-odd years in the attitude of the Spanish Crown and its officials
towards the Moorish population (documents V.5 and V.6). Two further
extracts provide interesting insights into the social organization of the
sixteenth-century Ottoman Empire and its treatment of *its* subject
peoples. An extract from the private correspondence of the Flemish
diplomat Ogier de Busbecq (document V.7) reveals how experience of
Turkish culture caused at least one European to express admiration for
it. The account of the French geographer Nicholas de Nicolay, meanwhile, provides evidence of how (in marked contrast to Christian Spain,
it may be noted) the Muslim Ottoman Empire extended a considerable
degree of toleration towards its Jewish subjects and their communities
(document V.8).

The remaining documents in section V concentrate upon South and

North America. Document V.11 provides a rare account of the implications of the Spanish conquest of Mexico from the perspective of the Aztec people themselves. Another group of extracts, by contrast, provides an insight into the experiences of early European explorers, conquerors and colonizers of the New World. Two of these descriptive accounts originate from the earliest and most famous of the sixteenth-century explorers, the Florentine Amerigo Vespucci (document V.12) and the Genoese Christopher Columbus (document V.13), the former probably having been written after the event as a letter to his patron, but also probably drawing on notes kept at the time of the voyage; the latter being an abstract made by the Spanish missionary and reformer Bishop Bartolomé de las Casas from Columbus's own log-book. The extract from John White's account of his 1590 voyage (again relying heavily on navigational records kept at the time of the voyage itself), provides an insight into the English initiative in colonizing North Carolina (document V.10). The extracts from the *True History of the Conquest of New Spain*, written in old age by the Spanish soldier Bernal Díaz record his first-hand experience of the campaign of Spanish conquest in Mexico (document V.9).

Each of these sources reveals the markedly hazardous nature of exploration, of military conquest (both for the invaders and the indigenous population), and of attempts at colonization. In the case of the European accounts, the reader also gains an insight into the mental set of the European observers regarding the Amerindians and especially their tendency to use their own culture's values and styles of behaviour as the standard by which to judge their encounters with other races and cultures.

The theme of the later American-orientated extracts shifts in emphasis to consider some of the varieties of philosophical debate prompted by the processes of discovery and colonization of the New World and the consequent subjugation of its indigenous peoples by the Spanish. This process of blatant exploitation received theoretical support from the pen of Juan Ginés de Sepúlveda, who in his treatise of *circa* 1547 utilized Aristotle's philosophical doctrine of natural slavery in order to furnish moral arguments in support both of the Spanish colonists' treatment of their Amerindian subjects and of the forced conversion of the latter to Christianity (document V.14). By contrast, the first-hand experience of Bishop Bartolomé de las Casas and the Franciscan Gerónimo de Mendieta as missionaries to the New World enabled these writers to present in their treatises (documents V.15 and V.16) a more sympathetic case for the human rights of the Amerindians – although as Christian missionaries and clerics both writers still perceived the Amerindians' best interests to lie in their wholehearted espousal of Christianity. In a similar spirit, the Dominican theologian Francisco de Vitoria, despite his lack of first-hand experience of the

New World and the Amerindians, addressed the political and moral issues arising from Spanish imperialism (document V.17). Using his considerable familiarity with the already existing body of classically and medievally derived judicial and theological knowledge on such matters, he attempted in his lectures *On the Indians* to give an impartial and just pronouncement on the evils and benefits of conquest and colonization.

Moral and political issues were not the only intellectual challenges posed to European traditions by the encounters with the Americas. In the extract from *The Natural and Moral History of the Indies* by the Spanish missionary José de Acosta (document V.18), the reader gains an insight into the further intellectual challenge presented by the discovery itself of the New World, with its exotic flora and fauna and indigenous peoples. Once again, as in the case of Francisco de Vitoria's moral and political theorizing, one can readily appreciate the intellectual debates that arose from setting the newly discovered data against existing knowledge based upon classical and medieval European texts.

Finally an official questionnaire (document V.19), issued by the government department responsible for the affairs of the Spanish empire overseas, gives an insight into the scale and nature of the practical problems involved in the administration of far-flung and relatively unknown subject territories.

1 Dürer: On the Netherlands (1520–1521)

Source: Albrecht Dürer, Diary of his Journey to the Netherlands, 1520–1521, translated by P. Trou and edited by J. A. Goris and G. Marlier (London: Lund Humphries, 1971), pp. 56–103 abridged.

On 12 July 1520, the celebrated Nuremberg artist Albrecht Dürer (1471–1528) left his home town for the Netherlands, where he spent just under a year. Although his ostensible reason for this journey was to meet the young Emperor Charles V in order to confirm his annual pension, he also used it for business purposes, securing the sale of books of woodcuts and engravings. The original manuscript of the diary is now lost but the text survives in two copies, one in Bamberg and the other in Nuremberg.

At Antwerp I went to Jobst Plankfelt's inn, and the same evening the Fuggers' Factor, Bernhard Stecher,[1] invited me and gave us a costly meal. My wife however dined at the inn. I paid the driver 3 gold florins for bringing us three,[2] and 1 st. I paid for carrying the goods. On Saturday after the feast of St Peter in Chains my host took me to see the Burgomaster's

---

[1] Head of the Antwerp branch of the famous Augsburg family business of the Fuggers.
[2] Dürer, his wife Agnes and their maidservant Susanna.

house at Antwerp.[3] It is newly built and beyond measure large, and very well ordered, with spacious and exceedingly beautiful chambers, a tower splendidly ornamented, a very large garden – altogether a noble house, the 𝒳 like of which I have nowhere seen in all Germany. The house also is reached from both sides by a very long street, which has been quite newly built according to the Burgomaster's liking and at his charges.

I paid 3 st. to the messenger, 2 pf. for bread, 2 pf. for ink. On Sunday, it was St Oswald's day, the painters invited me to the hall of their guild, with my wife and maid. All their service was of silver, and they had other splendid ornaments and very costly meats. All their wives also were there. And as I was being led to the table the company stood on both sides as if they were leading some great lord. And there were amongst them men of very high position, who all behaved most respectfully towards me with deep courtesy, and promised to do everything in their power agreeable to me that they knew of. And as I was sitting there in such honour the Syndic of Antwerp came, with two servants, and presented me with four cans of wine in the name of the Town Councillors of Antwerp, and they had bidden him say that they wished thereby to show their respect for me and to assure me of their good will. Wherefore I returned them my humble thanks and offered my humble service. After that came Master Peeter, the town-carpenter, and presented me with two cans of wine, with the offer of his willing services. So when we had spent a long and merry time together till late in the night, they accompanied us home with lanterns in great honour. And they begged me to be ever assured and confident of their good will, and promised that in whatever I did they would be all-helpful to me. So I thanked them and laid me down to sleep . . .

My host took me to the workshop in the Painters' warehouse at Antwerp, where they are making the Triumphal way through which King Charles is to make his entry.[4] It is four hundred arches long, and each arch is 40 feet wide. They are to be set up along both sides of the street, handsomely ordered and two storeys high. The plays are to be acted on them. It will cost the Painters and Joiners altogether 4,000 florins . . . , and the whole work is very splendidly done . . .

The Church of Our Lady at Antwerp is so very large that many masses are sung in it at one time without interfering with each other. The altars have wealthy endowments, and the best musicians are employed that can be had. The church has many devout services, much stonework, and in particular a beautiful tower. I have also been into the rich Abbey of St Michael. There are, in the choir there, splendid stalls of sculptured stonework. But at Antwerp they spare no cost on such things, for there is money enough . . .

On the Sunday after Our Dear Lady's Assumption I saw the great Procession from the Church of Our Lady at Antwerp, when the whole town of every craft and rank was assembled, each dressed in his best according to

---

[3] The Prinsenhof in Prinsestraat, built for the Burgomaster Aert van Liere (d. 1529).
[4] The newly crowned Holy Roman Emperor Charles V made his entrance into Antwerp on 23 September 1520.

his rank. And all ranks and guilds had their signs, by which they might be known. In the intervals great costly pole-candles were borne, and their long old Frankish trumpets of silver. There were also in the German fashion many pipers and drummers. All the instruments were loudly and noisily blown and beaten. I saw the Procession pass along the street, the people being arranged in rows, each man some distance from his neighbour, but the rows close one behind another. There were the Goldsmiths, the Painters, the Masons, the Broderers, the Sculptors, the Joiners, the Carpenters, the Sailors, the Fishermen, the Butchers, the Leatherers, the Clothmakers, the Bakers, the Tailors, the Cordwainers – indeed workmen of all kinds, and many craftsmen and dealers who work for their livelihood. Likewise the shopkeepers and merchants and their assistants of all kinds were there. After these came the shooters with guns, bows, and cross-bows and the horsemen and foot-soldiers also. Then followed the watch of the Lords Magistrates. Then came a fine troop all in red, nobly and splendidly clad. Before them however went all the religious Orders and the members of some foundations very devoutly, all in their different robes. A very large company of widows also took part in this procession. They support themselves with their own hands and observe a special rule. They were all dressed from head to foot in white linen garments, made expressly for the occasion, very sorrowful to see. Among them I saw some very stately persons. Last of all came the Chapter of Our Lady's Church with all their clergy, scholars, and treasurers. Twenty persons bore the image of the Virgin Mary with the Lord Jesus, adorned in the costliest manner, to the honour of the Lord God. In this Procession very many delightful things were shown, most splendidly got up. Waggons were drawn along with masques upon ships and other structures. Behind them came the company of the Prophets in their order and scenes from the New Testament, such as the Annunciation, the Three Holy Kings riding on great camels and on other rare beasts, very well arranged; also how Our Lady fled to Egypt – very devout – and many other things, which for shortness I omit. At the end came a great Dragon which St Margaret and her maidens led by a girdle; she was especially beautiful. Behind her came St George with his squire, a very goodly knight in armour. In this host also rode boys and maidens most finely and splendidly dressed in the costumes of many lands, representing various Saints. From beginning to end the Procession lasted more than two hours before it was gone past our house. And so many things were there that I could never write them all in a book, so I let it well alone . . .

I owe my host 7 fl. 20 st. 1 Heller – that was on Sunday before Bartholomew's. For sitting-room and bedroom and bedding I am to pay him 11 fl. a month. I came to a new agreement with my host on the 20th day of August – it was on Monday before Bartholomew's. I am to eat with him and to pay 2 st. for the meal and extra for what is drunk. My wife however and the maid can cook and eat up here . . .

On Sunday after Bartholomew's I travelled with Herr Tomasin from Antwerp to Mechlin, where we lay for the night . . . From Mechlin we passed through the little town [of] Vilvorde and came to Brussels on

Monday at midday ... At Brussels is a very splendid Townhall, large, and covered with beautiful carved stonework, and it has a noble, open tower ... I saw the things which have been brought to the King from the new land of gold,[5] a sun all of gold a whole fathom broad, and a moon all of silver of the same size, also two rooms full of the armour of the people there, and all manner of wondrous weapons of theirs, harness and darts, very strange clothing, beds, and all kinds of wonderful objects of human use, much better worth seeing than prodigies. These things were all so precious that they are ⟨᙭⟩ valued at 100,000 florins. All the days of my life I have seen nothing that rejoiced my heart so much as these things, for I saw amongst them wonderful works of art, and I marvelled at the subtle Ingenia of men in foreign lands. Indeed I cannot express all that I thought there ...

So then on Sunday after St Giles' day I travelled with Herr Tomasin to Mechlin ... and early on Monday I started away from the town and travelled to Antwerp.

I dined early with the Portuguese. He gave me three pieces of porcelain and Rodrigo gave me some Calicut feathers. I have spent 1 fl. and paid the messenger 2 st. I bought Susanna a mantle for 2 fl. 10 st. My wife paid 4 fl. Rhenish for a wash-tub, a bellows, a bowl, her slippers, fire-wood, knee-hose, a parrot-cage, two jugs, and 'trinkgelds' [tips]. She has spent besides for eating, drinking, and other necessaries 21 st.

I have paid 1 st. for the printed 'Entry into Antwerp'[6] telling how the King was received with a splendid triumph – the gates very costly adorned – and with plays, great joy, and graceful maidens whose like I have seldom seen. I changed 1 fl. for expenses. I saw at Antwerp the bones of the giant.[7] His leg above the knee is 5 1/2 ft. long and beyond measure heavy and very thick, so with his shoulder blades – a single one is broader than a strong man's back – and his other limbs. The man was 18 ft. high, had ruled at Antwerp and done wondrous great feats, as is more fully written about him in an old book, which the Lords of the Town possess ...

On Friday before Whitsunday in the year 1521, came tidings to me at Antwerp, that Martin Luther had been so treacherously taken prisoner ... And whether he yet lives I know not, or whether they have put him to death; if so, he has suffered for the truth of Christ and because he rebuked the unchristian Papacy, which strives with its heavy load of human laws against the redemption of Christ ... Call together again the sheep of Thy pasture, who are still in part found in the Roman Church, and with them also the Indians, Muscovites, Russians, and Greeks, who have been scattered by the oppression and avarice of the Pope and by false appearance of holiness. Oh God, redeem Thy poor people constrained by heavy bann and edict, which it nowise willingly obeys, continually to sin against its conscience if it disobeys them. Never, oh God, hast Thou so horribly burdened a people

---

[5] Mexico.

[6] A printed programme of the Triumphal Entry of Charles V composed by the Antwerp humanist Peter Gillis.

[7] The bones of the legendary giant Druon Antigon.

with human laws as us poor folk under the Roman chair, who daily long to be free Christians, ransomed by Thy blood ... We pray Thee, oh heavenly Father, that Thou wouldst again give Thy Holy Spirit to one, that he may gather anew everywhere together Thy Holy Christian Church, that we may again live free and in Christian manner, and so, by our good works, all unbelievers, as Turks, Heathen, and Calicuts, may of themselves turn to us and embrace the Christian faith ... Every man who reads Martin Luther's books may see how clear and transparent is his doctrine, because he sets forth the holy Gospel. Wherefore his books are to be held in great honour and not to be burnt; unless indeed his adversaries, who ever strive against the truth and would make gods out of men, were also cast into the fire, they and all their opinions with them, and afterwards a new edition of Luther's works were prepared. Oh God, if Luther be dead, who will henceforth expound to us the holy Gospel with such clearness? What, oh God, might he not still have written for us in ten or twenty years! Oh all ye pious Christian men, help me deeply to bewail this man, inspired of God, and to pray Him yet again to send us an enlightened man. Oh Erasmus of Rotterdam, where wilt thou stop? Behold how the wicked tyranny of worldly power, the might of darkness, prevails.

2 Montaigne: Travel Journal (1580–1581)

Source: *The Complete Works of Montaigne*, translated by D. M. Frame (London: Hamish Hamilton, 1958), pp. 890–962 abridged.

In June 1580, the French essayist Michel de Montaigne (1533–92) set out on a trip to Rome accompanied by his brother and several friends. This expedition lasted some eighteen months (22 June 1580 to 30 November 1581) and was made both for pleasure and for health since Montaigne suffered from kidney stones and hoped to obtain relief from the mineral baths of the countries that he visited. Not intended for publication, the original manuscript remained undiscovered until 1770; it was later published in Paris (1774). The following extracts from Montaigne's travel journal begin as Montaigne's secretary's record but continue as an autograph account.

Sunday [9 October 1580] after dinner we left Constance, and after crossing the lake one league away from the town, we came to sleep at Markdorf, two leagues, which is a little Catholic town, and we stayed at the Cologne, the posthouse which is situated here for the Emperor, for the trip from Italy into Germany.[1] Here, as in several other places, they fill the mattresses with leaves from a certain tree, which serve the purpose better than straw and last longer. It is a town surrounded by a vast region of vineyards, where very good wines are produced.

---

[1] A reference to the Holy Roman Emperor.

On Monday, October 10th, we left after breakfast; for Monsieur de
Montaigne was lured by the fine day to change his plan of going to
Ravensburg that day, and turned aside a day's journey to go to Lindau.
Monsieur de Montaigne never ate breakfast; but they would bring him a
piece of dry bread that he ate on the way, and this was sometimes helped
down by the grapes he found; for the vintage was still under way in that
region and the country was full of vines, especially around Lindau. They
raise them from the ground on trellises and thus leave a quantity of fine
roads surrounded by verdure, which are very beautiful. We passed a town
named Buchhorn,[2] which is Imperial and Catholic, on the shore of the Lake
of Constance, into which town all the merchandise from Ulm, Nuremberg,
and elsewhere is brought in wagons, and beyond there they take the Rhine
route across the lake. We arrived about three o'clock in the afternoon at
Lindau, three leagues, a small town situated a hundred paces into the lake,
which hundred paces you pass over a stone bridge; there is only this
entrance, all the rest of the town being surrounded by this lake . . .

Both religions are practised. We went to see the Catholic church, built in
the year 866 and preserved in its entirety; and we also saw the church used
by the [Protestant] ministers. All the Imperial towns are free to choose their
religion, Catholic or Lutheran, according to the wish of the inhabitants.
They attach themselves more or less to the one they favour. At Lindau there
are only two or three Catholics, from what the priest told Monsieur de
Montaigne. The priests do not fail for all that to receive their revenues freely
and to perform their service, as do also some nuns who are here. The said
sieur de Montaigne also spoke to the minister, from whom he did not learn
much of anything except that they feel the usual hatred of Zwingli and
Calvin. They say that in truth there are few towns that do not have
something particular in their belief; and under the authority of Martin
[Luther] whom they accept as their chief, they get up many disputes over the
interpretation of the meaning of Martin's writings . . .

Monsieur de Montaigne found three things lacking in his travels: one,
that he had not brought along a cook to instruct in their ways so that some
day the cook could try them at home; another, that he had not brought along
a German valet or sought the company of some gentleman of the country –
for to live at the mercy of some poor blockhead of a guide he found to be a
great inconvenience; the third, that before making the trip he had not looked
into the books that might have informed him about the rare and remarkable
things in each place, or that he did not have a Münster[3] or some other such
book in his coffers . . .

. . . [15–19 October] and came to Augsburg, four leagues, which is considered the most beautiful town in Germany, as Strasbourg is considered
the strongest.

The first thing we noticed on our arrival was a strange arrangement, and

[2] Now Friedrichshafen.
[3] Montaigne owned a copy of Sebastian Münster's *Cosmographie universelle* (Basel, 1554), an
important general geography of the world which appeared in numerous editions and six
languages.

one that shows their cleanliness: the steps of the staircase of our inn all covered with linen, on which we had to walk, so as not to dirty the steps, which they had just washed and scoured, as they do every Saturday. We have never noticed any cobwebs or mud in their inns. In some there are curtains for those who want to draw them over the windows.

There are hardly any tables in the bedrooms, except those that they attach to the foot of each bed, which hang there by hinges and may be raised or lowered as you wish. The footboards of the beds rise two or three feet above the frames, and often to the level of the headboard; the wood in them is very handsome and elaborately carved; but our walnut much surpasses their pine. Also they served here very shiny pewter plates underneath the wooden ones, out of disdain. They often hang against the wall, beside the beds, linen and curtains, so that people may not dirty their wall by spitting.

The Germans are much in love with coats of arms; for in all the inns there are thousands that the gentlemen of the country passing through leave on the walls, and all their windows are furnished with them.

The order of the courses is often changed. Here crayfish were served up first – which everywhere else are served just before the end – and of unusual size. In many hostelries, big ones, they serve everything covered. What makes their panes shine so much is that they have no windows fixed in our style, and that their frames can be taken out when they want, and they furbish their glasswork very often.

The next morning, which was Sunday, Monsieur de Montaigne went to see several churches; and in the Catholic ones, which are in great number, he found the service everywhere very well done. There are six Lutheran churches and sixteen ministers; two of the six are usurped from the Catholic churches, the other four they have built. He saw one this morning which resembles a great college hall: neither images, nor organs, nor crosses. The wall loaded with lots of writings in German, passages from the Bible; two pulpits, one for the minister – and there was one preaching then – and another below where the man is who leads the singing of the psalms. At each verse they wait for him to give the pitch for the following one; they sing pell-mell, whoever wishes, and whoever wishes remains covered. After that a minister who was in the crowd went up to the altar, where he read a lot of prayers out of a book; and at certain prayers the people rose and clasped their hands, and at the name of Jesus Christ made a low bow. After he had finished reading, uncovered, he turned to the altar, on which there was a napkin, a ewer, and a saucer with water in it; a woman, followed by ten or twelve other women, presented to him a child in swaddling clothes, its face uncovered. Three times the minister took water from this saucer with his fingers and sprinkled it over the child's face, saying certain words. This done, two men approached, and each of them put two fingers of his right hand on this child; the minister spoke to them, and it was done. Monsieur de Montaigne spoke to this minister on his way out. They receive no revenue from the churches; the Senate pays them publicly. There was much more of a crowd in this church alone than in two or three of the Catholic churches together.

We did not see one beautiful woman. Their clothes are very different from one another's. Among the men it is hard to distinguish the nobles, for their velvet bonnets are worn by all kinds of people, and everyone wears a sword at his side.

We were lodged at the sign of a tree called *Linden* in this country, next to the palace of the Fuggers.[4] One of this family, dying a few years ago, left two solid millions of French crowns to his heirs; and these heirs, to pray for his soul, gave the Jesuits here thirty thousand florins in ready money, with which they have set themselves up very well. The said house of the Fuggers is roofed with copper. In general the houses are much more beautiful, big, and tall than in any city of France, the streets much wider. Monsieur de Montaigne estimates the city to be of the size of Orléans . . .

Marriages between Catholics and Lutherans are common, and the more eager party submits to the laws of the other. There are a thousand such marriages; our landlord was Catholic, his wife Lutheran . . .

Monsieur de Montaigne said that all his life he had distrusted other people's judgement on the matter of the conveniences of foreign countries, since every man's taste is governed by the ordering of his habit and the usage of his village; and he had taken very little account of the information that travellers gave him; but in this spot he wondered even more at their stupidity, for he had heard, and especially on this trip, that the passes of the Alps in this region were full of difficulties, the manners of the people uncouth, roads inaccessible, lodgings primitive, the air insufferable. As for the air, he thanked God that he had found it so mild, for it inclined rather toward too much heat than too much cold; and in all this trip up to that time we had had only three days of cold and about an hour of rain. But that for the rest, if he had to take his daughter, who is only eight, for a walk, he would as soon do so on this road as on any path in his garden. And as for the inns, he had never seen a country where they were so plentifully distributed and so handsome, for he had always lodged in handsome towns well furnished with victuals and wine, and more reasonably than elsewhere . . .

I truly believe that if Monsieur de Montaigne had been alone with his own attendants he would rather have gone to Cracow or toward Greece by land than make the turn toward Italy; but the pleasure he took in visiting unknown countries, which he found so sweet as to make him forget the weakness of his age and of his health, he could not impress on any of his party, and everyone asked only to return home. Whereas he was accustomed to say that after spending a restless night, he would get up with desire and alacrity in the morning when he remembered that he had a new town or region to see. I never saw him less tired or complaining less of his pains; for his mind was so intent on what he encountered, both on the road and at his lodgings, and he was so eager on all occasions to talk to strangers, that I think this took his mind off his ailment.

If someone complained to him that he often led his party, by various roads and regions, back very close to where he had started (which he was likely to

---

[4] The wealthy Augsburg banking family.

do, either because he had been told about something worth seeing, or because he had changed his mind according to the occasions), he would answer that as for him, he was not going anywhere except where he happened to be, and that he could not miss or go off his path, since he had no plan but to travel in unknown places; and that provided he did not fall back upon the same route or see the same place twice, he was not failing to carry out his plan . . .

Through this sort of country we arrived at about eight in the evening on the last day of November, the feast of Saint Andrew, at the Porta del Popolo, in Rome, thirty miles. Here they made some difficulties for us, as elsewhere, because of the plague at Genoa . . .

On Christmas Day we went to hear the Pope's Mass at Saint Peter's, where Monsieur de Montaigne had a convenient place for seeing all the ceremonies at his ease. There are several particular forms: the Gospel and the Epistle are said first in Latin and then in Greek, as is also done on Easter Day and Saint Peter's Day. The Pope[5] gave Communion to several others, and with him at this service there officiated the cardinals Farnese, Medici, Caraffa, and Gonzaga. There is a certain instrument for drinking from the chalice, in order to provide safety from poison. It seemed novel to him, both at this Mass and others, that the Pope and cardinals and other prelates are seated, and, almost all through the Mass, covered, chatting and talking together. These ceremonies seem to be more magnificent than devout . . .

On the third day of January, 1581, the Pope passed in front of our window. In front of him walked about two hundred horses bearing persons of his court of one or the other robe.[6] Beside him was the Cardinal de' Medici, who was conversing with him covered and was taking him to dine with him. The Pope had on a red hat, his white apparel and red velvet hood, as usual, and was mounted on a white hackney harnessed with red velvet with gold fringes and lace. He mounts on horseback without the help of a groom, and yet is in his eighty-first year. Every fifteen steps he gave his benediction. After him came three cardinals, and then about a hundred men-at-arms, lance on thigh, in full armour except for the head. There was also another hackney with the same trappings, a mule, a handsome white charger, and a litter following him, and two robe bearers who carried valises at their saddlebow.

That same day Monsieur de Montaigne took some turpentine, without any reason except that he had a cold, and afterward he passed a lot of gravel.

On January 11th, in the morning, as Monsieur de Montaigne was leaving the house on horseback to go to the bankers', it happened that they were taking out of prison Catena, a famous robber and bandit captain who had kept all Italy in fear and to whom some monstrous murders were ascribed, especially those of two Capuchins whom he had made to deny God, promising on that condition to save their lives, and then massacred without any reason either of advantage or of vengeance. Monsieur de Montaigne

---

[5] Gregory XIII (1502–85; Pope 1572), until his death a strong adversary of Protestantism.
[6] Churchmen or laymen.

stopped to see this spectacle. Besides the formalities used in France, they carry in front of the criminal a big crucifix covered with a black curtain, and on foot go a large number of men dressed and masked in linen, who, they say, are gentlemen and other prominent people of Rome who devote themselves to this service of accompanying criminals led to execution and the bodies of the dead; and there is a brotherhood of them. There are two of these, or monks dressed and masked in the same way, who attend the criminal on the cart and preach to him; and one of them continually holds before his face a picture on which is the portrait of Our Lord, and has him kiss it incessantly; this makes it impossible to see the criminal's face from the street. At the gallows, which is a beam between two supports, they still kept this picture against his face until he was launched. He made an ordinary death, without movement or word; he was a dark man of thirty or thereabouts.

After he was strangled, they cut him into four quarters. They hardly ever kill men except by a simple death, and exercise their severity after death. Monsieur de Montaigne here remarked what he has said elsewhere, how much the people are frightened by the rigours exercised on dead bodies; for these people, who had appeared to feel nothing at seeing him strangled, at every blow that was given to cut him up cried out in a piteous voice. As soon as a criminal is dead, one or several Jesuits or others get up on some high spot and shout to the people, one in this direction, the other in that, and preach to them to make them take in this example . . .

On January 28th Monsieur de Montaigne had the colic, which did not keep him from any of his ordinary actions, and passed a rather biggish stone and other smaller ones.

On the 30th he went to see the most ancient religious ceremony there is among men, and watched it very attentively and with great profit: that is, the circumcision of the Jews.

He had already seen their synagogue at another time, one Saturday morning, and their prayers, in which they sing without order, as in the Calvinist churches, certain lessons from the Bible in Hebrew, that are suited to the occasion. They sing the same songs, but with extreme discord, because they do not keep time and because of the confusion of so many voices of every sort of age; for the children, even the very youngest, take part, and all without exception understand Hebrew. They pay no more attention to their prayers than we do to ours, talking of other affairs in the midst of them and not bringing much reverence to their mysteries. They wash their hands on coming in, and in that place it is an execrable thing to doff one's hat; but they bow the head and knees where their devotions ordain it. They wear over their shoulders or on their head a sort of cloth with fringes attached: the whole thing would be too long to describe. After dinner their doctors each in turn give a lesson on the Bible passage for that day, doing it in Italian. After the lesson some other doctor present selects some one of the hearers, and sometimes two or three in succession, to argue with the reader about what he has said. The one we heard seemed to him to argue with great eloquence and wit.

But as for the circumcision, it is done in private houses, in the most convenient and lightest room in the boy's house. Where he was, because the house was inconvenient, the ceremony was performed at the entrance door. They give the boys a godfather and a godmother, as we do; the father names the child . . . On the table where this godfather is seated there is also a great preparation of all the instruments necessary for this operation. Besides that, a man holds in his hands a phial full of wine and a glass. There is also a brazier on the ground, at which brazier this minister first warms his hands, and then, finding this child all stripped, as the godfather holds him on his lap with his head toward him, he takes his member and with one hand pulls back toward himself the skin that is over it, with the other pushing the glans and the member within. To the end of this skin which he holds towards the said glans he applies a silver instrument which stops the said skin there and keeps the cutting edge from injuring the glans and the flesh. After that, with a knife he cuts off this skin, which they immediately bury in some earth which is there in a basin among the other preparations for this mystery. After that the minister with his bare nails plucks up also some other particle of skin which is on this glans and tears it off by force and pushes the skin back beyond the glans. It seems there is much effort and pain in this; however, they find no danger in it, and the wound is always cured in four or five days. The boy's outcry is like that of ours when they are baptized . . .

[Hereafter Montaigne continues the journal himself.]

On Maundy Thursday in the morning, the Pope, in full pontificals, takes his stand on the first portico of Saint Peter's, on the second storey, attended by the cardinals, himself holding a torch in his hand. There, on one side, a canon of Saint Peter's reads aloud a Latin bull by which are excommunicated an infinite variety of people, among others the Huguenots, under that very name, and all the princes who have appropriated some part of the territories of the Church; at which articles the cardinals de' Medici and Caraffa, who were next to the Pope, laughed very hard . . .

On these days they show the Veronica, which is a disfigured face, of a dark and sombre colour, in a square frame like a big mirror.[7] It is shown with great ceremony from the height of a pulpit five or six paces wide. The hands of the priest who holds it are clad in red gloves, and there are two or three other priests who support him. There is nothing viewed with such great reverence as this, the people prostrate on the ground, most of them with tears in their eyes, with cries of commiseration. A woman who they said was possessed of a spirit became frantic on seeing this face, screamed, stretched out and twisted her arms. These priests, walking around this pulpit, display the image to the people, now this way, now that; and at every movement the people to whom it is presented cry out.

They also show at the same time and with the same ceremony the lance-head in a crystal bottle. Several times on this day this exhibition takes place,

---

[7] The cloth with which it is believed St Veronica wiped the face of Jesus on his way to the Crucifixion and which is reputed to have retained the imprint of his face.

with an assemblage of people so huge that even very far outside the church, as far as this pulpit can be seen, there is a tremendous crush of men and women.

It is a true papal court: the pomp of Rome, and its principal grandeur, lies in displays of devotion. It is fine to see the ardour for religion of so innumerable a people on these days.

They have a hundred brotherhoods and more, and there is hardly a man of quality who is not attached to some one of these; there are some for foreigners. Our kings belong to that of the Gonfalon. These private societies perform many acts of religious fellowship, which are principally practised in Lent; but on this day they walk in companies, dressed in linen; each company has its fashion, white, red, blue, green, or black; most of them have their faces covered.

The noblest and most magnificent thing I have seen here or elsewhere is the incredible number of people scattered throughout the city on this day at their devotions, and especially in these companies. For besides a large number of others that we had seen by day and who had come to Saint Peter's, as night began this city seemed to be all on fire: these companies marching in order toward Saint Peter's, each man carrying a torch, and almost all these of white wax. I think there passed before me twelve thousand torches at the least; for from eight in the evening until midnight the street was always full of this procession, conducted in such good and measured order that although there were various companies and parties, starting from various places, there was never a breach or interruption to be seen; each body having a large choir of music, always singing as they went, and in the centre of the ranks a file of Penitents, who scourge themselves with ropes; there were five hundred of them at least, their backs all flayed and bleeding in a piteous fashion ...

I used to say about the advantages of Rome, among other things, that it is the most universal city in the world, a place where strangeness and differences of nationality are considered least; for by its nature it is a city pieced together out of foreigners; everyone is as if at home. Its ruler embraces all Christendom with his authority; his princely jurisdiction is binding on foreigners in their own homes just as here. At his own election and that of all the princes and grandees of his court the consideration of their origin has no weight. The freedom of the government of Venice, and the advantages of its trade, people it with foreigners; but they are nevertheless as if at someone else's house. Here they hold their own offices, property, and responsibilities; for it is the seat of ecclesiastics. You see as many or more foreigners in Venice (for the influx of foreigners you see in France, in Germany, or elsewhere, does not come into comparison with the number here), but of resident, domiciled foreigners, far fewer. The common people are no more dismayed at our fashion in dress, or the Spanish or German fashion, than at their own; and you hardly see a beggar who does not ask alms of us in our own language.

I therefore sought, and employed all my five natural senses, to obtain the title of Roman citizen, were it only for the ancient honour and the religious memory of its authority. I found some difficulty in this; however, I surmounted it without any Frenchman's favour or even knowledge. The authority of the Pope was employed in it through the medium of Filippo Musotti,[8] his majordomo, who had taken a singular liking to me and went to great pains for this. And letters-patent were dispatched to me on 'the 3rd day before the Ides of March, 1581', which were delivered to me on the 5th of April, very authentic, in the same form and favourable terms as were used for the lord Giacomo Buoncompagno, duke of Sora, son of the Pope. It is a vain title; but at all events I received much pleasure in having obtained it.

3 Fynes Moryson, *An Itinerary* (1591–1597)

Source: Fynes Moryson, *An Itinerary* (Glasgow: James MacLehose & Sons, 1907), I, xxi–429, abridged; spelling modernized by A. Laurence.

Fynes Moryson (1566–1629) was an Englishman who travelled extensively throughout Europe and the Middle and Near East between 1591 and 1597. The work was originally written in Latin but first published in English (London, 1617).

Again, for the work in general, I profess not to write it to any curious wits, who can endure nothing but extractions and quintessences: nor yet to great statesmen, of whose reading I confess it is unworthy: but only into the inexperienced, who shall desire to view foreign kingdoms. And these may, the rather by this direction, make better use of what they see, hear, and read, than myself did . . .

1591. AT LAST, in the beginning of the year 1591, and upon the first day of May, I took ship at Leigh, distant from London twenty-eight miles by land, and thirty-six by water, where Thames in a large bed is carried into the sea
. . .

The next day [the eleventh day] we passed four miles to Wittenburg, which hath his name of Wittekindus, the first Christian Duke of Saxony, and is seated in a plain sandy ground, having on the north hills planted with vines yielding a sour grape plentifully; yet they make no wine thereof. One street lies the whole length of the town, being all the beauty thereof, and in the midst of this street is the cathedral church and a fair market place, in which the Senate house is built, and near the west gate is the duke's church; it is proverbially said that a man shall meet nothing at Wittenburg, but whores, students, and swine . . . In the study of Dr Wisinbechius this inscription is in Latin;

---

[8] Alessandro (not Filippo) Musotti, the current prefect of the Vatican.

HERE STOOD THE BED IN WHICH LUTHER GENTLY DIED

See how much they attribute to Luther, for this is not the place where he died, neither was there any bed, yet suffer they not the least memory of him to be blotted out ... Yet from his sudden death the malicious Jesuits took occasion to slander him, as if he died drunken; that by aspersions on his life and death, they might slander the reformation of religion which he first began ...

Being to take my journey to Prague, in the end of the year 1591 (after the English account, who began the year upon the twenty five of March[1]), I returned again to Dresden; from whence I wrote this letter concerning my journey, to a friend living at Leipzig.

'Honest M., know that after I parted from you at Torg [Torgau], by good hap, and beside my expectation, I lit upon a coach going to Dresden ... Will you know the companions of my journey? I was alone among a coach full of women, and those of the Elector's Duchess's chamber forsooth,[2] which you would have said to have been of the black guard. It was a comedy for me to hear their discourse; now declaiming against Calvinists, now brawling together, now mutually with tears bewailing their hard fortunes: and they fell into all these changes, while the wind blew from one and the same quarter. Is anything lighter than a woman? and lest the flock of geese should want matter, sometimes they charged me to be a Calvinist, sometimes a Jew; and I answered merrily, that if any of them were but a consul's wife, I would satisfy them for my religion.

'At eight o'clock in the night, the horses being spent, my self wearied, and only their tongues untired, we came to a village called Derwaldhan, where we should lodge. We entered a kind of barn, myself not without sighs. Lipsius[3] should here have had no cause to complain of stinking beer, brown bread, and often shaking hands. No man returned salutation to us: the women my companions, drew out victuals they had brought to eat, I being fasting to that hour, with great fear and trembling of heart, expected that at least they would give me some raw bacon, or dried puddings. But they thought nothing less. At last I desired an egg or two for my supper. The servant answered that the old woman was in bed, and that he knew not the mystery, whether any eggs were in the house or no ... To be brief, the women took compassion on me, and I without blushing was content to eat of free cost, and made them know that I was no Jew, for I made no religion to eat what was before me.

'The next morning before the day-star arose, I was walking in a meadow, what do you bless yourself with a cross? Sure I am no less sleepy than I was,

---

[1] In the Middle Ages, in many European countries, the year began on 25 March for legal and official purposes.

[2] Refers to the wife of the Elector of Saxony (one of the seven German princes entitled to vote for the Holy Roman Emperor).

[3] The Latinized name for the Flemish scholar Joest Lips (1547–1606).

but he is soon apparelled that hath a dog's bed in straw: yet this straw was clean, which is no small favour ... The women, virgins, men and maids, servants, all of us lay in one room, and myself was lodged furthest from the stove, which they did not for any favour, though contrary to their opinion I was glad of it, delighting more in sweet air, than the smoke of a dunghill. My companions laughed at me for babbling Dutch in my sleep: surely reason commanding me waking, had not power over me in sleep, to hinder me from revolving the pleasant passages of the day past ... Embrace in my name our common friend G.B. and of my loving host's family, let not a whelp go unsaluted. Farewell honest M. and return me love for love: from Dresden the seventh of March, 1591 ...'

1592. AFTER breakfast the next morning, we having hired a wagon for eighteen groats, passed four miles in the territory of the said Count [of Oldenburg] and one mile to Stickhausen in the territory of the Count of Emden, who had a castle there. Then because we could get no wagon in this place, we went one mile further on foot, which being very long, and my self having some gold guildens in my shoes, which I could not remove without suspicion; the way was very irksome to me, and we came to a country house, but we found good cheer, each man paying for his supper seven groats ...

While we lay at Leere for a night, a doctor of the civil law seeing me walk in the garden, and thinking my servile habit not fit for contemplation, commanded me to draw water for his horse, giving me no reward presently but only a nod; yet after when he had drunk with his friends, going out he said to me, 'Knecht dore hastu zu drincken', that is, 'sirrah drink you what is left'. After supper, having expected a bed almost till midnight, the maid at last told me I must lie upon the bench; but after, while I was washing my feet, which the gold in my shoes had galled, she espying my silk stockings, which I wore under my linen, ran to her mistress, and procured me a very good bed. This effect pleased me well, but I was afraid of the cause, by which lest I should be discovered, I hasted away early next morning. I paid here for my supper and breakfast, fifteen stivers, and giving the servant one for his pains, he would have restored it to me, seeming by my habit to have more need thereof than himself ...

In the spring of the year, 1594 (the Italians beginning the year the first of January), I began my journey to see Italy ... The city [of Venice] parted in the midst with the great channel, coming in from the sea bank near the two castles, is of old divided into six sextaries, or six parts, vulgarly sestieri; three on this side the channel, and three beyond the channel. The first sextary on this side the channel, is that of St Mark; for howsoever it be not the cathedral church, yet it is preferred before the rest, as well because the Duke [Doge] resides there, as especially because St Mark is the protecting saint of that city ...

The roof, in form of a globe, lies open at the very top, where the light comes in; for the church hath no windows, and the papist churches being commonly dark, to cause a religious horror, or to make their candles show better, this is more dark than the rest. I pass over the image of St Mark of brass in the form of a lion, gilded over, and holding a book of brass. Likewise the artificial images of the doctors of the church, and others. I would pass over the image of the Virgin Mary, painted a la mosaica, that is as if it were engraven, but that they attribute great miracles to it, so as women desirous to know the state of their absent friends, place a wax candle burning in the   ✗ open air before the image, and believe that if their friend be alive, it cannot be put out with any force of wind; but if he be dead, that the least breath of wind puts it out, or rather of itself it goes out; and besides for that I would mention that those who are adjudged to death, offer wax candles to this image, and as they pass by, fall prostrate to adore the same . . .

1594. As I WALKED about the church [of Loreto], behold in a dark chapel a priest, by his exorcisms casting a devil out of a poor woman: Good Lord what fencing and truly conjuring words he used! How much more skilful was he in the devil's names? than any ambitious Roman ever was in the   ╱ names of his citizens, whom he courted for their voices. If he had eaten a bushel of salt in hell; if he had been an inhabitant thereof, surely this art could never have been more familiar to him . . .

He [the French writer Villamont] sets it down for a maxim, and proves it by an example, that no man ever took anything out of this church, without great mischief befalling him; and that the robbers thereof are compelled to restore, as it were by infernal furies. Let me say truly (always reserving due reverence to the blessed Virgin, to whom the Scriptures teach such divine worship to be most unpleasing, as the papists yield her), I say let me with due reverence tell a truth. Myself and two Dutchmen my consorts, abhorring from this superstition, by leave entered the inner chapel, where we did see the Virgin's picture, adorned with precious jewels, and the place (to increase religious horror) being dark, yet the jewels shined by the light of wax candles. When we were entered, the priest courteously left us, to give us space for our devotion: but when we came forth (as the Italians proverbially speak of the priest's avarice, every psalm ends in, Glory be, etc. as if they should say, all religion to end in profit) it was necessary for us to cast alms into an iron chest behind the altar, covered with an iron grate. Therefore my consorts, of purpose to delight the priest's ears with the sound of money, as ╱ with music, did cast into that chest many brass quatrines, but of small value, ⌐ and myself being last, when my turn was to give alms, did instead thereof, gather some ten quatrines of theirs, which lay scattered upon the grate, and got that clear gain by that idol. God forbid I should brag of any contempt to religion; but since it appears, that such worship is unpleasing to God: and because papists will have all their miracles believed, I will freely say by experience, that having gotten these few quatrines in such sort as I said, yet after that, God of his mercy preserved me in my long and dangerous travel, and from that time to this day, by his grace, I have enjoyed, though no abundant, yet a competent estate, and more plentiful than in my former days . . .

1595. MYSELF after a few days' stay, finding no consorts for my journey into France, was admonished by some honest gentlemen in this city that this journey would be very dangerous to me, in respect that the army being broken up, all France would be full through all parts of scattering troops of soldiers, returning to their own homes. But when they perceived that I was obstinate in my purpose to pass through France into England, they persuaded me at least to sell my horse and go on foot; for they said, the booty of a good horse would surely cause me to be robbed by those, who might perhaps let me pass quietly on foot, disguised in poor apparel; for they seeing me well mounted, would surely set upon me . . .

Being to take my journey towards Paris on foot, I hired a poor man to guide me in Châlons, and to carry my cloak, and my little baggage . . . Our way was very dirty, through fruitful fields of corn, and we often heard the cries of the country people, driving their cattle to fortified places, upon the seeing of some scattered troops of soldiers, which made me much afraid, and that not without just cause: but God delivered us from this danger . . .

We had now scarce entered France, when suddenly the mischiefs fell upon me, which my friends at Metz had foretold me. When I had passed half this day's journey I met with a dozen horsemen, whose captain demanded of me my name and country. I answered that I was a Dutch man, and the servant of a Dutch merchant, who stayed for me at Châlons, whither I was then going. He (as it seemed to me) thinking it dishonourable to him, if he should himself assault a poor fellow, and a stranger, did let me pass, but before I came to the bottom of the hill, I might see him send two horsemen after me, who wheeling about the mountains, that I might not know they were of his company, suddenly rushed upon me, and with fierce countenance threatening death, presented their carbines to my breast. I having no ability to defend me, thought good not to make any the least show of resistance, so they took my sword from my guide, and were content only to rob me of my money . . .

One thing in this misery made me glad. I formerly said, that I sold my horse for 16 French crowns at Metz, which crowns I put in the bottom of a wooden box, and covered them with stinking ointment for scabs. The other French crowns, for the worst event, I lapped in cloth, and thereupon did wind divers coloured threads, wherein I sticked needles, as if I had been so good a husband, as to mend my own clothes. This box and this ball of thread, I had put in my hose, as things of no worth; and when in spoiling me they had searched my pockets, they first betook the box, and smelling the stink of the ointment, they cast it away on the ground; neither were they so frugal to take my ball of thread to mend their hose, but did tread it likewise under their feet. Then they rode swiftly to their companions, and I with some spark of joy in my greater loss, took up the box and ball of thread, thinking myself less miserable, that by the grace of God I had some money left, to keep me from begging in a strange country.

This tragedy thus acted, I and my guide (very sad because he despaired of my ability to pay him his hire) went forward our journey, he wondering that I was no more dejected in the danger I had passed, and for my miserable want of money, thinking that I had never a penny left, whom he did see so narrowly searched, and yet perceived that I was in some sort merry. At last we did see the city of Châlons not far distant, and upon our left hand was a fair spring, which had seven heads, to which we went to drink, being both very thirsty. Here I put under the water the hat which the thieves had given me, by unequal exchange for mine, being greasy to the very top, and deep according to the French fashion, and filling it up with water thrice, drunk it up greedily. Then I filled it the fourth time, and broke into it the crumbs of the brown loaf, the crust whereof had to that time kept my mouth with some moisture, which I devoured, and thought I had never eaten better brewess [broth]; but three days' sickness of vomiting and looseness made me repent this intemperance . . .

From my tender youth I had a great desire to see foreign countries, not to get liberty (which I had in Cambridge in such measure, as I could not well desire more), but to enable my understanding, which I thought could not be done so well by contemplation as by experience; nor by the ear or any sense so well, as by the eyes. And having once begun this course, I could not see any man without emulation, and a kind of virtuous envy, who had seen more cities, kingdoms, and provinces, or more courts of princes, kings, and emperors, than myself. Therefore having now wandered through the greatest part of Europe, and seen the chief kingdoms thereof, I sighed to myself in silence, that the kingdom of Spain was shut from my sight, by the long war between England and Spain, except I would rashly cast myself into danger, which I had already inadvisedly done, when I viewed the city and fort of Naples, and the city of Milan. And howsoever now being newly returned home, I thought the going into more remote parts would be of little use to me, yet I had an itching desire to see Jerusalem, the fountain of religion, and Constantinople, of old the seat of Christian emperors, and now the seat of the Turkish Ottoman.

Being of this mind when I returned to England, it happened that my brother Henry was then beginning that voyage . . . I liked his counsel, and made myself his consort in that journey . . .

In the same year 1595, wherein (some few months past) I returned into England from my former journey, I now set forth again towards Jerusalem, and upon the twenty-ninth of November (after the old style), I and my brother consort of my journey, went by water twenty miles (which are seventeen miles by land) from London to Gravesend, in a boat with two oars, for which we paid two shillings sixpence. At last the wind serving us, upon the seventh of December in the evening, we set sail at an ebbing water, and upon the eighth of December in the afternoon, having passed the River Thames, we cast anchor, upon the shore of England, right before the village Margate.

Then in the twilight of the evening, we put to sea.

4 Spenser, *A View of the Present State of Ireland* (1590s)

Source: *A View of the Present State of Ireland*, edited by W. L. Renwick (Oxford, Clarendon Press, 1970), pp. 49–75 abridged.

Edmund Spenser, the English poet (1552–99), migrated in 1580 to Ireland, where he remained, as government official and landowner, for the rest of his life. Drawing on his experience of this country, Spenser wrote in the mid-1590s an imaginary dialogue between two people, one named 'Eudoxus' and the other 'Irenius', who conduct a discussion on the state of the country and its indigenous people. This work was first circulated in manuscript form and printed in Dublin only in 1633, in an edition edited by Sir James Ware. These extracts display the deep prejudice entertained by English colonists like Spenser against Gaelic culture, which seemed to them lawless.

Irenius: I will then begin to count their customs in the same order that I counted their nations, and first with the Scythian,[1] or Scottish manners, of the which there is one use amongst them to keep their cattle and to live themselves the most part of the year in Bollies,[2] pasturing upon mountain and waste wild places, and removing still to fresh land as they have depastured the former days; the which appeareth plain to be the manner of the Scythians as ye may read in Olaus Magnus et [and] Johannes Boemus,[3] and yet is used amongst all the Tartarians and the people about the Caspian Sea which are naturally Scythians, to live in herds as they call them, being the very same that the Irish Bollies are, driving their cattle continually with them and feeding only on their milk and white meats.

Eudoxus: What fault can ye find with this custom, for though it be an old Scythian use, yet it is very behoveful in this country of Ireland where there are great mountains and waste deserts full of grass, that the same should be eaten down and nourish many thousand of cattle, for the good of the whole realm, which cannot, methinks, well be any other way than by keeping those Bollies as there ye have showed?

Iren: But by this custom of Bollyng there grow in the meantime many great enormities unto that commonwealth. For, first, if there be any outlaws or loose people, as they are never without some which live upon stealths and spoils, they are ever more succoured and find relief only in these Bollies being upon the waste places; where else they should be driven shortly to starve, or to come down to the towns to seek relief, where by one means or another they would soon be caught. Besides, such stealths of cattle as they make they bring commonly to those Bollies where they are received readily,

---

[1] A name given by classical geographers to a people of a vague 'northern' nation, to whom nearly all sixteenth-century writers attribute the origins of the Irish.

[2] Temporary summer dwellings which the nomadic Irish would use for habitation while grazing their cattle on highland pastures.

[3] A reference to Olaeus Magnus's work *Historia de Gentibus Septentrionalibus* (1555), and to Johannes Boemus's work *Mores, Leges, et Ritus Omnium Gentium* (1561).

and the thief harboured from danger of law or such officers as might light upon him. Moreover, the people that live thus in these Bollies grow thereby the more barbarous and live more licentiously than they could in towns, using what means they list, and practising what mischiefs and villainies they will, either against the government there generally by their combinations, or against private men, whom they malign by stealing their goods or murdering themselves; for there they think themselves half exempted from law and obedience, and having once tasted freedom do, like a steer that hath been long out of his yoke, grudge and repine ever after to come under rule again.

Eudox: By your speech, Irenius, I perceive more evil come by these Bollies than good by their grazing, and therefore it may well be reformed, but that must be in his due course. Do you proceed to the next.

Iren: They have another custom from the Scythians, that is the wearing of mantles and long glibs, which is a thick curled bush of hair hanging down over their eyes, and monstrously disguising them, which are both very bad and hurtful.

Eudox: Do ye think that the mantle cometh from the Scythians? I would surely think otherwise, for by that which I have read it appeareth that most nations in the world anciently used the mantle, for the Jews used it as ye may read of Elias' mantle of ——.[4] The Caldees[5] also used it, as ye may read in Diodorus, the Egyptians likewise used it, as ye may read in Herodotus[6] and may be gathered by the description of Berenice in the Greek commentaries upon Callimachus. The Greeks also used it anciently, as appeareth by Venus' mantle lined with stars, though afterwards they changed the form thereof into their cloaks called *pallia*, as some of the Irish also use. And the ancient Latins and Romans also used it, as ye may read in Virgil who was a very great antiquary, that Evander, when Aeneas came to him at his feast, did entertain and feast him sitting on the ground, and lying on mantles. Insomuch as he useth the very word *mantile* for a mantle, *mantilia humi sternunt*,[7] so that it seemeth that the mantle was a general habit to most nations, and not proper to the Scythians only as ye suppose.

Iren: I cannot deny but anciently it was common to most, and yet sithence [since] disused and laid away. But in this latter age of the world since the decay of the Roman Empire, it was renewed and brought in again by those northern nations, when breaking out of their cold caves and frozen habitation into the sweet soil of Europe, they brought with them their usual weeds, fit to shield the cold and that continual frost to which they had at home been enured; the which yet they left not off, by reason that they were in perpetual wars with the nations where they had invaded, but still removing from place to place carried always with them that weed as their house, their

---

[4] A reference to 2 Kings 13–14. The following word is illegible in the original manuscript.

[5] Chaldeans, an ancient Semitic people who controlled south Babylonia from the late eighth century to the late seventh century BC.

[6] Herodotus gives an extensive account of the Egyptians and seems to have been the first classical author to describe the wandering life of the Scythians.

[7] Possibly Spenser is here referring to Virgil's description of the napkins used at Dido's feast (*Aeneid* I, 701–2).

bed and their garment, and coming lastly into Ireland they found there more special use thereof, by reason of the raw cold climate, from whom it is now grown into that general use in which that people now have it; afterward the Africans succeeding, yet finding the like necessity of that garment, continued the like use thereof.

Eudox: Since then the necessity thereof is so commodious as ye allege, that it is instead of housing, bedding, and clothing, what reason have you then to wish so necessary a thing cast off?

Iren: Because the commodity doth not countervail the discommodity. For the inconveniences which thereby do arise are much more many, for it is a fit house for an outlaw, a meet bed for a rebel, and an apt cloak for a thief. First the outlaw being for his many crimes and villainies banished from the towns and houses of honest men, and wandering in waste places far from danger of law, maketh his mantle his house, and under it covereth himself from the wrath of heaven, from the offence of the earth, and from the sight of men: when it raineth it is his pentice [shed], when it bloweth it is his tent, when it freezeth it is his tabernacle; in summer he can wear it loose, in winter he can wrap it close; at all times he can use it, never heavy, never cumbersome. Likewise for a rebel it is as serviceable: for in his war that he maketh (if at least it deserve the name of war) when he still flyeth from his foe and lurketh in the thick woods and straight passages waiting for advantages), it is his bed, yea and almost all his household stuff. For the wood is his house against all weathers, and his mantle is his cave to sleep in. There he wrappeth his self round and ensconceth himself strongly against the gnats, which in the country do more annoy the naked rebels whilst they keep the woods, and do more sharply wound them than all their enemies' swords or spears which can seldom come nigh them; yea and oftentimes their mantle serveth them when they are near driven, being wrapped about their left arm instead of a target, for it is hard to cut through it with a sword; besides, it is light to bear, light to throw away, and being as they then commonly are naked, it is to them all in all. Lastly, for a thief it is so handsome, as it may seem it was first invented for him, for under it he can cleanly convey any fit pillage that cometh handsomely in his way, and when he goeth abroad in the night on freebooting it is his best and surest friend, for lying as they often do, two or three nights together abroad to watch for their booty, with that they can prettily shroud themselves under a bush or a bankside till they may conveniently do their errand. And when all is done he can, in his mantle, pass through any town or company, being close hooded over his head as he useth from knowledge of any to whom he is endangered. Besides all this he or any man else that is disposed to mischief or villainy may, under his mantle, go privily, armed without suspicion of any, carry his headpiece, his skene [short dagger] or pistol, if he please to be always in a readiness. Thus necessary and fitting is a mantle for a bad man. And surely for a bad housewife it is no less convenient. For some of them that be these wandering women, called of them *Monashut*, it is half a wardrobe, for in summer ye shall find her arrayed commonly but in her smock and mantle to be more ready for her light services; in winter and in her travel it is her cloak and safeguard,[8] and also a coverlet for her lewd exercise, and when she hath filled her vessel, under it she can hide both her burden and her blame; yea, and when her bastard is born it serves instead of all her swaddling clothes, her mantles, her cradles with which others are vainly cumbered, and as for all other good women which love to do but little work, how handsome it is to lie in and sleep, or to louse themselves in the sunshine, they that have been but a while in Ireland can well witness. Sure I am that ye will think it very unfit for good housewives to stir in or to busy herself about the housewifery in sort as they should. These be some of the abuses for which I would think it meet to forbid all mantles.

Eudox: O evil minded man, that having reckoned up so many uses of mantles, will yet wish it to be abandoned. Sure I think Diogenes' dish did never serve his master more turns, notwithstanding that he made his dish his cup, his measure, his waterpot,[9] then a mantle doth an Irishman, but I see they be all to bad intents, and therefore I will join with you in abolishing it. But what blame lay you to their glib? Take heed, I pray you, that you be not too busy therewith, for fear of your own blame, seeing our Englishmen take it up in such a general fashion, to wear their hair so unmeasurably long that some of them exceed the longest Irish glibs.

Iren: I fear not the blame of any undeserved mislikes, but for the Irish glibs I say that besides their savage brutishness and loathly filthiness, which is not to be named, they are fit masks as a mantle is for a thief, for whensoever he hath run himself into that peril of law that he will not be known, he either cutteth off his glib quite, by which he becometh nothing like himself, or pulleth it so low down over his eyes that it is very hard to discern his thievish countenance, and therefore fit to be trussed up with the mantle . . .

Iren: There is amongst the Irish a certain kind of people called the bards, which are to them instead of poets, whose profession is to set forth the praises and dispraises of men, in their poems or rhymes, the which are had in so high regard and estimation amongst them that none dare displease them for fear to run into reproach through their offence and to be made infamous in the mouths of all men; for their verses are taken up with a general applause, and usually sung at all feasts and meetings by certain other persons whose proper function that is, which also receive for the same great rewards, and reputation besides.

Eudox: Do you blame this in them, which I would otherwise have thought to have been worthy of good account, and rather to have been maintained and augmented amongst them, than to have been disliked? For I have read that in all ages, poets have been had in special reputation, and that meseems not without great cause, for besides their sweet inventions and most witty lays, they are always used to set forth the praises of the good and virtuous, and to beat down and disgrace the bad and vicious, so that many brave young minds have oftentimes, through the hearing the praises and famous

[8] An outer skirt for riding and travel.
[9] A reference to the ascetic mode of life of the Greek philosopher Diogenes.

eulogies of worthy men sung and reported to them, been stirred up to affect like commendations, and so to strive unto the like deserts. So they say that the Lacedemonians were more inclined to desire of honour with the excellent verses of the poet Tyrtaeus,[10] than with all the exhortations of their captains, or authority of their rulers and magistrates.

Iren: It is most true that such poets as in their writing do labour to better the manners, and through the sweet bait of their numbers to steal into the young spirits a desire of honour and virtue, are worthy to be had in great respect, but these Irish bards are for the most part of another mind, and so far from instructing young men in moral discipline, that they themselves do more deserve to be sharply disciplined, for they seldom use to choose unto themselves the doings of good men for the ornaments of their poems, but whomsoever they find to be most licentious of life, most bold and lawless in his doings, most dangerous and desperate in all parts of disobedience and rebellious disposition, him they set up and glorify in their rhymes, him they praise to the people, and to young men make an example to follow.

Eudox: I marvel what kind of speeches they can find or what face they can put on to praise such lewd persons as live so lawlessly and licentiously upon stealths and spoils as most of them do, or how can they think that any good mind will applaud the same?

Iren: There is none so bad, Eudoxus, but that shall find some to favour his doings, but such licentious parts as these, tending for the most part to the hurt of the English, or maintenance of their own lewd liberty, they themselves being most desirous thereof, do most allow, besides these evil things being decked and suborned with the gay attire of goodly words, may easily deceive and carry away the affection of a young mind that is not well stayed, but desirous by some bold adventure to make proof of himself. For being (as they all be) brought up idly without awe of parents, without precepts of masters, without fear of offence, not being directed nor employed in any course of life which may carry them to virtue, will easily be drawn to follow such as any shall set before them, for a young mind cannot rest if he be not still busied in some goodness. He will find himself such business as shall soon busy all about him, in which, if he shall find any to praise him and to give him encouragement, as those bards and rhymers do for little reward or a share of a stolen cow, then waxeth he most insolent and half mad, with the love of himself and his own lewd deeds. And as for words to set forth such lewdness it is not hard for them to give a goodly gloss and painted show thereunto, borrowed even from the praises which are proper unto virtue itself, as of a most notorious thief and wicked outlaw, which had lived all his lifetime of spoils and robberies, one of their bards in his praise said that he was none of those idle milksops that was brought up by the fireside, but that most of his days he spent in arms and valiant enterprises, that he did never eat his meat before he had won it with his sword, that he lay not slugging all night in a cabin under his mantle, but used commonly to

---

[10] A reference to the poetry of Tyrtaeus, who wrote elegies to the Spartans exhorting them to virtuous deeds.

keep others waking, to defend their lives, and did light his candle at the flame of their houses to lead him in the darkness, that the day was his night and the night his day; that he loved not to lie long wooing of wenches to yield to him, but where he came he took by force the spoil of other men's love, and left but lamentation to their lovers; that his music was not the harp nor lays of love, but the cries of people and clashing of armour, and that finally he died, not bewailed of many, but made many wail when he died, that dearly bought his death. Do you not think, Eudoxus, that many of these praises might be applied to men of best desert? Yet are they all yielded to a most notable traitor. And amongst some of the Irish not smally accompted of, for the song when it was first made, and sung unto a person of high degree, there was bought as their manner is for forty crowns.

Eudox: And well worthy sure, but tell me, I pray you, have they any art in their compositions or be they anything witty or well savoured, as poems should be?

Iren: Yea, truly, I have caused diverse of them to be translated unto me, that I might understand them, and surely they savoured of sweet wit and good invention, but skilled not of the goodly ornaments of poetry. Yet were they sprinkled with some pretty flowers of their own natural devise, which gave good grace and comeliness unto them, the which it is great pity to see so abused to the gracing of wickedness and vice, which would with good usage serve to beautify and adorn virtue. This evil custom, therefore, needeth reformation.

5 Letter from Isabella and Ferdinand to the Moorish King (1491)

Source: Luis de Mármol Carvajal, *Historia del rebelión y castigo de los moriscos del reino de Granada* (Málaga, 1600), in Biblioteca de autores españoles, 21 (Madrid: M. Rivadeneyra, 1852), pp. 147–50, abridged and translated by D. Goodman.

The final phase of the long Christian reconquest of Spain occurred in the reign of Isabella (1474–1504) and Ferdinand (1479–1504). Their armed forces had captured Almería and Málaga, and by 1491 the city of Granada remained the last stronghold in Moorish hands. From their armed camp close to the walls of Granada, the Catholic monarchs despatched this letter on 28 November 1491, to the Moorish king Abí Abdilehi, the population of Granada and its surrounding localities.

First, the Moorish King, fakirs,[1] officials and other leaders, and the entire population of the city of Granada and its surroundings, shall within forty days surrender to Their Highnesses, or to the person they appoint, the fortress of the Alhambra and the Alhizán[2] with all its towers and gates, and

---

[1] Religious mendicants or ascetics.
[2] Palace and fortress of the Moorish rulers of Granada.

all other fortresses, towers and gates of the city of Granada and its surroundings so that they may be taken over in Their Highnesses' name and with their men and at their will. And justices will be ordered not to permit Christians to go up to the wall which lies between the Alcazaba and the Albaicín [3] from where the houses of Moors could be observed; anyone doing this shall be severely punished.

After the forty days have elapsed all Moors are to surrender to Their Highnesses and fulfil what all kings and lords demand of loyal vassals. And as a guarantee of surrender, the day before the fortresses are to be handed over, the [Moorish] official Yussef Aben Comixa and 500 members of the leading families will be given as hostages, Their Highnesses keeping them in custody for ten days while the fortresses are taken over, manned and provisioned. The hostages during this time shall be given all the sustenance they need, and once the surrender has been effected they shall be released.

And after the fortresses have been surrendered, Their Highnesses and Prince Don Juan, their Son, give their word that they and successive monarchs will receive as their vassals and protect King Abí Abdilehi, [Moorish] officials, fakirs, military leaders, nobles and the entire population, great or humble, men and women, residents of Granada and its Albaicín of the surroundings, fortified places, towns and localities, and of the Alpujarra [4] and of all other places which fall under this agreement and capitulation. All will be allowed to remain in their homes and estates, now and for all time. They shall suffer no harm and this shall be guaranteed by justice; nor shall their possessions or property be taken from them. Instead they shall be honoured and respected as subjects and vassals just like all others who live under Their government and rule . . .

Their Highnesses and Their successors shall forever permit King Abí Abdilehi, his officials, and all the population, great or humble, to live by their own law; and They shall not allow their mosques to be taken from them, nor their towers and muezzins; income reserved for these things shall not be touched; nor shall their existing customs be interfered with.

Moors will be judged according to their law and according to their own justices . . .

And all Moors wishing to leave for Barbary [5] or other lands shall be given free and safe passage by Their Highnesses, along with their families, moveable goods, merchandise, jewels, gold, silver and all types of arms except for powder weapons. To expedite their passage, Their Highnesses shall provide ten large ships which for a period of seventy days shall wait in appropriate ports and then carry them free and safely to the Barbary ports where Christian merchants' ships customarily sail to for trade. In addition all those who shall wish to leave within a period of three years may do so after giving fifty days' notice, Their Highnesses ordering ships wherever they are requested, giving them free and safe passage.

[3] A specific quarter of the city.
[4] The highlands around Granada.
[5] The western part of North Africa.

After the expiry of the three years' period, passage to Barbary will continue to be permitted but only on payment to Their Highnesses of one ducat per head and the cost of freight . . .

Neither Their Highnesses, nor their son Prince Don Juan, nor those who succeed them, shall ever order their Moorish vassals to wear badges on their clothing as the Jews do . . .

During the surrender of the city and localities the Moors shall be obliged to deliver to Their Highnesses all Christian captives, male and female, so that they regain their freedom, without asking for anything in return or receiving anything for this; and should a Moor have sold some captives in Barbary, provided he swears and gives evidence that the sale was effected prior to this surrender, he will be under no obligation to return them . . .

Christians will not be allowed to enter mosques, where Moors pray, without the permission of the fakirs; whoever fails to obey this shall be punished.

Their Highnesses will not permit Jews to have any authority over Moors, nor may they collect any rent from them.

King Abdilehi, his officials, fakirs, military chiefs, nobles and the entire population of the city of Granada, the Albaicín and its environs, the Alpujarra and other localities will be respected and well treated by Their Highnesses and Their ministers. Customs and rites will be protected, their voice shall be heard, and all officials and fakirs will be permitted to collect income and enjoy their privileges and liberties as is their custom, and which it is just to maintain . . .

Suits arising between Moors are to be decided according to their law, known as Sunna, and by their own justices, as they customarily do. And if the dispute shall be between Christian and Moor, it shall be judged by a Christian magistrate and a Moorish cadi,[6] so that the parties can have no complaints about the verdict . . .

Moors will pay Their Highnesses no more tribute than what they have been accustomed to give to Moorish kings . . .

Should the King or any other Moor find after settling in Barbary that he is unhappy in that land and wants to return to Spain, Their Highnesses shall give him licence within three years to return, enjoying the same terms of these capitulations as the others.

Moors wishing to go with their merchandise to trade in Barbary will be given freedom to do so, and the same applies to all places in Castile and Andalusia, without payment of tolls or duties normally paid by Christians.

No person shall be allowed to maltreat by word or deed those Christians who have become Moors;[7] and if such renegades are the wives of Moors they will not be forced against their will to return to Christianity, but they will be interrogated in the presence of Christians and Moors and their wishes respected; the same shall apply to the children born of a Christian woman and a Moor.

[6] A judge in a Muslim community.

[7] i.e. Muslims.

Neither shall any Moors be compelled to become Christian against their will. Any maiden, married woman or widow wishing to convert to Christianity for amorous reasons will not be accepted until she has been interrogated . . .

Neither Their Highnesses, nor their successors, will at any time require King Abdilehi or any who enter into these capitulations, to restore horses, beasts of burden, livestock, gold, silver, jewels, or anything else acquired in whatever way during the war . . .

If any Moor shall have wounded or killed a Christian captive there shall be no investigation . . .

The justices, magistrates and governors appointed by Their Highnesses in and around the city of Granada will be persons who respect the Moors, treat them with affection and observe the terms of this capitulation. Any who fail to do this will be dismissed and punished . . .

As a gesture of goodwill to King Abí Abdilehi and to the residents of Granada and its environs, orders will be given for all captive Moors, men or women, held by Christians, to be set free without any payment; those in Andalusia within five months and those in Castile within eight months. And two days after the Moors have delivered Christian captives held in Granada, Their Highnesses will order the handing over of two hundred Moorish men and women . . .

The donations and income of the mosques, and the alms and other things normally given to the schools where they teach their children will continue to be administered by the fakirs for distribution as they think fit; and in this neither Their Highnesses nor Their ministers shall interfere, nor at any time order any confiscation.

Their Highnesses will issue orders for all ships of Barbary which shall be in the ports of the kingdom of Granada to leave freely, but without carrying any Christian captive; and while the ships remain in those ports no damage shall be done to them nor any valuables taken from them . . .

Moors will not be compelled against their will for military service . . .

The meat supplies of Christians shall be kept apart from those of the Moors; their provisions will not be mixed. Those who disobey will be punished . . .

All that is contained in these capitulations will, on the orders of Their Highnesses, be observed from the day that the fortresses of the city of Granada are surrendered. Which they have ordered by Their royal letter signed by Their names and under Their seal, countersigned by Hernando de Zafra, Their secretary, in the royal camp, Vega de Granada, 28th day of the month of November, in the year of 1491.

6 Petition from Francisco Núñez Muley, Morisco Noble (1567)

Source: Luis de Mármol Carvajal, *Historia del rebelión y castigo de los moriscos del reino de Granada* (Málaga, 1600), in Biblioteca de autores españoles, 21 (Madrid: M. Rivadeneyra, 1852), pp. 163–5 abridged and translated by D. Goodman.

After their subjugation and forced conversion to Christianity, the Moors of Spain, now known as 'Moriscos', continued with few exceptions to adhere to their Islamic traditions. The existence of an unassimilated minority was a matter of increasing concern to Philip II (1556–98) and his government, particularly in view of its links with Spain's enemies: kinship with the Barbary corsairs and religious affiliation with the Ottoman Turks. The growing intolerance of the Spanish Crown was apparent in the Draconian measures proclaimed in Granada in January 1567. The new prohibitions sought to obliterate the Moorish traditions, outlawing the use of Arabic, and the minority's distinctive dress and music. Filled with dismay, the Moriscos turned to their elder Francisco Núñez Muley to intercede on their behalf with Pedro de Deza, president of the high court of justice in Granada.

When the naturals of this kingdom were converted to the Christian faith, there was no regulation compelling them to abandon their dress, language or customs associated with their festivities; and indeed that conversion was forced and against the agreed surrender terms when King Abdilehi gave up this city to the Catholic Monarchs ... And now these new pragmatics, seemingly easy to fulfil, in reality create great difficulties which I will relate to Your Lordship so that he may be filled with pity, love and charity for this miserable people and solicit their protection with His Majesty, as presidents have always done in the past. The dress of our women is not Moorish but merely provincial, just as in Castile and other regions it is usual for the inhabitants to have distinctive headdress, skirts and hose. Who can deny that our dress is very different from the apparel of Moors and Turks? And even that varies: the dress of Fez differs from what is worn in Tlemcen [Barbary states]; nor is dress the same in Tunis and Morocco; and the same variation occurs in Turkey and other kingdoms. Yet all of these would be identical if there really was a dress peculiar to Mohammedans. We are visited by Christian clergy and laymen from Syria and Egypt clothed like Turks in their caftans and headdress; they speak Arabic and Turkish, know neither Latin nor Castilian, yet they are nonetheless Christians ... Our women inherit bridal and other dresses from three or four generations and keep them until they are needed. What advantage can anyone derive from prohibiting our dress, which we have paid for with many ducats? Why should they want us to forfeit over three millions in gold which we have invested in it [the manufacture of clothes], thereby ruining traders, merchants, silversmiths and other craftsmen who make a living through the manufacture of garments, hose and jewellery for Morisco women? If the 200,000 women of this kingdom are to change their dress from head to foot where will they find the money? And how much will also be lost in the Moriscos' jewellery and clothes which have to be destroyed? . . . And Crown income from Moriscos' [taxes] will also fall.

We are persecuted by ecclesiastical and secular courts; yet we are all loyal vassals, obedient to His Majesty and ready to serve him with our wealth. Never could it be said that we have committed treason from the day we surrendered . . . Our wedding feasts, dances and celebrations are no obstacle to becoming Christian . . . Our music is not found in Africa or Turkey, but is a provincial custom; whereas if it were the ceremony of a sect it would be found elsewhere . . .

There is even less reason for regarding the women's use of henna as a Moorish rite; it is only a tradition for cleansing the head and is therefore healthy . . . This is not against the faith but beneficial to the body . . .

And what good would come from forcing us to keep the doors of our houses open? It would allow thieves to rob us and the lustful to have access to women . . . If anyone wanted to be a Moor and follow their ceremonies couldn't they do so at night? Of course they could! Mohammedanism requires solitude and retreat. Therefore it matters little whether doors are open or closed if the intention is there; there is punishment for him who does what he should not, for nothing is concealed from God.

But what of our baths, are they for rituals? Certainly not! Many people come to them and they are mostly Christians. The baths are dens of filth; by contrast Moorish ritual requires cleanliness and solitude . . . There have always been baths throughout the world, and if they were once prohibited in Castile it was because they sapped the strength and courage of warriors. The natives of this kingdom do not have to fight, nor do the women need strength, but only to be clean: if they do not wash there, or in rivers and streams . . . where are they to wash? . . .

To require our women to unveil their faces is only to provide opportunity for men to sin after beholding the beauty of those they are attracted to; while the ugly will find no one willing to marry them. They cover themselves because they do not want to be known, just like Christian women: it is an act of modesty to avoid molestation . . .

Our ancient surnames serve to identify people and preserve lineage. What could be gained by losing these records? . . .

But the greatest inconvenience of all would be the loss of our Arabic language. How can a language be taken away from a people, the natural language in which they are reared? The Egyptians, Syrians, Maltese and other Christian peoples speak, read and write Arabic, yet are Christian like us . . . Our people are born and grow up in small communities where Castilian has never been spoken or understood – except by the priest, curate or sacristan, and even they speak always in Arabic. It will be difficult and practically impossible for the old to learn Castilian in the years remaining to them, and all the more so in the [stipulated] brief period of three years, even if they did nothing else but go to school. This is clearly a measure designed to weaken us . . . and those who could not sustain such hardship would leave the land or become brigands . . . What people in the world are more vile and despicable than the negroes of Guinea? Yet they are allowed to speak their language, play their instruments and dance, in order to keep them content.

What I have written here is without malice; my intentions are good. I have always served the Lord our God, the Crown, and the naturals of this kingdom . . . and for over sixty years I have negotiated on these matters. May Your Lordship have mercy on us and not desert those who are powerless. May he undeceive His Majesty, remedy these ills and do what is required of a Christian gentleman; that God and His Majesty may be served and this kingdom be forever in your debt.

7 Ogier Ghiselin de Busbecq: Impressions of Turkey (1556–1564)

Source: *The Turkish Letters of Ogier Ghiselin de Busbecq*, translated by E. S. Forster (Oxford: Clarendon Press, 1927), pp. 58–61.

Ogier Ghiselin de Busbecq (1522–92), Flemish diplomat, traveller and antiquarian scholar, spent approximately eight years in Constantinople as ambassador of the Holy Roman Emperor, Ferdinand I (reigned 1556–64). While resident in Turkey, he not only provided official diplomatic intelligence on Turkish affairs but also sent back private correspondence of a more informal nature to Nicholas Michault, a friend from student days. A Latin edition of these letters was published in the 1580s and an English translation in 1694.

In the extract below, Busbecq describes his summons to Anatolia to meet Suleiman the Magnificent (1520–66), an outstanding leader, lawgiver and patron of the arts. Under his rule, the Ottoman Empire doubled its size.

On reaching Amasia we were taken to pay our respects to Achmet, the Chief Vizier, and the other Pashas[1] (for the Sultan[2] himself was away), and we opened negotiations with them in accordance with the Emperor's injunctions. The Pashas, anxious not to appear at this early stage prejudiced against our cause, displayed no opposition but postponed the matter until their master could express his wishes. On his return we were introduced into his presence; but neither in his attitude nor in his manner did he appear very well disposed to our address, or the arguments which we used, or the instructions which we brought.

The Sultan was seated on a rather low sofa, not more than a foot from the ground and spread with many costly coverlets and cushions embroidered with exquisite work. Near him were his bow and arrows. His expression, as I have said, is anything but smiling, and has a sternness which, though sad, is full of majesty. On our arrival we were introduced into his presence by his chamberlains, who held our arms – a practice which has always been observed since a Croatian sought an interview and murdered the Sultan

---

[1] Turkish officers of high rank such as a military commander or governor of a province.
[2] Suleiman the Magnificent.

Amurath in revenge for the slaughter of his master, Marcus the Despot of Serbia. After going through the pretence of kissing his hand, we were led to the wall facing him backwards, so as not to turn our backs or any part of them towards him. He then listened to the recital of my message, but, as it did not correspond with his expectations (for the demands of my imperial master[3] were full of dignity and independence, and, therefore, far from acceptable to one who thought that his slightest wishes ought to be obeyed), he assumed an expression of disdain, and merely answered 'Giusel, Giusel', that is, 'Well, Well'. We were then dismissed to our lodging.

The Sultan's head-quarters were crowded by numerous attendants, including many high officials. All the cavalry of the guard were there, the Spahis, Ghourebas, Ouloufedjis, and a large number of Janissaries. In all that great assembly no single man owed his dignity to anything but his personal merits and bravery; no one is distinguished from the rest by his birth, and honour is paid to each man according to the nature of the duty and offices which he discharges. Thus there is no struggle for precedence, every man having his place assigned to him in virtue of the function which he performs. The Sultan himself assigns to all their duties and offices, and in doing so pays no attention to wealth or the empty claims of rank, and takes no account of any influence or popularity which a candidate may possess; he only considers merit and scrutinizes the character, natural ability, and disposition of each. Thus each man is rewarded according to his deserts, and offices are filled by men capable of performing them. In Turkey every man has it in his power to make what he will of the position into which he is born and of his fortune in life. Those who hold the highest posts under the Sultan are very often the sons of shepherds and herdsmen, and, so far from being ashamed of their birth, they make it a subject of boasting, and the less they owe to their forefathers and to the accident of birth, the greater is the pride which they feel. They do not consider that good qualities can be conferred by birth or handed down by inheritance, but regard them partly as the gift of heaven and partly as the product of good training and constant toil and zeal. Just as they consider that an aptitude for the arts, such as music or mathematics or geometry, is not transmitted to a son and heir, so they hold that character is not hereditary, and that a son does not necessarily resemble his father, but his qualities are divinely infused into his bodily frame. Thus, among the Turks, dignities, offices, and administrative posts are the rewards of ability and merit; those who are dishonest, lazy, and slothful never attain to distinction, but remain in obscurity and contempt. This is why the Turks succeed in all that they attempt and are a dominating race and daily extend the bounds of their rule. Our method is very different; there is no room for merit, but everything depends on birth; considerations of which alone open the way to high official position. On this subject I shall perhaps say more in another place, and you must regard these remarks as intended for your ears only.

[3] Ferdinand I of Austria, King of Bohemia and Hungary, and Holy Roman Emperor.

8 Nicholas de Nicolay, *Navigations Made into Turkey* (1567)

Source: *Navigations, Peregrinations and Voyages Made into Turkey*, translated by T. Washington (1585), in *A Collection of Voyages and Travels Compiled from the Library of the Earl of Oxford* (London, 1774), I, 605–24, abridged and spelling modernized by D. Norman.

Nicholas de Nicolay was geographer royal to the King of France and in that capacity travelled to the Levant. His first-hand account of the Ottoman Empire was published in French (Lyons, 1567), translated into English (London, 1585) and reprinted several times.

Of the physicians of Constantinople

In Turkey, and principally at Constantinople, are found divers physicians professing the art of physic, and exercising the practice thereof, but a greater number of the Jews than Turks, amongst which there are many that are skilful in the theory, and experimented in practice; and the reason wherefore, in this art, they commonly exceed all other nations is the knowledge which they have in the language and letters, Greek, Arabian, Chaldee, and Hebrew. In which languages as to them partly peculiar and original, have written the principal authors of physic, natural philosophy, and astronomy, being the sciences meet and necessary for those that study physic. Besides the common physicians, which the Turks called Echim, the great lord hath of his own proper and ordinary, waged with great stipends, and entertainments, whereof part are Turks and part Jews. He, who in the time when I was in Levant, had the first dignity and authority amongst the order of physicians, was by nation a Hebrew, called Amon, of age above sixty years, a personage great of authority, and much-esteemed, as well for his goods, knowledge, and renown, as for honour and portliness. There are, moreover, besides those aforesaid, within the seraglio of the great Turk,[1] ten common physicians, which, for their salary, have every one of them ten aspers[2] a day, and meat and drink, their charge being such, that, so soon as there falleth any sick within the seraglio, one of them goeth unto the great Turk to ask licence to heal him (for otherwise they dare not take him in hand) which having obtained, he causeth the patient to be brought into a place, which within the seraglio is ordained for sick folk, and is bound to visit him four times a day, until such time as he have recovered his health; but if it chance the sick to wax daily worse and worse, then all the other physicians are bound to come to his assistance. As for the apparel of the physicians of Turkey, it doth not differ much from that of the common people; but yet from that of the Jewish physicians, for, instead of a yellow

---

[1] A reference to Suleiman the Magnificent.
[2] A silver Turkish coin.

turban, very like unto the Jewish nation, they wear a high topped cap, dyed of red scarlet.

OF THE MERCHANT-JEWS DWELLING IN CONSTANTINOPLE, AND OTHER PLACES OF TURKEY AND GREECE

The number of the Jews dwelling throughout all the cities of Turkey and Greece, and principally at Constantinople, is so great, that it is a thing marvellous and incredible; for the number of these, using trade and traffic of merchandise, like money at usury, doth there multiply so from day to day, that the bringing of merchandises which arrive there from all parts, as well by sea as by land, is such, that it may be said with good reason, that at this present day they have in their hands the most and greatest traffic of merchandise and ready money, that is in all the Levant. And likewise the shops and warehouses, the best furnished with all rich sorts of merchandises, which are in Constantinople, are those of the Jews. Likewise they have amongst them workmen of all arts and handicrafts most excellent, and especially of the Maranes [Marranos],[3] of late banished and driven out of Spain and Portugal, who, to the great detriment and damage of Christianity, have taught the Turks divers inventions, crafts, and engines of war, as to make artillery, harquebuses, gunpowder, shot, and other ammunition: they have also there set up printing, not before seen in those countries, by which, in fair characters, they put in light divers books in divers languages, as Greek, Latin, Italian, Spanish, and the Hebrew tongue, being to them natural, but are not permitted to print the Turkish or Arabian tongue: they have also the commodity and usage to speak and understand all other sorts of languages used in the Levant; which serveth them greatly for the communication and traffic, which they have with other strange nations, to whom oftentimes they serve for dragomans or interpreters. Besides, this detestable nation of the Jews are men full of all malice, fraud, deceit, and subtle dealing, exercising execrable usuries amongst the Christians, and other nations, without any conscience, or reprehension, but have free licence, paying the tribute, a thing which is great ruin unto the country and people, where they are conversant. They are marvellous obstinate and stubborn in their infidelity, attending daily their Messiah promised, by whom they hope to be brought again into the land of promise: they have the veil of Moses so knit before the eyes of their understanding, that they will not, nor can by any manner of means see or acknowledge the brightness and light of Jesus Christ, whom, through misbelief, envy and unmeasured rage, they condemned, and caused to die on the cross, and, charging themselves with the offence and sin committed towards his person, wrote unto Pilate, 'His blood be upon us, and on our children'; and therefore their sin hath

---

[3] A name applied in Spain to a Jew or Moor converted to Christianity especially to one who merely professed conversion in order to avoid persecution.

followed them and their successors throughout all generations, so as, whereas they would not receive his salvation, the fame for ever shall be kept from them, to their great mischief and confusion, for, since their extermination, and the vengeance upon Jerusalem unto this present day, they had at no time any certain dwelling-place upon the face of the earth, but have always gone straying, dispersed and driven away from country to country: and yet even at this day, in what region soever they are permitted to dwell under tribute, they are abhorred of God and men, and more persecuted by the Turks, who, in derision, call them Chifont, than of any other nation, who have them in such disdain and hatred, that by no means they will eat in their company, and much less marry any of their wives or daughters, notwithstanding that often times they do marry with Christians, whom they permit to live according to their law, and have a pleasure to eat [with] and be conversant with Christians; and that which is worse, if a Jew would become a mussulman [Muslim], he should not be received, except first, leaving his Judaical sect, he became a Christian. The Jews, which dwell in Constantinople, Adrianople, Bursia, Salonica, Gallipoli, and other places of the dominions of the great Turk, are all apparelled with long garments, like unto the Grecians, and other nations of the Levant, but, for their mark and token to be known from others, they wear a yellow turban. Those that dwell in the isle of Chios (which are in great number, under the tribute of the seignior) instead of a turban, wear a great cap of credit, which some do call a bonnet of arbalest, being also of a yellow colour.

9 Bernal Díaz: Accounts of Mexico (c. 1568)

Source: Bernal Díaz *The Conquest of New Spain*, translated and edited by J. M. Cohen (Harmondsworth: Penguin Books, 1963), pp. 20–239 abridged.

Bernal Díaz del Castillo (*c*.1492–*c*.1580), Spanish explorer and soldier, participated in the early exploration of the Mexican coast and took part in Hernán Cortés's 1519 march on the Aztec capital and the final conquest of this island city. He wrote in his old age an account of his experiences under the title *The True History of the Conquest of New Spain* (*Historia verdadera de la conquista de la nueva España*, first published in 1632) partly as a refutation of such works as Francisco López de Gómara's glowing account of the campaign.

In the extracts below Díaz describes an expedition undertaken in 1517 to explore the coast of Mexico.

We disembarked near the town, where there was a pool of good water, at which the inhabitants were accustomed to drink. For as far as we could see, there were no rivers in this country. We landed the casks, intending to fill them and re-embark. But when we were ready to go a company of about fifty Indians, dressed in good cotton cloaks ... came peacefully out of the town, and asked us by signs what we were looking for. We gave them to understand that we had come for water, and were going straight back to our ships. They asked us by gesture whether we came from the east, and repeated the word '*Castilan, Castilan*'. But we did not understand what they meant. Then they invited us to go with them to their town, and after some discussion among ourselves we decided to go, but in good formation and very cautiously.

They led us to some very large buildings of fine masonry which were the prayer-houses of their idols, the walls of which were painted with the figures of great serpents and evil-looking gods. In the middle was something like an altar, covered with clotted blood, and on the other side of the idols were symbols like crosses, and all were coloured. We stood astonished, never having seen or heard of such things before.

It appears that they had just sacrificed some Indians to their idols, so as to ensure victory over us. However, many Indian women were strolling about most peacefully, as it seemed, laughing and amusing themselves. But as the men were gathered in such numbers, we were afraid that there might be another ambush, like that at Catoche.[1] At this point many more Indians came up ... At that moment there came from another house, which was the temple of their idols, ten Indians ... These were the priests of their gods, who in New Spain are generally called *papas* ... By means of signs they gave us to understand that we must leave their land before the firewood that they had piled there burnt out. Otherwise they would attack us and kill us ...

When we saw these great bands of Indians threatening us so boldly we were afraid. For we had not yet recovered from the wounds received at Cape Catoche, and had just thrown overboard the bodies of two soldiers who had died. So we decided to retire to the coast in good order, and began to march along the shore towards a large rock which rose out of the sea, while the boats and the small ship laden with the water-casks coasted along close to the shore. We had not dared to embark near the town, where we had landed, since a great number of Indians were waiting for us there, and we were sure they would attack as we did so ...

We sailed on for six days and nights in good weather. Then we were struck by a *norther*, which is a cross-wind on that coast. It lasted four days and nights, and was so strong that it almost drove us ashore, and forced us to anchor. In doing so we broke two cables, and one ship began to drag. Our danger was very great, for if the last cable had broken we should have been driven ashore and destroyed. But, thank God, we were able to ease the strain by lashing it with ropes and hawsers.

When the weather had improved, we continued to follow the coast, going ashore as often as we could, to take fresh water. For, as I have said, our casks were not watertight. They gaped and we could not repair them ...

As we sailed on our course we sighted another town ... Then we went ashore in our boats and the smallest ship, carrying all our casks and well provided with weapons. We landed a little after midday three miles from the

---

[1] The name given by the expeditionary force to the place where they earlier made landfall and encountered Amerindians.

town, where there were some pools, some maize plantations, and a few small stone houses. As we were filling our casks, many bands of Indians came along the coast from the town of Champoton, as it is called, wearing cotton armour to the knees, and carrying bows and arrows, lances and shields, swords which appeared to be two-handed, slings and stones. They wore the habitual feathered crests, their faces were painted black and white and rust-red, and they approached us silently. They came straight towards us, as if in peace, and asked us by signs whether we came from the east. We replied also by signs that we did. We were puzzled by the words that they then called out to us, which were the same as the Indians at Lazaro had used. But we could not make out what they meant. All this happened about nightfall, and the Indians then went off to some near-by village. We posted sentinels as a precaution, for we mistrusted these great assemblies of Indians.

As we watched through the night, we heard a great band of warriors approaching from the farms and the town, and we well knew that this boded us no good. We discussed what we should do, and some were for embarking immediately. As is usual in such cases, there was no agreement . . . A few of us were for attacking them in the night, for, as the proverb goes, the first blow is half the battle.

While we were still debating, the dawn broke, and we saw that we were outnumbered by two hundred to one. So wishing one another a stout heart for the fight, we commended ourselves to God and did our best to save our lives.

Once it was daylight we could see many more warriors advancing along the coast with banners raised and plumes and drums, to join the others who had gathered during the night. After forming up in squadrons and surround-ing us on all sides, they assailed us with such a shower of arrows and darts and stones from their slings that more than eighty of our soldiers were wounded. Then they attacked us hand to hand, some with lances and some shooting arrows, and others with their two-handed cutting swords. Though we fought back with swords and muskets and crossbows they brought us to a bad pass . . .

Our captain saw that good fighting did not help us, since so many bands surrounded us and so many more were coming up fresh from the town, bringing food and drink with them and a large supply of arrows. All our soldiers had received two or three arrows, three of them had their throats pierced by lance-thrusts, and our captain was bleeding from many wounds. Already fifty of our men had been killed, and we knew that we had no more strength to resist. So we determined with stout hearts to break through the Indian battalions and seek shelter in our boats, which lay off shore, not far away. Thus we saved ourselves . . .

Then we ran into another danger. As we all jumped into the boats at the same time, and there were many of us, they began to sink. Clinging to the sides of the waterlogged craft as best we could, and half swimming, we reached the vessel of shallowest draught, which came in haste to our assistance. Many of our men were wounded again as we embarked, especially those who were clinging to the stern of the boats, for they presented a good target. The Indians even waded into the sea with their lances, and attacked us with all their might. But, thank God, by a great effort we escaped with our lives from these people's clutches.

The battle had lasted an hour, and in addition to the fifty men or more killed and the two prisoners we threw five men overboard a few days later, who had died of their wounds and of the great thirst we suffered . . .

After attending to our wounds, we decided to return to Cuba. But as almost all the sailors were wounded we had not enough men to tend the sails. So we abandoned our smallest vessel and set fire to her after removing her sails, cables, and anchors and dividing her unwounded crew among the two larger vessels. But we had even worse trouble in our lack of fresh water . . . We had such a thirst that our mouths and tongues were cracked, and there was nothing to give us relief. Such are the hardships to be endured when discovering new lands in the manner that we set about it! No one can imagine their severity who has not himself endured them.

[Díaz describes Cortés's 1519 march from the coast to Mexico City, seat of the Aztec ruler Montezuma, through neighbouring towns.]

Next morning, we came to a broad causeway and continued our march towards Iztapalapa. And when we saw all those cities and villages built in the water, and other great towns on dry land, and that straight and level causeway leading to Mexico, we were astounded. These great towns and *cues* [temples] and buildings rising from the water, all made of stone, seemed like an enchanted vision from the tale of Amadis.[2] Indeed, some of our soldiers asked whether it was not all a dream . . .

When we arrived near Iztapalapa we beheld the splendour of the other *Caciques* who came out to meet us,[3] the lord of that city whose name was Cuitlahuac, and the lord of Culuacan, both of them close relations of Montezuma. And when we entered the city of Iztapalapa, the sight of the palaces in which they lodged us! They were very spacious and well built, of magnificent stone, cedar wood, and the wood of other sweet-smelling trees, with great rooms and courts, which were a wonderful sight, and all covered with awnings of woven cotton.

When we had taken a good look at all this, we went to the orchard and garden, which was a marvellous place both to see and walk in. I was never tired of noticing the diversity of trees and the various scents given off by each, and the paths choked with roses and other flowers, and the many local fruit-trees and rose-bushes, and the pond of fresh water. Another remarkable thing was that large canoes could come into the garden from the lake, through a channel they had cut, and their crews did not have to disembark. Everything was shining with lime and decorated with different kinds of stonework and paintings which were a marvel to gaze on. Then there were birds of many breeds and varieties which came to the pond. I say again that I stood looking at it, and thought that no land like it would ever be

[2] A prose romance which was very popular in sixteenth-century Spain.
[3] A tribe of Amerindians who began as the Spaniards' enemies but later became their allies.

discovered in the whole world, because at that time Peru was neither known ? reper
nor thought of. But today all that I then saw is overthrown and destroyed; ϰ
nothing is left standing . . .

[The Spaniards are courteously received by Montezuma.]

The great Montezuma had some fine gold jewels of various shapes in
readiness which he gave to Cortés after this conversation. And to each of our
captains he presented small gold objects and three loads of cloaks of rich
feather work; and to us soldiers he gave two loads of cloaks each, all with a
princely air. For in every way he was like a great prince . . .

He said that . . . we were in his house, which we might call our own. Here
we might rest and enjoy ourselves, for we should receive good treatment. If
on other occasions he had sent to forbid our entrance to his city, it was not of
his own free will, but because his vassals were afraid. For they told him we
shot out flashes of lightning, and killed many Indians with our horses, and
that we were angry *Teules* [gods], and other such childish stories . . .

We all thanked him heartily for his signal good will, and Montezuma
replied with a laugh, because in his princely manner he spoke very gaily:
'Malinche,[4] I know that these people of Tlascala with whom you are so
friendly have told you that I am a sort of god or *Teule*, and keep nothing in
any of my houses that is not made of silver and gold and precious stones. But
I know very well that you are too intelligent to believe this and will take it as
a joke. See now, Malinche, my body is made of flesh and blood like yours,
and my houses and palaces are of stone, wood, and plaster. It is true that I
am a great king, and have inherited the riches of my ancestors, but the lies
and nonsense you have heard of us are not true. You must take them as a
joke, as I take the story of your thunders and lightnings.'

Cortés answered also with a laugh that enemies always speak evil and tell
lies about the people they hate, but he knew he could not hope to find a
more magnificent prince in that land, and there was good reason why his
fame should have reached our Emperor . . .

As it was now past midday and he did not wish to be importunate, Cortés
said to Montezuma: 'My lord, the favours you do us increase, load by load,
every day, and it is now the hour of your dinner.' Montezuma answered that
he thanked us for visiting him. We then took our leave with the greatest
courtesy . . .

[The Spaniards explore Montezuma's city.]

On reaching the market-place, escorted by the many *Caciques* whom
Montezuma had assigned to us, we were astounded at the great number of
people and the quantities of merchandise, and at the orderliness and good
arrangements that prevailed, for we had never seen such a thing before. The
chieftains who accompanied us pointed everything out. Every kind of
merchandise was kept separate and had its fixed place marked for it.

Let us begin with the dealers in gold, silver, and precious stones, feathers,
cloaks, and embroidered goods, and male and female slaves who are also

---

[4] Montezuma's name for Cortés.

sold there. They bring as many slaves to be sold in that market as the Portuguese bring Negroes from Guinea . . . Next there were those who sold coarser cloth, and cotton goods and fabrics made of twisted thread, and there were chocolate merchants with their chocolate. In this way you could see every kind of merchandise to be found anywhere in New Spain . . .

There were sellers of kidney-beans and sage and other vegetables and herbs in another place, and in yet another they were selling fowls, and birds with great dewlaps [turkeys], also rabbits, hares, deer, young ducks, little dogs, and other such creatures . . . Elsewhere they sold timber too, boards, cradles, beams, blocks, and benches, all in a quarter of their own . . .

I must also mention, with all apologies, that they sold many canoe-loads of human excrement, which they kept in the creeks near the market. This was for the manufacture of salt and the curing of skins, which they say cannot be done without it . . .

They have a building there also in which three judges sit, and there are officials like constables who examine the merchandise . . .

[The Spaniards accompany Montezuma to the Aztec temple.]

On each altar was a giant figure, very tall and very fat. They said that the one on the right was Huichilobos, their war-god. He had a very broad face and huge terrible eyes . . .

There were some smoking braziers of their incense, which they call copal, in which they were burning the hearts of three Indians whom they had sacrificed that day; and all the walls of that shrine were so splashed and caked with blood that they and the floor too were black. Indeed, the whole place stank abominably . . .

 I have already described the manner of their sacrifices. They strike open the wretched Indian's chest with flint knives and hastily tear out the palpitating heart which, with the blood, they present to the idols in whose name they have performed the sacrifice. Then they cut off the arms, thighs, and head, eating the arms and thighs at their ceremonial banquets. The head they hang up on a beam, and the body of the sacrificed man is not eaten but given to the beasts of prey . . .

A little apart from the *cue* [temple] stood another small tower which was also an idol-house or true hell, for one of its doors was in the shape of a terrible mouth, such as they paint to depict the jaws of hell. This mouth was open and contained great fangs to devour souls. Beside this door were groups of devils and the shapes of serpents, and a little way off was a place of sacrifice, all blood-stained and black with smoke. There were many great pots and jars and pitchers in this house, full of water. For it was here that they cooked the flesh of the wretched Indians who were sacrificed and eaten by the *papas* [priests]. Near this place of sacrifice there were many large knives and chopping-blocks like those on which men cut up meat in slaughter-houses; and behind that dreadful house, some distance away, were great piles of brushwood, beside which was a tank of water that was filled and emptied through a pipe from the covered channel that comes into the city from Chapultepec. I always called that building Hell.

10 John White: Voyage to Virginia (1590)

Source: *The Virginia Voyages from Hakluyt*, edited by D. B. Quinn and A. M. Quinn (London: Oxford University Press, 1973), pp. 122–8, abridged and spelling modernized by A. Laurence.

John White (fl. 1577–93) took part in Sir Richard Grenville's 1585–6 expedition to Virginia and stayed with the shortlived colony on Roanoke Island off the coast of North Carolina. During this period he was commissioned to make sketches of the Indians and the indigenous flora and fauna. He was subsequently appointed governor of the second and even more tragic settlement of 1587, but left the colony in August of that year to return to England in order to secure supplies. He was not able to return to Virginia until 1590 whereupon he discovered the settlement abandoned. In 1593 he sent a copy of his journal of the 1590 voyage to the geographer Richard Hakluyt, who published it as part of volume 3 of his revised edition of *The Principal Navigations, Voyages and Discoveries of the English Nation* (1600).

The next morning being the 17 of August, our boats and company were prepared again to go up to Roanoake, but Captain Spicer had then sent his boat ashore for fresh water, by means whereof it was ten of the clock afternoon before we put from our ships which were then come to anchor within two miles of the shore . . . We had a sea break into our boat which filled us half full of water, but by the will of God and careful steerage of Captain Cooke we came safe ashore, saving only that our furniture, victuals, match and powder were much wet and spoiled . . . Captain Spicer came to the entrance of the breach[1] with his mast standing up, and was half passed over, but by the rash and indiscreet steerage of Ralph Skinner his master's mate, a very dangerous sea broke into their boat and overset them quite, [yet] the men kept the boat, some in it, some hanging on it. But the next sea set the boat on ground, where it beat to, so that some of them were forced to let go their hold, hoping to wade ashore, but the sea still beat them down so that they could neither stand nor swim, and the boat twice or thrice was turned keel upward; whereon Captain Spicer and Skinner hung on till they sunk, and [were] seen no more. But four that could swim a little kept themselves in deeper water and were saved by Captain Cooke's means . . . They were a [*sic*] 11 in all, and 7 of the chiefest were drowned . . . This mischance did so discomfit the sailors, that they were all of one mind not to go any further to seek the planters. But in the end by the commandment and persuasion of me and Captain Cooke, they prepared the boats: and seeing the Captain and me so resolute, they seemed much more willing. Our boats and all things fitted again, we put off from Hatorask, being the number of 19 persons in both boats . . . We therefore landed at daybreak . . . From hence we went through the woods to that part of the island directly over against Dasamongwepeuk, and from thence we returned by the water side, round about the north point of the island, until we came to the place where I left

---

[1] An inlet with water breaking on a bar or shoal nearby.

our colony in the year 1586.[2] In all this way we saw in the sand the print of the savages' feet of 2 or 3 sorts trodden that night, and as we entered up the sandy bank upon a tree, in the very brow thereof were curiously carved these fair Roman letters CRO: which letters presently we knew to signify the place where I should find the planters seated, according to a secret token agreed upon between them and me at my last departure from them, which was, that in any ways they should not fail to write or carve on the trees or posts of the doors the name of the place where they should be seated; for at my coming away they were prepared to remove from Roanoake 50 miles into the main [mainland]. Therefore at my departure from them in Anno 1587 I willed them, that if they should happen to be distressed in any of those places, that then they should carve over the letters or name, a cross in this form, but we found no such sign of distress. And having well considered of this, we passed toward the place where they were left in sundry houses, but we found the houses taken down, and the place very strongly enclosed with a high palisade of great trees . . . very fort-like, and one of the chief trees or posts on the right side of the entrance had the bark taken off, and 5 foot from the ground in fair capital letters was graven CROATOAN without any cross or sign of distress; this done, we entered into the palisade, where we found many bars of iron, two pigs of lead, four iron fowlers, iron sackershot,[3] and suchlike heavy things, thrown here and there, almost overgrown with grass and weeds. From thence we went along by the water side, towards the point of the creek, to see if we could find any of their boats or pinnace, but we could perceive no sign of them, nor any of the last falcons and small ordnance which were left with them, at my departure from them. At our return from the creek, some of our sailors meeting us, told us that they had found where divers chests had been hidden, and long sithence digged up again and broken up, and much of the goods in them spoiled and scattered about, but nothing left, of such things as the savages knew any use of, undefaced. Presently Captain Cooke and I went to the place, which was at the end of an old trench, made two years past by Captain Amadas: where we found five chests, that had been carefully hidden by the planters, and of the same chests three were my own, and about the place many of my things spoiled and broken, and my books torn from the covers, the frames of some of my pictures and maps rotten and spoiled with rain, and my armour almost eaten through with rust; this could be no other but the deed of the savages our enemies at Dasamongwepeuk, who had watched the departure of our men to Croatoan; and as soon as they were departed, digged up every place where they suspected anything to be buried: but although it much grieved me to see such spoil of my goods, yet on the other side I greatly joyed that I had safely found a certain token of their safe being in Croatoan, which is the place where . . . the savages of the island [are] our friends.

When we had seen in this place so much as we could, we returned to our boats . . . Therefore the same evening with much danger and labour, we got

---

[2] It was, in point of fact, 1587 when White left the colony to return to England.
[3] Cannon balls used in a small cannon (a sacker, saker).

ourselves aboard, by which time the wind and the seas were so greatly risen, that we doubted our cables and anchors would scarcely hold until morning: wherefore the Captain caused the boat to be manned with five lusty men, who could swim all well, and sent them to the little island on the right hand of the harbour, to bring aboard six of our men, who had filled our cask with fresh water: the boat the same night returned aboard with our men, but all our cask ready filled they left behind, impossible to be had aboard without danger of casting away both men and boats; for this night proved very stormy and foul.

The next morning it was agreed by the Captain and myself, with the Master and others, to weigh anchor, and go for the place at Croatoan where our planters were: for that then the wind was good for that place, and also to leave that cask with fresh water on shore in the island until our return. So then they brought the cable to the capstan, but . . . the cable broke, by means whereof we lost another anchor, wherewith we drove so fast into the shore, that we were forced to let fall a third anchor; which came so fast home that the ship was almost aground . . . so that we were forced to let slip the cable . . . And if it had not been chanced that we had fallen into a channel of deeper water, closer by the shore than we accounted of, we could never have gone clear of the point that lyeth to the southwards . . . Being thus clear of some dangers, and gotten into deeper waters, but not without some loss; for we had but one cable and anchor left us of four, and the weather grew to be fouler and fouler; our victuals scarce, and our cask and fresh water lost: it was therefore determined that we should go for Saint John[4] or some other island to the southward for fresh water. And it was further purposed, that if we could any ways supply our wants of victuals and other necessaries, either at Hispaniola, Saint John, or Trinidad, that then we should continue in the Indies all the winter following, with hope to make 2 rich voyages of one, and at our return to visit our countrymen at Virginia. The Captain and the whole company in the Admiral (with my earnest petitions) thereunto agreed, so that it rested only to know what the master of the Moon-light our consort[5] would do herein. But when we demanded them if they would accompany us in that new determination, they alleged that their weak and leaky ship was not able to continue it; wherefore the same night we parted, leaving the Moon-light to go directly for England, and the Admiral set his course for Trinidad, which course we kept two days.

[4] San Juan de Puerto Rico.
[5] A ship belonging to William Sanderson, a member of the syndicate which financed this expedition.

11 Aztec Account of the Conquest of Mexico (1519)

Source: *The Spanish Tradition in America*, edited by C. Gibson (New York: Harper & Row, 1968), pp. 90–2. Translated by A. M. Garibay and L. Kemp.

This extract is from a sixteenth-century manuscript. The narrators belong to the Tlatelolco community, a subdivision of the Aztec capital, Tenochtitlán. The text identifies the year as 3-House, which according to the European calendar would be 1519.

Now the Spaniards began to wage war against us. They attacked us by land for ten days, and then their ships appeared. Twenty days later, they gathered all their ships together near Nonohualco, off the place called Mazatzinta-malco. The allies from Tlaxcala and Huexotzinco set up camp on either side of the road.

Our warriors from Tlatelolco immediately leaped into their canoes and set out for Mazatzintamalco and the Nonohualco road. But no one set out from Tenochtitlán to assist us: only the Tlatelolcas[1] were ready when the Spaniards arrived in their ships. On the following day, the ships sailed to Xoloco.

The fighting at Xoloco and Huitzillan lasted for two days. While the battle was under way, the warriors from Tenochtitlán began to mutiny. They said: 'Where are our chiefs? They have fired scarcely a single arrow! Do they think they have fought like men?' Then they seized four of their own leaders and put them to death. The victims were two captains, Cuauhnochtli and Cuapan, and the priests of Amantlan and Tlalocan. This was the second time that the people of Tenochtitlán killed their own leaders.

The Spaniards set up two cannons in the middle of the road and aimed them at the city. When they fired them, one of the shots struck the Eagle Gate. The people of the city were so terrified that they began to flee to Tlatelolco. They brought their idol Huitzilopochtli with them, setting it up in the House of the Young Men. Their king Cuauhtemoc[2] also abandoned Tenochtitlán. Their chiefs said: 'Mexicanos! Tlatelolcas! All is not lost! We can still defend our houses. We can prevent them from capturing our storehouses and the produce of our lands. We can save the sustenance of life, our stores of corn. We can also save our weapons and insignia, our clusters of rich feathers, our gold earrings and precious stones. Do not be discouraged; do not lose heart. We are Mexicanos! We are Tlatelolcas!'

During the whole time we were fighting, the warriors of Tenochtitlán were nowhere to be seen. The battles at Yacacolco, Atezcapan, Coatlan, Nonohualco, Xoxohuitlan, Tepeyacac and elsewhere were all fought by ourselves, by Tlatelolcas. In the same way, the canals were defended solely by Tlatelolcas.

---

[1] The people of Tlatelolco.
[2] The Aztec leader.

The captains from Tenochtitlán cut their hair short, and so did those of lesser rank. The Otomies and the other ranks that usually wore headdresses did not wear them during all the time we were fighting. The Tlatelolcas surrounded the most important captains and their women taunted them: 'Why are you hanging back? Have you no shame? No woman will ever paint her face for you again!' The wives of the men from Tenochtitlán wept and begged for pity.

When the warriors of Tlatelolco heard what was happening, they began to shout, but still the brave captains of Tenochtitlán hung back. As for the Tlatelolcas, their humblest warriors died fighting as bravely as their captains . . .

The Spaniards made ready to attack us, and the war broke out again. They assembled their forces in Cuepopan and Cozcacuahco. A vast number of our warriors were killed by their metal darts. Their ships sailed to Texopan, and the battle there lasted three days. When they had forced us to retreat, they entered the Sacred Patio, where there was a four-day battle. Then they reached Yacacolco.

The Tlatelolcas set up three racks of heads in three different places. The first rack was in the Sacred Patio of Tlilancalco [Black House], where we strung up the heads of our lords the Spaniards. The second was in Acacolco, where we strung up Spanish heads and the heads of two of their horses. The third was in Zacatla, in front of the temple of the earth-goddess Cihuacoatl, where we strung up the heads of Tlaxcaltecas.

The women of Tlatelolco joined in the fighting. They struck at the enemy and shot arrows at them; they tucked up their skirts and dressed in the regalia of war.

The Spaniards forced us to retreat. Then they occupied the market place. The Tlatelolcas – the Jaguar Knights, the Eagle Knights, the great warriors – were defeated, and this was the end of the battle. It had lasted five days, and two thousand Tlatelolcas were killed in action. During the battle, the Spaniards set up a canopy for the Captain in the market place. They also mounted a catapult on the temple platform . . .

Cuauhtemoc was taken to Cortés along with three other princes. The Captain was accompanied by Pedro de Alvarado and La Malinche.[3]

When the princes were made captives, the people began to leave, searching for a place to stay. Everyone was in tatters, and the women's thighs were almost naked. The Christians searched all the refugees. They even opened the women's skirts and blouses and felt everywhere: their ears, their breasts, their hair. Our people scattered in all directions. They went to neighbouring villages and huddled in corners in the houses of strangers.

The city was conquered in the year 3-House. The date on which we departed was the day 1-Serpent in the ninth month.

---

[3] The Aztec name for Cortés.

12 Amerigo Vespucci: Letter to Piero Soderini (1504)

Source: A Book of Travellers' Tales, edited by E. Newby (London: Collins, 1985), pp. 453–4 abridged. Translated by G. Tyler Northup.

Amerigo Vespucci (1454–1512), the Florentine navigator after whom America was named, has been credited with four separate voyages to America. On the first (to which this extract refers), he probably set out from Cadiz in May 1497, sailed first to the Canaries and then possibly to the Gulf of Mexico and the southern seaboard of North America, reaching what was to become North Carolina. From the evidence of three surviving copies of Vespucci's account of this voyage, it seems likely that the original text was written in Spanish and presented to the explorer's principal patron, Ferdinand of Spain. Vespucci, as a good publicist, subsequently sent copies in translation to other European rulers, including Piero Soderini, then head of the Florentine government.

The manner of their living is very barbarous, because they do not eat at fixed times, but as often as they please. And it matters little to them that they should be seized with a desire to eat at midnight rather than by day, for at all times they eat ... They sleep in certain nets made of cotton, very big, and hung in the air. And although this their way of sleeping may appear uncomfortable, I say that it is a soft way to sleep; because it was very frequently our lot to sleep in them, and we slept better in them than in quilts. They are people neat and clean of person, owing to the constant washing they practise. When, begging your pardon, they evacuate the bowels, they do everything to avoid being seen; and just as in this they are clean and modest, the more dirty and shameless are they in making water (both men and women) ... They are not very jealous, and are libidinous beyond measure, and the women far more than the men ... They are so heartless and cruel that, if they become angry with their husbands, they immediately resort to a trick whereby they kill the child within the womb, and a miscarriage is brought about, and for this reason they kill a great many babies. They are women of pleasing person, very well proportioned, so that one does not see on their bodies any ill-formed feature or limb. And although they go about utterly naked, they are fleshy women, and that part of their privies which he who has not seen them would think to see is invisible ... They showed themselves very desirous of copulating with us Christians. While among these people we did not learn that they had any religion. They can be termed neither Moors nor Jews; and they are worse than heathen; because we did not see that they offered any sacrifice, nor yet did they have [any] house of prayer. I deem their manner of life to be Epicurean.[1] Their dwellings are in common, and their houses built after the fashion of huts, but stoutly wrought and constructed out of very large trees and thatched with palm leaves, safe against tempests and winds, and in some places of such breadth and length that in a single house we found there were 600 souls; and we saw

[1] i.e. devoted to refined, sensuous pleasure.

towns of only thirteen houses where there were 4,000 souls ... Their wealth consists of feathers of many-hued birds, or of little rosaries which they make out of fish bones, or of white or green stones which they stick through cheeks, lips, and ears, and of many other things to which we attach no value.

13 Columbus: First Voyage (1492–1493)

Source: *The Four Voyages of Christopher Columbus*, edited and translated by J. M. Cohen (Harmondsworth: Penguin Books, 1969), pp. 55–61 abridged.

Christopher Columbus (1451–1506), Genoese explorer, made four voyages of discovery to America which were recorded in a number of letters and dispatches written by him and the officers who sailed with him. His log-book for the voyages is now lost but for a time it was in the possession of Bartolomé de las Casas, who used it as a source for his history of the Indies, written *c*.1552. His editing is evident in the excerpt from the digest of Columbus's log-book of his first voyage undertaken between 1492 and 1493, when he made a landfall on the coast of Cuba.

In order to win their friendship,[1] since I knew they were a people to be converted and won to our holy faith by love and friendship rather than by force, I gave some of them red caps and glass beads which they hung round their necks, also many other trifles. These things pleased them greatly and they became marvellously friendly to us. They afterwards swam out to the ship's boats in which we were sitting, bringing us parrots and balls of cotton thread and spears and many other things, which they exchanged with us for such objects as glass beads, hawks and bells. In fact, they very willingly traded everything they had. But they seemed to me a people very short of everything. They all go naked as their mothers bore them, including the women, although I saw only one very young girl ... They should be good servants and very intelligent, for I have observed that they soon repeat anything that is said to them, and I believe that they would easily be made Christians, for they appeared to me to have no religion. God willing, when I make my departure I will bring half a dozen of them back to their Majesties,[2] so that they can learn to speak. I saw no animals of any kind on this island except parrots ...

I went to view all this [the east part of the island] this morning, in order to give an account to your Majesties and to decide where a fort could be built. I saw a piece of land which is much like an island, though it is not one, on which there were six huts. It could be made into an island in two days, though I see no necessity to do so since these people are very unskilled in arms, as your Majesties will discover from seven whom I caused to be taken and brought aboard so that they may learn our language and return.

[1] Here Columbus is describing the Indians of San Salvador (Watling Island), an island where he went ashore and of which he took possession in the name of the Spanish Crown.

[2] Ferdinand and Isabella of Spain, patrons of the explorer.

However, should your Highnesses command it all the inhabitants could be taken away to Castile or held as slaves on the island, for with fifty men we could subjugate them all and make them do whatever we wish . . .

As from this island I saw another larger one to the west, I hoisted sail to run all that day till night, since I should otherwise not have been able to reach its western point. I named this island Santa Maria de la Concepción.[3] And it was almost sunset when I reached this point. I wished to learn whether there was gold there, because the men I had taken aboard at the island at San Salvador told me that here they wore very large gold bracelets round their legs and arms. I thought that this tale was probably a lie told in the hope of getting away. Generally it was my wish to pass no island without taking possession of it. Though having annexed one it might be said that we had annexed all. I anchored and stayed there until today, Tuesday, when at daybreak I approached the shore with the armed boats and landed.

There were many people all naked and like those of San Salvador. They let us go about the island and gave us all that we asked for. But as the wind was blowing from the south-east I did not wish to delay and went back to the ship. A large canoe happening to lie alongside the *Niña*,[4] a little before midnight one of the men from San Salvador who was in the caravel[5] jumped overboard and went off in it. A few minutes later another threw himself overboard also and swam after the canoe, which went so fast that no boat could overtake it, for it had a considerable start.

So they came to land and left the canoe. Several members of my crew went ashore after them and they ran off like frightened hens. We took the canoe they had abandoned aboard the caravel *Niña*; it was approached by another small canoe with a man who had come to barter a ball of cotton. Since he would not board the caravel some sailors jumped down and seized him. Having seen all this from the forecastle where I was standing, I sent for him and gave him a red cap and some green glass beads which I put on his arm and two hawks' bells which I put in his ears. I told the sailors to give him back his canoe which they had taken on to the ship's boat, and sent him ashore. I then raised sail for the other large island which I saw to the west and ordered that the second canoe which the *Niña* was towing astern should be set adrift. Shortly afterwards I saw the man to whom I had given these gifts come ashore.

I had not taken the ball of cotton from him, although he wished to give it to me. The people gathered round him and he appeared astonished. It seemed to him that we were good people and that the man who had escaped in the canoe must have wronged us or we should not have carried him off.

It was to create this impression that I had him set free and gave him presents. I was anxious that they should think well of us so that they may not be unfriendly when your Majesties send a second expedition here. All I gave him was worth less than four *maravedis*.[6]

---

[3] Rum Kay, one of the islands in the Bahamas.
[4] One of the ships on the expedition.
[5] A small, light and fast ship.
[6] A small copper coin.

14 Sepúlveda: On the Indians (c.1547)

Source: Juan Ginés de Sepúlveda, *Democrates alter de justi belli causis apud Indos*, in *Latin American History: Select Problems. Identity, Integration, Nationhood*, edited by F. B. Pike; translations by J. L. Phenan (New York: Harcourt, Brace & World, 1969), pp. 47–51 abridged.

Juan Ginés de Sepúlveda, sixteenth-century Spanish theologian and champion of Spanish colonists, wrote this treatise (in Latin) as a justification for the Spanish imperial policies within the New World. Written *circa* 1547, the manuscript was circulated during the sixteenth century but not published until 1892.

You should remember that authority and power are not only of one kind but of several varieties, since in one way and with one kind of law the father commands his children, in another the husband commands his wife, in another the master commands his servants, in another the judge commands the citizens, in another the king commands the peoples and human beings confined to his authority … Although each jurisdiction may appear different, they all go back to a single principle, as the wise men teach. That is, the perfect should command and rule over the imperfect, the excellent over its opposite …

And thus we see that among inanimate objects, the more perfect directs and dominates, and the less perfect obeys its command. This principle is even clearer and more obvious among animals, where the mind rules like a mistress and the body submits like a servant. In the same way the rational part of the soul rules and directs the irrational part, which submits and obeys. All of this derives from divine and natural law, both of which demand that the perfect and most powerful rule over the imperfect and the weaker …

The man rules over the woman, the adult over the child, the father over his children. That is to say, the most powerful and most perfect rule over the weakest and most imperfect. This same relationship exists among men, there being some who by nature are masters and others who by nature are slaves. Those who surpass the rest in prudence and intelligence, although not in physical strength, are by nature the masters. On the other hand those who are dim-witted and mentally lazy, although they may be physically strong enough to fulfil all the necessary tasks, are by nature slaves. It is just and useful that it is this way. We even see it sanctioned in divine law itself, for it is written in the Book of Proverbs: 'He who is stupid will serve the wise man.' And so it is with the barbarous and inhumane people [the Indians] who have no civil life and peaceful customs. It will always be just and in conformity with natural law that such people submit to the rule of more cultured and humane princes and nations. Thanks to the virtues and the practical wisdom of their laws, the latter can destroy barbarism and educate these [inferior] people to a more humane and virtuous life. And if the latter reject such rule, it can be imposed upon them by force of arms. Such a war will be just according to natural law . . . One may believe as certain and undeniable, since it is affirmed by the wisest authors, that it is just and natural that prudent, upright, and humane men should rule over those who are not. On this basis the Romans established their legitimate and just rule over many nations, according to St Augustine in several passages of his work, *The City of God*,[1] which St Thomas [Aquinas] collected and cited in his work, *De regimine principum*.[2] Such being the case, you can well understand . . . if you know the customs and nature of the two peoples, that with perfect right the Spaniards rule over these barbarians of the New World and the adjacent islands, who in wisdom, intelligence, virtue, and humanitas[3] are as inferior to the Spaniards as infants to adults and women to men. There is as much difference between them as there is between cruel, wild peoples and the most merciful of peoples, between the most monstrously intemperate peoples and those who are temperate and moderate in their pleasures, that is to say, between apes and men.

You do not expect me to make a lengthy commemoration of the judgement and talent of the Spaniards . . . And who can ignore the other virtues of our people, their fortitude, their humanity, their love of justice and religion? I speak only of our princes and those who by their energy and industriousness have shown that they are worthy of administering the commonwealth. I refer in general terms only to those Spaniards who have received a liberal education. If some of them are wicked and unjust, that is no reason to denigrate the glory of their race, which should be judged by the actions of its cultivated and noble men and by its customs and public institutions, rather than by the actions of depraved persons who are similar to slaves . . .

Now compare these natural qualities of judgement, talent, magnanimity, temperance, humanity, and religion with those of these pitiful men [the Indians], in whom you will scarcely find any vestiges of humanness. These people possess neither science nor even an alphabet, nor do they preserve any monuments of their history except for some obscure and vague reminiscences depicted in certain paintings, nor do they have written laws, but barbarous institutions and customs. In regard to their virtues, how much restraint or gentleness are you to expect of men who are devoted to all kinds of intemperate acts and abominable lewdness, including the eating of human flesh? And you must realize that prior to the arrival of the Christians, they did not live in that peaceful kingdom of Saturn that the poets imagine,[4]

---

[1] One of the most celebrated works of this fifth-century saint. During the first decades of discovery and conquest, Spanish actions were largely justified by the view, identified with St Augustine, that only membership of the Church guaranteed the personal, political and economic rights of individuals.

[2] Thomas Aquinas, the Dominican theologian (1225–74), whose major works form the basis of much Catholic doctrine. He embraced in a single grand scheme the whole ideological world of the medieval Church including its views on politics as rehearsed in the *De regimine principum* (c.1265) cited here by Sepúlveda.

[3] The quality of mind and spirit which makes a given person competent to achieve civilization.

[4] A period when, according to some classical poets, Saturn, the god of agriculture, ruled and men lived without strife, labour and injustice.

but on the contrary they made war against one another continually and fiercely, with such fury that victory was of no meaning if they did not satiate their monstrous hunger with the flesh of their enemies . . . These Indians are so cowardly and timid that they could scarcely resist the mere presence of our soldiers. Many times thousands upon thousands of them scattered, fleeing like women before a very few Spaniards, who amounted to fewer than a hundred.

In regard to those [of the Aztec and other Indian civilizations] who inhabit New Spain and the province of Mexico, I have already said that they consider themselves the most civilized people [in the New World]. They boast of their political and social institutions, because they have rationally planned cities and non-hereditary kings who are elected by popular suffrage, and they carry on commerce among themselves in the manner of civilized people. But . . . I dissent from such an opinion. On the contrary, in those same institutions there is proof of the coarseness, barbarism, and innate servility of these men. Natural necessity encourages the building of houses, some rational manner of life, and some sort of commerce. Such an agreement merely proves that they are neither bears nor monkeys and that they are not totally irrational. But on the other hand they have established their commonwealth in such a manner that no one individually owns anything, neither a house nor a field that one may dispose of or leave to his heirs in his will, because everything is controlled by their lords, who are incorrectly called kings. They live more at the mercy of their king's will than of their own. They are the slaves of his will and caprice, and they are not the masters of their fate. The fact that this condition is not the result of coercion but is voluntary and spontaneous is a certain sign of the servile and base spirit of these barbarians . . .

War against these barbarians can be justified not only on the basis of their paganism but even more so because of their abominable licentiousness, their prodigious sacrifice of human victims, the extreme harm that they inflicted on innocent persons, their horrible banquets of human flesh, and the impious cult of their idols . . . What is more appropriate and beneficial for these barbarians than to become subject to the rule of those whose wisdom, virtue, and religion have converted them from barbarians into civilized men (insofar as they are capable of becoming so), from being torpid and licentious to becoming upright and moral, from being impious servants of the Devil to becoming believers in the true God? . . . For numerous and grave reasons these barbarians are obligated to accept the rule of the Spaniards by natural law . . . For them it ought to be even more advantageous than for the Spaniards, since virtue, humanity, and the true religion are more valuable than gold or silver. And if they refuse our rule, they may be compelled by force of arms to accept it.

15 Las Casas: On the Indians (1552)

Source: Bartolomé de las Casas, *Aquí se contienen treinta proposiciones muy jurídicas*, in *Latin American History*, edited by F. B. Pike (see document V. 14), pp. 52–7 abridged.

Bartolomé de las Casas (1475–1566), Dominican missionary, reformer, New World bishop, and friend of the Indians, wrote this treatise which contains thirty propositions as to why Christians (and in particular Christian rulers) had the right to convert the Indians to the Christian faith. The treatise was published in Spanish in Seville in 1552. As a result of his efforts the Council of the Indies framed a new legislative code for the New World – the New Laws.

PROPOSITION I

The Roman Pontiff, canonically chosen vicar of Jesus Christ and successor of St Peter, has the authority and the power of Christ himself, the Son of God, over all men in the world, believers or infidels, insofar as it is necessary to guide and direct men to the end of the eternal life and to remove any impediments to this goal. Although the Pontiff uses and ought to use such power in a special fashion with the infidels, who have never entered into holy baptism of the holy Church, especially those who never heard tidings of Christ nor of His faith, he uses another kind of authority with Christians and those who at one time were Christian.

PROPOSITION II

St Peter and his successors had and have a necessary duty by the injunctions of God to adopt measures with the greatest care that the gospel and faith of Jesus Christ may be preached to all men throughout the whole world, and in my opinion it is unlikely that anyone will resist the preaching of the gospel and the Christian doctrine . . .

PROPOSITION IV

. . . For the conversion of the infidels the Christian kings are very necessary for the Church; with their secular power, armed forces, and temporal wealth, they may help, protect, preserve, and defend the ecclesiastical and spiritual ministers . . .

PROPOSITION VII

In order to avoid confusion, the vicar of Christ with his divine authority can and has wisely and justly divided the kingdoms and provinces of all the infidels, of whatever infidelity or sect they may be, among the Christian princes, charging and entrusting those princes with the task of spreading the holy faith, the expansion of the universal Church and the Christian religion, and the conversion and health of their souls as the ultimate end.

Proposition VIII

This division, commission, or concession was not made (nor is it made, nor should the Sovereign Pontiff in the future make it) primarily or ultimately to concede grace or to increase the power of Christian states and to bestow on these princes honour, titles, and riches, but primarily and ultimately for the spread of the divine worship, the glory of God, and the conversion and salvation of the infidels, which is the purpose and final intention of the King of kings and the Master of masters, Jesus Christ. He imposed a most dangerous duty and office upon the Christian princes, about which they will have to give the most meticulous account before divine judgement at the end of their lives. Thus, the said division and grant is more for the well-being and profit of the infidels than of the Christian princes.

Proposition IX

It is a just and worthy thing that the primary reward of Christian kings for the services they render to God and the welfare of the universal Mother Church in their royal persons does not consist in worldly and earthly things – to which kings should not aspire, for they are transitory and of little value – but in co-reigning with Christ in heaven ... The Supreme Pontiff may concede and donate to Christian princes compensation in the kingdoms of the infidels in order to fulfil the purpose for which he originally entrusted those kingdoms to them. This is a just thing, which does not notably harm or damage the rights of those kings, princes, and notable individuals among the infidels.

Proposition X

Among the infidels who have distant kingdoms that have never heard the tidings of Christ or received the faith, there are true kings and princes. Their sovereignty, dignity, and royal pre-eminence derive from natural law and the law of nations ... Therefore, with the coming of Jesus Christ to such domains, their honours, royal pre-eminence, and so on, do not disappear either in fact or in right.

Proposition XI

The opinion contrary to that of the preceding proposition is erroneous and most pernicious. He who persistently defends it will fall into formal heresy. It is likewise most impious and iniquitous and has been the cause of innumerable thefts, violent disturbances, tyrannies, massacres, larcenies, irreparable damages, the gravest sins, infamy, stench, and hatred against the name of Christ and the Christian religion ...

PROPOSITION XII

The said infidels, monarchs or subjects, are not deprived of their domains, dignities, or other property by any sin of idolatry or any other sin, regardless of how grave or abominable it may be . . .

PROPOSITION XIII

Infidels, especially those whose paganism is a simple denial, cannot be punished by any judge in the world for the sin of idolatry or for any other sin they committed during their infidelity, regardless of how enormous, extensive, or abominable such sins may have been, until they voluntarily receive the sacrament of holy Baptism. The only exceptions are those infidels who maliciously obstruct the preaching of the gospel and who refuse to desist after they have been sufficiently warned.

PROPOSITION XIV

The Sovereign Pontiff, Alexander VI, during whose reign the vast new world that we call the West Indies was discovered, had the duty by divine injunction to select a Christian king to whom he could entrust the task of preaching the gospel in those lands. That Christian king was also to have the responsibility of establishing and spreading the divine cult and the universal Church in all the kingdoms of the Indies . . . In compensation for this undertaking, the Pope granted him the dignity and the imperial crown of [universal] sovereignty over all the kingdoms of the New World.

PROPOSITION XV

The kings of Castile and León, Ferdinand and Isabella, the Catholic kings, possessed more outstanding virtues than all the other Christian princes. For this reason, the Pope entrusted this task to them rather than to any other Christian prince . . . Among their notable virtues there are two in particular. First, inheriting from their royal ancestors the obligation to reconquer all of the Spanish kingdoms from the grip of the tyrannical Muslim enemies of our holy Catholic faith, with their own royal persons and at a heavy expense they reconquered the great kingdom of Granada and at long last restored it to Christ and the universal Church. Secondly, at their own expense and upon their own initiative they sponsored an expedition commanded by the eminent Christopher Columbus, whom they honoured and exalted with the title of First Admiral of the Indies, when he discovered the vast and extensive Indies.

PROPOSITION XVI

The Roman Pontiff, vicar of Jesus Christ, whose divine authority extends over all the kingdoms of heaven and earth, could justly invest the kings of Castile and León with the supreme and sovereign empire and dominion over the entire realm of the Indies, making them emperors over many kings ... If the vicar of Christ were to see that this was not advantageous for the spiritual well-being of Christianity, he could without doubt, by the same divine authority, annul or abolish the office of emperor of the Indies, or he could transfer it to another prince, as one Pope did when he transferred the imperial crown from the Greeks to the Germans [at the coronation of Charlemagne in 800]. With the same authority, the Apostolic See could prohibit, under penalty of excommunication, all other Christian kings from going to the Indies without the permission and authorization of the kings of Castile. If they do the contrary, they sin mortally and incur excommunication.

PROPOSITION XVII

The kings of Castile and León are true princes, sovereign and universal lords and emperors over many kings. The rights over all that great empire and the universal jurisdiction over all the Indies belong to them by the authority, concession, and donation of the said Holy Apostolic See and thus by divine authority. This and no other is the juridical basis upon which all their title is founded and established ...

PROPOSITION XIX

All the kings and princes, cities, communities, and towns of those Indies are obliged to recognize the kings of Castile as universal and sovereign lords and emperors in the said manner, after having received by their own free will our holy faith and the sacred Baptism. If before Baptism they do not wish to accept [the imperial sovereignty of Castile], they cannot be punished by any judge or justice.

PROPOSITION XX

The kings of Castile are obligated by the Apostolic See and also by divine law to procure, to provide, and to send with all diligence qualified ministers to preach the faith everywhere, calling and inviting the people in the Indies to come to the wedding and banquet of Christ ...

PROPOSITION XXII

The kings of Castile are obliged by divine law to ensure that the faith of Jesus Christ be preached in the same manner that He, the Son of God, established for His Church. [This method and this method only] was literally and without any change or diminution followed by His apostles, and the universal Church has made it customary law, enshrining it in its decrees and canons. The holy doctors expostulated and glorified it in their books. The gospel should be preached peacefully, with love, charity, sweetness, and affection, with meekness and good example. The infidels, especially the Indians (who by nature are very gentle, humble, and peaceful), should be persuaded by gifts and presents, and nothing should be taken away from them. And thus they will regard the God of the Christians as a good, gentle, and just God. Hence they will want to be His subjects and to receive His Catholic faith and holy doctrine.

PROPOSITION XXIII

To conquer them first by war is contrary to the law, gentle yoke, light load, and sweetness of Jesus Christ. It is the same approach that Mohammed and the Romans followed when they disturbed and plundered the world. It is the same manner that the Turks and Moors have adopted today . . . Therefore it is iniquitous, tyrannical, and infamous to the sweet name of Christ, causing infinite new blasphemies against the true God and against the Christian religion. And we have abundant evidence of the damage that this warlike approach has done and is still doing in the Indies. Since the Indians regard our God as the most cruel, unjust, and pitiless god of all, the conversion of the Indians has been hindered, and it has become impossible to convert infinite numbers of infidels . . .

PROPOSITION XXV

The kings of Castile have prohibited wars against the Indians of the Indies from the time that the First Admiral [Columbus] discovered them, but the Spaniards never honoured, observed, or fulfilled these orders and instructions that the kings issued . . .

PROPOSITION XXVI

Since our kings never sanctioned just wars against the innocent Indians . . . we affirm that all such wars that have taken place in the Indies since their discovery have been, are, and will be unjust, iniquitous, and tyrannical . . .

PROPOSITION XXVII

The kings of Castile are obliged by divine law to establish a government and administration over the native peoples of the Indies that will preserve their just laws and good customs and abolish the evil ones, which are very few . . . Whatever defects their society may have had can be removed and corrected with the preaching and the spread of the gospel . . .

PROPOSITION XXVIII

The Devil could invent no worse pestilence to destroy all that world and to kill all the people there ... than the *repartimiento*[1] and *encomienda*,[2] the institution used to distribute and entrust Indians to the Spaniards. This was like entrusting the Indians to a gang of devils or delivering herds of cattle to hungry wolves. The encomienda or repartimiento was the most cruel sort of tyranny that can be imagined, and it is most worthy of infernal damnation. The Indians were prevented from receiving the Christian faith and religion. The wretched and tyrannical Spanish encomenderos worked the Indians night and day in the mines and in other personal services. They collected unbelievable tributes. The encomenderos forced the Indians to carry burdens on their backs for a hundred and two hundred leagues, as if they were less than beasts. They persecuted and expelled from the Indian villages the preachers of the faith ... And I solemnly affirm, as God is my witness, that so long as these encomiendas remain, all the authority of the kings, even if they were resident in the Indies, will not be enough to prevent all the Indians from perishing.

16 Mendieta: On the Indians (1596)

Source: Gerónimo de Mendieta, *Historia eclesiástica indiana*, in *Latin American History*, edited by F. B. Pike (see document V.14), pp. 59–61.

Gerónimo de Mendieta (1525–1604) was a Spanish Franciscan who spent his life in Mexico and became a champion of his Indian parishioners. In 1596 he completed his chronicle *The Ecclesiastical History of Mexico* (*Historia eclesiástica indiana*), where he put forward a very personal view of what the conversion of the Indians signified. As an author Mendieta inherited the rich mystical tradition of the Franciscans and he therefore tended to express his thought in symbolic and poetic terms.

[MENDIETA'S EXEGESIS OF A PARABLE FROM LUKE 14]

As the hour of the supper approached (which symbolizes the end of the world), a certain man sent his servant out into the streets to invite the guests to the banquet. They excused themselves, each with a different pretext. It was therefore necessary to send the servant out a second time to the squares and streets to bring the poor, the weak, and the crippled so that they might be seated in the empty chairs at the supper. Yet there was still room for more guests, and so the host dispatched his servant for a third time to the highways and the hedgerows. He ordered his servant to compel people to

---

[1] The distribution of Indians among the Spanish colonists (*encomenderos*).

[2] An institution by which the Spanish Crown distributed the Indian population among the Spanish colonists, who in turn collected a yearly tribute from the Indians assigned to them. The colonists were obliged to provide protection to their Indian dependants but the system was subject to many abuses.

come to the supper so that his house might be filled. We well know (if we wish to consider the matter) that this business and task of searching, calling, and procuring souls for heaven is of such importance that our Almighty God ... has done nothing else (in our way of speaking) during the almost seven thousand years since He created the first man. By means of His illumina-tions, warnings, and punishments; by His servants, the patriarchs and prophets; by His own son in person, and later by the apostles, martyrs, preachers, and saints, God has been calling all the peoples of the earth to hasten to prepare themselves to enter and to enjoy that everlasting feast. This vocation of God will not cease until the number of the predestined is reached, which according to the vision of St John must include all nations, all languages, and all peoples. Although the servant in the parable ... symbolizes the preachers who announce the word of God and preach the holy gospel, with even more propriety ... we can say that the Pope symbolizes the servant[1] ... because to be sent by the king is the same as to be sent by the Pope. What the Pontiff does through the king is as if the Pontiff himself did it. Thus, the parable in the Holy Gospel about the servant being sent to call people for the banquet of the Lord has now come to pass literally in the person of the king of Spain. The hour of the banquet stands for the approaching end of the world ... And it should be emphasized that the three types of invitations issued by the servant in the parable coincide with the differences between those three nations ... In the case of the Jews, who are acquainted with the Holy Scriptures, they will sin only out of pure malice. Hence, it is enough that the preacher simply inform them of the truth of the word of God. This is an adequate summons for this nation. Thus in the parable, the first invitation was simply to tell the guests that they might come to the supper, that is, that the Messiah had arrived and that the prophecies were coming to pass. In the case of the Muslims, who can sin out of some (although gross) ignorance of the truth of the law of the Scriptures (for their knowledge has been perverted with the blind errors of the false prophet Mohammed), it is necessary that the priests not only preach to them the word of Christian truth but also persuade them with examples of the good life and with good works. The preachers must demonstrate to the Muslims that they are motivated by pure zeal to save their souls ... Therefore, the host ordered his servant in the second invitation to go out and lead the guests to the supper ... In the case of the Indian Gentiles, on the other hand, who not only are ignorant of the Truth but who also are likely to sin in matters of the faith and in observing the commandments of God out of sheer weakness, for they are very weak, for them the mere preaching of the gospel will not suffice, nor will the verification of the doctrine by the good example of the ministers, nor even good treatment on the part of the Spaniards ... For this reason, God said to His servant in reference to the Gentiles, 'Give them no choice but to come in.' He did not mean that the Gentiles should be compelled by harsh treatment (as some are, which only shocks and alienates

---

[1] Here Mendieta is referring to the Pope's delegation of missionary activity to Christian rulers.

them); He meant that the Gentiles should be compelled in the sense of being guided by the power and the authority of fathers, who have the right to discipline their children for committing evil and harmful actions and to reward them for good and beneficial deeds, especially in respect of all those matters relating to the obligations necessary for eternal salvation.

[MENDIETA'S FRANCISCAN VISION]

Some of the Indians, especially the old people and more often the women than the men, are of such simplicity and purity that they do not know how to sin. Our confessors, who are more perplexed by some of these Indians than they are by notorious sinners, search for some shred of sin by which they can grant them the benefit of absolution. And this difficulty does not arise because the Indians are stupid or ignorant, for they are well versed in the law of God. They answer well all the questions, even the trifles, that they are asked. The fact is, because of their simple and good nature they do not know how to hold a grudge, to say an unkind thing of anyone else, to complain even of mischievous boys, or to forget to fulfil one particle of the obligation that the Church has imposed on them. And in this case I do not speak from hearsay but from my own experience.

And thus I mean that they [the Indians] are made to be pupils, not teachers, parishioners, not priests; and for this they are the best in the world. Their disposition is so good for this purpose that I, a poor, useless good-for-nothing ... could rule with little help from associates a province of fifty thousand Indians organized and arranged in such good Christianity that it seemed as if the whole province were a monastery. And it was just like the island of Antillia of the ancients,[2] which some say is enchanted and which is located not far from Madeira. In our own times it has been seen from afar, but it disappears as one approaches it. In Antillia there is an abundance of all temporal goods, and the people spend their time marching in processions and praising God with hymns and spiritual canticles ... It would be equally appropriate to ask of Our Lord that the Indians be organized and distributed in islands like that of Antillia; for then they would live virtuously and peacefully serving God, as in a terrestrial paradise. At the end of their lives, they would go to heaven, and thus they would avoid all those temptations for which many of us go to hell.

17 Vitoria: Defence of the Indians (1537–1539)

Source: Francisco de Vitoria, De Indiis et de iure belli relectiones, translated by J. Pawley Bate in Classics of International Law, edited by E. Nys (Washington, DC: Carnegie Institution, 1917), pp. 116–28 abridged.

Francisco de Vitoria (c.1486–1546), one of the great Spanish theologians, never went to the New World, though as Dominican professor of theology at the University of

---

[2] Legendary island supposed to exist somewhere in the Atlantic.

Salamanca, he was consulted from time to time on colonial matters. He lectured (1537–9) on the political and moral problems of the conquest using the intellectual traditions and scholastic methods of the Catholic Church and summaries of two of his lecture courses were published in 1557. These were: *On the Indians* (*Relectio de Indiis* and *On the law of war* (*Relectio de iure belli*). The following extracts all come from section I of *On the Indians*.

'Teach all nations, baptizing them in the name of the Father and Son and Holy Spirit' (St Matthew, last ch.). This passage raises the question whether the children of unbelievers may be baptized against the wishes of their parents. This question is discussed by the doctors in the fourth book of the *Sententiae*, dist. 4,[1] and by St Thomas, Secunda Secundae, qu. 10, art. 12, and Tertia Pars, qu. 68, art. 10.[2] The whole of this controversy and discussion was started on account of the aborigines of the New World, commonly called Indians, who came forty years ago into the power of the Spaniards, not having been previously known to our world. This present disputation about them will fall into three parts. In the first part we shall inquire by what right these Indian natives came under Spanish sway. In the second part, what rights the Spanish sovereign obtained over them in temporal and civil matters. In the third part, what rights these sovereigns or the Church obtained over them in matters spiritual and touching religion, in the course of which an answer will be given to the question before us.

As regards the first part, it might seem at the very outset that the whole of this discussion is useless and futile, not only for us who have no concern either to inquire whether the men in question have conducted their administration with propriety in every detail or to raise any doubts about that business or to correct any fault that may have been committed, but also for those whose concern it is to attend to and administer these matters. Firstly, this may so seem because neither the sovereigns of Spain nor those at the head of their councils are bound to make completely fresh and exhaustive examination of rights and titles which have already been elsewhere discussed and settled, especially as regards things of which the sovereigns are in *bona fide* occupation and peaceful possession; this is so because, as Aristotle says (*Ethics*, bk. 3), 'if anyone were to be continually inquiring, settlement would be indefinitely postponed';[3] and sovereigns and their advisers could not attain security and certitude of conscience, and if they had to trace the title of their rule back to its origin, they could not keep anything they had discovered. Moreover, inasmuch as our

---

[1] A reference to the *Sentences* of the twelfth-century theologian Peter Lombard, a series of short reasoned expositions of the main tenets of Christian doctrine which became the main textbook of Catholic theology until superseded by Aquinas's *Summa Theologica*.

[2] References to Aquinas's magnum opus the *Summa Theologica*, which is divided into four parts with part II subdivided into two parts – hence Secunda Primae and Secunda Secundae. Each part is broken down into a series of questions (qu.) which in turn are subdivided into articles (art.). See also document I.6.

[3] A quotation from Aristotle's treatise on ethics *Nicomachean Ethics*.

sovereigns namely Ferdinand and Isabella, who were the first to occupy those regions, were most Christian, and the Emperor Charles V was a most just and scrupulous sovereign, it is not to be believed that they did not make a thoroughly complete and exact investigation into everything that could affect the security of their estate and conscience, especially in such a great matter. On these accounts, then, it may seem not only useless but also presumptuous to raise any question about the matter; it is like looking for a knot in a bulrush and for wickedness in the abode of the righteous.

In meeting this objection we must bear in mind what Aristotle says (*Ethics*, bk. 3), namely, that just as there can be no questioning or deliberation about matters either impossible or necessary, so also there can be no moral investigation about those which are certainly and notoriously lawful and seemly, or, on the other hand, about those which are certainly and notoriously unlawful and unseemly. For no one can properly raise a question whether we ought to live a temperate and brave and upright life or a wicked and base life, nor whether we ought to commit adultery or perjury, or cherish our parents, and other matters of this kind. Certainly such discussion would not be Christian. When, however, some project is on foot concerning which there is a genuine doubt whether it be good or bad, just or unjust, it is then advantageous to take advice and to deliberate and to abstain from premature action before finding out and determining how far it is or is not lawful ... For in order that an act, the goodness of which is otherwise uncertain, be good, it must be done in accordance with the investigation and determination of the wise, it being (*Ethics*, bk. 2) one of the conditions of a good act that it be done in accordance therewith. Accordingly, when, in a doubtful case, the doer omits to take the advice of the wise, he is without excuse. Nay, even if we grant that the act in question is lawful in itself, yet, if there be any doubt thereon, the doer is bound to take the advice, and to act in accordance with the award, of the wise, even though they be themselves in error ... in those matters which belong to his salvation a man is bound to yield credence to the teachers appointed by the Church, and in a doubtful matter their ruling is law. For just as in the contentious forum the judge is bound to judge in accordance with what is alleged and proved, so in the forum of conscience a man is bound to base his judgement, not on his own sentiments, but on demonstrable reason or on the authority of the wise; else his judgement is presumptuous and exposes him to the risk of going wrong, and indeed he does err in the very fact. This accords with what was laid down in the Old Testament (Deuteronomy 17):

'If there arise a matter too hard for thee in judgment, between blood and blood, between plea and plea, between leprosy and not leprosy, being matters of controversy within thy gates (saith the Lord), thou shalt arise and get thee up to the place which the Lord thy God shall choose, and thou shalt come unto the priests the Levites, and unto the judges that shall be in those days and enquire, and they shall show thee the sentence of judgment, and thou shalt do according to the sentence which they of authority in that place shall show thee, and according to the judgment which they shall tell thee thou shalt do, not declining to the right hand or to the left.'[4]

I accordingly assert that in doubtful matters a man is bound to seek the advice of those whom the Church has appointed for that purpose, such as prelates, preachers, and confessors, who are people skilled in divine and human law . . .

When, then, we return to the question before us, namely, the matter of the barbarians, we see that it is not in itself so evidently unjust that no question about its justice can arise, nor again so evidently just that no doubt is possible about its injustice, but that it has a look of both according to the standpoint. For, at first sight, when we see that the whole of the business has been carried on by men who are alike well-informed and upright, we may believe that everything has been done properly and justly. But then, when we hear of so many massacres, so many plunderings of otherwise innocent men, so many princes evicted from their possessions and stripped of their rule, there is certainly ground for doubting whether this is rightly or wrongly done. And in this way the discussion in question does not seem at all superfluous and so we get a clear answer to the objection . . .

But someone may come forward and say: Although there were at one time some elements of doubt in this business, yet they have now been discussed and settled by the wise and so everything is now being administered in accordance with their advice and we have no need of a fresh inquiry. To such a person I answer first, God be blessed if it is so; our discussion raises no obstacle thereto; nor would I raise any new complaints. Secondly, I assert that it is not for jurists to settle this question or at any rate not for jurists only, for since the barbarians in question, as I shall forthwith show, were not in subjection by human law, it is not by human, but by divine law that questions concerning them are to be determined. Now, jurists are not skilled enough in the divine law to be able by themselves to settle questions of this sort. Nor am I sure that in the discussion and determination of this question theologians have ever been called competent to pronounce on so grave a matter. And as the issue concerns the forum of conscience, its settlement belongs to the priests, that is, to the Church. Accordingly in Deuteronomy 17, it is enjoined on the king that he take a copy of the law from the hand of the priest. Thirdly, in order that the whole of the matter be adequately examined and assured, is it not possible that so weighty a business may produce other special doubts deserving of discussion? Accordingly I think I shall be doing something which is not only not futile and useless, but well worth the trouble, if I am enabled to discuss this question in a manner befitting its importance. ⁄

Returning now to our main topic, in order that we may proceed in order, I ask first whether the aborigines in question were true owners in both private and public law before the arrival of the Spaniards; that is, whether they were true owners of private property and possessions and also whether there were

---

[4] Deuteronomy 17: 8–11.

among them any who were the true princes and overlords of others. The answer might seem to be No, the reason being that slaves own no property, 'for a slave can have nothing of his own' (*Inst.*, 2.9.3, and *Dig.*, 29.2.79),[5] and so all his acquisitions belong to his master (*Inst.*, 1.8.1). But the aborigines in question are slaves. Therefore the matter is proved; for as Aristotle (*Politics*, bk. 1)[6] neatly and correctly says, 'Some are by nature slaves, those, to wit, who are better fitted to serve than to rule.' Now these are they who have not sufficient reason to govern even themselves, but only to do what they are bidden, and whose strength lies in their body rather than in their mind. But, of a surety, if there be any such, the aborigines in question are pre-eminently such, for they really seem little different from brute animals and are utterly incapable of governing, and it is unquestionably better for them to be ruled by others than to rule themselves. Aristotle says it is just and natural for such to be slaves. Therefore they and their like cannot be owners. And it is immaterial that before the arrival of the Spaniards they had no other masters; for there is no inconsistency in a slave having no master, as the glossator on *Dig.*, 40.12.23, notes. Nay, the statement is expressly made in that passage of the *Digest* and it is the expressed case set out in *Dig.*, 45.3.36, pr., where it is said that a slave who has been abandoned by his master and not taken into possession by anyone else can be taken into possession by anyone. If, then, these were slaves they could be taken into possession by the Spaniards.

On the opposite side we have the fact that the people in question were in peaceable possession of their goods, both publicly and privately. Therefore unless the contrary is shown, they must be treated as owners and not be disturbed in their possession unless cause be shown.

In the aid of a solution . . . let me . . . observe that, if the aborigines had not dominion, it would seem that no other cause is assignable therefore except that they were sinners or were unbelievers or were witless or irrational.

FIFTH. Now, some have maintained that grace is the title to dominion and consequently that sinners, at any rate those in mortal sin, have no dominion over anything. That was the error of the poor folk of Lyons, or Waldenses, and afterwards of John Wycliffe.[7] One error of his, namely, that 'no one is a civil owner, while he is in mortal sin,' was condemned by the Council of Constance.[8] This opinion is also held by Armachanus . . . Armachanus relies on the fact that such dominion is reprobated by God: 'They have set up Kings but not by me; they have made princes and I knew it not' (Hosea 8);[9]

---

[5] References to the *Institutes* of Justinian, a legal code of practice drawn up under the Roman Emperor Justinian (reigned AD 527–65) and to the *Digest*, a short manual or textbook for students extracted from the writings of Roman jurists.

[6] Here Vitoria provides the key reference to Aristotle's treatise on politics where the Greek philosopher argues his case for the existence of natural slavery.

[7] A reference to the small Christian community organized in the twelfth century by Peter Valdes (Waldo) of Lyons who were excommunicated and persecuted by the Church and to John Wycliffe (c.1329–84) whose teaching was likewise condemned by the Church.

[8] A Church Council (1414–18) which attempted to combat heresy by condemning over 200 propositions of John Wycliffe.

[9] Hosea 8: 4.

... Again (Genesis 1), 'Let us make man in our own image and Likeness that he may have dominion over the fish of the sea,' etc.[10] It appears therefore that dominion is founded on the image of God. But the sinner displays no such image. Therefore he has no dominion ... Wycliffe and Armachanus ... seem to have in view all kinds of dominion generally ... Those who would follow their teaching may, therefore, say that the barbarians had no dominion, because they were always in mortal sin.

SIXTH. But against this doctrine I advance the proposition that mortal sin does not hinder civil dominion and true dominion ... I employ against the opposing party their own argument: Dominion is founded on the image of God; but man is God's image by nature, that is, by his reasoning powers; therefore, dominion is not lost by mortal sin. The minor is proved from St Augustine (*De Trinitate*, bk 9)[11] and from the doctors ... And in the same way that God makes His sun rise on the good and on the bad, and sends rain on the just and on the unjust, so also He has given temporal goods alike to good and to bad. Nor is this subject discussed, because it is in doubt, but in order that from one crime, to wit, from this insensate heresy, we may learn the character of all heretics.

SEVENTH. Now it remains to consider whether at any rate dominion may be lost by reason of unbelief ... My answer is in the following propositions: The first proposition is that unbelief does not prevent anyone from being a true owner. This is the conclusion of St Thomas Aquinas (Secunda Secundae, qu. 10, art. 12). It is proved also ... by the fact that Scripture gives the name of king to many unbelievers, such as Sennacherib[12] and Pharaoh and many other kings. Also, St Paul (Romans 13) and St Peter (1 Peter 2) enjoin obedience to princes, all of whom at that time were unbelievers, and slaves are there bidden to obey their masters ... The proposition is also supported by the reasoning of St Thomas, namely: Unbelief does not destroy either natural law or human law; but ownership and dominion are based either on natural or on human law; therefore they are not destroyed by want of faith. In fine, this is as obvious an error as the foregoing. Hence it is manifest that it is not justifiable to take anything that they possess from either Saracens or Jews or other unbelievers as such, that is, because they are unbelievers; but the act would be robbery or theft no less than if it were done to Christians ...

TWENTIETH. It remains to ask whether the Indians lacked ownership because of want of reason or unsoundness of mind ... The Indian aborigines are not barred on this ground from the exercise of true dominion. This is proved from the fact that the true state of the case is that they are not of unsound mind, but have, according to their kind, the use of reason. This is clear, because there is a certain method in their affairs, for they have polities which are orderly arranged and they have definite marriage and magistrates,

---

[10] Genesis 1: 26.

[11] St Augustine's philosophical treatise on the Trinity.

[12] A reference to the Assyrian king (reigned 705–681 BC), who conquered as far west as the Ionian Greek islands (see, 2 Kings 18: 13; Isaiah 37: 21).

overlords, laws, and workshops, and a system of exchange, all of which call for the use of reason; they also have a kind of religion. Further, they make no error in matters which are self-evident to others; this is witness to their use of reason. Also, God and nature are not wanting in the supply of what is necessary in great measure for the race. Now, the most conspicuous feature of man is reason, and power is useless which is not reducible to action. Also, it is through no fault of theirs that these aborigines have for many centuries been outside the pale of salvation, in that they have been born in sin and void of baptism and the use of reason whereby to seek out the things needful for salvation. Accordingly I for the most part attribute their seeming so unintelligent and stupid to a bad and barbarous upbringing, for even among ourselves we find many peasants who differ little from brutes . . .

TWENTY-FOURTH. The upshot of all the preceding is, then, that the aborigines undoubtedly had true dominion in both public and private matters, just like Christians, and that neither their princes nor private persons could be despoiled of their property on the ground of their not being true owners. It would be harsh to deny those, who have never done any wrong, what we grant to Saracens and Jews, who are the persistent enemies of Christianity. We do not deny that these latter peoples are true owners of their property, if they have not seized lands elsewhere belonging to Christians.

It remains to reply to the argument of the opposite side to the effect that the aborigines in question seem to be slaves by nature because of their incapability of self-government. My answer to this is that Aristotle certainly did not mean to say that such as are not over-strong mentally are by nature subject to another's power and incapable of dominion alike over themselves and other things; for this is civil and legal slavery, wherein none are slaves by nature. Nor does the Philosopher mean that, if any by nature are of weak mind, it is permissible to seize their patrimony and enslave them and put them up for sale; but what he means is that by defect of their nature they need to be ruled and governed by others and that it is good for them to be subject to others, just as sons need to be subject to their parents until of full age, and a wife to her husband. And that this is the Philosopher's intent is clear from his corresponding remark that some are by nature masters, those, namely, who are of strong intelligence. Now it is clear that he does not mean hereby that such persons can arrogate to themselves a sway over others in virtue of their superior wisdom, but that nature has given them capacity for rule and government. Accordingly, even if we admit that the aborigines in question are as inept and stupid as is alleged, still dominion can not be denied to them, nor are they to be classed with the slaves of civil law. True, some right to reduce them to subjection can be based on this reason and title, as we shall show below. Meanwhile the conclusion stands sure, that the aborigines in question were true owners, before the Spaniards came among them, both from the public and the private point of view.

18 José de Acosta: On the Indians and Animals of the New World (1590)

Source: José de Acosta, *Historia natural y moral de las Indias*, edited and translated by B. Beddall (Gil Torrón, Valencia, 1977), pp. 112–29 abridged.

José de Acosta (*c*.1540–1600), a Spanish Jesuit, went as a missionary to Peru in 1571 and remained there for fifteen years. His acute observations on Peru and Mexico were recorded in his widely read book, first published in Latin (Salamanca, 1588) then in extended form in Spanish (Seville, 1590), and published in many other languages. The extracts which follow are amongst the most remarkable records of the reactions of an educated sixteenth-century European to the New World.

IN WHAT WAY COULD THE FIRST MEN HAVE COME TO THE INDIES, FOR THEY DID NOT SAIL TO THIS REGION ON PURPOSE

Now it is time to answer those who say that there are no antipodes and that this region in which we are living cannot be inhabited. The immensity of the ocean frightened Saint Augustine against believing that the human race might have crossed it to this new world. And since on the one hand we know for certain that there have been men in these regions for many hundreds of years, and on the other hand, we cannot contradict what the Divine Scripture clearly teaches, that all men have descended from one first man, we are without a doubt obliged to admit that men of Europe, or Asia, or Africa did cross over from there to here, but how and by what route they came we are still investigating and hope to find out.

It certainly cannot be thought that there was another Noah's Ark in which men reached the Indies, and even less that some angel carried the first settlers of this world, as the prophet Habacuc was carried, hanging by the hair[1] ... And thus two things must in truth be taken as marvellous and belonging to the secrets of God: one, that humankind should have been able to cross such an immensity of seas and lands; the other, that with there being such countless numbers of people here, they should be hidden from us for so many centuries ...

It is certain that the first Indians reached the land of Peru by one of three methods. Because they came either by sea or by land; and if by sea, either accidentally or on purpose: by accidentally, I mean driven by the great force of a storm, as happens in contrary and violent weather; by purposefully, I mean that they intended to sail and find new lands. Outside of these three methods, no other possibility occurs to me, if we are to reason in terms of the course of human events and not begin to fabricate poetic and fabulous fictions ...

---

[1] A reference to the legend associated with the Old Testament prophet Habakkuk, who was reputed to have been carried by his hair by an angel in order to bring food to Daniel in Babylon.

NEVERTHELESS, IT IS MORE IN ACCORDANCE WITH GOOD REASON TO THINK THAT
THE FIRST SETTLERS OF THE INDIES CAME BY LAND

I will conclude, then, by saying that it seems very probable that the first settlers reached the Indies as the result of a shipwreck and storm at sea. But here a difficulty arises that I have struggled to understand, and it is that since we have already proposed that men may have come to such remote lands by sea, and that the tribes we see have proliferated from them, yet I do not know how we can contrive to put the beasts and the predators, which are numerous and large in the New World, aboard ship and transport them by sea to the Indies. The reason we are forced to say that the men of the Indies were from Europe or Asia is so as not to contradict the Sacred Scripture, which clearly teaches that all men are descended from Adam, and therefore we cannot give any other origin to the men of the Indies. The same Divine Scripture also tells us that all the beasts and animals of the earth perished, except those that were preserved in Noah's Ark for the purpose of propagating their kind. Therefore, it is also required that the propagation of all the said animals be confined to those that came out of the Ark on Mount Ararat, where it came to rest, so that as for men, thus also for the beasts, it is necessary for us to look for a route by which they might have passed from the Old World to the New.

Saint Augustine discussed the question, how it is that wolves, tigers, and other wild animals that are of no use to men are found on some islands. Because there is no obstacle to thinking that elephants, horses, oxen, dogs, and other animals that serve men were transported by sea in ships through men's efforts, as we see today that they are carried from the East to Europe, and from Europe to Peru in lengthy voyages. But in what manner might the animals that are of no use at all, and on the contrary are very dangerous, have crossed over to the islands, if it is true, as it is, that the Flood covered the whole earth? In discussing this, the above-mentioned saint and most learned man tried to free himself of these anxieties by saying that such beasts swam to the islands, or that someone who wanted to hunt them took them there, or that it was ordained by God that they should be produced from the earth in the manner that God proclaimed the first Creation: 'Let the earth bring forth living creatures according to their kinds: cattle and creeping things and beasts of the earth according to their kinds.'[2]

But assuredly if we wish to apply this solution to our question, the more puzzling the matter becomes. Because, beginning with the last point, it is not in accordance with the order of nature, nor in accordance with the order of government that God has arranged, that perfect animals, like lions, tigers, and wolves, should be produced from the earth without generation. Frogs and mice and wasps and other imperfect animals are produced in this way. But for what purpose does the Scripture say in such detail: 'Take with you seven pairs of all clean animals, the male and his mate; and seven pairs of the

---

[2] Here Acosta is citing Genesis 1: 24.

birds of the air also, male and female, to keep their kind alive upon the face of all the earth'[3] . . . That some of these animals may have been transported with the intention of hunting them, which was the other answer, I do not think incredible, for we often see that solely to arouse admiration princes and nobles are accustomed to keep lions, bears, and other wild animals in cages, especially when they have been brought from distant lands. But to believe this of wolves and foxes and such other lowly and useless animals, which are not remarkable in any way but only harm cattle, and to say that for the purpose of hunting they were brought by sea, certainly is not reasonable . . .

[margin, handwritten: universal-attitude for a Christian!]

Therefore, if these animals came by sea, the only remaining possibility is that they did so by swimming. This is possible and practicable with respect to some islands that are not far from others or from the mainland. Positive evidence, by which we see that sometimes out of grave necessity these animals swim whole days and nights, and in the end escape by swimming, cannot be denied. But this implies very small seas, because our ocean would make a mockery of swimmers like these, for even birds of strong flight lack wings to cross such an immense void. It is true that there are birds that fly more than a hundred leagues, as we have seen on different occasions while sailing, but to cross the whole ocean by flying is impossible, or at the least very difficult. If all this is so, where shall we find a route for the wild animals and birds to cross to the Indies? In what way could they go from one world to the other?

This argument that I have presented is for me a conjecture leading me to think that the New World, which we call the Indies, is not completely divided and separated from the other world. And to offer my opinion, I have recently thought that somewhere the two lands are joined and are continuous, or at least approach each other and are very close. Up to now, at least, there is no certainty of the contrary. Because in the direction of the arctic pole, which they call the North Pole, the full extent of the land has not been discovered and is not known, and there is no lack of those who affirm that above Florida the land runs for a very long distance to the north, which, they say, reaches to the Scottish Sea or even to the North Sea. Others add that there was a ship that reported that, while sailing there, it had seen cod running almost to the edges of Europe. Indeed, neither is it known in regard to Cape Mendocino [California] in the Pacific Ocean how far beyond it the land runs, other than that everyone says that it runs an immense distance.

Turning to the South Pole, there is no man who knows where the land on the other side of the Strait of Magellan comes to an end. A ship of the bishop of Plasencia, which passed through the strait, reported that land was always in sight, and the pilot Hernando Lamero, who was driven two or three degrees beyond the strait in a storm, related the same thing. There is, therefore, no reason to the contrary, nor any evidence that might destroy my supposition or thought that the whole earth is joined together and is continuous somewhere, or at least nearly continuous.

---

[3] Here Acosta is citing Genesis 7: 2–3.

If, as it seems to me, this is the truth, the very difficult question that we had presented, how the first settlers travelled to the Indies, has an easy answer, because it can be said that they went not so much by sailing on the sea as by walking on the land; and they made this journey without any plan, gradually shifting localities and territories; and as some of them settled the places already found and others looked for new places, they came over a period of time to fill the lands of the Indies with so many tribes, peoples, and languages.

The indications that are offered to those who examine with curiosity the Indians' mode of habitation strongly support the opinion already given. Because wherever there is an island distant from the mainland and also from other islands, as is Bermuda, there are no men at all. The reason is because the early men did not sail except along neighbouring beaches and almost always in sight of land. In this regard, it is alleged that nowhere in the Indies does one find the large boats required to cross great seas. What one finds are rafts, pirogues,[4] or canoes, which are all smaller than a long-boat. The Indians use only such vessels, with which they could not put out to sea without an obvious and certain danger of perishing, and if they had boats large enough to go out to sea, they were unfamiliar with the compass, or the astrolabe, or the quadrant. If they were to be out of sight of land for eighteen days, it was impossible for them not to become lost, not knowing where they were. We see islands densely populated by Indians, and the voyages they frequently make, but they were those that I mention, which the Indians could make by canoe or pirogue, and without a magnetic compass.

When the Indians who lived in Tumbes saw our Spaniards who were sailing to Peru for the first time, and observed the great size of the outstretched sails and the equally large ships, they were astonished. As they could not believe that they were ships, because they had never seen any of that shape and size, they say that their immediate thought was that they must be rocks or large stones on the sea. As they saw that they moved and did not sink, they were for a long time beside themselves with fear, until looking further they saw some bearded men, whom they believed must be gods or people from beyond the sky, walking around in the ships. From which it can easily be seen how foreign the use of large boats was to the Indians, when they had not even heard of them . . .

How is it possible for there to be animals in the Indies that are not found in any other part of the world?

It is more difficult to determine the origin of the various animals that are found in the Indies and are not found in the Old World. Because if the Creator brought them forth there, there was no need to have recourse to Noah's Ark, nor would it even have been necessary to save all the species of birds and animals then, if they were to be created anew afterwards; neither does it seem that with the six days of Creation God would leave the world

---

[4] Long narrow canoe made from a single tree trunk.

finished and perfect, if new species of animals remained to be formed, especially perfect animals that are no less excellent than the others known.

For if we say that all these species of animals were preserved in Noah's Ark, it follows that, as these other animals went to the Indies from this world here, so also did those others that are not found elsewhere in the world. And if this is so, I ask, how is it that their kinds did not remain here? How is it that they are found only where they are travellers and foreigners? Certainly this is a question that has perplexed me for a long time. I say, for example, if the llamas of Peru and those they call alpacas and guanacos are not found in any other region of the world, who took them to Peru? Or how did they go? For no trace of them remained anywhere else in the world, and if they did not come from another region, how were they formed and brought forth there? Did God, perhaps, bring about a new formation of animals?

What I say about these guanacos and alpacas I will affirm about the thousand differences of the birds and wild animals that have never been known either by name or shape, nor is there any record of them among the Romans and the Greeks, nor in any other country of the Old World. But let us say that although all the animals came from the Ark, through natural instinct and the providence of heaven various kinds went to various regions, and in some of them they succeeded so well that they did not wish to leave them, or if they left, they did not survive, or at some time they died out, as happens in many cases. And if one looks carefully, this is not a case peculiar to the Indies, but common in many other regions and provinces of Asia, Europe, and Africa, of which one reads that in some there are kinds of animals not found in others; and if they are found, it is known that they have been transported there. For as these animals came out of the Ark – for example, elephants, which are found only in eastern India and have been transferred from there to other places – we may say the same thing about the animals of Peru and the rest of the Indies that are not found in any other part of the world.

It must also be considered whether such animals differ specifically and essentially from all the others, or whether their difference is accidental, which could be caused by various accidents, as among the family of man some are white and others black, some giants and some dwarfs. Thus, for example, in the monkey family some are without tails and others do have tails, and in the sheep family some are smooth and some are woolly, some large and strong and with very long necks like those of Peru,[5] others small and weak and with short necks, as those of Castile. But to speak most truly, whoever by means of supposing only accidental differences would try to save the propagation of the animals of the Indies by reducing them to those of Europe, will take up a charge that will turn out badly. Because if we are to judge the species of animals by their characteristics, these are so dissimilar that to wish to reduce them to the species known in Europe will be to call an egg a chestnut.

---

[5] Llamas, which, however, are not sheep but members of the camel family.

19 Questionnaire on the Spanish American Empire (1577–1586)

Source: H. Cline, 'The *Relaciones Geográficas* of the Spanish Indies, 1577–1586', *Hispanic American Historical Review*, 44 (1964), 364–71.

It was not until the middle of Philip II's reign that systematic efforts were devoted to acquiring a fuller knowledge and greater exploitation of Spain's new territories in America. The first sign of this new determination on the part of the Crown was evident in the document here reproduced. Copies of these questions were sent to every town in Spanish America and the responses were to be used to improve administration. By this process the Spanish government accumulated much detailed information about the new colonial empire.

INSTRUCTION AND MEMORANDUM FOR PREPARING THE REPORTS WHICH ARE TO BE MADE FOR THE DESCRIPTION OF THE INDIES THAT HIS MAJESTY COMMANDS TO BE MADE, FOR THEIR GOOD GOVERNMENT AND ENNOBLEMENT

Firstly, the Governors, Corregidors, or Alcaldes Mayores to whom the Viceroys, Audiencias,[1] or other governmental or administrative officials, may send the printed Instruction and Memorandum are, before everything, to make a list and statement of the towns inhabited by Spaniards and by Indians within their jurisdictions, on which only the names of these towns are to appear, written clearly and legibly. This list is to be sent immediately to the officials of government, so that they may return it to His Majesty and the Council of the Indies, together with the reports prepared in each town.

They shall distribute this printed Instruction and Memorandum throughout their jurisdiction to all towns of Spaniards and Indians, sending them to the municipal councils of towns in which there are Spaniards, or, if these are lacking, to the parish priests or monks charged with religious instruction. They shall directly order the councils or recommend from his Majesty to the ecclesiastics, that within a short time they satisfactorily respond to the queries, as specified. The reports they make, together with this Instruction, are to be sent to the above official of government who ordered them. The latter shall redistribute the Instructions and Memoranda to other towns, to which none has been sent previously.

In the towns and cities where the Governors, Corregidors, or other administrative officials reside they are to write the reports themselves. Or they may encharge them to intelligent persons with knowledge of matters of the area, requiring them to follow the specifications of the Memorandum.

Persons in the towns to whom responsibility for each of them is given for

---

[1] Corregidors: Crown officials responsible for a certain geographical area (*corregimiento*); Alcaldes Mayores: Crown officials responsible for a larger jurisdiction (*alcaldía mayor*); Audiencias: judges.

preparing the particular report shall respond to the chapters of the Memorandum, in the following order and form:

Firstly, on a separate paper, as a cover sheet for their report, they are to write the date – day, month, year – with the name of the person or persons who aided in preparing it. Also the name of the Governor or other person who sent them the Instruction shall appear.

After carefully reading each paragraph of the Memorandum, they are to write down separately what they have to say, answering each one of the questions it contains, one after the other. Those questions to which they have nothing to answer are to be omitted without comment, passing on to the following ones, until all are read. The answers are to be short and clear. That which is certain shall be stated as such, and that which is not shall be declared doubtful, in such a way that the reports shall be valid, and in conformance with the following queries:

QUESTION 1

In the towns of Spaniards state the name of the district or province, also the meaning of the name in the native language and the reason it is so named.

QUESTION 2

State who was the discoverer and conqueror of said province and by whose order or mandate it was discovered. Give the year of its discovery and conquest and all that can be readily learned about it.

QUESTION 3

State in general the climate and quality of said province or district; whether it is cold or hot, dry or damp, with much rainfall or little and at what season there is more or less; and the prevailing winds, whether violent, and from what quarter and at what seasons of the year.

QUESTION 4

State whether the country is level, rough, flat or mountainous; with many or few rivers and fountains, with abundance or scarcity of water; whether fertile or lacking in pasture; with an abundance or scarcity of fruits and subsistence crops.

QUESTION 5

State whether the district is inhabited by many or few Indians and whether in former times it had a greater or lesser population; the causes for the increase or diminution and whether the inhabitants live permanently together in regular towns or not.

State also what is the character and condition of their intelligence, inclinations and modes of life; also whether different languages are spoken throughout the whole province or whether they have one which is spoken by all.

QUESTION 6

State the latitude in which these towns of Spaniards lie, if this has been taken or if known, or if there is anyone who knows how to take it. State on what days of the year the sun does not cast a shadow at noon.

QUESTION 7

State the distance in leagues between each city or town occupied by Spaniards and the city in which dwells the Audiencia in whose jurisdiction it belongs, or the residence of the governor to whom it is subject; state also the directions in which said cities and towns lie from each other.

QUESTION 8

Give also the distance in leagues between each city or town occupied by Spaniards and those which bound them in adjoining districts, stating in what direction they lie; whether the leagues are long or short, the country level or broken and mountainous; whether the roads are straight or winding and good or bad for travel.

QUESTION 9

State the name and surname that every city or town has or has had and the reason, if known, why it was so named; also who named it and who was the founder, and by whose order or mandate he made the settlement; the year of its foundation and the number of inhabitants at that and at the present time.

QUESTION 10

Describe the site and state the situation of said town, if it lies high or low or in a plain, and give a plan or coloured painting showing the streets, squares, and other places; mark the monasteries. This can be easily sketched on paper, and shall be done as well as possible. It is to be noted which parts of the town face North and which South.

QUESTION 11

In the case of Indian towns it is only to be stated how far they are from the capital, in what district and jurisdiction they lie, and which is the nearest centre (*cabecera*) for the teaching of religious doctrine. The names of all of the chief towns in its jurisdiction are to be given as well as those of their respective dependencies.

QUESTION 12

State also the distances between the other towns of Indians or of Spaniards that surround it and the directions in which they lie and whether the leagues are long or short and the roads level or straight or mountainous and winding.

QUESTION 13

State what the name of the Indian town means in the native tongue, why it was so named; what more there is to know about it; what it is in the language which the native inhabitants of the place actually speak.

QUESTION 14

State to whom the Indians belonged in heathen times and what dominion was exercised over them by their lords; what tribute they paid and the form of worship, rites and customs they had, good or bad.

QUESTION 15

State how they were governed; against whom they carried on warfare; how they fought; the clothes and costumes they wore and now wear and whether they used to be more or less healthy anciently than they are now, and what reasons may be learned for this.

QUESTION 16

State about all towns, of Spaniards or of Indians, whether the town is situated in a mountain, valley or open plain, and the names of the mountains or valleys and district in which it lies. Record the native meaning of each of these names.

QUESTION 17

State whether the town is situated in a healthful or unhealthful place and if unhealthful, the cause for this if it can be learned; note the kinds of illness that are prevalent and the remedies employed for curing them.

QUESTION 18

State how far or close is any nearby remarkable mountain or mountain range, in what direction it lies, and what it is called.

QUESTION 19

State what principal river or rivers pass near to the town; at what distance they do so; how abundant they are and whether there is anything remarkable about their sources, their waters, its water-supply and how banks are exploited; also whether it is employed or could be employed for various irrigation works on an important scale.

QUESTION 20

Mention the important lakes, lagoons and fountains within the bounds of the towns, and any notable things about them there may be.

QUESTION 21

Mention volcanoes, caves and all other remarkable and admirable works of nature there may be in the district, which are worthy of being known.

QUESTION 22

Describe the native trees that commonly grow wild in said district; and benefits to be gained from them, their fruits and their wood. State for what they are or might be useful.

QUESTION 23

Mention whether the cultivated trees and fruit trees in the district brought there from Spain or elsewhere grow well or not.

QUESTION 24

Mention the grains and seeds and other plants and vegetables which have served or serve as subsistence for the natives.

QUESTION 25

State what plants have been introduced there from Spain and whether wheat, barley, wines and the olive flourish; in what quantity they are harvested and whether there are silkworms or cochineal[2] in the district, and in what quantities.

---

[2] Dried bodies of female insects reared on cactus and used for making a very valuable commodity of scarlet dye.

QUESTION 26

Mention the herbs or aromatic plants with which the Indians cure themselves, and their medicinal or poisonous qualities.

QUESTION 27

Describe the native animals, birds of prey and domestic fowl and those introduced from Spain and state how well they breed and multiply.

QUESTION 28

Describe the gold and silver mines, and other veins of metal or minerals, and mineral dyes there may be in the district and within the confines of the town.

QUESTION 29

State the deposits of precious stones, jasper, marble, and other important and esteemed materials which likewise may exist.

QUESTION 30

State whether there are salt pans in or near said town and from where they obtain their supplies of salt and of all other things they lack for sustenance and clothing.

QUESTION 31

Describe the form and construction of their houses and the building materials for them that are found in the town or the other places from which they are brought.

QUESTION 32

Describe the fortresses in said town and the strongholds which are in their vicinity and within their confines.

QUESTION 33

Describe the trade and commerce and dealings by which the Spanish and native inhabitants of the town support themselves and state what they produce and how they pay their tributes.

QUESTION 34

State the diocese of the archbishopric or bishopric or abbey to which the town belongs; the district in which it is situated and its distance in leagues. State in what direction from it lies the cathedral town and the capital of the district and whether the leagues are long or short; the roads straight or winding and the country flat or rough.

QUESTION 35

Note the cathedral or parish church or churches in each town, with the number of benefices and prebends in each; if the town contains any chapel or noteworthy endowment, state what it is, and who was its founder.

QUESTION 36

Mention the monasteries of friars and convents of nuns of each Order there may be in each town; when and by whom they were founded and the number of friars and nuns therein. Mention also anything noteworthy there may be in the towns.

QUESTION 37

Mention also the hospitals, colleges and pious institutions there may be in said towns and by whom and when they were instituted.

QUESTION 38

If the towns are maritime, in addition to the above state in the report the nature of the sea which reaches them, if it is calm or stormy, and what sorts of storms, and other perils, and at what seasons, more or less, these commonly occur.

QUESTION 39

State whether the coasts have beaches or are *costa brava*[3] without them, and the significant reefs, and perils to navigation there may be along the coast.

QUESTION 40

Note the tides, and rising of the sea, and how high these are, and at what time they rise and ebb, on what days and hours of the day.

---

[3] In this context, a rough and rugged coastline.

QUESTION 41

State the main capes and points, and notable bays within the vicinity, with their names and extent, if these can be declared accurately.

QUESTION 42

State the ports and places of disembarkation there may be on the said coast, and provide a chart and map of them, as best possible, on a sheet of paper, through which it may be seen the form and size they have.

QUESTION 43

State their size and capacity, with approximate paces and leagues they may have in length and breadth, as near as possible, and how many vessels they can accommodate.

QUESTION 44

State their depth in *brazas*,[4] how clean is the bottom, special deeps and shallows in them and where; state if free of boring-worms and other inconveniences.

QUESTION 45

State the entrances and exits to them, and how they face, and the prevailing winds for entering and leaving them.

QUESTION 46

Note the ease or difficulties of obtaining firewood, fresh water, and supplies, and other good or bad features for entering and staying in them.

QUESTION 47

Give the names of islands belonging to the coast, why they are so named, their shapes and forms, and show them on the map, if possible, with length and breadth, and area, their soils, pastures, trees, and benefits they may offer, as well as the birds and animals on them, and their important rivers and watering spots.

---

[4] Fathoms.

QUESTION 48

State generally the sites of depopulated towns of Spaniards, when they were populated and when abandoned, and whatever may be learned of the reasons for their depopulation.

QUESTION 49

Mention any other notable thing about the natural features, and any effects of soil, air, sky, which may be found in any part and which are worthy of being noted.

QUESTION 50

Once this report is prepared, the persons who have aided in its preparation will sign it, and without delay send it, together with this Instruction, to the person who has dispatched it to them.

SECTION VI

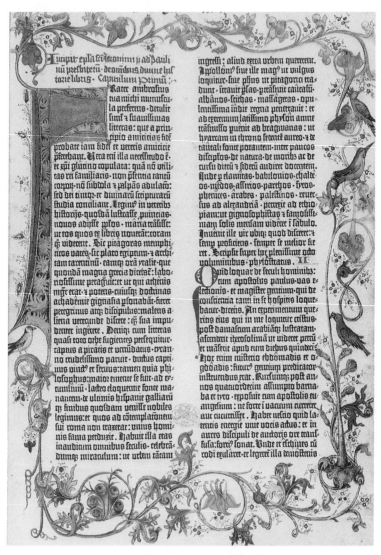

Page from Gutenberg 42-Line Bible of 1453–5.
Reproduced by kind permission of The British Library (British Library copy c.9.d.3).

SECTION VI

Print Culture

The hundred years from 1450 to 1550 saw the invention and establishment of nearly all the features that characterize modern printing. Before 1450, books were hand-produced, frequently on vellum, and consequently were expensive and scarce. With the invention of the adjustable metal type mould, the printing press, printer's ink, and the availability of cheap paper, all this changed, and the large-scale production of identical copies of printed books, at a reasonable price, became possible. Once the main processes had been developed, there was a veritable explosion of print throughout Europe. It has been calculated that between 1450 and 1500 some 20 million books were printed, representing up to 15,000 separate titles. During the sixteenth century the figure rose to something between 150 and 200 million books.

The consequences of this shift to a print culture were profound. Almost all the items in this anthology are themselves products of the new technology, and scholars have long debated such questions as how far the invention of printing made possible developments such as the Reformation. In this section, we have concentrated on three examples of printing. We begin with an extract from the most famous production of the first English printer, William Caxton: Sir Thomas Malory's *Le Morte d'Arthur*. First printed in 1485, Caxton's Malory was the earliest substantial work of prose fiction to be published in English. Its accounts of the exploits and adventures of King Arthur's knights of the Round Table have been vastly influential upon subsequent English literature.

The next piece is a fine example of the interaction between the older oral culture and the new medium of print. Hugh Latimer's famous 'Sermon on the Ploughers' was first delivered as a sermon and only subsequently written down and printed. Its vivid rhetorical style bears many traces of the preacher's art, and its outspoken condemnation of what Latimer regarded as social and ecclesiastical evils indicates why those in authority were quick to control the production of print.

We end with some chapters from the first great European novel, *Don Quixote*. In many respects this work tells us much about the impact of the new print culture. Its hero is a besotted reader of chivalric romances, and in Part II of the novel he discovers that his own story has been printed in a book and he and Sancho are now famous. We might even say that the novel, a new genre, written by an individual author to be read silently and alone by unknown individual readers, only became possible through the development of printing and bookselling.

1 Sir Thomas Malory, *Le Morte d'Arthur* (1485)

Source: *Caxton's Malory: A New Edition of Sir Thomas Malory's Le Morte d'Arthur, Based on the Pierpont Morgan Copy of William Caxton's Edition of 1485*, edited by James W. Spisak and William Matthews (Berkeley and Los Angeles: University of California Press, 1983), pp. 555–65 abridged. Spelling has been modernized by W. R. Owens.

Almost nothing is known about the Sir Thomas Malory who wrote *Le Morte d'Arthur*. In the text itself he tells us his name, that he is a 'knight prisoner', and that he finished the book in 1469–70, that is, during the Wars of the Roses. Several Thomas Malorys have been identified by scholars, but the most promising candidate is a Sir Thomas Malory from Newbold Revel in Warwickshire. After taking part in the wars between England and France which lasted from 1337 to 1453, he appears, in 1439, as a country landowner and member of parliament for Warwickshire. In 1450, however, he was charged with cattle-stealing, extortion and rape. By 1452 he was in prison in London, where he spent nearly eight years, escaping and being re-captured several times. He was never tried on any of the charges brought against him, and was eventually pardoned in 1460 by the Yorkists. After changing sides to support the Lancastrians, Malory seems to have ended up in prison again in the late 1460s, and may have been released in October 1470. He died in March 1471.

Whoever 'Sir Thomas Malory' may have been, the cycle of Arthurian tales which he put together was largely based on a number of French and English sources which had circulated from the twelfth century onwards. But Malory's book is a skilled and original re-arrangement and re-telling of the earlier tales, and stands in its own right as the greatest and most influential romance of chivalry in the English language.

It was first published by William Caxton in 1485. Caxton (*c*.1422–91) had started out as a highly successful merchant, and it was not till he was nearly 50 that he turned to printing and bookselling. His first books, printed in Bruges around 1474, were the earliest to have been printed in English. In 1476 he set up a press at Westminster, and before his death printed about 100 books. These included a number of translations from French, but also editions of works by English authors such as Chaucer, Lydgate and Gower. The *Morte d'Arthur* was his most ambitious production, and the publication for which he is most remembered. In his Prologue, Caxton tells us that he divided the work into twenty-one books and 507 chapters but otherwise he does not seem to have interfered much with Malory's text. The extracts that follow are from Book 20, which relates the discovery of Lancelot's adulterous affair with Queen Guenevere, and the subsequent break-up of the fellowship of the Round Table.

CHAPTER 1: HOW SIR AGGRAVAIN AND SIR MORDRED WERE BUSY UPON SIR GAWAIN FOR TO DISCLOSE THE LOVE BETWEEN SIR LANCELOT AND QUEEN GUENEVERE

In May, when every lusty heart flourisheth and burgeoneth, for as the season is lusty to behold and comfortable, so man and woman rejoice and gladden of summer coming with his fresh flowers, for winter with his rough winds and blasts causeth a lusty man and woman to cower and sit fast by the fire. So in this season, as in the month of May, it befell a great anger and unhap [misfortune] that stinted [ceased] not till the flower of chivalry of all the world was destroyed and slain, and all was long upon [because of] two unhappy knights, the which were named Sir Aggravain and Sir Mordred, that were brethren unto Sir Gawain. For this Sir Aggravain and Sir Mordred had ever a privy [secret] hate unto Queen Dame Guenevere and to Sir Lancelot, and daily and nightly they ever watched upon Sir Lancelot.

So it mishapped [happened by misfortune] that Sir Gawain and all his brethren were in King Arthur's chamber, and then Sir Aggravain said thus openly, and not in no council [secret council], that many knights might hear it: I marvel that we all be not ashamed both to see and to know how Sir Lancelot lieth daily and nightly by the queen. And all we know it so, and it is shamefully suffered of us all that we all should suffer so noble a king as King Arthur is so to be shamed. Then spake Sir Gawain and said, brother Sir Aggravain, I pray you and charge you move [suggest] no such matters no more afore me. For wit [know] you well, said Sir Gawain, I will not be of your counsel. So God me help, said Sir Gaheris and Sir Gareth, we will not be knowing [party], brother Aggravain, of your deeds. Then will I, said Sir Mordred. I leve [believe] well that, said Sir Gawain, for ever unto all unhappiness, brother Sir Mordred, thereto will you grant, and I would that you left all this and made you not so busy. For I know, said Sir Gawain, what will fall of it. Fall of it what fall may, said Sir Aggravain, I will disclose it to the king . . .

CHAPTER 2: HOW SIR AGGRAVAIN DISCLOSED THEIR LOVE TO KING ARTHUR, AND HOW KING ARTHUR GAVE THEM LICENCE TO TAKE HIM

And then Sir Arthur asked them what noise they made. My lord, said Aggravain, I shall tell you that I may keep no longer . . . Sir Lancelot holdeth your queen and hath done long. And we be your sister's sons and we may suffer it no longer. And all we wot that you should be above Sir Lancelot, and you are the king that made him knight; and therefore we will prove it, that he is a traitor to your person. If it be so, said Sir Arthur, wit you well, he is none other; but I would be loath to begin such a thing but [unless] I might have proof upon it, for Sir Lancelot is a hardy knight, and all you know he is the best knight among us all. And but if he be taken with the deed, he will fight with him that bringeth up the noise [rumour], and I know no knight that is able to match him. Therefore, and it be sooth as you say, I would he were taken with the deed.

For as the French book saith, the king was full loath thereto that any noise should be upon Sir Lancelot and his queen, for the king had a deeming [suspicion], but he would not hear of it. For Sir Lancelot had done so much for him and the queen so many times that, wit you well, the king loved him passingly [exceedingly] well. My lord, said Sir Aggravain, you shall ride to-morn [tomorrow] on hunting, and doubt you not Sir Lancelot will not go with you. Then when it draweth toward night, you may send the queen word that you will lie out all that night, and so may you send for your cooks. And then upon pain of death we shall take him that night with the queen, and other [either] we shall bring him to you dead or quick. I will well [readily agree], said the king. Then I counsel you, said the king, take with you sure fellowship. Sir, said Aggravain, my brother Sir Mordred and I will take with us twelve knights of the Round Table. Beware, said King Arthur, for I warn you, you shall find him wight [strong]. Let us deal [handle it], said Sir Aggravain and Sir Mordred . . .

CHAPTER 3: HOW SIR LANCELOT WAS ESPIED IN THE QUEEN'S CHAMBER, AND HOW SIR AGGRAVAIN AND SIR MORDRED CAME WITH TWELVE KNIGHTS TO SLAY HIM

So Sir Lancelot departed and took his sword under his arm . . . and so he passed till he came to the queen's chamber, and then Sir Lancelot was lightly put into the chamber. And then, as the French book saith, the queen and Sir Lancelot were together. And whether they were abed or at other manner of disports we list not hereof make no mention, for love that time was not as is nowadays.

But thus as they were together, there came Sir Aggravain and Sir Mordred with twelve knights with them of the Round Table, and they said with crying voice, traitor knight Sir Lancelot du Lake, now art thou taken! And thus they cried with a loud voice that all the court might hear it, and they all fourteen were armed at all points as they should fight in a battle. Alas, said Queen Guenevere, now are we mischieved [harmed] both. Madam, said Sir Lancelot, is there here any armour within your chamber that I might cover my poor body withal? And if there be any, give it me, and I shall soon stint their malice, by the grace of God. Truly, said the queen, I have none armour, shield, sword, nor spear, wherefore I dread me sore our long love is come to a mischievous end. For I hear by their noise there be many noble knights and well I wit they be surely armed. Against them you may make no resistance, wherefore you are likely to be slain and then shall I be burnt. For and you might escape them, said the queen, I would not doubt but that you would rescue me in what danger that ever I stood in. Alas, said Sir Lancelot, in all my life thus was I never bestad [afflicted] that I should be thus shamefully slain for lack of mine armour.

But ever in one [together] Sir Aggravain and Sir Mordred cried, traitor knight, come out of the queen's chamber, for wit thou well, thou art so beset that thou shalt not escape. Oh Jesu mercy, said Sir Lancelot, this shameful cry and noise I may not suffer, for better were death at once than thus to endure this pain. Then he took the queen in his arms and kissed her and said, most noble Christian queen, I beseech you as you have been ever my special good lady, and I at all times your true poor knight unto my power, and as I never failed you in right nor in wrong sithen [since] the first day King Arthur made me knight, that you will pray for my soul if that I here be slain. For well I am assured that Sir Bors, mine nephew, and all the remnant of my kin with Sir Lavaine and Sir Urry, that they will not fail you to rescue you from the fire . . .

Nay Lancelot, said the queen, wit thou well, I will never live after thy days, but and thou be slain I will take my death as meekly for Jesus Christ's sake as ever did any Christian queen. Well, madam, said Lancelot, sith [since] it is so that the day is come that our love must depart [end], wit you well, I shall sell my life as dear as I may. And a thousandfold, said Sir Lancelot, I am more heavy [sad] for you than for myself. And now I had lever [rather] than to be lord of all Christendom that I had sure armour upon me, that men might speak of my deeds or ever I were slain. Truly, said the queen, I would, and it might please God, that they would take me and slay me and suffer you to escape. That shall never be, said Sir Lancelot. God defend me from such a shame, but Jesu, be thou my shield and mine armour . . .

CHAPTER 4: HOW SIR LANCELOT . . . SLEW SIR AGGRAVAIN, AND TWELVE
OF HIS FELLOWS

Leave your noise, said Sir Lancelot unto Sir Aggravain, for wit you well, Sir Aggravain, you shall not prison me this night. And therefore and ye do by my counsel, go ye all from this chamber door and make not such crying and such manner of slander as ye do. For I promise you by my knighthood, and ye will depart and make no more noise, I shall as to-morn appear afore you all before the king, and then let it be seen which of you all other [or] else you all that will accuse me of treason. And there I shall answer you as a knight should, that hither I came to the queen for no manner of mal engine [evil design], and that will I prove and make it good upon you with my hands. Fie on thee, traitor! said Sir Aggravain and Sir Mordred. We will have thee maugre thy heed [in spite of your resistance] and slay thee if we list, for we let thee wit, we have the choice of King Arthur to save thee or to slay thee. Ah, sirs, said Sir Lancelot, is there none other grace with you? Then keep [guard] yourself.

So then Sir Lancelot set all open the chamber door and mightily and knightly he strode in amongst them. And anon at the first buffet he slew Sir Aggravain, and twelve of his fellows after. Within a little while he laid them cold to the earth, for there was none of the twelve that might stand Sir Lancelot one buffet. Also Sir Lancelot wounded Sir Mordred and he fled with all his might.

And then Sir Lancelot returned again unto the queen and said, madam now wit you well, all our true love is brought to an end, for now will King Arthur ever be my foe. And therefore, madam, and it like [please] you that I may have you with me, I shall save you from all manner of adventures dangerous. That is not best, said the queen; me seemeth [thinketh] now you have done so much harm, it will be best you hold you still with this. And if you see that as to-morn they will put me unto the death, then may you rescue me as you think best. I will well, said Sir Lancelot, for have you no doubt, while I am living I shall rescue you. And then he kissed her, and either gave other a ring, and so there he left the queen and went until his lodging.

CHAPTER 5: HOW SIR LANCELOT CAME TO SIR BORS, AND TOLD HIM HOW HE
HAD . . . ESCAPED

When Sir Bors saw Sir Lancelot he was never so glad of his homecoming as
he was then. Jesu mercy, said Sir Lancelot, why be you all armed? What
meaneth this? Sir, said Sir Bors, after you were departed from us, we all that
be of your blood and your well-willers [well-wishers] were so dretched
[troubled] that some of us leapt out of our beds naked, and some in their
dreams caught naked swords in their hands. Therefore, said Sir Bors, we
deemed [thought] there is some great strife at hand, and then we all deemed
that you were betrapped with some treason, and therefore we made us thus
ready; what need that ever ye were in. My fair nephew, said Sir Lancelot
unto Sir Bors, now shall ye wit all that this night I was more harder bestad
than ever I was in my life, and yet I escaped. And so he told them all how and
in what manner, as you have heard tofore [previously] . . .

My Lords, said Sir Lancelot, wit you well, I have been ever since I came
into this country well willed unto my lord King Arthur and unto my lady
Queen Guenevere unto my power. And this night because my lady the
queen sent for me to speak with her (I suppose it was made by treason, how
be it I dare largely excuse her person), notwithstanding I was there by a
forecast [plan] near slain. But as Jesu provided me, I escaped all their
malice and treason. And then that noble knight Sir Lancelot told them all
how he was hard bestad in the queen's chamber, and how and in what
manner he escaped from them. And therefore, said Sir Lancelot, wit you
well, my fair lords, I am sure there nis [is not] but war unto me and mine.
And for because I have slain this night these knights, I wot well (as is Sir
Aggravain, Sir Gawain's brother, and at the least twelve of his fellows), for
this cause now I am sure of mortal war, for these knights were sent and
ordained [commanded] by King Arthur to betray me. And therefore the
king will in his heat and malice judge the queen to the fire, and that may not
I suffer, that she should be burnt for my sake. For and I may be heard and
suffered and so taken, I will fight for the queen, that she is a true lady unto
her lord. But the king in his heat, I dread me, will not take me as I ought to
be taken.

CHAPTER 6: OF THE COUNSEL AND ADVICE WHICH WAS TAKEN BY SIR LANCELOT
AND BY HIS FRIENDS FOR TO SAVE THE QUEEN

My lord Sir Lancelot, said Sir Bors, by mine advice you shall take the woe
with the weal, and take it in patience, and thank God of it. And sithen it is
fallen as it is, I counsel you keep yourself, for and you will yourself, there is
no fellowship of knights christened that shall do you wrong. Also I will
counsel you, my lord Sir Lancelot, that and my lady Queen Guenevere be in
distress, in so much as she is in pain for your sake, that you knightly rescue
her. And you did otherways, all the world will speak of your shame to the

world's end, in so much as you were taken with her, whether you did right or wrong. It is now your part to hold with the queen that she be not slain and put to a mischievous death, for and she so die, the shame shall be yours. Jesu defend me from shame, said Sir Lancelot, and keep and save my lady the queen from villainy and shameful death, and that she never be destroyed in my default.

Wherefore my fair lords, my kin, and my friends, said Sir Lancelot, what will ye do? Then they said all, we will do as you will do. I put this to you, said Sir Lancelot, that if my lord Arthur by evil counsel will to-morn in his heat put my lady the queen to the fire there to be burnt, now I pray you counsel me what is best to do. Then they said all at once with one voice, sir, us thinketh best that you knightly rescue the queen. In so much as she shall be burnt, it is for your sake; and it is to suppose, and you might be handled [captured], you should have the same death or a more shameful death. And sir, we say all that you have many times rescued her from death for other men's quarrels; us seemeth it is more your worship [honour] that you rescue the queen from this peril, in so much she hath it for your sake.

Then Sir Lancelot stood still and said, my fair lords, wit you well, I would be loath to do that thing that should dishonour you or my blood, and wit you well, I would be loath that my lady the queen should die a shameful death. But and it be so that you will counsel me to rescue her, I must do much harm or I rescue her, and peradventure I shall there destroy some of my best friends; that should much repent me. And peradventure there be some, and they could well bring it about, or disobey my lord King Arthur, they would soon come to me, the which I were loath to hurt. And if so be that I rescue her, where shall I keep her?

That shall be the least care of us all, said Sir Bors. How did the noble knight Sir Tristram, by your good will? Kept not he with him La Belle Isode near three years in Joyous Garde, the which was done by your elthers device [by the planning of you all]? And that same place is your own, and in like wise may you do and you list and take the queen lightly [easily] away, if it so be the king will judge her to be burnt. And in Joyous Garde you may keep her long enough until the heat of the king be past. And then shall you bring again the queen to the king with great worship, and then peradventure you shall have thanks for her bringing home, and love and thanks where other shall have maugre [ill will].

That is hard to do, said Sir Lancelot, for by Sir Tristram I may have a warning. For when by means of treaties Sir Tristram brought again La Belle Isode unto King Mark from Joyous Garde, look what befell on the end, how shamefully that false traitor King Mark slew him. As he sat harping afore his lady La Belle Isode, with a ground glaive [sharp sword] he thrust him in behind to the heart. It grieveth me, said Sir Lancelot, to speak of his death, for all the world may not find such a knight. All this is truth, said Sir Bors, but there is one thing shall courage [encourage] you and us all: you know well King Arthur and King Mark were never like of conditions [characters], for there was never yet man could prove King Arthur untrue of his promise.

So to make short tale, they were all consented that for better other for worse, if so were that the queen were on that morn brought to the fire, shortly they all would rescue her . . .

[News of the affray, and of the death of Sir Aggravain, is brought to King Arthur; he determines that the queen shall be burnt.]

CHAPTER 8: HOW SIR LANCELOT AND HIS KINSMEN RESCUED THE QUEEN FROM THE FIRE, AND HOW HE SLEW MANY KNIGHTS

Then said the noble King Arthur to Sir Gawain, dear nephew, I pray you make ready in your best armour with your brethren, Sir Gaheris and Sir Gareth, to bring my queen to the fire, there to have her judgement and receive the death. Nay, my most noble lord, said Sir Gawain, that will I never do, for wit you well, I will never be in that place where so noble a queen as is my lady Dame Guenevere shall take a shameful end. For wit you well, said Sir Gawain, my heart will never serve me to see her die, and it shall never be said that ever I was of your counsel of her death . . .

Then was there one that Sir Lancelot had sent unto that place for to espy what time the queen should go unto her death, and anon as he saw the queen despoiled [undressed] into her smock, and so shriven, then he gave Sir Lancelot warning. Then was there but spurring and plucking up of horses, and right so they came to the fire, and who that stood against them, there were they slain. There might none withstand Sir Lancelot, so all that bare arms and withstood him, there were they slain, full many a noble knight . . .

Then when Sir Lancelot had thus done, and slain and put to flight all that would withstand him, then he rode straight unto Dame Guenevere and made a kirtle and a gown to be cast upon her, and then he made her to be set behind him and prayed her to be of good cheer. Wit you well, the queen was glad that she was escaped from the death, and then she thanked God and Sir Lancelot. And so he rode his way with the queen, as the French book saith, unto Joyous Garde, and there he kept her as a noble knight should do . . .

CHAPTER 9: OF THE SORROW AND LAMENTATION [OF KING ARTHUR] FOR THE DEATH OF HIS NEPHEWS AND OTHER GOOD KNIGHTS, AND ALSO FOR THE QUEEN, HIS WIFE

So turn we again unto King Arthur, that when it was told him how and in what manner of wise [fashion] the queen was taken away from the fire, and when he heard of the death of his noble knights, and in especial for Sir Gaheris' and Sir Gareth's death, then the king swooned for pure sorrow. And when he awoke of his swoon, then he said, alas that ever I bare crown upon my head. For now have I lost the fairest fellowship of noble knights that ever held Christian king together. Alas, my good knights be slain away from me. Now within these two days I have lost forty knights, and also the noble fellowship of Sir Lancelot and his blood, for now I may never hold them together no more with my worship. Alas, that ever this war began.

Now fair fellows, said the king, I charge you that no man tell Sir Gawain of the death of his two brethren. For I am sure, said the king, when Sir Gawain hears tell that Sir Gareth is dead, he will go nigh out of his mind. Mercy Jesu, said the king, why slew he Sir Gareth and Sir Gaheris? For I dare say, as for Sir Gareth, he loved Sir Lancelot above all men earthly. That is truth, said some knights, but they were slain in the hurtling [rush] as Sir Lancelot throng [clashed] in the thick of the press. And as they were unarmed, he smote them and wist not whom that he smote, and so unhappily they were slain. The death of them, said Arthur, will cause the greatest mortal war that ever was. I am sure, wist Sir Gawain that Sir Gareth were slain, I should never have rest of him till I had destroyed Sir Lancelot's kin and himself both, other else he to destroy me. And therefore, said the king, wit you well, my heart was never so heavy as it is now.

And much more I am sorrier for my good knights' loss than for the loss of my fair queen, for queens I might have enow [enough] but such a fellowship of good knights shall never be together in no company. And now I dare say, said King Arthur, there was never Christian king held such a fellowship together. And alas, that ever Sir Lancelot and I should be at debate [dispute]. Ah, Aggravain, Aggravain, said the king, Jesu forgive it thy soul, for thine evil will that thou and thy brother Sir Mordred hadst unto Sir Lancelot hath caused all this sorrow. And ever among these complaints the king wept and swooned.

2 Hugh Latimer, 'Sermon on the Ploughers' (1548)

Source: *Sermons by Hugh Latimer*, edited by G. E. Corrie (The Parker Society, Cambridge: Cambridge University Press, 1844), pp. 59–78 abridged.

Hugh Latimer (*c*.1485–1555), the son of a Leicestershire yeoman, was educated at Cambridge where he took orders as a Roman Catholic priest. Under the influence of reformers such as Thomas Bilney (who was burned for heresy in 1531), Latimer became a Protestant and devoted himself to preaching. In 1535 he was consecrated Bishop of Worcester, but resigned in 1539 because he could not support the Act of the Six Articles which reinstated elements of Catholic doctrine. During the reign of the young Protestant Edward VI, from 1547 to 1553, Latimer's influence was at its height. He preached his famous 'Sermon on the Ploughers' at St Paul's Cross in London in 1548. On the accession of Mary I in 1553 Latimer was immediately sent to the Tower. He was subsequently condemned and burned at the stake in Oxford on 16 October 1555, along with Nicholas Ridley, Bishop of London. Latimer behaved throughout with exemplary courage. His last words to Ridley as recorded – and immortalized – in John Foxe's *Acts and Monuments* (1570) were: 'Be of good comfort, Master Ridley, and play the man. We shall this day light such a candle by God's grace in England, as, I trust, shall never be put out.'

Only forty-one of Latimer's sermons have survived. Some of them, including probably the 'Sermon on the Ploughers', were taken down in a kind of shorthand by one Thomas Some. Others were prepared for the press by Latimer's 'servant', Augustine Bernher. It would seem that Latimer did not revise them for publication, and they are thus likely to be close to the spoken form. The 'Sermon on the Ploughers' was one of a series of four sermons based on Christ's Parable of the Sower. The clergy are the ploughers, who prepare the land (the people) to receive the seed (the Word of God). Much of the sermon is an attack on preachers (or 'prelates' as Latimer calls them) who are failing in their duty.

Quaecunque scripta sunt ad nostram doctrinam scripta sunt.
Romans 15: 4

'All things which are written, are written for our erudition and knowledge. All things that are written in God's book, in the Bible book, in the book of the holy scripture, are written to be our doctrine.'

I told you in my first sermon, honourable audience, that I purposed to declare unto you two things. The one, what seed should be sown in God's field, in God's plough land; and the other, who should be the sowers: that is to say, what doctrine is to be taught in Christ's church and congregation, and what men should be the teachers and preachers of it. The first part I have told you in the three sermons past, in which I have assayed to set forth my plough, to prove what I could do. And now I shall tell you who be the ploughers: for God's word is a seed to be sown in God's field, that is, the faithful congregation, and the preacher is the sower. And it is in the gospel: *Exivit qui seminat seminare semen suum:* 'He that soweth, the husbandman, the ploughman, went forth to sow his seed.'[1] So that a preacher is resembled to a ploughman, as it is in another place: *Nemo admota aratro manu, et a tergo respiciens, aptus est regno Dei:* 'No man that putteth his hand to the plough, and looketh back, is apt for the kingdom of God.'[2] That is to say, let no preacher be negligent in doing his office. Albeit this is one of the places that hath been racked,[3] as I told you of racking scriptures. And I have been one of them myself that hath racked it, I cry God mercy for it; and have been one of them that have believed and expounded it against religious persons that would forsake their order which they had professed, and would go out of their cloister:[4] whereas indeed it toucheth not monkery, nor maketh any thing at all for any such matter; but it is directly spoken of diligent preaching of the word of God.

For preaching of the gospel is one of God's plough-works, and the preacher is one of God's ploughmen. Ye may not be offended with my similitude, in that I compare preaching to the labour and work of ploughing, and the preacher to a ploughman . . . For heaven is in the gospel likened to a mustard-seed: it is compared also to a piece of leaven; and as Christ saith, that at the last day he will come like a thief: and what dishonour is this to God? or what derogation is this to heaven? Ye may not then, I say, be offended with my similitude, for because I liken preaching to a ploughman's labour, and a prelate to a ploughman. But now you will ask me, whom I call a

[1] Luke 8: 5.
[2] Luke 9: 62.
[3] Misinterpreted by straining the meaning.
[4] Before his 'conversion' Latimer had been an ardent anti-Protestant.

prelate? A prelate is that man, whatsoever he be, that hath a flock to be taught of him; whosoever hath any spiritual charge in the faithful congregation, and whosoever he be that hath cure of souls. And well may the preacher and the ploughman be likened together: first, for their labour of all seasons of the year; for there is no time of the year in which the ploughman hath not some special work to do: as in my country in Leicestershire, the ploughman hath a time to set forth, and to assay his plough, and other times for other necessary works to be done. And then they also may be likened together for the diversity of works and variety of offices that they have to do. For as the ploughman first setteth forth his plough, and then tilleth his land, and breaketh it in furrows, and sometime ridgeth it up again;[5] and at another time harroweth it and clotteth it,[6] and sometime dungeth it and hedgeth it, diggeth it and weedeth it, purgeth and maketh it clean: so the prelate, the preacher, hath many diverse offices to do. He hath first a busy work to bring his parishioners to a right faith, as Paul calleth it, and not a swerving faith; but to a faith that embraceth Christ, and trusteth to his merits; a lively faith, a justifying faith; a faith that maketh a man righteous, without respect of works: as ye have it very well declared and set forth in the Homily.[7] He hath then a busy work, I say, to bring his flock to a right faith, and then to confirm them in the same faith: now casting them down with the law, and with threatenings of God for sin; now ridging them up again with the gospel, and with the promises of God's favour: now weeding them, by telling them their faults, and making them forsake sin; now clotting them, by breaking their stony hearts, and by making them supplehearted, and making them to have hearts of flesh; that is, soft hearts, and apt for doctrine to enter in: now teaching to know God rightly, and to know their duty to God and their neighbours: now exhorting them, when they know their duty, that they do it, and be diligent in it; so that they have a continual work to do. Great is their business, and therefore great should be their hire. They have great labours, and therefore they ought to have good livings, that they may commodiously feed their flock; for the preaching of the word of God unto the people is called meat: scripture calleth it meat; not strawberries, that come but once a year, and tarry not long, but are soon gone: but it is meat, it is no dainties. The people must have meat that must be familiar and continual, and daily given unto them to feed upon. Many make a strawberry of it, ministering it but once a year; but such do not the office of good prelates. For Christ saith, *Quis putas est servus prudens et fidelis? Qui dat cibum in tempore:* 'Who think you is a wise and a faithful servant? He that giveth meat in due time.'[8] So that he must at all times convenient preach diligently: therefore saith he, 'Who trow ye is a faithful servant?' He speaketh it as though it were a rare thing to find such a one, and as though he should say, there be but a few of them to find in the world. And how few of them there be throughout this realm that give

---

[5] Throw it into ridges.

[6] Free it from clods.

[7] The first book of *Homilies*, including 'A Short Declaration of the True, Lively, and Christian Faith', was published in 1547.

[8] Matthew 24: 45.

meat to their flock as they should do, the Visitors can best tell.[9] Too few, too few; the more is the pity, and never so few as now.

By this, then, it appeareth that a prelate, or any that hath cure of soul, must diligently and substantially work and labour. Therefore saith Paul to Timothy, *Qui episcopatum desiderat, hic bonum opus desiderat*: 'He that desireth to have the office of a bishop, or a prelate, that man desireth a good work.'[10] Then if it be a good work, it is work; ye can make but a work of it. It is God's work, God's plough, and that plough God would have still going. Such then as loiter and live idly, are not good prelates, or ministers. And of such as do not preach and teach, nor do their duties, God saith by his prophet Jeremy, *Maledictus qui facit opus Dei fradulenter*: 'Cursed be the man that doth the work of God fraudulently, guilefully or deceitfully':[11] some books have it *negligenter*: 'negligently or slackly'. How many such prelates, how many such bishops, Lord, for thy mercy, are there now in England! And what shall we in this case do? shall we company with them? O Lord, for thy mercy! shall we not company with them? O Lord, whither shall we flee from them? But 'cursed be he that doth the work of God negligently or guilefully.' A sore word for them that are negligent in discharging their office, or have done it fraudulently; for that is the thing that maketh the people ill.

But true it must be that Christ saith, *Multi sunt vocati, pauci vero electi*: 'Many are called, but few are chosen.'[12] Here have I an occasion by the way somewhat to say unto you; yea, for the place I alleged unto you before out of Jeremy, the forty-eighth chapter. And it was spoken of a spiritual work of God, a work that was commanded to be done; and it was of shedding blood, and of destroying the cities of Moab. For, saith he, 'Cursed be he that keepeth back his sword from shedding of blood.' As Saul, when he kept back the sword from shedding of blood at what time he was sent against Amaleck, was refused of God for being disobedient to God's commandment, in that he spared Agag the king. So that that place of the prophet was spoken of them that went to the destruction of the cities of Moab, among the which there was one called Nebo,[13] which was much reproved for idolatry, superstition, pride, avarice, cruelty, tyranny, and for hardness of heart; and for these sins was plagued of God and destroyed.

Now what shall we say of these rich citizens of London? What shall I say of them? Shall I call them proud men of London, malicious men of London, merciless men of London? No, no, I may not say so; they will be offended with me then. Yet must I speak. For is there not reigning in London as much pride, as much covetousness, as much cruelty, as much oppression, and as much superstition, as was in Nebo? Yes, I think, and much more too. Therefore I say, repent, O London; repent, repent. Thou hearest thy faults told thee, amend them, amend them. I think, if Nebo had had the preaching

[9] In 1547 a general visitation of all churches was ordered. Thirty visitors, ten of them clerics and the rest laymen, were appointed.
[10] 1 Timothy 3: 1.
[11] Jeremiah 48: 10.
[12] Matthew 22: 14.
[13] Jeremiah 48: 1.

that thou hast, they would have converted. And, you rulers and officers, be wise and circumspect, look to your charge, and see you do your duties; and rather be glad to amend your ill living than to be angry when you are warned or told of your fault. What ado was there made in London at a certain man, because he said (and indeed at that time on a just cause), 'Burgesses!' quoth he, 'nay, Butterflies.' Lord, what ado there was for that word! And yet would God they were no worse than butterflies! Butterflies do but their nature: the butterfly is not covetous, is not greedy, of other men's goods; is not full of envy and hatred, is not malicious, is not cruel, is not merciless. The butterfly glorieth not in her own deeds, nor preferreth the traditions of men before God's word; it committeth not idolatry, nor worshippeth false gods. But London cannot abide to be rebuked; such is the nature of man. If they be pricked, they will kick; if they be rubbed on the gall, they will wince; but yet they will not amend their faults, they will not be ill spoken of. But how shall I speak well of them? If you could be content to receive and follow the word of God, and favour good preachers, if you could bear to be told of your faults, if you could amend when you hear of them, if you would be glad to reform that is amiss; if I might see any such inclination in you, that you would leave to be merciless, and begin to be charitable, I would then hope well of you, I would then speak well of you. But London was never so ill as it is now. In times past men were full of pity and compassion, but now there is no pity; for in London their brother shall die in the streets for cold, he shall lie sick at the door between stock and stock,[14] I cannot tell what to call it, and perish there for hunger: was there ever more unmercifulness in Nebo? I think not. In times past, when any rich man died in London, they were wont to help the poor scholars of the Universities with exhibition.[15] When any man died, they would bequeath great sums of money toward the relief of the poor. When I was a scholar in Cambridge myself, I heard very good report of London, and knew many that had relief of the rich men of London: but now I can hear no such good report, and yet I inquire of it, and hearken for it; but now charity is waxen cold, none helpeth the scholar, nor yet the poor. And in those days, what did they when they helped the scholars? Marry, they maintained and gave them livings that were very papists, and professed the pope's doctrine: and now that the knowledge of God's word is brought to light, and many earnestly study and labour to set it forth, now almost no man helpeth to maintain them.

Oh London, London! repent, repent; for I think God is more displeased with London than ever he was with the city of Nebo. Repent therefore, repent, London, and remember that the same God liveth now that punished Nebo, even the same God, and none other; and he will punish sin as well now as he did then: and he will punish the iniquity of London, as well as he did then of Nebo. Amend therefore. And ye that be prelates, look well to your office; for right prelating is busy labouring, and not lording. Therefore preach and teach, and let your plough be doing. Ye lords, I say, that live like

---

[14] Between door-posts.
[15] A grant for the maintenance of a student.

loiterers, look well to your office; the plough is your office and charge. If you live idle and loiter, you do not your duty, you follow not your vocation: let your plough therefore be going, and not cease, that the ground may bring forth fruit.

But now methinketh I hear one say unto me: Wot ye what you say? Is it a work? Is it a labour? How then hath it happened that we have had so many hundred years so many unpreaching prelates, lording loiterers, and idle ministers? Ye would have me here to make answer, and to shew the cause thereof. Nay, this land is not for me to plough; it is too stony, too thorny, too hard for me to plough. They have so many things that make for them, so many things to lay for themselves, that it is not for my weak team to plough them. They have to lay for themselves long customs, ceremonies and authority, placing in parliament, and many things more. And I fear me this land is not yet ripe to be ploughed: for, as the saying is, it lacketh weathering: this gear lacketh weathering; at least way it is not for me to plough. For what shall I look for among thorns, but pricking and scratching? What among stones, but stumbling? What (I had almost said) among serpents, but stinging? But this much I dare say, that since lording and loitering hath come up, preaching hath come down, contrary to the apostles' times: for they preached and lorded not, and now they lord and preach not. For they that be lords will ill go to plough: it is no meet office for them; it is not seeming for their estate. Thus came up lording loiterers: thus crept in unpreaching prelates; and so have they long continued. For how many unlearned prelates have we now at this day! And no marvel: for if the ploughmen that now be were made lords, they would clean give over ploughing; they would leave off their labour, and fall to lording outright, and let the plough stand: and then both ploughs not walking, nothing should be in the commonweal but hunger. For ever since the prelates were made lords and nobles, the plough standeth; there is no work done, the people starve. They hawk, they hunt, they card, they dice; they pastime in their prelacies with gallant gentlemen, with their dancing minions, and with their fresh companions, so that ploughing is set aside: and by their lording and loitering, preaching and ploughing is clean gone. And thus if the ploughmen of the country were as negligent in their office as prelates be, we should not long live, for lack of sustenance. And as it is necessary for to have this ploughing for the sustentation of the body, so must we have also the other for the satisfaction of the soul, or else we cannot live long ghostly.[16] For as the body wasteth and consumeth away for lack of bodily meat, so doth the soul pine away for default of ghostly meat . . . But they that will be true ploughmen must work faithfully for God's sake, for the edifying of their brethren. And as diligently as the husbandman plougheth for the sustentation of the body, so diligently must the prelates and ministers labour for the feeding of the soul: both the ploughs must still be going, as most necessary for man. And wherefore are magistrates ordained, but that the tranquillity of the commonweal may be confirmed, limiting both ploughs?

---

[16] Spiritually.

3rd extract

But now for the fault of unpreaching prelates, methink I could guess what might be said for excusing of them. They are so troubled with lordly living, they be so placed in palaces, couched in courts, ruffling in their rents, dancing in their dominions, burdened with ambassages,[17] pampering of their paunches, like a monk that maketh his jubilee;[18] munching in their mangers, and moiling in their gay manors and mansions, and so troubled with loitering in their lordships, that they cannot attend it. They are otherwise occupied, some in the king's matters, some are ambassadors, some of the privy council, some to furnish the court, some are lords of the parliament, some are presidents, and comptrollers of mints.[19]

Well, well, is this their duty? Is this their office? Is this their calling? Should we have ministers of the church to be comptrollers of the mints? Is this a meet office for a priest that hath cure of souls? Is this his charge? I would here ask one question: I would fain to know who controlleth the devil at home in his parish, while he controlleth the mint? If the apostles might not leave the office of preaching to the deacons, shall one leave it for minting? I cannot tell you; but the saying is, that since priests have been minters, money hath been worse than it was before. And they say that the evilness of money hath made all things dearer. And in this behalf I must speak to England. 'Hear, my country, England,' as Paul said in his first epistle to the Corinthians, the sixth chapter; for Paul was no sitting bishop, but a walking and a preaching bishop. But when he went from them, he left there behind him the plough going still; for he wrote unto them, and rebuked them for going to law, and pleading their causes before heathen judges: 'Is there,' saith he, 'utterly among you no wise man, to be an arbitrator in matters of judgement? What, not one of all that can judge between brother and brother; but one brother goeth to law with another, and that under heathen judges?' *Constituite contemptos qui sunt in ecclesia,* &c.: 'Appoint them judges that are most abject and vile in the congregation.'[20] Which he speaketh in rebuking them; 'For,' saith he, *ad erubescentiam vestram dico:* 'I speak it to your shame.' So, England, I speak it to thy shame: is there never a nobleman to be a lord president, but it must be a prelate? Is there never a wise man in the realm to be a comptroller of the mint? 'I speak it to your shame. I speak it to your shame.' If there be never a wise man, make a water-bearer, a tinker, a cobbler, a slave, a page, comptroller of the mint: make a mean gentleman, a groom, a yeoman, or a poor beggar, lord president.

Thus I speak, not that I would have it so; but 'to your shame', if there be never a gentleman meet nor able to be lord president. For why are not the noblemen and young gentlemen of England so brought up in knowledge of God, and in learning, that they may be able to execute offices in the

---

[17] Ambassadorships.

[18] Fiftieth year.

[19] The privilege of coining had long been delegated by the Crown to the Archbishops of Canterbury and York, and the Bishop of Durham. Cuthbert Tunstall, Bishop of Durham, was President of the Council of the North and master of the episcopal mint at Durham until 1547.

[20] 1 Corinthians 6: 4–6.

commonweal? The king hath a great many of wards, and I trow there is a Court of Wards:[21] why is there not a school for the wards, as well as there is a Court for their lands? Why are they not set in schools where they may learn? Or why are they not sent to the universities, that they may be able to serve the king when they come to age? If the wards and young gentlemen were well brought up in learning, and in the knowledge of God, they would not when they come to age so much give themselves to other vanities. And if the nobility be well trained in godly learning, the people would follow the same train. For truly, such as the noblemen be, such will the people be. And now, the only cause why noblemen be not made lord presidents, is because they have not been brought up in learning.

Therefore for the love of God appoint teachers and schoolmasters, you that have charge of youth; and give the teachers stipends worthy of their pains, that they may bring them up in grammar, in logic, in rhetoric, in philosophy, in the civil law, and in that which I cannot leave unspoken of, the word of God. Thanks be unto God, the nobility otherwise is very well brought up in learning and godliness, to the great joy and comfort of England; so that there is now good hope in the youth, that we shall another day have a flourishing commonweal, considering their godly education. Yea, and there be already noblemen enough, though not so many as I would wish, able to be lord presidents, and wise men enough for the mint. And as unmeet a thing it is for bishops to be lord presidents, or priests to be minters, as it was for the Corinthians to plead matters of variance before heathen judges. It is also a slander to the noblemen, as though they lacked wisdom and learning to be able for such offices, or else were no men of conscience, or else were not meet to be trusted, and able for such offices. And a prelate hath a charge and cure otherwise; and therefore he cannot discharge his duty and be a lord president too. For a presidentship requireth a whole man; and a bishop cannot be two men. A bishop hath his office, a flock to teach, to look unto; and therefore he cannot meddle with another office, which alone requireth a whole man: he should therefore give it over to whom it is meet, and labour in his own business; as Paul writeth to the Thessalonians, 'Let every man do his own business, and follow his calling.'[22] Let the priest preach, and the noblemen handle the temporal matters. Moses was a marvellous man, a good man: Moses was a wonderful fellow, and did his duty, being a married man: we lack such as Moses was. Well, I would all men would look to their duty, as God hath called them, and then we should have a flourishing christian commonweal.

And now I would ask a strange question: who is the most diligentest bishop and prelate in all England, that passeth all the rest in doing his office? I can tell, for I know him who it is; I know him well. But now I think I

---

[21] Minors inheriting land held from the Crown automatically came under royal guardianship: the Crown administered their lands and had the right to arrange their marriages, being entitled to remuneration for doing so. Henry VIII established the Court of Wards in 1540 to regulate and administer this profitable business of wardships (which was not solely a perquisite of the Crown).

[22] 1 Thessalonians 4: 11.

see you listening and hearkening that I should name him. There is one that passeth all the other, and is the most diligent prelate and preacher in all England. And will ye know who it is? I will tell you: it is the devil. He is the most diligent preacher of all other; he is never out of his diocess; he is never from his cure; ye shall never find him unoccupied; he is ever in his parish; he keepeth residence at all times; ye shall never find him out of the way, call for him when you will he is ever at home; the diligentest preacher in all the realm; he is ever at his plough: no lording nor loitering can hinder him; he is ever applying his business, ye shall never find him idle, I warrant you. And his office is to hinder religion, to maintain superstition, to set up idolatry, to teach all kind of popery. He is ready as he can be wished for to set forth his plough; to devise as many ways as can be to deface and obscure God's glory. Where the devil is resident, and hath his plough going, there away with books, and up with candles; away with bibles, and up with beads; away with the light of the gospel, and up with the light of candles, yea, at noon-days. Where the devil is resident, that he may prevail, up with all superstition and idolatry; censing, painting of images, candles, palms, ashes, holy water, and new service of men's inventing; as though man could invent a better way to honour God with than God himself hath appointed. Down with Christ's cross, up with purgatory pickpurse,[23] up with him, the popish purgatory, I mean. Away with clothing the naked, the poor and impotent; up with decking of images, and gay garnishing of stocks and stones: up with man's traditions and his laws, down with God's traditions and his most holy word. Down with the old honour due to God, and up with the new god's honour. Let all things be done in Latin: there must be nothing but Latin, not so much as *Memento, homo, quod cinis es, et in cinerem reverteris*: 'Remember, man, that thou art ashes, and into ashes thou shalt return':[24] which be the words that the minister speaketh unto the ignorant people, when he giveth them ashes upon Ash-Wednesday; but it must be spoken in Latin: God's word may in no wise be translated into English.

Oh that our prelates would be as diligent to sow the corn of good doctrine, as Satan is to sow cockle and darnel![25] And this is the devilish ploughing, the which worketh to have things in Latin, and letteth[26] the fruitful edification. But here some man will say to me, What, sir, are ye so privy of the devil's counsel, that ye know all this to be true? Truly I know him too well, and have obeyed him a little too much in condescending to some follies; and I know him as other men do, yea, that he is ever occupied, and ever busy in following his plough . . .

Wo worth[27] thee, O devil, wo worth thee, that hast prevailed so far and so long; that hast made England to worship false gods, forsaking Christ their Lord. Wo worth thee, devil, wo worth thee, devil, and all thy angels. If Christ

---

[23] A reference to the use made of the doctrine of Purgatory to extract payments for masses for departed souls.

[24] Genesis 3: 19.

[25] Weeds.

[26] Hindereth.

[27] A curse upon.

by his death draweth all things to himself, and draweth all men to salvation, and to heavenly bliss, that trust in him; then the priests at the mass, at the popish mass, I say, what can they draw, when Christ draweth all, but lands and goods from the right heirs? The priests draw goods and riches, benefices and promotions to themselves; and such as believed in their sacrifices they draw to the devil. But Christ is he that draweth souls unto him by his bloody sacrifice. What have we to do then but *epulari in Domino*: 'to eat in the Lord at his supper'? What other service have we to do to him, and what other sacrifice have we to offer, but the mortification of our flesh? What other oblation have we to make, but of obedience, of good living, of good works, and of helping our neighbours? But as for our redemption, it is done already, it cannot be better: Christ hath done that thing so well, that it cannot be amended. It cannot be devised how to make that any better than he hath done it. But the devil, by the help of that Italian bishop yonder,[28] his chaplain, hath laboured by all means that he might to frustrate the death of Christ and the merits of his passion. And they have devised for that purpose to make us believe in other vain things by his pardons; as to have remission of sins for praying on hallowed beads; for drinking of the bakehouse bowl; as a canon of Waltham Abbey once told me, that whensoever they put their loaves of bread into the oven, as many as drank of the pardon-bowl[29] should have pardon for drinking of it. A mad thing, to give pardon to a bowl! Then to pope Alexander's holy water,[30] to hallowed bells, palms, candles, ashes, and what not? And of these things, every one hath taken away some part of Christ's sanctification; every one hath robbed some part of Christ's passion and cross, and hath mingled Christ's death, and hath been made to be propitiatory and satisfactory, and to put away sin. Yea, and Alexander's holy water yet at this day remaineth in England, and is used for a remedy against spirits and to chase away devils; yea, and I would this had been the worst. I would this were the worst. But wo worth thee, O devil, that hast prevailed to evacuate Christ's cross, and to mingle the Lord's supper. These be the Italian bishop's devices, and the devil hath pricked[31] at this mark to frustrate the cross of Christ: he shot at this mark long before Christ came, he shot at it four thousand years before Christ hanged on the cross, or suffered his passion.

For the brasen serpent was set up in the wilderness, to put men in remembrance of Christ's coming; that like as they which beheld the brasen serpent were healed of their bodily diseases, so they that looked spiritually upon Christ that was to come, in him should be saved spiritually from the devil. The serpent was set up in memory of Christ to come; but the devil found means to steal away the memory of Christ's coming, and brought the people to worship the serpent itself, and to cense him, to honour him, and to offer to him, to worship him, and to make an idol of him. And this was done

[28] The Pope.

[29] A bowl venerated as the relic of a saint.

[30] Pope Alexander I (*c*.105–*c*.115) was thought to have introduced the use of a mixture of holy water and salt to clear evil spirits from Christian homes.

[31] Aimed.

by the market-men that I told you of.[32] And the clerk of the market did it for the lucre and advantage of his master, that thereby his honour might increase; for by Christ's death he could have but small worldly advantage. And so even now so hath he certain blanchers[33] belonging to the market, to let and stop the light of the gospel, and to hinder the king's proceedings in setting forth the word and glory of God. And when the king's majesty, with the advice of his honourable council, goeth about to promote God's word, and to set an order in matters of religion,[34] there shall not lack blanchers that will say, 'As for images, whereas they have used to be censed, and to have candles offered unto them, none be so foolish to do it to the stock or stone, or to the image itself; but it is done to God and his honour before the image.' And though they should abuse it, these blanchers will be ready to whisper the king in the ear, and to tell him, that this abuse is but a small matter; and that the same, with all other like abuses in the church, may be reformed easily. 'It is but a little abuse,' say they, 'and it may be easily amended. But it should not be taken in hand at the first, for fear of trouble or further inconveniences. The people will not bear sudden alterations; an insurrection may be made after sudden mutation, which may be to the great harm and loss of the realm. Therefore all things shall be well, but not out of hand, for fear of further business.' These be the blanchers, that hitherto have stopped the word of God, and hindered the true setting forth of the same. There be so many put-offs, so many put-byes, so many respects and considerations of worldly wisdom: and I doubt not but there were blanchers in the old time to whisper in the ear of good king Hezekiah, for the maintenance of idolatry done to the brasen serpent,[35] as well as there hath been now of late, and be now, that can blanch the abuse of images, and other like things. But good king Hezekiah would not be so blinded; he was like to Apollos, 'fervent in spirit'.[36] He would give no ear to the blanchers; he was not moved with the worldly respects, with these prudent considerations, with these policies; he feared not insurrections of the people: he feared not lest his people would not bear the glory of God; but he, without any of these respects, or policies, or considerations, like a good king, for God's sake and for conscience sake, by and by[37] plucked down the brasen serpent, and destroyed it utterly, and beat it to powder. He out of hand did cast out all images, he destroyed all idolatry, and clearly did extirpate all superstition. He would not hear these blanchers and worldly-wise men, but without delay followeth God's cause, and destroyeth all idolatry out of hand. Thus did good king Hezekiah; for he was like Apollos, fervent in spirit, and diligent to promote God's glory.

And good hope there is, that it shall be likewise here in England; for the

[32] Evidently in an earlier sermon, which has not been preserved.

[33] Perverters, obstructors.

[34] A reference to the Royal Injunctions of July 1547, which provided, among other things, that each parish should purchase a copy of the Great Bible and a copy of the *Paraphrase* of the Gospels and Acts by Erasmus, and that on Sundays the preacher should read from the *Homilies* when there was no other sermon.

[35] 2 Kings 18: 1–4.

[36] Acts 18: 24–8.

[37] Immediately.

king's majesty is so brought up in knowledge, virtue, and godliness, that it is not to be mistrusted but that we shall have all things well, and that the glory of God shall be spread abroad throughout all parts of the realm, if the prelates will diligently apply their plough, and be preachers rather than lords. But our blanchers, which will be lords, and no labourers, when they are commanded to go and be resident upon their cures, and preach in their benefices, they would say, 'What? I have set a deputy there; I have a deputy that looketh well to my flock, and the which shall discharge my duty.' 'A deputy,' quoth he! I looked for that word all this while. And what a deputy must he be, trow ye? Even one like himself: he must be a canonist; that is to say, one that is brought up in the study of the pope's laws and decrees; one that will set forth papistry as well as himself will do; and one that will maintain all superstition and idolatry; and one that will nothing at all, or else very weakly, resist the devil's plough: yea, happy it is if he take no part with the devil; and where he should be an enemy to him, it is well if he take not the devil's part against Christ.

But in the mean time the prelates take their pleasures. They are lords, and no labourers: but the devil is diligent at his plough. He is no unpreaching prelate: he is no lordly loiterer from his cure, but a busy ploughman; so that among all the prelates, and among all the pack of them that have cure, the devil shall go for my money, for he still applieth his business. Therefore, ye unpreaching prelates, learn of the devil: to be diligent in doing of your office, learn of the devil: and if you will not learn of God, nor good men, for shame learn of the devil; *ad erubescentiam vestram dico*: 'I speak it to your shame'; if you will not learn of God, nor good men, to be diligent in your office, learn of the devil. Howbeit there is now very good hope that the king's majesty, being by the help of good governance of his most honourable counsellors trained and brought up in learning, and knowledge of God's word, will shortly provide a remedy, and set an order herein; which thing that it may so be, let us pray for him. Pray for him, good people; pray for him. Ye have great cause and need to pray for him.

3 Cervantes, *Don Quixote* (1605, 1615)

Source: Miguel de Cervantes Saavedra, *The Adventures of Don Quixote*, translated by J. M. Cohen (Harmondsworth: Penguin Books, 1950), pp. 31–5, 68–9, 171–81, 485–92.

Cervantes (1547–1616) was born at Alcalà in Spain, the son of a poor doctor. After an irregular education, he became a soldier, losing the use of his left hand through a wound at the naval battle of Lepanto (1571). He saw further military action, but was captured by pirates in 1575 and spent five years as a prisoner in Algiers. For the remainder of his life he struggled to earn a livelihood. Unsuccessful in attempts to secure a good position under the Crown, he turned to writing, first of all plays and then a novel, *La Galatea*, which failed miserably. In the 1590s he was jailed several times and lived in great poverty. His greatest work, *Don Quixote*, was published (part

I) in 1605. It was an instant success – pirated editions appeared within weeks – but seems not to have brought him much money. In 1615, prompted by the appearance of a spurious continuation, Cervantes published his own part II. He died the following year, 'old, a soldier, a gentleman and poor', in the words of a French visitor.

CHAPTER 1: WHICH TREATS OF THE QUALITY AND WAY OF LIFE OF THE FAMOUS KNIGHT DON QUIXOTE DE LA MANCHA

In a certain village in La Mancha, which I do not wish to name, there lived not long ago a gentleman – one of those who have always a lance in the rack, an ancient shield, a lean hack and a greyhound for coursing. His habitual diet consisted of a stew, more beef than mutton, of hash most nights, boiled bones on Saturdays, lentils on Fridays, and a young pigeon as a Sunday treat; and on this he spent three-quarters of his income. The rest of it went on a fine cloth doublet, velvet breeches and slippers for holidays, and a homespun suit of the best in which he decked himself on weekdays. His household consisted of a housekeeper of rather more than forty, a niece not yet twenty, and a lad for the field and market, who saddled his horse and wielded the pruning-hook.

Our gentleman was verging on fifty, of tough constitution, lean-bodied, thin-faced, a great early riser and a lover of hunting. They say that his surname was Quixada or Quesada – for there is some difference of opinion amongst authors on this point. However, by very reasonable conjecture we may take it that he was called Quexana. But this does not much concern our story; enough that we do not depart by so much as an inch from the truth in the telling of it.

The reader must know, then, that this gentleman, in the times when he had nothing to do – as was the case for most of the year – gave himself up to the reading of books of knight errantry; which he loved and enjoyed so much that he almost entirely forgot his hunting, and even the care of his estate. So odd and foolish, indeed, did he grow on this subject that he sold many acres of corn-land to buy these books of chivalry to read, and in this way brought home every one he could get. And of them all he considered none so good as the works of the famous Feliciano de Silva.[1] For his brilliant style and those complicated sentences seemed to him very pearls, especially when he came upon those love-passages and challenges frequently written in the manner of: 'The reason for the unreason with which you treat my reason, so weakens my reason that with reason I complain of your beauty'; and also when he read: 'The high heavens that with their stars divinely fortify you in your divinity and make you deserving of the desert that your greatness deserves.'

These writings drove the poor knight out of his wits; and he passed sleepless nights trying to understand them and disentangle their meaning, though Aristotle himself would never have unravelled or understood them, even if he had been resurrected for that sole purpose. He did not much like

---

[1] Feliciano da Silva, author of sixteenth-century sequels to the famous Spanish romance, *Amadis of Gaul*, and to *Celestina*, a romantic novel in dialogue first published about 1499.

the wounds that Sir Belianis gave and received, for he imagined that his face and his whole body must have been covered with scars and marks, however skilful the surgeons who tended him. But, for all that, he admired the author for ending his book with the promise to continue with that interminable adventure, and often the desire seized him to take up the pen himself, and write the promised sequel for him. No doubt he would have done so, and perhaps successfully, if other greater and more persistent preoccupations had not prevented him.

Often he had arguments with the priest of his village, who was a scholar and a graduate of Siguenza, as to which was the better knight – Palmerin of England or Amadis of Gaul.[2] But Master Nicholas, the barber of that village, said that no one could compare with the Knight of the Sun. Though if anyone could, it was Sir Galaor, brother of Amadis of Gaul. For he had a very accommodating nature, and was not so affected nor such a sniveller as his brother, though he was not a bit behind him in the matter of bravery.

In short, he so buried himself in his books that he spent the nights reading from twilight till daybreak and the days from dawn till dark; and so from little sleep and much reading, his brain dried up and he lost his wits. He filled his mind with all that he read in them, with enchantments, quarrels, battles, challenges, wounds, wooings, loves, torments and other impossible nonsense; and so deeply did he steep his imagination in the belief that all the fanciful stuff he read was true, that to his mind no history in the world was more authentic. He used to say that the Cid Ruy Diaz must have been a very good knight, but that he could not be compared to the Knight of the Burning Sword, who with a single backstroke had cleft a pair of fierce and monstrous giants in two. And he had an even better opinion of Bernardo del Carpio for slaying the enchanted Roland at Roncesvalles, by making use of Hercules' trick when he throttled the Titan Antaeus in his arms.

He spoke very well of the giant Morgante; for, though one of that giant brood who are all proud and insolent, he alone was affable and well-mannered. But he admired most of all Reynald of Montalban, particularly when he saw him sally forth from his castle and rob everyone he met, and when in heathen lands overseas he stole that idol of Mahomet, which history says was of pure gold. But he would have given his housekeeper and his niece into the bargain, to deal the traitor Galaon a good kicking.

In fact, now that he had utterly wrecked his reason he fell into the strangest fancy that ever a madman had in the whole world. He thought it fit and proper, both in order to increase his renown and to serve the state, to turn knight errant and travel through the world with horse and armour in search of adventures, following in every way the practice of the knights errant he had read of, redressing all manner of wrongs, and exposing himself

---

[2] *Palmerin of England*, a very famous chivalric romance dealing with the exploits of Palmerin, has been attributed variously to the Portuguese Francisco de Moraes (*c*.1500–72) or the Spaniard Luis Hurtado (1530–79?); *Amadis of Gaul*, published early in the sixteenth century, but based on much older sources, relates the adventures of Amadis, a perfect flower of chivalry who achieves wonderful feats of arms.

to chances and dangers, by the overcoming of which he might win eternal honour and renown. Already the poor man fancied himself crowned by the valour of his arm, at least with the empire of Trebizond; and so, carried away by the strange pleasure he derived from these agreeable thoughts, he hastened to translate his desires into action.

The first thing that he did was to clean some armour which had belonged to his ancestors, and had lain for ages forgotten in a corner, eaten with rust and covered with mould. But when he had cleaned and repaired it as best he could, he found that there was one great defect: the helmet was a simple head-piece without a visor. So he ingeniously made good this deficiency by fashioning out of pieces of pasteboard a kind of half-visor which, fitted to the helmet, gave the appearance of a complete head-piece. However, to see if it was strong enough to stand up to the risk of a sword-cut, he took out his sword and gave it two strokes, the first of which demolished in a moment what had taken him a week to make. He was not too pleased at the ease with which he had destroyed it, and to safeguard himself against this danger, reconstructed the visor, putting some strips of iron inside, in such a way as to satisfy himself of his protection; and, not caring to make another trial of it, he accepted it as a fine jointed head-piece and put it into commission.

Next he went to inspect his hack, but though, through leanness, he had more quarters than there are pence in a groat, and more blemishes than Gonella's horse, which was nothing but skin and bone, he appeared to our knight more than the equal of Alexander's Bucephalus and the Cid's Babieca. He spent four days pondering what name to give him; for, he reflected, it would be wrong for the horse of so famous a knight, a horse so good in himself, to be without a famous name. Therefore he tried to fit him with one that would signify what he had been before his master turned knight errant, and what he now was; for it was only right that as his master changed his profession, the horse should change his name for a sublime and high-sounding one, befitting the new order and the new calling he professed. So, after many names invented, struck out and rejected, amended, cancelled and remade in his fanciful mind, he finally decided to call him Rocinante, a name which seemed to him grand and sonorous, and to express the common horse he had been before arriving at his present state: the first and foremost of all hacks in the world.

Having found so pleasing a name for his horse, he next decided to do the same for himself, and spent another eight days thinking about it. Finally he resolved to call himself Don Quixote. And that is no doubt why the authors of this true history, as we have said, assumed that his name must have been Quixada and not Quesada, as other authorities would have it. Yet he remembered that the valorous Amadis had not been content with his bare name, but had added the name of his kingdom and native country in order to make it famous, and styled himself Amadis of Gaul. So, like a good knight, he decided to add the name of his country to his own and call himself Don Quixote de la Mancha. Thus, he thought, he very clearly proclaimed his parentage and native land and honoured it by taking his surname from it.

Now that his armour was clean, his helmet made into a complete head-piece, a name found for his horse, and he confirmed in his new title, it struck him that there was only one more thing to do: to find a lady to be enamoured of. For a knight errant without a lady is like a tree without leaves or fruit and a body without a soul. He said to himself again and again: 'If I for my sins or by good luck were to meet with some giant hereabouts, as generally happens to knights errant, and if I were to overthrow him in the encounter, or cut him down the middle or, in short, conquer him and make him surrender, would it not be well to have someone to whom I could send him as a present, so that he could enter and kneel down before my sweet lady and say in tones of humble submission: "Lady, I am the giant Caraculiambro, lord of the island of Malindrania, whom the never-sufficiently-to-be-praised knight, Don Quixote de la Mancha, conquered in single combat and ordered to appear before your Grace, so that your Highness might dispose of me according to your will"?' Oh, how pleased our knight was when he had made up this speech, and even gladder when he found someone whom he could call his lady. It happened, it is believed, in this way: in a village near his there was a very good-looking farm girl, whom he had been taken with at one time, although she is supposed not to have known it or had proof of it. Her name was Aldonza Lorenzo, and she it was he thought fit to call the lady of his fancies; and, casting around for a name which should not be too far from her own, yet suggest and imply a princess and great lady, he resolved to call her Dulcinea del Toboso – for she was a native of El Toboso –, a name which seemed to him as musical, strange and significant as those others that he had devised for himself and his possessions.

[Don Quixote sets out in the manner of knights of old, but his various 'adventures' end in disaster. After being beaten up by a muleteer he is taken home by a neighbour and put to bed. His friends decide that reading too many romances has disordered his brain and they purge his library of the offending volumes, only *Palmerin of England* and *Amadis of Gaul* being excepted from the conflagration. Once recovered, however, Don Quixote attributes the loss of his books to the enchanter Friston. Undeterred, he repairs his armour and sets off on a second expedition, this time with his neighbour, Sancho Panza, as squire. They strike out across the plain of Montiel early in the morning.]

CHAPTER 8: OF THE VALOROUS DON QUIXOTE'S SUCCESS IN THE DREADFUL AND NEVER BEFORE IMAGINED ADVENTURE OF THE WINDMILLS, WITH OTHER EVENTS WORTHY OF HAPPY RECORD

At that moment they caught sight of some thirty or forty windmills, which stand on that plain, and as soon as Don Quixote saw them he said to his squire: 'Fortune is guiding our affairs better than we could have wished. Look over there, friend Sancho Panza, where more than thirty monstrous giants appear. I intend to do battle with them and take all their lives. With their spoils we will begin to get rich, for this is a fair war, and it is a great service to God to wipe out such a wicked brood from the face of the earth.'

'What giants?' asked Sancho Panza.

'Those you see there,' replied his master, 'with their long arms. Some giants have them about six miles long.'

'Take care, your worship,' said Sancho; 'those things over there are not giants but windmills, and what seem to be their arms are the sails, which are whirled round in the wind and make the millstone turn.'

'It is quite clear,' replied Don Quixote, 'that you are not experienced in this matter of adventures. They are giants, and if you are afraid, go away and say your prayers, whilst I advance and engage them in fierce and unequal battle.'

As he spoke, he dug his spurs into his steed Rocinante, paying no attention to his squire's shouted warning that beyond all doubt they were windmills and no giants he was advancing to attack. But he went on, so positive that they were giants that he neither listened to Sancho's cries nor noticed what they were, even when he got near them. Instead he went on shouting in a loud voice: 'Do not fly, cowards, vile creatures, for it is one knight alone who assails you.'

At that moment a slight wind arose, and the great sails began to move. At the sight of which Don Quixote shouted: 'Though you wield more arms than the giant Briareus, you shall pay for it!' Saying this, he commended himself with all his soul to his Lady Dulcinea, beseeching her aid in his great peril. Then, covering himself with his shield and putting his lance in the rest, he urged Rocinante forward at a full gallop and attacked the nearest windmill, thrusting his lance into the sail. But the wind turned it with such violence that it shivered his weapon in pieces, dragging the horse and his rider with it, and sent the knight rolling badly injured across the plain. Sancho Panza rushed to his assistance as fast as his ass could trot, but when he came up he found that the knight could not stir. Such a shock had Rocinante given him in their fall.

'O my goodness!' cried Sancho. 'Didn't I tell your worship to look what you were doing, for they were only windmills? Nobody could mistake them, unless he had windmills on the brain.'

'Silence, friend Sancho,' replied Don Quixote. 'Matters of war are more subject than most to continual change. What is more, I think – and that is the truth – that the same sage Friston who robbed me of my room and my books has turned those giants into windmills, to cheat me of the glory of conquering them. Such is the enmity he bears me; but in the very end his black arts shall avail him little against the goodness of my sword.'

'God send it as He will,' replied Sancho Panza, helping the knight to get up and remount Rocinante, whose shoulders were half dislocated . . .

[Don Quixote and Sancho have a series of unfortunate encounters and adventures on their subsequent travels.]

CHAPTER 22: HOW DON QUIXOTE SET AT LIBERTY MANY UNFORTUNATE
CREATURES WHO WERE BEING BORNE, MUCH AGAINST THEIR WILL, WHERE THEY
HAD NO WISH TO GO

Cide Hamete Benengeli,[3] the Arabian and Manchegan author, relates in his most grave, eloquent, meticulous, delightful, and ingenious history that after that conversation between the famous Don Quixote de la Mancha and Sancho Panza, his squire, which is set down at the end of the twenty-first chapter, Don Quixote raised his eyes and saw on the road which he was taking some dozen men on foot, strung by the neck like beads on a great iron chain, and all manacled. With them were two horsemen and two men on foot, the horsemen carrying firelocks, the footmen javelins and swords. And as soon as Sancho Panza saw them he said: – 'Here's a chain of galley-slaves, men forced by the King, going to serve in the galleys.'

'What! Men forced?' asked Don Quixote. 'Is it possible that the King uses force on anyone?'

'I don't say that,' answered Sancho; 'but they are men condemned for their crimes to serve the King in the galleys, and they go perforce.'

'In fact,' replied Don Quixote, 'however you put it, these men are taken, and go by force and not of their own free will.'

'That is so,' said Sancho.

'Then,' said his master, 'this is a case for the exercise of my profession, for the redressing of outrages and the succouring and relieving of the wretched.'

'Consider, your worship,' said Sancho, 'that justice – that is the King himself – is doing no wrong or outrage to such people, but only punishing them for their crimes.'

At this moment the chain of galley-slaves came up, and in most courteous terms Don Quixote begged the guards to be so kind as to inform him of the cause or causes why they were bearing those people off in that fashion. One of the horsemen replied that they were galley-slaves belonging to His Majesty on the way to the galleys, such was the truth of the matter and there was no more to say.

'Nevertheless,' replied Don Quixote, 'I should like to learn from each one of them separately the cause of his misfortune.' He went on in such very polite language to persuade them to give him the information he desired, that the other mounted guard replied: 'Although we have with us here the copies and certificates of the sentences on each of these wretches, there is no time to take them out and read them. But your worship may come and ask them themselves, and they may tell you, if they please – and they will, for they are the sort who not only enjoy acting the villain but boasting of it afterwards too.'

With this permission, which Don Quixote would have taken if it had not been granted, the knight went up to the chain, and asked the first man for what sins he was in that evil plight. He replied that it was for falling in love.

---

[3] In chapter 9 Cervantes describes how he found the story of Don Quixote in a parchment book by the (imaginary) Arab historian, Cide Hamete Benengeli.

'For no more than that?' cried Don Quixote. 'But if they send men to the galleys for falling in love, I should long since have been rowing there myself.'

'It isn't the kind of love your worship imagines,' said the galley-slave. 'Mine was an over-great affection for a basketful of white linen, which I clasped to me so tight that if the law hadn't wrested it from me by force I shouldn't have let it go of my own free will even to this day. I was taken red-handed; there was no need of the torture; the trial was short; they accommodated my shoulders with a hundred lashes, and three years in the *gurapas* thrown in, and the job was done.'

'What are the *gurapas*?' asked Don Quixote.

'*Gurapas* are galleys,' replied the galley-slave, who was a lad of about twenty-four, and came, as he said, from Piedranita.

Don Quixote asked the same question of the second man, who was too melancholy and dejected to answer a word. But the first man replied for him: 'This man is here for being a canary – I mean a musician and singer.'

'How is that?' asked Don Quixote. 'Do men go to the galleys for being musicians and singers?'

'Yes, sir,' replied the galley-slave: 'for there is nothing worse than singing in anguish.'

'I have always heard the opposite,' said Don Quixote. 'Sing away sorrow, cast away care.'

'Here it's the reverse,' said the galley-slave. 'If you sing once you weep for a lifetime.'

'I do not understand,' said Don Quixote. But one of the guards put in: 'Sir, singing in anguish with these ungodly people means confessing on the rack. They put this sinner to the torture, and he confessed his crime, which was cattle-thieving; and on his confession they sentenced him to six years in the galleys, besides two hundred lashes on the back; and the reason why he is dejected and melancholy is that the rest of the thieves back there, and these marching here, abuse him and bully him, and mock him and despise him, because he confessed and hadn't the courage to say no. For, as they say, *no* takes no longer to say than *yes*, and a crook is in luck if his life depends on his own tongue and not on witnesses and proofs; and I think that they are not far wrong.'

'I agree,' replied Don Quixote. Then, passing to the third man, he asked him the same question as the others, and the man answered very readily and calmly: 'I am going to their ladyships the *gurapas* for five years because I was short of ten ducats.'

'I will give you twenty with pleasure,' said Don Quixote, 'to free you from this distress.'

'That,' replied the galley-slave, 'looks to me like having money when you're in mid-ocean and dying of hunger, and there's nowhere to buy what you need. Because if I had had those twenty ducats your worship now offers me at the right time, I should have greased the clerk's pen with them and livened up my lawyer's wits to such effect that I should have been in the Zocodover square in Toledo today, and not dragging along this road like a greyhound on a leash. But God is great. Patience – that's enough.'

Don Quixote went on to the fourth, a man of venerable appearance with a white beard reaching below his chest who, when asked why he was there, began to weep and answered not a word. But the fifth convict lent him a tongue and said: 'This honest fellow is going to the galleys for four years after parading the town in state and on horseback.'

'I suppose you mean that he was exposed to public shame,' said Sancho Panza.

'That's right,' replied the galley-slave, 'and the offence for which he got his sentence was trafficking in ears, in fact in whole bodies. What I mean is that this gentleman is here for procuring, and also for having a touch of the wizard about him.'

'If it had not been for that touch,' said Don Quixote, 'and if it were merely for procuring, he would not deserve to go and row in the galleys, but to be their general and command them. For the office of procurer is no easy one. It requires persons of discretion and is a most essential office in a well-ordered state. Only men of good birth should exercise it. Indeed, there ought to be an overseer and controller of these procurers, as there are of other professions, and only a certain number should be appointed and recognized, like brokers on the Exchange. In that way a great many troubles would be avoided, which are caused through this office getting into the hands of idiots and people of little intelligence, such as half-witted servant-maids and little pages and buffoons, raw and inexperienced folk. Then, at the critical moment, when they have a really important affair to manage, they let the morsel freeze between their fingers and their mouth, and do not know their right hand from their left. I should like to go on and explain why it is necessary to select those who are to hold so necessary a position in the State; but this is no proper place. But some day I will put the matter before those who can furnish a remedy. Now I can only say that the grief caused me by the sight of these white hairs and this venerable countenance in such distress for procuring has been entirely removed by the mention of witchcraft, though I know very well that there are no wizards in the world capable of affecting or compelling the affections, as some simple people believe; for our will is free and there is no drug or spell that can control it. What such simple servant-maids and lying rogues generally do is to make up mixtures and poisons which drive a man crazy, under the pretence that they have the power to excite love; whereas, as I have said, it is impossible to compel the affections.'

'That is so,' said the old fellow, 'and really, sir, as to being a wizard, I was not guilty, though I can't deny the procuring. But I never thought that I was doing any harm. All I wanted was for everyone to have a good time and live in peace and quiet, without quarrels or troubles. But the best intentions didn't serve to keep me from going to a place I don't expect to come back from, being stricken in years and having a bladder complaint which never gives me a moment's rest.' Here he burst into tears once more, and Sancho was so sorry for him that he took a *real* from under his shirt and gave it to him out of charity.

Don Quixote passed on and asked another his crime, and this one replied with rather more freedom than the last: 'I am here for having a bit too much fun with two girl cousins of mine, and two other cousins who were not mine. In fact, I had such fun with them all that the result of the joke was an intricate tangle of relationships that is more than any devil of a clerk can make out. It was all proved against me; I had no friends; I had no money; I was within an inch of having my gullet squeezed; they sentenced me to six years on the galleys; I submitted; it's the punishment for my crime. I'm young; if only my life holds out, all may yet come right. But, sir, should your worship have anything about you to give us poor wretches, God will repay you in Heaven, and here on earth we'll be sure to beseech Him in our prayers that your worship's life and health may be as long and as prosperous as your good looks deserve.'

The fellow who spoke wore the dress of a student, and one of the guards said that he was a great talker and a very good Latin scholar. Behind the rest came a man of about thirty, of very good appearance except that he squinted when he looked at you. He was fettered in a different way from the others. For he had a chain on his leg so long that it was wound right round his body, and two collars about his neck, one secured to the chain and the other of the kind called a *keep friend* or *friend's foot*. From this two iron bars reached down to his waist, with two manacles attached in which his wrists were secured by a heavy padlock, so that he could neither lift his hands to his mouth nor bend his head down to his hands. Don Quixote asked why this man had so many more fetters than the rest, and the guard replied that it was because he had committed more crimes than all the others put together, and that he was so bold and desperate a criminal that even though he was chained in that way they were not sure of him, but feared he might escape.

'What crimes, then, can he have committed?' asked Don Quixote, 'if they have not earned him a heavier penalty than the galleys?'

'He is going for ten years,' replied the guard, 'which is a sort of civil death. I need tell you no more than that this fellow is the famous Gines de Pasamonte, alias Ginesillo de Parapilla.'

'Not so rough, sergeant,' put in the galley-slave. 'Don't let us be settling names and surnames now. I am called Gines, not Ginesillo, and Pasamonte is my surname, not Parapilla as you say. Let everyone have a good look in his own cupboard, and he'll not be doing too badly.'

'A little less insolence,' replied the sergeant, 'you double-dyed thief, or I may have to shut you up, and then you'll be sorry.'

'You may see,' replied the galley-slave, 'that man proposes and God disposes; but one day somebody may learn whether my name is Ginesillo de Parapilla or not.'

'Isn't that what they call you, then, rogue?' asked the guard.

'Yes, they do,' replied Gines, 'but I'll stop them calling me that or I'll pluck them – but no matter where. If, sir, you have anything to give us, give it us now, and go in God's name; for you weary me with your prying into other men's lives. But if you want to know about mine, I am Gines de Pasamonte, and I have written my life with these very fingers.'

'He is speaking the truth,' put in the sergeant. 'He has written his own story, as fine as you please, and left the book behind at the prison pawned for two hundred *reals.*'

'And I mean to redeem it,' said Gines, 'even if it were pledged for two hundred ducats.'

'Is it as good as that?' said Don Quixote.

'It's so good,' replied Gines, 'that Lazarillo de Tormes[4] will have to look out, and so will everything in that style that has ever been written or ever will be. One thing I can promise you is that it is all the truth, and such well-written, entertaining truth that there is no fiction that can compare with it.

'And what is the title of the book?' asked Don Quixote.

'*The Life of Gines de Pasamonte,*' replied that hero.

'Is it finished?' asked Don Quixote.

'How can it be finished,' replied the other, 'if my life isn't? What is written begins with my birth and goes down to the point when I was sent to the galleys this last time.'

'Then you have been there before?' said Don Quixote.

'Four years I was there before,' replied Gines, 'in the service of God and the King, and I know the taste of the biscuit and the lash already. I am not greatly grieved at going, for I shall have a chance there to finish my book. I have a lot more to say, and in the Spanish galleys there is more leisure than I shall require, though I shan't need much for what I have to write, because I know it by heart.'

'You seem a clever fellow,' said Don Quixote.

'And an unfortunate one,' replied Gines, 'for misfortunes always pursue men of talent.'

'They pursue rogues,' replied the sergeant.

'I have already requested you to use better language, sergeant,' replied Pasamonte, 'for your superiors did not give you that staff to maltreat us poor devils, but to guide and lead us where his Majesty commands. If you do not, by God – but enough! – perhaps one day the stains that were made at the inn will come out in the wash. And let everyone hold his tongue, live virtuously and speak better. Now let us get along, for this is a bit too much of a joke.'

The sergeant raised his staff to strike Pasamonte in return for his threats. But Don Quixote interposed and begged him not to ill-treat him, for it was no great matter if a man who had his hands tied let his tongue free a little. Then, addressing the whole chain-gang, the knight said: 'From all that you have told me, dearest brethren, I clearly gather that, although it is for your faults they have punished you, the penalties which you are to suffer give you little pleasure. You are going to them, it seems, very reluctantly and much against your wills; and possibly it is only lack of courage under torture in one, shortage of money in another, lack of friends in another – in short, the unfair decisions of the judge – that have been the cause of your undoing and of your failure to receive the justice which was your due. All of which is now so clear in my mind that it bids me, persuades me, and even compels me, to

---

[4] *Lazarillo de Tormes*, the earliest of the Spanish picaresque novels, was published in 1553. It is the autobiography of a miller's son who embarks on a life of crime.

demonstrate on you the purpose for which Heaven has sent me into the world and made me profess therein the order of chivalry which I follow, and the vow I made to succour the needy and those who are oppressed by the strong. Conscious, however, that it is the part of prudence not to do by foul means what can be done by fair, I would beg the gentlemen of the guard and the sergeant to be so good as to release you and let you go in peace, since there will be no lack of men to serve the King out of better motives; for it seems to me a hard case to make slaves of those whom God and nature made free. Furthermore, gentlemen of the guard,' added Don Quixote, 'these poor men have committed no wrong against you. Let everyone answer for his sins in the other world. There is a God in Heaven, who does not neglect to punish the wicked nor to reward the good, and it is not right that honourable men should be executioners of others, having themselves no concern in the matter. I make this request in a calm and gentle manner, so that I may have cause to thank you if you comply; but if you do not do so willingly, then this lance and this sword, together with the valour of my arm, will force you to do so under compulsion.'

'This is fine foolishness,' replied the sergeant. 'It is a good joke he has taken all this time hatching! He would like us to let the King's convicts go, as if we had authority to free them, or he had it to order us to! Get along with you, sir, and good luck to you! Put that basin straight on your head,[5] and don't go about looking for a cat with three legs.'

'You are the cat, the rat, and the rascal!' replied Don Quixote. Then, matching deeds to his words, he attacked him so swiftly that he had dealt him a serious wound with his lance and brought him to the ground before he had a chance to defend himself; and, luckily for Don Quixote, this was the man with the firelock. The rest of the guards were dumbfounded by this unexpected turn of events. They recovered themselves, however, and the horsemen drew their swords, while the men on foot seized their javelins and rushed at Don Quixote, who awaited them in complete calm. And no doubt things would have gone badly for him if the galley-slaves had not seen their chance of gaining their liberty and taken advantage of it to break the chain which linked them together. Such was the confusion, in fact, that the guards ran first to the galley-slaves, who were struggling loose, and then to deal with Don Quixote, who was attacking, and so achieved no good purpose. Sancho, for his part, helped in releasing Gines de Pasamonte, who was the first to leap free and unfettered into the open, where he attacked the fallen sergeant and seized his sword and firelock. Then, first levelling the gun at one man and then picking on another, without ever firing it he cleared the field of all the guards, who fled from Pasamonte's gun and from the showers of stones, as well, flung by the now liberated galley-slaves.

Sancho was much grieved at this business, for he guessed that the guards who had fled would report the matter to the Holy Brotherhood,[6] who would

[5] In the previous chapter, Don Quixote had 'captured' a barber's basin which he thought was the magic helmet of Mambrino, a character in Ariosto's epic poem *Orlando Furioso* (1532).

[6] The Spanish *Santa Hermandad*, a voluntary organization formed in 1476 which later was reorganized as a regular national police force.

sound the alarm and come out in pursuit of the criminals. This thought he communicated to his master, begging him that they might clear out immediately and hide in the nearby mountains.

'That is all very well,' said Don Quixote, 'but I know what is right for us to do now.' Then he called all the galley-slaves, who were running about excitedly and had stripped the sergeant to the skin; and when they had gathered around him to hear what his orders might be, he addressed them thus: 'It is a mark of well-born men to show gratitude for benefits received, and ingratitude is one of the sins which most offend God. I say this, gentle-men, because you have already had good experience of benefits received at my hands; as payment for which it is my will that you bear this chain which I have taken from your necks and immediately take the road to the city of El Toboso, there to present yourselves before the Lady Dulcinea del Toboso and tell her that her knight, the Knight of the Sad Countenance, presents his service to her. Then you are to tell her, point by point, every detail of this famous adventure up to the restoration of your long-coveted liberty; and when you have done so you may go wherever you will, and good luck go with you.'

Gines de Pasamonte answered for them all, and said: 'What your worship commands, lord and liberator, is of all impossibilities the most impossible for us to perform, since we cannot appear on the roads together, but must go singly and separately, each one on his own. And we must try to hide in the bowels of the earth for fear of being found by the Holy Brotherhood, for there is no doubt that they will come out in search of us. What your worship can do, and what you should do, is to substitute for this service and tribute to the lady Dulcinea del Toboso some number of Ave Marias and Credos, which we will say for your worship's benefit, this being a thing which can be performed by night and by day, on the run or resting, in peace or in war. But to think of our returning now to the flesh-pots of Egypt, I mean of our taking up our chain and setting out on the road for El Toboso, is to imagine that it is already night when it is not yet ten in the morning, and you can no more ask us for that than you can ask pears from an elm-tree.'

'Then I swear by Heaven,' cried Don Quixote in fury, 'sir son of a whore, Don Ginesillo de Parapillo, or whatever you are called, – that you shall go yourself alone, with your tail between your legs and the whole chain on your back!'

Pasamonte was quite certain from Don Quixote's crazy action in giving them their liberty that he was not right in the head; and being far from long-suffering, when he found himself treated in this way he tipped his companions the wink. They then drew back and began to rain such a shower of stones upon Don Quixote that he could not contrive to cover himself with his shield, and poor Rocinante took no more notice of the spur than if he had been made of brass. Sancho got behind his ass and used him as a defence against the cloud and hailstorm of stones which descended on the pair of them. But Don Quixote could not shield himself well enough, and was hurt by some of the pebbles, which struck him on the body with such force that they knocked him to the ground. The moment he was down the student leapt on him, and seizing the basin from his head, brought it down three or four times on his shoulders, and as many more on the ground, till it was almost smashed to pieces. They also stripped him of a jacket which he wore over his armour, and would have taken off his stockings too if his leg armour had not prevented them. While from Sancho they took his overcoat, and left him in his shirt. Then, dividing the rest of the spoils of battle, they fled, each in a separate direction, more intent on escaping from the dreaded Brotherhood than on loading themselves with the chain and going to present themselves to the lady Dulcinea del Toboso.

All that remained were the ass and Rocinante, Sancho and Don Quixote; the ass pensively hanging his head and shaking his ears now and then, imagining that the storm of stones which had whizzed by his head had not yet ceased; Rocinante prostrate beside his master, for he had also been brought down by a stone; Sancho in his shirt and terrified of the Holy Brotherhood; and Don Quixote much distressed at finding himself so vilely treated by the very men for whom he had done so much.

[After further adventures Don Quixote and Sancho return home, thus ending the first part of the novel. In 1615 Cervantes published his continuation, in which Sancho reports to Don Quixote that he has heard from a student, Sampson Carrasco, that their story has been published, the author being a Moor, Cide Hamete Benengeli.]

CHAPTER 3: OF THE RIDICULOUS CONVERSATION WHICH PASSED BETWEEN DON QUIXOTE, SANCHO PANZA AND THE BACHELOR SAMPSON CARRASCO

Don Quixote was very thoughtful as he waited for the Bachelor Carrasco, from whom he expected to hear how he had been put into a book, as Sancho had told him. He could not persuade himself that such a history existed, for the blood of the enemies he had slain was scarcely dry on his own sword-blade. Yet they would have it that his noble deeds of chivalry were already about in print. Nevertheless he imagined that some sage, either friendly or hostile, had given them to the Press by magic art; if a friend, to magnify and extol them above the most renowned actions of any knight errant; and if an enemy, to annihilate them and place them below the basest ever written of any mean squire – although, he admitted to himself, the deeds of squires were never written of. But if it were true that there was such a history, since it was about a knight errant it must perforce be grandiloquent, lofty, remarkable, magnificent and true. With this he was somewhat consoled; but it disturbed him to think that its author was a Moor, as that name of Cide suggested. For he could hope for no truth of the Moors, since they are all cheats, forgers and schemers. He was afraid too that his love affairs might have been treated with indelicacy, which would redound to the disparagement and prejudice of his lady, Dulcinea del Toboso. For he was anxious that it should be declared that he had always preserved his fidelity and reverence towards her, scorning Queens, Empresses, and damsels of all qualities, and curbing the violence of his natural appetites. And so Sancho found him, wrapt and involved in a thousand such fancies when he returned with Carrasco, whom the knight received with great courtesy.

The Bachelor was not very big in body, although his name was Sampson, but a great wag, of poor colour though of great intelligence. He must have been about twenty-four years old, with a round face, a flat nose, and a big mouth – all signs that he was of a mischievous disposition and fond of jokes and japes, as he showed, on seeing Don Quixote, by going down on his knees before him, and saying: 'Give me your hands, your Mightiness, Don Quixote de la Mancha. For by the habit of St Peter, which I wear – although I have taken no more than the first four orders – your worship is one of the most famous knights errant there has ever been on all the rotundity of the earth. Blessed be Cide Hamete Benengeli, who has left us the history of your great deeds recorded, and thrice blessed the man of taste who took the pains to have it translated out of the Arabic into our vulgar Castilian, for the universal entertainment of mankind!'

Don Quixote made him get up and said: 'So it is true, then, that there is a history of me, and that he was a Moor and a sage who composed it?'

'So true is it,' said Sampson, 'that it is my opinion there are more than twelve thousand copies of this history in print today. If not, let Portugal, Barcelona and Valencia speak; for there they were printed. There is even a report that it is being printed at Antwerp too. In fact, I am pretty sure that there cannot be any nation into whose tongue it will not be translated.'

'One of the things,' said Don Quixote at this, 'which must give the greatest pleasure to a virtuous and eminent man is to see himself, in his lifetime, printed and in the Press, and with a good name on people's tongues. I said a good name because, were it the opposite, no death could be so bad.'

'If it is a question of a good reputation and a good name,' said the Bachelor, 'your worship alone bears away the palm from all knights errant. For the Moor in his language, and the Christian in his, have carefully and accurately depicted for us your worship's gallantry, your great courage in confronting perils, your patience in adversity, your fortitude too under misfortune and wounds, and the chastity and continence of the most platonic loves of your worship and my lady, Doña Dulcinea del Toboso.'

'Never,' Sancho Panza broke in at this point, 'have I heard my lady Dulcinea called Doña, but simply The Lady Dulcinea del Toboso. There the history's wrong.'

'That is not an important objection,' replied Carrasco.

'No, surely,' replied Don Quixote; 'but tell me, Master Bachelor, which of my exploits are most highly praised in this history?'

'About that,' replied the Bachelor, 'there are different opinions, as there are different tastes. Some favour the adventure of the windmills which seemed to your worship Briareuses and giants. Others the adventure of the fulling mills. One man is for the description of the two armies, which proved afterwards to be two flocks of sheep. Another thinks most highly of the tale of the corpse which they were taking to Segovia for burial. Another says that the best of all is the freeing of the galley-slaves. And yet another that there is nothing equal to the two Benedictine giants and the combat with the valorous Basque.'

'Tell me, Master Bachelor,' put in Sancho, 'does the adventure with the Yanguesans come in, when our good Rocinante had a fancy to look for dainties at the bottom of the sea?'

'The sage left nothing in his ink-horn,' replied Sampson. 'He tells us everything and dwells on every point, even to the capers Sancho cut on the blanket.'

'I cut no capers on the blanket,' replied Sancho. 'But in the air I did, and more than I liked.'

'In my opinion,' said Don Quixote, 'there is no human history in the world which has not got its ups and downs, particularly those that treat of knight errantry. They can never be full of fortunate incidents.'

'For all that,' replied the Bachelor, 'some who have read your history say that they would have been glad if the authors had left out a few of the countless beatings which Don Quixote received in various encounters.'

'That's where the truth of the story comes in,' said Sancho.

'Yet they might in fairness have kept quiet about them,' said Don Quixote, 'for there is no reason to record those actions which do not change or affect the truth of the story, if they redound to the discredit of the hero. Aeneas was not as pious as Virgil paints him, I promise you, nor Ulysses as prudent as Homer describes him.'

'That is true,' replied Sampson; 'but it is one thing to write as a poet, and another as a historian. The poet can relate and sing things, not as they were but as they should have been, without in any way affecting the truth of the matter.'

'Well, if it's telling the truth this Moor's after,' said Sancho, 'and my master's beatings are all set down, then mine will be found amongst them. For they never took the measure of his worship's shoulders without taking it of my whole body. But that's not to be wondered at, for this same master of mine says the limbs have to take a share in the head's pain.'

'You are a sly fellow, Sancho,' answered Don Quixote. 'I swear your memory does not fail you when you want to remember anything.'

'Even if I'd a mind to forget the thrashings I got,' said Sancho, 'the marks wouldn't let me, for they're still fresh on my ribs.'

'Be quiet, Sancho,' said Don Quixote, 'and do not interrupt the Bachelor, whom I beg to proceed and tell me what is said of me in this history of his.'

'And of me,' said Sancho, 'for they say I'm one of the principal presonages in it.'

'Personages, not *presonages*, Sancho my friend,' said Sampson.

'So we have another vocabulary corrector!' said Sancho. 'If it goes on like this we shall never be done in this life.'

'Hang me, Sancho,' answered the Bachelor, 'if you are not the second person in the history. And there are some who think the parts where you talk are the best bits in the story; though there are others who say that you were excessively credulous in believing in the governorship of that isle Don Quixote here promised you.'

'There is still sun on the thatch,' said Don Quixote, 'and all the while Sancho is getting older. With the experience that years bring he will become more competent and fitter to be a governor than he is now.'

'By God, sir,' said Sancho, 'any isle I can't govern at my present age I shall never govern if I live to be as old as Methuselah. The trouble is that this isle of yours is hidden away, I don't know where, and not that I haven't the brains to govern it.'

'Leave it to God, Sancho,' said Don Quixote, 'and all will be well. Perhaps better than you think, for not a leaf stirs on a tree without God's will.'

'That is the truth,' said Sampson; 'for if God wills, Sancho will not lack a thousand isles to govern, let alone one.'

'I have seen governors about here,' said Sancho, 'who, to my thinking, don't come up to the sole of my shoe. Yet for all that they're called *your worship*, and served off silver.'

'Those are not governors of isles,' answered Sampson, 'but of more manageable territories. Governors of isles must at least be grammarians.'

'The "*gram*" I can easily manage,' said Sancho, 'but the "*marians*" I pass, for I don't understand them. But leaving this matter of a governorship in God's hands – and may He place me where I may serve Him best – let me say, Master Bachelor Sampson Carrasco, that I'm extraordinarily glad that the author of this history has spoken of me so nicely that what he says gives no offence. For, as I'm a good squire, if he'd said things about me unbefitting the old Christian I am, the deaf would be hearing of it.'

'That would be working miracles,' said Sampson.

'Miracles or no miracles,' said Sancho, 'let everyone mind how he speaks or writes about *presons*, and not put down helter-skelter the first thing that come into his head.'

'One of the faults they find in this history,' said the Bachelor, 'is that the author inserted a novel called *The Tale of Foolish Curiosity* – not that it is bad or badly told, but because it is out of place and has nothing to do with the story of his worship Don Quixote.'

'I'll bet the son of a dog has made a fine mix-up of everything,' put in Sancho.

'Now I believe that the author of my story is no sage but an ignorant chatterer,' said Don Quixote, 'and that he set himself to write it down blindly and without any method, and let it turn out anyhow, like Orbaneja, the painter of Ubeda, who, when they asked him what he was painting, used to answer "Whatever it turns out." Sometimes he would paint a cock, in such a fashion and so unlike one that he had to write in Gothic characters beside it: *This is a cock*. And so it must be with my history, which will need a commentary to be understood.'

'No,' replied Sampson, 'for it's so plain that there is nothing in it to raise any difficulty. Children finger it; young people read it; grown men know it by heart, and old men praise it. It is so dog-eared, in fact, and so familiar to all sorts of people that whenever they see a lean horse go by, they cry: "There goes Rocinante." Those who are most given to reading it are pages;

there is not a gentleman's antechamber in which you will not find a *Don Quixote*. When one lays it down, another picks it up; some rush at it; others beg for it. In fact, this story is the most delightful and least harmful entertainment ever seen to this day, for nowhere in it is to be found anything even resembling an indelicate expression or an uncatholic thought.'

'To write in any other way,' said Don Quixote, 'would be to write not the truth, but lies; and historians who resort to lies ought to be burnt like coiners of false money. But I do not know what induced the author to make use of novels and irrelevant stories, when he had so much of mine to write about. No doubt he felt bound by the proverb: "With hay or with straw, it is all the same." For really, if he had confined himself to my thoughts, my sighs, my tears, my worthy designs, and my undertakings, he could have made a volume greater than all the works of El Tostado, or at any rate as big. In fact my conclusion is, Master Bachelor, that to compose histories or books of any sort at all you need good judgement and ripe understanding. To be witty and write humorously requires great genius. The cunningest part in a play is the fool's, for a man who wants to be taken for a simpleton must never be one. History is like a sacred writing, for it has to be truthful; and where the truth is, in so far as it is the truth, there God is. But notwithstanding this there are some who compose books and toss them off like fritters.'

'There is no book so bad,' said the Bachelor, 'that there is not something good in it.'

'No doubt of that,' replied Don Quixote, 'but it very often happens that authors who have deservedly reaped and won great fame by their writings have lost it all, or somewhat diminished it, when they have given them to the Press.'

'The cause of that,' said Sampson, 'is that printed books are viewed at leisure, and so their faults are easily seen, and the greater the fame of their authors the more closely are they examined. Renowned men of genius, great poets and famous historians are always, or generally, envied by such as make it their pleasure and particular pastime to judge the writings of others, without having published any of their own.'

'That is not to be wondered at,' said Don Quixote, 'for there are many theologians who are not good in the pulpit, but excellent at recognizing the faults or excesses of those who preach.'

'All that is true, Don Quixote,' said Carrasco, 'but I should be glad if such censors would be more merciful and less scrupulous, and not scold at the specks in the bright sun of the work they review. For, though Homer sometimes nods, let them reflect how long he stayed awake to give us the light of his work with the least possible shadow. And it may well be that what seem faults to them are moles, which at times enhance the beauty of a face. In fact it is my opinion that an author runs a very great risk in printing a book. For it is the greatest of all impossibilities to write one that will satisfy and please every reader.'

'The one which treats of me,' said Don Quixote, 'must have pleased few.'

'Quite the opposite; for as there are an infinite number of fools in the world, an infinite number of people have enjoyed that history. But here are some who have found fault, and taxed the author's memory for forgetting who it was that robbed Sancho of his Dapple. For it is not stated there, but only from the context do we infer that it was stolen. Yet a little farther on we find Sancho riding on this same ass, and are never told how he turned up again. They also say that he forgot to put down what Sancho did with the hundred crowns he found in the leather bag in the Sierra Morena, for they were never mentioned again. Many people want to know what use he made of them, or what he spent them on – that is one of the essential points left out of the work.'

'I'm not prepared now, Master Sampson,' replied Sancho, 'to go into details or accounts, for I've got a stomach-ache, and if I don't cure it with two gulps of the old stuff, it will put me on St Lucy's thorn. I have a drop at home, and my old woman is waiting for me. I'll come back when I've had my dinner, and answer all your worship's questions, and all the world's besides, whether it's about my losing the ass or spending the hundred crowns.'

Then, waiting for no reply, he went off home without another word. Don Quixote begged and prayed the Bachelor to stop and take pot-luck with him, and he accepted the invitation and stayed to the meal, at which a pair of pigeons were added to the ordinary fare. Over table they talked of knight-errantry, Carrasco following the knight's humour, and when the banquet was ended they slept through the heat of the day, till Sancho came back and their previous discussion was resumed.

SECTION VII

The engraved title page to a Book of Hours
printed by the French printer Reginald Chauldière (Paris 1549).
Reproduced by kind permission of The British Library (C27 E14).

The Crisis of Authority: France

France in the second half of the sixteenth century was a nation in search of a sovereign. The basis of authority and obligation, called into question by the intellectual, religious and material transformations of the Renaissance and the Reformation, became the focus of anxious and intense debate as the centralized absolutism of Henry II disintegrated in the Wars of Religion. Between 1559 and 1594 the people of France were plunged into civil war and anarchy. Besides confessional conflict, there were sharp divisions between court and country and town and country; between plebeians and patricians; landlord and tenant; and between Paris and the provinces. Regional resistance to political and cultural domination from the centre, sustained by royal fiscality, was symptomatic of the crisis of the monarchy. That crisis was perceived by contemporaries in personal rather than structural terms; its conjunctural character, though, was readily understood. The Venetian ambassador in an interesting and insightful analysis of France on the eve of civil war, noted how royal authority, sapped by the brief reign of a juvenile king, followed by the minority of his brother and the regency of his mother, was unable to repress the unrest and disorder unleashed by religious dissidence and social radicalism (document VII.5). The ambassador had no doubt that Protestantism was fundamentally subversive of all authority, ecclesiastical and civil. Not all Catholics were so minded. For some the progress of Protestantism was a measure of their own failure. Attempts at spiritual renewal and Church reform, undertaken by the Meaux circle in the 1520s and 1530s, sought to distinguish humanism from heresy and revival from rebellion. The evangelical humanist perspective which informed their approach is presented here through the writings of Jacques Lefèvre d'Étaples (document VII.2). Alas, personal piety was not enough. Men of a moderate Erasmian disposition were censured and silenced; heretics were burned. But to no avail. Repression bred resistance; extremism excess.

The Calvinist challenge, which grew in strength and confidence during the 1540s and 1550s, required more than organization and doctrine. In an age in which the monarch was held to be God's vice-regent on earth, tyrannicide required elaborate justification. In the aftermath of the Massacre of St Bartholomew (1572) such justifications were not in short supply. Huguenot pamphleteers and polemicists appeared, to denounce an idolatrous and tyrannical government. Principles, though, were not the sole issue; personalities were equally important. Catherine de Medici's statecraft seemed to personify the precepts of Niccolò Machiavelli, another godless Italian, and helped to fuel the misogynism of her Huguenot critics. *Francogallia*, Hotman's influential treatise on popular sovereignty, supplies a good example of such sentiment (document VII.6).

To those who held a theocratic conception of the state, Machiavelli was outrageous and offensive. Innocent Gentillet, the best-known of such critics, assailed the concept of justification by 'reason of state' in a savage parody. His Anti-Machiavel (document VII.7), first published in Geneva in 1576, dismissed Machiavelli's maxims as 'vicious and detestable in the highest degree' and concluded with a warning to his audience that 'perfidy is so detestable to God and to the whole world, that God never allows the perfidious and the breakers of their word to go unpunished.'

In its emphasis upon popular sovereignty and representative institutions as a constraint on monarchy, Huguenot theory broke new ground that pointed to the future; in its emphasis upon the limitations on absolutism, and its insistence that the monarch be merciful and godly, it harked back to the constitutional thinkers of the early sixteenth century. The classic statement of these views, that of Claude de Seyssel, is given below in documents VII.1 and VII.4.

Seyssel emphasized the restraints on royal authority. Bodin, by contrast, asserted the necessity for compliance with the will of the sovereign. Bodin, like Hotman, was a jurist who believed in the application of historical methods to the solution of practical and pressing problems. The outcome, though, was radically different. For Bodin, history was the handmaiden of politics; its study enabled the student to identify the general laws of social development from which the best form of law and government could be determined. Not the least interesting aspect of Bodin's thought was his theory of climate as a determinant of political and social structures and disparities. Both these aspects are represented in document VII.8.

But it is the contrast between Bodin and the 'monarchomachs' (king killers) that is most striking. Those who valued order above liberty found in Bodin's *Six Books of the Commonwealth* an uncompromising defence of royal absolutism and a root and branch assault on the theory and practice of the Huguenot revolution. The salient features of the argument are summarized in document VII.9.

The items collected here are best considered as a commentary and reflection upon the troubled condition of sixteenth-century France. The texts, though, should be read as more than statements of abstract political thought; the theories and arguments contained therein, with their hidden values and inherited assumptions, illuminate the intel-

lectual and social landscape in which they arose. They enable us to⎫
penetrate the mentality and outlook of a world which is now remote and ⎬
increasingly inaccessible.

Political theorizing, however, was not the sole (or possibly even the
most important) means for the defence of royal authority, not at any rate
to contemporaries, the vast majority of whom could neither afford to
purchase nor read the learned treatises in which political arguments
were presented. Ocular evidence of princely power was provided by the
magnificence of the court, the focus of artistic effort, and by the
pageants, processions and progresses in which relations of dominance
and subordination were ritualized and celebrated (documents VII.3 and
VII.10).

1 Claude de Seyssel, *The Monarchy of France* (1519)

Source: Claude de Seyssel, *The Monarchy of France*, translated by J. H. Hexter, edited
by Donald R. Kelley (New Haven and London: Yale University Press, 1981),
pp. 46–7.

Bishop of Marseilles.

Claude de Seyssel (1450–1520) was a statesman, scholar and distinguished
churchman. *The Monarchy of France* was written in retirement by this former minister
of Louis XII for the new king, Francis I. It was composed in 1515 and published in
1519. In it Seyssel commends monarchy as the form of government least liable to
degeneration.

A single head and monarch can better remedy and obviate all dangers and
difficulties than can an assembly of folk elected to govern but nonetheless
subject to those whom they govern. He is always better obeyed, revered,
feared, and esteemed, whether the community be great or small, than a
temporary and removable head or one without full authority. Divine and
human, natural and political reasons all prove that it is always necessary to
revert to a single head in all things and that plurality of heads is pernicious.
Experience also shows that several monarchical states, as for example, those
of the Egyptians, the Assyrians and the Parthians,[1] have lasted longer than
any aristocratic, democratic or popular ones. And they have been more
peaceful and have had fewer changes and civil dissensions, although the
heads and monarchs often changed by death or otherwise. And the same is
true of the monarchies of our own time, the kingdoms of England, of Spain,
and especially of France, for these have already lasted longer as monarchical
orders than any great popular or aristocratic state that we know of.

---

[1] Parthian: from the ancient kingdom of Western Asia.

2 Lefèvre d'Étaples: Restoration of the Gospel (1522)

Source: *The Portable Renaissance Reader*, edited by James Bruce Ross and Mary Martin McLaughlin (Harmondsworth: Penguin Books, 1977), pp. 84–6.

Jacques Lefèvre d'Étaples (*c*.1460–1536), was a French Christian humanist much influenced by Ficino and the Florentine Neoplatonists. The philological and textual methods of the humanists characterized his *Quintuplex Psalterium*, a study of the Psalms, written in 1509, and a similar work on St Paul's Epistles published three years later. In this latter work he argued that man was dependent upon God's grace and in so doing supplied Luther with the idea of 'sola fide'. A critic from within of the Roman Catholic Church, he enjoyed the patronage of both Marguerite of Navarre and the circle around Briçonnet, Bishop of Meaux. The following extract was written in 1522.

O you whom God has truly loved, and who are especially dear to me in Christ, know that only those are Christians who love our Lord Jesus Christ and His Word with perfect purity . . .

For the Word of Christ is the Word of God, the Gospel of peace, liberty, and joy, the Gospel of salvation, redemption, and life; the Gospel of peace after continuous warfare, of liberty after the most harsh servitude, of joy after constant sadness, of salvation after complete perdition, of redemption after the most dreadful captivity, and finally of life itself as an escape from eternal death. If this Word is called the Gospel, the 'good news', it is because, for us, it is the herald of all good things, and of the infinite blessings which are prepared for us in heaven . . .

And pray God that the model of faith may be sought in the primitive Church, which offered to Christ so many martyrs, which knew no other rule than the Gospel, and no other end than Christ, and which rendered its devotion to only one God in three Persons! If we rule our life by this example, the eternal Gospel of Christ will flourish now, as it flourished then. The faithful then depended in everything on Christ; we ourselves should also depend entirely on Him . . .

Why may we not aspire to see our age restored to the likeness of the primitive Church, when Christ received a purer veneration, and the splendour of His Name shone forth more widely? . . . As the light of the Gospel returns, may He Who is blessed above all grant also to us this increase of faith, this purity of worship: as the light of the Gospel returns, I say, which at this time begins to shine again. By this divine light many have been so greatly illuminated that, not to speak of other benefits, from the time of Constantine, when the primitive Church, which had little by little declined, came to an end, there has not been greater knowledge of languages, more extensive discovery of new lands, or wider diffusion of the name of Christ in the more distant parts of the earth than in these times.

The knowledge of languages, and especially of Latin and Greek (for afterwards the study of Hebrew letters was stimulated by Johann Reuchlin),[1]

---

[1] Johann Reuchlin (1455–1522), German humanist.

began to return about the time when Constantinople was captured by the enemies of Christ, and when a few Greeks, notably Bessarion, Theodore of Gaza, George of Trebizond, and Manuel Chrysoloras, took refuge in Italy.[2]

Soon afterwards the new lands were discovered, and thereupon the name of Christ was propagated, by the Portuguese in the east, and in the southwest by the Spaniards, under the leadership of a Genoese, and in the northwest by the French. Would that the name of Christ might have been, and may henceforth be, proclaimed purely and sincerely so that soon the word may be fulfilled: 'O Lord, may the whole earth adore Thee.' Yes, may it offer Thee a religion evangelical and pure, a religion of the spirit and of truth! It is this above all which is to be desired.

3 Cellini, *Autobiography* (1559)

Source: Benvenuto Cellini, *Autobiography*, translated by George Bull (Harmondsworth: Penguin Books, 1956), pp. 269–304 abridged.

Benvenuto Cellini (1500–71), goldsmith, sculptor, medallist and jeweller, was born and died in Florence but passed much of his professional life in Rome in the service of the Popes Clement VII and Paul III and at Fontainebleau. He arrived in France in 1540. His description of his stay at the court of Francis I underscores the extent of French artistic dependence upon Italy. The commissions he secured through royal patronage are recorded in the exuberant and revealing autobiography for which he is now chiefly remembered. The text was in large part dictated by the author to a 14-year-old amanuensis; it was in first draft by 1559.

First of all I had made a model for the doorway of the palace of Fontainebleau, slightly correcting its proportions, as it was wide and squat in that bad French style of theirs. The opening of the doorway was almost square, and above it there was a half-circle, squashed like the handle of a basket. In this half-circle the King wanted to have a figure representing Fontainebleau. I made a beautifully-proportioned doorway, and then I placed over it an exact half-circle. At the sides I designed some charming projections, with socles underneath to match the cornices above. At each side, instead of the two columns usually found with this style, I had two satyrs. One of them stood out in rather more than half relief, and with one of his arms was making as if to hold up the part of the doorway which would have rested on the column; in the other hand he was grasping a heavy club. He looked very fierce and aggressive and was meant to strike terror into the beholder. The other satyr had the same stance, but the head and several things of that sort were

---

[2] Bessarion (c.1400–1472), Greek scholar who contributed to the revival of classical learning in the fifteenth century; Theodore of Gaza (c.1400–75), one of the Greek scholars who led the revival of ancient learning and whose patron was Bessarion; George of Trebizond (c.1396–1488), Greek philosopher and pioneer of the revival of ancient learning in the West; Manuel Chrysoloras (c.1355–1415), one of the Greek scholars who revived the study of Greek literature in the West.

different. He was holding a whip, with three balls attached to some chains. Although I call them satyrs, they had nothing of the satyr about them except for their little horns and goats' heads, otherwise they looked like humans.

In the half-circle I had made a woman reclining in a beautiful attitude; she had her left hand resting on the neck of a stag, which was one of the King's emblems. On one side I showed some little fawns in half relief, and there were some wild boars and other wild beasts in lower relief. On the other side there were hunting-dogs and hounds of various kinds, since these are found in that beautiful forest where the fountain springs.

I had enclosed the whole work in an oblong, and in each of the upper angles I had designed a Victory, in low relief, with torches in their hands as we see in representations left by the ancients. Above this I had shown the salamander, the King's own device, and a host of other charming ornaments all harmonizing with the work, which was in the Ionic style.

As soon as the King saw this model he brightened up, and it took his mind off the tiresome discussions he had been having for more than two hours. Seeing that he was as amiably disposed as I wanted, I uncovered the other model; and this he wasn't expecting at all as he thought he had seen all he could hope for.

This model was more than two cubits high; in it I had fashioned a fountain in the form of a perfect square, and around it there were some very fine flights of steps, intersecting each other, a thing which had never been seen in France before and which is rare in Italy. In the middle of the fountain I had constructed a pedestal, which was a little taller than the basin of the fountain itself: on the pedestal I had shown a nude figure, in correct proportion and full of beauty and grace. Its right hand was raised on high, holding a broken lance; and the left hand rested on the hilt of an exquisitely designed scimitar. With its weight resting on its left foot, its right had under it a rich and elaborately worked helmet. At the corners of the fountain I had fashioned four seated figures, each one of them raised up, with its own fanciful emblems.

The King began by asking me what was the idea behind the beautiful design, saying that without a word from me he understood all I had done as regards the doorway, but that though he appreciated that the model of the fountain was very beautiful he didn't understand it at all: and, he added, he was well aware that I hadn't worked like the kind of fool whose art had a certain amount of grace but was completely devoid of significance. At this I prepared to explain, for having pleased him by what I had done I wanted to please him with what I had to say.

'You must know, sacred Majesty, that this little work of mine is so exactly calculated to the last detail that when executed it will lose none of its present grace. This figure in the middle is to be fifty-four feet high' (at this the King made a tremendous gesture of amazement), 'and it is meant to represent the god Mars. The other four figures stand for the Arts and Sciences, which your Majesty protects and in which he finds such pleasure. This, on the right hand, is meant for the world of Learning; you see how she has her emblems, showing Philosophy and the various branches of philosophy. This other represents all the Arts of Design, that is, Sculpture, Painting, and Architecture. This other is for Music, which rightly accompanies all these branches of knowledge. Next, this gracious, kindly figure represents Liberality, for without her the splendid talents given us by God would be stifled. The great statue in the centre represents your Majesty himself, the god Mars, unique in valour: and you employ your valour justly and devoutly, in the defence of your glory.'

The King hardly had the patience to let me finish before he said in a loud voice: 'In very truth, I've found a man after my own heart.'

Then, calling the treasurers appointed to me, he said that they should provide all I needed no matter what it cost; then, tapping me on the shoulder, he said to me: '*Mon ami*' (that is, my friend), 'I don't know which is the greater, the pleasure of a prince at having found a man after his own heart, or the pleasure of an artist at having found a prince ready to provide him with all he needs to express his great creative ideas.'

I answered that if it was me his Majesty meant then my fortune was by far the greater. He answered with a laugh: 'Let's say that it's equal.' I left him in very high spirits, and went back to my work . . .

While I was forging ahead with this work I set aside certain hours of the day to work on the salt-cellar, and others to work on the Jupiter. As there were more men working on the salt-cellar than I could manage to employ on the Jupiter, by this time I had already finished it down to the last detail. The King had returned to Paris, and I went to find him, bringing the salt-cellar with me. As I have said before, it was oval in shape, about two-thirds of a cubit high, entirely in gold, and chased by means of a chisel. And, as I said when describing the model, I represented the Sea and the Land, both seated, with their legs intertwined just as some branches of the sea run into the land and the land juts into the sea: so, very fittingly, that was the attitude I gave them. I had placed a trident in the right hand of the Sea, and in his left hand, to hold the salt, I had put a delicately worked ship. Below the figure were his four sea-horses: the breast and front hoofs were like a horse, all the rest, from the middle back, was like a fish; the fishes' tails were interlaced together in a charming way. Dominating the group was the Sea, in an attitude of pride and surrounded by a great variety of fish and other marine creatures. The water was represented with its waves, and then it was beautifully enamelled in its own colour.

The Land I had represented by a very handsome woman, holding her horn of plenty in her hand, and entirely naked like her male partner. In her other hand, the left, I had made a little, very delicately worked, Ionic temple that I intended for the pepper. Beneath this figure I had arranged the most beautiful animals that the earth produces; the rocks of the earth I had partly enamelled and partly left in gold. I had then given the work a foundation, setting it on a black ebony base. It was of the right depth and width and had a small bevel on which I had set four gold figures, executed in more than half relief, and representing Night, Day, Twilight, and Dawn. Besides these there were four other figures of the same size, representing the four chief winds, partly enamelled and finished off as exquisitely as can be imagined.

When I set this work before the King he gasped in amazement and could not take his eyes off it. Then he instructed me to take it back to my house, and said that in due course he would let me know what I was to do with it. I took it home, and at once invited in some of my close friends; and with them I dined very cheerfully, placing the salt-cellar in the middle of the table. We were the first to make use of it. Then I set out to finish the silver Jupiter and the large vase I have mentioned before that was charmingly ornamented with a host of figures . . .

The following day, at the same hour, I went back to see him [the King]: and as soon as he set eyes on me he protested that he meant to come to my house at once. As usual he went to take his leave of Madame d'Étampes [the King's mistress], and when she realized that, for all her influence, she had not been able to change his mind for him, she began using her sharp tongue to slander me as much as if I were a mortal enemy of the throne. In reply to this the good King said that his intention in going to visit me was solely to give me a terrifying dressing-down, and he gave her his word of honour that this was what he would do. Immediately, he came to the house, and I led him into some large rooms on the ground floor where I had assembled the great door in its entirety. When the King saw it he was so stupefied that he could not see his way to giving me the dressing-down he had said he would. All the same he did not want to miss the opportunity of abusing me as he had promised, and so he began saying: 'There is one very important thing, Benvenuto, that you artists, talented as you are, must understand: you cannot display your talents without help; and your greatness only becomes perceptible because of the opportunities you receive from us. Now you should be a little more obedient and less arrogant and headstrong. I remember giving you express orders to make me twelve silver statues, and that was all I wanted. But you have set your mind on making me a salt-cellar, and vases, and busts, and doors, and so many other things that I'm completely dumbfounded when I consider how you've ignored my wishes and set out to satisfy yourself. If you think you can go on like this, I'll show you the way I behave when I want things done my way. So I warn you, make sure you obey my orders: if you persist in your own ideas you'll run your head against a wall.'

All the time he was talking, the noblemen with him remained very attentive, watching him as he shook his head, and frowned and gesticulated, now with one hand and now with the other. They were trembling with fear of what was going to happen to me, though for my part I was determined not to let myself panic in the slightest.

As soon as he was finished with the harangue that he had promised his Madame d'Étampes he would make, I knelt down on one knee, and kissing his robe just above his knee I said: 'Sacred Majesty, I admit that everything you say is true; all I can reply is that continually, day and night, with all my heart and soul I have been intent only on obeying and serving your Majesty; and as for anything that may appear to disprove what I say, your Majesty must blame it not on Benvenuto, but on my evil destiny or my bad fortune, which has tried to make me unworthy of serving the most splendid prince the world ever had. So I beg you to forgive me . . .

'Now that I see that God is unwilling to make me worthy of the honour of serving you, I beg your Majesty, in place of the honourable reward you intended to give me for my work, just to allow me a little of your good favour and to allow me to take my leave. And now, if you are good enough to allow it, I shall return to Italy, and I shall always give thanks to God and to your Majesty for the happy hours I have spent in your service.'

He took hold of me with his hand, and then, very graciously, raised me from my knees and said that I should be content to serve him, and that everything I had made was good and pleased him very much. Then he turned to the noblemen with him, and used these very words: 'I firmly believe that if doors had to be made for paradise, nothing finer than this could be achieved.'

I paused a little, after this forceful praise, and then with very great respect I thanked him once again, but because I was still angry I repeated that I would like to be given leave to go. When the great King realized that I had not received his unusually generous acts of kindness the way they deserved, in a loud, terrifying voice he ordered me not to say another word or it would be worse for me. And then he added that he would drown me in gold, and that he was quite content with my working on my own initiative in addition to the works commissioned by him, and that I would never again have any dispute with him, because now he understood me; and he said that for my part I should try to understand him in the way my duty commanded.

I replied that I gave thanks for everything to God and to his Majesty, and then I begged him to come and see the great statue and how far I had advanced it: so he came with me. I had it uncovered, and he was astonished beyond words. Straight away he ordered his secretary to give me without any delay all the money I had spent on it out of my own pocket, no matter what it was so long as I wrote the amount down myself. Then he left saying: 'Goodbye, *mon ami*' – words rarely spoken by a king.

4 Claude de Seyssel: Three Bridles on Princely Power (1519)

Source: Claude de Seyssel, *The Monarchy of France*, translated by J. H. Hexter, edited by Donald R. Kelley (New Haven and London: Yale University Press, 1981), pp. 51–4, 82–5 abridged.

Peace, order and justice, Seyssel argued, rested upon respect for ancient law and custom rather than divine right. The strength of the monarchy stemmed from its commitment to justice and the rule of law, its respect for the customary rights and privileges of classes and groups, cities and provinces, and its outward devotion to the Christian faith. These three bridles of religion, justice and of the polity were the real constraints upon tyranny and absolutism.

When the Christian faith appeared, France was among the first of the distant nations to receive it, and having received it kept it completely and constantly beyond all other realms and peoples without even nourishing any monster of heresy, as St Jerome bears witness. The English, the Germans, the Spaniards, and other neighbouring nations often and at divers times have received or reformed their faith after that of the Gauls and the French, and the princes and people of France always have been more ardent and more prompt than any others to wipe out heretics and infidels and to defend the Roman Catholic church. Even to this day all the nations of Christianity come to learn theology at the University of Paris, as the true fountain whence flows forth the perfect doctrine. Therefore, this realm is called most Christian and the kings most Christian.

So, it is essential that whosoever is king here make known to the people by example and by present and overt demonstration that he is a zealous observant of the Christian faith and wishes to maintain and augment it to the best of his ability. If the people had another opinion of him, they would hate him and perhaps obey him but ill. Moreover, this people would impute all the troubles that came to the realm to the erroneous creed and imperfect religion of the king. Thence might result many great scandals, as has happened several times formerly . . .

If the king lives in accordance with the Christian religion and law (at least in appearance) he can scarcely act tyrannically and if he does so act, it is permissible for any prelate or any other man of religion who leads a good life and holds the people in esteem to remonstrate with him and censure him and for a simple preacher to reprehend him publicly to his face. Truly, although the king might want to, he would not dare mistreat or harm the men who do this, for fear of provoking the ill will and indignation of the people . . . Moreover, the kings are so instructed and habituated in religion from their childhood with a traditional reverence that they can scarcely go so far astray that they cease to fear God and to reverence prelates and churchmen of good renown. This colour [sic] and appearance of religion and of having God on their side has always brought great favour [sic], obedience, and reverence to princes . . .

Understanding that they must live (in esteem and reputation) as good Christians in order to have the love and complete obedience of the people, even though they themselves were not sufficiently dedicated to devotion to God and fear of Him, the kings of France have avoided doing outrageous and reprehensible things, if not always and in everything at least ordinarily.

5 Suriano: Strength and Weakness of France (1561)

Source: *The Portable Renaissance Reader*, edited by James Bruce Ross and Mary Martin McLaughlin (Harmondsworth: Penguin Books, 1977), pp. 306–27 abridged.

Renaissance Venice possessed a worldwide diplomatic network which supplied the Republic with high-quality commercial and political intelligence. The reports of the

Venetian ambassadors are famous for their comprehensive coverage, cogent argument and convincing detail. That submitted by Michele Suriano on France in 1561 after an embassy of fourteen months is no exception. It provides an insight into the social structure of France, its monarchy, governing institutions, military status and material conditions.

To begin with, I say that the kingdom of France, by universal opinion, was reputed the first kingdom of Christendom by reason of its dignity and power and the authority of its kings. As to its dignity, it was independent from the very beginning and has never recognized any superior authority except God. ... Of its power there can be no doubt, because it is the most extensive kingdom and exceeds any other European kingdom in population, arms, and wealth ...

The population of France is very large. It has one hundred and forty episcopal cities, and an infinite number of other lands, castles, and villages, and every place is as full as it can be. In Paris alone there are believed to be from four hundred to five hundred thousand souls. The condition and quality of the people are threefold, and hence there are three estates of the realm. The first is that of the clergy; the second of the nobility; the third has no special name, but because it is composed of various ranks and professions one can give it the general name of 'the estate of the people'.

The clergy includes many of the third estate and many foreigners who, because of services to the crown or by special favour of the king, are named to benefices in the kingdom. A considerable part, however, comes from the nobility ...

By nobles are meant those who are free and do not pay any kind of tax to the king; they have only the obligation of personal service in time of war. Among ... the princes, those of the blood, because of their relationship to the crown, are of more importance than the others, although some of them, on account of poverty, cannot live in the splendour suitable to such high rank. Eighty years ago these princes of the blood were numerous, ... but now the house of Bourbon stands alone; all the others have either been united to the crown or extinguished ...

The estate of the people includes men of letters – who are called 'men of the robe' – merchants, artisans, plebeians, and peasants. Among the men of the robe, whoever has the rank of judge or councillor or a similar office is considered as noble and privileged and is so treated throughout his life. The merchants, being in these times the money-masters, are favoured and caressed, but they have no distinction of dignity because any pursuit of gain in this kingdom is held to be unworthy of the nobility ...

These three estates are used in various ways for the benefit of the kingdom. The third estate of the people always has in its hands four important offices, either by virtue of law or ancient custom, or because it does not seem honourable to the nobles to be burdened with such responsibilities ... Now since the people have in their hands all these offices, which carry with them reputation and riches, and since two of them always go to men of letters or 'of the robe' ... every father tries to send one of his sons to the university.

That is why there are so many students in France, more than in any other Christian kingdom . . . And for some time the princes also have been sending their sons to the university, especially the second and third born, not indeed to put them in these offices but to make clerics of them, because now some effort is being made not to give bishoprics to ignorant persons . . .

The government of the state is in the hands of the nobles and prelates. The prelates advise on affairs but do not carry them out, whereas the nobles do both . . . The nobles, who are usually not very rich, are ruined when they come to court, where everything is dear, by the great cost of servants, horses, food, and clothing. On the contrary, when they stay in their châteaux and lead a private and simple life, they have all they need without livery, sumptuous garments, expensive horses, banquets, and other things necessary to a courtier. For this reason there has grown up the service of the king 'by quarters'; whoever serves is obliged to stay at court only three months in the year . . .

The prelates, however, do not have to consider this aspect of expense because they have to bear the cost of their households and vestments wherever they are. Although living at court is more expensive, nevertheless their hope of constantly acquiring more wealth and reputation by always staying near the king leads them to disregard this loss . . .

The proper function of the nobles, and that which is of greatest value to king and people, is military service. Of this there are two kinds, on land and on sea . . . The heart of the military in France is the land force, and rather the cavalry than the infantry, because the ease of acquiring Germans and Swiss and the dislike of putting arms in the hands of plebeians and peasants have given the cavalry so much greater a reputation that it is composed entirely of nobles. It is, therefore, made up of men of courage and talent, unlike that of other countries, which is composed of persons of all conditions . . .

This is all I have to say about the number and character of the people of France and of the service which the crown derives from the three estates. As long as they were united, each performing its office without envying the others, and contributing its share to the public welfare and aiding the king, one estate by giving counsel, another by giving its wealth, and the last by giving its life, they made this kingdom invincible and formidable to all the world . . .

With regard to the authority of him who rules, I say that this most extensive and powerful kingdom . . . depends wholly on the supreme will of the king, who is the natural prince, loved and obeyed by the people, and of absolute authority. The king of France is a prince by natural right because this kind of government is ancient and not new; for more than a thousand years no other kind has ever been known in this kingdom. He does not succeed to the crown by the election of the people and therefore does not have to curry their favour; nor does he succeed by force, and hence he does not have to be cruel and tyrannical. The succession is rather by law of nature, from father to eldest son, or to that one who is most closely related, excepting bastards and women. The first-born succeeds, or, failing that, the nearest blood kin, because the kingdom does not suffer division but always goes to a single person ... Women are excluded by the Salic Law, as they call it, or by an established custom which has the force of law. And therefore the king of France is always a Frenchman and can never be of another nationality. For this reason there never happens here what often happens in other kingdoms where the succession through women causes uncertainty as to who will become king, and where often the king comes from a hated and hostile people ...

All these factors are the foundation and root of the love and obedience of the French. Accustomed for so long to being governed by a king, they have no desire for any other kind of government ... what best preserves and increases this affection of the people is their own interest and hope of something useful, for the king of France, being able to distribute so many places, offices, and magistracies, so much wealth of the Church, so many appointments, pensions, and emoluments, and so many other privileges and honours, which are infinite in this kingdom, divides everything among his own Frenchmen ...

For this reason there has never been a time in France when the people rebelled against the king to call another prince to the throne. Insurrections are very rare; as for conspiracies, none are known except the recent one of Amboise[1] ... In brief, the king is recognized as true monarch and absolute lord of everything.

And there is no council or magistrate of such authority as to circumscribe his actions, nor any prince or lord in the kingdom of such audacity as to oppose his will, as often happens in other kingdoms. The princes of the blood and the other great nobles are so poor and so lacking in authority, as compared to the king, that even if they tried to turn against him they would not be supported ...

As for the councillors and magistrates, it is enough to say that the king directs and chooses them at his will; and the council of affairs, which considers matters of state, is made up of few heads, and of those most close and dear to the king, sometimes of one only ... And to the private council, where formerly great matters were discussed, which are at present taken over by the council of affairs, are now referred only those things which have to be determined according to the constitution of the kingdom, or which the king turns over to it out of boredom. Thus in the council of affairs the king exercises his absolute power, whereas in the private council he exercises his ordinary power. And so it sometimes happens that the parliaments, which have supreme authority in the administration of justice and laws, especially the Parliament of Paris, modify, interpret, or even veto the decisions of the private council, but no one dares to touch those of the other council.

But if any authority in France can moderate the absolute authority of the king it is the assembly of the three estates, which represents the whole body

---

[1] Conspiracy of Amboise, 1560; a plot to displace the Guise party from its position of influence in the court of King Francis II, and to replace it with that of the Bourbons, notably Condé.

of the kingdom ... [Kings] have gradually discontinued the practice of holding the estates in order to free themselves little by little from this yoke ... [so that] it is likely that the estates will finally break down completely and the authority of the king will continue steadily to grow greater.

These are the foundations, these the columns, which support the great edifice of the kingdom of France. The great size of the state, the number of its cities and provinces, the strength of its location and frontiers, the number, unity, and obedience of the people and military forces, the supreme authority of the king and the unrestricted government – these are the chief reasons why this crown has reigned so long, has fought so many wars with such great glory, has acquired such reputation and dominion, has preserved its friends, frightened its enemies, and has become known in recent times as the sole refuge of the oppressed. And it would be able to achieve even greater things if there had not befallen those accidents and disorders of which I have to speak; these have weakened the strength on which was founded and established every aspect of the glory and greatness of this realm.

I must now speak of the defects and disorders in the kingdom of France, very great indeed and very grave, because if it is true, as reason and experience teach us, that every change and alteration in states is always perilous, what state was ever in greater peril than one which at the same time, and almost the same moment, experienced a change in its head, its principal members, and its whole body? As for the head of the kingdom of France, on the death of King Francis II, who possessed real authority, Charles IX succeeded, who has only the name of king. As for the members, the government of such a great kingdom has fallen into the hands of women or inexperienced men, and there is no agreement among them. And into the whole body there has been introduced the curse of the new sects which has totally confused the religion of the realm, which is the sole means of holding a people united and obedient to its prince. Since this is the subject which excites most interest, I shall speak first of religion ...

It will not be difficult for me to show how slight was the beginning of this evil, because everyone knows that it was one man alone [Martin Luther], and of very lowly condition, who revived the old heresies and was the source of the new sects of our times ... There is no part of Christianity which is free from this pestilence ...

Although it now seems that God may wish to give some hope of aid to this kingdom, nevertheless things are still in a very bad state, because this disease has too much strength and encounters too little resistance. Those who could, do not wish to repress it, and those who wish to repress it, cannot or know not how ...

First, it lessens the fear of God, which should always take precedence over all other considerations, because on that rests the rule of life, the concord of men, the preservation of the state, and all greatness. And how can there be fear of God where there is no observation of divine law, no obedience to magistrates, either ecclesiastical or civil; where everyone dares to conceive God after his own fashion, interpreting Holy Scripture not according to the ancient tradition of the Church and the Holy Fathers, but according to his own understanding, as if one whose vision reaches only a span should presume to measure things a thousand miles away?

The second evil consequence of this change in religion is that it destroys the control and order of the government, because from it springs a change in the usual habits and customs of life, contempt for the laws and authority of magistrates and finally even for the prince. Already in various parts of France judges have been driven out of the land and new ones set up at the will of the seditious. In other places they have not wished to permit the publication of royal edicts, and in others they have begun to disseminate among the crowd the idea that the king holds his authority from the people and that subjects are not obliged to obey the prince when he commands something which is not stated in the Holy Gospels. This is the path that is leading to the reduction of this land to a popular state like Switzerland and the destruction of the monarchy and kingdom.

To these two disorders is added a third, the division of the people, the seditions, and civil wars which always spring from religious confusion ... The insolence of these rebels has become so great that nature is turned upside down; where the head was wont to rule the members, the members now rule the head.

Although such serious effects have not yet been seen in France, one hears every day of murders and wounds and other acts of violence. In every part of the kingdom this sect is found organized and with connections in Flanders, England, Scotland, and other countries. It is known that it spends freely and supports not only its preachers and ministers, but also many princes and other great men who favour it. And so it grows every day in insolence and becomes more difficult to repress. And since the disturbance springs from the lower class, which, being envious and poor, aspires to the wealth and honours of the rich, everyone is in a state of suspicion; trade ceases, contracts are broken, and there is no merchant in Paris or Lyons or anywhere in the kingdom who feels secure in his house. Although not a tenth of the kingdom (according to calculation) is yet infected, everything is so disturbed that one can imagine what would happen if the corruption spread to the rest ...

I shall speak now of two other misfortunes of less importance that occurred at the same time. One concerns the head, which is the king; the other the chief members, who are those of authority in the government. It seems as if all the evils that cause the destruction of kingdoms have conspired together for the ruin of France.

As to the first, everyone knows that a change of kings always produces some alteration in kingdoms, because it rarely happens that a new king has the same ideas as the old ... All this breeds sedition and tumult. And when the new king lacks ability and authority, so much greater is the change. What happens to other kings from lack of wisdom has happened to the present king, Charles IX, because of his tender age, and because like an innocent lamb he is subject to the influence of those who control him. If it has always been considered a calamity for a kingdom to have a boy king ..., how much more miserable is a kingdom full of disorders, division, and rivalry, oppressed by debts and poverty, exhausted by a long and expensive war, and where one boy has succeeded another and neither of them was able to learn how to govern from the instruction and example of his father, owing to the brevity of the latter's life! Because when King Francis succeeded to the crown he was scarcely fifteen years, and the present king not yet ten; now he is eleven and a half. It is true that he is of fine and noble intelligence, that he shows in his actions gravity and modesty, in his words sweetness and humanity, in his countenance grace and gaiety, and indeed lacks no kingly quality. One can entertain great hope of his Majesty, if he lives and does not change . . . As for living, it is the opinion of many that he has not long to live, both because of his feeble and delicate constitution and because he is not taken care of as regularly as he should be . . .

Let us speak now of the particular defects of those who have the chief responsibility, the queen [Catherine de Medici] and the King of Navarre [Anthony of Bourbon]. As to the queen, it is enough to say that she is a woman, but, I should add, a foreigner as well, and even more, a Florentine, born in a private family, very unequal to the grandeur of the kingdom of France. On this account she does not have the reputation or authority which she would have, perhaps, if she had been born in the kingdom or of more illustrious blood. It cannot be denied that she is a woman of great worth and intelligence; and if she had greater experience in matters of state, and were a bit more firm, she might well achieve great things . . . Her Majesty has need of good advisers, but she has no one in whom she can trust; dissension in religion and discord among the great have made everyone suspect to her . . .

As for the intentions of her Majesty in matters of religion, opinions differ . . . I can affirm, however, from what I have seen, although I do not know what her Majesty's true sentiments are, that she does not suffer willingly these tumults in the kingdom. If she has not shown herself as zealous in repressing them as one could desire, she has been restrained by fear that the necessity of using force would tear France to pieces . . .

The King of Navarre, to speak freely, is a very weak character; although he is a gallant prince, gracious and agreeable, he does not have the experience or judgement essential for the burden of such an important government . . . But I say that in matters of religion he has shown himself neither firm nor wise, moving now in one direction, now in another, now favouring the Catholics in order to stand in well with the pope, now the Huguenots to secure a following in the kingdom, now the Lutherans to keep the friendship of Germany . . .

Such then is the present state of France: the king a boy, without experience or authority; the council full of discord; supreme authority in the hands of the queen, a wise woman, although timid and irresolute, and always a woman; the King of Navarre, a noble and gracious prince, but inconstant and little skilled in government; the people in open discord and disunity, full of insolent and seditious elements, who under pretext of religion have disturbed the public peace, corrupted the old customs and ways of life, spoiled discipline, stifled justice, defied the magistrates, and finally undermined the authority of the king and the safety of all. Anyone who wishes to compare the present state of the kingdom with the past, when it was so formidable to the great kings and emperors of the world, will find it so weak and infirm that there is not a single sound member left in it.

6 Hotman: Exclusion of Women (1573)

Source: François Hotman, *Francogallia*, translated by J. H. M. Salmon (Cambridge: Cambridge University Press, 1972), pp. 481–93.

François Hotman (1524–90) was a Calvinist jurist and polemicist. Hotman published the *Francogallia*, which he had been preparing for some years, in 1573. It was written in Latin. Further editions appeared in 1576 and 1586, the last adapted to the changing political situation. Later editions were also published in French. Some of the propagandists of the Catholic League had been using Hotman's own arguments to limit the power of Henry III, whom they no longer trusted. Hotman kept his anti-feminine sentiments in the later edition. He diluted the power of assemblies, however, in electing a monarch by introducing the argument that an heir should succeed through proximity of blood independently of all other factors.

If a woman does not have the personal right to be queen, neither does she have the right and power to rule. A woman cannot be a queen in her own right, nor can an hereditary claim to the kingdom be derived from her or her descendants. If they are termed queens it is only so accidentally and because they are married to kings, and we have already shown this from the ancient records for twelve hundred years. A point we have explained above may here be added, namely that, just as all power to appoint and depose kings lay with the public council, so also the supreme right to choose a regent or administrator of the commonwealth rested in that same council. Even after kings had been appointed, the supreme authority in government was retained by the council, and a century has not passed since thirty-six guardians were created by that same council to act as though they were ephors,[1] and this even occurred when Louis XI was reigning, cunning and crafty as he was. If we seek the authority of our ancestors in this matter, there exists the remarkable instance in the chronicle of Aimon,[2] where he writes as follows about Brunhild, the queen mother of King Childebert [Childebert II]: 'At the same time, because it was discovered that Brunhild wished to keep the sovereign administration of the kingdom in her own hands, the nobility of France, who for so long had disdained to be dominated and ruled by a woman ...' François Connan, a judge in the parlement, states: 'Panormitanus made a great mistake when he claimed that queens have any right among the French by our custom.[3] For there is no people less exposed

---

[1] Ephors, a council of five in ancient Sparta which exercised very wide powers.
[2] Aimon, Aimoin, *c*.960–*c*.1010. A French Benedictine chronicler who wrote the widely known *History of the Franks*.
[3] Panormitanus: see document II.7, n. 2.

Queen in Command, State in ruins

to the government of women, since the law of the Salians, that is to say the law of the French, excludes them from succession to the kingdom. Thus we see that on the death of their husbands queens are almost completely degraded in rank so that they do not retain even a shadow of the dignity of queen.' So writes Connan.[4]

Indeed it has so happened that, if ever women acquired control of the administration of the kingdom in the times of our ancestors, they always caused extraordinary calamities and subsequently a vast crop of troubles in our commonwealth. It may be appropriate to provide a number of examples of this. There was a time when Queen Clothild, the mother of the kings Childebert [Childebert I] and Lothar, held sway. She favoured with a love akin to madness the sons of another of her own sons, Chlodomir by name, who had died, and she caused a very great dispute by trying to exclude her surviving sons and promoting their nephews to royal dignity. Hence, because of the practice we have earlier described, she took the greatest care to nourish their long hair.[5] When the two royal brothers were informed of her intention, they at once sent a certain Arcadius to her, who offered her a naked sword and a pair of scissors and made her choose which she preferred to have applied to the heads of her grandsons. 'But she', says Gregory of Tours,[6] 'was choked by excess of gall, especially when she saw the unsheathed sword and the scissors, and in her bitterness replied: "I should rather see them dead than shorn if they are not to be raised to the throne."' Thus each of her grandsons was killed before her eyes. In another place the same author adds that this queen won the favour of the common people with the gifts and donations she bestowed upon the monastic orders.

As Cato used to say,[7] 'If you loose the reins with women, as with an unruly nature and an untamed beast, you must expect uncontrolled actions.' What an unbridled beast was that daughter of King Theuderic, of Italian birth, who fell madly in love with her own servant! When she found out that he had been killed by her mother's command, she pretended the appearance of reconciliation with her mother and feigned a wish to take the sacrament of the Lord's supper with her. She mixed some poison in the chalice, and offered it to her mother with both sacrilegious impiety and execrable cruelty. These are the words of Gregory of Tours: 'They lived under the Arian form of worship,[8] and, because it was their custom that the royal family should, on approaching the altar, take communion from one cup and people of lesser rank from another (and here it is worth noting the practice

---

[4] François Connan: the reference is to his commentaries published in 1557.

[5] Long hair: possession of long hair was a compulsory qualification for kingship amongst the Franks.

[6] St Gregory of Tours, c. AD 540–94. His *History of the Franks* was intended to show the inevitable advance of Christianity against the forces of paganism.

[7] Marcus Porcius Cato, 234–149 BC, the Censor, a statesman and writer. His moral works were very popular in Europe in the Middle Ages and still much quoted in the sixteenth century although most that survives was probably produced by later classical writers.

[8] The heresy of Arius, which he preached in the early fourth century, was that Christ was not truly divine and that his existence post-dated that of God the Father.

of giving the communion cup to the people), she placed poison in that chalice from which her mother was to communicate, which killed her as soon as she tasted it.'

Very well, let us look at the other examples. Fredegund, queen mother and widow of Chilperic I, obtained power at one time. While her husband was alive she had adopted the habit of living in adultery with a man named Lander. When she noticed that Chilperic had become aware of this she had him murdered, and as queen mother promptly undertook the administration of the kingdom in the name of her son, King Lothar, retaining it for thirteen years. First she poisoned her son's uncle, Childebert, and his wife. Then she stirred up the Huns against his sons and caused a civil war in the commonwealth. Finally she was the instigator of those conflagrations which consumed Francogallia for many years. This is related by Aimon on two occasions and also by the writer of the Dijon chronicle.

Queen Brunhild, the mother of Childebert and the widow of King Sigebert, also ruled. She had a certain Italian, Protadius by name, as her companion in vice, and she puffed him up with all possible honours. She brought up her sons Theudebert and Theuderic in such a vicious kind of life when they were youths that they became mortal enemies of one another, and they fought a fearful conflict in the course of a protracted war. She killed Merovech, the son of Theudebert and her own grandson, with her own hands. She poisoned Theuderic. Need we go on? As Cato said, 'If you loose the reins with women, as with an unruly nature and an untamed beast, you must expect uncontrolled actions.' She caused the death of ten royal princes. When she was reproved by a certain bishop and asked to be more temperate, she ordered him to be thrown into a river. In the end a council of the Franks was convoked, and she was summoned to judgement, condemned, and torn limb from limb by wild horses. This is attested by Gregory of Tours, Ado, Otto of Freising, Godfrey of Viterbo, and Aimon.[9] The following passage is taken from the appendix to Gregory of Tours: 'She was held responsible for the death of ten kings of the Franks, namely Sigebert, Merovech, his father Chilperic, Theudebert and his son Lothar, Merovech the son of Lothar, Theuderic and his three children who had been recently put to death. It was ordered that for three days she be tortured in various ways ...' ... [A monastic chronicle related:] 'She was placed upon a camel and taken on a circuit of the army. All shuddered with horror at her cries, as if she commanded body and soul to be taken down again to the infernal regions. She was tied to four wild horses and torn in pieces as they stampeded apart. Then a fire was lit and her remnants, together with her retinue of criminals, were thrust into it by the common people.' In another passage the same chronicler writes: 'So many evils and effusions of blood occurred in France as a result of the counsels of Brunhild that the prophecy of the Sibyl was fulfilled, namely "Bruna will come from distant

---

[9] Otto of Freising, 1111/12–1158: a German bishop and the author of several historical and philosophical works; Godfrey of Viterbo, 1125–c.1200, a chaplain to the German Emperor Frederick I Barbarossa, and author of several historical and moral works.

Spain and peoples will perish before her gaze. But she will be torn apart by the hooves of horses"' . . .

Let us look at other examples. Power was seized by the queen mother of Charles the Bald, Judith by name, who was the wife of Louis known as the Pious, the king of Francogallia and also the emperor of Italy and Germany. She stirred up a disastrous and fatal war between Louis and her stepsons, from which sprang so great a conspiracy against the king that they forced him to abdicate and cede them his office, to the great detriment of nearly all Europe. All historians place a large share of the blame for these troubles upon Judith, the queen mother, for instance the abbot of Ursperg, Michael Ritius, and Otto of Freising. 'Louis', writes Otto of Freising, 'was expelled from the kingdom because of the evil works of his wife Judith.' This is also the view of Regino in his chronicle for the year 838,[10] when he says: 'Louis was deprived of his government by his own people and was placed in solitary confinement, while the crown was bestowed upon his son Lothar by the election of the Franks. Moreover, this deposition was due mainly to the many adulterous liaisons of his wife Judith.'

In a later age power was exercised by Queen Blanche, who was Spanish by birth and the mother of Saint Louis.[11] When she first seized the helm of the ship of state, the nobility of France began to take up arms under Duke Philip, count of Bologne and uncle to the king. As that most excellent author Jean de Joinville writes,[12] the nobility protested that it was not to be borne that so great a kingdom should be governed by a woman, and she a foreigner. Thus the nobles repudiated Blanche and chose Count Philip as the regent of the kingdom. But Blanche persevered in her purpose nonetheless, and sought help wherever she could, finally arranging to ally herself in treaty and friendship with Ferdinand, the king of Spain. The duke of Brittany and the count of Evreux, his brother, allied themselves with Duke Philip, and suddenly seized a number of towns, making them secure with garrisons. Joinville describes this and explains how a most intense conflict flared up in France because the government of the kingdom had been taken over by the queen mother. It so happened that the king set out for Etampes at this time, having been sent there for military reasons by his mother. The nobility at once flocked there from all parts of France, and began to surround the king in the town, not for the sake of harming him or doing him violence, but, as Joinville says, to remove him from his mother's authority. This news was related to her when she was still in Paris, and she swiftly ordered the Parisians to arm themselves and march on Etampes. These

[10] Regino von Prüm (d. c.915), cleric and chronicler. His *Chronicon* covered the period from Christ's birth to the early tenth century; it was first published in 1521.

[11] St Louis: Louis IX (1214–70), most popular of the Capetian kings, who led the Seventh Crusade to the Holy Land in 1248–50. He was the only king of France to be numbered by the Roman Catholic Church among its saints. Queen Blanche: Blanche of Castile, daughter of Alfonso VIII of Castile, married Louis VIII of France in 1200 and was the mother of St Louis and regent during the latter's infancy.

[12] Sire Jean de Joinville, c.1224–1317. He wrote the *History of St Louis*, having accompanied the king on the Seventh Crusade.

forces had scarcely reached Montlhéry when the king, who had been freed from his restriction, joined them and returned with them to Paris. When Philip saw that he was equipped with too few troops of his own, he sought help from the queen of Cyprus, who had been conducting a certain legal suit in the kingdom. The latter invaded Champagne with strong forces and pillaged the province extensively. Nevertheless Blanche remained resolute in her purpose. In response the nobility finally called in the help of the English to the outlying provinces of the kingdom. They in turn caused great devastation in Aquitaine and other maritime provinces, and all these troubles arose from the passion and ambition of that queen mother, as Joinville records at length.

Since a very different opinion is held among us concerning Blanche's ability and habits – an opinion, one may believe, caused by the flattery of those who wrote at that time (for writers generally hesitate to criticize queen mothers, either out of fear of punishment or out of respect for the kings their sons) – it seems we should not omit to mention Joinville's remark that she had her son so much in her power, and had reduced him to such a state of timidity and despair, that she would rarely allow the king to converse with his wife Margaret, her own daughter-in-law, whom she hated. Thus when the king went on a journey, Blanche ordered those who laid out the lodgings to give the queen quarters apart from the king. Indeed, if ever the king secretly went to join his wife at night, he placed servants on watch. If they happened to learn that Blanche was approaching they were under orders to thrash some dogs, whose howls might remind him to hide himself. Need we say more? 'One day', writes Joinville, 'when Queen Margaret was ill through pregnancy, the king came to visit because of his fondness for her, and Blanche unexpectedly appeared. The king was warned by the howling of the dogs, and hid himself behind a corner of the bed, wrapping himself in some curtains. Nevertheless, the queen mother found him and, with everyone looking on, laid hold of him and dragged him out of the room. "You had no business to do here", she said. "Get out." But the pregnant queen reacted so strongly to this great insult that she fainted in her exasperation, and the servants were obliged to call back the king. At his return the queen was brought round and recovered consciousness.' Such is Joinville's literal account.

7 Innocent Gentillet: Anti-Machiavel (1576)

Source: Innocent Gentillet, *A Discourse upon the Meanes of Well Governing. Against Nicholas Machiavell the Florentine*, translated by Simon Patericke (London, 1602), pp. 235–9; spelling modernized by David Englander.

Innocent Gentillet (1535–88) was a prominent Huguenot pamphleteer. His *A Discourse upon the Meanes of Well Governing and Maintaining in Good Peace, a Kingdome, or other Principalitie, divided into three parts, namely, the Counsell, the Religion, the Policie, which a Prince ought to hold and follow. Against Nicholas Machiavell the Florentine* was published in Geneva in 1576. As the title suggests, the work was partly intended to reaffirm the three bridles upon absolute rule of counsel, religion and policy (or polity or police). The main purpose was to draw fifty maxims out of Machiavelli's writings, especially *The Prince* and the *Commentary on the Discourses of Livy*, and show the evil consequences of their application. The maxim discussed in the extract below is taken from the *Discourses*, book 2, chapter 2 and book 3, chapter 3.

15 Maxime

A virtuous tyrant,[1] *to maintain his tyranny, ought to maintain partialities and factions amongst his subjects, and to slay and take away such as love the commonwealth.*

It most commonly happeneth (sayeth Machiavell) in countries governed by princes, that that which is profitable to him, is damageable to subjects, and that which is profitable to his subjects, is damageable unto him: Which causeth oftentimes princes to become tyrants, better loving their profit, than their subjects: As also the contrary makes subjects often arise against their prince, not able to endure his tyranny and oppression. To keep subjects then, that they do not conspire and agree together to a rise against his tyranny, he must nourish and maintain partialities and factions amongst them: For, by that means shall you see, that distrusting one another, and fearing that one will accuse and disclose another, they will not dare to enterprise any thing: But herewithall he must cause all them to be slain, which love liberty, and the commonwealth and which are enemies to tyranny. If Tarquin, the last king of Rome, had well observed this Maxim, and had caused Brutus to be slain,[2] no man would have been found, that durst have enterprised any thing against him, and then might he always after, have exercised his tyranny at his pleasure without controlment.

Here before Machiavell hath showed, how a prince should best become a tyrant; namely, by exercising all manner of cruelty, impiety, and injustice, after the examples of Cesar Borgia, of Oliver de Ferme, and of Agathocles:[3] Now he shows how he in his tyranny, may maintain and conserve himself, that is, by feeding and maintaining partialities and divisions amongst his subjects, and in causing such to die, as appear to be curious lovers of the common weale, because none can love the good and utility of the common weale, but he must be an enemy of tyranny: as contrary, none can love tyranny, but he must needs be an enemy to the common weale: For, tyranny draweth all to himself, and dispoileth subjects of their goods and

---

[1] Virtuous: Machiavelli used 'virtue' in the sense of 'strong rule' rather than of 'goodness' or 'morality'.

[2] Lucius Brutus, who in the semi-legendary period of the sixth century BC led the Romans against the tyrannical rule of King Tarquin the Proud. Later, as consul, he condemned his own two sons to death for plotting to restore Tarquin.

[3] Cesar(e) Borgia, 1475/6–1507, Duke of Valentino and illegitimate son of Pope Alexander VI, infamous for his ruthless campaign to secure himself a principality; Oliver(otto) da Ferm(o), an Italian soldier of fortune (*condottiere*) who was murdered by Cesare Borgia; Agathocles, 361–289 BC, a tyrant of Syracuse.

commodities, to appropriate all to himself, making his particular good of that which belongs to all men, and applying to his own private profit and use, that which should serve to all men in general: So that it followeth, that whosoever loveth the profit of a tyrant, by consequent hateth the profit of his subjects, and he that loveth the common good of subjects, hateth also the particular profit of a tyrant. But thus speaking, I do not mean of tributes, which are lawfully levied upon subjects: for the exaction of taxes, may well be the work of a prince, and of a just ruler, but we speak of the proper and particular actions of tyrants.

Surely indeed if there be any proper and meet mean to maintain a tyranny, it seems well, that that which Machiavell teacheth is one. To maintain subjects in partialities and divisions: For as Quintius sayeth (when he exhorted the towns of Greece, to accord amongst themselves), Against a people which are in a good unity amongst themselves, tyrants can do nothing, but if there be discord amongst them, an overture is straight made, for him to do what he will: I freely then confess (and if I would deny it, experience proves it) that in this point Machiavell is a true doctor, who well understands the science of tyranny, and no man can set down more proper precepts, for so wicked a thing, than such as this Maxim containeth; namely, to slay all lovers of the commonwealth, and amongst other subjects to maintain partialities. Surely if anything serve to maintain a tyranny, these seem most proper and convenable: for they are made from the same mould that tyranny itself is, and drawn from one same spring, of most execrable wickedness and impiety.

An excellent wise man affirmeth [meaning Plato] that if tyrants' souls might be seen uncovered, a man should see them torn and wounded with blows of cruelty, riotousness, and wicked counsel, as we see bodies ulcerated with rods and cudgels. What pleasure could Denis the tyrant of Sicily have,[4] who trusted none? Also when one day a certain philosopher told him, that he could not be but happy, who was so rich, so well served at his table, and had so goodly a palace to dwell in, and so richly furnished: he answered him: Well, I will show you how happy I am: and withall he led that philosopher into a chamber gallantly hanged with tapestry, and caused him to be laid on a gilded rich bed to repose himself; there were also brought him exquisite and delicate viands, and excellent wines: but whilst certain servants made these provisions for Monsieur the philosopher, who was so desirous of a tyrannical felicity, another varlet [servant] fastened by the hilts to the upper bed feeling, a bright shining sharp sword, and this sword was hung only in a horse hair, the point of it right over the philosopher's face so newly happy, who incontinent as he saw the sword hang by so small a thread, and so right over his visage, lost all his appetite to eat, drink, or to muse at, or contemplate the excessive riches of the tyrant, but continually cast his sight upon that sword: And in the end he prayed Denis, to take him from the supposed beatitude [state of supreme blessedness or happiness], wherein he was laid: saying, that he had rather be a poor philosopher, than

---

[4] Dionysius, c.432–367 BC, a tyrant of Syracuse.

in that manner to be happy: Did not I then say well to thee (answered the tyrant) that we tyrants are not so happy as men think, for our lives depend always upon a small thread?

What repose could Nero also have?[5] who confessed, that often the likeness of his mother (whom he slew) appeared to him, which tormented and afflicted him; and that furies beat him with rods, and tormented him with burning torches? . . . And indeed it is one of the greatest wisdoms that can be in a tyrant, to take a good course for his death, when it is necessary and expedient for him: for they are often troubled, and do come short therein: as we see of Nero, who in his need could find no man that would slay him, but he was forced to slay himself: True it is, that his secretary held his hand, that with more strength and less fear he might dash the dagger into his throat, yet neither his secretary nor any other person would of themselves attempt it. If this secretary had been one of Machiavell's scholars, it is likely he would have proved more hardy.

. . .

But the example of Hieronimus (another tyrant of Sicily) is to this purpose well to be noted. This Hieronimus was the son of a good and wise king, called Hiero (whom also they well called tyrant, because he came not to that estate by a legitimate title, although he exercised it sincerely and in good justice)[6] who when he died, left this Hieronimus his son very young and under age: For the government therefore of him and of his affairs, he gave him fifteen tutors, and amongst them Andronodorus and Zoilus, his sons in law, and one Thraso, which he charged to maintain the country of Sicily in peace, as he himself had done by the space of fifty years of his reign: but especially that they should maintain the treaty and confederation, which he had, all the length of his time, duly observed with the Romans. The said tutors promised to perform his request, and to change nothing in the estate, but altogether to follow his footsteps. Straight after Hiero was dead, Andronodorus being angry because of so many tutors, caused the king (who was then but 15 years old) to be proclaimed of sufficient age to be dismissed of tutors, and so dispatched himself as well as others, of that dutiful care they ought to have had of their king and country: After, he got to himself alone the government of the kingdom, and to make himself to be feared under the king's authority, he took to him a great number of waiters for his guard, and to wear purple garments and a diadem upon his head, and to go in a coach drawn with white horses, altogether after the manner of Denis the tyrant, and contrary to the use of Hieronimus: yet was not this the worst; for, besides all this, Andronodorus caused the young king his brother in law, to be instructed in pride, and arrogancy, to condemn every man, to give audience to no man, to be quarrelous, and to take advantage at words; of hard access, given to all new fashions of effeminacy and riotousness, and to be immeasurably cruel, and thirsty after blood. After Andronodorus had

---

[5] Nero Claudius Caesar, AD 37–68, Emperor of Rome notorious for his cruelty and extravagance.

[6] Hiero, the name of two tyrants of Syracuse, one of the fifth, one of the third, century BC.

thus framed to his mind this young king, a conspiration was made against him (unto which Andronodorus was consenting) to dispatch and slay him, but it was discovered, but yet executed, which was strange: For one Theodorus was accused, and he confessed himself to be one of the conspiracy: but being tortured and racked to confess his complices [associates in crime] and partners in that conspiracy, knowing he must needs die, and by that means desiring to be revenged of that young tyrant, he accused the most faithful and trustiest servants of the king: This young tyrant rash and inconsiderate, straight put to death his friends and principal servants by the counsel of Andronodorus, who desired nothing more, because they hindered his designs: This execution performed, incontinent this young tyrant was massacred and slain upon a straight way by the conspirators themselves, which before had made the conjuration, the execution whereof was the more easy, by the discovery thereof, because (as is said) the tyrant's most faithful friends and servants were slain. Soon after the tyrant's death, Andronodorus obtained the fortress of Syracuse, a town of Sicily: but the tumults and stirs which he raised in the country (as he thought for his own profit) fell out so contrary to his expectation, that finally he, his wife, and all their race, and the race of Hieronimus were extermined, as well such as were innocent, as they that were culpable. And so doth it ordinarily happen to all young princes, which by corruption are degenerated into tyrants: So it falls out also to all them, which are corrupters of princes, to draw them into habits of all wickedness.

Lastly, here would not be omitted altogether this wickedness of Machiavell, who confounding good and evil together, yieldeth the title of Virtuous unto a tyrant: Is not this as much as to call darkness, full lightsome and bright, vice, good and honourable, and ignorance, learned? But it pleaseth this wicked man thus to say, to pluck out of the hearts of men, all hatred, horror, and indignation, which they might have against tyranny, and to cause princes to esteem tyranny, good, honourable and desirable.

8 Bodin, *Method* (1566)

Source: Jean Bodin, *Method for the Easy Comprehension of History*, translated by B. Reynolds (New York: Columbia University Press, 1945), pp. 92–101, 178–9 abridged.

Jean Bodin (1530–1596) was a French social and political philosopher, economist, occultist, necromancer and lawyer. His *Method for the Easy Comprehension of History* was written in Latin in 1565 and published a year later. Twelve more editions appeared during the following century. Bodin acquired his legal education at the University of Toulouse, where humanist scholarship was already influential. In his book he designed a systematic method of studying history with the purpose of establishing universal law. The following extract contains parts of his theory that climate and geographical features determined the character and, therefore, the political dispositions of men. Those who were born in temperate zones, such as the French, were predisposed to moderation and good sense in the conduct of affairs.

Let us therefore adopt this theory, that all who inhabit the area from the forty-fifth parallel to the seventy-fifth toward the north grow increasingly warmer within, while the southerners, since they have more warmth from the sun, have less from themselves. In winter the heat is collected within, but in summer it flows out. Whereby it happens that in winter we are more animated and robust, in summer more languid. The same reason usually makes us hungrier in winter so that we eat more than in summer, especially when the north wind blows. The south wind has the opposite effect, that is to say, living things are less hungry, as Aristotle wrote. So it comes to pass that when the Germans visit Italy, or the French, Spain, we observe that they eat more frugally or suffocate. This accident happened to Philip, duke of Austria,[1] when he dined according to his usual custom in Spain. But the Spanish, who live frugally in their fatherland, in France are more voracious than the French. Let it serve as evidence that the shepherds commonly say that when the herds and the flocks go down to the south they are wasted with fasting; they are more active in the north. Nor is it remarkable that Leo the African[2] wrote he had seen almost no herds of oxen or horses and only a few flocks of sheep in Africa; the ewes gave only a little milk. In contrast, the flocks of the Germans and the Scythians are praised by almost all writers.[3] This ought not to be attributed to the fact that they have better pastures than the southerners, as Pliny thought,[4] but to the climate. For the strength of inward heat brings it about that those who live in northerly lands are more active and robust than the southerners. Even in the opposite area, beyond Capricorn's circle, the same thing happens: the further men move from the equator, the larger they grow, as in the land of the Patagonians,[5] who are called giants, in the very same latitude as the Germans. This, then, is the reason why Scythians have always made violent attacks southward; and what seems incredible, but is nevertheless true, the greatest empires always have spread southward – rarely from the south toward the north. The Assyrians defeated the Chaldeans; the Medes, the Assyrians; the Greeks, the Persians; the Parthians, the Greeks; the Romans, the Carthaginians; the Goths, the Romans; the Turks, the Arabs; and the Tartars, the Turks. The Romans, on the contrary, were unwilling to advance beyond the Danube. After Trajan[6] had built a stone bridge of remarkable size across the Danube (for it is said that it had twenty pylons, of which the fragments even now remain), he did indeed conquer the Dacians completely.[7] But when Hadrian

---

[1] Philip the Fair, 1478–1506, husband of Joanna the Mad of Spain. He died suddenly soon after his arrival from his native Netherlands in Spain.

[2] Leo the African, c.1494–1552, a widely travelled Moorish convert to Christianity. His Italian *Description of Africa* and the Arabic classes he gave in Rome increased Western knowledge of Moorish culture. He finally returned to North Africa and the Islamic faith.

[3] Scythians, nomadic peoples from the area of south-west Russia.

[4] Pliny the Elder, AD 23–79, was killed during the eruption of Vesuvius. His *Natural History* is a great source of information about the ancient world.

[5] Patagonia is a name given to the southern part of South America.

[6] Trajan, AD 98–117, Roman emperor.

[7] Dacia, a Roman province beyond the River Danube which proved impossible to maintain.

understood that these tribes were not easily kept in subjection and did not submit to defeat, he ordered the bridge to be destroyed. Let us, however, cite more recent examples.

The French often suffered serious defeat at the hands of the English in France itself and almost lost their territory; they could never have penetrated into England, had they not been invited by the inhabitants. The English, on the other hand, were frequently overwhelmed by the Scots, and although they fought for control for more than 1,200 years, yet they could not drive the Scots from a small part of the island, even when in resources and numbers they were as much superior to the Scots as they were inferior to the French. It is not a fact, as the English complain, that the contest was unequal because of French hostility, for when the Roman Empire was tottering the South Britons were forced to call the Anglo-Saxons for protection, lest they should fall into servitude under the Scots. Yet the men who withstood the onslaughts of the Scots were not willing to attack at home. I omit the serious incursions into Europe and Asia of the Scythians, Parthians, Turks, Tartars, Muscovites, Goths, Huns, and Suessiones,[8] since the list is endless. Unless I err, this is what Ezekiel, Jeremiah, Isaiah, and the remaining Prophets threaten so many times: wars from the north, soldiers, horsemen, and the coming downfall of empires . . .

The Africans, with dry, cold, and very hard bodies, bear work and heat patiently . . . Yet they cannot bear the cold, since they have no internal heat, unlike the Scythians, who endure external heat with difficulty, since they are abundantly supplied within. In the same way horses, by their very nature warm and wet, live with difficulty in Ethiopia, but more easily in Scythia. On the other hand, asses, dry and cold, are lively in Africa, tired in Europe, nonexistent in Scythia . . .

The chief discussion is about the peoples who dwell from the thirtieth parallel to the sixtieth, because we know their history, about which we must form an opinion. We have almost no material for other peoples, but by this illustration we shall learn what must be believed about all. The Mediterranean peoples, then, as far as concerns the form of the body, are cold, dry, hard, bald, weak, swarthy, small in body, crisp of hair, black-eyed, and clear-voiced. The Baltic peoples, on the other hand, are warm, wet, hairy, robust, white, large-bodied, soft-fleshed, with scanty beards, bluish grey eyes, and deep voices. Those who live between the two show moderation in all respects. But this one thing is open to question: that the southerners, weak by the consent of all, are yet hard; the northerners, indeed, are robust, but soft. In opposition to this, Hippocrates[9] and almost all the other writers said that Scythians and mountaineers who resemble the type of the Scythians were hard, wild, and born to endure labour. Among these conflicting opinions of historians and philosophers, however, we shall judge correctly about history, as well as reconcile with Hippocrates and

---

[8] Suessiones, one of the 'barbarian' tribes of Gaul; they occupied the region around Soissons.

[9] Hippocrates of Cos, a physician of the fifth century BC.

Alexander, Livy, Tacitus, Polybius, Plutarch, and Caesar,[10] who reported that the French and the Germans were impatient of work, if we grant that the northerners in a cold region patiently bear labour, but in a warm region dissolve in sweat and languish. With this the account of Agathias about the Germans and of Krantz about the Scandinavians agree – that they wage war willingly in the winter, but rarely in the summer.

In contrast, the southerners easily endure heat suited to their nature, although they become more energetic in a cold region, languid in a warm one. And so, as I hear, in their language the Spanish women usually call the Germans 'soft fish'. But the Celts and the Belgae, when they come into Italy or Provence, are tortured by the mosquitoes and vermin to an unusual extent because of the softness of their skin. The natives, due to their toughness, are not annoyed so much . . .

The southerners are not so avaricious as they are parsimonious and stingy; the Scythians, on the other hand, are extravagant and rapacious. Since they know that they are at a disadvantage, they are usually suspicious. This trait our men formerly knew well enough. Holster related to me the additional fact that spies and listeners in Gothland hide in public inns, for suspicion arises from want of knowledge. They do not have intercourse with southerners unless they are sober, and when they feel themselves deceived, they draw back, or often anticipate by deceiving the strangers, or as a last resort use force. Whereby it happens that by universal consent they are supposed to be as perfidious as the southerners. (Of this fact the old historians were entirely ignorant, because they had no intercourse with the Scythians.) Later, when they left their homes, they revealed their character. Since the Franks came from Germany into France (for the Germans boast that the French are of Teutonic origin), it is in keeping that Procopius,[11] in speaking of the Franks, commented: 'This race is the most likely of all to betray their faith.' And Vopiscus said: 'It is customary for the Franks to break their faith laughingly.'[12] Hence, Alciati wrote that a scorpion's tail was tossed at the Germans.[13] This proverb we retain in France in the vulgar tongue – with due apologies, may it be said, lest our discourse should seem to harm the name of any race. I am not discussing this particular characteristic, but the inborn nature of each race. In this trait, however, the Germans are exceeded to a considerable degree by the Danes and the Norwegians, from whom they differ widely. Certainly greater perfidy or

[10] Alexander, the name of several Greek writers, but this may refer to one of the many histories of Alexander the Great of Macedon; Titus Livius (Livy), 59 BC–AD 17, author of a great history of Rome; Cornelius Tacitus, c.AD 56–120, historian of Rome of the first century AD; Polybius, c.200–118 BC, a Greek historian of Rome; Plutarch, see documents II.8, n. 3, and II.9, n. 7; Gaius Julius Caesar, 100–44 BC, Roman general, dictator and historian who wrote the Commentaries on the Gallic War and an unfinished work on the Civil War.
[11] Procopius of Caesarea, secretary to Belisarius the great general of Justinian in the sixth century AD. He wrote an official history of his times and unofficial Anecdotes relating most scandals.
[12] Flavius Vopiscus, one of the reputed authors of the Histories of the Emperors, AD 117–284.
[13] Andrea Alciati, 1492–1550, influential Italian jurist renowned for the Renaissance elegance of his style in, for example, his Commentaries on the Digest.

cruelty of people toward princes or of princes among themselves was never engendered than between Christian and Gustavus, between Danes and Swedes. From these races originate also the Normans, who, the common people believe, are unreliable.

But if from want of reasoning and wisdom the northerners cannot control their appetites and furthermore are regarded as intemperate, suspicious, perfidious, and cruel why are the southerners much more cruel and perfidious even than these? Here again I seek the decision in history. It is evident that by nature the southerners have the greatest gifts of ability; thus Columella, in Book I, chapter iii, declared: 'It is well known that the Carthaginians, a very acute race, said "the field must be weaker than the ploughman."'[14] Concerning the Egyptians who fought against Caesar, Hirtius said: 'These very clever men shrewdly constructed the things they saw made by us, so that our men seemed to imitate their work.'[15] A little later the same author added, 'The race of Egyptians is much given to treachery.' Moreover, who does not know how artfully and how long the Carthaginians eluded the power of the Romans? Nevertheless, they always practised incredible cruelty against the enemy, as may be seen in the Punic War[16] and also in that combat which the Spendii and the Carthaginians, both Phoenicians, waged against each other. As Polybius said, 'It far exceeded all wars of which we have heard in cruelty and all kinds of crimes.' Yet the things related by Polybius about the cruelty of the Carthaginians would seem ludicrous if anyone compared them with the history of Leo the African, or even with the unheard-of cruelty of Muley-Hasan and his sons, which not so long ago they practised against the citizens and then against each other.[17] For Muley-Hasan, driven from the kingdom whence he had driven his father, came as a suppliant to Emperor Charles, suffering from the loss of his eyes, which had been burnt out through the brutal violence of his brother.

[The passage below contains part of Bodin's claim that there was no such thing as a mixed constitution because sovereignty could not be shared. In the second paragraph Bodin, in pursuit of his main theme, dismissed Aristotle's six types of constitution, saying that there were only three – monarchy, aristocracy (rule of optimates) and democracy. The rule of bad versions of these – tyranny, oligarchy and ochlocracy (mob-rule) were not different kinds of constitution, only perversions of the three types.]

---

[14] Lucius Junius Moderatus Columella was born in Cadiz and wrote *Of Rural Matters*, a handbook for farmers, *c*. AD 65.

[15] Aulus Hirtius, *c*.90–43 BC, an associate of Julius Caesar, killed in the civil war which followed his assassination. He wrote part of the continuation of Caesar's Commentaries.

[16] Punic Wars: three wars – 264–241, 218–201 and 149–146 BC – in which Rome displaced Carthage as the dominant power in the western Mediterranean.

[17] Muley-Hasan: Al-Hasan ben Muhammad, sultan (muley or mawlay) of Tunisia; ruled 1526–42. He relied upon Spanish assistance to resist Ottoman aggression and from 1535 was kept in power by Charles V. He was hated by his subjects, particularly after the massacres that followed his reinstatement. His unpopularity enabled his son to depose and blind him in 1542.

Then the powers which are attributed to the senate or to magistrates have a significance distinct from sovereignty. Otherwise, it must be confessed, the sovereignty would be vested in those who had received it from others. If this seems absurd, what Polybius affirmed ought also to seem absurd – that the sovereignty of the state was partly in the people, partly in the senate, partly in the consuls. Furthermore, he thought that the form of government seemed to be mixed – aristocracy, monarchy, and democracy. This opinion Dionysius and Cicero adopted;[18] then Machiavelli, Contarini, Thomas More, Garimberto, and Manutius[19] vehemently approved it. We must refute them in debate, because this subject is of great importance for the thorough comprehension of the history of states. When the restoration of liberty to the people was mooted with bitter contention among the Florentines and it did not seem sage, and indeed was dangerous, to spread the secrets of empire among the throng, it was decided that after they had segregated the dregs of the plebs, who could not legally hold office, the laws must be ordained and the magistrates must be elected by the people. Other matters were to be regulated through the senate and the popular magistrates. For thus Guicciardini wrote.[20]

From this, also, it is made plain that the right of sovereignty is chiefly displayed in these specified attributes. Therefore, in every state one ought to investigate who can give authority to magistrates, who can take it away, who can make or repeal laws – whether one citizen or a small part of the citizens or a greater part. When this has been ascertained, the type of government is easily understood. There can be no fourth, and indeed none can be conceived, for virtue and viciousness do not create a type of rule. Whether the prince is unjust or worthy, nevertheless the state is still a monarchy. The same thing must be said about oligarchy and the rule of the people, who, while they have no powers but the creation of magistrates, still have the sovereignty, and on them the form of government necessarily depends. We shall then call the form one of optimates, or else popular (let us use these words in order that we may not rather often be forced to use the names aristocracy, oligarchy, democracy, ochlocracy, according to the type of virtue or vice); much more so if in addition to the creation of magistrates there is also power over war and peace, life and death. Moreover, it is evident that these things have always been so, not only in a monarchy but also in a government of optimates or in a popular state . . . But not to take endless examples from history, we shall use as examples Athenians, Romans, and Venetians, in order to show that what they taught about the mixed type of the Roman state is false.

---

[18] Dionysius of Halicarnassus, a Greek writer who lived in Rome under Augustus in the first century BC; Cicero, see document II.7, n. 11.

[19] Contarini see above, document II.1; Thomas More see above, document IV. 2; Paul Manutius, 1512–74, a member of the family which founded the Aldine press in Venice, who wrote a commentary on Cicero's orations.

[20] Francesco Guicciardini (1483–1540), Florentine historian; author of *History of Italy, 1492–1534*; friend of Machiavelli.

9 Bodin, *Six Books of the Commonwealth* (1576)

Source: Jean Bodin, *Six Books of the Commonwealth*, abridged and translated by M. J. Tooley (Oxford: Blackwell, 1955), pp. 41–9.

Bodin's *Six Books of the Commonwealth*, an inquiry into the nature of the state and of society, was published in French in 1576; nine more editions appeared in his lifetime and he brought out a slightly expanded Latin version in 1586. The extract printed below is taken from chapter 10 of Book 1. The first paragraph is typical of much which occurs elsewhere in the work and demonstrates how it became renowned not only as a justification for royal absolutism, but also for the claim that kings rule by divine right. He then reverts to his favourite subject: the impossibility that sovereignty could be shared. The remainder of the extract is devoted to proving his argument by listing the attributes of sovereignty.

CHAPTER 10: THE TRUE ATTRIBUTES OF SOVEREIGNTY

Because there are none on earth, after God, greater than sovereign princes, whom God establishes as His lieutenants to command the rest of mankind, we must enquire carefully into their estate, that we may respect and revere their majesty in all due obedience, speak and think of them with all due honour. He who contemns his sovereign prince, contemns God whose image he is . . .

Aristotle, Polybius, and Dionysius Halicarnassus alone among the Greeks discussed the attributes of sovereignty.[1] But they treated the subject so briefly that one can see at a glance that they did not really understand the principles involved. I quote Aristotle. 'There are', he says, 'three parts of a commonwealth. There must be provision for the taking and giving of counsel, for appointing to office and assigning to each citizen his duties, for the administration of justice.' If he did not mean by *parts* attributes of sovereignty, he never treated of the subject at all, since this is the only passage which has any bearing. Polybius does not define the rights and duties of sovereignty either, but he says of the Romans that their constitution was a mixture of monarchy, aristocracy, and popular government, since the people made law and appointed to office, the Senate administered the provinces and conducted great affairs of state, the consuls enjoyed the pre-eminence of honour accorded to kings, especially in the field, where they exercised supreme command. This passage appears to imply a treatment of sovereign rights, since he says that those who enjoyed those rights had sovereign power. Dionysius Halicarnassus however had a clearer and better understanding of the matter than the others. When he was explaining how the King Servius deprived the Senate of authority, he observed that he transferred to the people the power to make and unmake

---

[1] Aristotle see above, document II.9, n. 2; Polybius see above, document VII.8, n. 10; Dionysius of Halicarnassus see above, document VII.8, n. 18.

law, to determine war and peace, to institute and deprive magistrates, and the right of hearing appeals from all courts whatsoever. In another passage, when describing the third conflict between the nobles and the people, he reported how the Consul Marcus Valerius rebuked the people and said that they should be content with the powers of making law, appointing to office and hearing appeals.[2] Other matters should be left to the Senate.

Since ancient times civilians, and especially those of more recent years, have elaborated these rights, especially in their treatises on what they call regalian rights.[3] Under this heading they have collected an immense number of particular rights and privileges enjoyed by dukes, counts, bishops, and various officials, and even subjects of sovereign princes. As a result they describe dukes, such as those of Milan, Mantua, Ferrara, and Savoy, and even counts, as sovereign princes. However reasonable it may appear, this is an error. How can these rulers be regarded as anything but sovereign, they argue, when they make law for their subjects, levy war and conclude peace, appoint to all offices in their dominions, levy taxes, make a free man of whom they please, pardon those who have forfeited their lives? What other powers has any sovereign prince?

But we have already shown above that the Dukes of Milan, Mantua, Ferrara, Florence, and Savoy hold of the Empire. Their most honourable title is that of Imperial Vicar and Prince of the [Holy Roman] Empire . . . We have also pointed out the absurdities that ensue if one makes sovereigns of vassals, since the lord and his subject, the master and his servant, the man who makes the law and the man on whom it is imposed, the man who issues orders and the man who obeys them, are thereby placed on an equal footing. Since this cannot be, it follows that dukes, counts, and all those who hold of another, or are bound by his laws and subject to his commands, whether of right or by constraint, are not sovereign. The same holds good of the highest officers of state, lieutenant-generals of the king, governors, regents, dictators, whatever the extent of their powers. They are not sovereigns since they are subject to the laws and commands of another and may be appealed against.

The attributes of sovereignty are therefore peculiar to the sovereign prince, for if communicable to the subject, they cannot be called attributes of sovereignty . . . Just as Almighty God cannot create another God equal with Himself, since He is infinite and two infinities cannot co-exist, so the sovereign prince, who is the image of God, cannot make a subject equal with himself without self-destruction.

If this is so, it follows that rights of jurisdiction are not attributes of sovereignty since they are exercised by subjects as well as the prince. The same is true of the appointment and dismissal of officials, for this power also the prince shares with the subject, not only in regard to the lesser offices of

[2] Marcus Valerius: Roman consul of the fourth century BC; he occupied the curule chair twenty-one times; dictator in 342 and 301.
[3] Civilians: jurists expert in Civil (as opposed to Canon) Law. Regalian: rights which belong to a king.

justice, of police, of the armed forces, or of the revenues, but also in regard to responsible commanders in peace and war . . . The infliction of penalties and the bestowing of awards is not an attribute of sovereignty either, for the magistrate has this power, though it is true he derives it from the sovereign. Nor is taking counsel about affairs of state an attribute of sovereignty, for such is the proper function of the privy council or senate in the commonwealth, a body always distinct from that in which sovereignty is vested. Even in the popular state, where sovereignty lies in the assembly of the people, so far from it being the function of the assembly to take counsel, it ought never be permitted to do so, as I shall show later.

It is clear therefore that none of the three functions of the state that Aristotle distinguishes are properly attributes of sovereignty. As for what Halicarnassus says about Marcus Valerius' speech to the people of Rome, when trying to pacify them, that they should be content with the prerogatives of making law and appointing magistrates, he does not make the point sufficiently clear. As I have already said, appointing to office is not an attribute of sovereignty. Moreover some further explanation is necessary of the nature of the law-making power. A magistrate can make laws binding on those subject to his jurisdiction, provided such laws do not conflict with the edicts and ordinances of his sovereign prince.

Before going any further, one must consider what is meant by *law*. The word law signifies the right command of that person, or those persons, who have absolute authority over all the rest without exception, saving only the law-giver himself, whether the command touches all subjects in general or only some in particular. To put it another way, the law is the rightful command of the sovereign touching all his subjects in general, or matters of general application . . . As to the commands of the magistrate, they are not properly speaking laws but only edicts. 'An edict', says Varro, 'is an order issued by a magistrate.'[4] Such orders are only binding on those subject to his jurisdiction, and are only in force for his term of office.

The first attribute of the sovereign prince therefore is the power to make law binding on all his subjects in general and on each in particular. But to avoid any ambiguity one must add that he does so without the consent of any superior, equal, or inferior being necessary. If the prince can only make law with the consent of a superior he is a subject; if of an equal he shares his sovereignty; if of an inferior, whether it be a council of magnates or the people, it is not he who is sovereign. The names of the magnates that one finds appended to a royal edict are not there to give force to the law, but as witnesses, and to make it more acceptable . . . When I say that the first attribute of sovereignty is to give law to all in general and each in particular, I mean by this last phrase the grant of privileges. I mean by a privilege a concession to one or a small group of individuals which concerns the profit or loss of those persons only . . .

It may be objected however that not only have magistrates the power of issuing edicts and ordinances, each according to his competence and within

---

[4] Marcus Terentius Varro, 116–27 BC. A learned and prolific Roman writer.

his own sphere of jurisdiction, but private citizens can make law in the form of general or local custom. It is agreed that customary law is as binding as statute law. But if the sovereign prince is author of the law, his subjects are the authors of custom. But there is a difference between law and custom. Custom establishes itself gradually over a long period of years, and by common consent, or at any rate the consent of the greater part. Law is made on the instant and draws its force from him who has the right to bind all the rest. Custom is established imperceptibly and without any exercise of compulsion. Law is promulgated and imposed by authority, and often against the wishes of the subject. For this reason Dion Chrysostom compared custom to the king and law to the tyrant.[5] Moreover law can break custom, but custom cannot derogate from the law, nor can the magistrate, or any other responsible for the administration of law, use his discretion about the enforcement of law as he can about custom. Law, unless it is permissive and relaxes the severity of another law, always carries penalties for its breach. Custom only has binding force by the sufferance and during the good pleasure of the sovereign prince, and so far as he is willing to authorize it. Thus the force of both statutes and customary law derives from the authorization of the prince ... Included in the power of making and unmaking law is that of promulgating it and amending it when it is obscure, or when the magistrates find contradictions and absurdities ...

All the other attributes and rights of sovereignty are included in this power of making and unmaking law, so that strictly speaking this is the unique attribute of sovereign power. It includes all other rights of sovereignty, that is to say of making peace and war, of hearing appeals from the sentences of all courts whatsoever, of appointing and dismissing the great officers of state; of taxing, or granting privileges of exemption to all subjects, of appreciating or depreciating the value and weight of the coinage, of receiving oaths of fidelity from subjects and liege-vassals alike, without exception of any other to whom faith[6] is due ...

But because *law* is an unprecise and general term, it is as well to specify the other attributes of sovereignty comprised in it, such as the making of war and peace. This is one of the most important rights of sovereignty, since it brings in its train either the ruin or the salvation of the state. This was a right of sovereignty not only among the ancient Romans, but has always been so among all other peoples ... Sovereign princes are therefore accustomed to keep themselves informed of the smallest accidents and undertakings connected with warfare. Whatever latitude they may give to their representatives to negotiate peace or an alliance, they never grant the authority to conclude without their own express consent. This was illustrated in the negotiations leading up to the recent treaty of Câteaux-Cambrésis,[7] when the king's envoys kept him almost hourly informed of all proposals and counter-proposals ... In popular states and aristocracies the difficulty of

[5] Dio Chrysostom, *c.* AD 30–117, a celebrated Greek orator.
[6] Faith: loyalty.
[7] Treaty of Câteau-Cambrésis (1559) between France and Spain concluded a long period of intermittent warfare.

assembling the people, and the danger of making public all the secrets of diplomacy has meant that the people have generally handed responsibility over to the council. Nevertheless it remains true that the commissions and the orders that it issues in discharge of this function proceed from the authority of the people, and are despatched by the council in the name of the people . . .

The third attribute of sovereignty is the power to institute the great officers of state. It has never been questioned that the right is an attribute of sovereignty, at any rate as far as the great officers are concerned. I confine it however to high officials, for there is no commonwealth in which these officers, and many guilds and corporate bodies besides, have not some power of appointing their subordinate officials. They do this in virtue of their office, which carries with it the power to delegate. For instance, those who hold feudal rights of jurisdiction of their sovereign prince in faith and homage have the power to appoint the judges in their courts, and their assistants. But this power is devolved upon them by the prince . . . It is therefore not the mere appointment of officials that implies sovereign right, but the authorization and confirmation of such appointments. It is true however that in so far as the exercise of this right is delegated, the sovereignty of the prince is to that extent qualified, unless his concurrence and express consent is required.

The fourth attribute of sovereignty, and one which has always been among its principal rights, is that the prince should be the final resort of appeal from all other courts . . . Even though the prince may have published a law, as did Caligula,[8] forbidding any appeal or petition against the sentences of his officers, nevertheless the subject cannot be deprived of the right to make an appeal, or present a petition, to the prince in person. For the prince cannot tie his own hands in this respect, nor take from his subjects the means of redress, supplication, and petition, notwithstanding the fact that all rules governing appeals and jurisdictions are matters of positive law, which we have shown does not bind the prince. This is why the Privy Council, including the Chancellor de l'Hôpital, considered the action of the commissioners deputed to hold an enquiry into the conduct of the President l'Alemant irregular and unprecedented. They had forbidden him to approach within twenty leagues of the court, with the intention of denying him any opportunity of appeal. The king himself could not deny this right to the subject, though he is free to make whatsoever reply to the appeal, favourable or unfavourable, that he pleases . . . Were it otherwise, and the prince could acquit his subjects or his vassals from the obligation to submit their causes to him in the last instance, he would make of them sovereigns equal with himself . . . But if he would preserve his authority, the surest way of doing so is to avoid ever devolving any of the attributes of sovereignty upon a subject . . .

---

[8] 'Caligula' (little boots or *caligae*) was the nickname given to the Roman emperor Gaius Caesar, AD 12–41, whose short, violent reign (AD 37–41) ended with his murder by palace guards.

With this right is coupled the right of pardoning convicted persons, and so of overruling the sentences of his own courts, in mitigation of the severity of the law, whether touching life, property, honour, or domicile. It is not in the power of any magistrate, whatever his station, to do any of these things, or to make any revision of the judgement he has once given ... In a well-ordered commonwealth the right should never be delegated either to a special commission, or to any high officer of state, save in those circumstances where it is necessary to establish a regency, either because the king is abroad in some distant place, or in captivity, or incapable, or under age. For instance, during the minority of Louis IX, the authority of the Crown was vested in his mother Blanche of Castile as his guardian[9] ... Princes however tend to abuse this right, thinking that to pardon is pleasing to God, whereas to exact the utmost punishment is displeasing to Him. But I hold, subject to correction, that the sovereign prince cannot remit any penalty imposed by the law of God, any more than he can dispense any one from the operation of the law of God, to which he himself is subject. If the magistrate who dispenses anyone from obedience to the ordinance of his king merits death, how much more unwarrantable is it for the prince to acquit a man of the punishment ordained by God's law? If a sovereign prince cannot deny a subject his civil rights, how can he acquit him of the penalties imposed by God, such as the death penalty exacted by divine law for treacherous murder?

It may be objected that the prince can never show the quality of mercy if he cannot remit punishments prescribed by divine law. But in my opinion there are other means of showing clemency, such as pardoning breaches of positive laws. For instance, if the prince forbids the carrying of arms, or the selling of foodstuffs to the enemy in time of war, on pain of death, he can very properly pardon the offence of carrying arms if it was done in self-defence, or the selling of provisions if done under the pressure of extreme poverty. Again, the penalty for larceny under the civil law is death. A merciful prince can reduce this to fourfold restitution, which is what is required by divine law. It has always been the custom among Christian kings to pardon unpardonable offences on Good Friday. But pardons of this kind bring in their train pestilences, famine, war, and the downfall of states. That is why it is said in the law of God that in punishing those who have merited death one averts the curse on the whole people. Of a hundred criminals only two are brought to justice, and of those brought to justice only one half are proved guilty. If the few proven cases of guilt are pardoned, how can punishment act as a deterrent to evil-doers? ... The best way for a prince to exercise his prerogative of mercy is to pardon offences against his own person. Of all exercises of mercy none is more pleasing to God. But what can one hope of the prince who cruelly avenges all injuries to himself, but pardons those inflicted on others? ...

Faith and homage are also among the most important attributes of

[9] Louis IX and Blanche of Castile, see above document VII.6, n. 11.

sovereignty, as was made clear when the prince was described as the one to whom obedience was due without exception.

As for the right of coinage, it is contained within the law-making power, for only he who can make law can regulate currency. This is illustrated in the very terms used by Greeks, Romans, and French alike, for the word *nummus* comes from the Greek *nomos* signifying both law and alloy. There is nothing of more moment to a country, after the law, than the denomination, the value, and the weight of the coinage, as we have already shown in a separate treatise.[10] Therefore in every well-ordered commonwealth the prince reserves this right exclusively to himself ... And although in this kingdom many private persons, such as the Vicomte de Touraine, the Bishops of Meaux, Cahors, Agde, Ambrun and the Counts of St Pol, de la Marche, Nevers, Blois, and others enjoyed this right, Francis I in a general edict cancelled all such rights whatsoever, declaring the concessions null and void. This right and attribute of sovereignty ought not ever to be granted to a subject ...

The right of levying taxes and imposing dues, or of exempting persons from the payment of such, is also part of the power of making law and granting privileges. Not that the levying of taxation is inseparable from the essence of the commonwealth, for as President Le Maître has shown, there was none levied in France till the time of Louis IX. But if any necessity should arise of imposing or withdrawing a tax, it can only be done by him who has sovereign authority ... It is true that many seigneurs have prescriptive rights of levying tallages,[11] dues, and imposts. Even in this kingdom many seigneurs can levy tallage on four occasions in virtue of privileges confirmed by judgements in the courts, and by custom. Even seigneurs who have no rights of jurisdiction enjoy this privilege. But in my opinion the privilege started as an abuse which in consequence of long years of enjoyment acquired the dignity of a prescriptive right. But there is no abuse, of however long standing, that the law cannot amend, for the law exists to amend all abuses. Therefore, by the Edict of Moulins,[12] it was ordained that all rights of tallage claimed by seigneurs over their dependants could no longer be levied, notwithstanding immemorial prescription ...

I have left out of this discussion those lesser prerogatives that individual sovereign princes claim in their own particular realms, as I have confined myself to those general attributes of sovereignty proper to all sovereign princes as such, but which, being inalienable and imprescriptible, cannot, of their very nature, be communicated to subordinate persons such as feudal lords, magistrates, or subjects of any degree whatsoever. Whatever grant a sovereign prince makes of lands or jurisdiction, the rights of the crown are always reserved. This was implied in a judgement of the High Court relating to appanages in France,[13] that no passage of time could justify the

---

[10] *Response to the Paradox of Monsieur de Malestroict* (1568).
[11] Tallages: feudal taxes on dependants.
[12] Edict of Moulins, 1566.
[13] Appanages: provision made for the maintenance of the younger children of kings.

usurpation of royal rights. If common lands cannot be acquired by prescription, how can the rights and attributes of sovereignty? It is certain, on the evidence of various edicts and ordinances, that the public domain is inalienable, and cannot be acquired by prescription. Over two thousand years ago Themistocles,[14] in recovering common lands occupied by private persons, said in his speech to the people of Athens that men could acquire no prescriptive rights against God nor private citizens against the commonwealth ...

Such are the principal characteristics of sovereign majesty, treated as briefly as possible, since I have already written at greater length on the subject in my book *De Imperio*.[15] It is most expedient for the preservation of the state that the rights of sovereignty should never be granted out to a subject, still less to a foreigner, for to do so is to provide a stepping-stone whereby the grantee himself becomes the sovereign.

10 Entertainment at Antwerp (1582)

Source: J. Nichols, *The Progresses and Public Processions of Queen Elizabeth, among which are interspersed other solemnities, public expenditures, and remarkable events, during the reign of that illustrious princess* (London, 1788), II, 156–99.

Christopher Plantin (1514–89) was a French printer and publisher who set up his press in Antwerp. He is famed for his classical Hebrew and liturgical texts. The following extracts are from a translation of Plantin's contemporary account of the *joyeuse entrée* of the Duke of Anjou into Antwerp in February, 1582. He took the oath as Duke of Brabant on a platform or 'theatre' before entering the city and was invested with the traditional mantle by the Prince of Orange.

The Monsieur the Duke of Anjou departed from Lislo, and sailed towards Antwerp, having in his company but twenty ships, for the rest had gotten to Antwerp afore, as well to put themselves in a readiness, as for other affairs. And he came about eight of the clock nigh to the new town, and, passing along by the town side, left the foreland of Flanders on his right hand, and the town on his left, and passed beyond all the town and the place where the castle was. By the way he heard all the cannons shot off from that part of the town which faceth the river, and from a great number of ships which rode at anchor there: and he saw all the wharves furnished with men of war of the city, well armed, who welcomed him with their shot, and were answered again by the ships of war that accompanied him, conducted by monsieur de Treslon, and the vice-admirals, and diverse captains of Flushing. And so the first foot that he did set on land in Brabant, was at a village called Kiell,

[14] Themistocles: Athenian democratic statesman (*c*.528–462 BC).
[15] *De Imperio*. This has not survived. It was written whilst Bodin was still in Toulouse and may have contained some material which later appeared in the *Six Books*.

which is at the cannon wharf at Antwerp. The States of Brabant,[1] the magistrates of the city, and diverse other states, coming in like order on horseback to the same place with their trumpets, sergeants and heralds, apparelled in coats of the arms of Lothier, Brabant, and Limborough [Limburg], alighted there, and waited on foot at the wharf to receive his Highness . . . But the press of people was so great . . . that it was found better for them, by the advice of the Prince of Orange,[2] to return back, and to tarry for his Highness upon a theatre which was prepared for him.

This theatre was set up towards a corner of the castle, and opened towards the city, so as his Highness being there, might at one time view both the city and the castle, and behold the counterscarfes:[3] the deep ditches full of fair water clear to the very bottom of the channel, enclosed on either side with hewn stone: the great and fair buildings, the goodly walls, beautiful to look on and very thick: and the broad rampires[4] garnished with trees planted by hand, that it resembled a little forest. The Monsieur was brought up to this theatre, accompanied with the Prince Daphin [Dauphin], the only son of the duke of Montapuser [Montpensier]: the earl of Leicester, and other English lords, representing the Queen of England: the Princes of Orange and Espinoie, the count de Lavall, the other English lords, the count de Chateauroux, and a great sort of the barons, lords, and gentlemen, besides the chief magistrates and masters of the companies of the city of Antwerp.

. . . There was set for the Monsieur a chair covered with cloth of gold, wherein he sat him down. And upon the theatre there was likewise a traverse[5] of cloth of gold, and all the theatre was covered with tapistry. On the front of the theatre, on the highest part thereof, were the arms of the marqueship of the Holy Empire; and a little beneath them, on the right hand, did stand the arms of Brabant, with a wreath of fruits; and on the left hand stood the arms of the city of Antwerp. Also there were set up two banners of silk azured[6] with the arms of Anjou, and in one partition were written these same verses:

O noble Prince, whose footsteps faith and gentlenesse preserve:
Receive thou here the honour which thy vertue dooth deserve:
That these Low Countries maie at length take breath by meanes of thee,
And thou a Father to us all in name and dooings bee!

. . .

As soon as the ceremonies were ended, his Highness came down from the theatre, and mounted upon a white courser of Naples,[7] covered with a

[1] States: Assembly.
[2] Prince of Orange, 1553–84: William the Silent, leader of the Netherlands in its revolt against the rule of Spain. It had been his plan to offer the rule of Brabant to Francis of Alençon (later Duke of Anjou), the younger brother of the King of France.
[3] Counterscarfes: outer walls or slopes of fortification ditches.
[4] Rampires: ramparts.
[5] Traverse: covering.
[6] Azured: dyed in blue.
[7] Courser: charger.

caparison[8] of velvet richly embroidered with gold. And so he began to take his way towards the right renowned and rich city of Antwerp ...

... Over the gate where his Highness entered, there was a compartment of Dorrick [Doric] work, wherein was written this title: 'To Francis the son of Henry the Second, and only brother of Henry the Third King of France, called by God's singular providence to the sovereign principality of the Low Countries, and to the dukedom of Brabant, and the marqueship of the Sacred Empire, which God grant to be most happy and lucky unto him, as to their invested Prince whom they have most earnestly wished for, and who as now is happily come unto this his most serviceable city, his most harty favourers, the senate and people of Antwerp.'

The chariot of the maiden of Antwerp[9] could not go out of the city for want of room to turn in; and therefore it tarried for his Highness at the gate within the city. This chariot was called the chariot of alliance; wherein sat a damsel apparelled in satin red and white, which are the colours of Antwerp; who had in her left hand a branch of bay tree, and on her head a garland of laurel, in token of victory against the tyrannies of the King of Spain, and in token of the deliverance which the people hoped for by means of the new Prince, through his gracious goodness, faithfulness, victoriousness, and defense: to whom with her other hand she presented the keys of the town ... Before her were the arms of the marqueship of the Holy Empire. On her right hand was Religion apparelled like one of the Sibyls,[10] holding in her one hand an open book, named 'The Law and the Gospel'; and in her other hand a sword, named 'God's Word'; and on her left hand was Justice, holding a balance and a sword in her hand, and over the balance was written, 'Yea and Naie [Nay]'.
...

Six gentlemen of the city waited at the gate with a canopy of cloth of gold friezed,[11] which they afterward unfolded and carried it over the Duke's head, who went under it into the town in the forementioned order. All the streets from the gate to his lodging were set on either side with armed men under their ensigns, with their fifes and drums. The officers carried gilt targets and swords in their hands; and all the rest were armed after the best and goodliest manner that could be seen. His Highness proceeded forth on to the corner of the street called Easthouse-street, ... where was a show made in the likeness of a table, very great and high, which was made by one of the companies of their tragical and comical poets, commonly called amongst them Rhetoricians ... The show or table had three compartments or partitions. The first was the first book of Samuel, the fifteenth chapter, where Samuel chargeth Saule with his disobedience, and hath a piece of his garment rent off by him, in token that the kingdom should be plucked from

[8] Caparison: ornamental covering spread over the saddle of a horse.
[9] Maiden of Antwerp: a symbol of the city.
[10] Sibyls: women in ancient Greece reputedly endowed with powers of prophecy.
[11] i.e. furnished with a frieze.

Saule's house, and given to a better. Whereby was meant, that the sovereignty of those Low Countries was taken from the King of Spain, for his abominable perjuries, tyrannies, and extortions. In the second compartment was set forth, how Samuel commanded Ishaie [Jesse] the father of David to bring forth his sons; of whom God would make one the Prince of his people, that is, to wit, the youngest, which was David. In the third was showed how David, being annointed, fought with Goliath, and overcame him . . .

And at the foot of the table lay Discord, closed up in a prison of lattice-work, where she was tormented with hellhounds and serpents; and there were these verses following:

> Alanson, whom God cherish aie,
> Doeth chase all ire and wrath awaie.

His Highness passing forth . . . came to the street named Hwivetter-street, that is to say, the chandler's street, where was an other stately pageant with arms, torches,and cressets,[12] made by an other company of the Rhetoricians, called Painters or Violers, who had for their device, 'Knit together by single-ness'. In this pageant was painted the near alliance of David and Jonathan, to betoken the firmness of the oath mutually made by his Highness and the States of Brabant; and the magistrates, members, colonels, and captains of the city of Antwerp . . .

Then went he further to the end of the street, where the upholsterers shops are, which part was full of burning torches and barrels of burning pitch, and so came to the Meerebridge. At the entering thereof stood an elephant bearing a castle of stone with soldiers and artillery. Before the elephant were painted the arms of the marquesdom and of the city, and behind, a spear with a banner of taffeta, with the arms of Anjou in a wreath of laurel, and four other bannerets of crimson taffeta, pulled out, wherein were painted the hands of Antwerp, with this poesie, 'Cherisheth and Chaseth'. And upon his side of his belly were these verses manifestly written:

> Whome light of Phebee[13] heretofore did lead,
> I now am drawne awaie,
> Her brothers beames to follow in hir stead,
> A farre more certeine staie.
> I thinke my change right gainefull, fith I see,
> These Lower Countries under him to bee.

. . .

Vanderwerke[14] read the oath which the magistrate and people were to make, which was repeated word for word by the magistrates and a great number of

---

[12] Cresset: fire basket hoisted high for illumination.
[13] Phoebe: moon goddess of classical Greeks.
[14] Vanderwerke: the Grand Pensionary or chief magistrate.

people which were within the hearing of it. And this oath was exacted of the magistrate and people of Antwerp by the amptman,[15] . . . in the name, and by the commandment, of the Duke. Upon the finishing of these solemnities, the Duke himself did cast two or three handfuls of gold and silver among them, and then the heralds cried 'A larges',[16] and the drums and trumpets were sounded every where, and many instruments of music were played upon, as had been done afore at his first arrival . . . he went to the townhouse, with all the princes, lords and gentlemen, which were very many; where he was received by the worshipful of the city, and dined openly at a very sumptuous and royal feast prepared for him; and so that day passed in great joy, contentation, and admiration, as well of his Highness and his company, as of all the rest of the people. Towards night were shot off two peals of great ordinance again, and the fires of joy were continued much greater, and more in number than afore.

Thus ended the joyful and royal entertainment of the Right Noble Prince Francis, son and brother to the King of France, by the grace of God Duke of Brabant. The rest of the week and the days following, the lords of the privy council, the officers of the aides, of the exchequers, of the chambers of the accounts, and of the other corporations, colleges, and communalties, came to visit his Highness, and to offer him their humble service, promising all faithfulness and obedience; all whom he received very graciously to their contentation, answering them so advisedly, with so good grace and fitness, without omitting any point of that which he had purposed: that all men not only wondered at him, but also were enforced to honour and love him, and to set forth his praises among the people. Finally, the deputies of the Reformed churches of both the languages, being presented unto him by the Prince of Orange, were gently heard, and they spake to him as followeth: 'Sir, we be sent unto your Highness by the Reformed churches of this city, as well of the language of Low Dutchland, as of the French, to shew unto you with all humility, reverence, and subjection, that we have thanked, and still do thank, God, with all our heart, for vouchsafing to bring your Highness so happily hither. And this our joy is matched with the joy of all other folks, as we hope your Highness hath understood by the glad and joyful receiving and entertaining of you. Also, Sir, we hope, that as the great honour and felicity which these countries have attained unto (wherein few countries are able to match them) have been purchased under the sovereignty and government of the right renowned princes, the Dukes of Burgandy, which issued out of the most noble house of France; so under your guiding and governement, being of the same house, the ancient renown of the same dignity shall be recovered by your prowess, and mainteined by your wisdom . . . For the first duke of Orleans, of whome your Highnesse is lineally descended from the father to the son, was the son of King Charles the First; and as now there be no more heirs male of the said duke of Orleans, but only

[15] Chief legal officer.

[16] 'A larges', a traditional cry when princes scattered money or 'largesse' amongst their subjects.

your Highness and the King your brother. Whereby it falleth out, that the dukes of Burgandy are great uncles to your Highness by the father's side. And therefore we doubt not but you will follow the footsteps of their virtues, in restoring the state of the countrie to her ancient renown and dignity; and also maintain and increase the honour whereunto it hath been advanced by those noble princes your uncles.'

SECTION VIII

Portrait of Sir Philip Sidney by an unknown artist.
Reproduced by kind permission of the National Portrait Gallery, London.

SECTION VIII

Church, State and Literature in Britain

During the reign of Henry VIII the English Church was severed from Catholic Christendom and nationalized by the state. The impetus for this revolutionary change came from the King and his advisers: Henry wanted to divorce Catherine of Aragon and marry Anne Boleyn, and the Pope, as head of the Church, would not allow him to do so. The process of separation was not a sudden one, however. The early 1530s saw the passage of a series of Parliamentary statutes which, piece by piece, transferred authority from the Pope to the Crown. For example, the Act in Restraint of Appeals of 1533 prohibited ecclesiastical appeals being taken outside the jurisdiction of English courts, and so made it possible for Henry's divorce case to be decided by Cranmer in England.

The climax of this series of Acts came with the passage of the 1534 Act of Supremacy, by which Parliament recognized the monarch as 'supreme head in earth of the Church of England'. The way was now clear for the dissolution of the monasteries, which transferred much of the Church's wealth first of all to the Crown and later to the nobility and gentry.

As well as the Henrician Act, we have reprinted in this section passages from the Elizabethan Act of Supremacy of 1559. But although Elizabeth was recognized as 'supreme governor' of the Church, the achievement of a lasting religious settlement was not easy. The whole question of who controlled the Church was raised sharply in the so-called 'Vestiarian Controversy' of the 1560s. Elizabeth, and some of her bishops, demanded that priests wear the traditional clerical vestments, the round cap and the surplice. Many, perhaps a majority, of the clergy were resistant, believing that vestments had no place in a truly reformed ministry. In the end, the Queen got her way; but, as the letters printed below reveal, the affair touched on fundamental issues of authority.

The impact of the Protestant Reformation on subsequent cultural developments in England was profound, as can be seen in the work of the greatest writers of the age: Shakespeare, Spenser and Marlowe. But equally powerful as an influence on English culture in the late sixteenth century were the values of Renaissance humanism. The combination of advanced Protestantism and Renaissance humanism is nowhere more strikingly exemplified than in the life and work of Sir Philip Sidney. Born into a powerful, aristocratic family, Sidney was regarded by contemporaries as the very epitome of the Protestant Renaissance courtier. Before his death at the early age of thirty-two, he had been a diplomat, soldier, politician, scholar, poet and critic. With his sonnet sequence *Astrophil and Stella* he created not just a fashion for such sequences in the closing decades of the century but a vastly influential model for English lyric poetry. Equally, in his *Defence of Poetry*, he produced the first substantial work of literary theory and criticism in English.

In Scotland the struggle between Protestant and Catholic noblemen was often bloody, and Calvinism made slow progress. Mary Queen of Scots was a Catholic, but her son James VI was brought up as a Protestant. Under him, the Stuart court, which had always patronized poets and musicians, became the centre of a group of poets interested in technical experimentation, and much influenced by French poets like Marot and Ronsard. This 'courtly' tradition coexisted with, and to some extent drew upon, a much older tradition of Scottish ballad and folk song. The selection of poems reprinted here is intended to represent both traditions.

1 The Acts of Supremacy (1534, 1559)

Source: *The Tudor Constitution: Documents and Commentary*, edited by G. R. Elton, second edition (Cambridge: Cambridge University Press, 1982), pp. 364–5, 372–7 abridged.

The Acts of Supremacy of 1534 and 1559 are religious and constitutional landmarks. By the Act of 1534 Parliament declared that the monarch was head of the Church of England, thus effectively replacing the authority of the Pope with that of the King in all ecclesiastical affairs. In 1554, under Mary I, all Henry VIII's anti-papal legislation, including the Act of Supremacy, was repealed, but this attempt to end the schism with Rome was shortlived. Elizabeth's position, however, was weaker than her father's had been, and she was much less independent of Parliament. The 1559 Act gave to her the title 'supreme governor' rather than 'supreme head', and the change indicates a shift in the nature of royal supremacy from the highly personal and semi-spiritual legislative character it had under Henry, to the more external and administrative authority of the 'Queen-in-Parliament' under Elizabeth.

An Act concerning the King's Highness to be supreme head of the Church of England and to have authority to reform and redress all errors, heresies and abuses in the same (1534: 26 Henry VIII, c. 1)

Albeit the King's Majesty justly and rightfully is and oweth [ought] to be the supreme head of the Church of England, and so is recognised by the clergy of this realm in their Convocations; yet nevertheless for corroboration and confirmation thereof, and for increase of virtue in Christ's religion within this realm of England, and to repress and extirp [extirpate] all errors, heresies and other enormities and abuses heretofore used in the same, Be it enacted by authority of this present Parliament that the King our sovereign lord, his heirs and successors kings of this realm, shall be taken, accepted and reputed the only supreme head in earth of the Church of England called *Anglicana Ecclesia*, and shall have and enjoy annexed and united to the imperial crown of this realm as well the title and style thereof, as all honours, dignities, preeminences, jurisdictions, privileges, authorities, immunities, profits and commodities, to the said dignity of supreme head of the same Church belonging and appertaining. And that our said sovereign lord, his heirs and successors kings of this realm, shall have full power and authority from time to time to visit, repress, redress, reform, order, correct, restrain and amend all such errors, heresies, abuses, offences, contempts and enormities, whatsoever they be, which by any manner spiritual authority or jurisdiction ought or may lawfully be reformed, repressed, ordered, redressed, corrected, restrained or amended, most to the pleasure of Almighty God, the increase of virtue in Christ's religion, and for the conservation of the peace, unity and tranquillity of this realm: any usage, custom, foreign laws, foreign authority, prescription or any other thing or things to the contrary hereof notwithstanding.

AN ACT RESTORING TO THE CROWN THE ANCIENT JURISDICTION OVER THE STATE
ECCLESIASTICAL AND SPIRITUAL, AND ABOLISHING ALL FOREIGN POWER
REPUGNANT TO THE SAME (ACT OF SUPREMACY, 1559: 1 ELIZ. I, c. 1)

Most humbly beseeches your most excellent Majesty your faithful and obedient subjects the Lords spiritual and temporal and the Commons in this your present Parliament assembled: that where in time of the reign of your most dear father of worthy memory, King Henry the Eighth, divers good laws and statutes were made and established, as well for the utter extinguishment and putting away of all usurped and foreign powers and authorities out of this your realm and other your Highness' dominions and countries, as also for the restoring and uniting to the imperial crown of this realm the ancient jurisdictions, authorities, superiorities and preeminences to the same of right belonging and appertaining; by reason whereof we your most humble and obedient subjects, from the five and twentieth year of the reign of your said dear father, were continually kept in good order and were disburdened of divers great and intolerable charges and exactions before that time unlawfully taken and exacted by such foreign power and authority as before that was usurped, until such time as all the said good laws and statutes by one act of Parliament made in the first and second years of the reigns of the late King Philip and Queen Mary, your Highness' sister [1 & 2 Philip and Mary, c. 8], were all clearly repealed and made void, as by the same act of repeal more at large doth and may appear. By reason of which act of repeal your said humble subjects were eftsoons[1] brought under an usurped foreign power and authority and yet do remain in that bondage, to the intolerable charges of your loving subjects if some redress by the authority of this your High Court of Parliament with the assent of your Highness be not had and provided.

[I.] May it therefore please your Highness, for the repressing of the said usurped foreign power and the restoring of the rights, jurisdictions and preeminences appertaining to the imperial crown of this your realm, that it may be enacted by the authority of this present Parliament, That the said act ... and all and every branch, clauses and articles therein contained (other than such branches, clauses and sentences as hereafter shall be excepted) may from the last day of this session of Parliament, by authority of this present Parliament, be repealed, and shall from thenceforth be utterly void and of none effect.

II. And that also for the reviving of divers of the said good laws and statutes made in the time of your said dear father, it may also please your Highness [that the following statutes may be revived by authority of this present Parliament: 23 Henry VIII, c. 9, Foreign Citations; 24 Henry VIII, c. 12, Appeals to Rome; 23 Henry VIII, c. 20, Payment of Annates; 25 Henry VIII, c. 19, Submission of the Clergy; 25 Henry VIII, c. 20, Consecration of Bishops; 25 Henry VIII, c. 21, Exactions from Rome; 26 Henry VIII, c. 14, Suffragans; 28 Henry VIII, c. 16, Dispensations] ... And that the branches, sentences and words of the said several acts and every of them from thenceforth shall and may be judged, deemed and taken to extend to your Highness, your heirs and successors, as fully and largely as ever the same acts or any of them did extend to the said late King Henry the Eighth, your Highness' father.

...

IV. And that it may also please your Highness that it may be further enacted by the authority aforesaid, that all other laws and statutes, and the branches and clauses of any act or statute, repealed and made void by the said act of repeal ... and not in this present act specially mentioned and revived, shall stand, remain and be repealed and void in such like manner and form as they were before the making of this act; anything herein contained to the contrary notwithstanding.

[V revives 1 Edw. VI, c. 1 permitting communion in both kinds.[2]]

[VI repeals the heresy laws revived by Mary, and the act which revived them.]

VII. And to the intent that all usurped and foreign power and authority, spiritual and temporal, may for ever be clearly extinguished and never to be used nor obeyed within this realm or any other your Majesty's dominions or countries: May it please your Highness that it may be further enacted by the

---

[1] A second time, again.
[2] Both bread and wine.

authority aforesaid that no foreign prince, person, prelate, state or potentate, spiritual or temporal, shall at any time after the last day of this session of Parliament use, enjoy or exercise any manner of power, jurisdiction, superiority, authority, preeminence or privilege spiritual or ecclesiastical, within this realm or within any other your Majesty's dominions or countries that now be or hereafter shall be, but from thenceforth the same shall be clearly abolished out of this realm and all other your Highness' dominions for ever; any statute, ordinance, custom, constitutions or any other matter or cause whatsoever to the contrary in any wise notwithstanding.

VIII. And that also it may likewise please your Highness that it may be established and enacted by the authority aforesaid that such jurisdictions, privileges, superiorities and preeminences spiritual and ecclesiastical, as by any spiritual or ecclesiastical power or authority hath heretofore been or may lawfully be exercised or used for the visitation of the ecclesiastical state and persons, and for reformation, order and correction of the same and of all manner of errors, heresies, schisms, abuses, offences, contempts and enormities, shall for ever by authority of this present Parliament be united and annexed to the imperial crown of this realm. And that your Highness, your heirs and successors, kings or queens of this realm, shall have full power and authority, by virtue of this act, by letters patents under the great seal of England to assign, name and authorise, when and as often as your Highness, your heirs or successors, shall think meet and convenient, and for such and so long time as shall please your Highness, your heirs or successors, such person or persons being natural born subjects to your Highness, your heirs or successors, as your Majesty, your heirs or successors, shall think meet, to exercise, use, occupy and execute under your Highness, your heirs and successors, all manner of jurisdictions, privileges and preeminences in any wise touching or concerning any spiritual or ecclesiastical jurisdiction within these your realms ... and to visit, reform, redress, order, correct and amend all such errors, heresies, schisms, abuses, offences, contempts and enormities whatsoever which by any manner spiritual or ecclesiastical power, authority or jurisdiction can or may lawfully be reformed, ordered, redressed, corrected, restrained, or amended, to the pleasure of Almighty God, the increase of virtue, and the conservation of the peace and unity of this realm. And that such person or persons so to be named, assigned, authorised and appointed by your highness, your heirs or successors, after the said letters patents to him or them made and delivered as is aforesaid, shall have full power and authority, by virtue of this act and of the said letters patents, under your Highness, your heirs or successors, to exercise, use and execute all the premises according to the tenor and effect of the said letters patents; Any matter or cause to the contrary in any wise notwithstanding.

IX. And for the better observation and maintenance of this act, may it please your Highness that it may be further enacted by the authority aforesaid that all and every archbishop, bishop, and all and every other ecclesiastical person and other ecclesiastical officer and minister, of what estate, dignity, preeminence or degree soever he or they be or shall be, and all and every temporal judge, justicer, mayor, and other lay or temporal officer and minister, and every other person having your Highness' fee or wages within this realm or any your Highness' dominions, shall make, take and receive a corporal oath upon the evangelist,[3] before such person or persons as shall please your Highness, your heirs or successors, under the great seal of England to assign and name to accept and take the same, according to the tenor and effect hereafter following, that is to say: I, *A. B.*, do utterly testify and declare in my conscience that the Queen's Highness is the only supreme governor of this realm and of all other her Highness' dominions and countries, as well in all spiritual or ecclesiastical things or causes as temporal, and that no foreign prince, person, prelate, state or potentate hath or ought to have any jurisdiction, power, superiority, preeminence or authority ecclesiastical or spiritual within this realm, and therefore I do utterly renounce and forsake all foreign jurisdictions, powers, superiorities and authorities, and do promise that from henceforth I shall bear faith and true allegiance to the Queen's Highness, her heirs and lawful successors, and to my power shall assist and defend all jurisdictions, preeminences, privileges and authorities granted or belonging to the Queen's Highness, her heirs and successors, or united or annexed to the imperial crown of this realm: so help me God and by the contents of this Book.

[X attaches to refusal to take the oath the penalty of loss of 'every ecclesiastical and spiritual promotion, benefice, and office, and every temporal and lay promotion and office' which the person so refusing holds 'at the time of such refusal made', 'and that also all and every such person and persons so refusing to take the said oath shall immediately after such refusal be from thenceforth during his life disabled to retain or exercise any office or other promotion which he at the time of such refusal hath jointly or in common with any other person or persons.' Persons hereafter preferred 'to any archbishopric or bishopric, or to any other spiritual or ecclesiastical benefice, promotion, dignity, office or ministry, or . . . to any temporal or lay office, ministry or service,' are required to take the oath before they 'receive, use, exercise, supply or occupy' such office.]

. . .

[XII. Oath also to be taken by persons suing livery of lands and doing homage, and by anyone taking holy orders or degrees at the Universities.]
. . .

XIV. And for the more sure observation of this act and the utter extinguishment of all foreign and usurped power and authority, may it please your Highness that it may be further enacted by the authority aforesaid that if any person or persons dwelling or inhabiting within this

---

[3] An oath ratified by corporally touching the Gospels, or other sacred relic, as distinct from a verbal oath.

your realm or in any other your Highness' realms or dominions, of what estate, dignity or degree soever he or they be, after the end of thirty days next after the determination of this session of this present Parliament shall by writing, printing, teaching, preaching, express words, deed or act, advisedly, maliciously and directly affirm, hold, stand with,[4] set forth, maintain or defend the authority, preeminence, power or jurisdiction spiritual or ecclesiastical of any foreign prince, prelate, person, state or potentate whatsoever, heretofore claimed, used or usurped within this realm or any dominion or country being within or under the power, dominion or obeisance [obedience] of your Highness, or shall advisedly, maliciously and directly put in ure[5] or execute anything for the extolling, advancement, setting forth, maintenance or defence of any such pretended or usurped jurisdiction, power, preeminence or authority, or any part thereof, that then every such person and persons so doing and offending, their abettors, aiders, procurers and counsellors, being thereof lawfully convicted and attainted according to the due order and course of the common laws of this realm, [shall be subject to the following penalties: for the first offence, forfeiture of goods, or if these are not worth £20, one year's imprisonment, the benefices and promotions of ecclesiastics becoming void; for the second offence, the penalties of praemunire; the third offence is to be deemed high treason].

. . .

XX. Provided always and be it enacted by the authority aforesaid that such person or persons to whom your Highness, your heirs or successors, shall hereafter by letters patent under the great seal of England give authority to have or execute any jurisdiction, power or authority spiritual, or to visit, reform, order, or correct any errors, heresies, schisms, abuses or enormities by virtue of this act, shall not in any wise have authority or power to order, determine or adjudge any matter or cause to be heresy but only such as heretofore have been determined, ordered or adjudged to be heresy by the authority of the canonical Scriptures, or by the first four General Councils or any of them, or by any other General Council wherein the same was declared heresy by the express and plain words of the said canonical Scriptures, or such as hereafter shall be ordered, judged or determined to be heresy by the High Court of Parliament of this realm with the assent of the clergy in their Convocation; anything in this act contained to the contrary notwithstanding.

[XXI. Offences under this act shall be proved by two lawful witnesses, confronted with the accused.]

---

[4] Agree with.
[5] In or into use, practice or operation.

2 The Vestiarian Controversy: Laurence Humphrey, Thomas Sampson and Bishop Grindal (1563–1566)

Source: *The Zurich Letters, Comprising the Correspondence of Several English Bishops and Others, with some of the Helvetian Reformers, during the Early Part of the Reign of Queen Elizabeth*, edited by Hastings Robinson (The Parker Society; Cambridge: Cambridge University Press, 1842), pp. 133–4, 153–4, 168–9.

One of the most serious religious controversies of Elizabeth's reign centred on her insistence that there be uniformity of clerical dress. The more radical English Protestant churchmen had always objected to wearing the surplice, on the grounds that it was associated with popery and idolatry. Many of them had gone into exile in Europe during Mary I's reign, and they were heavily influenced by Continental reformers such as Peter Martyr, Heinrich Bullinger and Martin Bucer. When they returned to England at Elizabeth's accession, they kept in close contact with these European leaders, and continually referred to them for their opinions on the acceptability of various elements in the Elizabethan settlement.

The three letters reprinted here are all addressed to Heinrich Bullinger. Bullinger (1504–75) had succeeded Zwingli as the leader of the Protestant Church in Zurich, and was highly regarded as a mediator in the great quarrels which broke out between the different branches of the Reformation. In 1565, Archbishop Matthew Parker, at the Queen's insistence, ordered his clergy to wear the surplice and cap. Two of the leading objectors were Laurence Humphrey, President of Magdalen College, Oxford, and Thomas Sampson, Dean of Christ Church, and in letters to Bullinger they attempted to enlist his support. Unfortunately for them, as the letter from Edmund Grindal, Bishop of London, makes clear, Bullinger ultimately endorsed the bishops' case. His judgement was swiftly printed by the prelates, and many waverers decided to conform as a result. Although the immediate points of the vestiarian controversy may seem trivial, very important issues relating to the extent of royal authority over the Church were at stake.

LAURENCE HUMPHREY TO HENRY BULLINGER

Dated at Oxford, 16 August 1563

Health in Christ, and everlasting peace! I rejoice and congratulate you again and again that the tumult of war has subsided. I lament, however, that the affairs of religion have made so little progress. Jesus will at length afford us halcyon days, when the gospel shall meet with more acceptance, and the church, I hope, will have her sons, and the gospel its course, in spite of, and with the opposition of, all the powers of hell. For the truth will prevail, and no power or cunning of man shall be able to resist the divine will and operation. But to you and yours, our fathers and brethren, do we wish a long life, lest the christian commonwealth should be deprived of her parents, and patrons, and guardians.

Respecting the subject of the habits, I wish you would again write me your opinion, either at length, or briefly, or in one word: first, whether that appears to you as *indifferent* which has been so long established with so much superstition, and both fascinated the minds of the simple with its splendour, and imbued them with an opinion of its religion and sanctity: secondly, whether at the command of the sovereign, (the jurisdiction of the pope having been abolished,) and for the sake of order, and not of ornament, habits of this kind may be worn in church by pious men, lawfully and with a safe conscience. I am speaking of that round cap and popish surplice, which are now enjoined us, not by the unlawful tyranny of the pope, but by the just and legitimate authority of the queen. To the pure, then, can all these things be pure, and matters of indifference? I ask your reverence to let me know very exactly what is your opinion . . .

THOMAS SAMPSON TO HENRY BULLINGER

Dated at London, 16 February 1566

Reverend father in Christ, I wrote you a letter six months since, and should have satisfied the wishes of many of my brethren, if, as I then earnestly requested, I had received an answer from your worthiness. But since either my letter was not delivered to you, or yours (if you have written any) appears to have been intercepted, I am under the necessity of repeating what I before stated.

Our church remains in the same condition as was long since reported to you. For, after the expiration of seven years in the profession of the gospel, there has now been revived that contest about habits, in which Cranmer, Ridley, and Hooper, most holy martyrs of Christ, were formerly wont to skirmish.[1] The state of the question, however, is not in all respects the same, but the determination of those in power is more inflexible. This indeed is very gratifying to our adversaries at Louvaine,[2] for they praise these things up to the skies.

But that you may more readily understand the matter in controversy, I have thought it best to reduce it into certain questions, which are these:

I. Whether a peculiar habit, distinct from that of the laity, were ever assigned to the ministers of the gospel in better times, and whether it ought now to be assigned to them in the reformed church?

II. Whether the prescribing habits of this kind be consistent with ecclesiastical and christian liberty?

III. Whether the nature of things indifferent admits of coercion; and whether any violence should be offered to the consciences of the many who are not yet persuaded?

IV. Whether any new ceremonies may be instituted, or superadded to what is expressly commanded in the word?

---

[1] In 1550 John Hooper had initially refused to be consecrated Bishop of Gloucester wearing vestments, and had quarrelled with Archbishop Cranmer and Bishop Ridley over the issue.

[2] The theological faculty of the University of Louvain in Belgium was noted for its opposition to Protestant teachings.

V. Whether it be lawful to revive the Jewish ceremonies respecting the habit of the priesthood, and which were abolished by Christ?

VI. Whether it be expedient to borrow rites from idolaters or heretics, and to transfer such as are especially dedicated to *their* sect and religion to the use of the reformed church?

VII. Whether conformity and general agreement must of necessity be required in ceremonies of this kind?

VIII. Whether those ceremonies may be retained which occasion evident offence?

IX. Whether any ecclesiastical constitutions may be tolerated, which, though from their nature they are free from any thing impious, do not, nevertheless, tend to edification?

X. Whether any thing of a ceremonial nature may be prescribed to the church by the sovereign, without the assent and free concurrence of churchmen?

XI. Whether a man ought thus to obey the decrees of the church; or on account of non-compliance, supposing there is no alternative, to be cast out of the ministry?

XII. Whether good pastors, of unblemished life and doctrine, may rightfully be removed from the ministry on account of their non-compliance with such ceremonies?

Here you have, most esteemed Sir, our difficulties. Here many pious men are hesitating; for the sake of whom I again ask it as a favour from you, that, having well considered the matter with master Gualter[3] and the rest of your colleagues, with your wonted piety, you will plainly state your opinion, and send a written answer to each of the above questions. You will confer an exceeding kindness upon many, and on myself especially; and you will also confer an excellent benefit upon our church.

BISHOP GRINDAL TO HENRY BULLINGER

Dated at London, 27 August 1566

Health in Christ, most illustrious master Bullinger, and my very dear brother in Christ. Master John Abel gave me the letter from you, addressed to the bishops of Winchester and Norwich in common with myself, together with what you had written on the controversy about the habits; copies of all which I immediately forwarded to them. As to myself, I return you my best thanks, both for manifesting so much interest for our churches, and for acquainting me, a man personally unknown to you, with what has been written to our brethren concerning the matters in dispute.

It is scarcely credible how much this controversy about things of no importance has disturbed our churches, and still, in great measure, continues to do. Many of the more learned clergy seemed to be on the point of forsaking their ministry. Many of the people also had it in contemplation

---

[3] Rudolph Gualter, Bullinger's fellow pastor in Zurich.

to withdraw from us, and set up private meetings; but however most of them, through the mercy of the Lord, have now returned to a better mind. Your letter, replete with piety and wisdom, has greatly contributed to this result; for I have taken care that it should be printed, both in Latin and English. Some of the clergy, influenced by your judgment and authority, have relinquished their former intention of deserting their ministry. And many also of the laity have begun to entertain milder sentiments, now that they have understood that our ceremonies were by no means considered by you as unlawful, though you do not yourselves adopt them; but of this, before the publication of your letter, no one could have persuaded them. There are nevertheless some, among whom are masters Humphrey and Sampson, and others, who still continue in their former opinion. Nothing would be easier than to reconcile them to the queen, if they would but be brought to change their mind; but until they do this, we are unable to effect any thing with her majesty, irritated as she is by this controversy. We, who are now bishops, on our first return, and before we entered on our ministry, contended long and earnestly for the removal of those things that have occasioned the present dispute; but as we were unable to prevail, either with the queen or the parliament, we judged it best, after a consultation on the subject, not to desert our churches for the sake of a few ceremonies, and those not unlawful in themselves, especially since the pure doctrine of the gospel remained in all its integrity and freedom; in which, even to this day, (notwithstanding the attempts of many to the contrary,) we most fully agree with your churches, and with the confession you have lately set forth.[4] And we do not regret our resolution; for in the mean time, the Lord giving the increase, our churches are enlarged and established, which under other circumstances would have become a prey to the Ecebolians,[5] Lutherans, and semi-papists. But these unseasonable contentions about things which, as far as I am able to judge, are matters of indifference, are so far from edifying, that they disunite the churches, and sow discord among the brethren.

3 Scottish Ballads and Court Poetry (fifteenth to sixteenth centuries)

A. 'Sir Patrick Spens'

Source: *The Oxford Book of Scottish Verse*, edited by J. MacQueen and T. Scott (Oxford: Clarendon Press, 1966), pp. 282–4.

'Sir Patrick Spens' (or Spence) is widely regarded as one of the finest of all Scottish ballads. Although no record of a Sir Patrick Spens survives, the ballad seems to refer

---

[4] Bullinger's 'Second Helvetic Confession' was published in 1566.
[5] Ecebolus taught rhetoric to the emperor Julian in the fourth century; he followed Julian's apostasy but after the emperor's death attempted to come back into the Church.

to the death, on the return voyage, of courtiers who had accompanied the daughter of the Scottish King Alexander III to Norway where she was married to King Eric in 1281.

The king sits in Dumferling toune,
   Drinking the blude-reid wine:
'O whar will I get guid sailor,
   To sail this schip of mine?'

Up and spak an eldern knicht,   5
   Sat at the kings richt kne:
'Sir Patrick Spence is the best sailor
   That sails upon the se.'

The king has written a braid letter,
   And signd it wi his hand,   10
And sent it to Sir Patrick Spence,
   Was walking on the sand.

The first line that Sir Patrick red,
   A loud lauch lauched he;
The next line that Sir Patrick red,   15
   The teir blinded his ee.

'O wha is this has don this deid,
   This ill deid don to me,
To send me out this time o' the yeir,
   To sail upon the se!   20

'Mak hast, mak haste, my mirry men all,
   Our guid schip sails the morne:'
'O say na sae, my master deir,
   For I feir a deadlie storme.

'Late late yestreen I saw the new moone,   25
   Wi the auld moone in hir arme,
And I feir, I feir, my deir master,
   That we will cum to harme.'

O our Scots nobles wer richt laith
   To weet their cork-heild schoone;   30
Bot lang owre a' the play wer playd,
   Thair hats they swam aboone.

O lang, lang may their ladies sit,
   Wi thair fans into their hand,
Or eir they se Sir Patrick Spence   35
   Cum sailing to the land.

9 *braid*: informal
23 *na sae*: not so
30 *cork-heild schoone*: cork-
   heeled shoes
32 *aboone*: above

O lang, lang may the ladies stand,   38 *kems*: combs
  Wi thair gold kems in their hair,
Waiting for thair ain deir lords,
  For they'll se thame na mair.   40

Haf owre, haf owre to Aberdour,
  It's fiftie fadom deip,
And thair lies guid Sir Patrick Spence,
  Wi the Scots lords at his feit.

B. 'The Bonny Earl o' Murray'

Source: *The Oxford Book of Scottish Verse*, edited by J. MacQueen and T. Scott (Oxford: Clarendon Press, 1966), p. 296.

This very popular ballad refers to the assassination in 1592 of James Stewart, Earl of Moray, by his enemy George Gordon, Earl of Huntly. Huntly had been authorized by James VI to apprehend Moray because of rumours that he had been implicated in some of his cousin Bothwell's rebellious activities, but also, perhaps, because James was jealous of the queen's admiration for the handsome earl. Resentment over Moray's death ran so high that James had to remove the court to Glasgow.

Ye hielands and ye lawlands,   5 *braw callant*: brave young
  O whaur hae ye been?   man
They hae slain the Earl o Moray   12 *soondan*: sounding
And laid him on the green.   13 *wae*: woe
                                           14 *sae*: so

  He was a braw callant   5
    And he rid at the ring,[1]
  And the bonnie Earl o Moray,
    He micht hae been a king.

    O lang will his ladie look
      Owre the Castle Doune,[2]   10
    Ere she see the Earl o Moray
      Come soondan throu the toun.

Nou wae be tae ye, Huntly,
  And wharfore did ye sae?
I bad ye bring him wi ye,   15
  But forbad ye him to slay.

[1] The phrase 'riding at the ring' referred to a game in which riders attempted to carry off on the point of a lance a metal circle suspended from a post.
[2] Moray had been staying at his mother Lady Doune's castle of Donibristle in Fife when it was surrounded and set on fire by Huntly.

He was a braw callant,
    And he playd at the gluve,[3]
And the bonnie Earl o Moray,
    He wes the queen's true-love.   20

O lang will his ladie look, etc.

C. Alexander Scott, 'To luve unluvit'

Source: *Ballattis of Luve*, edited by John MacQueen (Edinburgh: Edinburgh University Press, 1970), pp. 104–5.

Alexander Scott (*c*.1515–83) seems to have been a professional musician as well as a poet, and to have had connections with the Scottish court. His poems of courtly love from the 1530s and 1540s skilfully blend humour, irony and passion, and he has been described as 'the finest Scottish love poet before Burns'.

1

To Luve unluvit it is ane pane,
for scho that is my soverane,
sum wantoun man so he hes set hir
that I can get no lufe agane
bot brekis my hairt and nocht the bettir.   5

2

Quhen that I went with that sweit may
to dance, to sing, to sport and pley,
and oft times in my armis plet hir,
I do now murne both nycht and day
and brekis my hart and nocht the bettir.   10

3

Quhair I wes wont to se hir go
rycht trimly passand to and fro,
with cumly smylis quhen that I met hir –
and now I leif in pane and wo
and brekis my hairt and nocht the bettir.   15

4

Quhattane ane glaikit fule am I
to slay my self with malancoly,
sen weill I ken I may nocht get hir,
or quhat suld be the caus and quhy
to brek my hairt and nocht the bettir.   20

1 *unluvit*: unloved
    ane: a
2 *scho*: she
6 *Quhen*: When
    sweit may: sweet maid
8 *plet*: entwined
11 *Quhair*: Where
12 *passand*: passing
16 *Quhattane ane*: What a
    glaikit: silly
18 *sen*: since
    weill I ken: well I know

---

[3] Possibly a reference to a race in which a glove set up on a post was the goal.

5

My hairt, sen thou may nocht hir pleis,
adew! – as gud lufe cumis as gais.
Go chus ane udir and foryet hir.
God gif him dolour and diseis
that brekis thair hairt and nocht the bettir.   25

D. Alexander Montgomerie, 'Hay, now the Day Dawis'

Source: *A Choice of Scottish Verse 1560–1600*, edited by R. D. S. Jack (London: Hodder
& Stoughton, 1978), pp. 96–8.

Alexander Montgomerie (*c*.1550–98) was the leading poet at the court of James VI.
He often set his lyrics to popular tunes of his time, and 'Hay, now the Day Dawis'
was in fact based on a folk song, adapted by Montgomerie and set to the tune 'Hey
tuttie taittie'.

1

Hay, now the day dawis,
The jolie cok crawis,
Now shroudis the shawis
    Throu Natur anone.
The thissell-cok cryis   5
On lovers wha lyis
Now skaillis the skyis,
    The nicht is neir gone.

2

The feilds ou'rflowis
With gowans that growis   10
Quhair lilies lyk low-is
    Als rid as the rone.
The turtill that trew is
With nots that renewis
Hir pairtie persewis,   15
    The night is neir gone.

3

Now hairtis with hyndis
Conforme to thair kyndis
Hie tursis their tyndis
    On grund whair they grone.   20
Now hurchonis with hairis
Ay passis in pairis,
Quhilk deuly declaris,
    The night is neir gone.

3 *shawis*: groves
4 *anone*: at once
5 *thissell-cok*: male mistle-
    thrush
7 *skaillis*: clears
11 *low-is*: flames
12 *rone*: rowan berry
15 *pairtie*: mate
19 *tursis*: tosses
    tyndis: antlers
21 *hurchonis*: hedgehogs

4

The sesone excellis   25
Thrugh sweetnes that smellis
Now Cupid compellis
    Our hairtis echone
On Venus wha waikis
To muse on our maikis   30
Syn sing for thair saikis,
    The night is neir gone.

5

All curageous knichtis
Aganis the day dichtis
The breist plate that bright is   35
    To feght with thair fone.
The stoned steed stampis
Throu curage and crampis
Syn on the land lampis,
    The night is neir gone.   40

6

The freikis on feildis
That wight wapins weildis
With shyning bright shieldis
    At Titan in trone,
Stiff speiris in reistis   45
Ouer cursoris cristis
Ar brok on thair breistis,
    The night is neir gone.

7

So hard ar their hittis
Some sweyis, some sittis   50
And some perforce flittis
    On grund whill they grone.
Syn groomis that gay is
On blonkis that brayis
With swordis assayis,   55
    The night is neir gone.

28 *echone*: each one
30 *maikis*: mates
34 *dichtis*: prepare
38 *crampis*: swaggers
39 *lampis*: strides along
41 *freikis*: soldiers
42 *wapins*: weapons
45 *reistis*: rests (for a lance or spear)
46 *cursoris*: war horses
    cristis: plumes
51 *flittis*: fall
54 *blonkis*: steeds

E. Mark Alexander Boyd, 'Fra banc to banc'

Source: *A Choice of Scottish Verse 1560–1600*, edited by R. D. S. Jack (London: Hodder & Stoughton, 1978), p. 158.

Mark Alexander Boyd (1563–1601) spent much of his life on the Continent, and is best known as a Latin scholar. 'Fra banc to banc' is one of the most famous of all Scottish sonnets.

Fra banc to banc, fra wod to wod, I rin
Ourhailit with my feble fantasie,
Lyc til a leif that fallis from a trie
Or til a reid ourblawin with the wind.
Twa gods gyds me; the ane of tham is blind, 5
Ye, and a bairn brocht up in vanitie;
The nixt a wyf ingenrit of the se
And lichter nor a dauphin with hir fin.
Unhappie is the man for evirmaire
That teils the sand and sawis in the aire; 10
Bot twyse unhappier is he, I lairn,
That feidis in his hairt a mad desyre
And follows on a woman throw the fyre,
Led be a blind and teichit be a bairn.

1 *Fra*: From
rin: run
2 *Ourhailit*: Overcome
5 *Twa gods*: i.e. Cupid and
Venus (who was said to have
sprung from the foam of the
sea)
6 *bairn*: child
7 *wyf*: waif
ingenrit: engendered
8 *lichter*: lighter
dauphin: dolphin
10 *teils*: tills
sawis: saws
12 *feidis*: feeds
14 *teichit*: taught

4 Sir Philip Sidney, *Astrophil and Stella* (c. 1582)

Source: *The Poems of Sir Philip Sidney*, edited by William A. Ringler, Jr. (Oxford: Clarendon Press, 1962). Spelling has been modernized by W. R. Owens.

Sir Philip Sidney (1554–86) was born at Penshurst, Kent, the eldest son of Sir Henry Sidney (later Lord Deputy of Ireland) and Lady Mary Sidney (sister of the Earls of Leicester and Warwick). He was educated at Shrewsbury School and at Christ Church, Oxford; he left in 1571 without taking a degree. For the next few years he travelled widely throughout Europe, assisting on diplomatic missions and meeting leading Protestant statesmen and scholars. He returned to England in 1575, received a minor court office, and spent some months in Ireland with his father. In 1577 he returned to Europe to explore the possibility of some form of Protestant alliance, but this came to nothing and Sidney lost the favour of Elizabeth. He retired for long periods to Wilton in Wiltshire, the home of his sister Mary, Countess of Pembroke, and it was here that he composed his long prose romance, the *Arcadia*. He was a member of the 'Areopagus', a circle of poets interested in the reform of English literature, and including Sidney's friends Fulke Greville, Edward Dyer and Edmund Spenser.

In 1581 Sidney became a Member of Parliament, and was partially reconciled with the Queen, though she disapproved of his marriage in 1583 to Frances, daughter of Sir Francis Walsingham. He was appointed governor of Flushing in 1584 and took part in military campaigns against the Spanish. He met his death from a wound sustained at the Battle of Zutphen in 1586. His father-in-law paid for a grand funeral in old St Paul's Cathedral, and numerous elegies mourned his passing.

The sequence of 108 sonnets, with eleven lyrics, making up *Astrophil and Stella* was probably completed in 1582. Manuscript copies circulated among friends, but the work was not published until after Sidney's death. Two unauthorized editions appeared in 1591, and in 1598 the Countess of Pembroke supervised the publication of a collected edition of her brother's works, including *Astrophil and Stella*.

Much influenced by Petrarch's famous sequence of love poems to the woman he called Laura, *Astrophil and Stella* is the poetic record of the love of a young courtier for a married woman. There are some autobiographical elements in the sequence: Sidney had been briefly engaged to a young woman called Penelope Devereux, the daughter of the Earl of Essex. She later married Lord Rich, and there are several puns on her married name. The central figure, however, is Astrophil, and the poems are addressed more to the reader than to the lady.

I

Loving in truth, and fain in verse my love to show,
That the dear she might take some pleasure of my pain:
Pleasure might cause her read, reading might make her know,
Knowledge might pity win, and pity grace obtain,
    I sought fit words to paint the blackest face of woe,
Studying inventions fine,[1] her wits to entertain:
Oft turning others' leaves, to see if thence would flow
Some fresh and fruitful showers upon my sun-burn'd brain.[2]
    But words came halting forth, wanting Invention's stay,
Invention, Nature's child, fled step-dame Study's blows,
And others' feet[3] still seem'd but strangers in my way.
Thus great with child to speak, and helpless in my throes,
    Biting my truand pen, beating myself for spite,
    'Fool,' said my Muse to me, 'look in thy heart[4] and write.'

still: always; *truand*: idle

5

It is most true, that eyes are form'd to serve
The inward light: and that the heavenly part
Ought to be king, from whose rules who do swerve,
Rebels to Nature, strive for their own smart.
    It is most true, what we call Cupid's dart,
An image is, which for ourselves we carve;
And, fools, adore in temple of our heart,
Till that good god make church and churchman starve.
    True, that true Beauty Virtue is indeed,
Whereof this beauty can be but a shade,
Which elements with mortal mixture breed:[5]
True, that on earth we are but pilgrims made,

---

[1] Inventions fine is a reference to the first of the three processes of literary composition laid down by Renaissance theorists: *inventio* (discovery of ideas and subject), *dispositio* (structure) and *elocutio* (style).

[2] Sun-burn'd brain: the sun may be both Stella's beauty and the writings of the ancients.

[3] Others' feet: the writings of others, with a play on metrical feet.

[4] Look in thy heart: i.e. at Stella's image there, which will provide sufficient inspiration.

[5] The Platonic doctrine that the pure 'form' or 'idea' of the Beautiful is also the Good; but physical beauty – a mixture of the four elements in the human body – is merely a shadow ('shade') of the Beautiful.

And should in soul up to our country move:
True, and yet true that I must Stella love.

inward light: reason

9

Queen Virtue's court, which some call Stella's face,
    Prepar'd by Nature's chiefest furniture,
    Hath his front built of alabaster pure;
Gold is the covering of that stately place.
The door by which sometimes comes forth her grace,
    Red porphyr is, which lock of pearl makes sure:
    Whose porches rich (which name of cheeks endure)
Marble mixt red and white do interlace.
    The windows now through which this heav'nly guest
Looks over the world, and can find nothing such,
Which dare claim from those lights the name of best,
Of touch[6] they are that without touch doth touch,
    Which Cupid's self from Beauty's mine did draw:
    Of touch they are, and poor I am their straw.

chiefest furniture: best furnishing; *front*: also, forehead

12

Cupid, because thou shin'st in Stella's eyes,
    That from her locks, thy day-nets,[7] none scapes free,
    That those lips swell, so full of thee they be,
That her sweet breath makes oft thy flames to rise,
That in her breast thy pap well sugared lies,
    That her grace gracious makes thy wrongs, that she
    What words soe'er she speaks persuades for thee,
That her clear voice lifts thy fame to the skies.
    Thou countest Stella thine, like those whose powers
Having got up a breach by fighting well,
Cry, 'Victory, this fair day all is ours.'
O no, her heart is such a citadel,
    So fortified with wit, stor'd with disdain,
    That to win it, is all the skill and pain.

That: Because (also ll. 3–6 and 8); *powers*: forces

---

[6] The touchstone: (1) a smooth, fine-grained black quartz used for testing the quality of gold and silver alloys by rubbing them on it, and (2) associated with black lignite or jet, which attracts light materials like straw when electrified by rubbing.

[7] Nets used to capture larks, to which they were lured by small pieces of mirror.

15

You that do search for every purling spring,
    Which from the ribs of old Parnassus flows,
    And every flower, not sweet perhaps, which grows
Near thereabout, into your poesy wring;
You that do dictionary's method[8] bring
    Into your rhymes, running in rattling rows;
    You that poor Petrarch's long deceasèd woes,
With new-born sighs and denizen'd wit do sing:
    You take wrong ways, those far-fet helps be such,
    As do bewray a want of inward touch,
And sure at length stol'n goods do come to light;
    But if (both for your love and skill) your name
    You seek to nurse at fullest breasts of Fame,
Stella behold, and then begin to indite.

purling: flowing with whirling motion; *Parnassus*: mountain in Greece, sacred to the Muses;
flower: also, rhetorical figure; *poesy wring*: twist into your posy, work into your poem; *denizen'd*:
naturalized into English; *far-fet*: far-fetched; *bewray*: betray; *inward touch*: true imagination;
indite: compose

20

Fly, fly, my friends, I have my death wound; fly,
See there that boy, that murth'ring boy I say,
Who like a thief, hid in dark bush doth lie,
Till bloody bullet get him wrongful prey.
    So tyrant he no fitter place could spy,
Nor so fair level in so secret stay,
As that sweet black which veils the heav'nly eye:
There himself with his shot he close doth lay.
    Poor passenger, pass now thereby I did,
And stayed pleas'd with the prospect of the place,
While that black hue from me the bad guest hid:
But straight I saw motions of lightning grace,
    And then descried the glist'ring of his dart:
    But ere I could fly thence, it pierc'd my heart.

level: aim; *stay*: stopping place; *close*: secretly; *passenger*: passer-by

27

Because I oft in dark abstracted guise,
    Seem most alone in greatest company,
    With dearth of words, or answers quite awry,
To them that would make speech of speech arise,
They deem, and of their doom the rumour flies,

---

[8] Dictionary's method: heavy alliteration (as in the following line).

That poison foul of bubbling pride doth lie
So in my swelling breast that only I[9]
Fawn on myself, and others do despise:
    Yet pride I think doth not my soul possess,
Which looks too oft in his unflatt'ring glass:
But one worse fault, ambition, I confess,
That makes me oft my best friends overpass,
    Unseen, unheard, while thought to highest place
Bends all his powers, even unto Stella's grace.

29

Like some weak lords, neighbour'd by mighty kings,
    To keep themselves and their chief cities free,
    Do eas'ly yield, that all their coasts may be
Ready to store their camps of needful things:
So Stella's heart, finding what power Love brings,
    To keep itself in life and liberty,
    Doth willing grant, that in the frontiers he
Use all to help his other conquerings:
And thus her heart escapes, but thus her eyes
    Serve him with shot, her lips his heralds are:
    Her breasts his tents, legs his triumphal car:
Her flesh his food, her skin his armour brave,
And I, but for because my prospect lies
Upon that coast, am giv'n up for a slave.

their: weak lords'; *their*: mighty kings' (l.4); *prospect*: view

31

With how sad steps, O moon, thou climb'st the skies,
    How silently, and with how wan a face,
    What, may it be that even in heav'nly place
That busy archer his sharp arrows tries?
Sure, if that long with love acquainted eyes
    Can judge of love, thou feel'st a lover's case;
    I read it in thy looks, thy languisht grace,
To me that feel the like, thy state descries.
    Then ev'n of fellowship, O moon, tell me
Is constant love deem'd there but want of wit?
Are beauties there as proud as here they be?
Do they above love to be lov'd, and yet
    Those lovers scorn whom that love doth possess?
Do they call Virtue there ungratefulness?[10]

---

[9] Only I: I do nothing except.
[10] The meaning may be either (1) do they, above, call (the lady's) ungratefulness a virtue? or (2) is the lover's Virtue considered 'ungrateful', i.e. unpleasant, above?

41

Having this day my horse, my hand, my lance
   Guided so well, that I obtain'd the prize,
   Both by the judgement of the English eyes,
And of some sent from that sweet enemy France;
Horsemen my skill in horsemanship advance,
    Town-folks my strength; a daintier judge applies
    His praise to sleight, which from good use doth rise;
Some lucky wits impute it but to chance;
    Others, because of both sides I do take
My blood from them, who did excel in this,[11]
Think nature me a man of arms did make.
How far they shoot awry! the true cause is,
    Stella look'd on, and from her heavenly face
    Sent forth the beams, which made so fair my race.

advance: praise; *daintier*: more fastidious; *sleight*: dexterity; *use*: practice; *race*: a course in a tournament

44

My words I know do well set forth my mind,
   My mind bemoans his sense of inward smart;
   Such smart may pity claim of any heart,
Her heart, sweet heart, is of no tiger's kind:
And yet she hears, yet I no pity find;
    But more I cry, less grace she doth impart,
    Alas, what cause is there so overthwart,
That nobleness itself makes thus unkind?
    I much do guess, yet find no truth save this,
That when the breath of my complaints doth touch
Those dainty doors unto the court of bliss,
The heav'nly nature of that place is such,
    That once come there, the sobs of mine annoys
    Are metamorphos'd straight to tunes of joys.

overthwart: perverse, contrary; *unkind*: also, unnatural; *annoys*: vexations

45

Stella oft sees the very face of woe
   Painted in my beclouded stormy face:
   But cannot skill to pity my disgrace,
Not though thereof the cause herself she know:
Yet hearing late a fable, which did show

---

[11] Both sides of his family (Sidney's father, grandfather and maternal uncles had frequently taken part in tournaments).

> Of lovers never known, a grievous case,
>   Pity thereof gat in her breast such place
> That, from that sea deriv'd, tears' spring did flow.
>   Alas, if Fancy drawn by imag'd things,
> Though false, yet with free scope more grace doth breed
> Than servant's wrack, where new doubts honour brings;[12]
> Then think my dear, that you in me do read
>   Of lover's ruin some sad tragedy:
>   I am not I, pity the tale of me.

cannot skill: is not able

47

> What, have I thus betrayed my liberty?
>   Can those black beams such burning marks engrave
>   In my free side? or am I born a slave,
> Whose neck becomes such yoke of tyranny?
> Or want I sense to feel my misery?
>   Or sprite, disdain of such disdain to have?
>   Who for long faith, tho' daily help I crave,
> May get no alms but scorn of beggary.
>   Virtue awake, Beauty but beauty is,
> I may, I must, I can, I will, I do
> Leave following that, which it is gain to miss.
> Let her go. Soft, but here she comes. Go to,
>   Unkind, I love you not: O me, that eye
>   Doth make my heart give to my tongue the lie.

black beams: Stella's glance; *burning marks*: brands denoting slavery; *becomes*: suits; *scorn of*: scorn for

52

> A strife is grown between Virtue and Love,
>   While each pretends that Stella must be his:
>   Her eyes, her lips, her all, saith Love do this,
> Since they do wear his badge, most firmly prove.
> But Virtue thus that title doth disprove,
>   That Stella (O dear name) that Stella is
>   That virtuous soul, sure heir of heav'nly bliss:
> Not this fair outside, which our hearts doth move.
>   And therefore, though her beauty and her grace
> Be Love's indeed, in Stella's self he may
> By no pretence claim any manner place.
> Well Love, since this demur[13] our suit doth stay,

[12] His honourable behaviour (which results in 'servant's wrack') only produces new doubts or fears in her.

[13] Demur: a legal plea which admits the facts as stated by the opponent but denies his right to relief, thus delaying the action until this point is determined.

Let Virtue have that Stella's self; yet thus,
That Virtue but that body grant to us.

pretends: brings a legal action; *his badge*: Love's livery; *That*: i.e. claiming that; *suit*: (1) legal; (2) courtship of Stella

54

Because I breathe not love to every one,
    Nor do not use set colours for to wear,
    Nor nourish special locks of vowèd hair,
Nor give each speech a full point of a groan,
The courtly nymphs, acquainted with the moan
    Of them, who in their lips Love's standard bear;
    'What he?' say they of me, 'now I dare swear,
He cannot love: no, no, let him alone.'
    And think so still, so Stella know my mind,
Profess in deed I do not Cupid's art;
But you fair maids, at length this true shall find,
That his right badge is but worn in the heart:
    Dumb swans, no chatt'ring pies, do lovers prove,
    They love indeed, who quake to say they love.

full point: full stop; *And*: i.e. let them; *pies*: magpies

59

Dear, why make you more of a dog than me?
    If he do love, I burn, I burn in love:
    If he wait well, I never thence would move:
If he be fair, yet but a dog can be.
Little he is, so little worth is he;
    He barks, my songs thine own voice oft doth prove:
    Bidd'n, perhaps he fetcheth thee a glove,
But I unbid, fetch even my soul to thee.
    Yet while I languish, him that bosom clips,
That lap doth lap, nay lets in spite of spite,
This sour-breath'd mate taste of those sug'red lips.
Alas, if you grant only such delight
    To witless things, then Love, I hope (since wit
    Becomes a clog) will soon ease me of it.

prove: try; *clips*: embraces; *clog*: heavy wooden fetter

63

O grammar rules, O now your virtues show;
    So children still read you with awful eyes,
    As my young dove may in your precepts wise
Her grant to me, by her own virtue know.
For late with heart most high, with eyes most low,

I crav'd the thing which ever she denies:
She lightning Love, displaying Venus' skies,
Least once should not be heard, twice said, No, No.
Sing then my Muse, now *Io Pean* sing,
Heav'ns envy not at my high triumphing:
But grammar's force with sweet success confirm:
For grammar says (O this dear Stella weigh,)
For grammar says (to grammar who says nay)
That in one speech two negatives affirm.

awful: respectful; *Io Pean*: hymn of praise to Apollo; *success*: also, result

68

Stella, the only planet of my light,
Light of my life, and life of my desire,
Chief good, whereto my hope doth only aspire,
World of my wealth, and heav'n of my delight.
Why dost thou spend the treasures of thy sprite,
With voice more fit to wed Amphion's lyre,[14]
Seeking to quench in me the noble fire,
Fed by thy worth, and kindled by thy sight?
And all in vain, for while thy breath most sweet,
With choicest words, thy words with reasons rare,
Thy reasons firmly set on Virtue's feet,
Labour to kill in me this killing care:
O think I then, what paradise of joy
It is, so fair a Virtue to enjoy.

planet of my light: sun that gives me light; *sprite*: spirit

71

Who will in fairest book of Nature know,
How Virtue may best lodg'd in beauty be,
Let him but learn of Love to read in thee,
Stella, those fair lines, which true goodness show.
There shall he find all vices' overthrow,
Not by rude force, but sweetest sovereignty
Of reason, from whose light those night-birds fly;
That inward sun in thine eyes shineth so.
And not content to be perfection's heir
Thyself, dost strive all minds that way to move,
Who mark in thee what is in thee most fair.
So while thy beauty draws the heart to love,
As fast thy Virtue bends that love to good:
'But ah,' Desire still cries, 'give me some food.'

night-birds: vices

[14] The sound of Amphion's lyre caused the stones of the walls of Thebes to rebuild themselves.

76

She comes, and straight therewith her shining twins do move
    Their rays to me, who in her tedious absence lay
    Benighted in cold woe, but now appears my day,
The only light of joy, the only warmth of love.
She comes with light and warmth, which like Aurora prove
    Of gentle force, so that mine eyes dare gladly play
    With such a rosy morn, whose beams most freshly gay
Scorch not, but only do dark chilling sprites remove.
    But lo, while I do speak, it groweth noon with me,
Her flamy glist'ring lights increase with time and place;
Her heart cries 'ah', it burns, mine eyes now dazzled be:
No wind, no shade can cool, what help then in my case,
    But with short breath, long looks, stay'd feet and walking head,
    Pray that my sun go down with meeker beams to bed.

Aurora: Roman goddess of the dawn; *walking*: agitated

87

When I was forc'd from Stella ever dear,
Stella food of my thoughts, heart of my heart,
Stella whose eyes make all my tempests clear,
By iron laws of duty to depart:
    Alas I found, that she with me did smart,
I saw that tears did in her eyes appear;
I saw that sighs her sweetest lips did part,
And her sad words my sadded sense did hear.
    For me, I wept to see pearls scattered so,
    I sigh'd her sighs, and wailèd for her woe,
Yet swam in joy, such love in her was seen.
    Thus while th'effect most bitter was to me,
    And nothing than the cause more sweet could be,
I had been vext, if vext I had not been.

sadded: saddened

89

Now that of absence the most irksome night,
    With darkest shade doth overcome my day;
    Since Stella's eyes, wont to give me my day,
Leaving my hemisphere, leave me in night,
Each day seems long, and longs for long-stay'd night,
    The night as tedious, woos th'approach of day;
    Tired with the dusty toils of busy day,
Languisht with horrors of the silent night;
Suffering the evils both of the day and night,
    While no night is more dark than is my day,

Nor no day hath less quiet than my night:
  With such bad mixture of my night and day,
That living thus in blackest winter night,
  I feel the flames of hottest summer day.

90

Stella think not that I by verse seek fame,
  Who seek, who hope, who love, who live but thee;
  Thine eyes my pride, thy lips my history:
If thou praise not, all other praise is shame.
Nor so ambitious am I, as to frame
  A nest for my young praise in laurel tree:[15]
  In truth I swear, I wish not there should be
Graved in mine epitaph a poet's name:
  Ne if I would, could I just title make,
That any laud to me thereof should grow,
Without my plumes from others' wings I take.
  For nothing from my wit or will doth flow,
  Since all my words thy beauty doth indite,
  And love doth hold my hand, and makes me write.

Graved: (1) Engraved, (2) Buried; *Ne*: Nor; *Without*: Unless; *indite*: dictate

93

O fate, O fault, O curse, child of my bliss,
  What sobs can give words grace my grief to show?
  What ink is black enough to paint my woe?
Through me, wretch me, even Stella vexèd is.
Yet truth (if caitiff's breath might call thee) this
  Witness with me, that my foul stumbling so,
  From carelessness did in no manner grow,
But wit confus'd with too much care did miss.
  And do I then myself this vain 'scuse give?
I have (live I and know this) harmèd thee,
Tho' worlds quite me, shall I myself forgive?
Only with pains my pains thus easèd be,
  That all thy hurts in my heart's wrack I read;
  I cry thy sighs; my dear, thy tears I bleed.

miss: fail to understand; *quite*: acquit

100

O tears, no tears, but rain from beauty's skies,
  Making those lilies and those roses grow,
  Which aye most fair, now more than most fair show,
While graceful pity beauty beautifies.

[15] A laurel wreath was the traditional reward of the poet.

O honey'd sighs, which from that breast do rise,
  Whose pants do make unspilling cream to flow,
  Wing'd with whose breath, so pleasing Zephyrs blow,
As can refresh the hell where my soul fries.
  O plaints conserv'd in such a sug'red phrase,
  That eloquence itself envies your praise,
While sobb'd out words a perfect music give.
  Such tears, sighs, plaints, no sorrow is, but joy:
  Or if such heavenly signs must prove annoy,
All mirth farewell, let me in sorrow live.

prove annoy: signify sorrow

106

O absent presence Stella is not here;
  False flattering hope, that with so fair a face,
  Bare me in hand, that in this orphan place,
Stella, I say my Stella, should appear.
What say'st thou now, where is that dainty cheer
  Thou told'st mine eyes should help their famisht case?
  But thou art gone, now that self felt disgrace
Doth make me most to wish thy comfort near.
  But here I do store of fair ladies meet,
  Who may with charm of conversation sweet,
Make in my heavy mould new thoughts to grow:
  Sure they prevail as much with me, as he
  That bade his friend, but then new maim'd, to be
Merry with him, and not think of his woe.

Bare me in hand: Deluded me; *mould*: body

108

When sorrow (using mine own fire's might)
  Melts down his lead into my boiling breast,
  Through that dark furnace to my heart oppresst,
There shines a joy from thee my only light;
But soon as thought of thee breeds my delight,
  And my young soul flutters to thee his nest,
  Most rude despair my daily unbidden guest,
Clips straight my wings, straight wraps me in his night,
  And makes me then bow down my head, and say,
Ah what doth Phoebus' gold[16] that wretch avail,
Whom iron doors do keep from use of day?
So strangely (alas) thy works in me prevail,
  That in my woes for thee thou art my joy,
  And in my joys for thee my only annoy.

annoy: disturbance of mind

[16] Sunshine: Phoebus was one of Apollo's names as the Sun-god.

5 Sir Philip Sidney, *A Defence of Poetry* (c. 1582)

Source: *Miscellaneous Prose of Sir Philip Sidney*, edited by Katherine Duncan-Jones and Jan van Dorsten (Oxford: Clarendon Press, 1973), pp. 73–121 abridged.

Sidney's *Defence of Poetry* cannot be dated with certainty, but it was probably composed in the early 1580s, a period of political inactivity which Sidney spent at Wilton. The occasion may have been the publication in 1579 of Stephen Gosson's *The School of Abuse*, a denunciation of poets and the public stage. Gosson, who had been converted by the arguments of Puritans, dedicated his work to Sidney, but, according to Edmund Spenser, it was 'received with scorn'.

There are no explicit references to Gosson, however, and Sidney clearly planned his work as an independent treatise. It is carefully organized within the rules of a classical oration, though the prose style ranges from elegant, witty irony and understatement to impassioned eloquence. Sidney's subject is the nature and scope of poetry (by which he means literature in general: he uses the word 'poesy' to denote verse), the responsibilities of poets, and the state of contemporary English poetry. He argues that poetry, because inspired, has a unique ability to inculcate virtue; the poet, as a creator of fictions, avoids both the generalities of the philosopher and the particularities of the historian.

The *Defence* was first published, after Sidney's death, in 1595. It was immediately recognized as a most distinguished work of literary theory and criticism, and was frequently reprinted.

Sidney opens the work in a lighthearted, gentlemanly, conversational tone, explaining, with seeming diffidence, that his purpose is to make 'a pitiful defence of poor poetry, which from almost the highest estimation of learning is fallen to be the laughing-stock of children'. He begins by reminding his reader of the antiquity of poetry:

And first, truly, to all them that, professing learning, inveigh against poetry may justly be objected that they go very near to ungratefulness, to seek to deface that which, in the noblest nations and languages that are known, hath been the first light-giver to ignorance, and first nurse, whose milk by little and little enabled them to feed afterwards of tougher knowledges. And will they now play the hedgehog that, being received into the den, drave out his host? Or rather the vipers, that with their birth kill their parents?

Let learned Greece in any of his manifold sciences be able to show me one book before Musaeus, Homer, and Hesiod,[1] all three nothing else but poets. Nay, let any history be brought that can say any writers were there before them, if they were not men of the same skill, as Orpheus, Linus,[2] and some other are named, who, having been the first of that country that made pens deliverers of their knowledge to the posterity, may justly challenge to be called their fathers in learning: for not only in time they had this priority

---

[1] Musaeus, legendary pre-Homeric poet; Homer, supposed author of the *Iliad* and *Odyssey*; Hesiod (eighth century BC), Greek didactic poet, author of *Works and Days*.

[2] Orpheus, legendary pre-Homeric poet and singer who by the time of the Renaissance had become a symbol of the inspired poet; Linus, supposed teacher of Orpheus.

(although in itself antiquity be venerable) but went before them, as causes to draw with their charming[3] sweetness the wild untamed wits to an admiration of knowledge. So, as Amphion was said to move stones with his poetry to build Thebes, and Orpheus to be listened to by beasts – indeed stony and beastly people – so among the Romans were Livius Andronicus and Ennius.[4] So in the Italian language the first that made it aspire to be a treasure-house of science were the poets Dante, Boccaccio, and Petrarch.[5] So in our English were Gower and Chaucer,[6] after whom, encouraged and delighted with their excellent fore-going, others have followed, to beautify our mother tongue, as well in the same kind as in other arts.

This did so notably show itself, that the philosophers of Greece durst not a long time appear to the world but under the masks of poets ... And truly even Plato whosoever well considereth shall find that in the body of his work, though the inside and strength were philosophy, the skin, as it were, and beauty depended most of poetry: for all standeth upon dialogues, wherein he feigneth many honest burgesses of Athens to speak of such matters, that, if they had been set on the rack, they would never have confessed them, besides his poetical describing the circumstances of their meetings, as the well ordering of a banquet, the delicacy of a walk,[7] with interlacing mere tales, as Gyges' ring[8] and others, which who knoweth not to be flowers of poetry did never walk into Apollo's garden.

And even historiographers (although their lips sound of things done, and verity be written in their foreheads) have been glad to borrow both fashion and, perchance, weight of the poets. So Herodotus entitled his History by the name of the nine Muses;[9] and both he and all the rest that followed him either stole or usurped of poetry their passionate describing of passions, the many particularities of battles, which no man could affirm; or, if that be denied me, long orations put in the mouths of great kings and captains, which it is certain they never pronounced.

So that truly neither philosopher nor historiographer could at the first have entered into the gates of popular judgements, if they had not taken a great passport of poetry, which in all nations at this day where learning

[3] Sung, incantatory.

[4] Amphion, son of Zeus and Antiope, whose playing on his lyre was said to have moved the stones of the walls of Thebes to rebuild themselves; the music of Orpheus held the wild beasts spellbound; Livius Andronicus (third century BC), the earliest Latin poet and playwright; Quintus Ennius (239–169 BC), Latin epic poet.

[5] Dante Alighieri (1265–1321), whose masterpiece the *Divina Commedia* was composed in Italian; Giovanni Boccaccio (1313–75), humanist scholar best known for his collection of tales, the *Decameron*; Petrarch: Francesco Petrarca (1304–74), poet and humanist scholar.

[6] John Gower (?1330–1408), poet who wrote in French and Latin as well as English; Geoffrey Chaucer (?1345–1400), author of the *Canterbury Tales* and other poems.

[7] Plato's *Symposium* and *Phaedrus*, works in dialogue form, were set at a banquet and on a walk, respectively.

[8] In the *Republic*, Plato relates the story of the shepherd Gyges who, having found a magic ring in the Underworld, uses it to become King of Lydia.

[9] Herodotus (c.484–c.425 BC), Greek historian whose great *History* was divided into nine books, each bearing the name of a Muse, by later Alexandrian editors.

flourisheth not, is plain to be seen; in all which they have some feeling of poetry.

In Turkey, besides their law-giving divines, they have no other writers but poets. In our neighbour country Ireland, where truly learning goeth very bare, yet are their poets held in a devout reverence. Even among the most barbarous and simple Indians where no writing is, yet have they their poets who make and sing songs, which they call *areytos*, both of their ancestors' deeds and praises of their gods: a sufficient probability that, if ever learning come among them, it must be by having their hard dull wits softened and sharpened with the sweet delights of poetry – for until they find a pleasure in the exercises of the mind, great promises of much knowledge will little persuade them that know not the fruits of knowledge. In Wales, the true remnant of the ancient Britons, as there are good authorities to show the long time they had poets, which they called bards, so through all the conquests of Romans, Saxons, Danes, and Normans, some of whom did seek to ruin all memory of learning from among them, yet do their poets even to this day last; so as it is not more notable in soon beginning than in long continuing ...

[Sidney reminds his reader that the Roman word for a poet was *vates*, meaning 'a diviner, foreseer or prophet', while the Greek word comes from the verb 'to make', and so in English a poet is called a maker. The glory of this title is apparent when one compares the work of the poet with that of, say, astronomers, physicians or scientists who are restricted to the study of nature as it is.]

Only the poet, disdaining to be tied to any such subjection, lifted up with the vigour of his own invention, doth grow in effect another nature, in making things either better than nature bringeth forth, or, quite anew, forms such as never were in nature, as the Heroes, Demigods, Cyclops, Chimeras, Furies, and such like: so as he goeth hand in hand with nature, not enclosed within the narrow warrant of her gifts, but freely ranging only within the zodiac of his own wit. Nature never set forth the earth in so rich tapestry as divers poets have done; neither with so pleasant rivers, fruitful trees, sweet-smelling flowers, nor whatsoever else may make the too much loved earth more lovely. Her world is brazen, the poets only deliver a golden.[10]

But let those things alone, and go to man – for whom as the other things are, so it seemeth in him her uttermost cunning is employed – and know whether she have brought forth so true a lover as Theagenes, so constant a friend as Pylades, so valiant a man as Orlando, so right a prince as Xenophon's Cyrus, so excellent a man every way as Virgil's Aeneas.[11] Neither let this be jestingly conceived, because the works of the one be

[10] A reference to the literary tradition of the declining four ages of man: from golden down through silver, brass and iron, in which we now live.

[11] Theagenes, lover of Charicleia in the Greek romance *Aethiopica* by Heliodorus (third century AD); Pylades, in Greek legend, devoted friend of Orestes; Orlando, the French Roland, hero of Ariosto's epic poem *Orlando Furioso* (1516); Cyrus, the exemplary hero of Xenophon's political treatise, the *Cyropaedia* (early fourth century BC); Aeneas, founder of Rome in Virgil's *Aeneid*.

essential,[12] the other[13] in imitation or fiction; for any understanding knoweth the skill of each artificer standeth in that *idea* or fore-conceit of the work, and not in the work itself.[14] And that the poet hath that *idea* is manifest, by delivering them forth in such excellency as he had imagined them. Which delivering forth also is not wholly imaginative,[15] as we are wont to say by them that build castles in the air; but so far substantially it worketh, not only to make a Cyrus, which had been but a particular excellency as nature might have done, but to bestow a Cyrus upon the world to make many Cyruses, if they will learn aright why and how that maker made him.

Neither let it be deemed too saucy a comparison to balance the highest point of man's wit with the efficacy of nature; but rather give right honour to the heavenly Maker of that maker,[16] who having made man to His own likeness, set him beyond and over all the works of that second nature;[17] which in nothing he[18] showeth so much as in poetry, when with the force of a divine breath[19] he bringeth things forth surpassing her[20] doings – with no small arguments to the credulous of that first accursed fall of Adam, since our erected wit maketh us know what perfection is, and yet our infected will keepeth us from reaching unto it. But these arguments will by few be understood, and by fewer granted. This much (I hope) will be given me, that the Greeks with some probability of reason gave him the name above all names of learning.

[Sidney proceeds to define poetry as 'an art of imitation ... a representing, counterfeiting, or figuring forth ... with this end, to teach and delight'. Its two main rivals for the title of the 'mistress-knowledge' are philosophy and history, but Sidney finds the former too abstract and the latter too bound by particulars.]

The philosopher, therefore, and the historian are they which would win the goal, the one by precept, the other by example. But both, not having both, do both halt.[21] For the philosopher, setting down with thorny arguments the bare rule, is so hard of utterance and so misty to be conceived, that one that hath no other guide but him shall wade in him till he be old before he shall find sufficient cause to be honest. For his knowledge standeth so upon the abstract and general, that happy is that man who may understand him, and more happy that can apply what he doth understand. On the other side, the historian, wanting[22] the precept, is so tied, not to what should be but to what

---

[12] Real, substantial.

[13] *The one ... the other*: i.e. nature ... the poet.

[14] The idea or 'fore-conceit' which is embodied in a work of fiction pre-exists it and has substance.

[15] Fanciful.

[16] Man.

[17] Physical nature.

[18] Man.

[19] Inspiration.

[20] Nature's.

[21] Because neither philosophers nor historians have both precept and example, they both stumble.

[22] Lacking.

is, to the particular truth of things and not to the general reason of things, that his example draweth no necessary consequence, and therefore a less fruitful doctrine.

Now doth the peerless poet perform both: for whatsoever the philosopher saith should be done, he giveth a perfect picture of it in someone by whom he presupposeth it was done, so as he coupleth the general notion with the particular example. A perfect picture I say, for he yieldeth to the powers of the mind an image of that whereof the philosopher bestoweth but a wordish description, which doth neither strike, pierce, nor possess the sight of the soul so much as that other doth. For as in outward things, to a man that had never seen an elephant or a rhinoceros, who[23] should tell him most exquisitely all their shapes, colour, bigness, and particular marks, or of a gorgeous palace the architecture, with declaring the full beauties, might well make the hearer able to repeat, as it were by rote, all he had heard, yet should never satisfy his inward conceit with being witness to itself of a true lively knowledge; but the same man, as soon as he might see those beasts well painted, or the house well in model, should straightways grow, without need of any description, to a judicial comprehending of them: so no doubt the philosopher with his learned definitions – be it of virtue, vices, matters of public policy or private government – replenisheth the memory with many infallible grounds of wisdom, which, notwithstanding, lie dark before the imaginative and judging power, if they be not illuminated or figured forth by the speaking picture of poesy.

[Sidney goes on to develop and illustrate the argument that poetry teaches more effectively than either philosophy or history.]

Now therein of all sciences (I speak still of human, and according to the human conceit) is our poet the monarch. For he doth not only show the way, but giveth so sweet a prospect into the way, as will entice any man to enter into it. Nay, he doth, as if your journey should lie through a fair vineyard, at the first give you a cluster of grapes, that full of that taste, you may long to pass further. He beginneth not with obscure definitions, which must blur the margin with interpretations, and load the memory with doubtfulness; but he cometh to you with words set in delightful proportion, either accompanied with, or prepared for, the well enchanting skill of music; and with a tale forsooth he cometh unto you, with a tale which holdeth children from play, and old men from the chimney corner. And, pretending no more, doth intend the winning of the mind from wickedness to virtue – even as the child is often brought to take most wholesome things by hiding them in such other as have a pleasant taste, which, if one should begin to tell them the nature of the aloes or rhubarb they should receive, would sooner take their physic at their ears than at their mouth. So is it in men (most of which are childish in the best things, till they be cradled in their graves): glad will they be to hear the tales of Hercules, Achilles, Cyrus, Aeneas; and, hearing them, must needs hear the right description of wisdom, valour, and justice; which,

---

[23] Whoever.

if they had been barely, that is to say philosophically, set out, they would swear they be brought to school again.

[Sidney gives further examples of the power of poetry to move, and thereby effectively to teach virtue. He answers various objections to the different kinds of poetry – pastoral, elegy, comedy, tragedy, lyric and epic. Finally, he rounds on the 'poet-haters' themselves, rejecting in turn their four most serious charges against poetry: that it is a waste of time; that it is lies; that it can corrupt; and that it was banished by Plato from his Republic:]

So that, since the excellencies of it may be so easily and so justly confirmed, and the low-creeping objections so soon trodden down: it not being an art of lies, but of true doctrine; not of effeminateness, but of notable stirring of courage; not of abusing man's wit, but of strengthening man's wit; not banished, but honoured by Plato: let us rather plant more laurels for to engarland the poets' heads (which honour of being laureate, as besides them only triumphant captains wear, is a sufficient authority to show the price they ought to be held in) than suffer the ill-favoured breath of such wrong-speakers once to blow upon the clear springs of poesy.

But since I have run so long a career[24] in this matter, methinks, before I give my pen a full stop, it shall be but a little more lost time to inquire why England, the mother of excellent minds, should be grown so hard a stepmother to poets, who certainly in wit ought to pass all other, since all only proceedeth from their wit, being indeed makers of themselves, not takers of others. How can I but exclaim

Musa, mihi causas memora, quo numine laeso?[25]

Sweet poesy, that hath anciently had kings, emperors, senators, great captains, such as, besides a thousand others, David, Adrian, Sophocles, Germanicus, not only to favour poets, but to be poets; and of our nearer times can present for her patrons a Robert, king of Sicily, the great King Francis of France, King James of Scotland; such cardinals as Bembus and Bibbiena; such famous preachers and teachers as Beza and Melanchthon; so learned philosophers as Fracastorius and Scaliger; so great orators as Pontanus and Muretus; so piercing wits as George Buchanan; so grave counsellors as, beside many, but before all, that Hospital of France,[26] than

---

[24] Course.

[25] 'Muse, relate to me the reason, through what offended power . . .' (Virgil, *Aeneid* I. 8).

[26] Adrian, the Roman emperor Hadrian (reigned AD 117–38), who wrote poetry; Germanicus, Germanicus Caesar (15 BC–AD 19), Roman general and writer; Robert, Robert II of Anjou (1309–43) patron of Petrarch; Francis, King Francis I (1494–1547), patron of French literature and art; James, either James I (1394–1437) or James VI (1566–1625) of Scotland (the latter became James I of England); Bembus, Cardinal Pietro Bembo (1470–1547), Italian humanist and Latin poet; Bibbiena, Cardinal Bernardo Dovizi of Bibbiena (1470–1520), humanist and author of a comedy; Beza, Théodore de Beze (1519–1605), French Calvinist leader and philologist; Melanchthon, Philip Melanchthon (1497–1560), professor of Greek at Wittenberg University and supporter of Luther; Fracastorius, Girolamo Fracastoro (1483–1553), natural philosopher and author of a medical poem; Scaliger, Julius Caesar Scaliger (1484–1558), physician and author of scientific and philosophical works; Pontanus, Giovanni Pontano (1426–1503), poet and scholar; Muretus, Marc-Antoine Muret (1526–85), elegant Latin stylist;

whom (I think) that realm never brought forth a more accomplished judgement, more firmly builded upon virtue: I say these, with numbers of others, not only to read others' poesies, but to poetize for others' reading – that poesy, thus embraced in all other places, should only find in our time a hard welcome in England, I think the very earth lamenteth it, and therefore decketh our soil with fewer laurels than it was accustomed. For heretofore poets have in England also flourished, and, which is to be noted, even in those times when the trumpet of Mars did sound loudest . . .

Chaucer, undoubtedly, did excellently in his *Troilus and Criseyde*; of whom, truly, I know not whether to marvel more, either that he in that misty time could see so clearly, or that we in this clear age go so stumblingly after him. Yet had he great wants, fit to be forgiven in so reverent an antiquity. I account the *Mirror of Magistrates*[27] meetly furnished of beautiful parts, and in the Earl of Surrey's[28] lyrics many things tasting of a noble birth, and worthy of a noble mind. The *Shepherds' Calendar*[29] hath much poetry in his eclogues, indeed worthy the reading, if I be not deceived. (That same framing of his style to an old rustic language I dare not allow,[30] since neither Theocritus[31] in Greek, Virgil in Latin, nor Sannazzaro[32] in Italian did affect it.) Besides these I do not remember to have seen but few (to speak boldly) printed that have poetical sinews in them; for proof whereof, let but most of the verses be put in prose, and then ask the meaning, and it will be found that one verse did but beget another, without ordering at the first what should be at the last; which becomes a confused mass of words, with a tingling[33] sound of rhyme, barely accompanied with reason.

Our tragedies and comedies (not without cause cried out against), observing rules neither of honest civility nor skilful poetry – excepting *Gorboduc*[34] (again, I say, of those that I have seen), which notwithstanding as it is full of stately speeches and well-sounding phrases, climbing to the height of Seneca's style,[35] and as full of notable morality, which it doth most delightfully teach, and so obtain the very end of poesy, yet in truth it is very defectuous in

---

George Buchanan (1506–82), Scottish Protestant poet and scholar and personal acquaintance of Sidney's; Hospital, Michel de l'Hôpital (1505–73), Chancellor of France (1560–8), author of Latin verse and patron of the arts.

[27] *A Mirror for Magistrates*, first published in 1559, in an enlarged edition in 1563, and thereafter frequently reprinted, was a collection of metrical tragedies by various authors dealing with the fall of princes.

[28] Henry Howard, Earl of Surrey (?1517–47), known for his sonnets and other lyrics, and for the introduction into English of blank verse.

[29] Spenser's *Shepheards Calender* (1579), consisting of twelve eclogues, was dedicated to Sidney.

[30] Commend.

[31] Theocritus, Greek pastoral poet of the third century BC.

[32] Jacopo Sannazzaro (1458–1530), author of *Arcadia* (1504), a series of verse eclogues.

[33] Tinkling.

[34] *Gorboduc*, by Thomas Sackville and Thomas Norton, was first performed in 1561 and is regarded as the earliest English dramatic tragedy.

[35] Lucius Annaeus Seneca (d. AD 65), Roman philosopher and author of nine tragedies, which were highly regarded in the Renaissance.

the circumstances,[36] which grieveth me, because it might not remain as an exact model of all tragedies. For it is faulty both in place and time, the two necessary companions of all corporal actions. For where the stage should always represent but one place, and the uttermost time presupposed in it should be, both by Aristotle's precept and common reason,[37] but one day, there is both many days, and many places, inartificially[38] imagined . . .

[Sidney goes on to complain that English drama offends against decorum by mixing genres, and then turns his attention to contemporary lyric poetry, which he condemns for its lack of feeling.]

Other sort of poetry almost have we none, but that lyrical kind of songs and sonnets: which, Lord, if He gave us so good minds, how well it might be employed, and with how heavenly fruit, both private and public, in singing the praises of the immortal beauty: the immortal goodness of that God who giveth us hands to write and wits to conceive; of which we might well want words, but never matter; of which we could turn our eyes to nothing, but we should ever have new-budding occasions. But truly many of such writings as come under the banner of unresistible love, if I were a mistress, would never persuade me they were in love: so coldly they apply fiery speeches, as men that had rather read lovers' writings – and so caught up certain swelling phrases which hang together like a man that once told my father that the wind was at north-west and by south, because he would be sure to name winds enough – than that in truth they feel those passions, which easily (as I think) may be betrayed by that same forcibleness or *energia* (as the Greeks call it) of the writer. But let this be a sufficient though short note, that we miss the right use of the material point of poesy.

Now, for the outside of it, which is words, or (as I may term it) diction,[39] it is even well worse. So is that honey-flowing matron Eloquence apparelled, or rather disguised, in a courtesan-like painted affectation: one time, with so far-fet[40] words that may seem monsters but must seem strangers to any poor Englishman; another time, with coursing of a letter,[41] as if they were bound to follow the method of a dictionary; another time, with figures and flowers,[42] extremely winter-starved. But I would this fault were only peculiar to versifiers, and had not as large possession among prose-printers; and (which is to be marvelled) among many scholars; and (which is to be pitied) among some preachers. Truly I could wish, if at least I might be so bold to wish in a thing beyond the reach of my capacity, the diligent imitators of Tully and Demosthenes[43] (most worthy to be imitated) did not so much

[36] Arrangement of narrative: time, place, setting, etc.

[37] Aristotle in his *Poetics* had recommended that the action should take place within the space of twenty-four hours.

[38] Unskilfully.

[39] Choice of words.

[40] Far-fetched.

[41] Hunting for alliteration.

[42] Rhetorical figures.

[43] Tully, Marcus Tullius Cicero (106–43 BC), Roman orator and writer on the art of rhetoric (see document II.7, n. 11); Demosthenes (c.383–322 BC), Athenian orator.

keep Nizolian paper-books of their figures and phrases,[44] as by attentive translation[45] (as it were) devour them whole, and make them wholly theirs: for now they cast sugar and spice upon every dish that is served to the table – like those Indians, not content to wear earrings at the fit and natural place of the ears, but they will thrust jewels through their nose and lips, because they will be sure to be fine . . .

[In addition to faulty 'diction', Sidney condemns contemporary poets for their excessive and inappropriate use of similes.]

Undoubtedly (at least to my opinion undoubtedly), I have found in divers smally learned courtiers a more sound style than in some professors of learning; of which I can guess no other cause, but that the courtier, following that which by practice he findeth fittest to nature, therein (though he know it not) doth according to art, though not by art: where the other, using art to show art, and not to hide art (as in these cases he should do), flieth from nature, and indeed abuseth art.

But what? Methinks I deserve to be pounded[46] for straying from poetry to oratory. But both have such an affinity in the wordish consideration,[47] that I think this digression will make my meaning receive the fuller understanding: which is not to take upon me to teach poets how they should do, but only, finding myself sick among the rest, to show some one or two spots of the common infection grown among the most part of writers, that, acknowledging ourselves somewhat awry, we may bend to the right use both of matter and manner: whereto our language giveth us great occasion, being indeed capable of any excellent exercising of it. I know some will say it is a mingled language.[48] And why not so much the better, taking the best of both the other? Another will say it wanteth grammar. Nay truly, it hath that praise, that it wants not grammar: for grammar it might have, but it needs it not, being so easy in itself, and so void of those cumbersome differences of cases, genders, moods, and tenses, which I think was a piece of the Tower of Babylon's curse,[49] that a man should be put to school to learn his mother-tongue. But for the uttering sweetly and properly the conceits of the mind (which is the end of speech), that hath it equally with any other tongue in the world; and is particularly happy in compositions of two or three words together,[50] near the Greek, far beyond the Latin, which is one of the greatest beauties can be in a language.

Now of versifying there are two sorts, the one ancient, the other modern: the ancient marked the quantity of each syllable,[51] and according to that

---

[44] A handbook of Ciceronian phrases, the *Thesarus Ciceronianus* compiled by Nizolius, had been slavishly followed by Cicero's imitators.

[45] Transformation, or transfer (in a legal sense).

[46] Impounded.

[47] In his subject matter: 'diction'.

[48] Derived from several other languages.

[49] Babylon was thought to have been built over the site of the Tower of Babel.

[50] Compound words.

[51] Length.

framed his verse; the modern, observing only number[52] (with some regard of the accent), the chief life of it standeth in that like sounding of the words, which we call rhyme. Whether[53] of these be the more excellent, would bear many speeches: the ancient (no doubt) more fit for music, both words and time observing quantity, and more fit lively to express diverse passions, by the low or lofty sound of the well-weighed syllable; the latter likewise, with his rhyme, striketh a certain music to the ear, and, in fine, since it doth delight, though by another way, it obtains the same purpose: there being in either sweetness, and wanting in neither majesty. Truly the English, before any vulgar language I know, is fit for both sorts. For, for the ancient, the Italian is so full of vowels that it must ever be cumbered with elisions;[54] the Dutch[55] so, of the other side, with consonants, that they cannot yield the sweet sliding, fit for a verse; the French in his whole language hath not one word that hath his accent in the last syllable saving two, called *antepenultima*; and little more hath the Spanish, and therefore very gracelessly may they use dactyls.[56] The English is subject to none of these defects. Now for the rhyme,[57] though we do not observe quantity, yet we observe the accent very precisely, which other languages either cannot do, or will not do so absolutely. That *caesura*, or breathing place in the midst of the verse, neither Italian nor Spanish have, the French and we never almost fail of. Lastly, even the very rhyme itself, the Italian cannot put it in the last syllable, by the French named the masculine rhyme, but still in the next to the last, which the French call the female, or the next before that, which the Italian term *sdrucciola*. The example of the former is *buono : suono*, of the *sdrucciola* is *femina : semina*. The French, of the other side, hath both the male, as *bon : son*, and the female, as *plaise : taise*, but the *sdrucciola* he hath not: where the English hath all three, as *due : true*, *father : rather*, *motion : potion* – with much more which might be said, but that already I find the triflingness of this discourse is much too much enlarged.

[Sidney ends the work in the tone in which be began it, lightheartedly promising immortality to the lovers of poetry and oblivion to its enemies.]

[52] Stress accent.
[53] Which.
[54] Contractions of sound when two vowels adjoin.
[55] German.
[56] Metrical feet of one stressed followed by two unstressed syllables.
[57] Modern accentual verse.

INDEX